The World of Literature

HENRY I. CHRIST

AMSCO

AMSCO SCHOOL PUBLICATIONS
315 Hudson Street, New York, N. Y. 10013

Henry I. Christ has had a long and distinguished career as writer, editor, teacher, and supervisor. A specialist in language, literature, and composition, he has written more than a hundred textbooks, many of which are published by Amsco. For nearly ten years, he was the editor of the magazine **High Points**. He has been active in professional organizations and has held office at the local, state, and national levels. A frequent speaker at conventions and workshops, he has also lectured on educational television and frequently participated in curriculum development and evaluation.

Marie E. Christ has worked with Henry I. Christ as a partner throughout his writing career. She has provided many practical suggestions and usable materials. As always, her good judgment, common sense, and hard work played a major role in the development and preparation of this book.

Cover Design: Meghan J. Shupe
Compositor: Northeastern Graphic, Inc.

Cover art includes these images from iStockphoto.com: Magnifying Glass/Duncan Walker, Fireworks/Chris Pendleton, Vase/Tracy Scott-Murray, Ball/Diane Diederich, Book/Diane Diederich, Dog/Michel Mory, Eagle/Kelly Shipp, Moon/Mark Bond, Leaf/Norman Pogson, Butterfly/Holger Wulschlaeger.

Please visit our Web site at ***www.amscopub.com***

When ordering this book, please specify:
either **R113P** or **THE WORLD OF LITERATURE**

ISBN: 978-1-56765-136-2

Printed in the United States of America

4 5 6 7 8 9 10 12

Contents

UNIT FOUR Can It Be Love?

UNIT FIVE For the Fun of It

UNIT SIX The Power of Poetry

UNIT SEVEN Actions and Motivations

UNIT EIGHT The World Over

To the Student

The World of Literature is an anthology of stories, plays, articles, essays, and poetry. All of these can be read for themselves alone, but enrichment material has been included to deepen appreciation and expand horizons.

The book has been divided into eight units, each with a special theme. Each unit has an introduction, with an appropriate quotation. The selections within the unit relate to the various themes. Each selection has a "teaser" to entice you to read the story. An introduction provides a helpful lead-in to each selection.

For deeper understanding and sharper reading skills, each selection has reading questions at the end. These focus on key reading skills like finding the main idea, identifying details, and drawing correct inferences. Words listed at grade 12 difficulty or above are tested. These are followed by questions designed to help you think about what you have just read. The section concludes with a "Language in Action" section that provides useful, lively information about language.

At the end of each unit, elements are tied together by questions that examine the selections with relation to each other. The Writing Portfolio helps you to gain valuable practice in writing, usually with relation to the selections you have just read. Then the section called "Other Areas of Communication" invites you to meet various creative challenges. The end-of-unit section concludes with a review of "Language in Action."

A glossary of words towards the end of the book provides additional information about the words tested in the text. An index of language items enables you to find a specific area of language that might interest you especially.

The World of Literature draws upon American sources, but also searches the world for stories from many countries: Third World countries as well as industrialized nations. The anthology reinforces the feeling that in a real sense, we belong to one world. The emotions of a disappointed young Syrian couple will be as completely understandable to you as those of an American teenager in love with an older man.

You will find a range of human emotions well represented in the selections that follow. Don't overlook the first goal: reading the selections for sheer enjoyment.

Acknowledgments

Grateful acknowledgment is made to the following sources for permission to reprint copyrighted materials. Every effort has been made to obtain permission to use previously published material; any errors or omissions are unintentional.

"Man in Hiding," by Vincent Starrett, copyright © 1964 by Davis Publications, Inc. © renewed, reprinted by permission of Penny Publications, LLC.

"The Crime in Nobody's Room," by John Dickson Carr. Reprinted by permission of Harold Ober Associates Incorporated. Copyright 1940 by William Morrow & Co. Copyright renewed 1968 by John Dickson Carr.

"Trifles," by Susan Glaspell. Reprinted with permission of the Walter H. Baker Company.

"Déjà Vu," by Mary Barrett. Reprinted by permission of the author.

"The Golden Kite, the Silver Wind," by Ray Bradbury, is reprinted by permission of Don Congdon Associates, Inc.
Copyright © 1953 by Epoch Associates, renewed 1981 by Ray Bradbury.

Tales from THE BEST-LOVED STORIES TOLD AT THE NATIONAL STORYTELLING FESTIVAL. Copyright © 1991 by the National Association for the Preservation and Perpetuation of Storytelling. "Cindy Ellie," by Mary Carter Smith. Reprinted by permission of the author. "A Fisherman and His Wife," by Carol L. Birch. Reprinted by permission of the author. "Could This Be Paradise?" by Steve Sanfield. Reprinted by permission of the author.

"Tortoise Learns a Lesson," from THINGS FALL APART, by Chinua Achebe. Reprinted by permission of Harcourt Education.

"The Mezcla Man," from TALES OF OLD TIME TEXAS by J. FRANK DOBIE. Copyright © 1928, 1930, 1931, 1935, 1936, 1938, 1939, 1941, 1947, 1949, 1950, 1951, 1952, 1955, 1960 by J. Frank Dobie. By permission of Little, Brown and Co., Inc.

"The Innkeeper's Wise Daughter," by Peninnah Schram. From JEWISH STORIES ONE GENERATION TELLS ANOTHER Retold by Peninnah Schram. Reprinted by permission of the publisher, Jason Aronson Inc., Northvale, NJ © 1987. Jason Aronson is an imprint of Rowman & Littlefield Publishers, Inc.

"All Summer in a Day," by Ray Bradbury, is reprinted by permission of Don Congdon Associates, Inc. Copyright © 1954, renewed 1982 by Ray Bradbury.

"The Sorrel Colt," by Benito Lynch. From SPANISH STORIES, edited by Angel Flores. Published by Dover Publications, Inc. New York. Copyright © 1960, 1987.

"The Work of One Day Is Gazed Upon for One Thousand Days," by Jade Snow Wong. From THE FIFTH CHINESE DAUGHTER, by Jade Snow Wong. Copyright © 1945, 1948, 1950, 1965, 1989 by Jade Snow Wong. Reprinted by permission of Curtis Brown, Ltd.

"Fifteen, Summer" (Mr. Cornelius, I Love You) from CRESS DELAHANTY, copyright 1952 and renewed 1980 by Jessamyn West. Reprinted with permission by Harcourt, Inc.

"Feuille d'Album," from THE SHORT STORIES OF KATHERINE MANSFIELD by Katherine Mansfield, copyright 1923 by Alfred A. Knopf, a division of Random House, Inc. and renewed 1951 by John Middleton Murry. Used by permission of Alfred A. Knopf, a division of Random House, Inc.

"Raymond's Run," copyright © 1971 by Toni Cade Bambara, from GORILLA, MY LOVE by Toni Cade Bambara. Used by permission of Random House, Inc.

"The Sojourner", from THE BALLAD OF THE SAD CAFÉ by Carson McCullers. Copyright 1936, 1941, 1942, 1950, © 1955 by Carson McCullers, © renewed 1979 by Floria V. Lasky, Executrix of the Estate of Carson McCullers. Reprinted by permission of Houghton Mifflin Company. All rights reserved.

"A Cap for Steve," Copyright © 1952, renewed 1980 by Morley Callaghan, reprinted by permission of the Estate of Morley Callaghan.

"Kiddie-Kar Travel" from INSIDE BENCHLEY by ROBERT BENCHLEY and DRAWINGS BY GLUYAS WILLIAMS. Copyright 1921, 1922, 1925, 1927, 1928, 1942 by Harper & Brothers. Copyright renewed © 1970 by Gertrude D. Benchley. Reprinted by permission of HarperCollins Publishers.

"Remember: Bills Are People, Too," by Mike Royko, published April 28, 1995. Copyright © 1995, Tribune Media Services. Reprinted with permission.

"Parents Should Choose Riskier Names for Babies," by Bill Tammeus. Copyright 1995, *The Kansas City Star*. Reproduced with permission of the Kansas City Star © Copyright 2005 The Kansas City Star. All rights reserved. Format differs from original publication. Not an endorsement.

"Banana Popsicles Good for What Ails You," by Benny Smith, reporter for the *Times-News* Hendersonville, NC. Copyright © June 30, 1995. Reprinted by permission of the *Times-News*, Hendersonville, NC.

"The Night the Ghost Got In," from MY LIFE AND HARD TIMES by James Thurber. Copyright © 1933, 1961 by James Thurber. Reprinted by arrangement with Rosemary Thurber and the Barbara Hogenson Agency, Inc. All rights reserved.

"The River Merchant's Wife: A Letter" by Ezra Pound, from PERSONAE, copyright © 1926 by Ezra Pound. Reprinted by permission of New Directions Publishing Corp.

"Up-Country" and "On an African Beach" by Abioseh Nicol. From AN AFRICAN TREASURY. Reprinted by permission of the author and David Higham Associates.

"Golden Bells," "Remembering Golden Bells," by Po Chü-i. From TRANSLATIONS FROM THE CHINESE by Arthur Waley, copyright 1919 and renewed 1947 by Arthur Waley. Used by permission of Alfred A. Knopf, a division of Random House, Inc.

"Women" from REVOLUTIONARY PETUNIAS & OTHER POEMS © 1970 and renewed 1998 by Alice Walker. Reprinted with permission by Harcourt, Inc.

Haiku from THE ESSENTIAL HAIKU: VERSIONS OF BASHO, BUSON & ISSA, EDITED AND WITH AN INTRODUCTION by ROBERT HASS. Introduction and selection copyright © 1994 by Robert Hass. Unless otherwise noted, all translations copyright © 1994 by Robert Hass. Reprinted by permission of HarperCollins Publishers. Ecco Press.

"Nine by Emily Dickinson," Reprinted by permission of the publishers and the Trustees of Amherst College from THE POEMS OF EMILY DICKINSON, Thomas H. Johnson, ed., Cambridge, Mass.: The Belknap Press of Harvard University Press, Copyright © 1951, 1955, 1979, 1983 by the President and Fellows of Harvard College.

"Anon." by R. J. Lowenherz. Originally appeared in PIEDMONT LITERARY REVIEW. Reprinted by permission of the author.

"A Quarter's Worth of Fireworks," by Norman Katkov. Copyright © 1954, © Renewed 1982 by Norman Katkov. Reprinted by permission of Harold Matson Company, Inc.

"The Lottery Ticket," reprinted from *The Wife and Other Stories* by Anton Chekhov, translated by Constance Garnett. (New York: Macmillan, 1918).

"A Story Told to the Dark." From STORIES OF GOD by Rainer Maria Rilke, translated by M. D. Herter Norton. Copyright 1932 by W. W. Norton & Company, Inc., renewed © 1960 by M. D. Herter Norton and Nora Purtscher-Wydenbruck. Used by permission of W. W. Norton & Company, Inc.

"Never," from COUNTRY TALES, by H. E. Bates. Reprinted by permission of Robinson Publishing, Laurence Pollinger Ltd., and the estate of H. E. Bates. Reproduced by permission of Pollinger Limited and the proprietor.

"A Worn Path" from A CURTAIN OF GREEN AND OTHER STORIES, copyright 1941 and renewed 1969 by Eudora Welty, reprinted by permission of Harcourt, Inc.

"Thank You, M'am" from SHORT STORIES by Langston Hughes. Copyright © 1996 by Ramona Bass and Arnold Rampersad. Copyright © 1996 by Ramona Bass and Arnold Rampersad. Reprinted by permission of Hill and Wang, a division of Farrar, Straus and Giroux, LLC.

"My Lord, the Baby," reprinted from *Hungry Stones and Other Stories* by Rabindranath Tagore. (New York: Macmillan, 1916).

"Bontsche the Silent," by Isaac Peretz. Translated from the Yiddish by Dr. Angelo S. Rappaport. Copyright © 1927 by Stanley Paul and Co., Ltd.

"He" from FLOWERING JUDAS AND OTHER STORIES, copyright 1930 and renewed 1958 by Katherine Anne Porter, reprinted by permission of Harcourt, Inc.

"The Person of the Moment" From I KNOW WHY THE CAGED BIRD SINGS by Maya Angelou, copyright © 1969 and renewed 1997 by Maya Angelou. Used by permission of Random House, Inc.

Photo Credits

All unit opening photos supplied by iStockphoto.com.

Unit 1 Candles
Unit 2 Antique Typewriter Black/Lauri Wiberg
Unit 3 Pleasure of Speed
Unit 4 Dancing/John Setzler
Unit 5 Look Before . . ./Darren Baker
Unit 6 Corvus Monedula (Jackdaw)/Gertjan Hooijer
Unit 7 Catch the Sky/Daniel Norman
Unit 8 Top of the World Fisheye/Kenneth C. Zirke

The World of Literature

UNIT ONE

I Love a Mystery

The most beautiful thing we can experience is the mysterious. It is the source of all true art and power.

Albert Einstein

Einstein was, of course, talking about larger and more important mysteries than those solved by Sherlock Holmes, Hercule Poirot, or Father Brown. Still, even a modest detective story contains a hint of the mysterious, a puzzle that seems too difficult to solve.

When the word **mystery** is mentioned, most people think of the detective story, but the mystery shelf in the average library contains a wide variety of types. There are, most of all, stories with detectives of all kinds. Then there are crime stories without a detective, like "Man in Hiding" (5). James Bond finds his way to these shelves, too, as do other spy and international-intrigue stories. Still, the most famous subcategory is the detective story.

"Why **do** people read detective stories?" asks the author Gladys Mitchell. Above all, she says, they have a definite plot. She adds, "Their writers must tidy up the loose ends, must supply a logical solution to the problem they have posed, must also, to hold the reader's attention, combine the primitive lust and energy of the hunter with the cold logic of the scholarly mind."

This unit contains a sampling of various types of mysteries. "Man in Hiding" and "Deja Vu" are crime stories without detectives. Both provide an unusual twist to the crimes. They suggest that punishment may come from circumstances, not the police. "Trifles" provides a sheriff and a county attorney, but the problem of the crime is solved by amateurs: two farm women.

The other stories introduce us to different detective types. Everybody's favorite, Sherlock Holmes, solves a puzzling mystery by assembling clues and coming to a conclusion. Jacques Futrelle's The Thinking Machine, demonstrates that "Nothing is impossible." The Man in the Corner solves a case from a distance. The blustering Colonel March overpowers the characters by his presence and insight.

Three stories deal with classic locked-room mysteries, each problem unique in its own way. Solutions depend upon small details, even the color blindness of a character.

This is a cross-section that will show you some possibilities within this popular literary type.

Man in Hiding

Vincent Starrett
American

Dr. Loxley closed the outer door behind him and almost ran for M. Boggs, Antiques. As he locked the door of the antique shop, still shaking, he was relieved to see that the corridor was empty. They would follow him, of course, in a matter of minutes. Every office in the building would be searched, every office in the vast Merchandise Exchange.

It had to be the chest!

Dr. B. Edward Loxley had committed the perfect murder. Secure in a new identity, he cultivates all new friendships and looks forward to a reunion in Paris with a young woman. He has planned the major strategy so flawlessly that nothing can harm him.

He hasn't anticipated a fatal flaw in himself, however. As you read this story, notice the clues suggesting that the good doctor is his own worst enemy. Notice the clever twist that ends the story. Then consider the many uses of irony, page (14).

Man in Hiding

DR. B. EDWARD LOXLEY (jocularly called "Bedward" by the Chicago gossip columnists), the wife-murderer for whom hundreds of police had been scouring the city for three weeks, sat quietly at his desk in the great Merchandise Exchange reading his morning mail. The frosted glass door of his outer office read simply: *William Drayham, Rare Books. Hours by Appointment.* After three weeks of security he was beginning to feel a little complacent. For three weeks he had not left his hiding place in the huge business complex and he had no intention of leaving it for the time being—except feet first.

It had all been carefully thought out beforehand. The office of "William Drayham" had been rented two months prior to the killing of his wife, and Loxley had quietly taken possession and created his new personality as a dealer in rare books. He had been accepted by all his neighbors in the sixth-floor corridor. The elevator starter was getting to know him. He breakfasted, lunched, and dined at the several restaurants in the building, was shaved by a favorite barber, and was—he had every reason to believe—an accepted fixture. His neighbors were inoffensive and unimaginative workers who did not for a moment question his identity, and the words *Rare Books* on the door were formidable enough to frighten away casual visitors.

Lora Loxley, murdered by suffocation, had been buried for nearly three weeks and even the newspapers were beginning to play down the sensational story. The feeling was growing that Dr. Loxley himself might also have been murdered and a desultory search for his body continued whenever the police had nothing more urgent to occupy them. Since Loxley's office window overlooked the river where, in addition to the normal traffic, police boats occasionally plied, he was able to watch the activities on the river with amused appreciation. He had now spent two lonely Saturdays and Sundays watching the weekend traffic with a pair of binoculars, waiting for any active renewal of police attention. He was on excellent terms with the watchmen in his part of the giant building, and they were now accustomed to seeing him at the most unlikely hours.

The Merchandise Exchange was actually a city within a city. It contained everything a man in hiding needed—restaurants, laundries, barber shops, tobacconists, dentists, newsstands, banking facilities, a gymnasium, even a postal station. He was already known by name in the restaurants and barber shops. He bought all the newspapers, morning and evening. Occasionally he dictated a letter to one of the public stenographers, ordering or declining rare books. As William Drayham he had a sufficient banking account downstairs for all his immediate needs. The rest of his wealth, in cash, was waiting in Paris—as was Gloria.

His principal bogies had been the watchmen and the cleaning women. But both fears had vanished. The watchmen had proved friendly, and the cleaning women, a friendly trio who liked candy, readily agreed to visit his office while he was having a late dinner. His domestic arrangements were simple. He slept on a couch in his inner office, which also contained a vault to which he could retire in an emergency. To date there had been no emergency.

Dr. Loxley pushed the mail aside impatiently. It was too early to expect a large response to the small rare-book advertisement he was running in a Sunday book-review supplement. But it was not too early for the coffee that Miss Marivole Boggs was willing to serve at all hours. What luck to have found so admirable a neighbor in the same corridor, and even, it might be said, in the same line! Rare books and antiques went very well together. Miss Boggs had been responsible for most of his infrequent customers. He glanced at his expensive wristwatch and left William Drayham's rare books without a pang.

The owner of *M. Boggs, Antiques,* as she described herself on the show window of her small shop at the end of the corridor, looked up at his entrance.

"Hello," she said. "I was hoping you'd come in."

"I couldn't resist," he said. His brown eyes took in the familiar room, resting for a moment on the suit of ancient armor that dominated one corner of the shop and the old Spanish chest that was Miss Boggs's pride and joy. "Well, I see nobody has bought either of them yet." It was one of their standing jokes that someday, when the rare-book business was better, he would buy them himself.

As Marivole Boggs poured his coffee she said, "The newspapers stories about that doctor are getting shorter every day. I'm beginning to believe he really *was* murdered."

They often discussed the missing Dr. Loxley, as indeed the whole city was doing. At first it had been Miss Boggs's idea that the "society doctor" had murdered his wife in favor of a more glamorous patient who was now living in sin with him somewhere on the French or Italian Riviera.

Dr. Loxley had thought not. "Too romantic, Miss Boggs. I still think his body is in the river or floating on its way to the Gulf of Mexico. That scarf they found on the river bank looks like it."

"Anyway, the police seem to have stopped looking," said Miss Boggs.

"Anyway, this is good coffee, my dear. I hope you'll give me your special recipe. Do you still plan to leave this month?"

"At once," she said. "I'm flying to New York tomorrow, if I can get away. I want to be in London for the Exhibition; then on to Paris, Rome, and Zurich. I'm enormously relieved that you'll be here to keep an eye on things, Bill. Coffee at all hours, eh?"

"Morning, noon, and night," he agreed, rising to leave. Her change of plan had startled him for a moment; but he was quick to see a distinct advantage in it for himself. "Never fear, I'll be here waiting for you when you return."

Strolling back to his own shop, humming a jaunty air, he became aware of a man leaving the doorway of the office directly opposite his own. Something about the man's carriage seemed familiar. The man was heading toward the elevators and walking fast. In an instant they would meet.

And suddenly Dr. Loxley realized that the man was indeed familiar. He was his own brother-in-law, Lawrence Bridewell.

Loxley's first instinct was to turn and flee, his second to return to *M. Boggs, Antiques.* His final decision, made in a split second, was to see the encounter through. His disguise had fooled better men than Larry Bridewell, although none who knew him better. With his former neat beard and mustache now gone, and his blue eyes transformed by brown contact lenses, Dr. Loxley was, to all appearances, another man. After that first appalling moment of indecision, he fumbled for a cigarette, realizing that after three weeks of growingly complacent safety, he was about to face the supreme test.

He tried and failed to light the cigarette. Then the two men were face to face, glancing at each other as men do in passing—and suddenly the test was over.

Or was it? Bridewell continued on his way to the elevators, still walking fast, and Loxley stumbled to his own door.

Did he dare look back? Had Bridewell turned to look back at *him?* Moving casually, Loxley stole a glance down the corridor. There was no doubt about it—Larry *was* looking back. Perhaps he had merely been troubled by an imagined resemblance.

Dr. Loxley had some difficulty opening his own door, and just before he closed it the thought occurred to him to look at the name on the door of the office from which his brother-in-law had emerged. Actually he knew very well what he would find there: *Jackson & Fortworth, Attorneys-at-Law*—and, below, the significant words: *Private Investigations.*

He tried to take himself in hand and was annoyed to find that he was shaking. Experimentally he ventured a drink to see what it would do for him. It helped considerably. But the whole incident haunted him the rest of the day and gave him a bad night. In the morning, however, his fears had evaporated. He was his confident self again—until, a few hours later, a second incident shook his nerve.

Returning from the cigar stand in the lobby, he passed the DeLuxe Dog Salon in one of the street-level corridors and, as he had often done before, paused to look into the windows at the fashionable dogs being barbered and prettified. It had always been an amusing spectacle, but this time, as he turned away, an appalling thing happened.

A well dressed woman was approaching the salon with a haughty French poodle on a leash. The woman looked familiar. Good Lord, she *was* familiar! She was Mrs. Montgomery Hyde, an old patient of his! Loxley's heart seemed to stop beating. Would she recognize him?

It was the dog that recognized him. With a refined little yelp the poodle jerked the leash from the woman's hand and flung himself against the doctor's legs.

With an effort, Loxley recovered his balance and somehow managed to recover his poise. It was his worst moment since the murder. Automatically he disengaged himself from the poodle's attentions and pulled the black ears.

"There, there, fellow," he said to the excited animal in a voice that he hoped was not his own. "I beg your pardon, Madam. Your dog appears to have made a mistake."

To his intense relief, Mrs. Montgomery Hyde agreed.

"Do forgive Toto's impulsiveness," she begged, snatching up the leash. "He loves everybody."

Dr. Loxley left the scene in almost a hurry. She had not recognized him! It seemed to him a miracle; but again he was annoyed to find himself shaking. And yet, wasn't it really a good omen? If Mrs. Hyde and his own brother-in-law had failed to recognize him, was there anything for him to fear?

Immediately he began to feel better. But when he had returned to his office, William Drayham again treated himself to a stiff drink.

In a moment of alert intelligence, he realized that for three weeks he had permitted himself to become too complacent. His meeting with Mrs. Hyde had taught him something that was important for him to remember: he had almost spoken her name! In the first onslaught of panic, he might well have betrayed himself. If it was important for him not to be recognized, it was equally important that *he* must not recognize anyone else.

It was clear to him now that this cat-and-mouse existence could not go on indefinitely. He must remain in hiding only until it was safe for him to emerge and get out of the country. Then William Drayham would ostentatiously pack his books and remove to New York. After that, the world was wide, with his immediate destination—Paris and Gloria.

For several days the chastened doctor lived cautiously, visiting *M. Boggs, Antiques* at intervals for coffee and to admire the suit of armor and the Spanish chest, which continued to fascinate him. He had promised Miss Boggs, now on her travels, not to cut the price on either if a buyer should turn up.

Twice, returning from the antique shop, he again caught a glimpse of his brother-in-law—both times entering the law office of Jackson & Fortworth—and had hurried to lock himself in his own office before Larry could emerge. What the devil did the fellow want with a firm of private investigators anyway?

The visit of Jackson, the senior lawyer of the firm, to the bookshop one morning took the doctor completely by surprise, or he might have locked the door.

"I've been intending to look in on you for some time, Mr. Drayham," said the lawyer cordially. "I'm Jackson, just across from you. Rare books have always interested me. Mind if I look around? I think that browse is the word."

Loxley rose from his chair abruptly, knocking a book from his desk to the floor. An icy fear had entered his heart. Was this the showdown at last, he wondered.

He shook hands effusively. "Glad to meet you, Mr. Jackson. By all means, browse. Is there anything special I can show you?"

But Jackson was already browsing. When he had finished, he strolled to the window. "Nice view of the river you have," he said appreciatively. "*My* windows all face an inner court." He walked to the door. "Just wanted to meet you, Mr. Drayham. I'll come in again when I have more time."

"Any time at all," said Loxley with warm courtesy.

Dr. Loxley sat down at his desk and reached for the lower drawer. Another little drink wouldn't hurt. What had the fellow really wanted? What had he hoped to learn? Or was he really one of those strange people who collected rare books?

One thing, however, was undeniably clear. Any day now he might have to leave the building and the city. If he was suspected, the blow would fall swiftly. At any minute the door might open again, and this time Jackson might not be alone. Why not get out of this trap immediately? What was there to stop him? His stock—300-odd volumes of miscellaneous volumes bought at a storage house—could be left behind if necessary.

What stopped him was Gloria's cable from Paris: TROUBLE HERE. PHONING FRIDAY NIGHT.

This was Thursday. Whatever else happened, he must wait for Gloria's call. His hand moved toward the lower drawer, then withdrew. Coffee, not whiskey, was what he needed; and after luncheon he spent most of the afternoon with Miss Boggs's weird collection of antiques. There he had an unobstructed view of Jackson's door, and was not himself visible. If Larry Bridewell was among the lawyer's visitors, Loxley did not see him.

Exploring the antique shop he paused, as always, to admire his two star exhibits, the almost frightening suit of armor and the massive Spanish chest. In a pinch, either would do as an emergency hiding place—if there was time enough to hide.

That evening he was startled to find his picture in the newspaper again—the face of Dr. B. Edward Loxley as he had looked with the neat little beard and moustache before he had murdered his wife. It seemed he'd been arrested by an alert Seattle policeman, but had denied his identity.

Dr. Loxley drew a long breath of relief. After all, perhaps he was still safe in this city within a city. But what could Gloria have to say to him that required a call from Paris? Bad news of some kind. Bad for somebody.

In spite of all his new fears, he hated to leave the building that had been his refuge. It had been his hope to live there indefinitely, undetected—never again to venture into the streets until Dr. Loxley was as forgotten as Dr. Crippen.

Again he slept off his fears and spent an uninterrupted forenoon with his view of the river and the morning newspapers. He was beginning to feel almost at ease again—indeed, when the insufferable Jackson knocked on his locked door and called a hearty greeting he almost welcomed having a visitor. But there was somebody with the attorney. Through the frosted pane Loxley could make out the shadowy outline of another man.

"May we come in?" the lawyer called out. "I've got a couple of friends here who want to talk to you."

Loxley rose uncertainly to his feet and moved to the door. So it had come at last! He had been right about his damned brother-in-law and this sneaking lawyer. This was the showdown. And suddenly Loxley knew what he had to do.

He unlocked the door and threw it open. "Come in, gentlemen," he said without emotion. "What can I do for you?"

Jackson was beaming. "These are my friends, Sergeants Coughlin and Ripkin, from headquarters. They hope you will come quietly." The lawyer laughed heartily at his own witticism.

"Come in, gentlemen, and sit down." Loxley forced a smile—he was panicking fast. He seated himself at his desk, trembling, and addressed and stamped an envelope. Then he stood up, shakily. "I was just going to the mail chute with an important letter. I'll be back in a few moments."

"Sure," said one of the two cops genially. "Take your time, Mr. Drayham."

Was there just the slightest emphasis on the name "Drayham" or was he merely imagining it?

Dr. Loxley closed the outer door behind him and almost ran for *M. Boggs, Antiques.* As he locked the door of the antique shop, still shaking, he was relieved to see that the corridor was empty. They would follow him, of course, in a matter of minutes. Every office in the building would be searched, every office in the vast Merchandise Exchange.

It *had* to be the chest!

It stood open as always, and he squeezed inside—an uncomfortable fit—then lowered the heavy lid until only a thin crack remained for air. Faintly now he thought he could hear footsteps in the corridor. He drew a deep breath and closed the lid.

There was a sharp "click," then only intense darkness.

Ten minutes later, Sergeant Ripkin said to his partner, "Wonder what's keeping that guy. We've still got about fifty tickets to sell, Pete."

"Oh, leave some with me," said Jackson. "I'll see that you get your money. Drayham's a good fellow—he'll buy a batch of them, I'm sure."

The two policemen, who had been hoping to dispose of all their remaining tickets for a benefit baseball game, departed leisurely.

The disappearance of William Drayham, a "rare-book dealer" with an office in the Merchandise Exchange, attracted less attention than the disappearance of Dr. B. Edward Loxley, but for a few days it was a mild sensation.

Returning from Europe a month later, Miss Boggs wondered idly when Bill would drop in for a cup of coffee. He had told her he would be here when she returned.

She puttered happily among her treasures. Some fool, she noted, had automatically locked the chest by closing it. One of these days she'd have to unlock it and raise the lid.

Reading for Understanding

Main Idea

1. The main idea may be suggested by which of the following common sayings?
   (a) It's an ill wind that blows nobody good.
   (b) Murder will out.
   (c) Empty barrels make the most noise.
   (d) Never leave till tomorrow what you can do today.

Details

2. A key element of Loxley's disguise was (a) a change of laugh (b) a large shoe size (c) formal clothes (d) eye color.
3. Loxley feared he might be recognized by (a) his brother-in-law (b) Miss Boggs (c) his tailor (d) none of these.
4. Bridewell visited the offices of (a) Dr. Crippen (b) an antique dealer (c) a private investigator (d) William Drayham.

Inferences

5. The most crucial element in the story proved to be (a) Miss Boggs' trip abroad (b) Toto's recognition of Loxley (c) Mrs. Montgomery Hyde's comments to him (d) good news from Gloria.
6. It is probable that the rare books (a) cost Loxley a small fortune (b) were not especially valuable (c) contained the best writing by English writers of the detective story (d) were the immediate cause of Loxley's fall.
7. The end of the mystery will occur when (a) Bridewell goes to the police (b) Drayham goes to New York (c) Miss Boggs opens the trunk (d) the police charge Loxley with murder.
8. William Drayham was (a) a policeman (b) a private detective (c) the husband of Lora (d) in love with Miss Boggs.

Order of Events

9. Arrange the items in the order in which they occurred. Use letters only.
   A. Drayham meets Miss Boggs.
   B. Loxley rents a bookstore.
   C. Drayham meets Mrs. Hyde.
   D. Drayham meets two policemen.
   E. Loxley murders his wife.

Fact or Opinion

Tell whether the following is a fact or an opinion.

10. Loxley placed most of his money in Paris to be with Gloria.

Words in Context

1. "After three weeks of security he was beginning to feel a little *complacent.*" **Complacent** (6) means (a) nervous (b) bored (c) irritated (d) self-satisfied.
2. "The words *Rare Books* on the door were *formidable* enough to frighten away casual visitors." **Formidable** (6) means (a) enticing (b) curious (c) evil (d) menacing.

3. "A *desultory* search for his body continued whenever the police had nothing more urgent to occupy them." **Desultory** (6) means (a) sluggish (b) mammoth (c) uninterrupted (d) well-publicized.
4. "He shook hands *effusively*." **Effusively** (10) means (a) gingerly (b) enthusiastically (c) warily (d) reluctantly.

Thinking Critically About the Story

1. What was Loxley's weakness? How did it finally defeat him?
2. Why does the author mention Paris as one of Miss Boggs' destinations?
3. Had Loxley committed the perfect crime? Is there such a thing as a perfect crime? Explain.
4. Does Loxley have a guilty conscience, or is he concerned solely with his own survival? Explain.
5. Have you ever read another story or seen a movie in which a criminal is defeated by his own weaknesses? Tell about it.
6. When Miss Boggs leaves (7), Loxley says, "Never fear, I'll be here waiting for you when you return." How does his expectation differ from the reality? How is it similar? See *Irony,* below.

Language in Action

Irony

A passenger whose fear of flying caused him to cancel a flight and take a train instead was involved in a fatal train accident.

"How ironic!" people said. "The very search for safety was in the end a source of disaster."

This is an example of situational irony. When the astronaut John Glenn returned from hazardous trips in space and injured himself in a bathroom fall, people exclaimed, "How ironic." **Irony** involves a clash between what is and what seems (or ought) to be. John Glenn's space trip should have been much more dangerous than the "safety" of home.

Irony prevails throughout "Man in Hiding." Loxley consistently misinterprets people's actions. Like guilty persons everywhere, he reads danger and disclosure all around him, even in the most unlikely circumstances. The reality is that returning to the police would have been safe. Entering the chest was fatal. How ironic!

Verbal irony is similar. When Antony kept saying at Julius Caesar's funeral that "Brutus is an honorable man," he meant quite the opposite. Irony says one thing and suggests another. On page 478, Sir Joseph Porter suggests, "Stick close to your desks and never go to sea and you all may be Rulers of the Queen's Navee." One would expect a "Ruler of the Queen's Navee" to be acquainted with the sea.

Sarcasm, satire, and verbal irony are members of the same family.

The Adventure of the Speckled Band

Arthur Conan Doyle
British

"It is not cold which makes me shiver," said the woman, in a low voice. "It is fear, Mr. Holmes. It is terror."

An impossible crime! Murder in a locked room, thoroughly barred on the inside! A mysterious whistle in the night . . . a wisp of cigar smoke . . . a dummy bellpull . . . a saucer of milk . . . the dying words "The speckled band" . . . these are a few of the clues in this powerful story of a puzzling murder case marked by suspense, terror, and a shocking climax.

Many critics consider this story one of the half dozen best detective stories ever written. It is a classic story of its kind. The author provides clue after clue and invites you to match wits with Sherlock Holmes

In this story, the author, Arthur Conan Doyle, is at his best. It suggests why Holmes is probably the most popular detective in all fiction. Here we see Holmes the powerful antagonist, the logical reasoner, the true friend, the dramatic entertainer. We understand why so many people thought of Holmes as a real person. (Many still do!) At one point Doyle tired of Holmes and decided to kill him off. In a story called "The Final Problem," Holmes apparently falls to his death in a raging waterfall. The readers were shocked and dismayed. They rebelled. "Bring Holmes back!" they insisted. Doyle at last relented. In "The Adventure of the Empty House," Doyle's readers learned that Holmes had not fallen into the waterfall after all.

Sherlock Holmes, it seems, is immortal. Are you ready to match your wits against so great a detective? Look sharp.

The Adventure of the Speckled Band

IN GLANCING OVER my notes of the seventy-odd cases in which I have during the last eight years studied the methods of my friend Sherlock Holmes, I find many tragic, some comic, a large number merely strange, but none commonplace; for, working as he did rather for the love of his art than for the acquirement of wealth, he refused to associate himself with any investigation which did not tend toward the unusual, and even the fantastic. Of all these varied cases, however, I cannot recall any which presented more singular features than that which was associated with the well-known Surrey family of the Roylotts of Stoke Moran. The events in question occurred in the early days of my association with Holmes, when we were sharing rooms as bachelors in Baker Street. It is possible that I might have placed them upon record before, but a promise of secrecy was made at the time, from which I have only been freed during the last month by the untimely death of the lady to whom the pledge was given. It is perhaps as well that the facts should now come to light, for I have reasons to know that there are widespread rumors as to the death of Dr. Grimesby Roylott which tend to make the matter even more terrible than the truth.

It was early in April in the year '83 that I woke one morning to find Sherlock Holmes standing, fully dressed, by the side of my bed. He was a late riser as a rule, and as the clock on the mantelpiece showed me that it was only a quarter past seven, I blinked up at him in some surprise, and perhaps just a little resentment, for I was myself regular in my habits.

"Very sorry to wake you up, Watson," said he, "but it's the common lot this morning. Mrs. Hudson has been stirred up, she retorted upon me, and I on you."

"What is it, then—a fire?"

"No; a client. It seems that a young lady has arrived in a considerable state of excitement, who insists upon seeing me. She is waiting now in the sitting room. Now, when young ladies wander about the metropolis at this hour of the morning, and knock sleepy people up out of their beds, I presume that it is something very pressing which they have to communicate. Should it prove to be an interesting case, you would, I am sure, wish to follow it from the outset. I thought, at any rate, that I should call you and give you the chance."

"My dear fellow, I would not miss it for anything."

I had no keener pleasure than in following Holmes in his professional investigations, and in admiring the rapid deductions, as swift as intuitions, and yet always founded on a logical basis, with which he unraveled the problems which were submitted to him. I rapidly threw on my clothes, and was ready in a few minutes to accompany my friend down to the sitting room. A lady dressed in black and heavily veiled, who had been sitting in the window, rose as we entered.

"Good morning madam," said Holmes, cheerily. "My name is Sherlock Holmes. This is my intimate friend and associate, Dr. Watson, before whom you can speak as freely as before myself. Ha! I am glad to see that Mrs. Hudson has had the good sense to light the fire. Pray draw up to it, and I shall order you a cup of hot coffee, for I observe that you are shivering."

"It is not cold which makes me shiver," said the woman, in a low voice, changing her seat as requested.

"What, then?"

"It is fear, Mr. Holmes. It is terror." She raised her veil as she spoke, and we could see that she was indeed in a pitiable state of agitation, her face all drawn and gray, with restless, frightened eyes, like those of some hunted animal. Her features and figure were those of a woman of thirty, but her hair was shot with premature gray, and her expression was weary and haggard. Sherlock Holmes ran her over with one of his quick, all-comprehensive glances.

"You must not fear," said he, soothingly, bending forward and patting her forearm. "We shall soon set matters right, I have no doubt. You have come in by train this morning, I see."

"You know me, then?"

"No, but I observe the second half of a return ticket in the palm of your left glove. You must have started early, and yet you had a good drive in a dogcart, along heavy roads, before you reached the station."

The lady gave a violent start, and stared in bewilderment at my companion.

"There is no mystery, my dear madam," said he, smiling. "The left arm of your jacket is spattered with mud in no less than seven places. The marks are perfectly fresh. There is no vehicle save a dogcart which throws up mud in that way, and then only when you sit on the left-hand side of the driver."

"Whatever your reasons may be, you are perfectly correct," said she. "I started from home before six, reached Leatherhead at twenty past, and came in by the first train to Waterloo. Sir, I can stand this strain no longer; I shall go mad if it continues. I have no one to turn to—none, save only one, who cares for me, and he, poor fellow, can be of little aid.

I have heard of you, Mr. Holmes; I have heard of you from Mrs. Farintosh, whom you helped in the hour of her sore need. It was from her that I had your address. Oh, sir, do you not think that you could help me, too, and at least throw a little light through the dense darkness which surrounds me? At present it is out of my power to reward you for your services, but in a month or six weeks I shall be married, with the control of my own income, and then at least you shall not find me ungrateful."

Holmes turned to his desk, and unlocking it, drew out a small casebook, which he consulted.

"Farintosh," said he. "Ah yes, I recall the case; it was concerned with an opal tiara. I think it was before your time, Watson. I can only say, madam, that I shall be happy to devote the same care to your case as I did to that of your friend. As to reward, my profession is its own reward; but you are at liberty to defray whatever expenses I may be put to, at the time which suits you best. And now I beg that you will lay before us everything that may help us in forming an opinion upon the matter."

"Alas!" replied our visitor, "the very horror of my situation lies in the fact that my fears are so vague, and my suspicions depend so entirely upon small points, which might seem trivial to another, that even he to whom of all others I have a right to look for help and advice looks upon all that I tell him about it as the fancies of a nervous woman. He does not say so, but I can read it from his soothing answers and averted eyes. But I have heard, Mr. Holmes, that you can see deeply into the manifold wickedness of the human heart. You may advise me how to walk amid the dangers which encompass me."

"I am all attention, madam."

"My name is Helen Stoner, and I am living with my stepfather, who is the last survivor of one of the oldest Saxon families in England, the Roylotts of Stoke Moran, on the western border of Surrey."

Holmes nodded his head. "The name is familiar to me," said he.

"The family was at one time amongst the richest in England, and the estates extended over the borders into Berkshire in the north and Hampshire in the west. In the last century, however, four successive heirs were of a dissolute and wasteful disposition, and the family ruin was eventually completed by a gambler in the days of the Regency. Nothing was left save a few acres of ground, and the two-hundred-year-old house, which is itself crushed under a heavy mortgage. The last squire dragged out his existence there, living the horrible life of an aristocratic pauper; but his only son, my stepfather, seeing that he must adapt himself to the new conditions, obtained an advance from a relative, which enabled him to take a medical degree, and went out to Calcutta, where, by his professional skill and his force of character, he established a large practice. In a fit of anger, however, caused by some robberies which had been perpetrated in the house, he beat his native butler to death, and narrowly escaped a capital sentence. As it was, he suffered a long term of imprisonment, and afterward returned to England a morose and disappointed man.

"When Dr. Roylott was in India he married my mother, Mrs. Stoner, the young widow of Major-General Stoner, of the Bengal Artillery. My sister Julia and I were twins, and we were only two years old at the time of my mother's remarriage. She had a considerable sum of money—not less than £ 1000 a year—and this she bequeathed to Dr. Roylott entirely while we resided with him, with a provision that a certain annual sum should be allowed to each of us in the event of our marriage. Shortly after our return to England my mother died—she was killed eight years ago in a railway accident near Crewe. Dr. Roylott then abandoned his attempts to establish himself in practice in London, and took us to live with him in the old ancestral house at Stoke Moran. The money which my mother had left was enough for all our wants, and there seemed to be no obstacle to our happiness.

"But a terrible change came over our stepfather about this time. Instead of making friends and exchanging visits with our neighbors, who had at first been overjoyed to see a Roylott of Stoke Moran back in the old family seat, he shut himself up in his house, and seldom came out save to indulge in ferocious quarrels with whoever might cross his path. Violence of temper approaching to mania has been hereditary in the men of the family, and in my stepfather's case it had, I believe, been intensified by his long residence in the tropics. A series of disgraceful brawls took place, two of which ended in the police court, until at last he became the terror of the village, and the folks would fly at his approach, for he is a man of immense strength, and absolutely uncontrollable in his anger.

"Last week he hurled the local blacksmith over a parapet into a stream, and it was only by paying over all the money which I could gather together that I was able to avert another public exposure. He had no friends at all save the wandering gypsies, and he would give these vagabonds leave to encamp upon the few acres of bramble-covered land which represent the family estate, and would accept in return the hospitality of their tents, wandering away with them sometimes for weeks on end. He has a passion also for Indian animals, which are sent over to him by a correspondent, and he has at this moment a cheetah and a baboon, which wander freely over his grounds, and are feared by the villagers almost as much as their master.

"You can imagine from what I say that my poor sister Julia and I had no great pleasure in our lives. No servant would stay with us, and for a long time we did all the work of the house. She was but thirty at the time of her death, and yet her hair had already begun to whiten, even as mine has."

"Your sister is dead, then?"

"She died just two years ago, and it is of her death that I wish to speak to you. You can understand that, living the life which I have described, we were little likely to see anyone of our own age and position. We had, however, an aunt, my mother's maiden sister, Miss Honoria Westphail, who lives near Harrow, and we were occasionally allowed to pay short visits at this lady's house. Julia went there at Christmas two years ago, and met there a half-pay major of marines, to whom she became engaged. My stepfather learned of the engagement when my sister returned, and offered no objection to the marriage; but within a fortnight of the day which had been fixed for the wedding, the terrible event occurred which has deprived me of my only companion."

Sherlock Holmes had been leaning back in his chair with his eyes closed and his head sunk in a cushion, but he half opened his lids now and glanced across at his visitor.

"Pray be precise as to details," said he.

"It is easy for me to be so, for every event of that dreadful time is seared into my memory. The manor house is, as I have already said, very old, and only one wing is now inhabited. The bedrooms in this wing are on the ground floor, the sitting rooms being in the central block of the buildings. Of these bedrooms the first is Dr. Roylott's, the second my sister's, and the third my own. There is no communication between them, but they all open out into the same corridor. Do I make myself plain?"

"Perfectly so."

"The windows of the three rooms open out upon the lawn. That fatal night Dr. Roylott had gone to his room early, though we knew that he had not retired to rest, for my sister was troubled by the smell of the strong Indian cigars which it was his custom to smoke. She left her room, therefore, and came into mine, where she sat for some time, chatting about her approaching wedding. At eleven o'clock, she rose to leave me, but she paused at the door and looked back.

" 'Tell me, Helen,' said she, 'have you ever heard anyone whistle in the dead of the night?'

" 'Never,' said I.

" 'I suppose that you could not possibly whistle, yourself, in your sleep?'

" 'Certainly not. But why?'

" 'Because during the last few nights I have always, about three in the morning, heard a low, clear whistle. I am a light sleeper, and it has awakened me. I cannot tell where it came from—perhaps from the next room, perhaps from the lawn. I thought that I would just ask you whether you had heard it.'

" 'No, I have not. It must be those wretched gypsies in the plantation.'

" 'Very likely. And yet if it were on the lawn, I wonder that you did not hear it also.'

" 'Ah, but I sleep more heavily than you.'

" 'Well, it is of no great consequence, at any rate.' She smiled back at me, closed my door, and a few moments later I heard her key turn in the lock."

"Indeed," said Holmes. "Was it your custom always to lock yourself in at night?"

"Always."

"And why?"

"I think that I mentioned to you that the doctor kept a cheetah and a baboon. We had no feeling of security unless our doors were locked."

"Quite so. Pray proceed with your statement."

"I could not sleep that that night. A vague feeling of impending misfortune impressed me. My sister and I, you will recollect, were twins, and you know how subtle are the links which bind two souls which are so closely allied. It was a wild night. The wind was howling outside, and the rain was beating and splashing against the windows. Suddenly, amid all the hubbub of the gale, there burst forth the wild scream of a terrified woman. I knew that it was my sister's voice. I sprang from my bed, wrapped a shawl round me, and rushed into the corridor. As I opened my door I seemed to hear a low whistle, such as my sister described, and a few moments later a clanging sound, as if a mass of metal had fallen. As I ran down the passage my sister's door was unlocked, and revolved slowly upon its hinges. I stared at it horror-stricken, not knowing what was about to issue from it. By the light of the corridor lamp I saw my sister appear at the opening, her face blanched with terror, her hands groping for help, her whole figure swaying to and fro like that of a drunkard. I ran to her and threw my arms round her, but at that moment her knees seemed to give way and she fell to the ground. She writhed as one who is in terrible pain, and her limbs were dreadfully convulsed. At first I thought that she had not recognized me, but as I bent over her she suddenly shrieked out, in a voice which I shall never forget: 'Oh, my God! Helen! It was the band! The speckled band!' There was something else which she would fain have said, and she stabbed with her finger into the air in the direction of the doctor's room, but a fresh convulsion seized her and choked her words. I rushed out, calling loudly for my stepfather, and I met him hastening from his room in his dressing gown. When he reached my sister's side she was unconscious, and though he poured brandy down her throat and sent for medical aid from the village, all efforts were in vain, for she slowly sank and died without having recovered her consciousness. Such was the dreadful end of my beloved sister."

"One moment," said Holmes; "are you sure about this whistle and metallic sound? Could you swear to it?"

"That was what the country coroner asked me at the inquiry. It is my strong impression that I heard it, and yet, among the crash of the gale and the creaking of an old house, I may possibly have been deceived."

"Was your sister dressed?"

"No, she was in her nightdress. In her right hand was found the charred stump of a match, and in her left a matchbox."

"Showing that she had struck a light and looked about her when the alarm took place. That is important. And what conclusions did the coroner come to?"

"He investigated the case with great care, for Dr. Roylott's conduct had long been notorious in the county, but he was unable to find any satisfactory cause of death. My evidence showed that the door had been fastened upon the inner side, and the windows were blocked by old-fashioned shutters with broad iron bars, which were secured every night. The walls were carefully sounded, and were shown to be quite solid all round, and the flooring was also thoroughly examined, with the same result. The chimney is wide, but is barred up by four large staples. It is certain, therefore, that my sister was quite alone when she met her end. Besides, there were no marks of any violence upon her."

"What about poison?"

"The doctors examined her for it, but without any success."

"What do you think that this unfortunate lady died of, then?"

"It is my belief that she died of pure fear and nervous shock, though what it was that frightened her I cannot imagine."

"Were there gypsies in the plantation at the time?"

"Yes, there are nearly always some there."

"Ah, and what did you gather from this allusion to a band—a speckled band?"

"Sometimes I have thought that it was merely the wild talk of delirium, sometimes that it may have referred to some band of people, perhaps to these very gypsies in the plantation. I do not know whether the spotted handkerchief which so many of them wear over their heads might have suggested the strange adjective which she used."

Holmes shook his head like a man who is far from being satisfied.

"These are very deep waters," said he; "pray go on with your narrative."

"Two years have passed since then, and my life has been until lately lonelier than ever. A month ago, however, a dear friend, whom I have known for many years, has done me the honor to ask my hand in marriage. His name is Armitage—Percy Armitage—the second son of Mr. Armitage, of Crane Water, near Reading. My stepfather has offered no opposition to the match, and we are to be married in the course of the spring. Two days ago some repairs were started in the west wing of the building, and my bedroom wall has been pierced, so that I have had to move into the chamber in which my sister died, and to sleep in the very bed in which she slept. Imagine, then, my thrill of terror when last night, as I lay awake, thinking over her terrible fate, I suddenly heard in the silence of the night the low whistle which had been the herald of her own death. I sprang up and lit the lamp, but nothing was to be seen in the room. I was too shaken to go to bed again, however, so I dressed, and as soon as it was daylight I slipped down, got a dogcart at the 'Crown Inn,' which is opposite, and drove to Leatherhead, from whence I have come on this morning with the one object of seeing you and asking your advice."

"You have done wisely," said my friend. "But have you told me all?"

"Yes, all."

"Miss Roylott, you have not. You are screening your stepfather."

"Why, what do you mean?"

For answer Holmes pushed back the frill of black lace which fringed the hand that lay upon our visitor's knee. Five little livid spots, the marks of four fingers and a thumb, were printed upon the white wrist.

"You have been cruelly used," said Holmes.

The lady colored deeply and covered over her injured wrist.

"He is a hard man," she said, "and perhaps he hardly knows his own strength."

There was a long silence, during which Holmes leaned his chin upon his hands and stared into the crackling fire.

"This is a very deep business," he said, at last. "There are a thousand details which I should desire to know before I decide upon our course of action. Yet we have not a moment to lose. If we were to come to Stoke Moran today, would it be possible for us to see over these rooms without the knowledge of your stepfather?"

"As it happens, he spoke of coming into town today upon some most important business. It is probable that he will be away all day, and that there would be nothing to disturb you. We have a housekeeper now, but she is old and foolish, and I could easily get her out of the way."

"Excellent. You are not averse to this trip, Watson?"

"By no means."

"Then we shall both come. What are you going to do yourself?"

"I have one or two things which I would wish to do now that I am in town. But I shall return by the twelve o'clock train, so as to be there in time for your coming."

"And you may expect us early in the afternoon. I have myself some small business matters to attend to. Will you not wait and breakfast?"

"No, I must go. My heart is lightened already since I have confided my trouble to you. I shall look forward to seeing you again this afternoon." She dropped her thick black veil over her face and glided from the room.

"And what do you think of it all, Watson?" asked Sherlock Holmes, leaning back in his chair.

"It seems to me to be a most dark and sinister business."

"Dark enough and sinister enough."

"Yet if the lady is correct in saying that the flooring and walls are sound, and that the door, window, and chimney are impassable, then her sister must have been undoubtedly alone when she met her mysterious end."

"What becomes, then, of these noctural whistles, and what of the very peculiar words of the dying woman?"

"I cannot think."

"When you combine the ideas of whistles at night, the presence of a band of gypsies who are on intimate terms with this old doctor, the fact that we have every reason to believe that the doctor has an interest in preventing his stepdaughter's marriage, the dying allusion to a band, and, finally, the fact that Miss Helen Stoner heard a metallic clang, which might have been caused by one of those metal bars which secured the shutters falling back into its place, I think that there is good ground to think that the mystery may be cleared along those lines."

"But what, then, did the gypsies do?"

"I cannot imagine."

"I see many objections to any such theory."

"And so do I. It is precisely for that reason that we are going to Stoke Moran this day. I want to see whether the objections are fatal, or if they may be explained away. But what in the name of the devil!"

The outburst had been drawn from my companion by the fact that our door had been suddenly dashed open, and that a huge man had framed himself in the aperture. His costume was a peculiar mixture of the professional and of the agricultural, having a black top hat, a long frock coat, and a pair of high gaiters, with a hunting crop swinging in his hand. So tall was he that his hat actually brushed the crossbar of the doorway, and his breadth seemed to span it across from side to side. A large face, seared with a thousand wrinkles, burned yellow with the sun, and marked with every evil passion, was turned from one to the other of us, while his deep-set, bile-shot eyes and his high, thin, fleshless nose gave him somewhat the resemblance to a fierce old bird of prey.

"Which of you is Holmes?" asked this apparition.

"My name, sir; but you have the advantage of me," said my companion, quietly.

"I am Dr. Grimesby Roylott, of Stoke Moran."

"Indeed, doctor," said Holmes, blandly. "Pray take a seat."

"I will do nothing of the kind. My stepdaughter has been here. I have traced her. What has she been saying to you?"

"It is a little cold for the time of the year," said Holmes.

"What has she been saying to you?" screamed the old man, furiously.

"But I have heard that the crocuses promise well," continued my companion, imperturbably.

"Ha! You put me off, do you?" said our new visitor, taking a step forward and shaking his hunting crop. "I know you, you scoundrel! I have heard of you before. You are Holmes, the meddler."

My friend smiled.

"Holmes, the busybody!"

His smile broadened.

"Holmes, the Scotland Yard Jack-in-office!"

Holmes chuckled heartily. "Your conversation is most entertaining," said he. "When you go out close the door, for there is a decided draft."

"I will go when I have said my say. Don't you dare to meddle with my affairs. I know that Miss Stoner has been here. I traced her! I am a dangerous man to fall foul of! See here." He stepped swiftly forward, seized the poker, and bent it into a curve with his huge brown hands.

"See that you keep yourself out of my grip," he snarled; and hurling the twisted poker into the fireplace, he strode out of the room.

"He seems a very amiable person," said Holmes, laughing. "I am not quite so bulky, but if he had remained I might have shown him that my grip was not much more feeble than his own." As he spoke he picked up the steel poker, and with a sudden effort straightened it out again.

"Fancy his having the insolence to confound me with the official detective force! This incident gives zest to our investigation, however, and I only trust that our little friend will not suffer from her imprudence in allowing this brute to trace her. And now, Watson, we shall order breakfast, and afterward I shall walk down to Doctors' Commons, where I hope to get some data which may help us in this matter."

It was nearly one o'clock when Sherlock Holmes returned from his excursion. He held in his hand a sheet of blue paper, scrawled over with notes and figures.

"I have seen the will of the deceased wife," said he. "To determine its exact meaning I have been obliged to work out the present prices of the investments with which it is concerned. The total income, which at the time of the wife's death was little short of £1100, is now, through the fall in agricultural prices, not more than £750. Each daughter can claim an income of £250, in case of marriage. It is evident, therefore, that if both girls had married, this beauty would have had a mere pittance, while even one of them would cripple him to a very serious extent. My morning's work has not been wasted, since it has proved that he has the very strongest motives for standing in the way of anything of the sort. And now, Watson, this is too serious for dawdling, especially as the old man is aware that we are interesting ourselves in his affairs; so if you are ready, we shall call a cab and drive to Waterloo. I should be very much obliged if you would slip your revolver into your pocket. An Eley's No. 2 is an excellent argument with gentlemen who can twist steel pokers into knots. That and a toothbrush are, I think, all that we need."

At Waterloo we were fortunate in catching a train for Leatherhead, where we hired a trap at the station inn, and drove for four or five miles through the lovely Surrey lanes. It was a perfect day, with a bright sun and a few fleecy clouds in the heavens. The trees and wayside hedges were just throwing out their first green shoots, and the air was full of the pleasant smell of the moist earth. To me at least there was a strange contrast between the sweet promise of spring and this sinister quest upon which we were engaged. My companion sat in front of the trap, his arms folded, his hat pulled down over his eyes, and his chin sunk upon his breast, buried in the deepest thought. Suddenly, however, he started, tapped me on the shoulder, and pointed over the meadows.

"Look there!" said he.

A heavily timbered park stretched up in a gentle slope, thickening into a grove at the highest point. From amid the branches there jutted out the gray gables and high rooftree of a very old mansion.

"Stoke Moran?" said he.

"Yes, sir, that be the house of Dr. Grimesby Roylott," remarked the driver.

"There is some building going on there," said Holmes; "that is where we are going."

"There's the village," said the driver, pointing to a cluster of roofs some distance to the left; "but if you want to get to the house, you'll find it shorter to get over this stile, and so by the footpath over the fields. There it is, where the lady is walking."

"And the lady, I fancy, is Miss Stoner," observed Holmes, shading his eyes. "Yes, I think we had better do as you suggest."

We got off, paid our fare, and the trap rattled back on its way to Leatherhead.

"I thought it as well," said Holmes, as we climbed the stile, "that this fellow should think we had come here as architects or on some definite business. It may stop his gossip. Good afternoon, Miss Stoner. You see that we have been as good as our word."

Our client of the morning had hurried forward to meet us with a face which spoke her joy. "I have been waiting so eagerly for you!" she cried, shaking hands with us warmly. "All has turned out splendidly. Dr.

Roylott has gone to town, and it is unlikely that he will be back before evening."

"We have had the pleasure of making the doctor's acquaintance," said Holmes, and in a few words he sketched out what had occurred. Miss Stoner turned white to the lips as she listened.

"Good heavens!" she cried. "He has followed me, then."

"So it appears."

"He is so cunning that I never know when I am safe from him. What will he say when he returns?"

"He must guard himself, for he may find that there is someone more cunning than himself upon his track. You must lock yourself up from him tonight. If he is violent, we shall take you away to your aunt's at Harrow. Now, we must make the best use of our time, so kindly take us at once to the rooms which we are to examine."

The building was of gray, lichen-blotched stone, with a high central portion, and two curving wings, like the claws of a crab, thrown out on each side. In one of these wings the windows were broken, and blocked with wooden boards, while the roof was partly caved in, a picture of ruin. The central portion was in little better repair, but the right-hand block was comparatively modern, and the blinds in the windows, with the blue smoke curling up from the chimneys, showed that this was where the family resided. Some scaffolding had been erected against the end wall, and the stonework had been broken into, but there were no signs of any workmen at the moment of our visit. Holmes walked slowly up and down the ill-trimmed lawn, and examined with deep attention the outsides of the windows.

"This, I take it, belongs to the room in which you used to sleep, the center one to your sister's, and the one next to the main building to Dr. Roylott's chamber?"

"Exactly so. But I am now sleeping in the middle one."

"Pending the alterations, as I understand. By the way, there does not seem to be any very pressing need for repairs at that end wall."

"There were none. I believe that it was an excuse to move me from my room."

"Ah! that is suggestive. Now, on the other side of this narrow wing runs the corridor from which these three rooms open. There are windows in it, of course?"

"Yes, but very small ones. Too narrow for anyone to pass through."

"As you both locked your doors at night, your rooms were unapproachable from that side. Now, would you have the kindness to go into your room and bar your shutters."

Miss Stoner did so, and Holmes, after a careful examination through the open window, endeavored in every way to force the shutter open, but without success. There was no slit through which a knife could be passed to raise the bar. Then with his lens he tested the hinges, but they were of solid iron, built firmly into the massive masonry. "Hum!" said he, scratching his chin in some perplexity; "my theory certainly presents some difficulties. No one could pass these shutters if they were bolted. Well, we shall see if the inside throws any light upon the matter."

A small side door led into the whitewashed corridor from which the three bedrooms opened. Holmes refused to examine the third chamber, so we passed at once to the second, that in which Miss Stoner was now sleeping, and in which her sister had met with her fate. It was a homely little room, with a low ceiling and a gaping fireplace, after the fashion of old country houses. A brown chest of drawers stood in one corner, a narrow white-counterpaned bed in another, and a dressing table on the left-hand side of the window. These articles, with two small wickerwork chairs, made up all the furniture in the room, save for a square of Wilton carpet in the center. The boards round and the paneling of the walls were of brown, worm-eaten oak, so old and discolored that it may have dated from the original building of the house. Holmes drew one of the chairs into a corner and sat silent, while his eyes traveled round and round and up and down, taking in every detail of the apartment.

"Where does that bell communicate with?" he asked, at last, pointing to a thick bell rope which hung down beside the bed, the tassel actually lying upon the pillow.

"It goes to the housekeeper's room."

"It looks newer than the other things."

"Yes, it was only put there a couple of years ago."

"Your sister asked for it, I suppose?"

"No, I never heard of her using it. We used always to get what we wanted for ourselves."

"Indeed, it seemed unnecessary to put so nice a bellpull there. You will excuse me for a few minutes while I satisfy myself as to this floor." He threw himself down upon his face with his lens in his hand, and crawled swiftly backward and forward, examining minutely the cracks between the boards. Then he did the same with the woodwork with which the chamber was paneled. Finally he walked over to the bed, and spent some time in staring at it, and in running his eye up and down the wall. Finally he took the bell rope in his hand and gave it a brisk tug.

"Why, it's a dummy," said he.

"Won't it ring?"

"No, it is not even attached to a wire. This is very interesting. You can see now that it is fastened to a hook just above where the little opening for the ventilator is."

"How very absurd! I never noticed that before."

"Very strange!" muttered Holmes, pulling at the rope. "There are one or two very singular points about this room. For example, what a fool a builder must be to open a ventilator into another room, when, with the same trouble, he might have communicated with the outside air!"

"That is also quite modern," said the lady.

"Done about the same time as the bell rope?" remarked Holmes.

"Yes, there were several little change carried out about that time."

"They seem to have been of a most interesting character—dummy bell ropes, and ventilators which do not ventilate. With your permission, Miss Stoner, we shall now carry our researches into the inner apartment."

Dr. Grimesby Roylott's chamber was larger than that of his step-daughter, but was as plainly furnished. A camp bed, a small wooden shelf full of books, mostly of a technical character, an armchair beside the bed, a plain wooden chair against the wall, a round table, and a large iron safe were the principal things which met the eye. Holmes walked slowly round and examined each and all of them with the keenest interest.

"What's in here?" he asked, tapping the safe.

"My stepfather's business papers."

"Oh! you have seen inside, then?"

"Only once, some years ago. I remember that it was full of papers."

"There isn't a cat in it, for example?"

"No. What a strange idea!"

"Well, look at this!" He took up a small saucer of milk which stood on the top of it.

"No; we don't keep a cat. But there is a cheetah and a baboon."

"Ah, yes, of course! Well, a cheetah is just a big cat, and yet a saucer of milk does not go very far in satisfying its wants, I dare say. There is one point which I should wish to determine." He squatted down in front of the wooden chair, and examined the seat of it with the greatest attention.

"Thank you. That is quite settled," said he, rising and putting his lens in his pocket. "Hello! Here is something interesting!"

The object which had caught his eye was a small dog leash hung on one corner of the bed. The leash, however, was curled upon itself, and tied so as to make a loop of whipcord.

"What do you make of that, Watson?"

"It's a common enough leash. But I don't know why it should be tied."

"That is not quite so common, is it? Ah, me! It's a wicked world, and when a clever man turns his brains to crime it is the worst of all. I think that I have seen enough now, Miss Stoner, and with your permission we shall walk out upon the lawn."

I had never seen my friend's face so grim or his brow so dark as it was when we turned from the scene of this investigation. We had walked several times up and down the lawn, neither Miss Stoner nor myself liking to break in upon his thoughts before he roused himself from his reverie.

"It is very essential, Miss Stoner," said he, "that you should absolutely follow my advice in every respect."

"I shall most certainly do so."

"The matter is too serious for any hesitation. Your life may depend upon your compliance."

"I assure you that I am in your hands."

"In the first place, both my friend and I must spend the night in your room."

Both Miss Stoner and I gazed at him in astonishment.

"Yes, it must be so. Let me explain. I believe that that is the village inn over there?"

"Yes, that is the 'Crown.'"

"Very good. Your windows would be visible from there?"

"Certainly."

"You must confine yourself to your room, on pretence of a headache, when your stepfather comes back. Then when you hear him retire for the night, you must open the shutters of your window, undo the hasp, put your lamp there as a signal to us, and then withdraw quietly with everything which you are likely to want into the room which you used to occupy. I have no doubt, that, in spite of the repairs, you could manage there for one night."

"Oh yes, easily."

"The rest you will leave in our hands."

"But what will you do?"

"We shall spend the night in your room, and we shall investigate the cause of this noise which has disturbed you."

"I believe, Mr. Holmes, that you have already made up your mind," said Miss Stoner, laying her hand upon my companion's sleeve.

"Perhaps I have."

"Then, for pity's sake, tell me what was the cause of my sister's death."

"I should prefer to have clearer proofs before I speak."

"You can at least tell me whether my own thought is correct, and if she died from some sudden fright."

"No, I do not think so. I think that there was probably some more tangible cause. And now, Miss Stoner, we must leave you, for if Dr. Roylott returned and saw us, our journey would be in vain. Good-bye, and be brave, for if you will do what I have told you, you may rest assured that we shall soon drive away the dangers that threaten you."

Sherlock Holmes and I had no difficulty in engaging a bedroom and sitting room at the "Crown Inn." They were on the upper floor, and from our window we could command a view of the avenue gate, and of the inhabited wing of Stoke Moran manor house. At dusk we saw Dr. Grimesby Roylott drive past, his huge form looming up beside the little figure of the lad who drove him. The boy had some slight difficulty in undoing the heavy iron gates, and we heard the hoarse roar of the doctor's voice, and saw the fury with which he shook his clinched fists at him. The trap drove on, and a few minutes later we saw a sudden light spring up among the trees as the lamp was lit in one of the sitting rooms.

"Do you know, Watson," said Holmes, as we sat together in the gathering darkness, "I have really some scruples as to taking you tonight. There is a distinct element of danger."

"Can I be of assistance?"

"Your presence might be invaluable."

"Then I shall certainly come."

"It is very kind of you."

"You speak of danger. You have evidently seen more in these rooms than was visible to me."

"No, but I fancy that I may have deduced a little more. I imagine that you saw all that I did."

"I saw nothing remarkable save the bell rope, and what purpose that could answer I confess is more than I can imagine."

"You saw the ventilator, too?"

"Yes, but I do not think that it is such a very unusual thing to have a small opening between two rooms. It was so small that a rat could hardly pass through."

"I knew that we should find a ventilator before ever we came to Stoke Moran."

"My dear Holmes!"

"Oh yes, I did. You remember in her statement she said that her sister could smell Dr. Roylott's cigar. Now, of course, that suggested at once that there must be a communication between the two rooms. It could only be a small one, or it would have been remarked upon at the coroner's inquiry. I deduced a ventilator."

"But what harm can there be in that?"

"Well, there is at least a curious coincidence of dates. A ventilator is made, a cord is hung, and a lady who sleeps in the bed dies. Does not that strike you?"

"I cannot as yet see any connection."

"Did you observe anything very peculiar about that bed?"

"No."

"It was clamped to the floor. Did you ever see a bed fastened like that before?"

"I cannot say that I have."

"The lady could not move her bed. It must always be in the same relative position to the ventilator and to the rope—for so we may call it, since it was clearly never meant for a bellpull."

"Holmes," I cried, "I seem to see dimly what you are hinting at! We are only just in time to prevent some subtle and horrible crime."

"Subtle enough and horrible enough. When a doctor does go wrong, he is the first of criminals. He has nerve and he has knowledge. Palmer and Pritchard were among the heads of their profession. This man strikes even deeper; but I think, Watson, that we shall be able to strike deeper still. But we shall have horrors enough before the night is over; for goodness' sake let us have a quiet pipe, and turn our minds for a few hours to something more cheerful."

About nine o'clock the light among the trees was extinguished, and all was dark in the direction of the manor house. Two hours passed slowly away, and then, suddenly, just at the stroke of eleven, a single bright light shone out in front of us.

"That is our signal," said Holmes, springing to his feet; "it comes from the middle window."

As we passed out he exchanged a few words with the landlord, explaining that we were going on a late visit to an acquaintance, and that it was possible that we might spend the night there. A moment later we were out on the dark road, a chill wind blowing in our faces, and one yellow light twinkling in front of us through the gloom to guide us on our somber errand.

There was little difficulty in entering the grounds, for unrepaired breaches gaped in the old park wall. Making our way among the trees, we reached the lawn, crossed it, and were about to enter through the window, when out from a clump of laurel bushes there darted what seemed to be a hideous and distorted child, who threw itself upon the grass with writhing limbs, and then ran swiftly across the lawn into the darkness.

"My God!" I whispered; "did you see it?"

Holmes was for the moment as startled as I. His hand closed like a vise upon my wrist in his agitation. Then he broke into a low laugh, and put his lips to my ear.

"It is a nice household," he murmured. "That is the baboon."

I had forgotten the strange pets which the doctor affected. There was a cheetah, too; perhaps we might find it upon our shoulders at any moment. I confess that I felt easier in my mind when, after following Holmes's example and slipping off my shoes, I found myself inside the bedroom. My companion noiselessly closed the shutters, moved the lamp onto the table, and cast his eyes round the room. All was as we had seen it in the daytime. Then creeping up to me and making a trumpet of his hand, he whispered into my ear again so gently that it was all that I could do to distinguish the words:

"The least sound would be fatal to our plans."

I nodded to show that I had heard.

"We must sit without light. He would see it through the ventilator."

I nodded again.

"Do not go asleep; your very life may depend upon it. Have your pistol ready in case we should need it. I will sit on the side of the bed, and you in that chair."

I took out my revolver and laid it on the corner of the table.

Holmes had brought up a long, thin cane, and this he placed upon the bed beside him. By it he laid the box of matches and the stump of a candle. Then he turned down the lamp, and we were left in darkness.

How shall I ever forget that dreadful vigil? I could not hear a sound, not even the drawing of a breath, and yet I knew that my companion sat open-eyed, within a few feet of me, in the same state of nervous tension in which I was myself. The shutters cut off the least ray of light, and we waited in absolute darkness. From outside came the occasional cry of a night bird, and once at our very window a long-drawn, catlike whine, which told us that the cheetah was indeed at liberty. Far away we could hear the deep tones of the parish clock, which boomed out every quarter of an hour. How long they seemed, those quarters! Twelve struck, and one and two and three, and still we sat waiting silently for whatever might befall.

Suddenly there was the momentary gleam of a light up in the direction of the ventilator, which vanished immediately, but was succeeded by a strong smell of burning oil and heated metal. Someone in the next room had lit a dark lantern. I heard a gentle sound of movement, and then all was silent once more, though the smell grew stronger. For half an hour I sat with straining ears. Then suddenly another sound became audible—a very gentle, soothing sound, like that of a small jet of steam escaping continually from a kettle. The instant that we heard it, Holmes sprang from the bed, struck a match, and lashed furiously with his cane at the bellpull.

"You see it, Watson?" he yelled. "You see it?"

But I saw nothing. At the moment when Holmes struck the light I heard a low, clear whistle, but the sudden glare flashing into my weary eyes made it impossible for me to tell what it was at which my friend lashed so savagely. I could, however, see that his face was deadly pale, and filled with horror and loathing.

He had ceased to strike, and was gazing up at the ventilator, when suddenly there broke from the silence of the night the most horrible cry to which I have ever listened. It swelled up louder and louder, a hoarse yell of pain and fear and anger all mingled in the one dreadful shriek. They say that away down in the village, and even in the distant parsonage, that cry raised the sleepers from their beds. It struck cold to our hearts, and I stood gazing at Holmes, and he at me, until the last echoes of it had died away into the silence from which it rose.

"What can it mean?" I gasped.

"It means that it is all over," Holmes answered. "And perhaps, after all, it is for the best. Take your pistol, and we will enter Dr. Roylott's room."

With a grave face he lit the lamp and led the way down the corridor. Twice he struck at the chamber door without any reply from within. Then he turned the handle and entered, I at his heels, with the cocked pistol in my hand.

It was singular sight which met our eyes. On the table stood a dark lantern with the shutter half open, throwing a brilliant beam of light upon the iron safe, the door of which was ajar. Beside this table, on the wooden chair, sat Dr. Grimesby Roylott, clad in a long gray dressing gown, his bare ankles protruding beneath, and his feet thrust into red heelless Turkish slippers. Across his lap lay the short stock with the long leash which we had noticed during the day. His chin was cocked upward and his eyes were fixed in a dreadful, rigid stare at the corner of the ceiling. Round his brow he had a peculiar yellow band, with brownish speckles, which seemed to be bound tightly round his head. As we entered he made neither sound nor motion.

"The band! the speckled band!" whispered Holmes.

I took a step forward. In an instant his strange headgear began to move, and there reared itself from among his hair the squat diamond-shaped head and puffed neck of a loathsome serpent.

"It is a swamp adder!" cried Holmes; "the deadliest snake in India. He has died within ten seconds of being bitten. Violence does, in truth, recoil upon the violent, and the schemer falls into the pit which he digs for another. Let us thrust this creature back into its den, and we can then remove Miss Stoner to some place of shelter, and let the county police know what has happened."

As he spoke he drew the dog whip swiftly from the dead man's lap, and throwing the noose round the reptile's neck, he drew it from its horrid perch, and carrying it at arm's length, threw it into the iron safe, which he closed upon it.

Such are the true facts of the death of Dr. Grimesby Roylott, of Stoke Moran. It is not necessary that I should prolong a narrative which has already run to too great a length, by telling how we broke the sad news to the terrified girl, how we conveyed her by the morning train to the care of her good aunt at Harrow, of how the slow process of official inquiry came to the conclusion that the doctor met his fate while indiscreetly playing with a dangerous pet. The little which I had yet to learn of the case was told me by Sherlock Holmes as we traveled back next day.

"I had," said he, "come to an entirely erroneous conclusion, which shows, my dear Watson, how dangerous it always is to reason from insufficient data. The presence of the gypsies, and the use of the word 'band,' which was used by the poor girl, no doubt to explain the appearance which she had caught a hurried glimpse of by the light of her match, were sufficient to put me upon an entirely wrong scent. I can only claim the merit that I instantly reconsidered my position when, however, it became clear to me that whatever danger threatened an occupant of the room could not come either from the window or the door. My attention was speedily drawn, as I have already remarked to you, to this ventilator, and to the bell rope which hung down to the bed. The discovery that this was a dummy, and that the bed was clamped to the floor, instantly gave rise to the suspicion that the rope was there as bridge for something passing through the hole and coming to the bed. The idea of a snake instantly occurred to me, and when I coupled it with my knowledge that the doctor was furnished with a supply of creatures from India, I felt that I was probably on the right track. The idea of using a form of poison which could not possibly be discovered by any chemical test was just such a one as would occur to a clever and ruthless man who had had an Eastern training. The rapidity with which such a poison would take effect would also, from his point of view, be an advantage. It would be a sharp-eyed coroner, indeed, who could distinguish the two little dark punctures which would show where the poison fangs had done their work. Then I thought of the whistle. Of course he must recall the snake before the morning light revealed it to the victim. He had trained it, probably by the use of the milk which we saw, to return to him when summoned. He would put it through this ventilator at the hour that he thought best, with the certainty that it would crawl down the rope and land on the bed. It might or might not bite the occupant, perhaps she might escape every night for a week, but sooner or later she must fall a victim.

"I had come to these conclusions before ever I had entered his room. An inspection of his chair showed me that he had been in the habit of standing on it, which of course would be necessary in order that he should reach the ventilator. The sight of the safe, the saucer of milk, and the loop of whipcord were enough to finally dispel any doubts which may have remained. The metallic clang heard by Miss Stoner was obviously caused by her stepfather hastily closing the door of his safe upon its terrible occupant. Having once made up my mind, you know the steps which I took in order to put the matter to the proof. I heard the creature hiss, as I have no doubt that you did also, and I instantly lit the light and attacked it."

"With the result of driving it through the ventilator."

"And also with the result of causing it to turn upon its master at the other side. Some of the blows of my cane came home, and aroused its snakish temper, so that it flew upon the first person it saw. In this way I am no doubt indirectly responsible for Dr. Grimesby Roylott's death, and I cannot say that it is likely to weigh very heavily upon my conscience."

Reading for Understanding

Main Idea

1. To solve the mystery of the speckled band, Sherlock Holmes had to rely heavily on observation and (a) luck (b) sentiment (c) reasoning (d) strength.

Details

2. A low, clear whistle was used to signal (a) the gypsies (b) the adder (c) the cheetah (d) the baboon.
3. Helen's wrist had been injured by (a) an animal (b) Holmes himself (c) her stepfather (d) a fall.
4. Holmes was called a busybody by (a) Watson (b) Mrs. Hudson (c) Miss Stoner (d) Dr. Roylott.
5. The odd fact about the ventilator was that (a) it was too high (b) it seemed unduly large (c) it didn't ventilate (d) it was made of a strange metal.

Inferences

6. In first speaking to Helen Stoner, Sherlock Holmes quickly showed that he was (a) indifferent (b) observant (c) unfriendly (d) humorous.
7. In his dealings with the townspeople, Dr. Roylott was (a) cruel and quarrelsome (b) calm and concerned (c) friendly but sometimes cross (d) creative and ingenious.

8. When Dr. Roylott heard of Helen Stoner's approaching marriage, he was (a) happy and relieved (b) eager to be best man (c) outspokenly opposed (d) inwardly furious.
9. The purpose of Dr. Roylott's visit to Holmes's office was to (a) welcome Holmes to Stoke Moran (b) meet Dr. Watson (c) threaten Sherlock Holmes (d) attend a convention.
10. In a word, the motive for the sister's murder was (a) jealousy (b) money (c) anger (d) power.

Order of Events

11. Arrange the items in the order in which they occurred. Use letters only.
    - A. Dr. Roylott marries Helen's mother.
    - B. Helen's sister dies mysteriously.
    - C. Helen's mother dies in a railway accident.
    - D. Helen visits Sherlock Holmes's office.
    - E. Helen's sister becomes engaged.
    - F. Dr. Roylott visits Sherlock Holmes's office.
    - G. Helen becomes engaged.

Outcome

12. If Holmes had come openly to Stoke Moran, he (a) would not have been admitted (b) would have prevented the murder more effectively (c) would have had no need of Dr. Watson (d) would have made Miss Stoner happy.

Cause and Effect

13. If Helen's sister had not become engaged, the sister (a) would have visited her aunt (b) would have disagreed violently with Dr. Roylott (c) would not have been murdered (d) would have moved into her sister's room.

Fact or Opinion

Tell whether each of the following is a fact or an opinion.

14. Despite her fears, Helen Stoner was unusually courageous.
15. Dr. Roylott had spent many years in India.

Words in Context

1. "Of all these varied cases, however, I cannot recall any which presented more *singular* features than that which was associated with the well-known Surrey family of the Roylotts of Stoke Moran." **Singular** (17) means (a) dramatic (b) unusual (c) low-key (d) violent.
2. "Her hair was shot with premature gray, and her expression was weary and *haggard*." **Haggard** (18) means (a) cheerful (b) animated (c) vicious (d) gaunt.
3. " 'You are at liberty to *defray* whatever expenses I may be put to, at the time which suits you best.' " **Defray** (19) means (a) overlook (b) pay (c) increase (d) report.
4. " 'My suspicions depend so entirely upon small points, which might seem *trivial* to another.' " **Trivial** (19) means (a) unimportant (b) exciting (c) unpopular (c) surprising.
5. " 'In the last century, however, four successive heirs were of a *dissolute* and wasteful disposition.' " **Dissolute** (19) means (a) enlightened (b) immoral (c) personable (d) mild.
6. " 'In a fit of anger, however, caused by some robberies which had been *perpetrated* in the house, he beat his native butler to death.' " **Perpetrated** (19) means (a) cleverly planned (b) observed (c) committed (d) prevented.
7. " 'He suffered a long term of imprisonment, and afterward returned to England a *morose* and disappointed man.' " **Morose** (20) means (a) optimistic (b) realistic (c) distinguished (d) sullen.
8. " 'A vague feeling of *impending* misfortune impressed me.' " **Impending** (22) means (a) menacing (b) unexpected (c) expected (d) annoying.
9. " 'By the light of the corridor lamp I saw my sister appear at the opening, her face *blanched* with terror.' " **Blanched** (22) means (a) slightly upset (b) made pale (c) smoothed (d) muddled.
10. " 'She *writhed* as one who is in terrible pain, and her limbs were dreadfully convulsed.'" **Writhed** (22) means (a) screamed (b) danced (c) twisted (d) stiffened.
11. " 'Dr. Roylott's conduct had long been *notorious* in the county.' " **Notorious** (23) means (a) unfavorably famous (b) mildly irritating (c) outstandingly brilliant (d) persistently curious.

12. " 'Ah, and what did you gather from this *allusion* to a band—a speckled band?' " **Allusion** (23) means (a) conversion (b) reference (c) challenge (d) presentation.
13. " 'You are not *averse* to this trip, Watson?' " **Averse** (24) means (a) warmly disposed (b) mildly prone (c) indifferent (d) unfavorably inclined.
14. " ' What becomes, then, of these *nocturnal* whistles, and what of the very peculiar words of the dying woman?' " **Nocturnal** (25) means (a) by day (b) at night (c) panicky (d) unexpected.
15. "Our door had been suddenly dashed open, and a huge man had framed himself in the *aperture*." **Aperture** (25) means (a) window (b) scene (c) outer room (d) opening.
16. " ' But I have heard that the crocuses promise well,' continued my companion, *imperturbably*.' " **Imperturbably** (26) means (a) hesitantly (b) angrily (c) coolly (d) dramatically.
17. " 'He seems a very *amiable* person,' said Holmes, laughing." **Amiable** (26) means (a) curious (b) agreeable (c) comical (d) unpredictable.
18. "We had walked several times up and down the lawn, neither Miss Stoner nor myself liking to break in upon his thoughts before he roused himself from his *reverie*." **Reverie** (31) means (a) anger (b) daydream (c) laziness (d) chair.
19. "How shall I ever forget that dreadful *vigil*?" **Vigil** (34) means (a) watch (b) chill (c) incident (d) exercise.
20. " 'The sight of the safe, the saucer of milk, and the loop of whipcord were enough to finally *dispel* any doubts which may have remained.'" **Dispel** (36) means (a) confirm (b) banish (c) enlarge (d) conceal.

Thinking Critically About the Story

1. List five adjectives that could be applied to Dr. Roylott—for example, *menacing*. How does the author show skill in describing the character of Dr. Roylott? (Hint: think of what he does.)
2. How would you describe Stoke Moran? Is Doyle's description vivid? Explain.
3. Once the mystery is solved, the story ends quickly. Is this a sound literary device? Why or why not?

4. Did the title arouse your curiosity? In each of the following pairs of titles, choose the one that seems superior. Tell why.
   1. The Red-headed League An Exciting Adventure
   2. A Jewel of a Story The Adventure of the Blue Carbuncle
   3. The Man with the Twisted Lip An Unusual Character
   4. An Unbelievable Story The Adventure of the Engineer's Thumb
   5. Was It a Ghost? The Hound of the Baskervilles

Language in Action

Inductive-Deductive Reasoning

Without being aware of the processes, you often use both inductive and deductive reasoning. If you enjoy Tom Hanks movies, you'll probably want to see the next one. Your reasoning runs something like this:

Major premise	All Tom Hanks movies are enjoyable.
Minor premise	This is a Tom Hanks movie.
Conclusion	This movie is enjoyable.

The pattern of the reasoning just illustrated is called a "*syllogism.*" The premises are assumptions leading to the conclusion. Deductive reasoning draws conclusions from premises, even if not actually stated. If you think eighteen-year-olds should retain the vote, your reasoning runs something like this:

Major premise	All responsible citizens should have the right to vote.
Minor premise	Eighteen-year-olds are responsible citizens.
Conclusion	Eighteen-year-olds should retain the right to vote.

The conclusion is valid, but you may dispute one of the premises or the conclusion drawn from the premises. Syllogisms are as good as the premises and resulting conclusions.

Inductive reasoning works the other way. Before a conclusion or generalization may be formulated, as much relevant information must be gained as possible. In "The Adventure of the Speckled Band," Holmes gathers many clues before deciding how Dr. Roylott performed his murderous act.

An inductive argument does not claim that its conclusions are absolutely true and certain. It claims merely that there is evidence for the truth of the conclusion. Many innocent victims have been cleared of a crime and released from prison when later evidence, often based on DNA tests, proves that the original conviction (conclusion) was wrong. The popularity of programs based on forensic evidence is a tribute to the fascination of inductive reasoning.

Inductive arguments are evaluated as probable or improbable. They are judged by questions like these:

1. How many experiences were considered?
2. Were these representative examples?
3. Were the experiences sufficiently similar?
4. Have times and conditions changed since the experiences were considered?

Fiction can afford to be more positive.

The Crime in Nobody's Room

Carter Dickson
American

"It's nobody's room, sir," the porter answered simply. "There's not a sitting room like that in the whole building."

Detective stories feature mysterious disappearances. Important clues vanish. Corpses seem to rise and walk away. Crucial articles of clothing suddenly become invisible. But to lose an entire room requires a special kind of ingenuity. It takes the genius of a Colonel March to "find" the room again.

Carter Dickson is a pen name of John Dickson Carr. He has created several sleuths. Under the **Carter Dickson** name, he introduced Colonel March and "The Old Man," Sir Henry Merrivale. Under the **John Dickson Carr** name, he gave us Gideon Fell. Though March, Merrivale, and Fell are very much alike, Carr's fans don't mind the similarities.

Colonel March, the detective in this story, is head of the Department of Queer Complaints, the Ragbag Department or the "Crazy House." He tackles problems that the regular police force is unable or unwilling to meddle with. Colonel March stories are filled with the kinds of puzzles presented in our story.

Carr is the master of the locked-room murder-mystery. In one of his stories, he actually discusses all the ways a murder can be committed within a seemingly locked room. Many of his stories seem to include supernatural elements, which are logically explained at the end. Though Carr plays fair and includes clues for the perceptive reader, his ingenious cleverness foils most puzzle solvers. Try to match wits with Colonel March in "The Crime in Nobody's Room."

The Crime in Nobody's Room

BANDS WERE PLAYING and seven suns were shining; but this took place entirely in the head and heart of Mr. Ronald Denham. He beamed on the car-park attendant at the Regency Club, who assisted him into the taxi. He beamed on the taxidriver. He beamed on the night porter who helped him out at his flat in Sloane Street, and he felt an irresistible urge to hand banknotes to everyone in sight.

Now, Ronald Denham would have denied that he had taken too many drinks. It was true that he had attended an excellent bachelor party, to celebrate Jimmy Bellchester's wedding. But Denham would have maintained that he was upheld by spiritual things; and he had proved his exalted temperance by leaving the party at a time when many of the guests were still present.

As he had pointed out in a speech, it was only a month before his own wedding to Miss Anita Bruce. Anita, in fact, lived in the same block of flats and on the same floor as himself. This fact gave him great pleasure on the way home. Like most of us, Denham in this mood felt a strong urge to wake people up in the middle of the night and talk to them. He wondered whether he ought to wake up Anita. But in his reformed state he decided against it, and felt like a saint. He would not even wake up Tom Evans, who shared the flat with him—though that stern young business man usually worked so late at the office that Denham got in before he did.

At a few minutes short of midnight, then, Denham steered his way into the foyer of Medici Court. Pearson, the night porter, followed him to the automatic lift.

"Everything all right, sir?" inquired Pearson in a stage whisper. Denham assured him that it was, and that he was an excellent fellow.

"You—er—don't feel like singing, do you, sir?" asked Pearson with some anxiety.

"As a matter of fact," said Denham, who had not previously considered this, "I do. You are full of excellent ideas, Pearson. But let us sing nothing improper, Pearson. Let it be something of noble sentiment, like——"

"Honestly, sir," urged Pearson, "if it was me, I wouldn't do it. *He's* upstairs, you know. We thought he was going to Manchester this afternoon, to stay a week, but he changed his mind. He's upstairs now."

This terrible hint referred to the autocrat of Medici Court, Cellini Court, Bourbon Court, and half a dozen other great hives. Sir Rufus Armingdale, high khan of builders, not only filled London with furnished flats which really were the last word in luxury at a low price: he showed his pride in his own merchandise by living in them.

"No special quarters for me," he was quoted as saying, with fist upraised for emphasis. "No castle in Surrey or barracks in Park Lane. Just an ordinary flat; and not the most expensive of 'em either. That's where I'm most comfortable, and that's where you'll find me."

Considering all the good things provided in Armingdale's Furnished Flats, even his autocratic laws were not much resented. Nor could anyone resent the fact that all flats in a given building were furnished exactly alike, and that the furniture must be kept in the position Rufus Armingdale gave it. Medici Court was "Renaissance," as Bourbon Court was "Louis XV": a tower of rooms like luxurious cells, and only to be distinguished from each other by an ornament on a table or a picture on a wall.

But Sir Rufus's leases even discouraged pictures. Considering that he was something of an art collector himself, and had often been photographed in his own flat with his favourite Greuze or Corot, some annoyance was felt at this. Sir Rufus Armingdale did not care. You either leased one of his flats, or you didn't. He was that that sort of man.

Otherwise, of course, Ronald Denham's adventure could not have happened. He returned from the bachelor party; he took Pearson's advice about the singing; he went up in the automatic lift to the second floor; and he walked into what the champagne told him was his own flat.

That he went to the second floor is certain. Pearson saw him put his finger on the proper button in the lift. But nothing else is certain, since the hall upstairs was dark. Pushing open a door—either his key fitted it or the door was open—Denham congratulated himself on getting home.

Also, he was a little giddy. He found himself in the small foyer, where lights were on. After a short interval he must have moved into the sitting room, for he found himself sitting back in an armchair and contemplating familiar surroundings through a haze. Lights were turned on here as well: yellow-shaded lamps, one with a pattern like a dragon on the shade.

Something began to trouble him. There was something odd, he thought, about those lamp shades. After some study, it occurred to him that he and Tom Evans hadn't any lamp shades like that. They did not own any bronze book ends either. As for the curtains . . .

Then a picture on the wall swam out of oblivion, and he stared at it. It was a small dull-coloured picture over the sideboard. And it penetrated into his mind at last that he had got into the wrong flat.

Everything now showed itself to him as wrong: it was as though a blur had come into focus.

"Here, I'm sorry!" he said aloud, and got up.

There was no reply. The heinousness of his offence partly steadied him. Where in the name of sanity was he? There were only three other flats on the second floor. One of these was Anita Bruce's. Of the others, one was occupied by a brisk young newspaper man named Conyers, and the other by the formidable Sir Rufus Armingdale.

Complete panic caught him. He felt that at any moment a wrathful occupant might descend on him, to call him a thief at worst or a snooper at best. Turning round to scramble for the door, he almost ran into another visitor in the wrong flat.

This visitor sat quietly in a tall chair near the door. He was a thin, oldish, well-dressed man, wearing thick-lensed spectacles, and his head was bent forward as though in meditation. He wore a soft hat and a thin oilskin waterproof coloured green: a jaunty and bilious-looking coat for such a quiet figure. The quiet light made it gleam.

"Please excuse——" Denham began in a rush, and talked for some seconds before he realized that the man had not moved.

Denham stretched out his hand. The coat was one of those smooth, almost seamless American waterproofs, yellowish outside and green inside; and for some reason the man was now wearing it inside out. Denham was in the act of telling him this when the head lolled, the smooth oilskin gleamed again, and he saw that the man was dead.

Tom Evans, stepping out of the lift at a quarter past one, found the hall of the second floor in complete darkness. When he had turned on the lights from a switch beside the lift, he stopped short and swore.

Evans, lean and swarthy, with darkish eyebrows merging into a single line across his forehead, looked a little like a Norman baron in a romance. Some might have said a robber baron, for he carried a brief case and was a stern man of business despite his youth. But what he saw now made him momentarily forget his evening's work. The hall showed four doors, with their microscopic black numbers, set some distance apart. Near the door leading to Anita Bruce's flat, Ronald Denham sat hunched on an oak settle. There was a lump at the base of his skull, and he was breathing in a way Evans did not like.

It was five minutes more before Denham had been whacked and pounded into semi-consciousness; and to such a blinding headache that its pain helped to revive him. First he became aware of Tom's lean, hook-nosed face bending over him, and Tom's usual fluency at preaching.

"I don't mind you getting drunk," the voice came to him dimly. "In fact, I expected it. But at least you ought to be able to carry your liquor decently. What the devil have you been up to, anyway? Hoy!"

"He had his raincoat on inside out," was the first thing Denham said. Then memory came back to him like a new headache or a new explosion, and he began to pour out the story.

"——and I tell you there's a dead man in one of those flats! I think he's been murdered. Tom, I'm not drunk; I swear I'm not. Somebody sneaked up behind and bashed me over the back of the head just after I found him."

"Then how did you get out here?"

"Oh, God, how should I know? Don't argue; help me up. I suppose I must have been dragged out here. If you don't believe me, feel the back of my head. Just feel it."

Evans hesitated. He was always practical, and there could be no denying the bruise. He looked uncertainly up and down the hall.

"But who is this dead man?" he demanded. "And whose flat is he in?"

"I don't know. He was an oldish man with thick glasses and a green raincoat. I never saw him before. Looked a bit like an American, somehow."

"Nonsense! Nobody wears a green raincoat."

"I'm telling you, he was wearing it inside out. If you ask me why, I'm going to bat my head against the wall and go to sleep again." He wished he could do this, for he could not see straight and his head felt like a printing press in full blast. "We ought to be able to identify the flat easily enough. I can give a complete description of it——"

He paused, for two doors had opened simultaneously in the hall. Anita Bruce and Sir Rufus Armingdale came out, in different stages of anger or curiosity at the noise.

If Evans had been more of a psychologist, he might have anticipated the effect this would have on them. As it was, he stood looking from one to the other, thinking whatever thoughts you care to attribute to him. For he was an employee of Sir Rufus, as manager of the Sloane Square Office of Armingdale Flats, and he could risk no trouble.

Anita seemed to take in the situation at a glance. She was small, dark, plump, and fluffy-haired. She was wearing a négligé and smoking a cigarette. Seeing the expressions of the other three, she removed the cigarette from her mouth in order to smile. Sir Rufus Armingdale did not look so much formidable as fretful. He had one of those powerful faces whose features seem to have run together like a bull pup's. But the old dressing gown, fastened up at the throat as though he were cold, took away the suggestion of an autocrat and made him only a householder.

He breathed through his nose, rather helplessly, until he saw an employee. His confidence returned.

"Good morning, Evans," he said. "What's the meaning of this?"

Evans risked it. "I'm afraid it's trouble, sir. Mr. Denham—well, he's found a dead man in one of the flats."

"Ron!" cried Anita.

"A dead man," repeated Armingdale, without surprise. "Where?"

"In one of the flats. He doesn't know which."

"Oh? why doesn't he know which?"

"He's got a frightful bump on the back of his head," said Anita, exploring. She looked back over her shoulder and spoke swiftly. "It's quite all right, Tom. Don't get excited. He's d-r-u-n-k."

"I am not drunk," said Denham, with tense and sinister calmness. "May I also point out that I am able to read and write, and that I have not had words spelled out in front of me since I was four years old? Heaven give me s-t-r-e-n-g-t-h! I tell you, I can describe the place."

He did so. Afterwards there was a silence. Anita, her eyes shining curiously, dropped her cigarette on the autocrat's hardwood floor and ground it out. The autocrat seemed too abstracted to notice.

"Ron, old dear," Anita said, going over and sitting down beside him, "I'll believe you if you're as serious as all that. But you ought to know it isn't *my* flat."

"And I can tell you it isn't mine," grunted Armingdale. "There certainly isn't a dead man in it. I've just come from there, and I know."

If they had not known Armingdale's reputation so well, they might have suspected him of trying to make a joke. But his expression belied it as well. It was heavy and lowering, with more than a suggestion of the bull pup.

"This picture you say you saw," he began. "The one over the sideboard. Could you describe it?"

"Yes, I think so," said Denham desperately. "It was a rather small portrait of a little girl looking sideways over some roses, or flowers of some kind. Done in that greyish-brown stuff; I think they call it sepia."

Armingdale stared at him.

"Then I know it isn't mine," he said. "I never owned a sepia drawing in my life. If this young man is telling the truth, there's only one flat left. I think I shall just take the responsibility of knocking, and——"

His worried gaze moved down towards the door of the flat occupied by Mr. Hubert Conyers, of the *Daily Record*. But it was unnecessary to knock at the door. It opened with such celerity that Denham wondered whether anyone had been looking at them through the slot of the letter box; and Hubert Conyers stepped out briskly. He was an unobtrusive, sandy-haired little man, very different from Denham's idea of a journalist. His only extravagance was a taste for blended shadings in his clothes, from suit to shirt to necktie; though he usually contrived to look rumpled. He was always obliging, and as busy as a parlour clock. But his manner had a subdued persuasiveness which could worm him through narrower places than you might have imagined.

He came forward drawing on his coat, and with a deft gesture he got into the middle of the group.

"Sorry, sorry, sorry," he began, seeming to propitiate everyone at once. "I couldn't help overhearing, you know. Good evening, Sir Rufus. The fact is, it's not my flat either. Just now, the only ornaments in my sitting room are a lot of well-filled ashtrays and a bottle of milk. Come and see, if you like."

There was a silence, while Conyers looked anxious.

"But it's got to be somebody's flat!" snapped Sir Rufus Armingdale, with a no-nonsense air. "Stands to reason. A whole confounded sitting room can't vanish like smoke. Unless—stop a bit—unless Mr. Denham got off at some other floor."

"I don't know. I may have."

"And I don't mind admitting——" said Armingdale, hesitating as everyone looked at him curiously. The autocrat seemed worried. "Very well. The fact is, *I've* got a picture in my flat something like the one Mr. Denham described. It's Grueze's 'Young Girl with Primroses.' But mine's an oil painting, of course. Mr. Denham is talking about a sepia drawing. That is, if he really saw anything. Does this dead man exist at all?"

Denham's protestations were cut short by the hum of an ascending lift. But it was not the ordinary lift in front of them; it was the service lift at the end of the hall. The door was opened, and the cage grating pulled back, to show the frightened face of the night porter.

"Sir," said Pearson, addressing Armingdale as though he were beginning an oration. "I'm glad to see *you,* sir. You always tell us that if something serious happens we're to come straight to you instead of the manager. Well, I'm afraid this is serious. I—the fact is, I found something in this lift."

Denham felt that they were being haunted by that phrase, "the fact is." Everybody seemed to use it. He recalled a play in which it was maintained that anyone who began a sentence like this was usually telling a lie. But he had not time to think about this, for they had found the elusive dead man.

The unknown lay on his face in one corner of the lift. A light in the roof of the steel cage shone down on his grey felt hat, on an edge of his thick spectacles, and on his oilskin waterproof. But the coat was no longer green, for he was now wearing it right-side-out in the ordinary way.

Anita, who had come quietly round beside Denham, seized his arm. The night porter restrained Tom Evans as the latter bent forward.

"I shouldn't touch him, sir, if I was you. There's blood."

"Where?"

Pearson indicated a stain on the grey-rubber floor. "And if I'm any judge, sir, he died of a stab through the heart. I—I lifted him up a bit. But I don't see any kind of knife that could have done it."

"Is this the man you saw?" Armingdale asked Denham quietly. Denham nodded. Something tangible, something to weigh and handle, seemed to have brought the force back to Armingdale's personality.

"Except," Denham added, "that he's now wearing his raincoat right-side-out. Why? Will somebody tell me that? Why?"

"Never mind the raincoat," Anita said close to his ear. "Ron, you don't know him, do you? You'll swear you don't know him?"

He was startled. She had spoken without apparent urgency, and so low that the others might not have heard her. But Denham, who knew her so well, knew that there was urgency behind the unwinking seriousness of her eyes. Unconsciously she was shaking his arm. His wits had begun to clear, despite the pain in his skull; and he wondered.

"No, of course I don't know him. Why should I?"

"Nothing! Nothing at all. Ss-t!"

"Well, I know him," said Hubert Conyers.

Conyers had been squatting down at the edge of the lift, and craning his neck to get a close view of the body without touching it. Now he straightened up. He seemed so excited that he could barely control himself, and his mild eye looked wicked.

"I interviewed him a couple of days ago," said Conyers. "Surely you know him, Sir Rufus?"

" 'Surely' is a large word, young man. No, I do not know him. Why?"

"That's Dan Randolph, the American real-estate king," said Conyers, keeping a watchful eye on Armingdale. "All of you will have heard of him: he's the fellow who always deals in spot cash, even if it's a million. I'd know those spectacles anywhere. He's as near-sighted as an owl. Er—am I correctly informed, Sir Rufus, that he was in England to do some business with you?"

Armingdale smiled bleakly. "You have no information, young man," he said. "And so far as I'm concerned you're not getting any. So that's Dan Randolph! I knew he was in England; but he's certainly not made any business proposition to me."

"Maybe he was coming to do it."

"Maybe he was," said Armingdale, with the same air of a parent to a child. He turned to Pearson. "You say you found him in that lift. When did you find him? And how did you come to find him?"

Pearson was voluble. "The lift was on the ground floor, sir. I just happened to glance through the little glass panel, and I see him lying there. So I thought I'd better run the lift up here and get you. As for putting him there——" He pointed to the recall button on the wall outside the lift. "Somebody on any floor, sir, could have shoved him in here, and pressed this button, and sent him downstairs. He certainly wasn't put in on the ground floor. Besides, I saw him come into the building to-night."

"Oh?" put in Conyers softly. "When was this?"

"Might have been eleven o'clock, sir."

"Whom was he coming to see?"

Pearson shook his head helplessly and with a certain impatience. "These ain't service flats, sir, where you telephone up about every visitor. You ought to know we're not to ask visitors anything unless they seem to need help, or unless it's somebody who has no business here. I don't know. He went up in the main lift, that's all I can tell you."

"Well, what floor did he go to?"

"I dunno." Pearson ran a finger under a tight collar. "But excuse me, sir, may I ask a question, if you please? What's wrong exactly?"

"We've lost a room," said Ronald Denham, with inspiration. "Maybe you can help. Look here, Pearson: you've been here in these flats a long time. You've been inside most of them—in the sitting rooms, for instance?"

"I think I can say I've been in all of 'em, sir."

"Good. Then we're looking for a room decorated like this," said Denham. For the third time he described what he had seen, and Pearson's expression grew to one of acute anguish. At the end of it he shook his head.

"It's nobody's room, sir," the porter answered simply. "There's not a sitting room like that in the whole building."

At three o'clock in the morning, a sombre group of people sat in Sir Rufus Armingdale's flat, and did not even look at each other. The police work was nearly done. A brisk divisional detective-inspector, accompanied by a sergeant, a photographer, and a large amiable man in a top hat, had taken a statement from each of those concerned. But the statements revealed nothing.

Denham, in fact, had received only one more mental jolt. Entering Armingdale's flat, he thought for a second that he had found the missing room. The usual chairs of stamped Spanish leather, the refectory table, the carved gewgaws, greeted him like a familiar nightmare. And over the sideboard hung a familiar picture—that of a small girl looking sideways over an armful of roses.

"That's not it?" said Anita quickly.

"It's the same subject, but it's not the same picture. That's in oils. What sort of game do you suppose is going on in this place?"

Anita glanced over her shoulder. She had dressed before the arrival of the police; and also, he thought, she had put on more make-up than was necessary.

"Quick, Ron; before the others get here. Were you telling the truth?"

"Certainly. You don't think——?"

"Oh, I don't know and I don't care; I just want you to tell me. Ron, you didn't kill him yourself?"

He had not even time to answer before she stopped him. Sir Rufus Armingdale, Conyers, and Evans came through from the foyer; and with them was the large amiable man who had accompanied Divisional Inspector Davidson. His name, it appeared, was Colonel March.

"You see," he explained, with a broad gesture, "I'm not here officially. I happened to be at the theatre, and I dropped in on Inspector Davidson for a talk, and he asked me to come along. So if you don't like any of my questions, just tell me to shut my head. But I do happen to be attached to the Yard——"

"I know you, Colonel," said Conyers, with a crooked grin. "You're the head of the Ragbag Department, D-3. Some call it the Crazy House."

Colonel March nodded seriously. He wore a dark overcoat, and had a top hat pushed back on his large head; this, with his florid complexion, sandy moustache, and bland blue eyes, gave him something of the look of a stout colonel in a comic paper. He was smoking a large-bowled pipe with the effect of seeming to sniff smoke from the bowl rather than draw it through the stem. He appeared to be enjoying himself.

"It's a compliment," he assured them. "After all, somebody has got to sift all the queer complaints. If somebody comes in and reports (say) that the Borough of Stepney is being terrorized by a blue pig, I've got to decide whether it's a piece of lunacy, or a mistake, or a hoax, or a serious crime. Otherwise good men would only waste their time. You'd be surprised how many such complaints there are. But I was thinking, and so was Inspector Davidson, that you had a very similar situation here. If you wouldn't mind a few extra questions——"

"As many as you like," said Sir Rufus Armingdale. "Provided somebody's got a hope of solving this damned——"

"As a matter of fact," said Colonel March, frowning, "Inspector Davidson has reason to believe that it is already solved. A good man, Davidson."

There was a silence. Something unintentionally sinister seemed to have gathered in Colonel March's affable tone. For a moment nobody dared to ask him what he meant.

"Already solved?" repeated Hubert Conyers.

"Suppose we begin with you, Sir Rufus," said March with great courtesy. "You have told the inspector that you did not know Daniel Randolph personally. But it seems to be common knowledge that he was in England to see you."

Armingdale hesitated. "I don't know his reasons. He may have been here to see me, among other things. Probably was. He wrote to me about it from America. But he hasn't approached me yet, and I didn't approach him first. It's bad business."

"What was the nature of this business, Sir Rufus?"

"He wanted to buy an option I held on some property in—never mind where. I'll tell you in private, if you insist."

"Was a large sum involved?"

Armingdale seemed to struggle with himself. "Four thousand, more or less."

"So it wasn't a major business deal. Were you going to sell?"

"Probably."

Colonel March's abstracted eye wandered to the picture over the sideboard. "Now, Sir Rufus, that Greuze, 'Young Girl with Primroses.' I think it was recently reproduced, in its natural size, as a full-page illustration in the *Metropolitan Illustrated News*."

"Yes, it was," said Armingdale. He added, "In—sepia."

Something about this afterthought made them all move forward to look at him. It was like the puzzle of a half truth: nobody knew what it meant.

"Exactly. Just two more questions. I believe that each of these flats communicates with a fire escape leading down into the mews behind?"

"Yes. What of it?"

"Will the same key open the front door of each of the flats?"

"No, certainly not. All the lock patterns are different."

"Thank you. Now, Mr. Conyers—a question for you. Are you married?"

Hitherto Conyers had been regarding him with a look of watchful expectancy, like an urchin about to smash a window and run. Now he scowled.

"Married? No."

"And you don't keep a valet?"

"The answer to that, Colonel, is loud and prolonged laughter. Honestly, I don't like your 'social' manner. Beston, our crime news man, knows you. And it's always, 'Blast you, Beston, if you print one hint about the Thingummy case I'll have your hide.' What difference does it make whether I'm married or not, or whether I have a valet or not?"

"A great deal," said March seriously. "Now, Miss Bruce. What is your occupation, Miss Bruce?"

"I'm an interior decorator," answered Anita.

She began to laugh. It may have been with a tinge of hysteria; but she sat back in a tall chair and laughed until there were tears in her eyes.

"I'm terribly sorry," she went on, holding out her hand as though to stop them, "but don't you see? The murder was done by an interior decorator. That's the whole secret."

Colonel March cut short Armingdale's shocked protest.

"Go on," he said sharply.

"I thought of it first off. Of course there's no 'vanishing room.' Some sitting room has just been redecorated. All the actual furnishings, tables and chairs and sideboards, are just the same in every room. The only way you can tell them apart is by small movable things—pictures, lamp shades, book ends—which could be changed in a few minutes.

"Ron accidentally walked into the murderer's flat just after the murderer had killed that old man. That put the murderer in a pretty awful position. Unless he killed Ron too, he was caught with the body and Ron could identify his flat. But he thought of a better way. He sent that man's body down in the lift and dragged Ron out into the hall. Then he simply altered the decorations of his flat. Afterwards he could sit down and dare anyone to identify it as the place where the body had been."

Anita's face was flushed with either defiance or fear.

"Warm," said Colonel March. "Unquestionably warm. That is why I was wondering whether you couldn't tell us what really happened."

"I don't understand you."

"Well, there are objections to the redecoration. You've got to suppose that nobody had ever been in the flat before and seen the way it was originally decorated. You've also got to suppose that the murderer could find a new set of lamp shades, pictures, and book ends in the middle of the night.——Haven't you got it the wrong way round?"

"The wrong way round?"

"Somebody," said March, dropping his courtesy, "prepared a dummy room to begin with. He put in the new lamp shades, the book ends, the copy of a well-known picture, even a set of new curtains. He entertained Randolph in that dummy room. He killed Randolph there. Afterwards, of course, he simply removed the knick-knacks and set the place right again. But it was the dummy room into which Ronald Denham walked. That, Mr. Denham, was why you did not recognize——"

"Recognize what?" roared Denham. "Where was I?"

"In the sitting room of your own flat," said Colonel March gravely. "If you had been sober you might have made a mistake; but you were so full of champagne that your instinct brought you home after all."

There were two doors in the room, and the blue uniform of a policeman appeared in each. At March's signal, Inspector Davidson stepped forward. He said:

"Thomas Evans, I arrest you for the murder of Daniel Randolph. I have to warn you that anything you say will be taken down in writing and may be used in evidence at your trial."

"Oh, look here," protested Colonel March, when they met in Armingdale's flat next day, "the thing was simple enough. We had twice as much trouble over that kid in Bayswater, who pinched all the oranges. And you had all the facts.

"Evans, as one of Sir Rufus's most highly placed and trusted employees, was naturally in a position to know all about the projected business deal with Randolph. And so he planned an ingenious swindle. A swindle, I am certain, was all he intended.

"Now you, Sir Rufus, had intended to go to Manchester yesterday afternoon, and remain there for a week. (Mr. Denham heard that from the night porter, when he was advised against singing.) That would leave your flat empty. Evans telephoned to Randolph, posing as you. He asked Randolph to come round to your flat at eleven o'clock at night, and settle the deal. He added that you *might* be called away to Manchester; but, in that event, his secretary would have the necessary papers ready and signed.

"It would have been easy. Evans would get into your empty flat by way of the fire escape and the window. He would pose as your secretary. Randolph—who, remember, always paid spot cash even if it involved a million—would hand over a packet of banknotes for a forged document.

"Why should Randolph be suspicious of anything? He knew, as half the newspaper-reading world knows, that Sir Rufus lived on the second floor of Medici Court. He had seen photographs of Sir Rufus with his favourite Greuze over the sideboard. Even if he asked the hall porter for directions, he would be sent to the right flat. Even if the hall porter said Sir Rufus was in Manchester, the ground had been prepared and Randolph would ask for Sir Rufus's secretary.

"Unfortunately, a hitch occurred. Sir Rufus decided not to go to Manchester. He decided it yesterday afternoon, after all Evans's plans had been made and Randolph was due to arrive. But Evans needed that money; as we have discovered to-day, he needed it desperately. He wanted that four thousand pounds.

"So he hit on another plan. Sir Rufus would be at home and his flat could not be used. But, with all the rooms exactly alike except for decorations, why not an *imitation* of Sir Rufus's flat? The same plan would hold good, except that Randolph would be taken to the wrong place. He would come up in the lift at eleven. Evans would be waiting with the door of the flat open, and would take him to a place superficially resembling Sir Rufus's. The numbers on the doors are very small; and Randolph, as we know, was so near-sighted as to be almost blind. If Evans adopted some disguise, however clumsy, he could never afterwards be identified as the man who swindled Randolph. And he ran no risk in using the flat he shared with Denham."

Anita interposed. "Of course!" she said. "Ron was at a bachelor party, and ordinarily it would have kept him there whooping until two or three o'clock in the morning. But he reformed, and came home early."

Denham groaned. "But I still can't believe it," he insisted. "Tom Evans? A murderer?"

"He intended no murder," said Colonel March. "But, you see, Randolph suspected something. Randolph showed that he suspected. And Evans, as a practical man, had to kill him. You can guess why Randolph suspected?"

"Well?"

"Because Evans is colour-blind," said Colonel March.

"It's too bad," Colonel March went on sadly, "but the crime was from the first the work of a colour-blind man. Now, none of the rest of you could qualify for that deficiency. As for Sir Rufus, I can think of nothing more improbable than a colour-blind art collector—unless it is a colour-blind interior decorator. Mr. Conyers here shows by the blended hues of brown or blue in his suits, shirts, and ties that he has a fine eye for colour effect; and he possesses no wife or valet to choose them for him.

"But Evans? He is not only partially, but wholly colour-blind. You gave us a spirited account of it. Randolph's body was sent up in the lift by Pearson. When Evans stepped forward, Pearson warned him not to touch the body, saying that there was blood. Evans said, 'Where?'—though he was staring straight down in a small, brightly lighted lift at a red bloodstain on a grey-rubber floor. Red on any surface except green or yellow is absolutely invisible to colour-blind men.

"That was also the reason why Randolph's waterproof was put on inside out. Randolph had removed his hat and coat when he first came into the flat. After Evans had stabbed him with a clasp knife, Evans put the hat and coat back on the body previous to disposing of it. But he could not distinguish between the yellowish outside and the green inside of that seamless oilskin.

"You, Mr. Denham, let yourself into the flat with your own key: which in itself told us the location of the 'vanished' room, for no two keys are alike. I also think that Miss Bruce could have told us all along where the 'vanished' room was. I am inclined to suspect she saw Randolph going into your flat, and was afraid you might be concerned in the murder."

"Oh, well," said Anita philosophically.

"Anyway, you spoke to a corpse about his coat being inside-out; and Evans rectified the error before he put the body in the lift. He had to knock you out, of course. But he genuinely didn't want to hurt you. He left the building by way of the fire escape into the mews. He disposed of his stage properties, though he was foolish enough to keep the money and the clasp knife on his person, where they were found when we searched him. When he came back here, he used the main lift in the ordinary way as though he were returning from his office. And he was genuinely concerned when he found you still unconscious on the bench in the hall."

There was a silence, broken by Armingdale's snort.

"But colour blindness! What's that got to do with the solution? How did you come to think the murderer must have been colour-blind to begin with?"

Colonel March turned to stare at him. Then he shook his head, with a slow and dismal smile.

"Don't you see it even yet?" he asked. "That was the starting point. We suspected it for the same reason Randolph suspected an imposture. Poor old Randolph wasn't an art critic. Any sort of coloured daub, in the ordinary way, he would have swallowed as the original 'Young Girl with Primroses' he expected to see. But Evans didn't allow for the one thing even a near-sighted man does know: colour. In his effort to imitate the decorations of Sir Rufus's flat, the fool hung up as an oil painting nothing more than a sepia reproduction out of an illustrated weekly."

Reading for Understanding

Main Idea

1. The main idea can best be expressed by which of the following statements?
   (a) The race is to the swift.
   (b) First impressions are soundest.
   (c) Check your assumptions.
   (d) Never trust an eyewitness.

Details

2. All the following statements about Anita Bruce are accurate EXCEPT
   (a) Denham was to marry her in a month.
   (b) She lived on the same floor as Denham.
   (c) She worried at first that Denham might have committed the murder.
   (d) She had been in love with Tom Evans.
3. Tom Evans was (a) an employee of Armingdale (b) a frustrated interior designer (c) a journalist (d) a friend of Colonel March's.

4. The most important clue in the story was (a) the character of Dan Randolph (b) Denham's drunkenness (c) the curiosity of Anita (d) color blindness.
5. The murder was actually committed in the room of (a) Conyers (b) Denham (c) Armingdale (d) Bruce.
6. The robbery was planned because Randolph (a) was American (b) disliked Armingdale (c) scorned British hospitality (d) always paid cash.

Inferences

7. The "lost-room" trick was dependent on (a) Denham's entering the room early (b) small items that could be replaced quickly (c) Armingdale's unpleasant manner (d) Anita Bruce's trust in Denham.
8. The plan also counted on (a) Armingdale's absence for a week (b) Denham's being a guest at a bachelor party (c) Anita's skill as an interior designer (d) Conyers' fussiness.

Order of Events

9. Arrange the items in the order in which they occurred. Use letters only.
   A. Denham leaves the party.
   B. The porter discovers the body in the lift.
   C. Colonel March points out the murderer.
   D. Conyers identifies the body.
   E. Denham discovers the body in the room.

Fact or Opinion

Tell whether the following is a fact or an opinion.

10. Tom Evans struck the man who shared his flat.

Words in Context

1. "The *heinousness* of his offense partly steadied him." **Heinousness** (46) means (a) nastiness (b) real meaning (c) results (d) extent.

2. "Evans, lean and *swarthy,* with darkish eyebrows merging into a single line across his forehead, looked a little like a Norman baron in a romance." **Swarthy** (46) means (a) with imperfect skin (b) of a dark complexion (c) menacing (d) yellowish.

3., 4. "Sir Rufus Armingdale did not look so much *formidable* as *fretful.*" **Formidable** (47) means (a) arousing fear (b) likely to disagree (c) strange looking (d) stimulating curiosity. **Fretful** (47) means (a) ill (b) violent (c) irritated (d) questioning.

5., 6. "The *autocrat* seemed too *abstracted* to notice." **Autocrat** (48) means (a) builder (b) banker (c) leader (d) tyrant. **Abstracted** (48) means (a) angry (b) inattentive (c) confused (d) thoughtless.

7. "His expression *belied* it as well." **Belied** (48) means (a) confirmed (b) represented (c) overlooked (d) contradicted.

8. "It was heavy and *lowering,* with more than a suggestion of the bull pup." **Lowering** (48) means (a) dropping (b) grinning (c) frowning (d) smirking.

9. "He was an *unobtrusive,* sandy-haired little man, very different from Denham's idea of a journalist." **Unobtrusive** (48) means (a) inconspicuous (b) unreliable (c) indecisive (d) unimportant.

10. " 'Sorry, sorry, sorry,' he began, seeming to *propitiate* everyone at once." **Propitiate** (49) means (a) arouse (b) catch the attention of (c) soothe (d) attract.

11. "Pearson was *voluble.* 'The lift was on the ground floor, sir.' " **Voluble** (50) means (a) excited (b) defensive (c) resentful (d) talkative.

12. "A brisk divisional detective-inspector, accompanied by a sergeant, a photographer, and a large *amiable* man in a top hat, had taken a statement from each of those concerned." **Amiable** (51) means (a) overweight (b) agreeable (c) menacing (d) busy.

13. "Something unintentionally sinister seemed to have gathered in Colonel March's *affable* tone." **Affable** (52) means (a) hesitant (b) friendly (c) softspoken (d) hostile.

14. "Hitherto Conyers had been regarding him with a look of watchful expectancy, like an *urchin* about to smash a window and run." An **urchin** (53) is a (a) hardened criminal (b) mischievous youngster (c) kind of messenger (d) leader of a club.

Thinking Critically About the Story

1. The traditional puzzle-type detective story requires the author to play fair with the reader. All needed clues should be presented but they may be concealed. "Red herring" possibilities may also be presented. Does Carter Dickson play fair with the reader? Should you have guessed the murderer before March reveals him? The author has to make one, and only one, character the murderer. The proof must have three parts: A, B, and C. Study the following analysis and then decide for yourself whether this is a classic "play fair" detective story.

   A. *The murderer is color-blind.*
   (a) He put up a sepia picture, assuming it resembled the original oil.
   (b) He got the raincoat on inside out.
   (c) The near-sighted Mr. Randolph could tell whether a picture was in color or sepia, even if the murderer couldn't.

   B. *All but one are innocent.*
   (a) Conyers wasn't color-blind. He dressed colorfully, with no wife or valet to help.
   (b) Anita Bruce was an interior decorator, certainly not color-blind.
   (c) Armingdale was an art collector, certainly not color-blind.
   (d) Denham had been struck and injured by the murderer.

   C. *The murderer is Tom Evans.*
   (a) He *was* color-blind as proved when he couldn't see the red blood against the gray floor.
   (b) He had motivation (cash) and opportunity (Armingdale employee), access to his and Denham's flat. Well, there you have it. Was it fair? Too tricky? Too ingenious?

2. Carter Dickson's detectives ask questions that seem to be unimportant, irrelevant. Yet, in the explanation, they turn out to be significant. What was the significance in asking Conyers if he were married or had a valet (53)?

3. Writers of detective stories try to make their detectives distinctive, different from others. Hercule Poirot, for example, constantly calls upon his "little gray cells." Sherlock Holmes has his rapid, incredibly accurate deductions from tiny clues. The Old Man in the Corner (99) solves mysteries from the corner table in a London tea room. Colonel March can be set apart by his physical appearance so unlike that of a typical fictional detective. What other characteristics does the author apply to March?

4. Is "The Crime in Nobody's Room" an effective title? Can you think of other possibilities?
5. Are the characters in the story well drawn or are they merely props to advance the plot? Explain.

Language in Action

Paradox

"If you had been sober, you might have made a mistake; but you were so full of champagne that your instincts brought you home after all."

Colonel March's statement may be called a *paradox,* defined in one sense as "a statement seemingly contradictory or opposed to common sense but perhaps true." Another example is the advice sometimes offered to parents: "If you would hold onto your children, let them go." Religious teachings sometimes seem paradoxical. Zen, for example, suggests that the more you seek absolute safety and security, the less secure you feel.

Some paradoxical statements are humorous.

Apathy is our greatest problem—but who cares.

I'm sorry I keep apologizing.

I hate people who hate others.

One of the most famous is a mind-boggler.

All generalizations are untrue—including this one.

Some paradoxes are matters of definition.

What happens when an irresistible force meets an immovable body?

If there is an irresistible force, by definition there is no immovable object . . . and vice versa.

The Problem of Cell 13

Jacques Futrelle
American

"Nothing is impossible," declared The Thinking Machine. "The mind is master of all things. When science fully recognizes that fact, a great advance will have been made."

As you've learned, the "locked room" is a standard set for a great many crime stories. "The Problem of Cell 13" is a crime story with a difference. True, there is a locked room, a maximum-security prison cell from which no one could escape. Or so it was thought. This time, however, there is no crime.

Suppose you had made the rash statement quoted above and your friends took you up on it. Then suppose that, as part of a wager, they placed you in a bare prison cell and challenged you to make your brain get you out of there in a week—if it could! That is just the situation that Professor Van Dusen, nicknamed "The Thinking Machine," found himself in. Yet, by using his brain, he escaped with ease. How did he do it? Read the story to find out.

If you like puzzles, suspense, and surprises, and if you like to match wits with a brilliant detective of fiction, you'll enjoy "The Problem of Cell 13" by Jacques Futrelle. Keep your eyes open. All the clues are presented. Can you outguess the warden? Step up and meet that astounding character, Professor Augustus S.F.X. Van Dusen, Ph.D., LL.D., F.R.S., M.D., M.D.S., etc., better known as "The Thinking Machine."

There is a sad postscript to the story, a bitter irony. The author, Jacques Futrelle, through his main character, declared that nothing is impossible for the brain, that no prison cell can hold a person who keeps his or her thinking processes working. On the night of

April 14–15, 1912, Jacques Futrelle went to his death on the luxury steamship *Titanic,* which had been struck by an iceberg.

The Problem of Cell 13

PRACTICALLY ALL THOSE LETTERS remaining in the alphabet after Augustus S. F. X. Van Dusen was named were afterward acquired by that gentleman in the course of a brilliant scientific career, and, being honorably acquired, were tacked on to the other end. His name, therefore, taken with all that belonged to it, was a wonderfully imposing structure. He was a Ph.D., an LL.D., an F.R.S., an M.D., and an M.D.S. he was also some other things—just what he himself couldn't say—through recognition of his ability by various foreign educational and scientific institutions.

In appearance he was no less striking than in nomenclature. He was slender with the droop of the student in his thin shoulders and the pallor of a close, sedentary life on his clean-shaven face. His eyes wore a perpetual, forbidding squint—of a man who studies little things—and when they could be seen at all through his thick spectacles, were mere slits of watery blue. But above his eyes was his most striking feature. This was a tall, broad brow, almost abnormal in height and width, crowned by a heavy shock of bushy, yellow hair. All these things conspired to give him a peculiar, almost grotesque, personality.

Professor Van Dusen was remotely German. For generations his ancestors had been noted in the sciences; he was the logical result, the master mind. First and above all he was a logician. At least thirty-five years of the half-century or so of his existence had been devoted exclusively to proving that two and two always equal four, except in unusual cases, where they equal three or five, as the case may be. He stood broadly on the general proposition that all things that start must go somewhere, and was able to bring the concentrated mental force of his forefathers to bear on a given problem. Incidentally it may be remarked that Professor Van Dusen wore a No. 8 hat.

The world at large had heard vaguely of Professor Van Dusen as The Thinking Machine. It was a newspaper catch-phrase applied to him at the time of a remarkable exhibition at chess; he had demonstrated then that a stranger to the game might, by the force of inevitable logic, defeat a champion who had devoted a lifetime to its study. The Thinking Machine! Perhaps that more nearly described him than all his honorary initials, for he spent week after week, month after month, in the seclusion of his small laboratory from which had gone forth thoughts that staggered scientific associates and deeply stirred the world at large.

It was only occasionally that The Thinking Machine had visitors, and these were usually men who, themselves high in the sciences, dropped in to argue a point and perhaps convince themselves. Two of these men, Dr. Charles Ransome and Alfred Fielding, called one evening to discuss some theory which is not of consequence here.

"Such a thing is impossible," declared Dr. Ransome emphatically, in the course of the conversation.

"Nothing is impossible," declared The Thinking Machine with equal emphasis. He always spoke petulantly. "The mind is master of all things. When science fully recognizes that fact a great advance will have been made."

"How about the spaceship?" asked Dr. Ransome.

"That's not impossible at all," asserted The Thinking Machine. "It will be invented some time. I'd do it myself, but I'm busy."

Dr. Ransome laughed tolerantly.

"I've heard you say such things before," he said. "But they mean nothing. Mind may be master of matter, but it hasn't yet found a way to apply itself. There are some things that can't be *thought* out of existence, or rather which would not yield to any amount of thinking."

"What, for instance?" demanded The Thinking Machine.

Dr. Ransome was thoughtful for a moment as he smoked. "Well, say prison walls," he replied. "No man can *think* himself out of a cell. If he could, there would be no prisoners."

"A man can so apply his brain and ingenuity that he can leave a cell, which is the same thing," snapped The Thinking Machine.

Dr. Ransome was slightly amused.

"Let's suppose a case," he said, after a moment. "Take a cell where prisoners under sentence of death are confined—men who are desperate and, maddened by fear, would take any chance to escape—suppose you were locked in such a cell. Could you escape?"

"Certainly," declared The Thinking Machine.

"Of course," said Mr. Fielding, who entered the conversation for the first time, "you might wreck the cell with an explosive—but inside, a prisoner, you couldn't have that."

"There would be nothing of that kind," said The Thinking Machine. "You might treat me precisely as you treated prisoners under sentence of death, and I would leave the cell."

"Not unless you entered it with tools prepared to get out," said Dr. Ransome.

The Thinking Machine was visibly annoyed and his blue eyes snapped.

"Lock me in any cell in any prison anywhere at any time, wearing only what is necessary, and I'll escape in a week," he declared, sharply.

Dr. Ransome sat up straight in the chair, interested. Mr. Fielding lighted a new cigar.

"You mean you could actually *think* yourself out?" asked Dr. Ransome.

"I would get out," was the response.

"Are you serious?"

"Certainly I am serious."

Dr. Ransome and Mr. Fielding were silent for a long time.

"Would you be willing to try it?" asked Mr. Fielding, finally.

"Certainly," said Professor Van Dusen, and there was a trace of irony in his voice. "I have done more asinine things than that to convince other men of less important truths."

The tone was offensive and there was an undercurrent strongly resembling anger on both sides. Of course it was an absurd thing, but Professor Van Dusen reiterated his willingness to undertake the escape and it was decided upon.

"To begin now," added Dr. Ransome.

"I'd prefer that it begin tomorrow," said The Thinking Machine, "because—"

"No, now," said Mr. Fielding, flatly. "You are arrested, figuratively, of course, without any warning locked in a cell with no chance to communicate with friends, and left there with identically the same care and attention that would be given to a man under sentence of death. Are you willing?"

"All right, now, then," said The Thinking Machine, and he arose.

"Say, the death-cell in Chisholm Prison."

"The death-cell in Chisholm Prison."

"And what will you wear?"

"As little as possible," said The Thinking Machine. "Shoes, stockings, trousers and a shirt."

"You will permit yourself to be searched, of course?"

"I am to be treated precisely as all prisoners are treated," said The Thinking Machine. "No more attention and no less."

There were some preliminaries to be arranged in the matter of obtaining permission for the test, but all three were influential men and everything was done satisfactorily by telephone, albeit the prison commissioners, to whom the experiment was explained on purely scientific grounds, were sadly bewildered. Professor Van Dusen would be the most distinguished prisoner they had ever entertained.

When The Thinking Machine had donned those things which he was to wear during his incarceration he called the little old woman who was his housekeeper, cook, and maidservant all in one.

"Martha," he said, "it is now twenty-seven minutes past nine o'-clock. I am going away. One week from tonight, at half past nine, these gentlemen and one, possibly two, others will take supper with me here. Remember Dr. Ransome is very fond of artichokes."

The three men were driven to Chisholm Prison, where the warden was awaiting them, having been informed of the matter by telephone. He understood merely that the eminent Professor Van Dusen was to be his prisoner, if he could keep him, for one week; that he had committed no crime, but that he was to be treated as all other prisoners were treated.

"Search him," instructed Dr. Ransome.

The Thinking Machine was searched. Nothing was found on him; the pockets of the trousers were empty; the white, stiff-bosomed shirt had no pocket. The shoes and stockings were removed, examined, then replaced. As he watched all these preliminaries—the rigid search and noted the pitiful, childlike physical weakness of the man, the colorless face, and the thin, white hands—Dr. Ransome almost regretted his part in the affair.

"Are you sure you want to do this?" he asked.

"Would you be convinced if I did not?" inquired The Thinking Machine in turn.

"No."

"All right. I'll do it."

What sympathy Dr. Ransome had was dissipated by the tone. It nettled him, and he resolved to see the experiment to the end; it would be a stinging reproof to egotism.

"It will be impossible for him to communicate with anyone outside?" he asked.

"Absolutely impossible," replied the warden. "He will not be permitted writing materials of any sort."

"And your jailers, would they deliver a message from him?"

"Not a word, directly or indirectly," said the warden. "You may rest assured of that. They will report anything he might say or turn over to me anything he might give them."

"That seems entirely satisfactory," said Mr. Fielding, who was frankly interested in the problem.

"Of course, in the event he fails," said Dr. Ransome, "and asks for his liberty, you understand you are to set him free?"

"I understand," replied the warden.

The Thinking Machine stood listening, but had nothing to say until this was all ended, then:

"I should like to make three small requests. You may grant them or not, as you wish."

"No special favors, now," warned Mr. Fielding.

"I am asking none," was the stiff response. "I would like to have some tooth powder—buy it yourself to see that it is tooth powder—and I should like to have one five-dollar and two ten-dollar bills."

Dr. Ransome, Mr. Fielding and the warden exchanged astonished glances. They were not surprised at the request for tooth powder, but were at the request for money.

"Is there any man with whom our friend would come in contact that he could bribe with twenty-five dollars?" asked Dr. Ransome of the warden.

"Not for twenty-five hundred dollars," was the positive reply.

"Well, let him have them," said Mr. Fielding. "I think they are harmless enough."

"And what is the third request?" asked Dr. Ransome.

"I should like to have my shoes polished."

Again the astonished glances were exchanged. This last request was the height of absurdity, so they agreed to it. These things all being attended to, The Thinking Machine was led back into the prison from which he had undertaken to escape.

"Here is Cell 13," said the warden, stopping three doors down the steel corridor. "This is where we keep condemned murderers. No one can leave it without my permission; and no one in it can communicate with the outside. I'll stake my reputation on that. It's only three doors back of my office and I can readily hear any unusual noise."

"Will this cell do, gentlemen?" asked The Thinking Machine. There was a touch of irony in his voice.

"Admirably," was the reply.

The heavy steel door was thrown open, there was a great scurrying and scampering of tiny feet, and The Thinking Machine passed into the gloom of the cell. Then the door was closed and double locked by the warden.

"What is that noise in there?" asked Dr. Ransome, through the bars.

"Rats—dozens of them," replied The Thinking Machine, tersely.

The three men, with final good nights, were turning away when The Thinking Machine called:

"What time is it exactly, warden?"

"Eleven seventeen," replied the warden.

"Thanks. I will join you gentlemen in your office at half past eight o'clock one week from tonight," said The Thinking Machine.

"And if you do not?"

"There is no 'if' about it."

Chisholm Prison was a great, spreading structure of granite, four stories in all, which stood in the center of acres of open space. It was surrounded by a wall of solid masonry eighteen feet high and so smoothly finished inside and out as to offer no foothold to a climber, no matter how expert. Atop of this fence, as a further precaution, was a five-foot fence of steel rods, each terminating in a keen point. This fence in itself marked an absolute deadline between freedom and imprisonment, for, even if a man escaped from his cell, it would seem impossible for him to pass the wall.

The yard, which on all sides of the prison building was twenty-five feet wide, that being the distance from the building to the wall, was by day an exercise ground for those prisoners to whom was granted the boon of occasional semi-liberty. But that was not for those in Cell 13.

At all times of the day there were armed guards in the yard, four of them, one patrolling each side of the prison building.

By night the yard was almost as brilliantly lighted as by day. On each of the four sides was a great arc light which rose above the prison wall and gave to the guards a clear sight. The lights, too, brightly illuminated the spiked top of the wall. The wires which fed the arc lights ran up the side of the prison building on insulators and from the top story led out to the poles supporting the arc lights.

All these things were seen and comprehended by The Thinking Machine, who was only enabled to see out his closely barred cell window by standing on his bed. This was on the morning following his incarceration. He gathered, too, that the river lay over there beyond the wall somewhere, because he heard faintly the pulsation of a motorboat and high up in the air saw a river bird. From that same direction came the shouts of boys at play and the occasional crack of a batted ball. He knew then that between the prison wall and the river was an open space, a playground.

Chisholm Prison was regarded as absolutely safe. No man had ever escaped from it. The Thinking Machine, from his perch on the bed, seeing what he saw, could readily understand why. The walls of the cell, though built he judged twenty years before, were perfectly solid, and the window bars of new iron had not a shadow of rust on them. The window itself, even with the bars out, would be a difficult mode of egress because it was small.

Yet, seeing these things, The Thinking Machine was not discouraged. Instead, he thoughtfully squinted at the great arc light—there was bright sunlight now—and traced with his eyes the wire which led from it to the building. That electric wire, he reasoned, must come down the side of the building not a great distance from his cell. That might be worth knowing.

Cell 13 was on the same floor with the offices of the prison— that is, not in the basement, nor yet upstairs. There were only four steps up to the office floor, therefore the level of the floor must be only three or four feet above the ground. He couldn't see the ground directly beneath his window, but he could see it further out toward the wall. It would be an easy drop from the window. Well and good.

Then The Thinking Machine fell to remembering how he had come to the cell. First, there was the outside guard's booth, a part of the wall. There were two heavily barred gates there, both of steel. At this gate was one man always on guard. He admitted persons to the prison after much clanking of keys and locks, and let them out when ordered to do so. The warden's office was in the prison building, and in order to reach that official from the prison yard one had to pass a gate of solid steel with only a peephole in it. Then coming from the inner office to Cell 13, where he was now, one must pass a heavy wooden door and two steel doors into the corridors of the prison; and always there was the double-locked door to Cell 13 to reckon with.

There were then, The Thinking Machine recalled, seven doors to be overcome before one could pass from Cell 13 into the outer world, a free man. But against this was the fact that he was rarely interrupted. A jailer appeared at his cell door at six in the morning with a breakfast of prison fare; he would come again at noon, and again at six in the afternoon. At nine o'clock at night would come the inspection tour. That would be all.

"It's admirably arranged, this prison system," was the mental tribute paid by The Thinking Machine. "I'll have to study it a little when I get out. I had no idea there was such great care exercised in the prisons."

There was nothing, positively nothing, in his cell, except his iron bed, so firmly put together that no man could tear it to pieces save with sledges or a file. He had neither of these. There was not even a chair, or a small table, or a bit of tin or crockery. Nothing! the jailer stood by when he ate, then took away the wooden spoon and bowl which he had used.

One by one these things sank into the brain of The Thinking Machine. When the last possibility had been considered he began an examination of his cell. From the roof, down the walls on all sides, he examined the stones and the cement between them. He stamped over the floor carefully time after time, but it was cement, perfectly solid. After the examination he sat on the edge of the iron bed and was lost in thought for a long time. For Professor Augustus S. F. X. Van Dusen, The Thinking Machine, had something to think about.

He was disturbed by a rat, which ran across his foot, then scampered away into a dark corner of the cell, frightened at its own daring. After a while The Thinking Machine, squinting steadily into the darkness of the corner where the rat had gone, was able to make out in the gloom many little beady eyes staring at him. He counted six pair, and there were perhaps others; he didn't see very well.

Then The Thinking Machine, from his seat on the bed, noticed for the first time the bottom of his cell door. There was an opening there of two inches between the steel bar and the floor. Still looking steadily at this opening, The Thinking Machine backed suddenly into the corner where he had seen the beady eyes. There was a great scampering of tiny feet, several squeaks of frightened rodents, and then silence.

None of the rats had gone out the door, yet there were none in the cell. Therefore there must be another way out of the cell, however small. The Thinking Machine, on hands and knees, started a search for this spot, feeling in the darkness with his long, slender fingers.

At last his search was rewarded. He came upon a small opening in the floor, level with the cement. It was perfectly round and somewhat larger than a silver dollar. This was the way the rats had gone. He put his fingers deep into the opening; it seemed to be a disused drainage pipe and was dry and dusty.

Having satisfied himself on this point, he sat on the bed again for an hour, then made another inspection of his surroundings through the small cell window. One of the outside guards stood directly opposite, beside the wall, and happened to be looking at the window of Cell 13 when the head of The Thinking Machine appeared. But the scientist didn't notice the guard.

Noon came and the jailer appeared with the prison dinner of repulsively plain food. At home The Thinking Machine merely ate to live; here he took what was offered without comment. Occasionally he spoke to the jailer who stood outside the door watching him.

"Any improvements made here in the last few years?" he asked.

"Nothing particularly," replied the jailer. "New wall was built four years ago."

"Anything done to the prison proper?"

"Painted the woodwork outside, and I believe about seven years ago a new system of plumbing was put in."

"Ah!" said the prisoner. "How far is the river over there?"

"About three hundred feet. The boys have a baseball ground between the wall and the river."

The Thinking Machine had nothing further to say just then, but when the jailer was ready to go he asked for some water.

"I get very thirsty here," he explained. "Would it be possible for you to leave a little water in a bowl for me?"

"I'll ask the warden," replied the jailer, and he went away.

Half an hour later he returned with water in a small earthen bowl.

"The warden says you may keep this bowl," he informed the prisoner. "But you must show it to me when I ask for it. If it is broken, it will be the last."

"Thank you," said The Thinking Machine. "I shan't break it."

The jailer went on about his duties. For just the fraction of a second it seemed that The Thinking Machine wanted to ask a question, but he didn't.

Two hours later this same jailer, in passing the door of Cell No. 13, heard a noise inside and stopped. The Thinking Machine was down on his hands and knees in a corner of the cell, and from that same corner came several frightened squeaks. The jailer looked on interestedly.

"Ah, I've got you," he heard the prisoner say.

"Got what?" he asked, sharply.

"One of these rats," was the reply. "See?" And between the scientist's long fingers the jailer saw a small gray rat struggling. The prisoner brought it over to the light and looked at it closely. "It's a water rat," he said.

"Ain't you got anything better to do than to catch rats?" asked the jailer.

"It's disgraceful that they should be here at all," was the irritated reply. "Take this one away and kill it. There are dozens more where it came from."

The jailer took the wriggling, squirmy rodent and flung it down on the floor violently. It gave one squeak and lay still. Later he reported the incident to the warden, who only smiled.

Still later that afternoon the outside armed guard on Cell 13 side of the prison looked up again at the window and saw the prisoner looking out. He saw a hand raised to the barred window and then something white fluttered to the ground, directly under the window of Cell 13. It was a little roll of linen, evidently of white shirting material, and tied around it was a five-dollar bill. The guard looked up at the window again, but the face had disappeared.

With a grim smile he took the little linen roll and the five-dollar bill to the warden's office. There together they deciphered something which was written on it with a queer sort of ink, frequently blurred. On the outside was this:

"Finder of this please deliver to Dr. Charles Ransome."

"Ah," said the warden, with a chuckle. "Plan of escape number one has gone wrong." Then, as an afterthought: "But why did he address it to Dr. Ransome?"

"And where did he get the pen and ink to write with?" asked the guard.

The warden looked at the guard and the guard looked at the warden. There was no apparent solution of that mystery. The warden studied the writing carefully, then shook his head.

"Well, let's see what he was going to say to Dr. Ransome," he said at length, still puzzled, and he unrolled the inner piece of linen.

"Well, if that—what—what do you think of that?" he asked, dazed.

The guard took the bit of linen and read this:

"Epa cseot d'net niiy awe htto n'si sih. 'T.'"

written note on 5 dollar bill

The warden spent an hour wondering what sort of cipher it was, and half an hour wondering why his prisoner should attempt to communicate with Dr. Ransome, who was the cause of his being there. After this the warden devoted some thought to the question of where the prisoner got writing materials, and what sort of writing materials he had. With the idea of illuminating this point, he examined the linen again. It was a torn part of a white shirt and had ragged edges.

Now it was possible to account for the linen, but what the prisoner had used to write with was another matter. The warden knew it would have been impossible for him to have either pen or pencil, and, besides, neither pen nor pencil had been used in this writing. What, then? The warden decided to personally investigate. The Thinking Machine was his prisoner; he had orders to hold his prisoners; if this one sought to escape by sending cipher messages to persons outside, he would stop it, as he would have stopped it in the case of any other prisoner.

The warden went back to Cell 13 and found The Thinking Machine on his hands and knees on the floor, engaged in nothing more alarming than catching rats. The prisoner heard the warden's step and turned to him quickly.

"It's disgraceful," he snapped, "these rats. There are scores of them."

"Other men have been able to stand them," said the warden. "Here is another shirt for you—let me have the one you have on."

"Why?" demanded The Thinking Machine, quickly. His tone was hardly natural, his manner suggested actual perturbation.

"You have attempted to communicate with Dr. Ransome," said the warden severely. "As my prisoner, it is my duty to put a stop to it."

The Thinking Machine was silent for a moment.

"All right," he said, finally. "Do your duty."

The warden smiled grimly. The prisoner arose from the floor and removed the white shirt, putting on instead a striped convict shirt the warden had brought. The warden took the white shirt eagerly, and then and there compared the pieces of linen on which was written and cipher with certain torn places in the shirt. The Thinking Machine looked on curiously.

"The guard brought *you* those, then?" he asked

"He certainly did," replied the warden triumphantly. "And that ends your first attempt to escape."

The Thinking Machine watched the warden as he, by comparison, established to his own satisfaction that only two pieces of linen had been torn from the white shirt.

"What did you write this with?" demanded the warden.

"I should think it a part of your duty to find out," said The Thinking Machine, irritably.

The warden started to say some harsh things, then restrained himself and made a minute search of the cell and of the prisoner instead. He found absolutely nothing; not even a match or toothpick which might have been used for a pen. The same mystery surrounded the fluid with which the cipher had been written. Although the warden left Cell 13 visibly annoyed, he took the torn shirt in triumph.

"Well, writing notes on a shirt won't get him out, that's certain," he told himself with some complacency. He put the linen scraps into his desk to await developments. "If that man escapes from that cell I'll—hang it—I'll resign."

On the third day of his incarceration The Thinking Machine openly attempted to bribe his way out. The jailer had brought his dinner and was leaning against the barred door, waiting, when The Thinking Machine began the conversation.

"The drainage pipes of the prison lead to the river, don't they?" he asked.

"Yes," said the jailer.

"I suppose they are very small?"

"Too small to crawl through, if that's what you're thinking about," was the grinning response.

There was silence until The Thinking Machine finished his meal. Then:

"You know I'm not a criminal, don't you?"

"Yes."

"And that I've a perfect right to be freed if I demand it?"

"Yes."

"Well, I came here believing that I could make my escape," said the prisoner, and his squint eyes studied the face of the jailer. "Would you consider a financial reward for aiding me to escape?"

The jailer, who happened to be an honest man, looked at the slender, weak figure of the prisoner, at the large head with its mass of yellow hair, and was almost sorry.

"I guess prisons like these were not built for the likes of you to get out of," he said, at last.

"But would you consider a proposition to help me get out?" the prisoner insisted, almost beseechingly.

"No," said the jailer, shortly.

"Five hundred dollars," urged the Thinking Machine. "I am not a criminal."

"No," said the jailer.

"A thousand?"

"No," again said the jailer, and he started away hurriedly to escape further temptation. Then he turned back. "If you should give me ten thousand dollars I couldn't get you out. You'd have to pass through seven doors, and I only have the keys to two."

Then he told the warden all about it.

"Plan number two fails," said the warden, smiling grimly. "First a cipher, then bribery."

When the jailer was on his way to Cell 13 at six o'clock, again bearing food to The Thinking Machine, he paused, startled by the unmistakable scrape, scrape of steel against steel. It stopped at the sound of his steps, then craftily the jailer, who was beyond the prisoner's range of vision, resumed his tramping, the sound being apparently that of a man going away from Cell 13. As a matter of fact he was in the same spot.

After a moment there came again the steady scrape, scrape, and the jailer crept cautiously on tiptoes to the door and peered between the bars. The Thinking Machine was standing on the iron bed working at the bars of the little window. He was using a file, judging from the backward and forward swing of his arms.

Cautiously the jailer crept back to the office, summoned the warden in person, and they returned to Cell 13 on tiptoes. The steady scrape was still audible. The warden listened to satisfy himself and then suddenly appeared at the door.

"Well?" he demanded, and there was a smile on his face.

The Thinking Machine glanced back from his perch on the bed and leaped suddenly to the floor, making frantic efforts to hide something. The warden went in, with hand extended.

"Give it up," he said.

"No," said the prisoner, sharply.

"Come, give it up," urged the warden. "I don't want to have to search you again."

"No," repeated the prisoner.

"What was it, a file?" asked the warden.

The Thinking Machine was silent and stood squinting at the warden with something very nearly approaching disappointment on his face—nearly, but not quite. The warden was almost sympathetic.

"Plan number three fails, eh?" he asked, good-naturedly. "Too bad, isn't it?"

The prisoner didn't say.

"Search him," instructed the warden.

The jailer searched the prisoner carefully. At last, artfully concealed in the waistband of the trousers, he found a piece of steel about two inches long, with one side curved like a half moon.

"Ah," said the warden, as he received it from the jailer. "From your shoe heel," and he smiled pleasantly.

The jailer continued his search and found, on the other side of the trousers waistband, another piece of steel identical with the first. The edges showed where they had been worn against the bars of the window.

"You couldn't saw a way through those bars with these," said the warden.

"I could have," said The Thinking Machine firmly.

"In six months, perhaps," said the warden, good-naturedly.

The warden shook his head slowly as he gazed into the slightly flushed face of his prisoner.

"Ready to give it up?" he asked.

"I haven't started yet," was the prompt reply.

Then came another exhaustive search of the cell. Carefully the two men went over it, finally turning out the bed and searching that. Nothing. The warden in person climbed upon the bed and examined the bars of the window where the prisoner had been sawing. When he looked he was amused.

"Just made it a little bright by hard rubbing," he said to the prisoner, who stood looking on with a somewhat crestfallen air. The warden grasped the iron bars in his strong hands and tried to shake them. They were immovable, set firmly in the solid granite. He examined each in turn and found them all satisfactory. Finally he climbed down from the bed.

"Give it up, professor," he advised.

The Thinking Machine shook his head and the warden and jailer passed on again. As they disappeared down the corridor The Thinking Machine sat on the edge of the bed with his head in his hands.

"He's crazy to try to get out of that cell," commented the jailer.

"Of course he can't get out," said the warden. "But he's clever. I would like to know what he wrote that cipher with."

It was four o'clock next morning when an awful, heart-racking shriek of terror resounded through the great prison. It came from a cell, somewhere about the center, and its tone told a tale of horror, agony, terrible fear. The warden heard and with three of his men rushed into the long corridor leading to Cell 13.

As they ran there came again that awful cry. It died away in a sort of wail. The white faces of prisoners appeared at cell doors upstairs and down, staring out wonderingly, frightened.

"It's that fool in Cell 13," grumbled the warden.

He stopped and stared in as one of the jailers flashed a lantern. "That fool in Cell 13" lay comfortably on his cot, flat on his back with his mouth open, snoring. Even as they looked there came again the piercing cry, from somewhere above. The warden's face blanched a little as he started up the stairs. There on the top floor he found a man in Cell 43, directly above Cell 13, but two floors higher, cowering in a corner of his cell.

"What's the matter?" demanded the warden.

"Thank God you've come," exclaimed the prisoner, and he cast himself against the bars of his cell.

"What is it?" demanded the warden again.

He threw open the door and went in. The prisoner dropped on his knees and clasped the warden about the body. His face was white with terror, his eyes were widely distended, and he was shuddering. His hands, icy cold, clutched at the warden's.

"Take me out of this cell, please take me out," he pleaded.

"What's the matter with you, anyhow?" insisted the warden, impatiently.

"I heard something—something," said the prisoner, and his eyes roved nervously around the cell.

"What did you hear?"

"I—I can't tell you," stammered the prisoner. Then, in a sudden burst of terror: "Take me out of this cell—put me anywhere—but take me out of here."

The warden and the three jailers exchanged glances.

"Who is this fellow? What's he accused of?" asked the warden.

"Joseph Ballard," said one of the jailers. "He's accused of throwing acid in a woman's face. She died from it."

"But they can't prove it," gasped the prisoner. "They can't prove it. Please put me in some other cell."

He was still clinging to the warden, and that official threw his arms off roughly. Then for a time he stood looking at the cowering wretch, who seemed possessed of all the wild, unreasoning terror of a child.

"Look here, Ballard," said the warden, finally, "if you heard anything, I want to know what it was. Now tell me."

"I can't, I can't," was the reply. He was sobbing.

"Where did it come from?"

"I don't know. Everywhere—nowhere. I just heard it."

"What was it—a voice?"

"Please don't make me answer," pleaded the prisoner.

"You must answer," said the warden, sharply.

"It was a voice—but—but it wasn't human," was the sobbing reply.

"Voice, but not human?" repeated the warden, puzzled.

"It sounded muffled and—and far away—and ghostly," explained the man.

"Did it come from inside or outside the prison?"

"It didn't seem to come from anywhere—it was just here, there, everywhere. I heard it. I heard it."

For an hour the warden tried to get the story, but Ballard had become suddenly obstinate and would say nothing—only pleaded to be placed in another cell, or to have one of the jailers remain near him until daylight. These requests were gruffly refused.

"And see here," said the warden, in conclusion, "if there's any more of this screaming I'll put you in the padded cell."

Then the warden went his way, a sadly puzzled man. Ballard sat at his cell door until daylight, his face, drawn and white with terror, pressed against the bars, and looked out into the prison with wide, staring eyes.

That day, the fourth since the incarceration of The Thinking Machine, was enlivened considerably by the volunteer prisoner, who spent most of his time at the little window of his cell. He began proceedings by throwing another piece of linen down to the guard, who picked it up dutifully and took it to the warden. On it was written:

"Only three days more."

The warden was in no way surprised at what he read; he understood that The Thinking Machine meant only three days more of his imprisonment, and he regarded the note as a boast. But how was the thing written? Where had The Thinking Machine found this new piece of linen? Where? How? He carefully examined the linen. It was white, of fine texture, shirting material. He took the shirt which he had taken and carefully fitted the two original pieces of the linen to the torn places. This third piece was entirely superfluous; it didn't fit anywhere, and yet it was unmistakably the same goods.

"And where—where does he get anything to write with?" demanded the warden of the world at large.

Still later on the fourth day The Thinking Machine, through the window of his cell, spoke to the armed guard outside.

"What day of the month is it?" he asked.

The fifteenth," was the answer.

The Thinking Machine made a mental astronomical calculation and satisfied himself that the moon would not rise until after nine o'clock that night. Then he asked another question:

"Who attends to those arc lights?"

"Man from the company."

"You have no electricians in the building?"

"No."

"I should think you could save money if you had your own man."

"None of my business," replied the guard.

The guard noticed The Thinking Machine at the cell window frequently during that day, but always the face seemed listless and there was a certain wistfulness in the squint eyes behind the glasses. After a while he accepted the presence of the leonine head as a matter of course. He had seen other prisoners do the same thing; it was the longing for the outside world.

That afternoon, just before the day guard was relieved, the head appeared at the window again, and The Thinking Machine's hand held something out between the bars. It fluttered to the ground and the guard picked it up. It was a five-dollar bill.

"That's for you," called the prisoner.

As usual, the guard took it to the warden. That gentleman looked at it suspiciously; he looked at everything that came from Cell 13 with suspicion.

"He said it was for me," explained the guard.

"It's a sort of a tip, I suppose," said the warden. "I see no particular reason why you shouldn't accept—"

Suddenly he stopped. He had remembered that The Thinking Machine had gone into Cell 13 with one five-dollar bill and two ten-dollar bills; twenty-five dollars in all. Now a five-dollar bill had been tied around the first pieces of linen that came from the cell. The warden still had it, and to convince himself he took it out and looked at it. It was five dollars; yet here was another five dollars, and The Thinking Machine had only had ten-dollar bills.

"Perhaps somebody changed one of the bills for him," he thought at last, with a sigh of relief.

But then and there he made up his mind. He would search Cell 13 as a cell was never before searched in this world. When a man could write at will, and change money, and do other wholly inexplicable things, there was something radically wrong with his prison. He planned to enter the cell at night—three o'clock would be an excellent time. The Thinking Machine must do all the weird things he did some time. Night seemed the most reasonable.

Thus it happened that the warden stealthily descended upon Cell 13 that night at three o'clock. He paused at the door and listened. There was no sound save the steady, regular breathing of the prisoner. The keys unfastened the double locks with scarcely a clank, and the warden entered, locking the door behind him. Suddenly he flashed his dark lantern in the face of the recumbent figure.

If the warden had planned to startle The Thinking Machine he was mistaken, for that individual merely opened his eyes quietly, reached for his glasses and inquired, in a most matter-of-fact tone:

"Who is it?"

It would be useless to describe the search that the warden made. It was minute. Not one inch of the cell or the bed was overlooked. He found the round hole in the floor, and with a flash of inspiration thrust his thick fingers into it. After a moment of fumbling there he drew up something and looked at it in the light of his lantern.

"Ugh!" he exclaimed.

The thing he had taken out was a rat—a dead rat. His inspiration fled as a mist before the sun. But he continued to search.

The Thinking Machine, without a word, arose and kicked the rat out of the cell into the corridor.

The warden climbed on the bed and tried the steel bars in the tiny window. They were perfectly rigid; every bar of the door was the same.

Then the warden searched the prisoner's clothing, beginning at the shoes. Nothing hidden in them! Then the trousers waistband. Still nothing! Then the pockets of the trousers. From one side he drew out some paper money and examined it.

"Five one-dollar bills," he gasped.

"That's right," said the prisoner.

"But the—you had two tens and a five—what the—how do you do it?"

"That's my business," said The Thinking Machine.

"Did any of my men change this money for you—on your word of honor?"

The Thinking Machine paused just a fraction of a second.

"No," he said.

"Well, do you make it?" asked the warden. He was prepared to believe anything.

"That's my business," again said the prisoner.

The warden glared at the eminent scientist fiercely. He felt—he knew—that this man was making a fool of him, yet he didn't know how. If he were a real prisoner he would get the truth—but, then, perhaps, those inexplicable things which had happened would not have been brought before him so sharply. Neither of the men spoke for a long time, then suddenly the warden turned fiercely and left the cell, slamming the door behind him. He didn't dare to speak, then.

He glanced at the clock. It was ten minutes to four. He had hardly settled himself in bed when again came that heartbreaking shriek through the prison. With a few muttered words, which, while not elegant, were highly expressive, he relighted his lantern and rushed through the prison again to the cell on the upper floor.

Again Ballard was crushing himself against the steel door, shrieking, shrieking at the top of his voice. He stopped only when the warden flashed his lamp in the cell.

"Take me out, take me out," he screamed. "I did it, I did it, I killed her. Take it away."

"Take what away?" asked the warden.

"I threw the acid in her face—I did it—I confess. Take me out of here."

Ballard's condition was pitiable; it was only an act of mercy to let him into the corridor. There he crouched in a corner, like an animal at bay, and clasped his hands to his ears. It took half an hour to calm him sufficiently for him to speak. Then he told incoherently what had happened. On the night before at four o'clock he had heard a voice—a sepulchral voice, muffled and wailing in tone.

"What did it say?" asked the warden, curiously.

"Acid—acid—acid!" gasped the prisoner. "It accused me. Acid! I threw the acid, and the woman died. Oh!" It was a long, shuddering wail of terror.

"Acid?" echoed the warden, puzzled. The case was beyond him.

"Acid. That's all I heard—that one word, repeated several times. There were other things, too, but I didn't hear them."

"That was last night, eh?" asked the warden. "What happened tonight—what frightened you just now?"

"It was the same thing," gasped the prisoner. "Acid—acid—acid." He covered his face with his hands and sat shivering. "It was acid I used on her, but I didn't mean to kill her. I just heard the words. It was something accusing me—accusing me." He mumbled, and was silent.

"Did you hear anything else?"

"Yes—but I couldn't understand—only a little bit—just a word or two."

"Well, what was it?"

"I heard 'acid' three times, then I heard a long, moaning sound, then—then—I heard 'No. 8 hat.' I heard that voice."

"No. 8 hat," repeated the warden. "What the devil—No. 8 hat? Accusing voices of conscience have never talked about No. 8 hats, so far as I ever heard."

"He's insane," said one of the jailers, with an air of finality.

"I believe you," said the warden "He must be. He probably heard something and got frightened. He's trembling now. No. 8 hat! What the—"

When the fifth day of The Thinking Machine's imprisonment rolled around the warden was wearing a hunted look. He was anxious for the end of the thing. He could not help but feel that his distinguished prisoner had been amusing himself. And if this were so, The Thinking Machine had lost none of his sense of humor. For on this fifth day he flung down another linen note to the outside guard, bearing the words: "Only two days more." Also he flung down half a dollar.

Now the warden knew—he *knew*—that the man in Cell 13 didn't have any half-dollars—he *couldn't* have any half-dollars, no more than he could have pen and ink and linen, and yet he did have them. It was a condition, not a theory; that is one reason why the warden was wearing a hunted look.

That ghastly, uncanny thing, too, about "Acid" and "No. 8 hat" clung to him tenaciously. They didn't mean anything, of course, merely the ravings of an insane murderer who had been driven by fear to confess his crime, still there were so many things that "didn't mean anything" happening in the prison now since The Thinking Machine was there.

On the sixth day the warden received a postal stating that Dr. Ransome and Mr. Fielding would be at Chisholm Prison on the following evening, Thursday, and in the event Professor Van Dusen had not yet escaped—and they presumed he had not because they had not heard from him—they would meet him there.

"In the event he had not yet escaped!" The warden smiled grimly. Escaped!

The Thinking Machine enlivened this day for the warden with three notes. They were on the usual linen and bore generally on the appointment at half past eight o'clock Thursday night, which appointment the scientist had made at the time of his imprisonment.

On the afternoon of the seventh day the warden passed Cell 13 and glanced in. The Thinking Machine was lying on the iron bed, apparently sleeping lightly. The cell appeared precisely as it always did from a casual glance. The warden would swear that no man was going to leave it between that hour—it was then four o'clock—and half past eight o'clock that evening.

On his way back past the cell the warden heard the steady breathing again, and coming close to the door looked in. He wouldn't have done so if The Thinking Machine had been looking, but now—well, it was different.

A ray of light came through the high window and fell on the face of the sleeping man. It occurred to the warden for the first time that his prisoner appeared haggard and weary. Just then The Thinking Machine stirred slightly and the warden hurried on up the corridor guiltily. That evening after six o'clock he saw the jailer.

"Everything all right in Cell 13?" he asked.

"Yes sir," replied the jailer. "He didn't eat much, though."

It was with a feeling of having done his duty that the warden received Dr. Ransome and Mr. Fielding shortly after seven o'clock. He intended to show them the linen notes and lay before them the full story of his woes, which was a long one. But before this came to pass the guard from the river side of the prison yard entered the office.

"The arc light in my side of the yard won't light," he informed the warden.

"Confound it, that man's a hoodoo," thundered the official. "Everything has happened since he's been here."

The guard went back to his post in the darkness, and the warden 'phoned to the electric light company.

"This is Chisholm Prison," he said through the 'phone. "Send three or four men down here quick, to fix an arc light."

The reply was evidently satisfactory, for the warden hung up the receiver and passed out into the yard. While Dr. Ransome and Mr. Fielding sat waiting, the guard at the outer gate came in with a special delivery letter. Dr. Ransome happened to notice the address, and, when the guard went out, looked at the letter more closely.

"By George!" he exclaimed.

"What is it?" asked Mr. Fielding.

Silently the doctor offered the letter. Mr. Fielding examined it closely.

"Coincidence," he said. "It must be."

It was nearly eight o'clock when the warden returned to his office. The electricians had arrived in a wagon, and were now at work. The warden pressed the buzz-button communicating with the man at the outer gate in the wall.

"How many electricians came in?" he asked, over the short 'phone. "Four? Three workmen in jumpers and overalls and the manager? Frock coat and silk hat? All right? Be certain that only four go out. That's all."

He turned to Dr. Ransome and Mr. Fielding. "We have to be careful here—particularly," and there was broad sarcasm in his tone, "since we have scientists locked up."

The warden picked up the special delivery letter carelessly, and then began to open it.

"When I read this I want to tell you gentlemen something about how—Great Caesar!" he ended, suddenly, as he glanced at the letter. He sat with mouth open, motionless, from astonishment.

"What is it?" asked Mr. Fielding.

"A special delivery letter from Cell 13," gasped the warden. "An invitation to supper."

"What?" and the two others arose, unanimously.

The warden sat dazed, staring at the letter for a moment, then called sharply to a guard outside in the corridor.

"Run down to Cell 13 and see if that man's in there."

The guard went as directed, while Dr. Ransome and Mr. Fielding examined the letter.

"It's Van Dusen's handwriting; there's no question of that," said Dr. Ransome. "I've seen too much of it."

Just then the buzz on the telephone from the outer gate sounded, and the warden, in a semi-trance, picked up the receiver.

"Hello! Two reporters, eh? Let 'em come in." He turned suddenly to the doctor and Mr. Fielding. "Why, the man *can't* be out. He must be in his cell."

Just at that moment the guard returned.

"He's still in his cell, sir," he reported. "I saw him. He's lying down."

"There, I told you so," said the warden, and he breathed freely again. "But how did he mail that letter?"

There was a rap on the steel door which led from the jail yard into the warden's office.

"It's the reporters," said the warden. "Let them in," he instructed the guard; then to the two other gentlemen: "Don't say anything about this before them, because I'd never hear the last of it."

The door opened, and the two men from the front gate entered.

"Good evening, gentlemen," said one. That was Hutchinson Hatch; the warden knew him well.

"Well?" demanded the other, irritably. "I'm here."

That was The Thinking Machine.

He squinted belligerently at the warden, who sat with mouth agape. For the moment that official had nothing to say. Dr. Ransome and Mr. Fielding were amazed, but they didn't know what the warden knew. They were only amazed; he was paralyzed. Hutchinson Hatch, the reporter, took in the scene with greedy eyes.

"How—how—did you do it?" gasped the warden, finally.

"Come back to the cell," said The Thinking Machine, in the irritated voice which his scientific associates knew so well.

The warden, still in a condition bordering on trance, led the way.

"Flash your light in there," directed The Thinking Machine.

The warden did so. There was nothing unusual in the appearance of the cell, and there—there on the bed lay the figure of The Thinking Machine. Certainly! There was the yellow hair! Again the warden looked at the man beside him and wondered at the strangeness of his own dreams.

With trembling hands he unlocked the cell door and The Thinking Machine passed inside.

"See here," he said.

He kicked at the steel bars in the bottom of the cell door and three of them were pushed out of place. A fourth broke off and rolled away in the corridor.

"And here, too," directed the erstwhile prisoner as he stood on the bed to reach the small window. He swept his hand across the opening and every bar came out.

"What's this in the bed?" demanded the warden, who was slowly recovering.

"A wig," was the reply. "Turn down the cover."

The warden did so. Beneath it lay a large coil of strong rope, thirty feet or more, a dagger, three files, ten feet of electric wire, a thin, powerful pair of steel pliers, a small tack hammer with its handle, and—and a Derringer pistol.

"How did you do it?" demanded the warden.

"You gentlemen have an engagement to supper with me at half past nine o'clock," said The Thinking Machine. "Come on, or we shall be late."

"But how did you do it?" insisted the warden.

"Don't ever think you can hold any man who can use his brain," said The Thinking Machine. "Come on; we shall be late."

It was an impatient supper party in the rooms of Professor Van Dusen and a somewhat silent one. The guests were Dr. Ransome, Albert Fielding, the warden, and Hutchinson Hatch, reporter. The meal was served to the minute, in accordance with Professor Van Dusen's instructions of one week before; Dr. Ransome found the artichokes delicious. At last the supper was finished and The Thinking Machine turned full on Dr. Ransome and squinted at him fiercely.

"Do you believe it now?" he demanded.

"I do," replied Dr. Ransome.

"Do you admit that it was a fair test?"

"I do."

With the others, particularly the warden, he was waiting anxiously for the explanation.

"Suppose you tell us how—" began Mr. Fielding.

"Yes, tell us how," said the warden.

The Thinking Machine readjusted his glasses, took a couple of preparatory squints at his audience and began the story. He told it from the beginning logically; and no man ever talked to more interested listeners.

"My agreement was," he began, "to go into a cell, carrying nothing except what was necessary to wear, and to leave that cell within a week. I had never seen Chisholm Prison. When I went into the cell I asked for tooth powder, two ten- and one five-dollar bills, and also to have my shoes blacked. Even if these requests had been refused it would not have mattered seriously. But you agreed to them.

"I knew there would be nothing in the cell which you thought I might use to advantage. So when the warden locked the door on me I was apparently helpless, unless I could turn three seemingly innocent things to use. They were things which would have been permitted any prisoner under sentence of death, were they not, warden?"

"Tooth powder and polished shoes, yes, but not money," replied the warden.

"Anything is dangerous in the hands of a man who knows how to use it," went on The Thinking Machine. "I did nothing that first night but sleep and chase rats." He glared at the warden. "When the matter was broached I knew I could do nothing that night, so suggested next day. You gentlemen thought I wanted time to arrange an escape with outside assistance, but this was not true. I knew I could communicate with whom I pleased, when I pleased."

The warden stared at him a moment, then went on smoking solemnly.

"I was aroused next morning at six o'clock by the jailer with my breakfast," continued the scientist. "He told me dinner was at twelve and supper at six. Between these times, I gathered, I would be pretty much to myself. So immediately after breakfast I examined my outside surroundings from my cell window. One look told me it would be useless to try to scale the wall, even should I decide to leave my cell by the window, for my purpose was to leave not only the cell, but the prison. Of course, I could have gone over the wall, but it would have taken me longer to lay my plans that way. Therefore, for the moment, I dismissed all idea of that.

"From this first observation I knew the river was on that side of the prison, and that there was also a playground there. Subsequently these surmises were verified by a keeper. I knew then one important thing—that anyone might approach the prison wall from that side if necessary without attracting any particular attention. That was well to remember. I remembered it.

"But the outside thing which most attracted my attention was the feed wire to the arc light which ran within a few feet—probably three or four—of my cell window. I knew that would be valuable in the event I found it necessary to cut off that arc light."

"Oh, you shut it off tonight, then?" asked the warden.

"Having learned all I could from that window," resumed The Thinking Machine, without heeding the interruption, "I considered the idea of escaping through the prison proper. I recalled just how I had come into the cell, which I knew would be the only way. Seven doors lay between me and the outside. So, also for the time being, I gave up the idea of escaping that way. And I couldn't go through the solid granite walls of the cell."

The Thinking Machine paused for a moment and Dr. Ransome lighted a new cigar. For several minutes there was silence, then the scientific jailbreaker went on:

"While I was thinking about these things a rat ran across my foot. It suggested a new line of thought. There were at least half a dozen rats in the cell—I could see their beady eyes. Yet I had noticed none come under the cell door. I frightened them purposely and watched the cell door to see if they went out that way. They did not, but they were gone. Obviously they went another way. Another way meant another opening.

"I searched for this opening and found it. It was an old drain pipe, long unused and partly choked with dirt and dust. But this was the way the rats had come. They came from somewhere. Where? Drain pipes usually lead outside prison grounds. This one probably led to the river, or near it. The rats must therefore come from that direction. If they came a part of the way, I reasoned that they came all the way, because it was extremely unlikely that a solid iron or lead pipe would have any hole in it except at the exit.

"When the jailer came with my luncheon he told me two important things, although he didn't know it. One was that a new system of plumbing had been put in the prison seven years before; another that the river was only three hundred feet away. Then I knew positively that the pipe was a part of an old system; I knew, too, that it slanted generally toward the river. But did the pipe end in the water or on land?

"This was the next question to be decided. I decided it by catching several of the rats in the cell. My jailer was surprised to see me engaged in this work. I examined at least a dozen of them. They were perfectly dry; they had come through the pipe, and, most important of all, they were *not house rats, but field rats.* The other end of the pipe was on land, then, outside the prison walls. So far, so good.

"Then, I knew that if I worked freely from this point I must attract the warden's attention in another direction. You see, by telling the warden that I had come there to escape you made the test more severe, because I had to trick him by false scents."

The warden looked up with a sad expression in his eyes.

"The first thing was to make him think I was trying to communicate with you, Dr. Ransome. So I wrote a note on a piece of linen I tore from my shirt, addressed it to Dr. Ransome, tied a five-dollar bill around it and threw it out the window. I knew the guard would take it to the warden, but I rather hoped the warden would send it as addressed. Have you that first linen note, warden?"

The warden produced the cipher.

"What the deuce does it mean, anyhow?" he asked.

"Read it backward, beginning with the 'T' signature and disregard the division into words," instructed The Thinking Machine.

The warden did so.

"T-h-i-s, this," he spelled, studied it a moment, then read it off, grinning:

"This is not the way I intend to escape."

"Well, now what do you think o' that?" he demanded, still grinning.

"I knew that would attract your attention, just as it did," said The Thinking Machine, "and, if you really found out what it was, it would be a sort of gentle rebuke."

"What did you write it with?" asked Dr. Ransome, after he had examined the linen and passed it to Mr. Fielding.

"This," said the erstwhile prisoner, and he extended his foot. On it was the shoe he had worn in prison, though the polish was gone—scraped off clean. "The shoe blacking, moistened with water, was my ink; the metal tip of the shoelace made a fairly good pen."

The warden looked up and suddenly burst into a laugh, half of relief, half of amusement.

"You're a wonder," he said, admiringly. "Go on."

"That precipitated a search of my cell by the warden, as I had intended," continued The Thinking Machine. "I was anxious to get the warden into the habit of searching my cell, so that finally, constantly finding nothing, he would get disgusted and quit. This at last happened, practically."

The warden blushed.

"He then took my white shirt away and gave me a prison shirt. He was satisfied that those two pieces of the shirt were all that was missing. But while he was searching my cell I had another piece of that same shirt, about nine inches square, rolled into a small ball in my mouth."

"Nine inches of that shirt?" demanded the warden. "Where did it come from?"

"The bosoms of all stiff white shirts are of triple thickness," was the explanation. "I tore out the inside thickness, leaving the bosom only two thicknesses. I knew you wouldn't see it. So much for that."

There was a little pause, and the warden looked from one to another of the men with a sheepish grin.

"Having disposed of the warden for the time being by giving him something else to think about, I took my first serious step toward freedom," said Professor Van Dusen. "I knew, within reason, that the pipe led somewhere to the playground outside; I knew a great many boys played there; I knew that rats came into my cell from out there. Could I communicate with someone outside with these things at hand?

"First was necessary, I saw, a long and fairly reliable thread, so—but here," he pulled up his trousers legs and showed that the tops of both stockings, of fine, strong lisle, were gone. "I unraveled those—after I got them started it wasn't difficult—and I had easily a quarter of a mile of thread that I could depend on.

"Then on half of my remaining linen I wrote, laboriously enough, I assure you, a letter explaining my situation to this gentleman here," and he indicated Hutchinson Hatch. "I knew he would assist me—for the value of the newspaper story. I tied firmly to this linen letter a ten-dollar bill—there is no surer way of attracting the eye of anyone—and wrote on the linen: 'Finder of this deliver to Hutchinson Hatch, *Daily American,* who will give another ten dollars for the information.'

"The next thing was to get this note outside on that playground where a boy might find it. There were two ways, but I chose the best. I took one of the rats—I became adept in catching them—tied the linen and money firmly to one leg, fastened my lisle thread to another, and turned him loose in the drain pipe. I reasoned that the natural fright of the rodent would make him run until he was outside the pipe and then out on earth he would probably stop to gnaw off the linen and money.

"From the moment the rat disappeared into that dusty pipe I became anxious. I was taking so many chances. The rat might gnaw the string, of which I held one end; other rats might gnaw it; the rat might run out of the pipe and leave the linen and money where they would never be found; a thousand other things might have happened. So began some nervous hours, but the fact that the rat ran on until only a few feet of the string remained in my cell made me think he was outside the pipe. I had carefully instructed Mr. Hatch what to do in case the note reached him. The question was: Would it reach him?

"This done, I could only wait and make other plans in case this one failed. I openly attempted to bribe my jailer, and learned from him that he held the keys to only two of seven doors between me and freedom. Then I did something else to make the warden nervous. I took the steel supports out of the heels of my shoes and made a pretense of sawing the bars of my cell window. The warden raised a pretty row about that. He developed, too, the habit of shaking the bars of my cell window to see if they were solid. They were—then."

Again the warden grinned. He had ceased being astonished.

"With this one plan I had done all I could and could only wait to see what happened," the scientist went on. "I couldn't know whether my note had been delivered or even found, or whether the rat had gnawed it up. And I didn't dare to draw back through the pipe that one slender thread which connected me with the outside.

"When I went to bed that night I didn't sleep, for fear there would come the slight signal twitch at the thread which was to tell me that Mr. Hatch had received the note. At half past three o'clock, I judge, I felt this twitch, and no prisoner actually under sentence of death ever welcomed a thing more heartily."

The Thinking Machine stopped and turned to the reporter.

"You'd better explain just what you did," he said.

"The linen note was brought to me by a small boy who had been playing baseball," said Mr. Hatch. "I immediately saw a big story in it, so I gave the boy another ten dollars, and got several spools of silk, some twine, and a roll of light, pliable wire. The professor's note suggested that I have the finder of the note show me just where it was picked up, and told me to make my search from there, beginning at two o'clock in the morning. If I found the other end of the thread I was to twitch it gently three times, then a fourth.

"I began to search with a small bulb electric light. It was an hour and twenty minutes before I found the end of the drain pipe, half hidden in weeds. The pipe was very large there, say twelve inches across. Then I found the end of the lisle thread, twitched it as directed and immediately I got an answering twitch.

"Then I fastened the silk to this and Professor Van Dusen began to pull it into his cell. I nearly had heart disease for fear the string would break. To the end of the silk I fastened the twine, and when that had been pulled in I tied on the wire. Then that was drawn into the pipe and we had a substantial line, which the rats couldn't gnaw, from the mouth of the drain into the cell."

The Thinking Machine raised his hand and Hatch stopped.

"All this was done in absolute silence," said the scientist. "But when the wire reached my hand I could have shouted. Then we tried another experiment, which Mr. Hatch was prepared for. I tested the pipe as a speaking tube. Neither of us could hear very clearly, but I dared not speak loud for fear of attracting attention in the prison. At last I made him understand what I wanted immediately. He seemed to have great difficulty in understanding when I asked for nitric acid, and I repeated the word 'acid' several times.

"Then I heard a shriek from a cell above me. I knew instantly that someone had overheard, and when I heard you coming, Mr. Warden, I feigned sleep. If you had entered my cell at that moment that whole plan of escape would have ended there. But you passed on. That was the nearest I ever came to being caught.

"Having established this improvised trolley it is easy to see how I got things in the cell and made them disappear at will. I merely dropped them back into the pipe. You, Mr. Warden, could not have reached the connecting wire with your fingers; they are too large. My fingers, you see, are longer and more slender. In addition I guarded the top of that pipe with a rat—you remember how."

"I remember," said the warden, with a grimace.

"I thought that if anyone were tempted to investigate that hole the rat would dampen his ardor. Mr. Hatch could not send me anything useful through the pipe until next night, although he did send me change for ten dollars as a test, so I proceeded with other parts of my plan. Then I evolved the method of escape, which I finally employed.

"In order to carry this out successfully it was necessary for the guard in the yard to get accustomed to seeing me at the cell window. I arranged this by dropping linen notes to him, boastful in tone, to make the warden believe, if possible, one of his assistants was communicating with the outside for me. I would stand at my window for hours gazing out, so the guard could see, and occasionally I spoke to him. In that way I learned that the prison had no electricians of its own, but was dependent upon the lighting company if anything should go wrong.

"That cleared the way to freedom completely. Early in the evening of the last day of my imprisonment, when it was dark, I planned to cut the feed wire which was only a few feet from my window, reaching it with an acid-tipped wire I had. That would make that side of the prison perfectly dark while the electricians were searching for the break. That would also bring Mr. Hatch into the prison yard.

"There was only one more thing to do before I actually began the work of setting myself free. This was to arrange final details with Mr. Hatch through our speaking tube. I did this within half an hour after the warden left my cell on the fourth night of my imprisonment. Mr. Hatch again had serious difficulty in understanding me, and I repeated the word 'acid' to him several times, and later the words: 'Number eight hat'—that's my size— and these were the things which made a prisoner upstairs confess to murder, so one of the jailers told me next day. This prisoner heard our voices, confused of course, through the pipe, which also went to his cell. The cell directly over me was not occupied, hence no one else heard.

"Of course the actual work of cutting the steel bars out of the window and door was comparatively easy with nitric acid, which I got through the pipe in thin bottles, but it took time. Hour after hour on the fifth and sixth and seventh days the guard below was looking at me as I worked on the bars of the window with the acid on a piece of wire. I used the tooth powder to prevent the acid spreading. I looked away abstractedly as I worked and each minute the acid cut deeper into the metal. I noticed that the jailers always tried the door by shaking the upper part, never the lower bars, therefore I cut the lower bars, leaving them hanging in place by thin strips of metal. But that was a bit of daredeviltry. I could not have gone that way so easily."

The Thinking Machine sat silent for several minutes.

"I think that makes everything clear," he went on. "Whatever points I have not explained were merely to confuse the warden and jailers. These things in my bed I brought in to please Mr. Hatch, who wanted to improve the story. Of course, the wig was necessary in my plan. The special delivery letter I wrote and directed in my cell with Mr.

Hatch's fountain pen, then sent it out to him and he mailed it. That's all, I think."

"But your actually leaving the prison grounds and then coming in through the outer gate to my office? asked the warden.

"Perfectly simple, " said the scientist. "I cut the electric light wire with acid, as I said, when the current was off. Therefore when the current was turned on the arc didn't light. I knew it would take some time to find out what was the matter and make repairs. When the guard went to report to you the yard was dark. I crept out the window—it was a tight fit, too—replaced the bars by standing on a narrow ledge and remained in a shadow until the force of electricians arrived. Mr. Hatch was one of them.

"When I saw him I spoke and he handed me a cap, a jumper and overalls, which I put on within ten feet of you, Mr. Warden, while you were in the yard. Later Mr. Hatch called me, presumably as a workman, and together we went out the gate to get something out of the wagon. The gate guard let us pass out readily as two workmen who had just passed in. We changed our clothing and reappeared, asking to see you. We saw you. That's all."

There was silence for several minutes. Dr. Ransome was first to speak.

"Wonderful!" he exclaimed. "Perfectly amazing."

"How did Mr. Hatch happen to come with the electricians?" asked Mr. Fielding.

"His father is manager of the company," replied The Thinking Machine.

"But what if there had been no Mr. Hatch outside to help?"

"Every prisoner has one friend outside who would help him escape if he could."

"Suppose—just suppose—there had been no old plumbing system there?" asked the warden, curiously.

"There were two other ways out," said the Thinking Machine, enigmatically.

Ten minutes later the telephone bell rang. It was a request for the warden.

"Light all right, eh?" the warden asked, through the 'phone. "Good. Wire cut beside Cell 13? Yes, I know. One electrician too many? What's that? Two came out?"

The warden turned to the others with a puzzled expression.

"He only let in four electricians, he has let out two and says there are three left."

"I was the odd one," said The Thinking Machine.

"Oh," said the warden. "I see." Then through the 'phone: "Let the fifth man go. He's all right."

Reading for Understanding

Main Idea

1. Professor Van Dusen is a man of (a) many quirks and bad habits (b) high intelligence and incredible resourcefulness (c) unexpected good luck and foolishness (d) pleasing personality and friendly manner.

Details

2. One of the objects requested by Van Dusen was (a) tooth powder (b) an explosive device (c) a telephone (d) a mousetrap.
3. Cell 13 was usually reserved for (a) political prisoners (b) petty thieves (c) embezzlers (d) condemned murderers.
4. Van Dusen's "coded message" to his friend Ransome was supposed to be read (a) in bright light (b) with the help of a dictionary (c) with a secret code devised by the warden (d) backwards.
5. The mysterious "extra electrician" was (a) Hatch (b) Ransome (c) Van Dusen (d) Fielding.

Inferences

6. The rats could reasonably be called (a) deadly enemies of the prisoner (b) Van Dusen's helpers (c) subjects of Dr. Ransome's experiments (d) pets of Mr. Hatch.
7. Which of the following statement is NOT true?
   (a) The Thinking Machine outguessed the warden.
   (b) He irritated Ransome.
   (c) He meant to drive the man above him into a confession of murder.
   (d) He used the guard for his own ends.
8. For his plan of escape, Van Dusen cleverly used (a) the location of the prison (b) the thickness of the walls (c) Dr. Ransome's stupidity (d) the guard's willingness to accept a bribe.
9. At the end, the warden's attitude toward Van Dusen was one of (a) hatred (b) extreme anger (c) indifference (d) respect.
10. The drain (a) led to the warden's office (b) distorted Van Dusen's voice (c) was free of rats (d) was fully operational.

Order of Events

11. Arrange the items in the order in which they occurred. Use letters only.
    A. Hatch begins to help Van Dusen. E
    B. The lights go out in the prison. D
    C. Van Dusen walks in with Hatch. A
    D. Van Dusen catches a rat. B
    E. Van Dusen declares nothing is impossible. C

Outcome

12. If there had been no drain in the cell, Van Dusen probably would have (a) given up (b) smuggled in a file for cutting the bars (c) succeeded in bribing a guard (d) found still another way. d

Cause and Effect

13. As a direct result of using the drain for a speaking tube, (a) the lighting system was blacked out (b) a prisoner confessed to murder (c) the warden caught on to Van Dusen's plans. (d) Ransome and Fielding called the challenge off. b

Fact or Opinion

Tell whether each of the following is a fact or opinion.

14. There was a playground near the prison. f
15. Van Dusen took unfair advantage of the warden's good nature. O

Words in Context

1. "In appearance he was no less striking than in *nomenclature*." **Nomenclature** (63) means (a) physique (b) name (c) temperament (d) features.

2., 3. "He was slender with the droop of the student in his thin shoulders and *pallor* of a close, *sedentary* life on his clean-shaven face." **Pallor** (63) means (a) appearance (b) glow (c) paleness

(d) strength. **Sedentary** (63) means (a) inactive (b) violent (c) unhappy (d) colorful.

4. "His eyes wore a *perpetual,* forbidding squint—of a man who studies little things." **Perpetual** (63) means (a) unpleasant (b) invisible (c) uncertain (d) continuing.
5. "All these things conspired to give him a peculiar, almost *grotesque,* personality." **Grotesque** (63) means (a) gloomy (b) strange (c) distracted (d) weak.
6. "He always spoke *petulantly.*" **Petulantly** (64) means (a) slowly (b) clearly (c) crossly (d) seriously.
7. " 'I have done more *asinine* things than that to convince other men of less important truths.' " **Asinine** (65) means (a) hasty (b) profound (c) unexpected (d) stupid.
8. "Professor Van Dusen *reiterated* his willingness to undertake the escape and it was decided upon." **Reiterated** (65) means (a) repeated (b) rejected (c) reported (d) re-evaluated.
9. "The Thinking Machine had donned those things which he was to wear during his *incarceration.*" **Incarceration** (65) means (a) lecture (b) imprisonment (c) investigation (d) period of schooling.
10. "What sympathy Dr. Ransome had was *dissipated* by the tone." **Dissipated** (66) means (a) driven off (b) increased (c) untouched (d) misdirected.
11. "It *nettled* him, and he resolved to see the experiment to the end." **Nettled** (66) means (a) interested (b) pleased (c) awakened (d) annoyed.
12. " 'Rats—dozens of them,' replied The Thinking Machine *tersely.*" **Tersely** (67) means (a) loudly (b) eagerly (c) briefly (d) sweetly.
13. "Atop of this fence, as a further precaution, was a five-foot fence of steel rods, each *terminating* in a keen point." **Terminating** (68) means (a) blossoming (b) ending (c) decorating (d) unwinding.
14. "Noon came and the jailer appeared with the prison dinner of *repulsively* plain food." **Repulsively** (70) means (a) disgustingly (b) unattractively (c) unusually (d) wholesomely.
15. "His tone was hardly natural, his manner suggested actual *perturbation.*" **Perturbation** (72) means (a) application (b) serenity (c) arbitration (d) anxiety.
16. " 'Well, writing notes on a shirt won't get him out, that's certain,' he told himself with some *complacency.*" **Complacency** (73) means (a) irritation (b) heat (c) self-satisfaction (d) hesitancy.

17. " 'But would you consider a proposition to help me get out?' the prisoner insisted, almost *beseechingly*." **Beseechingly** (73) means (a) in a begging manner (b) with considerable pride (c) without hesitation (d) in somewhat of a hurry.

18. "Then came another *exhaustive* search of the cell." **Exhaustive** (75) means (a) weary (b) thorough (c) confidential (d) bitterly angry.

19. "His face was white with terror, his eyes were widely *distended*, and he was shuddering." **Distended** (76) means (a) bloodshot (b) scarred (c) expanded (d) vibrating.

20. "When a man could write at will, and change money, and do other wholly *inexplicable* things, there was something radically wrong with his prison." **Inexplicable** (78) means (a) bad-tempered (b) easily understood (c) improper (d) unexplainable.

21. "Thus it happened that the warden *stealthily* descended upon Cell 13 that night at three o'clock." **Stealthily** (78) means (a) noisily (b) wearily (c) happily (d) slyly.

22. "Suddenly he flashed his dark lantern in the face of the *recumbent* figure." **Recumbent** (78) means (a) unconscious (b) recovering (c) lying down (d) untidy.

23. "Then he told *incoherently* what had happened." **Incoherently** (80) means (a) unclearly (b) calmly (c) ungrammatically (d) logically.

24. " 'When the matter was *broached* I knew I could do nothing that night, so suggested next day.' " **Broached** (85) means (a) disapproved (b) introduced (c) analyzed (d) uncovered.

25. "Subsequently these *surmises* were verified by a keeper." **Surmises** (85) means (a) errors (b) guesses (c) difficulties (d) bad thoughts.

26. " 'If you really found out what it was, it would be a sort of gentle *rebuke*.' " **Rebuke** (87) means (a) salute (b) reply (c) touch of humor (d) scolding.

27. " 'That *precipitated* a search of my cell by the warden, as I had intended.' " **Precipitated** (87) means (a) caused (b) avoided (c) reported (d) concealed.

28. " 'When I heard you coming, Mr. Warden, I *feigned* sleep.' " **Feigned** (89) means (a) sought (b) avoided (c) pretended (d) enjoyed.

29. " 'Having established this *improvised* trolley it is easy to see how I got things in the cell and made them disappear at will.' " **Improvised** (89) means something that is invented (a) after great difficulty

(b) without extensive preparation (c) with the help of other people (d) only by a genius.

30. " 'I thought that if anyone were tempted to investigate that hole the rat would dampen his *ardor*.' " **Ardor** (89) means (a) fingertips (b) enthusiasm (c) cowardice (d) hesitancy.

Thinking Critically About the Story

1. How does The Thinking Machine compare with Sherlock Holmes, Colonel March, and the Man in the Corner in method, personality, and appearance? Why does a writer try to make his or her detective as distinctive as possible, different from other sleuths?
2. There are at least five important steps in the thought process:

   (a) Identifying the Problem
   (b) Exploring the Problem
   (c) Narrowing the Problem
   (d) Considering Possible Solutions
   (e) Making the Decision and Acting on It.

   Point out how The Thinking Machine followed the five steps in solving his problem.
3. How do we use similar thinking in our everyday living? Mention a typical personal problem that can be solved by careful thought.
4. "There were two other ways out," declared The Thinking Machine. Do you think the author had in mind other possibilities? Have you any? Explain.
5. Why does the author make the warden so puzzled and confused? (Hint: put yourself in the warden's place.) What other detectives had assistants or associates whose ignorance was important to the progress of the plot?
6. On page (64), Dr. Ransome asks, "How about the spaceship?" and The Thinking Machine replies, "That's not impossible at all. It will be invented some time. I'd do it myself, but I'm busy."

   This story was written half a century before space flight was achieved, but The Thinking Machine's prediction came true. Mention one achievement now considered impossible with modern technology but possible in the future.

Language in Action

Codes and Ciphers

The guard took the bit of linen and read this:

"Epa cseot d'net niiy awe htto n'si sih. 'T.'"

There is a fascination with secret messages. Children's play often involves secrets decipherable only by the recipient. Secret messages may generally be divided into two groups: codes and ciphers, with variations and combinations. Codes require a prearranged set of symbols interpreted only by the intended recipient. Sometimes complicated code books are required to interpret the messages.

Ciphers are self-contained. In simple ciphers, one letter or symbol may be substituted for another. Or the words or letters may be rearranged. In the Thinking Machine's cryptic message, he merely reversed the letters and word order.

Secret messages have played a major role in history. Mary, Queen of Scots, was beheaded because secret messages to supporters outside the castle/prison were intercepted, deciphered, and shown to Queen Elizabeth. Because Mary had been plotting to replace her on the throne, Elizabeth felt that she had no option but to acquiesce in her execution.

Though much progress has been made in interpreting ancient languages, there are still some that defy translation. These are secret messages that have tantalized scholars for generations.

The Glasgow Mystery

Baroness E. Orczy
British

"No key or bolt was found on the inside of the door; the murderer, therefore, having accomplished his ghastly deed, must have locked his victim in, and probably taken the key away with him."

The Baroness Orczy is most famous as the author of *The Scarlet Pimpernel,* popular as a novel, a play, a film, and a television production. Besides her novels, she wrote a number of short stories with the Man in the Corner as the detective. Writing at the same time as A. Conan Doyle, she provides a special, old-fashioned flavor to her stories. In some ways, the Old Man resembles Sherlock Holmes in his method.

The Old Man solves crimes away from the scene, from his table in a London tearoom. "The Glasgow Mystery" provides another crime beyond the capacity of the police to solve. At the conclusion of an ideal mystery, the reader should say, "Oh, yes. I should have seen that!" Will you say that after you finish this story?

The Glasgow Mystery

I

"IT HAS OFTEN been declared," remarked the man in the corner, "that a murder—a successful murder, I mean—can never be committed single-handed in a busy city, and that on the other hand, once a murder *is* committed by more than one person, one of the accomplices is sure to betray the other, and that is the reason why comparatively so few crimes remain undetected. Now I must say I quite agree with this latter theory."

It was some few weeks after my first introduction to the man in the corner and the inevitable bit of string he always played with when unravelling his mysteries, and some time before he recounted to me his grim version of the tragedy in Percy-street, which I have already retold in the ROYAL.

Now I had made it a hard and fast rule whenever he made an assertion of that kind to disagree with it. This invariably irritated him; he became comically excited, produced his bit of string, and started off at rattling speed, after a few rude remarks directed at lady journalists in general and myself in particular, on one of his madly bewildering, true cock-and-bull stories.

"What about the Glasgow murder, then?" I remarked skeptically.

"Ah, the Glasgow murder," he repeated "Yes, what about the Glasgow murder? I see you are one of those people who, like the police, believe that Yardley was an accomplice to that murder, and you still continue to hope, as they do, that sooner or later he, and the other man, Upton, will meet, divide the spoils, and throw themselves into the expectant arms of the Glasgow police."

"Do you mean to tell me that you don't think Yardley had anything to do with that murder?"

"What does it matter what a humble amateur like myself thinks of that or any other case? Pshaw!" he added, breaking his bit of string between his bony fingers in his comical excitement. "Why, think a moment how simple is the whole thing! There was Mrs. Carmichael, the widow of a medical officer, young, good-looking, and fairly well-off, who for the sake of company, more than for actual profit-making, rents one of the fine houses in Woodbine Crescent with a view to taking in 'paying guests.' Her house is beautifully furnished—I told you she was fairly well-off. She has no difficulty in getting boarders.

"The house is soon full. At the time of which I am speaking she had ten or eleven 'guests'—mostly men out at business all day, also a married couple, an officer's widow with her daughter, and two journalists. At first she kept four female servants; then one day there was a complaint among the gentlemen boarders that their boots were insufficiently polished and their clothes very sketchily brushed. Chief among these complainants was Mr. Yardley, a young man who wrote verses for magazines, called himself a poet, and, in consequence, indulged in sundry eccentric habits which furnished food for gossip both in the kitchen and in the drawing-room over the coffee-cups.

"As I said before, it was he who was loudest in his complaint on the subject of his boots; it was he, again, who, when Mrs. Carmichael expressed herself willing to do anything to please her boarders, recommended her a quiet, respectable man named Upton to come in for a couple of hours daily, clean boots, knives, windows, and what-nots, and make himself 'generally useful'—I believe that is the technical expression. Upton, it appears, had been known to Mr. Yardley for some time, had often run errands and delivered messages for him, and had even been intrusted with valuable poetical MSS, to be left at various editorial offices.

"It was in July of last year, was it not, that Glasgow—honest, stodgy, busy Glasgow—was thrilled to its very marrow by the recital in its evening papers of one of the most ghastly and most dastardly crimes?

"At two o'clock that afternoon, namely, Mrs. Carmichael, of Woodbine Crescent, was found murdered in her room. Her safe had been opened, and all its contents—which were presumed to include a good deal of jewellery and money—had vanished. The evening papers had also added that the murderer was known to the police, and that no doubt was entertained as to his speedy arrest.

"It appears that in the household at Woodbine Crescent it was the duty of Mary, one of the maids, to take up a cup of tea to Mrs. Carmichael every morning at seven o'clock. The girl was not supposed to go into the room, but merely to knock at the door, wait for a response from her mistress, and then leave the tray outside on the mat.

"Usually Mrs. Carmichael took the tray in immediately, and was down to breakfast with her boarders at half-past eight. But on that eventful morning Mary seems to have been in a hurry. She could not positively state afterwards whether she had heard her mistress's answer to her knock or not; against that, she was quite sure that she had taken up the tray at seven o'clock precisely.

"When everybody went down to breakfast a couple of hours or so later, it was noticed that Mrs. Carmichael had not taken in her tea-tray as usual. A few anxious comments were made as to the genial hostess being unwell, and then the matter was dropped. The servants did not seem to have been really anxious about their mistress during the morning. Mary, who had been in the house two years, said that once before Mrs. Carmichael had stayed in bed with a bad headache until one o'clock.

"However, when the lunch hour came and went, Mrs. Tyrrell, one of the older lady boarders, became alarmed. She went up to her hostess's door and knocked at it loudly and repeatedly, but received no reply. The door, mind you, was locked or bolted, presumably, of course, from the inside. After consultation with her fellow boarders, Mrs. Tyrrell at last, feeling that something must be very wrong, took it upon herself to call in the police. Constable Rae came in; he too knocked and called, shook the door, and finally burst it open.

"It is not for me," continued the man in the corner, "to give you a description of that room as it appeared before the horrified eyes of the constable, the servants, and lady boarders; that lies more in your province than in mine.

"Suffice it to say that the unfortunate lady lay in her bed with her throat cut.

"No key or bolt was found on the inside of the door; the murderer, therefore, having accomplished his ghastly deed, must have locked his victim in, and probably taken the key away with him. Hardly had the terrible discovery been made than Emma the cook, half hysterical with fear and horror, rushed up to Constable Rae, and, clutching him wildly by the arm, whispered under her breath, 'Upton, Upton; he did it. I know . . . My poor mistress; he cut her throat with that fowl carver this morning. I saw it in his hand . . . It is him, constable!'

" 'Where is he?' asked the constable peremptorily. 'See that no one leaves the house. Who has seen this man?'

"But neither the constable, nor anyone else for that matter, was much surprised to find that on searching the house throughout, the man Upton had disappeared."

II

"AT FIRST, OF COURSE, the case seemed simplicity itself. No doubt existed, either in the public mind or that of the police, as to Upton being the author of the grim and horrible tragedy. The only difficulty, so far, was the fact that Upton had managed not only to get away on the day of the murder, but also had contrived to evade the rigorous search instituted throughout the city after him by the police—a search, I assure you, in which many an amateur detective readily joined.

"The inquest had been put off for a day or two in the hope that Upton might be found before it occurred. However, three days had now elapsed, and it could not be put off any longer. Little did the public expect the sensational developments which the case suddenly began to assume.

"The medical evidence revealed nothing new. On the contrary, it added its usual quota of vague indefiniteness which so often helps to puzzle the police. The medical officer had been called in by Constable Rae, directly after his discovery of the murder. That was about two o'clock in the afternoon. Death had occurred a good many hours before that time, stated Dr. Dawlish—possibly nine or ten hours; but it might also have been eleven or twelve hours previously.

"Then Emma the cook was called. Her evidence was, of course, most important, as she had noticed and talked to the man Upton the very morning of the crime. He came as usual to his work, about a quarter to seven, but the cook immediately noticed that he seemed very strange and excited.

" 'What do you mean by strange?' asked the coroner.

" 'Well, it was strange of him, sir, to start first thing in the morning cleaning knives when we had as many knives as we wanted clean for breakfast.'

" 'Yes? He started cleaning knives, and then what did he do?'

" 'Oh, he turned and turned that there knife machine so as I told him he would be turning all the edges. Then he suddenly took up the fowl carver and said to me; "This fowl carver is awful blunt—where's the steel?" I says to him: "In the sideboard, of course, in the dining-room," and he goes off with the fowl carver in his hand, and that is the last I ever saw of that carver and of Upton himself.'

" 'Have you known Upton long?' asked the coroner.

" 'No, sir, he had only been in the house two days. Mr. Yardley gave him a character, and the mistress took him on, to clean boots and knives. His hours were half-past six to ten, but he used to turn up about a quarter to seven. He seemed obliging and willing, but not much up to his work, and didn't say much. But I hadn't seen him so funny except that morning when the poor missus was murdered.'

" 'Is this the carver you speak of?' asked the coroner, directing a constable to show one he held in his hand to the witness.

"With renewed hysterical weeping Emma identified the carver as the one she had last seen in Upton's hand. It appears that Detective McMurdoch had found the knife, together with the key of Mrs. Carmichael's bedroom door, under the hall mat. Sensational, wasn't it?" laughed the man in the corner; "quite in the style of the penny novelette—sensational, but not very mysterious.

"Then Mrs. Tyrrell had to be examined, as it was she who had first been alarmed about Mrs. Carmichael, and who had taken it upon herself to call in the police. Whether through spite or merely accidentally Mrs. Tyrrell insisted in her evidence on the fact that it was Mr. Yardley who was indirectly responsible for the awful tragedy, since it was he who had introduced the man Upton into the house.

"The coroner felt more interested. He thought he would like to put a few questions to Mr. Yardley. Now Mr. Yardley when called up did not certainly look prepossessing; and from the first most persons present were prejudiced against him. He was, as I think I said before, that *rara avis*[1] a successful poet: he wrote dainty scraps for magazines and weekly journals.

"In appearance he was a short, sallow, thin man, with no body and long limbs, and carried his head so much to one side as to almost appear deformed. Here is a snapshot I got of him some time subsequently. He is no beauty, is he?

"Still his manner, his small shapely hands, and quiet voice undoubtedly proclaimed him a gentleman.

"It was very well known throughout the household that Mr. Yardley was very eccentric; being a poet he would enjoy the privilege with impunity. It appears that his most eccentric habit was to get up at unearthly hours in the morning—four o'clock sometimes—and wander about the streets of Glasgow.

" 'I have written my best pieces,' he stated in response to the coroner's astonished remark upon this strange custom of his, 'leaning against a lamp post in Sauchiehall Street at five o'clock in the morning. I spend my afternoons in the various public libraries, reading. I have only boarded and lodged in this house for two or three months, but, as the servants will tell you, I leave it long before they are up in the morning. I am never in to breakfast or luncheon, but always in to dinner. I go to bed early, naturally, as I require several hours sleep.'

"Mr. Yardley was then very closely questioned as to his knowledge of the man Upton.

" 'I first met the man,' replied Mr. Yardley, 'about a year ago. He was loafing in Buchanan Street, outside the *Herald* office, and spoke to me, telling me a most pitiable tale—namely, that he was an ex-compositor, had had to give up his work owing to failing eyesight, that he had striven for weeks and months to get some other kind of employment, spending in the meanwhile the hard-earned savings of many years' toil; that he had come to his last shilling two days ago, and had been reduced to begging, not for money, but for some kind of job—anything to earn a few honest coins.

" 'Well, I somehow liked the look of the man; moreover, as I just happened to want to send a message to the other end of the city, I sent Upton. Since then I have seen him almost every day. He takes my manuscripts for me to the editorial offices, and runs various errands. I have recommended him to one or two of my friends, and they have always found him honest and sober. He has eked out a very meagre livelihood in this way, and when Mrs. Carmichael thought of having a man in the

[1]rare bird

house to do odd jobs, I thought I should be doing a kind act by recommending Upton to her. Little did I dream then what terrible consequences such a kind act would bring in its trail. I can only account for the man's awful crime by thinking that perhaps his mind had become suddenly unhinged.'

"All this seemed plain and straightforward enough. Mr. Yardley spoke quietly, without the slightest nervousness or agitation. The coroner and jury both pressed him with questions on the subject of Upton, but his attitude remained equally self-possessed throughout. Perhaps he felt, after a somewhat severe cross-examination on the part of the coroner, who prided himself on his talent in that direction, that a certain amount of doubt might lurk in the minds of the jury and consequently the public. Be that as it may, he certainly begged that two or three of the servants might be recalled in order to enable them to state definitely that he was out of the house, as usual, when they came downstairs that morning.

"One of the housemaids, recalled, fully corroborated that statement. Mr. Yardley's room, she said, was on the ground floor, next to the dining-room. She went into it soon after half-past six, turned down the bed, and began tidying it up generally.

"There was only one other witness of any importance to examine. One other boarder—Mr. James Lucas, a young journalist, employed on the editorial staff of the *Glasgow Banner.*

"The reason why he had been called specially was because he was well known to be one of the privileged guests of the house, and had been more intimate with the deceased than any of her other boarders. This privilege, it appears, chiefly consisted in being admitted to coffee, and possibly whiskey and soda after dinner, in Mrs. Carmichael's special private sitting-room. Moreover, there was a generally accepted theory among the other boarders that Mr. James Lucas entertained certain secret hopes with regard to his amiable hostess, and that, but for the fact that he was several years her junior, she might have encouraged these hopes.

"Now, Mr. James Lucas was the exact opposite of Mr. Yardley, the poet; tall, fair, athletic, his appearance would certainly prepossess everyone in his favour. He seemed very much upset, and recounted with much, evidently genuine, feeling, his last interview with the unfortunate lady—the evening before the murder.

" 'I spent about an hour with Mrs. Carmichael in her sitting-room,' he concluded, 'and parted from her about ten o'clock. I then went to my club, where I stayed pretty late, until closing time, in fact. After that I went for a stroll, and it was a quarter past two by my watch when I came in. I let myself in with my latch-key.

" 'It was pitch dark in the outer hall, and I was groping for my candle, when I heard the sound of a door opening and shutting on one of the floors above, and directly after someone coming down the stairs.

As you have seen yourself, the outer hall is divided from the inner one by a glass door, which on this occasion stood open. In the inner hall there was a faint glimmer of light, which worked its way down from a skylight on one of the landings, and by this glimmer I saw Mr. Yardley descending the stairs, cross the hall, and go into his room. He did not see me, and I did not speak.'

"An extraordinary, almost breathless, hush had descended over all those assembled there. The coroner sat with his chin buried in his hand, his eyes resting searchingly on the witness who had just spoken. The jury had not uttered a sound. At last the coroner queried:

" 'Is the jury to understand, Mr. Lucas, that you can swear positively that at a quarter-past two in the morning, or thereabouts, you saw Mr. Yardley come down the stairs from one of the floors above and go into his own room, which is on the ground floor?'

" 'Positively.'

"That was enough. Mr. Lucas was dismissed and Mr. Yardley was recalled. As he once more stood before the coroner, his curious one-sided stoop, his sallowness, and length of limb seemed even more marked than before. Perhaps he was a shade or two paler, but certainly neither his hands nor his voice trembled in the slightest degree.

"Questioned by the coroner, he replied quietly:

" 'Mr. Lucas was obviously mistaken. At the hour he names I was in bed and asleep.'

"There had been excitement and breathless interest when Mr. James Lucas had made his statement, but that excitement and breathlessness was as nothing compared with the absolutely dumbfounded awe which fell over everyone there, as the sallow, half-deformed, little poet, gave the former witness so completely, so emphatically the lie.

"The coroner himself hardly knew how to keep up his professional dignity as he almost gasped the query:

" 'Then is the jury to understand that you can swear positively that at a quarter-past two o'clock on that particular morning you were in bed and asleep?'

" 'Positively.'

"It seemed as if Mr. Yardley had repeated purposely the other man's emphatic and laconic assertion. Certainly his voice was as steady, his eye as clear, his manner as calm as that of Mr. Lucas. The coroner and jury were silent, and Mr. Yardley turned to where young Lucas had retired in a further corner of the room. The eyes of the two met, almost like the swords of two duellists before the great attack; neither flinched. One or the other was telling a lie. A terrible lie since it might entail loss of honour, or life perhaps to the other, yet *neither* flinched. One was telling a lie, remember, and in everyone's mind there arose at once the great all absorbing queries 'Which?' and 'Wherefore!' "

III

I HAD BEEN so absorbed in listening to the thrilling narrative of that highly dramatic inquest that I really had not noticed until then that the man in the corner was recounting it as if he had been present at it himself.

"That is because I heard it all from an eye-witness," he suddenly replied with that eerie knack he seemed to possess of reading my thoughts, "but it must have been very dramatic, and, above all, terribly puzzling. You see there were two men swearing against one another, both in good positions, both educated men; it was impossible for any jury to take either evidence as absolutely convincing, and it could not be proved that either of them lied. Mr. Lucas might have done so from misapprehension. There was just a possibility that he had had more whiskey at his club than was good for him. Mr. Yardley, on the other hand, if he lied, lied because he had something to hide, something to hide in that case which might have been terrible.

"Of course Dr. Dawlish was recalled, and with wonderful learning and wonderful precision he repeated his vague medical statements:

" 'When I examined the body with my colleague, Dr. Swanton, death had evidently supervened several hours ago. Personally, I believe that it must have occurred certainly more like twelve hours ago than seven.'

"More than that he could not say. After all, medical science has its limits.

"Then Emma, the cook, was again called. There was an important point which, oddly enough, had been overlooked up to this moment. The question, namely, of the doormat under which the knife (which, by the way, was blood-stained) and also the key of Mrs. Carmichael's bedroom door was found. Emma, however, could make a very clear and very definite statement on that point. She had cleaned the hall and shaken the mat at half-past six that morning. At that hour the housemaid was making Mr. Yardley's bed; he had left the house already. There certainly was neither key nor knife under the mat then.

"The balance of evidence, which perhaps for one brief moment had inclined oh, ever so slightly, against Mr. Yardley, returned to its original heavy weight against the man Upton. Of course there was practically nothing to implicate Mr. Yardley seriously. The coroner made a résumé of the case before his jury worthy of a judge in the High Courts.

"He recapitulated all the evidence. It was very strong, undeniable, damning against Upton, and the jury could arrive but at one conclusion with regard to him. Then there was the medical evidence. That certainly favoured Upton a very little, if at all. Remember that both the medical gentlemen refused to make a positive statement as to the time;

their evidence could not, therefore, be said to weigh either for or against anyone.

"There was then the strange and unaccountably conflicting evidence between two gentlemen of the house—Mr. Lucas and Mr. Yardley. That was a matter which for the present must rest between either of these gentlemen and their conscience. There was also the fact that the man Upton—the evident actual murderer—had been introduced into the house by Mr. Yardley. The jury knew best themselves if this fact should or should not weigh with them in their decision.

"That was the sum total of the evidence. The jury held but a very brief consultation. Their foreman pronounced their verdict of 'Wilful murder against Upton.' Not a word about Mr. Yardley. What could they have said? There was really no evidence against him—not enough, certainly, to taint his name for ever with so hideous a blight.

"In a case like that, remember, the jury are fully aware that the police would never for a moment lose sight of a man who had so narrowly escaped a warrant as Yardley had done. Relying on the certainty that very soon Upton would be arrested, it was not to be doubted for a moment but that he would betray his accomplice, if he had one. Criminals in such a plight nearly always do. In the meanwhile, every step of Yardley's would be dogged, unbeknown to himself, even if he attempted to leave the country. As for Upton——."

The man in the corner paused. He was eyeing me through his great bone-rimmed spectacles, watching with ironical delight my evident breathless interest in his narrative. I remembered that Glasgow murder so well. I remember the talks, the arguments, the quarrels that would arise in every household. Was Yardley an accomplice? Did he kill Mrs. Carmichael at two in the morning? Did he tell a lie? If so, why? Did Mr. James Lucas tell a lie? Many people, I remember, held this latter theory, more particularly as Mrs. Carmichael's will was proved some days later, and it was found that she had left all her money to him.

For a little while public opinion veered dead against him. Some people thought that if he were innocent he would refuse to touch a penny of her money; others, of a more practical turn of mind, did not see why he should not. He was a struggling young journalist; the lady had obviously been in love with him, and intended to marry him; she had a perfect right—as she had no children or any near relative—to leave her money to whom she choose, and it would indeed be hard on him, if, through the act of some miscreant, he should at one fell swoop be deprived both of wife and fortune.

Then, of course, there was Upton—Upton! Upton! whom the police could not find! who must be guilty, seeing that he so hid himself, who never would have acted the hideous comedy with the carver. Why should he have wilfully drawn attention to himself, and left, as it were, his visiting card on the scene of the murder?

Why? why? why?

"Ah, yes, why?" came as a funny, shrill echo from my eccentric *vis-a-vis*.[1] "I see that in spite of my earnest endeavour to teach you to think out a case logically and clearly, you start off with a preconceived notion, which naturally leads you astray *because* it is preconceived, just like any blundering detective in these benighted islands."

"Preconceived?" I retorted indignantly. "There is no question of preconception. Whether Mr. Yardley knew of the contemplated murder or not, whether he was an accomplice or Mr. Lucas, there is one thing very clear—namely, that Upton was not innocent in the matter."

"What makes you say that?" he asked blandly.

"Obviously, because if he were innocent he would not have acted the hideous tragic comedy with the carver; he would not, above all, have absolutely damned himself by disappearing out of the house and out of sight at the very moment when the discovery of Mrs. Carmichael's murdered body had become imminent."

"It never struck you, I suppose," retorted the man in the corner with quiet sarcasm, "how *very* damning Upton's actions were on that particular morning?"

"Of course they were *very* damning. That is just my contention."

"And you have never then studied my methods of reasoning sufficiently to understand that when a criminal—a clever criminal, mind you—appears to be damning himself in the most brainless fashion, that is the time to guard against the clever pitfalls he is laying up for the police?"

"Exactly. That is why I, as well as many people connected with journalism, believe that Upton was acting a comedy in order to save his accomplice. The question only remains as to who the accomplice was."

"He must have been singularly unselfish and self-sacrificing, then."

"How do you mean?"

"According to your argument, Upton heaped up every conceivable circumstantial evidence against himself in order to shield his accomplice. Firstly he acts the part of strange, unnatural excitement, he loudly proclaims the fact that he leaves the kitchen with the fowl carver in his hand, thirdly he deposits that same blood-stained knife and the key of Mrs. Carmichael's room under the mat a few moments before he leaves the house. You must own that the man must have been singularly unselfish since, if he is ever caught, nothing would save him from the gallows, whilst, unless a great deal more evidence can be brought up, his accomplice could continue to go free."

---

[1]person opposite

"Yes, that might be," I said thoughtfully; "it was of course a part of the given plan. Many people held that Upton and Yardley were great friends—they might have been brothers, who knows?"

"Yes, who knows?" he repeated scornfully, as getting more and more excited his long thin fingers wound and unwound his bit of string, making curious complicated knots, and then undoing them feverishly.

"Do brothers usually so dote on each other, that they are content to swing for one another? And have you never wondered why the police never found Upton? How did he get away? Where is he? Has the earth swallowed him up?

"Surely a clumsy brute like that, who gives himself hopelessly away on the very day when he commits a murder, cannot have brains enough to hide altogether away from the police—a man who before a witness selects the weapon with which he means to kill his victim, and who then deliberately leaves it blood-stained there where it is sure to be found at once? Why imagine such a consummate fool evading the police, not a day, not a week, not a month, but nearly two years now, which means altogether? Why, such a fool as you, the public, and the police have branded him would have fallen into a trap within twenty-four hours of his attempt at evasion; whereas the man who planned and accomplished that murder was a genius before he became a blackguard."

"That's just what I said. He was doing it to shield his accomplice."

"His accomplice!" gasped the funny creature, with ever increasing excitement. "Yes, the accomplice he loved and cherished above all—his brother you say, perhaps. No, someone he would love ten thousand times more than any brother."

"Then you mean——"

"*Himself*, of course! Didn't you see it all along? Lord bless my soul! The young man—poet or blackguard, what you will—who comes into a boarding-house, then realises that its mistress is wealthy. He studies the rules of the house, the habits of its mistress, finds out about her money, her safe, her jewels, and then makes his plans. Oh, they were magnificently laid! That man ought to have been a great diplomatist, a great general—he was only a great scoundrel.

"The sort of disguise he assumed is so easy to manage. Only remember one thing: When a fool wishes to sink his identity he does so *after* he has committed a crime and is wanted by the police; he is bound, therefore, for the best part of the remainder of his life, to keep up the disguise he has selected at all times, every hour, every minute of the day; to alter his voice, his walk, his manners. On the other hand, how does a clever man like Yardley proceed?

"He chooses his disguise and assumes it *before* the execution of his crime: it is then only a matter of a few days, and when all is over, the individual, the known criminal, disappears; and, mind you, he takes great care that the criminal shall be known. Now in this case Upton is introduced into the house; say he calls one evening on Mr. Yardley's recommendation; Mrs. Carmichael sees him in the hall for a few moments, arranges the question of work and wages, and after that he comes every morning, with a dirty face, towzled hair, false beard and moustache—the usual type of odd job man very much down in his luck—his work lies in the kitchen, no one sees him upstairs, whilst the cook and kitchen folk never see Mr. Yardley.

"After a little while something—carelessness perhaps—might reveal the trick, but the deception is only carried on two days. Then the murder is accomplished and Upton disappears. In the meanwhile Mr. Yardley continues his eccentric habits. He goes out at unearthly hours; he is a poet; he is out of the house while Upton carries on the comedy with the carving knife. He knows that there never will be any evidence against him as Yardley; he has taken every care that all should be against Upton, all; hopeless, complete, absolute, damning!

"Then he leaves the police to hunt for Upton. He 'lies low' for a time, after a little while he will go abroad, I dare say he has done so already. A jeweller in Vienna, or perhaps St. Petersburg, will buy some loose stones of him, the stones he has picked out of Mrs. Carmichael's brooches and rings, the gold he will melt down and sell, the notes he can cash at any foreign watering-place, without a single question being asked of him. English banknotes find a very ready market abroad, and 'no questions asked.'

"After that he will come back to his friends in Glasgow and write dainty bits of poetry for magazines; the only difference being that he will write them at more reasonable hours. And during all the time the police will hunt for Upton.

"It was clever, was it not? You have his photo? I gave it you just now. Clever-looking, isn't he? As Upton he wore a beard and dyed his hair very black; it must have been a great trouble every morning, mustn't it?"

Reading for Understanding

Central Point

d 1. The central point of the story is a question of (a) accuracy in reporting (b) police efficiency (c) identity (d) curiosity.

Details

2. Mrs. Carmichael (a) expected to marry Yardley (b) was old and feeble (c) was jilted by Upton (d) took in boarders.
3. The first one to suspect that something was wrong was (a) Emma (b) Mrs. Tyrell (c) Constable Rae (d) Mary.
4. Upton was introduced into the household by (a) Emma (b) Mary (c) Mr. Yardley (d) Mrs. Tyrell.
5. Mr. Yardley insisted that he was a (a) retired army officer (b) journalist (c) poet (d) relative of Upton's.

Inferences

6. One important clue to the solution of the mystery was that (a) Lucas had been a favorite of Mrs. Carmichael's (b) Upton and Yardley were never seen together (c) Emma and Mary knew much more than they told (d) Detective McMurdoch found the knife under the hall mat.
7. The murderer succeeded because (a) he knew the routines of the house (b) the police falsified evidence (c) Yardley was basically an honest, if naive, young man (d) Lucas covered up for Yardley.
8. Of the characters in the story, the liar was (a) Lucas (b) Yardley (c) Mary (d) the coroner

Order of Events

9. Arrange the items in the order in which they occurred. Use letters only.

   A. Upton disappears.
   B. Yardley recommends Upton.
   C. Mrs. Carmichael does not take in her tea tray.
   D. The Old Man identifies the murderer.
   E. The jury identifies Upton.

Author's Attitude

10. The author's attitude toward her creation, the Man in the Corner, is one of (a) unwitting scorn (b) ill-concealed embarrassment (c) girlish awe (d) affectionate respect.

Words in Context

1.,2. "It was in July of last year, was it not, that Glasgow—honest, *stodgy*, busy Glasgow—was thrilled to its very marrow by the recital in its evening papers of one of the most ghastly and *dastardly* crimes." **Stodgy** (100) means (a) boring (b) colorful (c) overworked (d) exciting. **Dastardly** (100) means (a) intriguing (b) puzzling (c) unexpected (d) cowardly.

3. "'Where is he?'" asked the constable *peremptorily*." **Peremptorily** (101) means (a) swiftly (b) arrogantly (c) cautiously (d) heartlessly.

4., 5., 6. "Upton had managed not only to get away on the day of the murder, but also had *contrived* to *evade* the *rigorous* search instituted throughout the city after him by the police." **Contrived** (101) means (a) planned ingeniously (b) deceived unintentionally (c) accidentally achieved (d) obviously attempted. **Evade** (101) means (a) follow (b) dodge (c) counteract (d) resist. **Rigorous** (101) means (a) relentless (b) casual (c) evil (d) requested.

7. "Mr. Yardley when called up did not certainly look *prepossessing*." **Prepossessing** (103) means (a) attractive (b) gaudy (c) tiresome (d) greedy.

8. "In appearance he was a short, *sallow*, thin man, with no body and long limbs." **Sallow** (103) means (a) stocky and muscular (b) pale and sickly (c) well tanned (d) disagreeable.

9. "Being a poet he would enjoy the privilege with *impunity*." **Impunity** (103) suggests a lack of (a) enthusiasm (b) attentiveness (c) vitality (d) punishment.

10. "'Perhaps his mind had become suddenly *unhinged*.'" **Unhinged** (104) means (a) flabby (c) uncertain (c) unusually keen (d) confused.

11. "That excitement and breathlessness was as nothing compared with the absolutely *dumbfounded* awe which fell over everyone there." **Dumbfounded** (105) means (a) obvious (b) unwarranted (c) groundless (d) bewildered.

12. "It seemed as if Mr. Yardley had repeated purposely the other man's emphatic and *laconic* assertion." **Laconic** (105) means (a) vivid and memorable (b) extensive and meaningful (c) short and pointed (d) contradictory.

13. "The coroner made a *résumé* of the case before his jury worthy of a judge in the High Courts." A **résumé** (106) is a (a) critical review (b) summary (c) mockery (d) plea.
14. "He *recapitulated* all the evidence." **Recapitulated** (106) means (a) reviewed (b) challenged (c) glossed over (d) omitted.
15. "There was really no evidence against him—not enough, certainly, to taint his name for ever with so hideous a *blight*."A **blight** (107) is a kind of (a) illumination (b) disease (c) reputation (d) discovery.
16. "For a little while public opinion *veered* dead against him." **Veered** (107) means (a) protested loudly (b) changed direction (c) followed the course (d) bumped along.
17. "It is preconceived, just like any blundering detective in these *benighted* islands." **Benighted** (108) means (a) unenlightened (b) blessed (c) spacious (d) repressed.
18. "You must own that the man must have been *singularly* unselfish since, if he is ever caught, nothing would save him from the gallows." **Singularly** (108) means (a) cleverly (b) thoughtfully (c) remarkably (d) wearily.
19. "Do brothers usually so *dote on* each other that they are content to swing for one another." **Dote on** (109) means (a) imitate closely (b) fear irrationally (c) question sharply (d) love excessively.
20. "Why imagine such a *consummate* fool evading the police?" **Consummate** (109) means (a) foolish (b) complete (c) eager (d) original.
21. "Such a fool as you, the public, and the police have branded him would have fallen into a trap within twenty-four hours of his attempt at *evasion*." **Evasion** (109) means (a) repetition (b) disclosure (c) escape (d) success.

Thinking Critically About the Story

1. What crucial clues helped the Man in the Corner to a solution of the mystery?
2. Why did Upton take such pains to make himself appear so guilty?
3. What possible motive for the slaying was given to Lucas? Was it misleading?

4. The Man in the Corner agreed that Upton had an accomplice . . . but who? Why?
5. Why was it crucial for the murderer to change his identity before the crime, not after?
6. What was Yardley's motive in complaining about the polishing of his boots?
7. Yardley was short; Lucas, tall. Did this difference play a role in the solution of the crime? Explain.
8. The title "The Glasgow Mystery" is rather commonplace. Can you think of a better?

Language in Action

Concealed Metaphors

> "It was very well known throughout the household that Mr. Yardley was very eccentric."

Metaphor compares unlike objects and adds a touch of poetry to speech and writing. The flower name *foxglove* is, for example, particularly apt. Some metaphors are almost as colorful, even though they are concealed in their etymologies, or word histories. *Eccentric,* for example, derives from the root *center* and the prefix *ec; out, out of,* or *off.* Someone who is *eccentric* is "off center," a rather clever way of labeling a deviation from the normal.

Like most of the stories in this book, "The Glasgow Mystery" has a great many concealed metaphors.

An *amateur* is a "lover," someone who loves a hobby as a pastime, not a profession.

Humble comes from *humus, earth.* A humble person is literally "down to earth."

A *manuscript* was once written by hand. Now a manuscript may come in many forms.

A *constable* was once an *officer of the stable.*

Crescent means *growing.* The *crescent* moon is *growing* toward full. The shape of the crescent moon has been extended to streets.

Widow comes from a root *to divide, to separate,* a grim reminder of the loss of a spouse.

Gossip is *god-sibb,* a sponsor of a child at baptism. We may suspect that baptismal get-togethers provide an opportunity for talk about others, or *gossip.*

Trifles

Susan Glaspell
American

Mr. Henderson said coming out that what was needed for the case was a motive; something to show anger, or—sudden feeling.

This is a classic. Consider these achievements. It describes a murder, but without violence or gore. Little by little, it reveals the murderer. It presents major clues, subtly and tellingly. It has seven characters. Five actively appear in the play. The other two, though absent from the stage, are very much present in their impact on the plot. All seven characters are sharply distinguished. It has a subtle theme ridiculing the traditional attitude toward women and their capabilities. It has an ingenious, powerful climax—all in the space of a one-act play.

The "detectives" in this case are amateurs, unskilled in the ways of investigation and interrogation. Yet, this sharp observation and compassionate understanding "solve" a case impossible for the professionals. Don't miss the irony in the final sentence.

Trifles

SCENE: *The kitchen in the now abandoned farmhouse of* JOHN WRIGHT, *a gloomy kitchen, and left without having been put in order—the walls covered with a faded wallpaper.* D. R. *is a door leading to the parlor. On the* R. *wall above this door is a built-in kitchen cupboard with shelves in the upper portion and drawers below. In the rear wall at* R., *up two steps is a door opening onto stairs leading to the second floor. In the rear wall at* L. *is a door to the shed and from there to the outside. Between these two doors is an old-fashioned black iron stove. Running along the* L. *wall from the shed door is an old iron sink and sink shelf, in which is set a hand pump. Downstage of the sink is an uncurtained window. Near the window is an old wooden rocker. Center stage is an unpainted wooden kitchen table with straight chairs on either side. There is a small chair* D. R. *Unwashed pans under the sink, a loaf of bread outside the breadbox, a dish towel on the table—other signs of incompleted work. At the rear the shed door opens and the* SHERIFF *comes followed by the* COUNTY ATTORNEY *and* HALE. *The* SHERIFF *and* HALE *are men in middle life, the* COUNTY ATTORNEY *is a young man; all are much bundled up and go at once to the stove. They are followed by the two women—the* SHERIFF'S *wife,* MRS. PETERS, *first; she is a slight wiry woman, a thin nervous face.* MRS. HALE *is larger and would ordinarily be called more comfortable looking, but she is disturbed now and looks fearfully about as she enters. The women have come in slowly, and stand close together near the door.*

CAST OF CHARACTERS:

MR. PETERS, SHERIFF
MR. HENDERSON, COUNTY ATTORNEY
MR. HALE, NEIGHBOR OF THE WRIGHTS
MRS. PETERS, THE SHERIFF'S WIFE
MRS. HALE, WIFE TO MR. HALE

COUNTY ATTORNEY (*at stove rubbing his hands*). This feels good. Come up to the fire, ladies.

MRS. PETERS (*after taking a step forward*). I'm not—cold.

SHERIFF (*unbuttoning his overcoat and stepping away from the stove to right of table as if to mark the beginning of official business*). Now, Mr. Hale, before we move things about, you explain to Mr. Henderson just what you saw when you came here yesterday morning.

COUNTY ATTORNEY (*crossing down to left of the table*). By the way, has anything been moved? Are things just as you left them yesterday?

SHERIFF (*looking about*). It's just the same. When it dropped below zero last night I thought I'd better send Frank out this morning to make a fire for us—(*sits right of center table*) no use getting pneumonia with a big case on, but I told him not to touch anything except the stove—and you know Frank.

COUNTY ATTORNEY. Somebody should have been left here yesterday.

SHERIFF. Oh—yesterday. When I had to send Frank to Morris Center for that man who went crazy—I want you to know I had my hands full yesterday. I knew you could get back from Omaha by today and as long as I went over everything here myself—

COUNTY ATTORNEY. Well, Mr. Hale, tell just what happened when you came here yesterday morning.

HALE (*crossing down to above table*). Harry and I had started to town with a load of potatoes. We came along the road from my place and as I got here I said, "I'm going to see if I can't get John Wright to go in with me on a party telephone." I spoke to Wright about it once before and he put me off, saying folks talked too much anyway, and all he asked was peace and quiet—I guess you know about how much he talked himself; but I thought maybe if I went to the house and talked about it before his wife, though I said to Harry that I didn't know as what his wife wanted made much difference to John—

COUNTY ATTORNEY. Let's talk about that later, Mr. Hale. I do want to talk about that, but tell now just what happened when you got to the house.

HALE. I didn't hear or see anything; I knocked at the door, and still it was all quiet inside. I knew they must be up, it was past eight o'clock. So I knocked again, and I thought I heard somebody say, "Come in." I wasn't sure, I'm not sure yet, but I opened the door—this door (*indicating the door by which the two women are still standing*) and there in that rocker—(*pointing to it*) sat Mrs. Wright. (*They all look at the rocker* D. L.)

COUNTY ATTORNEY. What—was she doing?

HALE. She was rockin' back and forth. She had her apron in her hand and was kind of—pleating it.

COUNTY ATTORNEY. And how did she—look?

HALE. Well, she looked queer.

COUNTY ATTORNEY. How do you mean—queer?

HALE. Well, as if she didn't know what she was going to do next. And kind of done up.

COUNTY ATTORNEY (*takes out notebook and pencil and sits left of center table*). How did she seem to feel about your coming?

HALE. Why, I don't think she minded—one way or other. She didn't pay much attention. I said, "How do, Mrs. Wright, it's cold, ain't it?"

And she said, "Is it?"—and went on kind of pleating at her apron. Well, I was surprised; she didn't ask me to come up to the stove, or to set down, but just sat there, not even looking at me, so I said, "I want to see John." And then she—laughed. I guess you would call it a laugh. I thought of Harry and the team outside, so I said a little sharp: "Can't I see John?" "No," she says, kind o' dull like. "Ain't he home?" says I. "Yes," says she, "he's home." "Then why can't I see him?" I asked her, out of patience. "'Cause he's dead," says she. "*Dead?*" says I. She just nodded her head, not getting a bit excited, but rockin' back and forth. "Why—where is he?" says I, not knowing what to say. She just pointed upstairs—like that. (*Himself pointing to the room above*). I started for the stairs, with the idea of going up there. I walked from there to here—then I says, "Why, what did he die of?" "He died of a rope round his neck," says she, and just went on pleatin' at her apron. Well, I went out and called Harry. I thought I might—need help. We went upstairs and there he was lyin'—

COUNTY ATTORNEY. I think I'd rather have you go into that upstairs, where you can point it all out. Just go on now with the rest of the story.

HALE. Well, my first thought was to get that rope off. It looked . . . (*stops, his face twitches*) . . . But Harry, he went up to him, and he said, "No, he's dead all right, and we'd better not touch anything." So we went back downstairs. She was still sitting that same way. "Has anybody been notified?" I asked. "No," says she, unconcerned. "Who did this, Mrs. Wright?" said Harry. He said it business-like—and she stopped pleatin' of her apron. "I don't know," she says. "You don't *know?*" says Harry. "No," says she. "Weren't you sleepin' in the bed with him?" says Harry. "Yes," says she, "but I was on the inside." "Somebody slipped a rope round his neck and strangled him and you didn't wake up?" says Harry. "I didn't wake up," she said after him. We must 'a' looked as if we didn't see how that could be, for after a minute she said, "I sleep sound." Harry was going to ask her more questions but I said maybe we ought to let her tell her story first to the coroner, or the sheriff, so Harry went fast as he could to Rivers' place, where there's a telephone.

COUNTY ATTORNEY And what did Mrs. Wright do when she knew that you had gone for the coroner?

HALE. She moved from the rocker to that chair over there (*pointing to a small chair in the* D. R. *corner*) and just sat there with her hands held together and looking down. I got a feeling that I ought to make some conversation, so I said I had come in to see if John wanted to put in a telephone, and at that she started to laugh, and then she stopped and looked at me—scared (*The* COUNTY AT-

TORNEY, *who has had his notebook out, makes a note*). I dunno, maybe it wasn't scared. I wouldn't like to say it was. Soon Harry got back, and then Dr. Lloyd came, and you, Mr. Peters, and so I guess that's all I know that you don't.

COUNTY ATTORNEY (*rising and looking around*). I guess we'll go upstairs first—and then out to the barn and around there. (*To the* SHERIFF). You're convinced that there was nothing important here—nothing that would point to any motive?

SHERIFF. Nothing here but kitchen things. (*The* COUNTY ATTORNEY, *after again looking around the kitchen, opens the door of a cupboard closet in* R. *wall. He brings a small chair from* R.*—gets up on it and looks on a shelf. Pulls his hand away, sticky.*)

COUNTY ATTORNEY. Here's a nice mess. (*The women draw nearer* U. C.)

MRS. PETERS (*to the other woman*). Oh, her fruit; it did freeze. (*To the LAWYER*). She worried about that when it turned so cold. She said the fire'd go out and her jars would break.

SHERIFF (*rises*). Well, can you beat the women! Held for murder and worryin' about her preserves.

COUNTY ATTORNEY (*getting down from chair*). I guess before we're through she may have something more serious than preserves to worry about. (*Crosses down* R. C.)

HALE. Well, women are used to worrying over trifles. (*The two women move a little closer together.*)

COUNTY ATTORNEY (*with the gallantry of a young politician*). And yet, for all their worries, what would we do without the ladies? (*The women do not unbend. He goes below the center table to the sink, takes a dipperful of water from the pail and pouring it into a basin, washes his hands. While he is doing this the* SHERIFF *and* HALE *cross to cupboard, which they inspect. The* COUNTY ATTORNEY *starts to wipe his hands on the roller towel, turns it for a cleaner place.*) Dirty towels! (*Kicks his foot against the pans under the sink*). Not much of a housekeeper, would you say, ladies?

MRS. HALE (*stiffly*). There's a great deal of work to be done on a farm.

COUNTY ATTORNEY. To be sure. And yet (*with a little bow to her*) I know there are some Dickson County farmhouses which do not have such roller towels. (*He gives it a pull to expose its full length again.*)

MRS. HALE. Those towels get dirty awful quick. Men's hands aren't always as clean as they might be.

COUNTY ATTORNEY. Ah, loyal to your sex, I see. But you and Mrs. Wright were neighbors. I suppose you were friends, too.

MRS. HALE (*shaking her head*). I've not seen much of her of late years. I've not been in this house—it's more than a year.

COUNTY ATTORNEY (*crossing to women* U. C.). And why was that? You didn't like her?

MRS. HALE. I liked her all well enough. Farmers' wives have their hands full, Mr. Henderson. And then—

COUNTY ATTORNEY. Yes—?

MRS. HALE (*looking about*). It never seemed a very cheerful place.

COUNTY ATTORNEY. No—it's not cheerful. I shouldn't say she had the homemaking instinct.

MRS. HALE. Well, I don't know as Wright had, either.

COUNTY ATTORNEY. You mean that they didn't get on very well?

MRS. HALE. No, I don't mean anything. But I don't think a place'd be any cheerfuller for John Wright's being in it.

COUNTY ATTORNEY. I'd like to talk more of that a little later. I want to get the lay of things upstairs now. (*He goes past the women to* U. R. *where steps lead to a stair door.*)

SHERIFF. I suppose anything Mrs. Peters does'll be all right. She was to take in some clothes for her, you know, and a few little things. We left in such a hurry yesterday.

COUNTY ATTORNEY. Yes, but I would like to see what you take, Mrs. Peters, and keep an eye out for anything that might be of use to us.

MRS. PETERS. Yes, Mr. Henderson. (*The men leave by* U. R. *door to stairs. The women listen to the men's steps on the stairs, then look about the kitchen.*)

MRS. HALE (*crossing* L. *to sink*). I'd hate to have men coming into my kitchen, snooping around and criticizing. (*She arranges the pans under sink which the* LAWYER *had shoved out of place.*)

MRS. PETERS. Of course it's no more than their duty. (*Crosses to cupboard* U. R.)

MRS. HALE. Duty's all right, but I guess that deputy sheriff that came out to make the fire might have got a little of this on. (*Gives the roller towel a pull*). Wish I'd thought of that sooner. Seems mean to talk about her for not having things slicked up when she had to come away in such a hurry. (*crosses* R. *to* MRS. PETERS *at cupboard.*)

MRS. PETERS (*who has been looking through cupboard, lifts one end of a towel that covers a pan*). She had bread set. (*Stands still.*)

MRS. HALE (*eyes fixed on a loaf of bread beside the breadbox, which is on a low shelf of the cupboard*). She was going to put this in there. (*Picks up loaf, then abruptly drops it. In a manner of returning to familiar things*). It's a shame about her fruit. I wonder if it's all gone. (*Gets up on the chair and looks*). I think there's some here that's all right, Mrs. Peters. Yes—here; (*holding it toward the window*) this is cherries, too. (*Looking again*). I declare I believe that's the only one.

(*Gets down, jar in her hand. Goes to the sink and wipes it off on the outside*). She'll feel awful bad after all her hard work in the hot weather. I remember the afternoon I put up my cherries last summer. (*She puts the jar on the big kitchen table, center of the room. With a sigh, is about to sit down in the rocking chair. Before she is seated realizes what chair it is; with a slow look at it, steps back. The chair which she touched rocks back and forth.* MRS. PETERS *moves to center table and they both watch the chair rock for a moment or two.*)

MRS. PETERS (*shaking off the mood which the empty rocking chair has evoked. Now in a businesslike manner she speaks*). Well, I must get those things from the front room closet. (*She goes to the door at the* R., *but, after looking into the other room, steps back*). You coming with me, Mrs. Hale? You could help me carry them. (*They go in the other room; reappear,* MRS. PETERS *carrying a dress, petticoat and skirt,* MRS. HALE *following with a pair of shoes*). My, it's cold in there. (*She puts the clothes on the big table, and hurries to the stove.*)

MRS. HALE (*right of center table examining the skirt*). Wright was close. I think maybe that's why she kept so much to herself. She didn't even belong to the Ladies' Aid. I suppose she felt she couldn't do her part, and then you don't enjoy things when you feel shabby. I heard she used to wear pretty clothes and be lively, when she was Minnie Foster, one of the town girls singing in the choir. But that—oh, that was thirty years ago. This all you was to take in?

MRS. PETERS. She said she wanted an apron. Funny thing to want, for there isn't much to get you dirty in jail, goodness knows. But I suppose just to make her feel more natural. (*Crosses to cupboard*). She said they was in the top drawer in this cupboard. Yes, here. And then her little shawl that always hung behind the door. (*Opens stair door and looks*). Yes, here it is. (*Quickly shuts door leading upstairs.*)

MRS. HALE (*abruptly moving toward her*). Mrs. Peters?

MRS. PETERS. Yes, Mrs. Hale? (*At* U. R. *door.*)

MRS. HALE. Do you think she did it?

MRS. PETERS (*in a frightened voice*). Oh, I don't know.

MRS. HALE. Well, I don't think she did. Asking for an apron and her little shawl. Worrying about her fruit.

MRS. PETERS (*starts to speak, glances up, where footsteps are heard in the room above. In a low voice*). Mr. Peters says it looks bad for her. Mr. Henderson is awful sarcastic in a speech and he'll make fun of her sayin' she didn't wake up.

MRS. HALE. Well, I guess John Wright didn't wake when they was slipping that rope under his neck.

MRS. PETERS (*crossing slowly to table and placing shawl and apron on table with other clothing*). No, it's strange. It must have been done awful crafty and still. They say it was such a—funny way to kill a man, rigging it all up like that.

MRS. HALE (*crossing to left of* MRS. PETERS *at table*). That's just what Mr. Hale said. There was a gun in the house. He says that's what he can't understand.

MRS. PETERS. Mr. Henderson said coming out that what was needed for the case was a motive; something to show anger, or—sudden feeling.

MRS. HALE (*who is standing by the table*). Well, I don't see any signs of anger around here. (*She puts her hand on the dish towel which lies on the table, stands looking down at table, one-half of which is clean, the other half is messy*). It's wiped here. (*Makes a move as if to finish work, then turns and looks at loaf of bread outside of the breadbox. Drops towel. In that voice of coming back to familiar things*). Wonder how they are finding things upstairs. (*Crossing below table to* D. R.). I hope she had it a little more readied-up up there. You know, it seems kind of *sneaking*. Locking her up in town and then coming out here and trying to get her own house to turn against her!

MRS. PETERS. But, Mrs. Hale, the law is the law.

MRS. HALE. I s'pose 'tis. (*Unbuttoning her coat*). Better loosen up your things, Mrs. Peters. You won't feel them when you go out. (MRS. PETERS *takes off her fur tippet, goes to hang it on chair back left of table, stands looking at the work basket on floor near* D. L. *window.*)

MRS. PETERS. She was piecing a quilt. (*She brings the large sewing basket to the center table and they look at the bright pieces,* MRS. HALE *above the table and* MRS. PETERS *left of it.*)

MRS. HALE. It's a log cabin pattern. Pretty, isn't it? I wonder if she was goin' to quilt it or just knot it? (*Footsteps have been heard coming down the stairs. The* SHERIFF *enters followed by* HALE *and* COUNTY ATTORNEY.)

SHERIFF. They wonder if she was going to quilt it or just knot it! (*The men laugh, the women look abashed.*)

COUNTY ATTORNEY (*rubbing his hands over the stove*). Frank's fire didn't do much up there, did it? Well, let's go out to the barn and get that cleared up. (*The men go outside by* U. L. *door.*)

MRS. HALE (*resentfully*). I don't know as there's anything so strange, our takin' up our time with little things while we're waiting for them to get the evidence. (*She sits in chair right of table smoothing out a block with decision*). I don't see as it's anything to laugh about.

MRS. PETERS (*apologetically*). Of course they've got awful important things on their minds. (*Pulls up a chair and joins* MRS. HALE *at the left of the table.*)

MRS. HALE (*examining another block*). Mrs. Peters, look at this one. Here, this is the one she was working on, and look at the sewing! All the rest of it has been so nice and even. And look at this! It's all over the place! Why, it looks as if she didn't know what she was about! (*After she has said this they look at each other, then start to glance back at the door. After an instant* MRS. HALE *has pulled at a knot and ripped the sewing.*)

MRS. PETERS. Oh, what are you doing, Mrs. Hale?

MRS. HALE (*mildly*). Just pulling out a stitch or two that's not sewed very good. (*Threading a needle*). Bad sewing always made me fidgety.

MRS. PETERS (*with a glance at door, nervously*). I don't think we ought to touch things.

MRS. HALE. I'll just finish up this end. (*Suddenly stopping and leaning forward*). Mrs. Peters?

MRS. PETERS. Yes, Mrs. Hale?

MRS. HALE. What do you suppose she was so nervous about?

MRS. PETERS. Oh—I don't know. I don't know as she was nervous. I sometimes sew awful queer when I'm just tired. (MRS. HALE *starts to say something, looks at* MRS. PETERS, *then goes on sewing*). Well, I must get these things wrapped up. They may be through sooner than we think. (*Putting apron and other things together*). I wonder where I can find a piece of paper, and string. (*Rises.*)

MRS. HALE. In that cupboard, maybe.

MRS. PETERS (*crosses* R. *looking in cupboard*). Why here's a bird cage. (*Holds it up*). Did she have a bird, Mrs. Hale?

MRS. HALE. Why, I don't know whether she did or not—I've not been here for so long. There was a man around last year selling canaries cheap, but I don't know as she took one; maybe she did. She used to sing real pretty herself.

MRS. PETERS (*glancing around*). Seems funny to think of a bird here. But she must have had one, or why would she have a cage? I wonder what happened to it?

MRS. HALE. I s'pose maybe the cat got it.

MRS. PETERS. No, she didn't have a cat. She's got that feeling some people have about cats—being afraid of them. My cat got in her room and she was real upset and asked me to take it out.

MRS. HALE. My sister Bessie was like that. Queer, ain't it?

MRS. PETERS (*examining the cage*). Why look at this door. It's broke. One hinge is pulled apart. (*Takes a step down to* MRS. HALE'S *right.*)

MRS. HALE (*looking too*). Looks as if someone must have been rough with it.

MRS. PETERS. Why, yes. (*She brings the cage forward and puts it on the table.*)

MRS. HALE (*glancing toward* U. L. *door*). I wish if they're going to find any evidence they'd be about it. I don't like this place.

MRS. PETERS. But I'm awful glad you came with me, Mrs. Hale. It would be lonesome for me sitting here alone.

MRS. HALE. It would, wouldn't it? (*Dropping her sewing*). But I tell you what I do wish, Mrs. Peters. I wish I had come over sometimes when *she* was here. I—(*looking around the room*)—wish I had.

MRS. PETERS. But of course you were awful busy, Mrs. Hale—your house and your children.

MRS. HALE (*rises and crosses* L.). I could've come. I stayed away because it weren't cheerful—and that's why I ought to have come. I—(*looking out* L. *window*)—I've never liked this place. Maybe because it's down in a hollow and you don't see the road. I dunno what it is, but it's a lonesome place and always was. I wish I had come over to see Minnie Foster sometimes. I can see now—(*Shakes her head.*)

MRS. PETERS (*left of table above it*). Well, you mustn't reproach yourself, Mrs. Hale. Somehow we just don't see how it is with other folks until—something turns up.

MRS. HALE. Not having children makes less work—but it makes a quiet house, and Wright out to work all day, and no company when he did come in. (*Turning from window*). Did you know John Wright, Mrs. Peters?

MRS. PETERS. Not to know him; I've seen him in town. They say he was a good man.

MRS. HALE. Yes—good; he didn't drink, and kept his word as well as most, I guess, and paid his debts. But he was a hard man, Mrs. Peters. Just to pass the time of day with him—(*Shivers*). Like a raw wind that gets to the bone. (*Pauses, her eye falling on the cage*). I should think she would 'a' wanted a bird. But what do you suppose went with it?

MRS. PETERS. I don't know, unless it got sick and died. (*She reaches over and swings the broken door, swings it again, both women watch it.*)

MRS. HALE. You weren't raised round here, were you? (MRS. PETERS *shakes her head*). You didn't know—her?

MRS. PETERS. Not till they brought her yesterday.

MRS. HALE. She—come to think of it, she was kind of like a bird herself—real sweet and pretty, but kind of timid and—fluttery. How—she—did—change. (*Silence; then as if struck by a happy thought and relieved to get back to everyday things. Crosses* R. *above* MRS. PETERS *to cupboard, replaces small chair used to stand on to its orig-*

inal place D. R.). Tell you what, Mrs. Peters, why don't you take the quilt in with you? It might take up her mind.

MRS. PETERS. Why, I think that's a real nice idea, Mrs. Hale. There couldn't possibly be any objection to it, could there? Now, just what would I take? I wonder if her patches are in here—and her things. (*They look in the sewing basket.*)

MRS. HALE (*crosses to right of table*). Here's some red. I expect this has got sewing things in it. (*Brings out a fancy box*). What a pretty box. Looks like something somebody would give you. Maybe her scissors are in here. (*Opens box. Suddenly puts her hand to her nose*). Why—(MRS. PETERS *bends nearer, then turns her face away*). There's something wrapped up in this piece of silk.

MRS. PETERS. Why, this isn't her scissors.

MRS. HALE (*lifting the silk*). Oh, Mrs. Peters—it's—(MRS. PETERS *bends closer.*)

MRS. PETERS. It's the bird.

MRS. HALE. But, Mrs. Peters—look at it! Its neck! Look at its neck! It's all—other side *to.*

MRS. PETERS. Somebody—wrung—its—neck. (*Their eyes meet. A look of growing comprehension, of horror. Steps are heard outside.* MRS. HALE *slips box under quilt pieces, and sinks into her chair. Enter* SHERIFF *and* COUNTY ATTORNEY. MRS. PETERS *steps* D. L. *and stands looking out of window.*

COUNTY ATTORNEY (*as one turning from serious things to little pleasantries*). Well, ladies, have you decided whether she was going to quilt it or knot it? (*Crosses to* C. *above table.*)

MRS. PETERS. We think she was going to—knot it. (SHERIFF *crosses to right of stove, lifts stove lid and glances at fire, then stands warming hands at stove.*)

COUNTY ATTORNEY. Well, that's interesting, I'm sure. (*Seeing the birdcage.*) Has the bird flown?

MRS. HALE (*putting more quilt pieces over the box*). We think the—cat got it.

COUNTY ATTORNEY (*preoccupied*). Is there a cat? (MRS. HALE *glances in a quick covert way at* MRS. PETERS.)

MRS. PETERS (*turning from window takes a step in*). Well, not *now*. They're superstitious, you know. They leave.

COUNTY ATTORNEY (*to* SHERIFF PETERS, *continuing an interrupted conversation*). No sign at all of anyone having come from the outside. Their own rope. Now let's go up again and go over it piece by piece. (*They start upstairs*). It would have to have been someone who knew just the— (MRS. PETERS *sits down left of table. The two women sit there not looking at one another, but as if peering into something and at the same time holding back. When they talk now it is in the manner of feeling their way over strange ground, as if afraid of what they are saying, but as if they cannot help saying it.*)

MRS. HALE (*hesitatively and in a hushed voice*). She liked the bird. She was going to bury it in that pretty box.

MRS. PETERS (*in a whisper*). When I was a girl—my kitten—there was a boy took a hatchet, and before my eyes—and before I could get there—(*Covers her face an instant*). If they hadn't held me back I would have—(*catches herself, looks upstairs where steps are heard, falters weakly*)—hurt him.

MRS. HALE (*with a slow look around her*). I wonder how it would seem never to have had any children around. (*Pause*). No, Wright wouldn't like the bird—a thing that sang. She used to sing. He killed that, too.

MRS. PETERS (*moving uneasily*). We don't know who killed the bird.

MRS. HALE. I knew John Wright.

MRS. PETERS. It was an awful thing was done in this house that night, Mrs. Hale. Killing a man while he slept, slipping a rope around his neck that choked the life out of him.

MRS. HALE. His neck. Choked the life out of him. (*Her hand goes out and rests on the bird-cage.*)

MRS. PETERS (*with rising voice*). We don't know who killed him. We don't *know*.

MRS. HALE (*her own feeling not interrupted*). If there'd been years and years of nothing, then a bird to sing to you, it would be awful—still, after the bird was still.

MRS. PETERS (*something within her speaking*). I know what stillness is. When we homesteaded in Dakota, and my first baby died—after he was two years old, and me with no other then—

MRS. HALE (*moving*). How soon do you suppose they'll be through looking for evidence?

MRS. PETERS. I know what stillness is. (*Pulling herself back*). The law has got to punish crime, Mrs. Hale.

MRS. HALE (*not as if answering that*). I wish you'd seen Minnie Foster when she wore a white dress with blue ribbons and stood up there in the choir and sang. (*A look around the room*). Oh, I wish I'd come over here once in a while! That was a crime! That was a crime! Who's going to punish that?

MRS. PETERS (*looking upstairs*). We mustn't—take on.

MRS. HALE. I might have known she needed help! I know how things can be—for women. I tell you, it's queer, Mrs. Peters. We live close together and we live far apart. We all go through the same things—it's all just a different kind of same thing. (*Brushes her eyes, noticing the jar of fruit, reaches out for it*). If I was you I wouldn't tell her her fruit was gone. Tell her it *ain't*. Tell her it's all right. Take this in to prove it to her. She—she may never know whether it was broke or not.

MRS. PETERS (*takes the jar, looks about for something to wrap it in; takes petticoat from the clothes brought from the other room, very nervously begins winding this around the jar. In a false voice*). My, it's a good thing the men couldn't hear us. Wouldn't they just laugh! Getting all stirred up over a little thing like a—dead canary. As if that could have anything to do with—with—wouldn't they *laugh*! (*The men are heard coming downstairs.*)

MRS. HALE (*under her breath*). Maybe they would—maybe they wouldn't.

COUNTY ATTORNEY. No, Peters, it's all perfectly clear except a reason for doing it. But you know juries when it comes to women. If there was some definite thing. (*Crosses slowly to above table.* SHERIFF *crosses* D. R. MRS. HALE *and* MRS. PETERS *remain seated at either side of table*). Something to show—something to make a story about—a thing that would connect up with this strange way of doing it—(*The women's eyes meet for an instant. Enter* HALE *from outer door.*)

HALE (*remaining* U. L. *by door*). Well, I've got the team around. Pretty cold out there.

COUNTY ATTORNEY. I'm going to stay a while by myself. (*To the* SHERIFF). You can send Frank out for me, can't you? I want to go over everything. I'm not satisfied that we can't do better.

SHERIFF. Do you want to see what Mrs. Peters is going to take in? (*The* LAWYER *picks up the apron, laughs.*)

COUNTY ATTORNEY. Oh, I guess they're not very dangerous things the ladies have picked out. (*Moves a few things about, disturbing the quilt pieces which cover the box. Steps back*). No, Mrs. Peters doesn't need supervising. For that matter a sheriff's wife is married to the law. Ever think of it that way, Mrs. Peters?

MRS. PETERS. Not—just that way.

SHERIFF (*chuckling*). Married to the law. (*Moves to* D. R. *door to the other room*). I just want you to come in here a minute, George. We ought to take a look at these windows.

COUNTY ATTORNEY (*scoffingly*). Oh, windows!

SHERIFF. We'll be right out, Mr. Hale (HALE *goes outside. The* SHERIFF *follows the* COUNTY ATTORNEY *into the other room. Then* MRS. HALE *rises, hands tight together, looking intensely at* MRS. PETERS, *whose eyes make a slow turn, finally meeting* MRS. HALE'S. *A moment* MRS. HALE *holds her, then her own eyes point the way to where the box is concealed. Suddenly* MRS. PETERS *throws back quilt pieces* and *tries to put the box in the bag she is carrying. It is too big. She opens box, starts to take bird out, cannot touch it, goes to pieces, stands there helpless. Sound of a knob turning in the other room,* MRS. HALE *snatches the box and puts it in the pocket of her big coat. Enter* COUNTY ATTORNEY *and* SHERIFF, *who remains* D. R.)

COUNTY ATTORNEY (*crosses to* U. L. *door facetiously*). Well, Henry, at least we found out that she was not going to quilt it. She was going to—what is it you call it, ladies?

MRS. HALE (*standing* C. *below table facing front, her hand against her pocket*). We call it—knot it, Mr. Henderson.

CURTAIN

Reading for Understanding

Main Idea

1. The main idea of the play is that (a) tiny details often reveal the truth (b) men are more direct and observant than women (c) homicides in the countryside are more difficult to solve than those in the city (d) farm life often drives men mad.

Details

2. The sheriff's name is (a) Wright (b) Hale (c) Peters (d) Henderson.
3. The person who spoke first to Mrs. Wright was (a) the County Attorney (b) the sheriff (c) Mrs. Peters (d) Hale.
4. The sticky mess in the kitchen was caused by (a) blood (b) frozen and thawed fruit preserves (c) a broken honey jar (d) dirty dishes.
5. Mrs. Peters volunteered to (a) get a lawyer for Mrs. Wright (b) bring clothes to Mrs. Wright (c) do all the needed laundry (d) tell the name of the murderer.
6. Minnie Foster is (a) Dr. Lloyd's wife (b) Mrs. Peters' maiden name (c) Mrs. Wright's maiden name (d) the coroner.

Inferences

7. Mrs. Hale may best be characterized as (a) indifferent (b) cruel (c) neighborly (d) irritable.

8. The County Attorney may best be characterized as (a) sympathetic (b) self-important (c) untidy (d) brilliant.
9. When the directions say that Mrs. Hale replied *stiffly*, we can assume that she (a) disapproves of the County Attorney's comments (b) wishes to present an opinion in a formal fashion (c) is shy in the presence of a representative of the legal profession (d) disagrees with her own husband.
10. In speaking to each other, Mrs. Peters and Mrs. Hale (a) inwardly disagree with each other (b) try to outdo each other in cleverness (c) agree with the men's attitude toward Mrs. Wright (d) observe a certain formality toward each other.
11. "They wonder if she was going to quilt it or just knot it." When the sheriff says this, he (a) is being sarcastic (b) displays a courteous interest in his wife's crafts (c) considers the answer a clue to the murder (d) is impressed by the women's shrewdness.

Figurative Language

12. All the following are examples of figurative language EXCEPT (a) "Wright was close" (b) "Like a raw wind that gets to the bone" (c) "For that matter a sheriff's wife is married to the law" (d) "We ought to take a look at these windows."

Outcome

13. At the end of the play, probably (a) the County Attorney will find the canary (b) the women will keep their secret (c) Mrs. Peters will have a nervous breakdown (d) Mrs. Wright will confess.

Author's Purpose

14. A major purpose of the author is to (a) comment on quirks of the American legal system (b) show the sisterhood of women who share a demanding lifestyle (c) pass severe judgment on any violence as a solution to problems (d) hold up to gentle ridicule the focus of some people on trivial things.

Author's Attitude

15. The author's attitude toward Mrs. Wright is one of (a) dismay (b) disgust (c) sympathy (d) bafflement.

Words in Context

1. "Shaking off the mood which the empty rocking chair has *evoked.*" **Evoked** (121) means (a) dampened (b) demonstrated (c) frightened (d) called forth.
2. "'Well, you mustn't *reproach* yourself, Mrs. Hale.'" **Reproach** (124) means (a) congratulate (b) refuse (c) blame (d) puzzle.
3. "Mrs. Hale glances in a quick *covert* way at Mrs. Peters." **Covert** (125) means (a) secretive (b) questioning (c) upsetting (d) sorrowful.
4. "Crosses to U.L. door *facetiously.*" **Facetiously** (128) means (a) in a lively manner (b) jokingly (c) dramatically (d) somberly.

Thinking Critically About the Play

1. If there is a key sentence in the play, it is Hale's comment (119), "Well, women are used to worrying over trifles." Why is this so important as a key to the play? How does it, in ironic fashion, identify the intelligent persons in the play?
2. How many clues can you find as you follow the two women in their concern for trifles? What is the final clue that clearly reveals the murderer? Why do the women conceal this crucial clue?
3. The County Attorney is officious and not particularly perceptive. His impatience is revealed by his interruptions. His tactlessness is revealed by his criticism of Mrs. Wright's housekeeping, a job he has never had to worry about. Point out examples in the play in which he shows his petty weaknesses.
4. Mrs. Hale and Mrs. Peters turn out to be co-conspirators, but they are quite different personalities. Describe them, pointing out how they differ from each other. Show how their handling of the dead bird provides a clue to their characters.
5. John Wright never appears, yet his personality is clearly and objectively revealed. Point out, especially in the comments by Mrs. Hale, what kind of man he was. How did his actions, either described or implied, further reveal him to us?

6. The County Attorney tried to get Mrs. Hale to make some unfavorable comments about Mrs. Wright, thus implying a possible motive for the murder. She constantly foils his attempts and proves herself a worthy adversary. Point out examples from the play.
7. How did Mrs. Hale's comments contrast the bright happy girl that Mrs. Wright once was with the pitiable woman now in the county jail?
8. Mrs. Peters says, "The law is the law." Why is her part in the cover-up more difficult than Mrs. Hale's?
9. What physical clues tell us that Mrs. Wright's breakdown was sudden?
10. On page (126), Mrs. Peters says, "We don't know who killed the bird." Mrs. Hale replies, "I knew John Wright." What does she mean?
11. What is the similarity between the way in which the bird was killed and the way in which the man was killed? Is this intentional? Explain.
12. The County Attorney says, "No, Peters, it's all perfectly clear except a reason for doing it." Why is this statement ironic?

Language in Action

Stories in Words

Motive (119) comes ultimately from the Latin verb *movere*, "to move." A *motive* is an *impulse*, an *inner drive*, something that *propels* us to action. Related words are *motion*, *motivation*, *motor*, *motorize*, *commotion*, *emotion*, and a host of others. Then there are the *mov* words: *move*, *movement*, *movies*, *moving*, *immovable*, *remove* and others. *Automobile* is a hybrid word. *Auto*, "self," is Greek. *Mob* is Roman: the *mov* root again. An *automobile* is *self-moving*.

Sarcastic (121) is, perhaps, not a pretty word, but its origin is fascinating. The Greek root *sarx* meant "flesh." The second half comes from an Indo-European root meaning "cut, tear." Thus, in figurative fashion, a *sarcastic* remark *cuts the flesh*. *Sarcophagus*, a coffin or tomb, has an equally unusual root. The Greek root *phagein* meant *to eat*. Thus, with a grisly kind of humor, a *sarcophagus* is a *flesh-eater*! A *bacteriophage eats* bacteria. A *phagocyte* is a white-blood cell that *eats* harmful intruders.

Canaries (123) has a surprising derivation, too. *Canary* comes from the Latin root for *dog*, as in *canine*. How did the root for *dog* become associated with a *bird*? *Canaries* came from the Canary Islands, becoming popular in England in the 16th century. They were called *canary birds*. But the Canary Islands got their name in Roman times because of a large breed of dog found there: the dog islands.

Déjà Vu

Mary Barrett
American

Mrs. Oliver's panic was now beginning to overwhelm her. There was only one gift left—the last one John had given her. She knew what it would mean if that one came back.

Déjà vu is a convenient French phrase that has become fairly common. Have you ever seen a place for the first time and had the strange feeling you'd seen it before? That's **déjá vu**—translated as "already seen." It's also applied to something heard or experienced.

In our story, Mrs. Oliver is experiencing a chilling case of **déjà vu**. She encounters a series of events that recall a series of events in the past. Though the gifts she receives should make her happy, they terrify her. There is a sense of mystery here, as in the other stories in the unit, but this provides a special shiver of horror.

Déjà Vu

MRS. OLIVER WAS PUZZLED. She always liked to pay cash, now that she could, and she no longer kept in touch with anyone out of town. Therefore she received almost no mail. The package which the mailman handed her was a surprise, and, like many surprises, unwelcome.

"There must be a mistake," Mrs. Oliver said uncertainly.

"No mistake, lady." And the mailman walked away.

Mrs. Oliver inspected the parcel. It was wrapped in brown paper and sealed with tape. Her name and address were clearly spelled out in neat block letters. The stamps were canceled with the local postmark.

She put the parcel down on the dining table. For some reason she was reluctant to open it. At the edge of awareness, the sensation gnawed at her that she had experienced this same event before. *Déjà vu.*

Don't be a fool, Mrs. Oliver said sternly to herself. She hoped that she wasn't getting eccentric, living alone as she had been since John died. Surely a package in the mail was nothing to be so upset about.

She pulled at the sealing tape. Under the paper was a plain white box bearing no identification. Its very impersonality somehow increased Mrs. Oliver's uneasiness.

The box was lined with white tissue paper. Lying in the center, like a cherished treasure, was a little music box with a dainty lady dancer on top.

Mrs. Oliver gasped. She picked up the box. She wound the little key. The lady dancer turned slowly, gracefully, and the music box tinkled "The Blue Danube Waltz."

It was impossible!

Mrs. Oliver sat down. Her hands were suddenly cold and her heart was beating fast.

It was the very first gift that John had sent to her. It came before they were married, when John was still courting her. The little Bavarian music box had arrived, then as now, in a parcel in the mail. Then, as now, it had been carefully wrapped and sealed. John was always a careful man.

She looked again at the address on the wrapping paper. It told her nothing. The printed words were impersonal, unrevealing.

Panic hit Mrs. Oliver like a sonic boom. She knew very well where she had last seen the music box—in Mr. Stover's store, where she had taken it to be sold.

She stood up shakily and forced herself into action.

"Mr. Stover, I would like to see the Bavarian music box which I sold to you."

Mr. Stover had been afraid of this. How much of the truth could he tell her? He looked at her closely. No, he decided, she was too agitated; even part of the truth would be too great a shock.

"I remember it," he said. "Had a little dancing girl, didn't it? That was sold some time ago."

Mrs. Oliver was uncertain whether to feel relief or apprehension.

"Do you remember who bought it?"

"No. I didn't know the man. He was a stranger who happened in. A young fellow. Didn't quibble about the price."

Mrs. Oliver felt dizzy. That would have been John's style.

"A young man, you said?"

"That's right. In his early thirties, I'd say."

Mrs. Oliver slept restlessly that night. She had distressing dreams from which she woke perspiring, her heart pounding, the thought of her dead husband vivid in her mind.

John. *He* was in his early thirties when they first met. He was handsome and ambitious, already a successful lawyer. It was inevitable that he would become an important man in state politics.

He was a good catch for any woman. And how persuasively he had courted her, showering her with attention and presents!

He had this house built for her, and had it furnished with the finest things. She appreciated all this. There was no passion on her part, but she couldn't, finally, resist him. Her family was an old one, far more distinguished than his, but their money had long ago trickled away. She could not afford not to marry for money. So it might as well be John.

If he was ever disappointed he was too gentlemanly to let it show.

She hid the music box in a drawer under the linen tablecloths and tried to forget it. It was not that simple. Whoever was manipulating Mrs. Oliver's state of mind was not only very clever but astonishingly well informed.

Only a week after the arrival of the music box another parcel was delivered. It, too, was carefully wrapped and sealed. The box was, again, disquieting in its impersonality.

Mrs. Oliver opened it and felt her knees go weak. Deep in tissue paper the box held the exquisite emerald brooch which John had given her on the day they were married. It was a lovely thing, of superb craftsmanship. Mr. Stover had given her a very good price for it. Now it lay in her hand, as sparkling as it was the day John had pinned it so tenderly on her bridal dress.

Mrs. Oliver tried to slow the beating of her heart. It wasn't good for her to be so upset. The doctor would be cross with her.

If this eerie procedure continued, she would receive many packages. John had been very generous with gifts. His practice brought in a great deal of money. To outside observers she seemed a very lucky woman. She had only to drop the smallest hint and John would buy her whatever she wanted.

Still, as time went by, she had felt more and more like a kept slave. She yearned for a little cash of her own. Not much. Just enough so that she could be free to buy some small things for herself. He never let her have a personal checking or bank account, and he gave her a minimum of pocket money.

"I would rather take care of you myself, dear," he said.

John overlooked nothing. He established charge accounts with the grocery store, the milkman, the dry cleaners. He bought all her clothes himself. In all the days of her marriage she never had more than a five-dollar bill of her own. Of course, John paid all the bills himself.

The packages continued to come. Mrs. Oliver lived in a state of constant agitation. The parcels arrived with no regularity, and she never knew on which day one would be delivered. There was, however, one thing she could be certain of ahead of time—the contents of each box. For the presents were coming back to her in the exact order John had given them to her.

Her birthday present, the diamond bracelet, was followed by the matching earrings John had given her for Christmas.

At first, when she was a new bride, she had been charmed by John's generosity. She had never owned beautiful things before, and the shower of extravagant gifts was like a dream come true. It was only in time that the longing for the illusion of financial independence came to sit on her soul like a lead weight; and in time the longing became an obsession.

John refused even to consider the possibility of her looking for a job.

"We're rich, dear," he said. "It would be ridiculous for you to work. You know that I'll get you anything you want."

As time passed, John's gifts brought her no joy. They seemed merely symbols of her bondage. She even had trouble pretending to be pleased.

Now, receiving them a second time, she felt even less pleasure. She felt only horror and repugnance. As each gift arrived she quickly hid it away.

His anniversary present of silver demitasse spoons came only shortly before the hand-blown crystal vase which John had brought back from a short trip out of town.

Mrs. Oliver's panic was now beginning to overwhelm her. There was only one gift left—the last one John had given her. She knew what it would mean if that one came back. And she knew with dreadful certainty that though it had been, in life, John's last gift, it would not now be. She knew that the final gift would come to her from the grave.

Mrs. Oliver, never a hardy woman, was not well. She hardly ever slept. When, finally, she did drop off, her dreams were terrifying, and she often woke up screaming.

She no longer had any appetite. She had lost so much weight that her dresses hung like bags. She hardly recognized herself in the mirror. Her eyes stared back at her from sunken sockets like glass globes in a skull.

The package came.

John's last gift.

She knew very well what the package contained even before she opened it. He had brought this gift on no special occasion—it had been a sudden whim. He had seen it in a store window and, on impulse, had gone in and bought it for her.

Her hands shook. She could hardly tear off the paper. Inside the white box lay the gift. It was a beautiful little emerald pillbox, made by an expert craftsman. It was truly a work of art. Mrs. Oliver put it out of sight as quickly as she could.

She tried to brace herself for what she knew was bound to come next. But what could she do? There was no way to anticipate how it would come, or in what form. There was no way to protect herself.

That night she went to bed early and lay there, wide-awake. Her eyes were open, staring unseeingly at the ceiling.

There was a knock at the door. It was not imperative—simply firm and sure.

Mrs. Oliver stepped into her bedroom slippers and put on her robe. She went silently down the stairs. She could no more have ignored that self-assured knock than she could have left the packages unopened. She was moved by an irresistible compulsion.

The knock sounded again—no louder than before, but still firm and self-confident.

Mrs. Oliver went to the door. She stood there, dizzy. Her hand was on the doorknob.

She was faint with panic and fatigue. Her body shook, out of control. She sank to the floor and her face pressed against the hard wood of the door.

Again the knock sounded.

There was a pounding in her ears. The hall seemed to tilt, first one way, then another.

"John," she whispered, "how did you know?"

It was John on the other side of the door. She was certain of that. And somehow he had learned the truth.

She had taken the poison out of the little enamel pillbox. She had put it in his demitasse. She was sure he hadn't seen her do it. She had sat there calmly and watched him drink the coffee, and die. And, finally, she had money of her own.

She should have known better, she thought fuzzily. She should have known she couldn't outwit John, that he would never stop giving her things.

She lay, a crumpled disorderly heap, on the floor of the hall. She was shrunken and unadorned. She looked old. She sighed, a long sigh, and then she died.

There was a final knock on the door, and then the sound of footsteps going away.

Mr. Stover was disappointed. He had waited until he had sent back all her lovely things, in the same order she had sold them, to tell her he loved her. Well, he would call again tomorrow.

Reading for Understanding

Central Idea

1. The central idea of the story is *best* expressed by which of the following quotations?
   (a) The only cure for grief is action.
   —G.H. Lewes
   (b) Every guilty person is his own hangman.
   —Seneca
   (c) Do not suppose opportunity will knock twice at your door.
   —Sebastien Chamfort
   (d) The mind grows by what it feeds on.
   —J.G. Holland

Details

2. Mrs. Oliver realized that the packages were mailed (a) a long time in the past (b) without a clear address (c) locally (d) by a friend.
3. The first gift she received was (a) a pillbox (b) an emerald brooch (c) a music box (d) none of these.
4. The gifts were actually (a) a labor of love (b) John's revenge (c) sent to the wrong address (d) those she had never seen before.

Inferences

5. Mrs. Oliver's death might be ascribed to (a) cancer (b) muscular dystrophy (c) pneumonia (d) heart failure.
6. Mr. Stover had (a) apparently saved the gifts to return to Mrs. Oliver (b) probably been asked by John to send the gifts to Mrs. Oliver (c) taken an extreme dislike to Mrs. Oliver (d) probably cheated Mrs. Oliver in buying the little treasures.

7. Mrs. Oliver objected most strenuously to John's (a) affairs with other women (b) need for control (c) physical cruelty and abuse (d) stinginess.

Cause and Effect

8. John's excessive generosity and love (a) pleased Mrs. Oliver throughout the marriage (b) aroused the jealousy of Mr. Stover (c) brought on his poisoning (d) almost bankrupted him.

Mood of the Story

9. The mood of the story is one of (a) joyous expectation (b) threatening disaster (c) alert curiosity (d) understated enthusiasm.

Fact or Opinion

Tell whether the following is a fact or an opinion.

10. Mrs. Oliver was responsible for the death of her husband John.

Words in Context

1. "Mrs. Oliver was uncertain whether to feel relief or *apprehension.*" **Apprehension** (134) means (a) confusion (b) anxiety (c) understanding (d) jubilation.
2. "In time the longing became an *obsession.*" **Obsession** (136) means (a) passing fancy (b) weird interpretation (c) something owned (d) fixed conviction.
3. "She felt only horror and *repugnance.*" **Repugnance** (136) means (a) disgust (b) anger (c) fear (d) resistance.

Thinking Critically About the Story

1. This is a story that seems to bring in the supernatural. Were you taken in by the eerie suggestion? If not, at what point did you begin to suspect that the haunting was in Mrs. Oliver's head?
2. A great many stories that seem to tell of the supernatural have logical, reasonable endings. Others, however, leave the possibility in the

air. Do you prefer your stories to have reasonable endings, or would you rather have an unexplained mystery? Explain.

3. What was Mr. Stover's strategy in sending the gifts to Mrs. Oliver? How did that strategy ultimately destroy Mrs. Oliver?
4. What kind of person was John? Pleasant? Loving? Generous? Obnoxious? Hateful? How do you see him?
5. Does true love seek to control? How would you have felt if you had been treated so generously but with so many restrictions?
6. Some authorities explain déjà vu by saying that it is caused by a brief time lapse between the first sighting and the feeling, "I've been here before." What do you think? Have you had an experience of déjà vu? Tell about it.

Language in Action

New Words

Panic hit Mrs. Oliver like a sonic boom.

Your great-grandfather would have been puzzled by the words *sonic boom* . . . for good reason. A sonic boom did not exist before airplanes went faster than the speed of sound. The loud noise is a shock wave produced by the noise of an aircraft traveling at supersonic speeds. The Merriam-Webster *Collegiate Dictionary* lists the dates of the introduction of a word into the language. The date 1952 for *sonic boom* tells us about technology as well as about language.

English, unlike many other languages, is extremely receptive to new words. If there is a need and the need is met by a new word, English will adopt it freely. As the study of subatomic physics progressed, for example, English adopted many colorful new words for the various particles: *quark*, *meson*, *gluon*, *psion*, and *hadron*. As specialized words these are not in common use, but a great many new words *have* passed into everyday speech.

The world of computers has supplied a great many new words: USB flashdrive, DVD-RW, Wi-Fi, BlackBerry, iPod.

As you read this, dozens of new words are clamoring to enter the language.

I Love a Mystery

ACTIVITIES

Thinking Critically About the Stories

1. What do you think Albert Einstein had in mind (3) when he talked of the mysterious? Are there mysteries in life that are beyond the power of the human mind to comprehend? Comment.
2. What is the single common thread that links "Man in Hiding" and "Déjà Vu"?
3. Compare or contrast the three great detectives: Sherlock Holmes ("The Adventure of the Speckled Band") Colonel March ("The Crime in Nobody's Room"), the Man in the Corner ("The Glasgow Mystery"). Do you have a favorite? Explain.
4. Do you like to match wits with the detective? Do you try to guess the murderer before the great revelation, or do you just sit back and enjoy the puzzle? Explain.
5. Which one of the stories had no murder? Did you find it equally interesting, however? Present your point of view.
6. Which of the stories came closest to satisfying your own taste in detective stories? Why?

The Writing Portfolio

Writing Good Sentences

A writing portfolio is a helpful guide for you right now, for college preparation, and for the years beyond secondary school. A writing portfolio provides direction, helps you take charge of your writing, collect it with a purpose, and refer to it over and over. Your writing reflects you. Though the process is challenging and sometimes formidable, the results are rewarding.

A portfolio is a collection of your accomplishments, principally your writing. An applicant for a job may take a portfolio of descriptions of school or work experiences to Human Resources to suggest the range of the applicant's abilities. A photographer may either display his skills on a website, or carry a portfolio of his pictures to display his skills. An advertiser may take a portfolio of his ads to a prospective client and give a presentation to stimulate interest in the advertiser's ideas.

Throughout this book, you will be gathering materials for your own portfolio. It will suggest who you are, what your interests and talents are. The units in this book will provide writing activities to include in your portfolio, but you are encouraged to add personal items to this collection, too—for example, observations of people, bits of dialogue, descriptions of memorable experiences. This course of action enriches your life and opens your ears and eyes.

Decide upon the format and container for your material. On your computer, you can create your own files and folders. You can also do it the old-fashioned way. Stationery stores sell useful folders. Look beyond this book. Continue the portfolio after the book has become a memory. The portfolio will become one of your treasured possessions.

Now let's begin. Most of the questions, as well as those at the end of later units, are based upon reading experiences. Do not be limited by these, however. The more writing you do, the more relaxed and skillful you become.

The heart of writing is the sentence. All kinds of writing depend on the single sentence. Henry David Thoreau once wrote, " A sentence should read as if its author, had he held a plough instead of a pen, could have drawn a furrow deep and straight to the end." Good sentences don't ramble. They waste no words. They come to the point swiftly and directly. They allow the reader to follow the thought without confusion. "Haste makes waste" is a better sentence than "Impetuous and rash actions often result in extravagant expenditure of energy."

Now try your hand at writing thoughtful, clear English sentences.

1. Each evening for a week, write a single sentence presenting some idea you had during the day.

   Example

   Monday—I wonder why the old bank building is being torn down.

   Tuesday—That roaming terrier shouldn't be allowed loose on a busy street.

   Wednesday—I think I'll take Creative Writing next semester.

2. Write a follow-up sentence to this one: "I have planned the ideal vacation."

3. Pick up an object such as an iPod or cell phone. Touch it as though you can not see it. Pretend you picked it up in the dark. How would you describe it? Write a sentence describing it in such a way that your

fellow students will be able to identify it. Try to appeal only to the sense of touch.

4. Boil down the following sentence into the original simple proverb. "It's best not to lose control over your emotions when for some reason or other the milk has been carelessly spilled."
5. Complete the following sentence:

   A crowded city is like . . .

   Rain on the roof sounds like . . .

   Biting into ice cream is like . . .
6. In a brief sentence, sum up the character of Dr. Watson, the narrator of "The Adventure of the Speckled Band."
7. Write a sentence explaining whether you think there is a flaw in the escape plan from "Cell 13."
8. In one sentence, compare or contrast the two women in "Trifles."
9. Write a sentence, giving your opinion of another detective story like "The Crime in Nobody's Room."
10. Write a single sentence identifying the appeal of Sherlock Holmes. (Manner? Eccentricities? Deductive powers?)

Other Areas of Communication

1. Read another Sherlock Holmes short story, or a Carter Dickson (John Dickson Carr) short story or novel. Prepare to report to the class.
2. Which is your favorite television mystery (detective story, crime story, suspense, spy story, fantasy)? Be ready to tell why you enjoy it. Consider such things as plot, characterization, mood, dialogue, setting, and theme.
3. Watch a television program dealing with crime and law enforcement. Use these standards in judging the program.
   - (a) Did the program refrain from making crime attractive, profitable, or even cute?
   - (b) Was the story presented in a way so that the listener tends to identify himself with the forces of law and order?
   - (c) Were the procedures used in solving the crime realistic and believable?

(d) Were the characters complex and human or mere cardboard figures?

Report to the class, giving your own opinion of the standards set up.

4. The selections in this unit have sections that lend themselves to dramatizations—for example, the revelation scene in "The Crime in Nobody's Room" or the confrontation scene in "The Adventure of the Speckled Band" (Sherlock Holmes and Dr. Roylott). With a classmate or classmates, select a scene and prepare to dramatize it for the class. "Trifles" is a one-act play and may be dramatized intact.
5. The power of TV and films is demonstrated in many ways—for example, when watching the fictional show *Lost*, you may get caught up in the latest problems of people stranded on the island. You empathize with them. On the other hand, while watching the "Reality" show, *Survivor*, you may root for your favorite character to win the big prize. Set up a panel discussion of 4–6 participants on the topic, "How TV (or Film) Influences Our Daily Lives."
6. An explosive trend in television was set off when CSI ("Crime Scene Investigation") first went on the air. It sparked a renewed interest in forensics as a crime-solving tool and spawned many programs like *Cold Case Files* featuring forensic insights and discoveries. Some programs are fictional; others are documentaries. Debate the relevant powers of each.
7. How many television detectives can you mention? What is the distinctive characteristic of each? Draw up a class list.

Language in Action—a Review

You may refer to the preceding pages to answer these questions.

1. If I say, "I'm just too lucky" after sitting on a just-painted seat, I am using (a) metaphor (b) simile (c) irony (d) personification.
2. A code differs from a cipher in (a) level of difficulty (b) motivation of its writer (c) use of a book to interpret (d) use of symbols
3. The essence of paradox is (a) agreement (b) contradiction (c) drama (d) illness.
4. The word *canary* ultimately comes from a Latin word for (a) dog (b) bird (c) island (d) plant.
5. Inductive reasoning requires (a) a valid major premise (b) a valid minor premise (c) continuous observation (d) psychic abilities.

6. For information about when words entered the language, consult (a) Roget's Thesaurus (b) Samuel Johnson's *Dictionary of the English Language* (c) *Merriam-Webster's Collegiate Dictionary* (d) *Encyclopedia of Words and Phrases.*
7. *Eccentric* is an example of (a) flowery writing (b) poor definition (c) antagonistic reporting (d) concealed metaphor.
8. The basis of all metaphor is (a) comparison (b) irony (c) paradox (d) conflict.

UNIT TWO

The Creative Imagination

Imagination is more important than knowledge.

Albert Einstein

In one sense, **neoteny** (nee-OT-e-nee) is not a new word. It is used when an insect retains in maturity some of the characteristics of its larval state. Later, the word extended its meaning to human activities and personalities. **Neoteny** can be applied when an adult human being retains some of the desirable qualities of childhood: a creative imagination, a sense of awe and wonder, an openness to new things and ideas.

The poet William Wordsworth tried to capture that childhood joy in these lines:

There was a time when meadow, grove, and

stream,

The earth and every common sight,

To me did seem

Apparelled in celestial light,

The glory and the freshness of a dream.

Then he adds wistfully:

It is not now as it hath been of yore.

Why not? What has happened? Where has that "celestial light" gone?

Growing up is a difficult challenge. When you were a child, all things were possible. Every new day was a new experience. Alas, as you grow, you discover limitations, some of them necessary. You learned that you can't fly by jumping off a barn roof! But the real limitations tended to create imagined ones. "I'll never be able to pass math." "I'm giving up the clarinet. It's too hard for me." "I can't . . . I can't . . . I can't." You may not become an antarctic explorer, an astronaut, or a movie star, but there are still thousands of options open to you, if you keep the alertness and imagination of childhood.

The positive childhood qualities are especially visible in creative adults. Inventors, artists, writers, research scientists, composers—all of these exemplify the childhood sense of wonder, of adventure, of ever searching for new horizons. Were you surprised to read on the previous page that Albert Einstein valued imagination above knowledge?

The stories that follow demonstrate imagination in many forms. Ray Bradbury departs from science fiction to tell an amazing parable, a tale with a moral. Carol Birch and Steve Sanfield tell folk stories with imaginative details. Mary Carter Smith charms with a warm retelling of the Cinderella story. Chinua Achebe brings to life Tortoise, imaginative trickster, who ultimately outsmarts himself. Storyteller J. Frank Dobie tells of another trickster, who fooled everyone but a simple shepherd. There is magic in "The Innkeeper's Wise Daughter." You will be delighted with her solutions to problems that may stump you.

The Golden Kite, The Silver Wind

Ray Bradbury
American

One without the other is nothing. Together, all will be beauty and cooperation and a long and enduring life.

There is an old childhood saying: "Sticks and stones may break my bones, but words can never hurt me." Like some folk wisdom, this statement is sadly untrue. Words **can** hurt. Indeed, much of the pain in the world is caused by words, not actual deeds. Hurtful words shouted in an argument do inflict lasting harm.

Words are symbols (156–157). Like words, symbols influence our lives. Some symbols like the Star of David, the Cross, and the Crescent may have positive effects on worshipers. Other symbols, like the swastika of Nazi Germany, may lead to disastrous results. Mickey Mouse is a happy symbol of Disneyland. The skull and crossbones is a warning symbol of poison. Symbols can run us or ruin us.

In this story, Ray Bradbury imagines neighboring cities that get into a catastrophic competition for the silliest of reasons. The rulers are obsessed by symbols, not reality. They almost destroy their lands because mere symbols, not they, are the masters of their fate. This is a parable, a story with a moral. What message is Bradbury trying to convey to us?

The Golden Kite, The Silver Wind

IN THE SHAPE of a *pig?*" cried the Mandarin.

"In the shape of a pig," said the messenger, and departed.

"Oh, what an evil day in an evil year," cried the Mandarin. "The town of Kwan-Si, beyond the hill, was very small in my childhood. Now it has grown so large that at last they are building a wall."

"But why should a wall two miles away make my good father sad and angry all within the hour?" asked his daughter quietly.

"They build their wall," said the Mandarin, "in the shape of a pig! Do you see? Our own city wall is built in the shape of an orange. That pig will devour us, greedily!"

"Ah."

They both sat thinking.

Life was full of symbols and omens. Demons lurked everywhere, Death swam in the wetness of an eye, the turn of a gull's wing meant rain, a fan held *so*, the tilt of a roof, and, yes, even a city wall was of immense importance. Travelers and tourists, caravans, musicians, artists, coming upon these two towns, equally judging the portents, would say, "The city shaped like an orange? No! I will enter the city shaped like a pig and prosper, eating all, growing fat with good luck and prosperity!"

The Mandarin wept. "All is lost! These symbols and signs terrify. Our city will come on evil days."

"Then," said the daughter, "call in your stonemasons and temple builders. I will whisper from behind the silken screen and you will know the words."

The old man clapped his hands despairingly. "Ho, stonemasons! Ho, builders of towns and palaces!"

The men who knew marble and granite and onyx and quartz came quickly. The Mandarin faced them most uneasily, himself waiting for a whisper from the silken screen behind his throne. At last the whisper came.

"I have called you here," said the whisper.

"I have called you here," said the Mandarin aloud, "because our city is shaped like an orange, and the vile city of Kwan-Si has this day shaped theirs like a ravenous pig——"

Here the stonemasons groaned and wept. Death rattled his cane in the outer courtyard. Poverty made a sound like a wet cough in the shadows of the room.

"And so," said the whisper, said the Mandarin, "you raisers of walls must go bearing trowels and rocks and change the shape of *our* city!"

The architects and masons gasped. The Mandarin himself gasped at what he had said. The whisper whispered. The Mandarin went on: "And you will change our walls into a club which may beat the pig and drive it off!"

The stonemasons rose up, shouting. Even the Mandarin, delighted at the words from his mouth, applauded, stood down from his throne. "Quick!" he cried. "To work!"

When his men had gone, smiling and bustling, the Mandarin turned with great love to the silken screen. "Daughter," he whispered, "I will embrace you." There was no reply. He stepped around the screen, and she was gone.

Such modesty, he thought. She has slipped away and left me with a triumph, as if it were mine.

The news spread through the city; the Mandarin was acclaimed. Everyone carried stone to the walls. Fireworks were set off and the demons of death and poverty did not linger, as all worked together. At the end of the month the wall had been changed. It was now a mighty bludgeon with which to drive pigs, boars, even lions, far away. The Mandarin slept like a happy fox every night.

"I would like to see the Mandarin of Kwan-Si when the news is learned. Such pandemonium and hysteria; he will likely throw himself from a mountain! A little more of that wine, oh Daughter-who-thinks-like-a-son."

But the pleasure was like a winter flower; it died swiftly. That very afternoon the messenger rushed into the courtroom. "Oh, Mandarin, disease, early sorrow, avalanches, grasshopper plagues, and poisoned well water!"

The Mandarin trembled.

"The town of Kwan-Si," said the messenger, "which was built like a pig and which animal we drove away by changing our walls to a mighty stick, has now turned triumph to winter ashes. They have built their city's walls like a great bonfire to burn our stick!"

"The Mandarin's heart sickened within him, like an autumn fruit upon an ancient tree. "Oh, gods! Travelers will spurn us. Tradesmen, reading the symbols, will turn from the stick, so easily destroyed, to the fire, which conquers all!"

"No," said a whisper like a snowflake from behind the silken screen.

"No," said the startled Mandarin.

"Tell my stonemasons," said the whisper that was a falling drop of rain, "to build our walls in the shape of a shining lake."

The Mandarin said this aloud, his heart warmed.

"And with this lake of water," said the whisper and the old man, "we will quench the fire and put it out forever!"

The city turned out in joy to learn that once again they had been saved by the magnificent Emperor of ideas. They ran to the walls and built them nearer to this new vision, singing, not as loudly as before, of course, for they were tired, and not as quickly, for since it had taken a month to rebuild the wall the first time, they had had to neglect business and crops and therefore were somewhat weaker and poorer.

There then followed a succession of horrible and wonderful days, one in another like a nest of frightening boxes.

"Oh, Emperor," cried the messenger, "Kwan-Si has rebuilt their walls to resemble a mouth with which to drink all our lake!"

"Then," said the Emperor, standing very close to his silken screen, "build our walls like a needle to sew up that mouth!"

"Emperor!" screamed the messenger. "They make their walls like a sword to break your needle!"

The Emperor held, trembling, to the silken screen. "Then shift the stones to form a scabbard to sheathe that sword!"

"Mercy," wept the messenger the following morn, "they have worked all night and shaped their walls like lightning which will explode and destroy that sheath!"

Sickness spread in the city like a pack of evil dogs. Shops closed. The population, working now steadily for endless months upon the changing of the walls, resembled Death himself, clattering his white bones like musical instruments in the wind. Funerals began to appear in the streets, though it was the middle of summer, a time when all should be tending and harvesting. The Mandarin fell so ill that he had his bed drawn up by the silken screen and there he lay, miserably giving his architectural orders. The voice behind the screen was weak now, too, and faint, like the wind in the eaves.

"Kwan-Si is an eagle. Then our walls must be a net for that eagle. They are a sun to burn our net. Then we build a moon to eclipse their sun!"

Like a rusted machine, the city ground to a halt.

At last the whisper behind the screen cried out:

"In the name of the gods, send for Kwan-Si!"

Upon the last day of summer the Mandarin Kwan-Si, very ill and withered away, was carried into our Mandarin's courtroom by four starving footmen. The two mandarins were propped up, facing each other. Their breaths fluttered like winter winds in their mouths. A voice said:

"Let us put an end to this."

The old men nodded.

"This cannot go on," said the faint voice. "Our people do nothing but rebuild our cities to a different shape every day, every hour. They have no time to hunt, to fish, to love, to be good to their ancestors and their ancestors' children."

"This I admit," said the mandarins of the towns of the Cage, the Moon, the Spear, the Fire, the Sword and this, that, and other things.

"Carry us into the sunlight," said the voice.

The old men were borne out under the sun and up a little hill. In the late summer breeze a few very thin children were flying dragon kites in all the colors of the sun, and frogs and grass, the color of the sea and the color of coins and wheat.

The first Mandarin's daughter stood by his bed.

"See," she said.

"Those are nothing but kites," said the two old men.

"But what is a kite on the ground?" she said. "It is nothing. What does it need to sustain it and make it beautiful and truly spiritual?"

"The wind, of course!" said the others.

"And what do the sky and the wind need to make *them* beautiful?"

"A kite, of course—many kites, to break the monotony, the sameness of the sky. Colored kites, flying!"

"So," said the Mandarin's daughter. "You, Kwan-Si, will make a last rebuilding of your town to resemble nothing more nor less than the wind. And we shall build like a golden kite. The wind will beautify the kite and carry it to wondrous heights. And the kite will break the sameness of the wind's existence and give it purpose and meaning. One without the other is nothing. Together, all will be beauty and cooperation and a long and enduring life."

Whereupon the two mandarins were so overjoyed that they took their first nourishment in days, momentarily were given strength, embraced, and lavished praise upon each other, called the Mandarin's daughter a boy, a man, a stone pillar, a warrior, and a true and unforgettable son. Almost immediately they parted and hurried to their towns, calling out and singing, weakly but happily.

And so, in time, the towns became the Town of the Golden Kite and the Town of the Silver Wind. And harvestings were harvested and business tended again, and the flesh returned, and disease ran off like a frightened jackal. And on every night of the year the inhabitants in the Town of the Kite could hear the good clear wind sustaining them. And those in the Town of the Wind could hear the kite singing, whispering, rising, and beautifying them.

"So be it," said the Mandarin in front of his silken screen.

Reading for Understanding

Main Idea

1. The main idea of the story is (a) how vain men make mistakes (b) the importance of kite flying in Imperial China (c) the wisdom of women (d) how symbols can disguise reality.

Details

2. The town of Kwan-Si at first built the walls in the shape of (a) an orange (b) a bludgeon (c) a pig (d) a bonfire.
3. The whisper from behind the silken screen came from (a) the Mandarin (b) the stonemason (c) the daughter (d) the messenger.
4. The shape built to counteract the lake was (a) a mouth (b) an orange (c) a bludgeon (d) a golden kite.
5. The problem was finally resolved by (a) the daughter (b) the son (c) the prime minister (d) the Mandarin Kwan-Si.

Inferences

6. The Mandarin considered the orange (a) a last resort (b) an unlucky symbol (c) the mainstay of the economy (d) the principal color of the Mandarin's coat of arms.
7. The Mandarin Kwan-Si was (a) a stronger leader than the Mandarin of the neighboring city (b) a cruel leader who rose to power on deception (c) as silly as his neighbor (d) a suitor to the Mandarin's daughter.
8. The people "have no time to hunt, to fish" because they (a) are off to war (b) are constantly building walls (c) are too much involved in the affairs of state (d) have incurred the wrath of Kwan-Si.

Author's Tone

9. The author's tone is one of (a) unquenched hilarity (b) unrelieved gloom (c) studied indifference (d) tolerant affection.

Order of Events

10. Arrange the items in the order in which they occurred. Use letters only.
    A. The kite
    B. The pig
    C. The bludgeon
    D. The orange
    E. The lake

Words in Context

1. "The news spread through the city; the Mandarin was *acclaimed.*" **Acclaimed** (151) means (a) blamed (b) summoned (c) applauded (d) terrified.
2. "It was now a mighty *bludgeon* with which to drive pigs, boars, even lions, far away." A **bludgeon** (151) is a (a) sword (b) stick (c) gun (d) loud noise.
3. " 'Such *pandemonium* and hysteria; he will likely throw himself from a mountain.' " **Pandemonium** (151) means (a) uproar (b) weeping (c) joy (d) confrontation.

Thinking Critically About the Story

1. The person who finally turned things around had done everything possible to help her father. What would have happened if she hadn't stepped in at the end?
2. It isn't the symbol that governs people's lives. It's the meaning applied to the symbols that has an effect. How could the problem have been solved at any moment by giving a different interpretation to the symbols? Here's a hint: why not interpret the lake and the bonfire cooperatively? Sometimes water is needed to douse a bonfire. Sometimes a bonfire is needed to provide warmth, heat water, and cook food.
3. There are many fine descriptive touches in the story—for example,

"Poverty made a sound like a wet cough in the shadows of the room." Find other examples.

4. How could the moral of the story be applied to other problems of the human race—for example, bigotry, religious intolerance, war?
5. List five other symbols that play a role in human affairs. Do not use the symbols listed below.
6. How does superstition play a role in our lives even though this is supposedly a reasonable, sane society?
7. Is rivalry between countries good, bad, a little of both? Explain.
8. At the Olympic Games, the avowed purpose is the appreciation of individual achievement. Yet the media always emphasize the nationalism, listing how many medals each participating country has received. Should the national totals be eliminated? Why or why not?
9. Why is the title "The Golden Kite, The Silver Wind" instead of "The Lake and The Mouth"?

Language in Action

Symbols

> "They build their wall," said the Mandarin, "in the shape of a pig! Do you see? Our own city wall is built in the shape of an orange. That pig will devour us, greedily."
>
> Life was full of symbols and omens.

"How ridiculous," you rightly say. "How could the shape of the two cities have anything to do with the deteriorating relations?"

The story demonstrates in an amusing and somewhat exaggerated way the power of symbols in our lives. The American flag, a preeminent symbol, stirs the heart of all Americans. Symbols *stand for* things and ideas, but they *are not* the things or ideas. Other symbols include punctuation marks, the + sign, the judge's robe, an Olympic medal, a wedding ring, a graduation diploma, a traffic sign.

You recognize that a wedding ring is not the marriage; it stands for the marriage. You sometimes fail to realize, though, that words are symbols, not reality. If the word *snake* gives you a queasy feeling, you are being affected by a symbol, not by the real thing. If your mouth waters when you hear *a steak smothered with onions,* you are reacting to the symbols.

Here are two examples revealing the symbolic nature of language.

(a) "Your house is not legally in Minnesota. This survey puts it 20 yards over the Wisconsin line." "Really? That's wonderful. Now I won't have any more of those cold Minnesota winters!"

(b) A century ago a Hungarian scholar decided that Hungarian must be the original language because the Hungarian word for scissors, *ollo,* actually looks like a pair of scissors.

Cindy Ellie

Mary Carter Smith
American

"Something mighty strange happened tonight. As the clock at City Hall began to strike 12, that African princess began to run like crazy. She ran so fast, she ran right out of one of her golden sandals. The mayor's son found it and kept it. He's really upset over that sister.

The Cinderella folktale is one of the world's oldest. It has been traced all the way back to the ninth century in China. There are more than 500 European versions of the tale, but the best-known is by Charles Perrault in 1669. Rossini made it into the opera *La Cenerentola.* Prokoviev created a ballet. Walt Disney made it into an animated film. In addition, there are various movie versions, some with *Cinderella* in the title. There is something universally satisfying about a rags-to-riches story, especially one in which the downtrodden heroine gives her tormentors their comeuppance.

Mary Carter Smith, the author of "Cindy Ellie," is the official griot of the state of Maryland. A griot is a hereditary storyteller in West Africa whose function is to keep an oral history of the tribe or village, entertaining with stories, poems, songs, and dances. Ms. Smith is also co-founder of the Association of Black Storytellers. Her imagination has added a charming tale to the ever-growing **Cinderella** treasure trove.

Why another version of the Cinderella story? This is a special retelling, warm and delightful. Though it is written in colorful language, with some slang, "Cindy Ellie" is warmhearted, humorous, and recognizably human. Though varying from other versions in details, it retains the spirit and outline of the traditional folktale down to the "fairy godmother." Indeed, the new and different details provide many of the chuckles you'll experience as you ride with Cindy Ellie in her "solid gold Mercedes-Benz about half a block long"!

Cindy Ellie

ONCE UPON A TIME, over in East Baltimore, there lived a happy family: Sam Johnson, his wife, Lula, and their daughter, Ellie. Lula was good and kind—a quiet, church-going woman—but mighty puny and sickly. One day Lula called Ellie to her bedside and said, "Child, Mama ain't feeling so well. One of these days I might leave you."

"Oh, Mama, don't say that," Ellie said, with tears in her eyes. "Don't cry, child," her mama answered. "All of us go sometime, and I'd rather it be me than you. So there are a few things I want to tell you. Always mind your daddy. Stay in church, go to school, and learn that book. Remember what I'm telling you."

"All right, Mama, I'll remember."

One day not long after that, the poor woman just up and died, real peaceful-like and quiet.

Honey, let me tell you, she had a beautiful funeral. Sam sure put her away nice. The Senior Choir turned out full force. The Junior Choir was there. And the Gospel Chorus just sang their hearts out. The church was *crowded.* Folks all on the outside too, with loudspeakers going. Lula's lodge sisters was there in their white dresses and them purple sashes all edged in gold. Ellie was on the front row beside her daddy, just as cute as she could be in a white dress and her hair in a fine bush. Ellie was one purty young black sister, with skin like black velvet.

Child, let me tell you, that poor woman's body wasn't hardly cold before them church sisters was after Sam Johnson like flies after honey! 'Cause he had a good job down Sparrow's Point, with lots of seniority. And they had just paid for one of them big pretty houses on Broadway, with them pretty white marble steps.

That poor man, like so many good men, was weak for a pretty face and big legs and big hips. One hussy, the boldest of 'em all, had a heart as hard as a rock. The milk of human kindness had curdled in her breast. But she did have a pretty face, big legs, and great big hips. Ooh-wee! She could put on! Made like she loved Ellie so and was always bringing barbecued ribs, collard greens, cracklin' bread, and jelly layercake to Ellie and Sam. Well, that man fell right into her trap. She had him cornered and married before you could say Jackie Robinson.

Then bless my soul. You ain't never seen such a change in nobody. First off, that woman went down to South Car'lina to get her two big-footed ugly gals that her mama'd been keeping. Brought them back to Baltimore, put poor Ellie out of her pretty room with the canopied bed, and let her ugly gals sleep in that pretty room. Made poor little Ellie sleep on a pallet in the cellar.

Now, Ellie's mama had been wise. When everybody else was converting their furnaces to oil and gas, she said, "Uh uh. One day they gon' be hard to get." She had kept her coal furnace. Poor little Ellie had to do all the cooking, cleaning, washing, and ironing. She had to scrub them marble steps twice a day too and wait on them ugly gals hand and foot. Not only that, but in the winter she had to keep the fire going and clean out the ashes and cinders. So they got to calling her Cindy Ellie.

Tell you the truth, I believe that woman had put some roots on that man. 'Cause no matter how she mistreated Cindy Ellie, he never said a word—he was just crazy 'bout that big-legged woman.

That November the good white folks, the good Asian folks, and the good black folks all turned out and voted for a good black brother who was running for mayor, and he won the election by a landslide. He was going to have his inauguration ball down at the Convention Center, and so many folks had voted for him that they had to hold it for two nights running. The mayor's son had come home from Harvard to go to the ball.

Oh, them stepsisters was primping and buying designer gowns to go to the ball. Poor Cindy Ellie had to give one of 'em a perm, the other a jheri curl, and both of them facials—not that it helped much. Honey, them gals was ugly from the inside out.

"Cindy Ellie, don't you wish you could go to the ball?" they teased.

"Oh, you're making fun of me," Cindy Ellie said.

So Cindy Ellie's daddy, her stepmother, and them two ugly gals all went to the ball and left poor Cindy Ellie at home. Now, Cindy Ellie had a godmama. She had been her dear mama's best friend, and she still had a key to the house. She came to the house that night, as she often did, to sneak food to poor Cindy Ellie and found the child lying on her hard pallet, just crying her heart out.

"Why are you crying, child?" she asked her.

"Be-because I want to go to the ball."

Now, this godmama had been born with a veil over her face, down in New Orleans. She knew a thing or two about voodoo and hoodoo. Besides that, she had a High John the Conqueror root that she always used for good. The godmama told Cindy Ellie, "Go upstairs to the kitchen, child. Look in the kitchen-cabinet drawer, and bring me the biggest white onion you can find." Cindy Ellie was an obedient child, so she didn't ask why. She just did what her godmama told her to do. Cindy Ellie brought the onion to her godmama. Then the two of them went out in the back yard. The godmama lay that onion on the ground, and then she stepped back and waved that root over it. And right before their eyes that onion turned into a long white Cadillac that parked itself in the back alley.

"Cindy Ellie, go up to the third floor, and bring me that mouse trap." Cindy Ellie brought it down. In its cage were two little black mice. The godmama told Cindy Ellie to open the cage door, and them mice started out. But that godmama waved that root over them, and they turned into two six-foot-tall black chauffeurs dressed in shining white uniforms with fancy white caps. They had on tall black boots, and they was bowing and scraping. "All right, Cindy Ellie, you can go to the ball now."

"But Godmama, look at me. I'm clean, but I'm ragged."

"Don't worry 'bout it," her godmama said. Then she stepped back and waved that root over Cindy Ellie. Her rags turned into a dazzling dress of pink African lace. Her hair was braided into a hundred shining braids, and on the end of each braid were beads of pure gold. Her eyes were beautifully shaded, and her skin shone like polished ebony. On each ear hung five small diamond earrings. On her tiny feet were dainty golden sandals encrusted with dazzling jewels. Cindy Ellie was laid back!

As one of the chauffeurs helped her into the white Cadillac, her godmama told her, "Be sure you leave before midnight, or you'll be as you was. Your Cadillac will turn back into an onion, your chauffeurs into mice, and your clothes into rags." Cindy Ellie promised that she would leave before midnight. And away she went, as happy as could be.

At the ball, not long afterward, the mayor's son heard that a beautiful girl who looked like an African princess had arrived. He came out to see her and said to himself, "This sure is one fine fox." He asked her, "May I escort you into the ballroom?" Cindy Ellie replied in tones soft and low, "I don't mind if you do." He helped her out of her limousine and escorted her into the ballroom and to the head table.

Every eye was on Cindy Ellie. You could have heard a pin drop. Then voices could be heard, whispering, "Gorgeous," "Lovely," "Devastating," "Elegant." Even the mayor himself could not take his eyes off her. His wife agreed that she was indeed a charming young woman. The other ladies were looking at her clothes and wishing their own gowns were half as beautiful as Cindy Ellie's.

Although the table was loaded with sumptuous food, Toussaint, the mayor's son, couldn't eat a bite—he was too busy looking at Cindy

Ellie. Then the band started to play, and Cindy Ellie and Toussaint danced as if they had been dancing together all their lives. Cindy Ellie was friendly and courteous to everyone she met. She even sat beside her stepsisters, who had no idea who she was, and invited them to come back the next night. For Toussaint had begged Cindy Ellie to return for the second night of the ball.

Then Cindy Ellie heard the clock strike 11:45. She murmured to Toussaint, "Really, I must be getting home," and rushed out as fast as she could go. As soon as she was home, Cindy Ellie called her godmama and thanked her for such a splendid time. Then the doorbell rang, and she heard her stepsisters' voices: "Hurry, stupid! Open the door!"

Cindy Ellie came out, yawning and rubbing her eyes as if she'd been asleep. "Did you have a good time?" she asked. "Oh, it was all right, but we didn't get to dance with the mayor's son. He danced only with some new girl nobody had ever seen before. She had on some ol' African clothes. But on her they did look good. She had the good sense to recognize what quality people we are, and she asked the mayor's son to invite all of us to come tomorrow night."

"What was her name?" asked Cindy Ellie.

"No one knows. The mayor's son is dying to find out who she is."

Cindy Ellie said, "You don't mean it. Oh, how I wish I could go to the ball tomorrow night. Lillie, won't you lend me your old blue gown so I can go too?" The sisters almost split their sides laughing. "You, with your ragged self, go to the inauguration ball? Wouldn't that be something else! Of course not. Come and help us get undressed and turn back the covers on the bed so we can go to sleep."

And the next night, as on the night before, poor little Cindy Ellie was left behind while the rest of them went to the ball again. Her godmama came in and heard the child crying again. "Why you crying, child? You want to go to that ball again?"

"Yes, ma'am."

"I thought so. You've been a good child all your life, and you always respect your elders. So don't worry. You can go to the ball again. Now dry your eyes, and get your face together. Look in that kitchen-cabinet drawer, and bring me the biggest yellow onion you can find." Cindy Ellie came back with the biggest yellow onion you ever laid eyes on. Then the two of them went out in the back yard. The godmama laid that onion on the ground, and then she stepped back and waved the root over it. And right before their eyes, that onion turned into a solid gold Mercedes-Benz about half a block long and parked itself in the back alley.

"Cindy Ellie, go up on the third floor, and bring me that rat trap," said her godmama. Cindy Ellie brought it down, and in its cage were two big white rats. You see, the family lived so close to Johns Hopkins Hospital that mice and rats from the laboratories up there used to escape and get into the house. They took that cage out in the back yard, and the godmama stood back and waved that High John the Conqueror root over them, and they turned into two seven-foot-tall white chauffeurs dressed in shining gold uniforms with fancy gold caps. They had on long white boots, and they was bowing and scraping.

"All right, Cindy Ellie, you can go to the ball now."

"But Godmama, look at me. I'm clean, but I'm ragged."

"Don't worry 'bout it," her godmama said. Then she stepped back and waved that root over Cindy Ellie. Her rags turned into a dress made of pure silk kente, the royal cloth from Ghana, and worth thousands of dollars. On her head was a headdress of the rarest taffeta, standing tall and just gorgeous. Her big pretty eyes were beautifully shaded, and her skin was shining like polished ebony. Golden bracelets covered her arms clean up to her shoulders. On each ear hung five small diamond earrings. On her tiny feet were dainty golden sandals encrusted with dazzling jewels. She was cool!

As one of the chauffeurs helped her into that gold Mercedes-Benz, her godmama told her, "Be sure you leave before midnight, or you'll be as you was. That Mercedes-Benz will turn back into an onion, your chauffeurs into rats, and your clothes into rags." Cindy Ellie promised that she would leave before midnight. Away she went, as happy as could be.

As they drove up, Toussaint was waiting for her. She went into the ballroom draped on his arm. Oh, they was having such a good time, laughing and talking and waltzing and boogieing. That poor child forgot all about the time. Then she heard the clock as it began to strike 12. She ran out of there as fast as her legs could carry her—so fast that she ran out of one of her sandals. Toussaint ran behind her, but he couldn't see where she had gone. He picked up the golden sandal.

He asked the security people, "Did you see an African princess run by you?"

"No," they said. "We did see a girl dressed in rags run out of the door. We thought she had stole something. But that chick was gone!"

That night when the family came home from the ball, they told Cindy Ellie, "Something mighty strange happened tonight. As the clock at City Hall began to strike 12, that African princess began to run like crazy. She ran so fast, she ran right out of one of her golden sandals. The mayor's son found it and kept it. He's really upset over that sister."

Child, the next day the mayor's son came on television, came on the radio, and announced to every paper in Baltimore that he would marry the girl whose foot fit that sandal he had picked up. Now, a lot of folks who had supported the mayor lived in the places surrounding Baltimore. So first all them sorority girls and debutantes and folks like that tried to fit their foot in that sandal. Wouldn't fit none of them girls in Columbia, Cockeysville, Randallstown, and all the places like that. Then they went to them rich folks' houses up on Cadillac Row. Wouldn't fit none of them girls neither. Then they went to all them condominiums downtown by the Inner Harbor and them fancy townhouses. Wouldn't fit none of them neither. Finally they come to East Baltimore.

Length and long they came to Broadway and knocked at the Johnson's residence. The mayor's men came in with that golden sandal on a red velvet pillow. Them two stepsisters tried their best to put on that shoe. They pushed, and they jugged, but their big feet would not get into that shoe. No way, José!

"May I try?" asked Cindy Ellie.

"No, stupid. It's not for the likes of you," the sisters said.

"Yes, you may try on the sandal," the mayor's representative said. "For the proclamation issued by the mayor said that any girl in Baltimore and surrounding areas may try." He spoke kindly to Cindy Ellie. "Sit down, miss, and see if it fits you." And do you know, that sandal just slid on Cindy Ellie's little foot as smooth as silk. Then she pulled the other sandal from the pocket in her clean but ragged dress.

As soon as she put it on her foot, right there before their very eyes, Cindy Ellie was transformed into the African princess they had seen the two nights before. Them sisters had a fit.

"Oh, Cindy Ellie, we didn't mean you no harm! Oh, Cindy Ellie, please forgive us!" They was on the floor, rolling around and carrying on.

Cindy Ellie told them, "Get up off that floor, and stop all that whooping and hollering. I forgive you."

Then Cindy Ellie was transported to the mayor's mansion in his private limousine. Toussaint was there, waiting to welcome her with open arms. Cindy Ellie was true to her word. For she forgave her stepsisters not only in word but also in deed: she found them two ugly councilmen for husbands. Toussaint and Cindy Ellie were married in the biggest Baptist church in East Baltimore, and the reception was held in the Convention Center. And they lived happily, happily, forever after.

Reading for Understanding

Main Idea

1. The main idea can best be expressed by which of the following sayings?

   (a) Where there's smoke there's fire.

(b) Once bitten, twice shy.
(c) Virtue will triumph.
(d) The proof of the pudding is in the eating.

Details

2. Lula was (a) one of the stepsisters (b) the wife of Sam Johnson (c) the stepmother (d) Cindy Ellie's godmama.
3. The stepsisters had been staying (a) in North Carolina (b) with their father (c) with their grandma (d) next door to Cindy Ellie's family.
4. The godmama had been born in (a) East Baltimore (b) Sparrow's Point (c) South Carolina (d) New Orleans.
5. The mayor's son went to (a) Columbia (b) Harvard (c) Princeton (d) Temple.

Inferences

6. Ellie's father (a) failed in his responsibility for Ellie (b) was a respected member of the city council (c) was sought after only by the stepmother (d) arranged for the mayor's son to meet his daughter.
7. Ellie's mother's choice of heating (a) was no help to Ellie (b) failed to heat the house (c) was a last-minute idea (d) was objected to by her husband.
8. Apparently, being born with a veil over the face (a) prophesied a life of hard work (b) conferred certain magical powers on the owner (c) was fairly common in some areas of the country (d) was bad luck.

Author's Style

9. The style of "Cindy Ellie" is (a) warm and relaxed (b) nervous and upsetting (c) argumentative and wordy (d) serious and sober.

Fact or Opinion

Tell whether the following is a fact or an opinion.

10. Cindy Ellie was the most beautiful girl in East Baltimore.

Word in Context

"Made poor little Ellie sleep on a *pallet* in the cellar." A **pallet** (160) is a (a) kind of hammock (b) foldaway mattress (c) overstuffed sofa (d) crude bed.

Thinking Critically About the Story

1. Does the manner of telling the story satisfy you? Did you find the slang helpful to the story? Explain.
2. How many parallels to the usual version of *Cinderella* can you find in the story—for example, the coach and the Cadillac?
3. This version replaces the glass slippers with golden. Which do you prefer?
4. Mary Carter Smith, the author, introduced this story with a comment: "I tell 'Cindy Ellie' because of my desire to give urban audiences stories they can relate to." Has she succeeded? Explain.
5. The author adds, "The tale incorporates satire, humor, and African-American traditions and encourages voting, cleanliness, and forgiveness." Point out examples of each quality she mentions.
6. "Ethnic, cultural, and racial diversity is a source of America's strength." How do you feel about the quotation?
7. If this story were converted into a TV sitcom episode, what qualities would inevitably be lost?

Language in Action

Judgment Words

> Every eye was on Cindy Ellie. You could hear a pin drop. Then voices could be heard, whispering, "Gorgeous," "Lovely," "Devastating," "Elegant."

What wonderful words to describe the heroine of "Cindy Ellie"! They help us to visualize the radiant dancer as she was observed by the assembled guests. Words like these enrich our lives and imaginations, but they present some pitfalls, too. Above all, we must realize that the words are not tied forever with Cindy Ellie. They are judgment words that exist only in the minds of the speakers and the listeners.

Some labels are more verifiable than others. If we say, "Santos was a member of the baseball team," the statement is verifiable. If we say "Santos was egotistical," we use a judgment word that cannot be checked.

The flavor or connotation of a word is individual. To some voters, the word *liberal* is a red flag, arousing strong negative feelings. To other voters, the same word is an acceptable label for their own beliefs.

Judgment words are individual. *Lazy, bungling, incompetent, stupid,* and *reckless* are negative words that may be applied to individuals who are rated *energetic, steady, competent, wise,* and *careful* by others. How can that be? The words exist in the brain, not "out there."

When you listen to the next political debate or campaign speech, notice how many words are judgment words, expressing only the *opinions* of the speakers.

A Fisherman and His Wife

Carol L. Birch
American

Could This Be Paradise?

Steve Sanfield
American

"What do you wish?" the fish inquired. "Oh, my wish is not so simple. I want my wife and me to find contentment, and I do not know where it is." "Go in peace," said the fish. "Your wish has come true." Then the fish disappeared, never to be seen again.

In *Man and Superman*, the playwright George Bernard Shaw said, "There are two tragedies in life. One is to lose your heart's desire. The other is to gain it." These two stories support Shaw's comment.

The tales have been paired because they have similar themes. In both, there is dissatisfaction with ordinary life. In both, characters attempt to remedy the problem, to find a newer and better way of life. How they fare is the subject of both folktales.

Though superficially similar, the stories are different, as you will see. The end of one is clearcut, with a strong moral. The end of the other is left hanging. You, the reader, must decide if it is a happy ending or not. How you decide may be a reflection of your own philosophy of life.

Both Carol L. Birch and Steve Sanfield are famous storytellers. They have discovered engaging folktales and have retold them charmingly for modern readers and listeners. Anyone who has ever heard a skilled storyteller weave a yarn can remember the experience with pleasure.

A Fisherman and His Wife

ONCE UPON A TIME there was a fisherman named Jacques, who lived with his wife, Monique, in the south of France, where days are warm and nights are balmy. From Jacques they had fresh fish to eat, and from Monique's garden there were fresh vegetables on their table. Fragrant herbs and wildflowers of every hue grew in sweet profusion around their cottage.

But they were not happy. They could not enjoy what they had because they were so bitterly aware of what they did not have. Try as they might, they could not get ahead, so they greeted each day with fear and anxiety. Fear narrowed their vision, and anxiety left them with a bitter taste in their mouths.

One day Jacques caught a magic fish who promised three wishes over a year and a day, and they believed that they would finally know true contentment in their lives. Monique and Jacques talked late into the night, and the next morning at dawn Jacques went down to the sea and called out as he had been instructed:

Fishy, fishy in the sea,
Prithee cometh unto me.
Monique and her husband, Jacques,
Have a wish for you to grant.

The fish leaped above the dazzling sea and asked. "What do you wish?" "My wife and I wish to be prosperous vineyard owners!" replied Jacques. "Go in peace," called out the fish. "It is just as you wish."

Jacques ran down the road, past the small cottage that had once been home, eagerly searching for Monique. He saw her in the distance, pacing, wearing a nervous smile and a lovely gown. Together they gave the laborers in the fields and the servants in their new mansion the day off so that the two could revel privately in their new-found luxuries.

The next day Jacques began the life of a prosperous vineyard owner. He had known such cold from his days at sea that he looked forward to working on warm and dry land. And at first he was happy. He said the chill was finally gone from his bones. But soon the dust of the earth filled his eyes and mouth. The sun seemed to beat relentlessly upon his back. Eventually, he became more miserable than he had ever been as a fisherman.

Now, Monique was also happy with her new life—at first. But she had never managed servants before, and she was uncertain in her role. Worst of all, the women in town would not receive her, while the wives of the fishermen were suspicious of her new wealth and ways.

After six months of this life the dissatisfied couple decided to use their second wish. and Jacques once again called on the magic fish at the break of day:

Fishy, fishy in the sea,
Prithee cometh unto me.
Monique and her husband, Jacques,
Have a wish for you to grant.

"Are you happy?" asked the fish. "No, my wife and I wish that I would be the mayor of the village." "Go in peace," said the fish. "Your wish is granted."

Jacques passed their small cottage and looked at it longingly. As he passed the vineyard, he spat on the ground. About a mile from town he saw a crowd of people waiting . . . for him? One wanted to know what he intended to do about a land dispute, another demanded an appointment in private, and a third shrieked at him for failing to find more water for the town.

Jacques and Monique had dreams of what their lives would now be like. Which dreams came true? Oh, they seemed to be treated less suspiciously, but behind their backs the gossiping went on relentlessly. Now the women in town had to receive Monique, but they did not accept her. As for Jacques, he was free from the chill of the sea and the dust of the land, but his office brought unforeseen demands. He wanted to be a good mayor, so he spent hours hearing disputes and still longer hours considering them. When he wasn't at work, he was thinking of work. It seemed that someone was always unhappy. And most often it was his wife.

Feeling more and more isolated, Monique began visiting the small cottage where she and Jacques had lived. She transplanted wildflowers and herbs from the hills to their yard. She twined wild roses about the door. She enjoyed the labors that she had abhorred—hoeing the garden, whitewashing the cottage, weaving covers and curtains and carpets. If she just sat in the mayor's residence, the hours dragged on. At the cottage, while she worked, the time flew. But her thoughts always went back to the final wish that dangled enticingly before her. She wondered what would release them from their fear and anxiety, which had only deepened.

After just three months Monique suggested a final wish. "Go to the fish, and ask to be the King of France! You'll have councilors for all the tiresome duties, and we'll have parties. When you have to work, I will have the theater, the opera, and ballets to attend. No one will dare to talk against us!"

Because Jacques did not oppose her, Monique thought he agreed with her. The next day Jacques called out a final time:

Fishy, fishy in the sea,
Prithee cometh unto me.
Monique and her husband, Jacques,
Have a wish for you to grant.

"Are you happy?" asked the fish. "No," said Jacques sorrowfully, "this is not the life for us." "What do you seek?" the fish called out above the swelling sea. "Well, my wife wants me to be the King of France, but I do not think I am any better suited to that life." "What do you wish?" the fish inquired. "Oh, my wish is not so simple. I want my wife and me to find contentment, and I do not know where it is." "Go in peace," said the fish. "Your wish has come true." Then the fish disappeared, never to be seen again.

Jacques walked slowly back toward town. When he came to the small cottage where he and Monique had lived, he saw her there with her back bent over the garden. Once again she wore an old and shabby dress. But when Monique looked up, her smile was radiant. She ran to Jacques, and they kissed and kissed again. "Oh, Husband, you wished well! I had forgotten all that we had."

So Jacques and Monique began to live their old lives anew. They enjoyed living in the south of France, where the days are warm and the nights are balmy. They savored the fresh fish and vegetables on their table. They reveled in the fragrant herbs and wildflowers of every hue that grew in sweet profusion around their cottage. And, oh, they lived contentedly and much more happily ever after.

Could This Be Paradise?

THERE WAS ONCE a man who was unhappy with his life. Nothing seemed to be right. He had to work much too hard for far too little. Neither his friends nor his neighbors gave him the respect he felt he deserved. His wife was always complaining, and his children were never satisfied.

Despite his hopes, his condition did not improve, so he spent most of his time dreaming about Paradise. Whether he was alone or with others, whether at work or at rest, the idea of Paradise filled his head. "Someday," he kept telling himself, "someday I'm going to go to Paradise."

And one day—no different from any other—he decided that this was the day he was going to set off for Paradise.

Rising from his morning table, without saying a word to his wife and his two children, he went out the front door, past the gate with the broken latch, and through the open fields, until he came to the edge of the marketplace. He already knew which women would buy what goods from which merchants at what price and what they would argue about. He passed a bakery opposite a butcher shop, went on through the center of town with its synagogue and town hall, and continued out through another set of fields to the base of a long, steep hill.

He climbed the hill until he reached the beginning of a broad plateau. There he paused and took one last look at his village below. He was sure he would never see it again. He was a man bound for Paradise.

All day he walked along that plateau, and when the sun was setting in the west, he decided to take shelter under a tall pine tree. Before going to sleep, he removed his shoes and pointed them in the direction he was sure Paradise lay.

But how was he to know that in the darkest hour of the night a demon, an imp, would come and—either to punish him or to save him or to teach him a lesson or maybe just to play a joke on him—take his shoes and turn them around? No way for the man to know that.

The next morning the man rose early, said his prayers, and stepped into his shoes, certain that they would lead him to Paradise. Off he went, his head filled with dreams. Suddenly, there he was at the edge of the plateau, and just below him, Paradise. He had arrived.

Strange, he thought, *it's not much bigger than my own village. Oh well.*

He descended the hill and walked through the fields to the center of town. Here in Paradise there were also a synagogue and a town hall. As he stood there looking at them, the man thought, *They've been lying to me all these years—or at least exaggerating. They said that everything in Paradise would shine and gleam, but these buildings, why, they're almost as shabby as those in my own village.*

He passed a bakery that stood opposite a butcher shop. He began to suspect that when he entered the marketplace, he would know which women would buy what goods from which merchants at what price and what they would argue about—and he did.

Now more sad than angry, he was sure that if he continued through the fields in front of him, he would come to a gate with a broken latch—and he did.

As he stood there pondering his situation, he heard a whining voice from the house. "Come in and eat your food."

It was enough to drive a man mad. It sounded just like his own wife. But never having said no to his wife and being a bit hungry, he went into the house. He sat down, ate some black bread and some herring, and had a cup of coffee.

Two children came running up to him and jumped into his lap. Playing with his beard, the youngest one asked, "You'll stay with us this time, won't you, Papa?"

Not wanting to say no to the children, he agreed.

And to this very day, that man sits at that table every morning, drinking his coffee, trying to figure out whether he's in Paradise or not.

Reading for Understanding

Main Idea

1. Which proverb best summarizes a main point of both selections?
   (a) Habit, if not resisted, becomes necessity.
   (b) All happiness is in the mind.
   (c) Never trouble trouble till trouble troubles you.
   (d) The wise are too smart to deny their own ignorance.

Details

2. The first wish of Monique and Jacques was to (a) become celebrities (b) go to Paris (c) own a vineyard (d) own a large ship.
3. A major problem of Monique's was (a) learning to be a gardener (b) her negative feelings toward Jacques (c) managing servants (d) trying to enjoy fishing.

4. The suggestion about becoming King of France was (a) the fish's (b) Jacques' (c) the mayor's (d) Monique's.
5. The item of clothing that turned the man around was (a) a pair of shoes (b) a hunting cap (c) a woolen coat (d) a shirt embroidered by his wife.
6. The gate with the broken latch stood (a) at the butcher's (b) at the entrance to Paradise (c) on the plateau (d) at his own house.

Inferences

7. If Jacques had been given the original third wish (a) he'd have been miserable (b) the fish would have congratulated him (c) Monique would have divorced him (d) he might have been given three others.
8. The paradise seeker's actions toward his wife and children were (a) protective (b) inconsiderate (c) intentionally cruel (d) merited.
9. The one who knew best after all was (a) Monique (b) Jacques (c) the fish (d) the mayor.

Fact or Opinion

Tell whether the following is a fact or an opinion.

10. By the end of "Could This Be Paradise?" the seeker had found his goal.

Words in Context

1. "Fragrant herbs and wildflowers of every *hue* grew in sweet profusion around their cottage." **Hue** (169) means (a) shape (b) kind (c) color (d) taste.
2. "Together they gave the laborers in the fields and the servants in their new mansion the day off so that the two could *revel* privately in their new-found luxuries." **Revel** (170) means (a) celebrate (b) take stock (c) discover anew (d) think about.
3. "The sun seemed to beat *relentlessly* upon his back." **Relentlessly** (170) means (a) warmly (b) unpityingly (c) humidly (d) at regular intervals.

Thinking Critically About the Stories

1. Though the stories have been paired for their similar theme, there are many differences. Point these out.
2. Folktales arise from the folk, the people. As *The Standard Dictionary of Folklore* has put it, "Folklore materials thrive in a society in which there are people of considerable native intelligence, artistic appreciation, memory, imagination, and creative urge, who can comprehend, value, remember, and recreate their native folklore and thus propagate it as living tradition." What elements in the two stories suggest that these tales did originate with the people, not with a famous author?

   For example, the story of three wishes appears over and over again in folklore. It reflects a common human daydream. The lure of instant wealth sustains state lotteries. The advertising for the lotteries stresses the theme of wish fulfilment and appeals to a universal human longing.
3. Proverbs like those on page 173 express folk wisdom. They express in a single sentence a generalization that makes a point about people and life. They have their limitations, of course. Life is far too complicated to sum up in a sentence. Then, too, proverbs sometimes give conflicting advice:

   > Look before you leap.
   >
   > He who hesitates is lost.

   What other one-sentence message, other than the answer on page 171, can you supply as a bit of folk wisdom to take with you after you've finished the stories?
4. In *The Blue Bird*, Maurice Maeterlinck also suggests a search for happiness. Two children, Tyltyl and Mytyl, go on a quest to find the Blue Bird of Happiness. They fail and then discover that the Blue Bird has been in their garden all along. At the end of Voltaire's *Candide*, the hero, after many adventures, declares, "We must cultivate our garden." Which of the two folk stories most closely resembles the two just mentioned? Explain.
5. "The grass is always greener in the next man's yard." What contributes to this human failing? How do the characters in these stories display those failings?
6. The perennial Christmas movie *It's a Wonderful Life* shows us a man like the seeker in "Could This Be Paradise?" How does he a

learn a lesson that is also similar to a lesson learned by Monique and Jacques?

7. The title "Could This Be Paradise?" states the central question of the story. Has the man found Paradise? Explain.
8. English writer Somerset Maugham tells a fable about a Baghdad merchant whose servant came home trembling from the marketplace.

> "Master," cried the servant, "just now when I was in the marketplace I was jostled by a woman in the crowd and when I turned I saw it was Death that jostled me. She looked at me and made a threatening gesture."
>
> Terrified the servant asked the master for a horse to escape Death. After the servant had ridden off to Samarra, the merchant became annoyed at losing the services of his servant. He went down to the market place to question Death and complain.
>
> Death explained that the gesture was not a threat but rather an expression of surprise. "I was astonished to see him in Baghdad, for I had an appointment with him tonight in Samarra."

What similarity is there between the anecdote and "Could This Be Paradise?"?

Language in Action

Generalizations

> Neither his friends nor his neighbors gave him the respect he felt he deserved. His wife was always complaining, and his children were never satisfied.

Generalizations can be useful if we keep in mind their limitations. "All poison ivy plants should be avoided" is a pretty useful generalization, as is "Never drive a car with faulty brakes." But generalizations can be hazardous, too.

Sound advice is to use absolute words sparingly. Words like *all, always, every, never,* and *entirely* should carry red flags to alert you to their frequent misuse. "All participants had a chance to speak" is a sound comment. "Real-estate agents are never interested in the buyer's needs" is unfair. It's certain that the wife of "Could This Be Paradise?" was not *always* complaining. His children were *sometimes* satisfied. It's easy to fall into the *always, never* trap.

Hasty generalizations can lead to errors in thinking. "Six of the boys in the class refused to try out for track. All the boys in that class have no class spirit." Perhaps they show class spirit in other ways.

Here are some typical generalizations:

Every girl in the senior class is stuck-up (*stuck-up* is an idiom, 401).

All Italians (Spaniards, Japanese, whatever) are alike.

Every man has his price.

Nobody is ever nice to me.

Tortoise Learns a Lesson

Chinua Achebe
Nigerian

"There is one important thing which we must not forget," he said as they flew on their way. "When people are invited to a great feast like this, they take new names for the occasion." When they had all taken, Tortoise also took one. He was to be called *All of you.*

In Homer's *Odyssey*, Odysseus on his way home from Troy is captured by the one-eyed Cyclops Polyphemus. When asked to give his name, Odysseus calls himself *No-man*. After blinding the giant, Odysseus and the surviving crew flee on their ships. Polyphemus calls for help. When the other Cyclopes arrive, they ask who has afflicted him. "No-man," he cries in agony, and the other giants decide that the gods are punishing Polyphemus, and they leave him.

Odysseus is a bit of a trickster. The role of the trickster appears in folklore around the world. Coyote is the trickster of North America. Spider is the trickster of the West Coast of Africa. Though trickster is deceptive and slippery, he has a certain charm and is often the protagonist of the tale. In this tale by the African writer Chinua Achebe, tortoise plays the trickster role.

There is another folk element in this tale. In Greek mythology, deserts were created when Phaethon, son of the god Apollo, drove the chariot of the sun too close to earth. Winter was created because Persephone ate six pomegranate seeds during her captivity in Pluto's realm. Echos were created because of a goddess who wasted away. This selection tells how the tortoise got his wrinkled shell.

Tortoise Learns a Lesson

LOW VOICES, BROKEN now and again by singing, reached Okonkwo from his wives' huts as each woman and her children told folk stories. Ekwefi and her daughter, Ezinma, sat on a mat on the floor. It was Ekwefi's turn to tell a story.

'Once upon a time,' she began, 'all the birds were invited to a feast in the sky. They were very happy and began to prepare themselves for the great day. They painted their bodies with red cam wood and drew beautiful patterns on them with *uli*.

'Tortoise saw all these preparations and soon discovered what it all meant. Nothing that happened in the world of the animals ever escaped his notice; he was full of cunning. As soon as he heard of the great feast in the sky his throat began to itch at the very thought. There was a famine in those days and Tortoise had not eaten a good meal for two moons. His body rattled like a piece of dry stick in his empty shell. So he began to plan how he would go to the sky.'

'But he had no wings,' said Ezinma.

'Be patient,' replied her mother. 'That is the story. Tortoise had no wings, but he went to the birds and asked to be allowed to go with them.

'"We know you too well," said the birds when they had heard him. "You are full of cunning and you are ungrateful. If we allow you to come with us you will soon begin your mischief."

'"You do not know me," said Tortoise. "I am a changed man. I have learned that a man who makes trouble for others is also making it for himself."

'Tortoise had a sweet tongue, and within a short time all the birds agreed that he was a changed man, and they each gave him a feather, with which he made two wings.

'At last the great day came and Tortoise was the first to arrive at the meeting place. When all the birds had gathered together, they set off in a body. Tortoise was very happy and voluble as he flew among the birds, and he was soon chosen as the man to speak for the party because he was a great orator.

'"There is one important thing which we must not forget," he said as they flew on their way. "When people are invited to a great feast like this, they take new names for the occasion. Our hosts in the sky will expect us to honor this age-old custom."

'None of the birds had heard of this custom but they knew that Tortoise, in spite of his failings in other directions, was a widely-traveled man who knew the customs of different peoples. And so they each took a new name. When they had all taken, Tortoise also took one. He was to be called *All of you.*

'At last the party arrived in the sky and their hosts were very happy to see them. Tortoise stood up in his many-colored plumage and thanked them for their invitation. His speech was so eloquent that all the birds were glad they had brought him, and nodded their heads in approval of all he said. Their hosts took him as the king of the birds, especially as he looked somewhat different from the others.

'After kola nuts had been presented and eaten, the people of the sky set before their guests the most delectable dishes Tortoise had ever seen or dreamed of. The soup was brought out hot from the fire and in the very pot in which it had been cooked. It was full of meat and fish. Tortoise began to sniff aloud. There was pounded yam and also yam pottage cooked with palm-oil and fresh fish. There were also pots of palm-wine. When everything had been set before the guests, one of the people of the sky came forward and tasted a little from each pot. He then invited the birds to eat. But Tortoise jumped to his feet and asked: "For whom have you prepared this feast?"

'"For all of you," replied the man.

'Tortoise turned to the birds and said: "You remember that my name is *All of you.* The custom here is to serve the spokesman first and the others later. They will serve you when I have eaten."

'He began to eat and the birds grumbled angrily. The people of the sky thought it must be their custom to leave all the food for their king. And so Tortoise ate the best part of the food and then drank two pots of palm-wine, so that he was full of food and drink and his body filled out in his shell.

'The birds gathered round to eat what was left and to peck at the bones he had thrown all about the floor. Some of them were too angry to eat. They chose to fly home on an empty stomach. But before they left each took back the feather he had lent to Tortoise. And there he stood in his hard shell full of food and wine but without any wings to fly home. He asked the birds to take a message for his wife, but they all refused. In the end Parrot, who had felt more angry than the others, suddenly changed his mind and agreed to take the message.

'"Tell my wife," said Tortoise, "to bring out all the soft things in my house and cover the compound with them so that I can jump down from the sky without very great danger."

'Parrot promised to deliver the message, and then flew away. But when he reached Tortoise's house he told his wife to bring out all the hard things in the house. And so she brought out her husband's hoes, machetes, spears, guns and even his cannon. Tortoise looked down from the sky and saw his wife bringing things out, but it was too far to see what they were. When all seemed ready he let himself go. He fell and fell and fell until he began to fear that he would never stop falling. And then like the sound of his cannon he crashed on the compound.'

'Did he die?' asked Ezinma.

'No,' replied Ekwefi. 'His shell broke into pieces. But there was a great medicine man in the neighborhood. Tortoise's wife sent for him and he gathered all the bits of shell and stuck them together. That is why Tortoise's shell is not smooth.'

'There is no song in the story,' Ezinma pointed out.

'No,' said Ekwefi. 'I shall think of another one with a song. But it is your turn now.'

'Once upon a time,' Ezinma began, 'Tortoise and Cat went to wrestle against Yams—no, that is not the beginning. Once upon a time there was a great famine in the land of animals. Everybody was lean except Cat, who was fat and whose body shone as if oil was rubbed on it. . . .'

She broke off because at that very moment a loud and high-pitched voice broke the outer silence of the night.

Reading for Understanding

Main Idea

1. The main idea in the selection can best be expressed by the following statement.
   (a) Virtue is its own reward.
   (b) Selfishness sometimes backfires.
   (c) A true friend is more precious than diamonds.
   (d) Birds of a feather flock together.

Details

2. Tortoise was chosen to speak for the birds because of his (a) outstanding courage (b) history of good deeds (c) skill in speaking (d) basic sincerity.
3. All the following were mentioned as foods at the feast EXCEPT (a) yams (b) palm oil (c) fish (d) bananas.
4. The bird who took the message to Tortoise's wife was (a) Macaw (b) Parrot (c) Crane (d) Raven.

Inferences

5. An adjective that might reasonably and appropriately be applied to Tortoise is (a) deceitful (b) hesitant (c) appreciative (d) reliable.
6. The people of the sky were (a) cruel and unreasonable (b) taken in by Tortoise (c) disappointed (d) mighty orators.

Author's Attitude

7. We might infer that Ezinma (a) was a good listener (b) had heard the story many times before (c) was frightened by the personality of Tortoise (d) was another name for Ekwefi.
8. The author's attitude toward Tortoise is one of (a) complete disapproval (b) unqualified acceptance (c) amused affection (d) studied indifference.

Outcome

9. The events in the story probably (a) made Parrot rejoice (b) brought about a reformation of Tortoise (c) was a later source of pride for Tortoise (d) had little permanent effect on Tortoise's character.

Fact or Opinion

Tell whether the following is a fact or an opinion.

10. Tortoise ate most of the food being offered.

Words in Context

1. "Tortoise was very happy and *voluble* as he flew among the birds." **Voluble** (179) means (a) humorous (b) swift (c) considerate (d) talkative.
2. "After kola nuts had been presented and eaten, the people of the sky set before their guests the most *delectable* dishes Tortoise had ever seen or dreamed of." **Delectable** (180) means (a) varied (b) colorful (c) delicious (d) spicy.

Thinking Critically About the Story

1. There are two conversations in the story: between storyteller and listener and between Tortoise and the birds. How do these two conversations make the selection more readable and interesting?
2. Why do so many folktales and fairy stories begin with "Once upon a time"?
3. Many contemporary movies feature an antihero, rather than a hero. "Conspicuously absent in traditional heroic qualities," the antihero sometimes wins over the audience despite his or her faults. The TV and movie character, the Incredible Hulk, is a good example of this. Can you think of others? Why does an antihero sometimes appeal? Is Tortoise likable? Why or why not?
4. Why do you think folktales from around the world often seem so much alike?
5. Which of the author's touches definitely set this tale in Africa rather than in some other region?

Language in Action

Stories in Words

Tortoise (179) has a fascinating and unexpected history. Appropriately, it traces its history through the word *turtle*. A tortoise tends to be a creature of the land. *Turtle* is a broader term referring to water creatures as well. The word can be traced through various changes all the way back to the Greek *Tartarus*. Tartarus has two explanations. In early Greek mythology, it was located beneath Hades, the abode of the dead. Later it was frequently linked with Hades. It was the place where Zeus sent the rebellious Titans, like Tantalus and Sisyphus. In ancient times, the turtle was considered an infernal creature.

Patient (179) contains the Latin root *pati*, "to suffer." The word was originally narrowly connected to the concept of suffering. Another form of the same root is found in the word *passion*. It too was once narrowly tied to suffering. But both *patient* and *passion* have broadened their meanings, as words so often do. An operagoer, for example, may have a *passion* for music, an intense interest. A *patient* person may show great restraint and self-control. Ezinma is urged to be patient. Her impatience is a sure sign that the storyteller's magic is working.

Cunning (179) has many interesting ancestors. Like the word *can*, it traces its heritage to Middle English, Old Norse, and Old English. The most common words frequently have the most varied and surprising derivations. So it is with *can* and *cunning*. At the base of the root is the concept of *know*. In fact, an obsolete meaning of *can* is "to know, understand." A *cunning* person, by derivation, is one who *knows*, one who possesses keen insight. As so often happens, words sometimes go downhill in meaning. Though *cunning*, in some senses retains the idea of keen insight, in other, and perhaps more frequent, senses, it has a negative connotation: trickery. The birds rightfully suspect Tortoise of trickery when they call him *cunning*.

The Mezcla Man

J. Frank Dobie
American

He stood with his arms stretched to the east and west, and across his chest was this writing: "Dig out to the east and the west the way my hands are pointing and you will find the gold."

Booker T. Washington tells the anecdote of a sea captain and his men dying of thirst fifty miles out to sea off Brazil. The captain of a passing ship cries out, "Drop your buckets where you are."

The men do so and find fresh water, for the mighty Amazon carries fresh water far out to the sea from its mouth. Sometimes we can look too far afield for answers. In "The Purloined Letter," Edgar Allan Poe shows how the best hiding place is sometimes no hiding place at all.

Folktales enjoy playing with the theme of the secret hiding place. Often, learned men and ruthless villains fail to unlock the secret. It takes a simple, often unlettered man to find the answer. Luck may play a part in discovering the Mezcla man's secret, but once again an unassuming person solves the riddle.

The Mezcla Man

THERE WERE NO BANKS in the country then, so when the rich rancheros sold their wool and sheep, they brought the money home. It was gold, with some silver. Often they hid it in holes in the rock walls of their houses or buried it in the floors of dirt cemented with bull blood. Sometimes they put it outside.

Now one ranchero had more sheep and wool than any other. This rich old ranchero had more gold also than any other man, and he was very cunning. One time, after he had sold thousands of sheep and had conducted a caravan of carts loaded with wool to San Antonio, he brought home more gold than he had ever had before. But now, instead of hiding it in his house he carried it to the highest hill on his ranch. On its upper slopes black chaparral and catsclaw and other thorned brush grew so dense, a *javelina* (wild pig) could hardly squeeze through it. The top of the hill was flat, and in the middle of the thicket was a small natural clearing. The trail to it was dim and thorny, for hardly anybody but wildcats ever traveled it.

The cunning old *rico* (rich one) knew it, though. It must have been right after a rain, for he found mud. There in the middle of the clearing, he made a great big man out of mezcla, which is a mixture of mud and straw or little sticks, the same as adobe. Big sticks supported the legs and neck and arms of the mezcla man. He was as big as a giant, and he was natural like a picture. He stood with his arms stretched to the east and west, and across his chest was this writing: "Dig out to the east and the west the way my hands are pointing and you will find the gold." Oh, but this mezcla man was strange, and his stomach was so big that anybody who looked at him would laugh.

After the cunning old rico had finished making the mezcla man, he kept his secret. He raised more sheep and the shearers sheared more wool for him and he got more gold and hid it. They say that when he snored at night, his snores said, "*Más oro, más oro.*" Then one night when he was snoring for "more gold, more gold," the bandits came as quietly as the owl flies and went into the snoring room. They grasped the rico. "Your gold," the chief of the bandits said. "There is none," the rico replied. "You had better say," the *bandido* said. "There is none," the rico repeated.

"Hang him," the chief of bandidos ordered. The others tied his hands behind him and took a hair rope, so that it would not cut his skin too much, and noosed him by the neck. Then they drew the other end of the rope over a beam and pulled him up until his feet were kicking nothing but air. When he went to breathing like a lassoed wild horse choking down, they lowered him.

"What is the name of the dance you are doing for us?" one of the bandits laughed. The rico said nothing. Again the leader asked and the rico refused to tell where the gold was. "All right," the leader cried, "hang him up again." Again he danced and again he strangled, but the dance was weaker, and the sound of the little air passing through the tight noose was shriller. The bandits let him down again. "For the last time," the bandit chief said, "I ask where is the gold." The rico was purple in the face and coughing, but he wheezed out, "There is none."

"May you go with God!" one bandit called. "And all you to the *infierno*," the rico gasped back. "That's where you will snore now for more gold," another bandit taunted. After the rico's legs had made their last jerk, the taunter observed, "He loved his gold better than his life." "It was his pride that he loved," the bandit chief said, "even better than the Holy Virgin."

Then all went to searching. They looked everywhere there was to look inside the house and found not one piece of gold. When daylight came, they went to digging holes outside. One found the trail going up through the brush on the hill and followed it and came to the mezcla man. He came back yelling, "Now it is found!" What joy the bandits had! Quickly they dug under the hands of the mezcla man but found nothing. Now the bandits ran east and west the way the hands pointed, looking for likely places to dig. They were in a hurry, not only from eagerness for the gold but from knowledge that before long honest people would find out about the murder of the rico, a very important man, and begin trailing them down.

With all that traveling up and down the hill, from digging, to water and food, and back, the trail became as plain as the road to Laredo. On the afternoon of the second day the bandits heard horses galloping. They left the country.

When the ranchmen who were after the bandits came to the thicket and saw the strange mezcla man and read that writing on his breast, they forgot all about murder and justice. They thought only about finding the gold. Nobody was after them, so they could dig as deep and as far out as they wanted to. They would sight along the mezcla man's shoulders and along his arms and out his forefinger and out his middle finger, trying, trying to locate the right place on the ground to dig for gold. They even sighted out to a hill five miles away and dug a hole there. They cut paths through the brush east and west. But after they had dug and dug and found nothing, they became disgusted and quit.

Then the *pastores* (shepherds) began grazing their sheep up to the *Cerro del Rico* (Hill of the Rich One). These pastores would leave their dogs to care for the sheep and go up the hill and dig all day long. They dug new holes and they dug the old holes deeper. But they did not find anything, and after a while they became disgusted and quit.

Only one old *pastor* did not quit. He was very astute, very wise. So he kept on coming to that high hill and digging. Every morning he would put his gourd of water down at the mezcla man's feet, take his grubbing hoe and spade, and then for hours dig, dig, dig. One day after he had been working very hard and was thirsty and tired, the pastor regarded the writing for a long time. At last he said to the man of mud and sticks:

"Why, robbers came here and found you and read what you say and dug out to the east and west, and they did not find any gold. Then all the rich and important rancheros came. They had confidence in your word, and they dug out to the east and the west, and they did not find gold. Then after they quit, the pastores still believed you and they dug more holes. And I? Well, here I have been listening to you and digging my arms off for over a year, and I have never so much as found a copper *centavo*. Why you are just a billy goat of a liar!" He slapped him on his mouth.

The pastor was very indignant. "Shameless one," he said, "it is not with your mouth that you deceive. Right now your lying to honest people will end." He seized his spade and hacked off the head of the mezcla man with his wide-open mouth. Then he chopped off the arms. And then, wow! he came with all his might down through the words on the mezcla man's breast and into his enormous stomach.

And when he did, gold coins, and some silver coins too, just poured out on the ground. They were so heavy that the pastor could not carry them all. You see, the cunning old ranchero had built the man to hold plenty, and then he fed him through his open mouth until he was full.

The pastor gave his master some of the money, and he kept the rest, and he never had to herd sheep any more. He went back on the other side of the river into his own country, and there he made a home and lived *muy contento* all the rest of his life.

Reading for Understanding

Main Idea

1. The main idea of the story can best be expressed by (a) "the simplest solution is often the best" (b) "you can't teach an old dog new tricks" (c) "haste makes waste" (d) "a friend in need is a friend indeed."

Details

2. Mezcla (a) is another name for *giant* (b) is a mixture of mud and straw (c) suggests great wealth (d) means "bandit or robber."

3. The victim referred to in "Hang him" is (a) the bandit chief (b) the pastor (c) a ranchero (d) the rich man.
4. A javelina is a kind of (a) thorned bush (b) weapon (c) pig (d) horse.
5. According to the bandit chief, the rico refused to yield because of (a) greed (b) nastiness (c) pride (d) fear.

Inferences

6. The bandits' treatment of their victim might best be characterized as (a) cold-blooded (b) sympathetic (c) resourceful (d) mild.
7. The inscription on the mezcla man was intended to (a) enlighten (b) deceive (c) amuse (d) destroy.
8. *Muy contento* (page 188) probably means (a) boldly (b) intelligently (c) warily (d) happily.

Order of Events

9. Arrange the items in the order in which they occurred. Use letters only.
   A. The old man builds the mezcla man.
   B. The pastor shares his wealth with his master.
   C. The ranchmen begin to dig for gold.
   D. The pastor destroys the mezcla man.
   E. The bandits flee.

Figurative Language

10. From the description of the bandits' arrival, we may assume that they were (a) boisterous (b) bragging (c) noiseless (d) fearful.

Words in Context

1. "'That's where you will snore now for more gold,' another bandit *taunted.*" **Taunted** (187) means (a) mocked (b) repeated (c) shouted (d) declared.
2. "He was very *astute.*" **Astute** (187) means (a) vigorous (b) shrewd (c) persistent (d) greedy.

3. "The pastor was very *indignant.*" **Indignant** (188) means (a) involved (b) talkative (c) curious (d) angry.

Thinking Critically About the Story

1. Sherlock Holmes told Dr. Watson, "How often have I said to you that when you have eliminated the impossible, whatever remains, *however improbable*, must be the truth." How does this tale bear out the truth of Holmes's statement?
2. Greed is a dominating theme in the tale. Identify all those who are motivated by greed. Why was the *pastor* rewarded?
3. Irony (14) suggests that things are not quite as they seem. How did irony play a part in the resolution of this story?
4. One of the most famous moments in Classic TV comedy is associated with the late comedian, Jack Benny. A supposed tightwad, he was accosted by a robber who said, "Your money or your life." Benny hesitated. After a few moments, the robber repeated more harshly, "Your money or your life." Benny answered, "I'm thinking. I'm thinking." This brought forth some of the most sustained laughter ever heard for a television skit. How did the old rich man in our story carry Benny's skit to the ultimate?
5. In Greek legend, the sculptor Pygmalion falls in love with the statue he has created. He prays that the statue will come to life. Venus grants his prayer and Galatea steps from the pedestal. In Jacques Offenbach's opera *The Tales of Hoffmann*, the leading character Hoffmann falls in love with Olympia, the beautiful daughter of the inventor Spalanzani. At a party, she dances him into exhaustion, and her father rushes her away. Olympia proves to be a mechanical doll, who is eventually smashed by Hoffmann's enemy. In "The Mezcla Man," another human figure is created, but the purpose and outcome are different. How?

Language in Action

Stories in Words

Caravan (186) comes originally from a Persian word meaning "group of desert travelers." In the 17th century it meant "vehicle." In the 19th century it was used for a kind of railway carriage. By the end of the 19th century, it had come to mean a mobile home. In modern British usage, it may mean a trailer pulled by an automobile. Though the word *car* appears in *caravan*, the derivation of *car* is not related to *caravan*. This seemingly obvious but incorrect explanation of a word's history is called *folk etymology*. By derivation, a *belfry* has nothing to do with *bell* and *forlorn hope* did not come from *hope*.

Eagerness (187) is derived from the Latin *acer*, "sharp." When Horatio in Hamlet says, "It is a nipping and an eager air," he is agreeing with Hamlet that the night is indeed cold. Here, the earlier meaning of *eager* as "sharp" is apparent. The word *vinegar* also comes from *acer* and means "sharp wine."

Disgusted (187), by derivation, means "not to one's taste." The basic root of *disgusted* is the Latin *gustare*, "to taste." The root appears in *gusto* and *gustatory*, associated with the sense of taste. Though limited originally to the sense of taste, *disgust* has broadened its meaning to include other senses, as in a *disgusting sight* or *disgusting smell*. It may even refer to a state of mind, as in "I was *disgusted* by his actions." English is extending meanings all the time, adding new meanings to older words.

The Innkeeper's Wise Daughter

Peninnah Schram
American

When the nobleman had heard the case, he said to the two men, "Whoever answers these three questions correctly will be the one who knows more about life. What is the quickest thing in the world? What is the fattest thing in the world? And what is the sweetest? Return in three days' time with your answers, and I will settle your disagreement."

Riddles are a familiar element in folktales. They appeal to a sense of wonder and bring the "A-HA!" response when they are explained.

In the Greek legends of the hero Oedipus, the Sphinx was a monster who terrorized travelers with the famous riddle: "What animal is it that in the morning goes on four feet, at noon on two, and at night on three?" Those who failed to answer were killed. Until Oedipus came along, no one had succeeded. He answered, "Man, who crawls on all fours as a baby, walks on two feet as a mature adult, and uses a cane as an old man." The Sphinx was so upset, she threw herself from a rock and perished.

In this tale, the innkeeper's daughter has a keen sense of logic that solves riddles—and capitalizes on one of her own.

The Innkeeper's Wise Daughter

MANY YEARS AGO in a small village in Russia, there were two friends—a tailor and an innkeeper. One day as they were drinking glasses of tea, they began to talk about their philosophies of life. As their discussion went on, they began to argue more and more intensely, each one claiming to know more about life than the other, and they almost came to blows. They realized that neither one would win the argument, so they decided to bring the matter to the local nobleman, who was respected for his wisdom and honesty and who often served as a judge in disputes. The two friends finished their tea in silence and set out to see the nobleman.

When the nobleman had heard the case, he said to the two men, "Whoever answers these three questions correctly will be the one who knows more about life: What is the quickest thing in the world? What is the fattest thing in the world? And what is the sweetest? Return in three days' time with your answers, and I will settle your disagreement."

The tailor returned home and spent the three days thinking about these riddles, but found no answers to them. When the innkeeper returned to his home, he sat down, holding his head in his hands. Just then, his daughter saw him and cried out, "What's wrong, Father?" The innkeeper told her about the three questions. She answered, "Father, when you go back to the nobleman, give him these answers: The quickest thing in the world is thought. The fattest thing is the earth itself. The sweetest is sleep."

When three days had passed, the tailor and the innkeeper came before the nobleman. "Have you found answers to my questions?" He asked. The tailor stood there silently.

But when the innkeeper gave his answers, the nobleman exclaimed, "Wonderful! Those are wonderful answers! But tell me, how did you think of those answers?"

"I must tell you truthfully that those answers were told to me by my daughter," replied the innkeeper.

"Since your daughter knows so much about life," said the nobleman, "I will test her further. Give her this dozen eggs, and see if she can hatch them all in three days. If she does so, she will have a great reward."

The innkeeper carefully took the eggs and returned home. When his daughter saw him carrying a large basket, and she also saw how he trembled, she asked him, "What is wrong, Father?" He showed her the eggs and told her what she must do in order to receive a reward and prove her wisdom again.

The daughter took the eggs, and she weighed them, each one, in her hands. "Dear Father, how can these eggs be hatched when they are cooked? Boiled eggs indeed! But wait, Father, I have a plan as to how to answer this riddle." The daughter boiled some beans and waited three days. Then she instructed her father to go to the nobleman's house and ask permission to plant some special beans.

"Beans?" asked the nobleman. "What sort of special beans?" Taking the beans from his pocket, the innkeeper showed them to the nobleman and said, "These are boiled beans, Your Honor, that I want to plant."

The nobleman burst out laughing and said, "Well, you certainly are not wise to the ways of the world if you don't even know that beans can't grow from boiled beans—only from seeds."

"Well, then," replied the innkeeper, "neither can chickens hatch from boiled eggs!"

The nobleman immediately sensed the clever mind of the innkeeper's daughter in the answer. So he said to the innkeeper, "Tell your daughter to come here in three days. And she must come neither dressed nor undressed, neither walking nor riding, neither hungry nor overfed, and she must bring me a gift that is not a gift."

The innkeeper returned home even more perplexed than before. When his daughter heard what she had to do in three days' time, she laughed and said, "Father, tomorrow I will tell you what to do."

The next day the daughter said to her father, "Go to the marketplace, and buy these things: a large net, some almonds, a goat, and a pair of pigeons." The father was puzzled by these requests, but as he loved his daughter and knew her to be wise, he did not question her. Instead, he went to the marketplace and bought all that she had requested.

On the third day the innkeeper's daughter prepared for her visit to the nobleman. She did not eat her usual morning meal. Instead, she got undressed and wrapped herself in the transparent net, so she was neither dressed nor undressed.

Then she took two almonds in one hand and the pair of pigeons in the other. Leaning on the goat, she held on so that one foot dragged on the ground while she hopped on the other one. In this way, she was neither walking nor riding.

As she approached the nobleman's house, he saw her and came out to greet her.

At the gate she ate the two almonds to show that she was neither hungry nor overfed.

Then the innkeeper's daughter extended her hand, showing the pigeons she intended to give as a gift. The nobleman reached out to take them, but just at that moment the young woman opened her hand to release the pigeons—and they flew away. So she had brought a gift that was not a gift.

The nobleman gave a laugh of approval and called out, "You are a clever woman! I want to marry you, but on one condition. You must promise never to interfere with any of my judgments."

"I will marry you," said the innkeeper's daughter, "but I also have one condition: If I do anything that will cause you to send me away, you must promise to give me whatever I treasure most in your house." They each agreed to the other's condition, and they were married.

Some time passed, and one day a man came to speak with the young wife, who had become known for her wisdom. "Help me, please," the man begged, "for I know you are wise and understand things in ways your husband does not."

"Tell me what is wrong, for you look very troubled, sir," she answered. And the man told her his story.

"Last year," said the man, "my partner and I bought a barn that we now share. He keeps his wagon there, and I keep my horse there. Well, last night my horse gave birth to a foal under the wagon. So my partner says the foal belongs to him. We began to argue and fight, so we brought our dispute to the nobleman. The nobleman judged that my partner was right. I protested but to no avail. What can I do?"

The young woman gave him certain advice and instructions to follow. As she had told him to do, he took a fishing pole, went over to the nobleman's well, and pretended he was fishing there. The nobleman rode by the well, just as his wife had predicted, and when he saw the man, he stopped and asked, "What are you doing?" The man replied, "I am fishing in the well." The nobleman started to laugh and said, "Are you really so stupid that you do not know that you can't catch fish in a well?" "No, sir," said the man, "not any more than I know that a wagon cannot give birth to a foal."

At this answer, the nobleman stopped laughing. Understanding that his wife must be involved in the case, he got out of his carriage and went looking for her. When he found his wife, he said. "You did not keep your promise not to interfere with my judgments, so I must send you back to your father's home."

"You are right, my husband," she said. "But before I leave, let us dine together one last time." The nobleman agreed to this request.

At dinner the nobleman drank a great deal of wine, for his wife kept refilling his cup, and as a result he soon became very sleepy. As soon as he was asleep, the wife signaled to the servants to pick him up and put him in the carriage next to her, and so they returned to her father's home.

The next morning when the nobleman woke up, he looked around and realized where he was. "But how did I get here? What is the meaning of this?" he shouted.

"You may remember, dear husband, that you also made an agreement with me," she answered. "You promised that if you sent me away, I would be able to pick whatever I treasured most in your house to take with me. There is nothing I treasure more than you. So that is how you came to be here with me."

The nobleman laughed, embraced his wife, and said, "Knowing how much you love me, I now realize how much I love you. Let us return to our home."

And they did go home, where they lived with love and respect for many happy years.

Reading for Understanding

Main Idea

1. The major point of the story is that (a) nobles may be unfair and too demanding (b) in a difficult or puzzling situation, logic prevails (c) foolish questions sometimes provoke foolish answers (d) the disagreement between two people may be trivial and pointless.

Details

2. According to the daughter, the sweetest thing is (a) truth (b) love (c) sleep (d) thought.
3. To counter the nobleman's trickery with boiled eggs, the daughter used (a) beans (b) fresh eggs (c) tea (d) chickens.
4. "The gift that was not a gift" proved to be (a) almonds (b) a net (c) a wagon (d) pigeons.
5. The daughter's most treasured possession was (a) her child (b) a pearl necklace (c) her father (d) her husband.

Inferences

6. To solve the riddles, the daughter used (a) magic (b) common sense (c) deceit (d) books.
7. The nobleman's conditions for the girl's arrival at his house seemed (a) self-contradictory (b) not too difficult (c) encouraging (d) trivial.

Cause and Effect

8. The nobleman presented a second set of riddles for the innkeeper's daughter because (a) he was fond of the innkeeper (b) he was basically mean and ill-tempered (c) her ability aroused his interest (d) he was a foolish man.

Order of Events

9. Arrange the items in the order in which they occurred. Use letters only.
   A. A visitor asks advice of the daughter about a foal.
   B. The innkeeper and the tailor take their problem to the nobleman.
   C. The innkeeper's daughter and the nobleman are married.
   D. The nobleman gives the innkeeper a dozen boiled eggs.
   E. The daughter eats two almonds.

Fact or Opinion

Tell whether the following is a fact or an opinion.

10. The daughter set up a condition that eventually won her husband back.

Word in Context

"The innkeeper returned home even more perplexed than before." **Perplexed** (194) means (a) surprised (b) sorrowful (c) puzzled (d) angry.

Thinking Critically About the Story

1. In storytelling, three is a magic number. When you listen to someone tell a joke, notice how often just three items are mentioned. Point out examples of threes in this story.
2. What qualities does the innkeeper's daughter possess that make her sympathetic as a protagonist?

3. Did you anticipate the strategy of the daughter in saving her marriage? Did you expect her somehow to win the day? Explain.
4. The nobleman is introduced to show off the daughter's cleverness. What are some of his good qualities that balance his occasional mean-spiritedness?
5. "I lie all the time" is an example of *paradox* (61). If I lie all the time, the statement is false, but if the statement is false, then I don't lie all the time. Paradox is apparently self-contradictory. There are elements of paradox in the nobleman's challenge to visit—and in the daughter's clever solution. Point out apparent contradictions that are resolved by the daughter's cleverness.

Language in Action

Stories in Words

Tea (193) comes from the Chinese, as you might expect, but surprisingly it comes from the Amoy dialect of southeast China, not from the Mandarin. Mandarin is the official or main dialect spoken in about nine tenths of mainland China. How did a minor dialect affect the form of the word English and many Western European languages prefer? *Tea* came from southeastern China through Dutch and Malay. Most traders learned the product's name in this area. Because the Portuguese made contact with a different part of China, the Portuguese word for tea is *cha*, the Mandarin version of the word.

Almond (194) shows a surprising change from a Latin ancestor, *amandula*. Note that the Latin word does not have an *l* before the *m*. Where did the extra *l* come from? After all, the French, Portuguese, Italian, and German versions do not have such an unnecessary addition. The Latin prefix *al* is fairly common. The guess is that someone added *al* when the Latin passed into old French. Oddly enough, the French dropped that unnecessary *l*, but English retained it. English contains other oddities. *Light* has nothing to do with *delight*, but perhaps the one spelling influenced the other. At any rate, English has kept the more complicated spelling of *delight* even though Middle English had *deliten*. Logic doesn't always operate in language and language history

Embraced (196) contains a warm and loving metaphor. By derivation, to *embrace* someone is to "put your arms around" him or her. At Mont-St.-Michel, a famous French cathedral, tidal waters enclose the land on which it stands. Twice a day, except for a narrow causeway linking the cathedral to the mainland, the tidal waters flood the beaches where cars park to visit the area. To warn owners of the limitations of parking, the authorities post signs warning drivers to remove their cars before the tide comes sweeping in. In French, the signs tell the times when the sea comes in and "embraces" the land, a particularly poetic use of the basic concept.

The Creative Imagination

ACTIVITIES

Thinking Critically About the Stories

1. How did Albert Einstein's life prove that imagination is more important that knowledge (147)?
2. Joseph Joubert said, "He who has imagination without learning has wings and no feet." Does this contradict the Einstein quotation (147), or does it supplement it?
3. Read each of the following definitions of imagination and decide with which of these you agree.

> The lunatic, the lover, and the poet
> Are of imagination all compact.
>
> —William Shakespeare

> If the greatest philosopher in the world found himself upon a plank wider than actually necessary, but hanging over a precipice his imagination would prevail, though his reason convinces him of his safety.
>
> —Blaise Pascal

> Man consists of body, mind, and imagination. His body is faulty, his mind is untrustworthy, but his imagination has made his life on this planet an intense practice of all the lovelier energies.
>
> —John Masefield

> Memory is the mother of invention, reason, and skill.
>
> —Mark Van Doren

4. Which of the stories seems to you to be most imaginative? Justify your choice.
5. Three of the stories were written by women; four by men. Is there a difference in the style and emotional content? Do women tend to write differently, or are the supposed differences a myth?

The Writing Portfolio

The Paragraph

Often in writing, the hardest part is beginning. How do you start the juices flowing? How do you overcome indecision and distraction? Writing is a lot like eating peanuts. Once you start, it's easy to keep going. Like the first peanut, the first sentence can lead the way to more sentences.

Experienced writers know that there are two strategies. The first method is to jot down at random any and all ideas that come. This method, called brainstorming, may lead to an outline. The second method is just to begin, realizing that later you'll want to revise the first draft.

In Unit One, you had practice creating single, effective sentences. The next step is the paragraph. In writing a theme, when do you begin a new paragraph?

1. In an explanation—when you go to a new step or idea.
2. In a description—when you change the mood, setting, or point of view.
3. In a narrative—when you change the time, the place of the action.
4. In written conversation—when you change the speaker.

Many paragraphs may consist of a sentence or two, as in writing dialogue. Other paragraphs, especially explanatory or expository paragraphs, may consist of a number of sentences that stick to one topic. Often the topic is announced at the beginning of the paragraph. This topic sentence is a signpost telling the reader what to expect. An effective paragraph often includes a clincher, which sums up the topic.

These are some common ways of developing a paragraph:

1. Giving examples
2. Providing details
3. Comparing and contrasting
4. Giving reasons
5. Defining

Choose those activities (202) that you are most interested in. The topic sentence has been provided. For each topic sentence you choose, write a solid paragraph developing the topic suggested.

1. When I choose a subject to take in school, I usually have a good reason.
2. By the time I graduate from high school, there is one skill I hope to develop.
3. "The Mezcla Man" illustrates the popular saying, "Expect the Unexpected."
4. "Could This Be Paradise?" confirms the old proverb that the grass is always greener on the other side of the fence.
5. Though different in details, "Cindy Ellie" caught the spirit of the traditional Cinderella story.
6. One story in this unit affected me strongly.
7. In some ways, a folktale is like a country ballad.
8. A bitter truth may be more acceptable if told in a fable or folktale.
9. My room at home is a treasure house of objects I love.

Other Areas of Communication

1. Check the computer (or card-index file) in your local library and find out how many books by Ray Bradbury are available. Borrow one and report to the class on both the computer results and the book you chose.
2. Seven students, each choosing a different story, will present its special qualities and solicit votes for calling it the best story in the unit. After all have been presented, the class will take a vote and crown the winning story.
3. If possible, borrow a DVD or tape of the opera *La Cenerentola* from the library or a video store. Screen it at home and prepare to play portions in class. Then compare it with "Cindy Ellie." It certainly differs in details, but is it similar in spirit? Explain.
4. Study the following quotation.

> Michelangelo's famous statue of David was fashioned from a block of marble that had been spoiled in the quarrying and cast away as of no value. The great creative artist used his imagination; first he built up in his mind's eyes a vision of what could be done with that spoiled block of marble. Working patiently over a long period of time he brought into existence the beauty and wonder that he had built up in his mind.
>
> —Jacob M. Braude

Read the biographical entry on Michelangelo on-line or in a good encyclopedia and report to the class. If possible, bring to class a book of Michelangelo's sculptures.

5. Select from *TV Guide* or a newspaper summary of a week's programs a program that strikes you as possibly imaginative. Watch it and then report to the class. Did it show the kind of imagination that we have been reading about? Did it justify the time you spent on it?

Language in Action—a Review

1. You may refer to the preceding sections to answer these questions. The oak tree is often used as a symbol of (a) flexibility (b) strength (c) family life (d) fickleness.
2. The best example of a judgment word is (a) coward (b) president (c) driver (d) pitcher.
3. "Harriet and Barb passed me in the hall without saying *hello.* The whole stage crew is made up of snobs." This is best considered an example of (a) hasty generalization (b) false comparison (c) bandwagon (d) learning by doing.
4. All the following may be considered absolute words EXCEPT (a) *always* (b) *possibly* (c) *everyone* (d) *all.*
5. In the following group, which one contains a metaphor?
   (a) That's as cool as the other side of the pillow.
   (b) In manufacturing chlorophyll, the leaf is a sun trap.
   (c) Scrooge was as pitiless as the driving sleet.
   (d) Elaine was as graceful as a gazelle.
6. Each of the following is a metaphor EXCEPT
   (a) The trees were two sentinels against the sky.
   (b) Janice is secretary of the junior class.
   (c) Jeremy's thinking was muddy.
   (d) The scientist stumbled upon the discovery.
7. How did the following words acquire their present meanings?

almond	disgusted	patient
caravan	eagerness	tea
cunning	embraced	tortoise

UNIT THREE

Life Is an Adventure

Life is either a daring adventure or nothing. To keep our faces toward change and behave like free spirits in the presence of fate is strength undefeatable.

Helen Keller

"The game is afoot!" With this cry, Sherlock Holmes rallied his friend Dr. Watson to action and new adventures. The stories in this unit deal with adventure, but in each a different kind of adventure is displayed. "The Horse of the Sword," for example, is a romantic, wish-fulfillment story, always popular in books and movies.

Quite different is "The Work of One Day Is Gazed Upon for One Thousand Days." Taking a chance, starting a new venture after many discouragements, is an adventure of the spirit. Physically different but similar in many ways is the realistic "Love of Life," Jack London's description of a harrowing escape in northern Canada.

The strangest setting for adventure is the alien planet in "All Summer in a Day," where sunshine is a rare and beautiful experience. "The Sorrel Colt" sensitively describes the adventure of a young child with a beloved colt.

All five stories deal in some way with adventure, but the adventure goes beyond the physical.

The Horse of the Sword

Manuel Buaken
Filipino

MoroGlory had always obeyed me. He always responded to my lightest touch. But this time my sharp pull at the bridle brought no response. He had the bit between his teeth. Whip or no whip, he would not break his stride.

This unit includes two powerful horse stories. There are similarities and differences. Both were written by non-English writers: Buaken, a Filipino, educated in American universities, and Benito Lynch, a native Argentinian.

MoroGlory was called a bandit's horse. Unmanageable, he was given up as worthless until Maning, the narrator of the story, recognized in this fiery animal a kindred spirit and a true champion. This is the story of how MoroGlory changed from a mangy, disreputable, unkempt reject to a sparkling racer, filled with pride as well as strength.

At the Olympic Games, the equestrian events are grueling and sometimes terrifying. There is always the danger of a severe spill, like the kind that paralyzed the late Christopher Reeve. To avoid disaster, horse and rider must form a bond. If the rider lacks confidence, the horse will refuse to jump. But when horse and rider are in perfect harmony, the results are electrifying.

"The Horse of the Sword" tells of such a bonding.

The Horse of the Sword

"BOY, GET RID of that horse," said one of the wise old men from Abra where the racing horses thrive on the good Bermuda grass of Luzon uplands. "That's a bandit's horse. See that Sign of Evil on him. Something tragic will happen to you if you keep him."

But another one of the old horse traders who had gathered at that auction declared: "That's a good omen. The Sword he bears on his shoulder means leadership and power. He's a true mount for a chieftain. He's a free man's fighting horse."

As for me, I knew this gray colt was a wonder horse the moment I saw him. These other people were blind. They only saw that this gray, shaggy horse bore the marks of many whips, that his ribs almost stuck through his mangy hide, that his great eyes rolled in defiance and fear as the auctioneer approached him. They couldn't see the meaning of that Sword he bore—a marking not in the color, which was a uniform gray, but in the way that the hair had arranged itself permanently: it was parted to form an outline of a sword that was broad on his neck and tapered to a fine point on his shoulder.

Father, too, was blind against this horse. He argued with me and scolded: "Maning, when I promised you a pony as a reward for good work in high school English, I thought you'd use good judgment in choosing. It is true, this horse has good blood, for he came from the Santiago stables—they have raised many fine racers, but this colt has always been worthless. He is bad-tempered, would never allow himself to be bathed and curried, and no one has ever been able to ride him. Now, that black over there is well trained—"

"Father, you promised I could choose for myself," I insisted. "I choose this horse. None of them can tame him, but I can. He's wild because his mouth is very tender—see how it is bled. That's his terrible secret."

My father always kept his promises, so he paid the few *pesos* they asked for this outlaw colt and made arrangements to have the animal driven, herded, up to our summer home in the hills.

"I used to play, but now I have work to do," I told Father. "I'll show you and everybody else what a mistake you made about my horse."

Father agreed with me solemnly, and smiled over my head at Mother, but she wasn't agreeing at all. "Don't you go near that bad horse your father foolishly let you buy. You know he has kicked so many people."

It hurt me to disobey Mother, and I consoled myself with the thought she'd change her mind when I had tamed my Horse of the Sword.

But could I win where all others, smart grown men, had failed? I could, if I was right. So early in the morning I slipped off to the meadow. The Horse of the Sword was cropping the grass industriously, but defiantly, alert for any whips. He snorted a warning at me, and backed away skittishly as I approached. "What a body you have," I said, talking to accustom him to my voice and to assure him of my peaceful intentions. "Wide between the shoulders—that's for strength and endurance. Long legs for speed, and a proud arched neck, that's some Arabian aristocracy you have in you, Sword Horse."

I kept walking slowly toward him and talking softly, until he stopped backing away. He neighed defiance at me, and his eyes rolled angrily, those big eyes that were so human in their dare and their appeal. He didn't move now as I inched closer, but I could see his muscles twitch. Very softly and gently I put my hand on his shoulder. He jumped away. I spoke softly and again put my hand on the Sword of his shoulder. This time he stood. I kept my hand on his shaggy shoulder. Then slowly I slipped it up to his head, then down again to his shoulder, down his legs to his fetlocks. It was a major victory.

That very day I began grooming him, currying his coat, getting out the collection of insects that had burrowed into his skin. He sometimes jumped away, but he never kicked at me. And next day I was able to lead my gray horse across the meadow to the spring, with my hand on his mane as his only guide—this "untamable outlaw" responded to my light touch. It was the simple truth—his mouth was too tender for a jerking bridle bit. The pain just drove him wild; that's all that had made him an outlaw. Gentle handling, no loud shouts, no jerks on his tender mouth, good food and a cleaned skin—these spelled health and contentment. Kindness had conquered. In a few days the gaunt hollows filled out with firm flesh to give the gray horse beauty. Reckless spirit he always had.

Every morning I slipped off to the meadow—Mother was anxious to have the house quiet so Father could write his pamphlet on the language and Christianization of the Tinggians, so I had a free hand. It didn't take more than a month to change my find from a raging outlaw to a miracle of glossy horseflesh. But was his taming complete? Could I ride him? Was he an outlaw at heart?

In the cool of a late afternoon, I mounted to his back. If he threw me I should be alone in my defeat and my fall would be cushioned by the grass. He trembled a little as I leaped to his back. But he stood quiet. He turned his head, his big eyes questioning me. Then, obedient to my "*Kiph*"—"Go"—he trotted slowly away.

I knew a thrill then, the thrill of mastery and of fleet motion on the back of this steed whose stride was so smooth, so much like flying. He ran about the meadow eagerly, and I turned him into the mountain lane. "I know how a butterfly feels as he skims along," I crowed delightedly. Down the lane where the trees made dappled shade around our high-roofed bungalow we flew along. Mother stood beside her cherished flame tree, watching sister Dominga as she pounded the rice.

The Horse of the Sword pranced into the yard. Mother gasped in amazement. "Mother, I disobeyed you," I blurted out quickly. "I'm sorry, but I had to show you, and you were wrong, everybody was wrong about this horse."

Mother tried to be severe with me, but soon her smile warmed me, and she said, "Yes, I was wrong, Maning. What have you named your new horse?"

"A new name for a new horse, that's a good idea. Mother, you must name him."

Mother's imagination was always alive. It gave her the name at once. "Glory, that's his name. *MoroGlorioso.* Gray Glory." So MoroGlory it was.

Too soon, vacation was over and I had to go back to school. But MoroGlory went with me. "You take better care of that horse than you do of yourself," Father complained. "If you don't stop neglecting your lessons, I'll have the horse taken up to the mountain pasture again."

"Oh, no, Father, you can't do that," I exclaimed. "MoroGlory must be here for his lessons too. Every day I teach him and give him practice so that next spring, at the Feria, he is going to show his heels to all those fine horses they boast about so much."

Father knew what I meant. Those boasts had been mosquito bites in his mind too; for our barrio was known to be horse-crazy.

For instance, it was almost a scandal the way the Priest, Father Anastacio, petted his horse Tango. Tango ate food that was better than the priest's, they said. He was a beauty, nobody denied that, but the good Father's boasts were a little hard to take, especially for the Presidente.

The Presidente had said in public, "My Bandirado Boyo is a horse whose blood lines are known back to an Arabian stallion imported by the Conquistadores—these others are mere plow animals."

But the horse that really set the tongues wagging in Santa Lucia and in Candon was Allahsan, a gleaming sorrel who belonged to Bishop Aglipay and was said to share the Bishop's magic power. There were magic wings on his hooves, it was said, that let him carry the Bishop from Manila to Candon in one flying night.

Another boaster was the Municipal Treasurer—the Tesero, who had recently acquired a silver-white horse, Purao, the horse with the speed and power of the foam-capped waves.

The Chief of Police hung his head in shame now. His Castano had once been the pride of Santa Lucia, had beaten Katarman—the black satin horse from the near-by barrio of Katarman who had so often humbled Santa Lucia's pride. Much as the horses of Santa Lucia set their owners to boasting against one another, all united against Katarman. Katarman, so the tale went, was so enraged if another horse challenged him that he ran until the muscles of his broad withers parted and blood spattered from him upon his rider, but he never faltered till his race was won.

These were the boasts and boasters I had set out to dust with defeat.

Winter was soon gone, the rice harvested and the sugar cane milled. Graduation from high school approached. At last came the Feria day, and people gathered, the ladies in sheer flowing gowns of many colors, the men in loose flowing shirts over cool white trousers. Excitement was a wild thing in the wind at the Feria, for the news of the challenge of the wonder horse MoroGlory had spread. I could hear many people shouting "*Caballo a Bintuangin*—The Horse of the Sword." These people were glad to see the once despised outlaw colt turn by magic change into the barrio's pride. They were cheering for my horse, but the riders of the other horses weren't cheering. I was a boy, riding an untried and yet feared horse. They didn't want me there, so they raised the entrance fee. But Father had fighting blood also, and he borrowed the money for the extra fee.

As we paraded past the laughing, shouting crowds in the Plaza, the peddlers who shouted "Sinuman—Delicious Cascarones" stopped selling these coconut sweets and began to shout the praises of their favorite. I heard them calling: "Allahsan for me. Allahsan has magic hooves." The people of Katarman's village were very loud. They cried out: "Katarman will win. Katarman has the muscles of the carabao.[1] Katarman has the speed of the deer."

The race was to be a long-distance trial of speed and endurance—run on the Provincial Road for a racetrack. A mile down to the river, then back to the Judge's stand in the Plaza.

MoroGlory looked them over, all the big-name horses. I think he measured his speed against them and knew they didn't have enough. I looked them over too. I was so excited, yet I knew I must be on guard as the man who walks where the big snakes hide. These riders were experienced; so were their horses. MoroGlory had my teaching only. I had run him this same course many times. MoroGlory must not spend his strength on the first mile; he must save his speed for a sprint. In the high school, I had made the track team. An American coach had taught me, and I held this teaching in my head now.

[1]water buffalo

The starter gave his signal and the race began. Allahsan led out at a furious pace; the other horses set themselves to overtake him. It hurt my pride to eat the dust of all the others—all the way out the first mile. I knew it must be done. "Oomh, Easy," I commanded, and MoroGlory obeyed me as always. We were last, but MoroGlory ran that mile featherlight on his feet.

At the river's bank all the horses turned quickly to begin the fateful last mile. The Flagman said, "Too late, Boy," but I knew Moro-Glory.

I loosened the grip I held and he spurted ahead in flying leaps. In a few space-eating strides he overtook the tiring Allahsan. The pacesetter was breathing in great gasps. "Where are your magic wings?" I jeered as we passed.

"Kiph," I urged MoroGlory. I had no whip. I spoke to my horse and knew he would do his best. I saw the other riders lashing their mounts. Only MoroGlory ran as he willed.

Oh, it was a thrill, the way MoroGlory sped along, flew along, his hooves hardly seeming to touch the ground. The wind whipped at my face and I yelled just for pleasure. MoroGlory thought I was commanding more speed and he gave it. He flattened himself closer to the ground as his long legs reached forward for more and more. Up, and up. Past the strong horses from Abra, past the bright Tango. Bandirado Boyo was next in line. "How the Presidente's daughter will cry to see her Bandirado Boyo come trailing home, his banner tail in the dust," I said to myself as MoroGlory surged past him. The Tesero's Purao yielded his place without a struggle.

Now there was only Katarman, the black thunder horse ahead, but several lengths ahead. Could MoroGlory make up this handicap in this short distance, for we were at the Big Mango tree—this was the final quarter.

"Here it is, MoroGlory. This is the big test." I shouted. "Show Katarman how your Sword conquers him."

Oh, yes, MoroGlory could do it. And he did. He ran shoulder to shoulder with Katarman.

I saw that Katarman's rider was swinging his whip wide. I saw it came near to MoroGlory's head. I shouted to the man and the wind brought his answering curse at me. I must decide now—decide between Moro-Glory's danger and the winning of the race. That whip might blind him. I knew no winning was worth that. I pulled against him, giving up the race.

MoroGlory had always obeyed me. He always responded to my lightest touch. But this time my sharp pull at his bridle brought no response. He had the bit between his teeth. Whip or no whip, he would not break his stride. And so he pulled ahead of Katarman.

"MoroGlory—The Horse of the Sword," the crowd cheered as the gray horse swept past the judges, a winner by two lengths.

I leaped from his back and caught his head. Blood streamed down the side of his head, but his eyes were unharmed. The Sword on his shoulder was touched with a few drops of his own blood.

Men also leaped at Katarman, dragged his rider off and punished him before the Judges could interfere. The winner's wreath and bright ribbon went to MoroGlory, and we paraded in great glory. I was so proud. The Horse of the Sword had run free, without a whip, without spurs. He had proved his leadership and power. He had proved himself a "true mount for a chieftain, a free man's fighting horse," as the old Wise Man had said.

Golden days followed for MoroGlorioso. Again and again we raced,—in Vigan, in Abra, and always MoroGlory won.

Then came the day when my Father said, "The time has come for you, my son, to prove your Sword, as MoroGlory proved his. You must learn to be a leader," Father said.

And so I sailed away to America, to let the world know my will. As MoroGlory had proved himself, so must I.

Reading for Understanding

Main Idea

1. A major point made in the story can best be expressed in which of the following expressions?
   (a) An ounce of prevention is worth a pound of cure.
   (b) None so blind as those that will not see.
   (c) Appearances can be deceiving.
   (d) Good fences make good neighbors.

Details

2. Some of the men considered the horse's mark, the Sword, (a) a religious symbol (b) an ownership mark (c) a sign of evil (d) an indication of a meek temperament.
3. At Maning's first approach, the Horse of the Sword was (a) untroubled (b) vicious (c) indifferent (d) nervous.
4. In the race, the last horse to beat was (a) Tango (b) Bandirado Boyo (c) Allahsan (d) Katarman.

5. At the end of the race, MoroGlory (a) showed whip marks (b) dropped from exhaustion (c) turned on his master (d) broke away and raced off.

Inferences

6. MoroGlory was a raging outlaw because of (a) a tender mouth (b) Maning's cruelty (c) his defeat by Purao (d) bad bloodlines.
7. *Moro* is a word for (a) Moor (b) bandit (c) gray (d) speed.
8. The riders of the other horses were especially annoyed because (a) the Horse of the Sword wasn't a thoroughbred (b) they didn't want to lose to a boy (c) someone raised the entrance fee (d) Maning's father was a peasant.
9. The story emphasizes the importance of (a) having enough money for a good horse (b) having a horse with a long pedigree (c) using the whip skillfully (d) kindness and patience.

Order of Events

10. Arrange the items in the order in which they occurred. Use letters only.

    A. Allahsan goes out in front of the race.
    B. Maning leaves for America.
    C. Maning first approaches MoroGlory.
    D. MoroGlory pulls ahead of Tango.
    E. Father argues against buying MoroGlory.

Words in Context

1. "Down the lane where the trees made *dappled* shade around our high-roofed bungalow we flew along." **Dappled** (209) means marked with (a) small spots or patches (b) stripes running across the back (c) four or five different colors (d) brands or ownership marks.
2. "The horse that really set the tongues wagging was Allahsan, a gleaming *sorrel* who belonged to Bishop Aglipay. A **sorrel** (209) is generally (a) jet black (b) wholly white with a black tail (c) light brown (d) high-spirited.

Thinking Critically About the Selection

1. Why was the father able to buy the horse for just "a few pesos"? How did this purchase show his love for his son?

2. True story: Snowman, a famous jumper, was destined for slaughter when he was picked up for a small sum. The new owner wanted a safe horse for his children to ride. Snowman proved to be no ordinary horse. He soon began to jump fences on his own. He was entered in competition and proved to be a constant winner. How does the real story of Snowman match the events in this story? What conclusion can be drawn about the treatment of animals?

3. What does the following sentence mean? "Those boasts had been mosquito bites in his mind too." (209) *Mosquito bites* is a metaphor here. What is the comparison suggested?

4. The author has provided brief character sketches of various people: Father, Mother, Father Anastacio, the Presidente, Bishop Anglipay, the Tesero, the Chief of Police. How is each one distinguished from the others?

5. How does Maning tame the Horse of the Sword? Point out the slow steps he takes to win the horse's confidence.

6. How does the author build suspense in describing the race?

7. Would you have preferred an unhappy ending—perhaps a bad fall by MoroGlory or the loss of the race? Why or why not? See also "Thinking Critically About the Stories," item 4 on page 267.

8. What is the appeal of racing—horse racing, auto racing, trotting racing? Why do spectators get so caught up in the action, even if they have no personal stake in the outcome? Why are sports fans physically depressed if their teams lose? The win or loss doesn't affect their personal well-being.

9. The setting of the story is the Philippines. Do any elements show that this is in a special place? Is the plot possible anywhere? Explain.

10. Why did the author leave for America? After all, he had just had the peak experience of his life.

Language in Action

The Apostrophe

> The winner's wreath and bright ribbon went to MoroGlory, and we paraded in great glory.

You probably have little trouble with the apostrophe to show possession—if the word is singular. You correctly write *Nancy's ingenuity, the book's torn cover,* and *my sister-in-law's baby shower.* The rule is simple: to form the possessive singular of a noun, add *'s.*

The possessive plural sometimes provides difficulties. To form the possessive plural of a noun, first write the plural. If the plural ends in *s,* add an apostrophe. Boys' swim meet. If the plural does not end in *s,* add *'s: children's* toys. If you follow this simple rule, you'll never incorrectly write *mens'.* The plural of *man* is *men.* It doesn't end in *s;* therefore it takes *'s.*

Although some names ending in *s* may take the apostrophe only (*Thomas'*), you will also be correct if you add *'s* (*Thomas's*).

To show joint possession, use only one apostrophe: *Essie and Doug's mineral collection.*

Never use the apostrophe to form the possessive of a personal pronoun: *This is its stable. The camera is ours.*

The apostrophe has another important function: in contractions. An apostrophe indicates one or more missing letters:

It's time. (The apostrophe takes the place of a missing letter *i: it is.*)

Perry couldn't make it. (Missing *o*)

I'm satisfied. (Missing *a*)

Sometimes the apostrophe takes the place of more than one letter:

Where'd you put the tickets? (Missing *di*)

Sam should've called. (Missing *ha*)

How'd you like to eat early? (Missing letters *oul*)

There is an exception:

Janet won't get here on time. (Contraction for *will not*)

When using contractions, don't confuse these pairs:

you're—your	they're—their
it's—its	there's—theirs

All Summer in a Day

Ray Bradbury
American

The sun came out.

It was the color of flaming bronze and it was very large. And the sky around it was a blazing blue tile color. And the jungle burned with sunlight as the children, released from their spell, rushed out, yelling, into the springtime.

Suppose you lived in a land where the sun shone on only one day in seven years. How would you look forward to that magnificent sight that we all take for granted?

"All Summer in a Day" is set on Venus—not the barren, unlivable planet of recent knowledge, but a land of perennial rain forests and violent storms. Earth pioneers have settled this drenched land and live underground away from the turbulence of the surface. Most children cannot recall ever seeing the sun. One Earth-born child remembers from her childhood and lives for the moment when she can see the sun once more.

This is a science fiction story, a work of the creative imagination (147), but it is also a study of how people behave. A recognizable classroom is contrasted with the exotic external setting. The events are all so strange . . . and so familiar.

All Summer in a Day

"READY?"

"Ready."

"Now?"

"Soon."

"Do the scientists really know? Will it happen today, will it?"

"Look, look; see for yourself!"

The children pressed to each other like so many roses, so many weeds, intermixed, peering out for a look at the hidden sun.

It rained.

It had been raining for seven years; thousands upon thousands of days compounded and filled from one end to the other with rain, with the drum and gush of water, with the sweet crystal fall of showers and the concussion of storms so heavy they were tidal waves come over the islands. A thousand forests had been crushed under the rain and grown up a thousand times to be crushed again. And this was the way life was forever on the planet Venus, and this was the schoolroom of the children of the rocket men and women who had come to a raining world to set up civilization and live out their lives.

"It's stopping, it's stopping!"

"Yes, yes!"

Margot stood apart from them, from these children who could never remember a time when there wasn't rain and rain and rain. They were all nine years old, and if there had been a day, seven years ago, when the sun came out for an hour and showed its face to the stunned world, they could not recall. Sometimes, at night, she heard them stir, in remembrance, and she knew they were dreaming and remembering gold or a yellow crayon or a coin large enough to buy the world with. She knew they thought they remembered a warmness, like a blushing in the face, in the body, in the arms and legs and trembling hands. But then they always awoke to the tatting drum, the endless shaking down of clear bead necklaces upon the roof, the walk, the gardens, the forests, and their dreams were gone.

All day yesterday they had read in class about the sun. About how like a lemon it was, and how hot. And they had written small stories or essays or poems about it:

I think the sun is a flower,
That blooms for just one hour.

That was Margot's poem, read in a quiet voice in the still classroom while the rain was falling outside.

"Aw, you didn't write that!" protested one of the boys.

"I did," said Margot. "I *did*."

"William!" said the teacher.

But that was yesterday. Now the rain was slackening, and the children were crushed in the great thick windows.

"Where's teacher?"

"She'll be back."

"She'd better hurry, we'll miss it!"

They turned on themselves, like a feverish wheel, all tumbling spokes.

Margot stood alone. She was a very frail girl who looked as if she had been lost in the rain for years and the rain had washed out the blue from her eyes and the red from her mouth and the yellow from her hair. She was an old photograph dusted from an album, whitened away, and if she spoke at all her voice would be a ghost. Now she stood, separate, staring at the rain and the loud wet world beyond the huge glass.

"What're *you* looking at?" said William.

Margot said nothing.

"Speak when you're spoken to." He gave her a shove. But she did not move; rather she let herself be moved only by him and nothing else.

They edged away from her, they would not look at her. She felt them go away. And this was because she would play no games with them in the echoing tunnels of the underground city. If they tagged her and ran, she stood blinking after them and did not follow. When the class sang songs about happiness and life and games her lips barely moved. Only when they sang about the sun and the summer did her lips move as she watched the drenched windows.

And then, of course, the biggest crime of all was that she had come here only five years ago from Earth, and she remembered the sun and the way the sun was and the sky was when she was four in Ohio. And they, they had been on Venus all their lives, and they had been only two years old when last the sun came out and had long since forgotten the color and heat of it and the way it really was. But Margot remembered.

"It's like a penny," she said once, eyes closed.

"No it's not!" the children cried.

"It's like a fire," she said, "in the stove."

"You're lying, you don't remember!" cried the children.

But she remembered and stood quietly apart from all of them and watched the patterning windows. And once, a month ago, she had refused to shower in the school shower rooms, had clutched her hands to her ears and over her head, screaming the water mustn't touch her head.

So after that, dimly, dimly, she sensed it, she was different and they knew her difference and kept away.

There was talk that her father and mother were taking her back to Earth next year; it seemed vital to her that they do so, though it would mean the loss of thousands of dollars to her family. And so, the children hated her for all these reasons of big and little consequence. They hated her pale snow face, her waiting silence, her thinness, and her possible future.

"Get away!" The boy gave her another push. "What're you waiting for?"

Then, for the first time, she turned and looked at him. And what she was waiting for was in her eyes.

"Well, don't wait around here!" cried the boy savagely. "You won't see nothing!"

Her lips moved.

"Nothing!" he cried. "It was all a joke, wasn't it?" He turned to the other children. "Nothing's happening today. *Is* it?"

They all blinked at him and then, understanding, laughed and shook their heads. "Nothing, nothing!"

"Oh, but," Margot whispered, her eyes helpless. "But this is the day, the scientists predict, they say, they *know,* the sun . . ."

"All a joke!" said the boy, and seized her roughly. "Hey, everyone, let's put her in a closet before teacher comes!"

"No," said Margot, falling back.

They surged about her, caught her up and bore her, protesting, and then pleading, and then crying, back into a tunnel, a room, a closet, where they slammed and locked the door. They stood looking at the door and saw it tremble from her beating and throwing herself against it. They heard her muffled cries. Then, smiling, they turned and went out and back down the tunnel, just as the teacher arrived.

"Ready, children?" She glanced at her watch.

"Yes!" said everyone.

"Are we all here?"

"Yes!"

The rain slackened still more.

They crowded to the huge door.

The rain stopped.

It was as if, in the midst of a film concerning an avalanche, a tornado, a hurricane, a volcanic eruption, something had, first, gone wrong with the sound apparatus, thus muffling and finally cutting off all noise, all of the blasts and repercussions and thunders, and then, second, ripped the film from the projector and inserted in its place a peaceful tropical slide which did not move or tremor. The world ground to a standstill. The silence was so immense and unbelievable that you felt your ears had been stuffed or you had lost your hearing altogether. The children put their hands to their ears. They stood apart. The door slid back and the smell of the silent, waiting world came in to them.

The sun came out.

It was the color of flaming bronze and it was very large. And the sky around it was a blazing blue tile color. And the jungle burned with sunlight as the children, released from their spell, rushed out, yelling, into the springtime.

"Now, don't go too far," called the teacher after them. "You've only two hours, you know. You wouldn't want to get caught out!"

But they were running and turning their faces up to the sky and feeling the sun on their cheeks like a warm iron; they were taking off their jackets and letting the sun burn their arms.

"Oh, it's better than the sun lamps, isn't it?"

"Much, much better!"

They stopped running and stood in the great jungle that covered Venus, that grew and never stopped growing, tumultuously, even as you watched it. It was a nest of octopi, clustering up great arms of fleshlike weed, wavering, flowering in this brief spring. It was the color of rubber and ash, this jungle, from the many years without sun. It was the color of stones and white cheeses and ink, and it was the color of the moon.

The children lay out, laughing, on the jungle mattress, and heard it sigh and squeak under them, resilient and alive. They ran among the trees, they slipped and fell, they pushed each other, they played hide-and-seek and tag, but most of all they squinted at the sun until tears ran down their faces, they put their hands up to that yellowness and that amazing blueness and they breathed of the fresh, fresh air and listened and listened to the silence which suspended them in a blessed sea of no sound and no motion. They looked at everything and savored everything. Then, wildly, like animals escaped from their caves, they ran and ran in shouting circles. They ran for an hour and did not stop running.

And then—

In the midst of their running one of the girls wailed.

Everyone stopped.

The girl, standing in the open, held out her hand.

"Oh, look, look," she said, trembling.

They came slowly to look at her opened palm.

In the center of it, cupped and huge, was a single raindrop.

She began to cry, looking at it.

They glanced quietly at the sky.

"Oh. Oh."

A few cold drops fell on their noses and their cheeks and their mouths. The sun faded behind a stir of mist. A wind blew cool around them. They turned and started to walk back toward the underground house, their hands at their sides, their smiles vanishing away.

A boom of thunder startled them and like leaves before a new hurricane, they tumbled upon each other and ran. Lightning struck ten miles away, five miles away, a mile, a half mile. The sky darkened into midnight in a flash.

They stood in the doorway of the underground for a moment until it was raining hard. Then they closed the door and heard the gigantic sound of the rain falling in tons and avalanches, everywhere and forever.

"Will it be seven more years?"

"Yes. Seven."

Then one of them gave a little cry.

"Margot!"

"What?"

"She's still in the closet where we locked her."

"Margot."

They stood as if someone had driven them, like so many stakes, into the floor. They looked at each other and then looked away. They glanced out at the world that was raining now and raining and raining steadily. They could not meet each other's glances. Their faces were solemn and pale. They looked at their hands and feet, their faces down.

"Margot."

One of the girls said, "Well . . . ?"

No one moved.

"Go on," whispered the girl.

They walked slowly down the hall in the sound of cold rain. They turned through the doorway to the room in the sound of the storm and thunder, lightning on their faces, blue and terrible. They walked over to the closet door slowly and stood by it.

Behind the closet door was only silence.

They unlocked the door, even more slowly, and let Margot out.

Reading for Understanding

Main Idea

1. A main idea of the story is that (a) childhood cruelty can blast the life of a classmate (b) Venus is actually too uninhabitable to be colonized from Earth (c) children everywhere love sunlight (d) the storms of Venus are beneficial, supporting life.

Details

2. The children (a) dreamed about the sun (b) were proud that they had locked Margot up (c) hated their teacher (d) were born on Earth and transported to Venus.
3. To the children, the rain was (a) deadly (b) joyous (c) a fact of life (d) the basis of their songs.
4. The first sad sight in the open was (a) a crushed flower (b) a fallen tree (c) an injured classmate (d) a single raindrop.

Inferences

5. A child asks, "Will it happen today?" *It* refers to (a) Margot's release from the closet (b) the arrival of a spaceship from Earth (c) a surprise (d) sunshine.
6. "They edged away from her" (218) because Margot was (a) partially paralyzed (b) different (c) mean-spirited (d) teacher's pet.
7. The children tell Margot it's not the day because (a) the teacher told them to (b) they're being mean (c) Margot has lied to them (d) it isn't the day.
8. One color missing from the vegetation of Venus was (a) ash (b) white (c) green (d) ink.

Outcome

9. When Margot is released from the closet, she'll probably be (a) happy (b) curious (c) pathetic (d) talkative.

Fact or Opinion

Tell whether the following is a fact or an opinion.

10. The children were justified in teaching Margot a lesson.

Words in Context

1. "It was as if, in the midst of a film concerning an avalanche, a tornado, a hurricane, a volcanic eruption, something had, first, gone

wrong with the sound apparatus, thus muffling and finally cutting off all noise, all of the blasts and *repercussions* and thunders." **Repercussions** (219) are sounds which are (a) noisy (b) repeated (c) wearying (d) frightening.

2. "They stopped running and stood in the great jungle that covered Venus, that grew and never stopped growing, *tumultuously,* even as you watched." **Tumultuously** (220) means (a) steadily (b) unexpectedly (c) frighteningly (d) violently.

Thinking Critically About the Story

1. There are two main aspects of this story: the alien setting and the thoughtless cruelty of children. Would this story have been as effective if set on some cloud-shrouded area on earth? Why or why not?
2. Is it a human characteristic to take for granted all the blessings of life? Can we consciously train ourselves to appreciate what we have? How?
3. In an article in *Psychology Today,* Robin Westen said, "Kids' gossip is decidedly different from adults'; it's more innocent and more cruel. Children will gossip in front of the kids they're talking about." How can children be both "more innocent and more cruel"? Were Margot's classmates both innocent and cruel? Explain.
4. What was the root of Margot's inability to relate to her classmates? What experiences set her apart? How old was she when she last saw the sun? How old were her classmates?
5. How did the author contrast the ominous rainy setting with the vision of the brilliant sun? Point out examples of good description.
6. What is the significance of this line: "Behind the closet door was only silence"?
7. What effect will the experience probably have upon Margot?
8. Why did the author choose the title "All Summer in a Day"? Is it an appropriate title? Does the word *summer* have good connotations?
9. What picture does the following line paint for you? "They turned on themselves, like a feverish wheel, all tumbling spokes."

Language in Action

Simile

> "It's like a penny," she said once, eyes closed.
> "It's like a fire in the stove."

Figurative language (436) depends heavily upon comparison. The most obvious comparison device is the simile, which generally uses *like* or *as* to make the comparison. The metaphor omits these words.

An effective simile can be powerful. Samuel Taylor Coleridge created a vivid picture with "as idle as a painted ship upon a painted ocean." Jim Bishop described people "chattering like excited birds pulling at a conversational worm." William T. Polk described "a baby waving its arms and legs like a capsized beetle." Elizabeth Bishop said, "Think of a storm roaming the sky uneasily like a dog looking for a place to sleep in."

These are literary similes, but folk language is also filled with imaginative similes. A visitor to the South Islands of the Chesapeake Bay heard many expressions that go all the way back to Elizabethan English. When a native met the visitor's son, he commented, "Why I can see the muscles a 'swellin' under that young skin like yeast in the bakin' pan."

One trouble with similes, as with any expression, is the loss of effectiveness with overuse. The person who first created the following similes made a contribution to language: *dry as dust, red as a rose, teeth like pearls, quiet as a mouse.* When it was first created, the following extended simile was especially effective: *March came in like a lion and went out like a lamb.* Though it is still used occasionally to suggest March's unpredictable weather, the comparison has lost some of its freshness.

By all means, use similes to make your writing more colorful, but try to be original. If you want to suggest nervousness, for example, you might find *nervous as a candle flame* more effective than *as a student taking a test.*

Love of Life

Jack London
American

"I say, Bill, I've sprained my ankle,"

Bill staggered on through the milky water. He did not look around. The man watched him go, and though his face was as expressionless as ever, his eyes were like the eyes of a wounded deer.

The other man limped up the farther bank and continued straight on without looking back.

Literature broadens your experiences, allowing you to live many lives in one. You identify yourself with the characters and thus live vicariously—through others. You can walk on the moon with Neil Armstrong, or even be Neil Armstrong. With imaginative participation, you expand your own horizons and enrich your experiences.

"Love of Life" provides the perfect example of a vicarious experience. In the warmth and comfort of your own room, you can share the terrifying suffering of the unnamed narrator. From the sprained ankle through the long trek to safety, you can sympathetically endure the incredible hardships of a cold, bleak, and unforgiving land.

Jack London knew the Far North through personal experience. In 1897, he joined the gold rush, seeking fortune in the Klondike. His mining efforts were unsuccessful, but they turned into pure gold when he mined the experiences and set some of his best stories in the Far North. Perhaps his most famous story is *Call of the Wild,* but he wrote a great many more novels and short stories.

Jack London was a born storyteller. He had the writer's gift of bringing actions, setting, and characters to life. You will find every slight detail in the following story a model of keen observation. You will find some of the details horrifying, but you will marvel at the strength of the human spirit.

For an adventure you won't soon forget, join Bill's deserted comrade as he struggles just to keep alive.

Love of Life

"This out of all will remain—
They have lived and have tossed:
So much of the game will be gain,
Though the gold of the dice has been lost."

THEY LIMPED PAINFULLY down the bank, and once the foremost of the two men staggered among the rough-strewn rocks. They were tired and weak, and their faces had the drawn expression of patience which comes of hardship long endured. They were heavily burdened with blanket packs which were strapped to their shoulders. Head-straps, passing across the forehead, helped support these packs. Each man carried a rifle. They walked in a stooped posture, the shoulders well forward, the head still farther forward, the eyes bent upon the ground.

"I wish we had just about two of them cartridges that's layin' in that cache of ourn," said the second man.

His voice was utterly and drearily expressionless. He spoke without enthusiasm; and the first man, limping into the milky stream that foamed over the rocks, vouchsafed no reply.

The other man followed at his heels. They did not remove their footgear, though the water was icy cold—so cold that their ankles ached and their feet went numb. In places the water dashed against their knees, and both men staggered for footing.

The man who followed slipped on a smooth boulder, nearly fell, but recovered himself with a violent effort, at the same time uttering a sharp exclamation of pain. He seemed faint and dizzy and put out his free hand while he reeled, as though seeking support against the air. When he had steadied himself he stepped forward, but reeled again and nearly fell. Then he stood still and looked at the other man, who had never turned his head.

The man stood still for fully a minute, as though debating with himself. Then he called out:

"I say, Bill, I've sprained my ankle."

Bill staggered on through the milky water. He did not look around. The man watched him go, and though his face was expressionless as ever, his eyes were like the eyes of a wounded deer.

The other man limped up the farther bank and continued straight on without looking back. The man in the stream watched him. His lips trembled a little, so that the rough thatch of brown hair which covered them was visibly agitated. His tongue even strayed out to moisten them.

"Bill!" he cried out.

It was the pleading cry of a strong man in distress, but Bill's head did not turn. The man watched him go, limping grotesquely and lurching forward with stammering gait up the slow slope toward the soft sky-line of the low-lying hill. He watched him go till he passed over the crest and disappeared. Then he turned his gaze and slowly took in the circle of the world that remained to him now that Bill was gone.

Near the horizon the sun was smouldering dimly, almost obscured by formless mists and vapors, which gave an impression of mass and density without outline or tangibility. The man pulled out his watch, the while resting his weight on one leg. It was four o'clock, and as the season was near the last of July or first of August,—he did not know the precise date within a week or two,—he knew that the sun roughly marked the northwest. He looked to the south and knew that somewhere beyond those bleak hills lay the Great Bear Lake; also, he knew that in that direction the Arctic Circle cut its forbidding way across the Canadian Barrens. This stream in which he stood was a feeder to the Coppermine River, which in turn flowed north and emptied into Coronation Gulf and the Arctic Ocean. He had never been there, but he had seen it, once, on a Hudson Bay Company chart.

Again his gaze completed the circle of the world about him. It was not a heartening spectacle. Everywhere was soft sky-line. The hills were all low-lying. There were no trees, no shrubs, no grasses—naught but a tremendous and terrible desolation that sent fear swiftly dawning into his eyes.

"Bill!" he whispered, once and twice; "Bill!"

He cowered in the midst of the milky water, as though the vastness were pressing in upon him with overwhelming force, brutally crushing him with its complacent awfulness. He began to shake as with a fever, till the gun fell from his hand with a splash. This served to rouse him. He fought with his fear and pulled himself together, groping in the water and recovering the weapon. He hitched his pack farther over on his left shoulder, so as to take a portion of its weight from off the injured ankle. Then he proceeded, slowly and carefully, wincing with pain, to the bank.

He did not stop. With a desperation that was madness, unmindful of the pain, he hurried up the slope to the crest of the hill over which his comrade had disappeared—more grotesque and comical by far than that limping, jerking comrade. But at the crest he saw a shallow valley, empty of life. He fought with his fear again, overcame it, hitched the pack still farther over on his left shoulder, and lurched on down the slope.

The bottom of the valley was soggy with water, which the thick moss held, spongelike, close to the surface. This water squirted out from under his feet at every step, and each time he lifted a foot the action culminated in a sucking sound as the wet moss reluctantly released its grip. He picked his way from muskeg[1] to muskeg, and followed the other man's footsteps along and across the rocky ledges which thrust like islets through the sea of moss.

Though alone, he was not lost. Farther on he knew he would come to where dead spruce and fir, very small and withered, bordered the shore of a little lake, the *titchin-nichilie*, in the tongue of the country, the "land of little sticks." And into that lake flowed a small stream, the water of which was not milky. There was rush-grass on that stream—this he remembered well—but no timber, and he would follow it till its first trickle ceased at a divide. He would cross this divide to the first trickle of another stream, flowing to the west, which he would follow until it emptied into the river Dease, and here he would find a cache under an upturned canoe and piled over with many rocks. And in this cache would be ammunition for his empty gun, fish-hooks and lines, a small net—all the utilities for the killing and snaring of food. Also, he would find flour,—not much,—a piece of bacon, and some beans.

Bill would be waiting for him there, and they would paddle away south down the Dease to the Great Bear Lake. And south across the lake they would go, ever south, till they gained the Mackenzie. And south, still south, they would go, while the winter raced vainly after them, and the ice formed in the eddies, and the days grew chill and crisp, south to some warm Hudson Bay Company post, where timber grew tall and generous and there was grub without end.

These were the thoughts of the man as he strove onward. But hard as he strove with his body, he strove equally hard with his mind, trying to think that Bill had not deserted him, that Bill would surely wait for him at the cache. He was compelled to think this thought, or else there would not be any use to strive, and he would have lain down and died. And as the dim ball of the sun sank slowly into the northwest he covered every inch—and many times—of his and Bill's flight south before the downcoming winter. And he conned the grub of the cache and the grub of the Hudson Bay Company post over and over again. He had not eaten for two days; for a far longer time he had not had all he wanted to eat. Often he stooped and picked pale muskeg berries, put them into

[1]bog

his mouth, and chewed and swallowed them. A muskeg berry is a bit of seed enclosed in a bit of water. In the mouth the water melts away and the seed chews sharp and bitter. The man knew there was no nourishment in the berries, but he chewed them patiently with a hope greater than knowledge and defying experience.

At nine o'clock he stubbed his toe on a rocky ledge, and from sheer weariness and weakness staggered and fell. He lay for some time, without movement, on his side. Then he slipped out of the pack-straps and clumsily dragged himself into a sitting posture. It was not yet dark, and in the lingering twilight he groped about among the rocks for shreds of dry moss. When he had gathered a heap he built a fire,—a smouldering, smudgy fire,—and put a tin pot of water on to boil.

He unwrapped his pack and the first thing he did was to count his matches. There were sixty-seven. He counted them three times to make sure. He divided them into several portions, wrapping them in oil paper, disposing of one bunch in his empty tobacco pouch, of another bunch in the inside band of his battered hat, of a third bunch under his shirt on the chest. This accomplished, a panic came upon him, and he unwrapped them all and counted them again. There were still sixty-seven.

He dried his wet foot-gear by the fire. The moccasins were in soggy shreds. The blanket socks were worn through in places, and his feet were raw and bleeding. His ankle was throbbing, and he gave it an examination. It had swollen to the size of his knee. He tore a long strip from one of his two blankets and bound the ankle tightly. He tore other strips and bound them about his feet to serve for both moccasins and socks. Then he drank the pot of water, steaming hot, wound his watch, and crawled between his blankets.

He slept like a dead man. The brief darkness around midnight came and went. The sun arose in the northeast—at least the day dawned in that quarter, for the sun was hidden by gray clouds.

At six o'clock he awoke, quietly lying on his back. He gazed straight up into the gray sky and knew that he was hungry. As he rolled over on his elbow he was startled by a loud snort, and saw a bull caribou regarding him with alert curiosity. The animal was not more than fifty feet away, and instantly into the man's mind leaped the vision and the savor of a caribou steak sizzling and frying over a fire. Mechanically he reached for the empty gun, drew a bead, and pulled the trigger. The bull snorted and leaped away, his hoofs rattling and clattering as he fled across the ledges.

The man cursed and flung the empty gun from him. He groaned aloud as he started to drag himself to his feet. It was a slow and arduous task. His joints were like rusty hinges. They worked harshly in their sockets, with much friction, and each bending or unbending was accomplished only through a sheer exertion of will. When he finally gained his feet, another minute or so was consumed in straightening up, so that he could stand erect as a man should stand.

He crawled up a small knoll and surveyed the prospect. There were no trees, no bushes, nothing but a gray sea of moss scarcely diversified by gray rocks, gray lakelets, and gray streamlets. The sky was gray. There was no sun nor hint of sun. He had no idea of north, and he had forgotten the way he had come to this spot the night before. But he was not lost. He knew that. Soon he would come to the land of the little sticks. He felt that it lay off to the left somewhere, not far—possibly just over the next low hill.

He went back to put his pack into shape for travelling. He assured himself of the existence of his three separate parcels of matches, though he did not stop to count them. But he did linger, debating, over a squat moose-hide sack. It was not large. He could hide it under his two hands. He knew that it weighed fifteen pounds,—as much as all the rest of the pack,—and it worried him. He finally set it to one side and proceeded to roll the pack. He paused to gaze at the squat moose-hide sack. He picked it up hastily with a defiant glance about him, as though the desolation were trying to rob him of it; and when he rose to his feet to stagger on into the day, it was included in the pack on his back.

He bore away to the left, stopping now and again to eat muskeg berries. His ankle had stiffened, his limp was more pronounced, but the pain of it was as nothing compared with the pain of his stomach. The hunger pangs were sharp. They gnawed and gnawed until he could not keep his mind steady on the course he must pursue to gain the land of little sticks. The muskeg berries did not allay this gnawing, while they made his tongue and the roof of his mouth sore with their irritating bite.

He came upon a valley where rock ptarmigan rose on whirring wings from the ledges and muskegs. Ker—ker—ker was the cry they made. He threw stones at them, but could not hit them. He placed his pack on the ground and stalked them as a cat stalks a sparrow. The sharp rocks cut through his pants' legs till his knees left a trail of blood; but the hurt was lost in the hurt of his hunger. He squirmed over the wet moss, saturating his clothes and chilling his body; but he was not aware of it, so great was his fever for food. And always the ptarmigan rose, whirring, before him, till their ker—ker—ker became a mock to him, and he cursed them and cried aloud at them with their own cry.

Once he crawled upon one that must have been asleep. He did not see it till it shot up in his face from its rocky nook. He made a clutch as startled as was the rise of the ptarmigan, and there remained in his hand three tail-feathers. As he watched its flight he hated it, as though it had done him some terrible wrong. Then he returned and shouldered his pack.

As the day wore along he came into valleys or swales where game was more plentiful. A band of caribou passed by, twenty and odd animals, tantalizingly within rifle range. He felt a wild desire to run after them, a certitude that he could run them down. A black fox came toward him, carrying a ptarmigan in his mouth. The man shouted. It was a fearful cry, but the fox, leaping away in fright, did not drop the ptarmigan.

Late in the afternoon he followed a stream, milky with lime, which ran through sparse patches of rush-grass. Grasping these rushes firmly near the root, he pulled up what resembled a young onion-sprout no larger than a shingle-nail. It was tender, and his teeth sank into it with a crunch that promised deliciously of food. But its fibers were tough. It was composed of stringy filaments saturated with water, like the berries, and devoid of nourishment. He threw off his pack and went into the rush-grass on hands and knees, crunching and munching, like some bovine creature.

He was very weary and often wished to rest—to lie down and sleep; but he was continually driven on—not so much by his desire to gain the land of little sticks as by his hunger. He searched little ponds for frogs and dug up the earth with his nails for worms, though he knew in spite that neither frogs nor worms existed so far north.

He looked into every pool of water vainly, until, as the long twilight came on, he discovered a solitary fish, the size of a minnow, in such a pool. He plunged his arm in up to the shoulder, but it eluded him. He reached for it with both hands and stirred up the milky mud at the bottom. In his excitement he fell in, wetting himself to the waist. Then the water was too muddy to admit of his seeing the fish, and he was compelled to wait until the sediment had settled.

The pursuit was renewed, till the water was again muddied. But he could not wait. He unstrapped the tin bucket and began to bale the pool. He baled wildly at first, splashing himself and flinging the water so short a distance that it ran back into the pool. He worked more carefully, striving to be cool, though his heart was pounding against his chest and his hands were trembling. At the end of half an hour the pool was nearly dry. Not a cupful of water remained. And there was no fish. He found a hidden crevice among the stones through which it had escaped to the adjoining and larger pool—a pool which he could not empty in a night and a day. Had he known of the crevice, he could have closed it with a rock at the beginning and the fish would have been his.

Thus he thought, and crumpled up and sank down upon the wet earth. At first he cried softly to himself, then he cried loudly to the pitiless desolation that ringed him around; and for a long time after he was shaken by great dry sobs.

He built a fire and warmed himself by drinking quarts of hot water, and made camp on a rocky ledge in the same fashion he had the night before. The last thing he did was to see that his matches were dry and to wind his watch. The blankets were wet and clammy. His ankle pulsed with pain. But he knew only that he was hungry, and through his restless sleep he dreamed of feasts and banquets and of food served and spread in all imaginable ways.

He awoke chilled and sick. There was no sun. The gray of earth and sky had become deeper, more profound. A raw wind was blowing, and the first flurries of snow were whitening the hilltops. The air about him thickened and grew white while he made a fire and boiled more water. It was wet snow, half rain, and the flakes were large and soggy. At first they melted as soon as they came in contact with the earth, but ever more fell, covering the ground, putting out the fire, spoiling his supply of moss-fuel.

This was a signal for him to strap on his pack and stumble onward, he knew not where. He was not concerned with the land of little sticks, nor with Bill and the cache under the upturned canoe by the river Dease. He was mastered by the verb "to eat." He was hunger-mad. He took no heed of the course he pursued, so long as that course led him through the swale bottoms. He felt his way through the wet snow to the watery muskeg berries, and went by feel as he pulled up the rush-grass by the roots. But it was tasteless stuff and did not satisfy. He found a weed that tasted sour and he ate all he could find of it, which was not much, for it was a creeping growth, easily hidden under the several inches of snow.

He had no fire that night, nor hot water, and crawled under his blanket to sleep the broken hunger-sleep. The snow turned into a cold rain. He awakened many times to feel it falling on his upturned face. Day came—a gray day and no sun. It had ceased raining. The keenness of his hunger had departed. Sensibility, as far as concerned the yearning for food, had been exhausted. There was a dull, heavy ache in his stomach, but it did not bother him so much. He was more rational, and once more he was chiefly interested in the land of little sticks and the cache by the river Dease.

He ripped the remnant of one of his blankets into strips and bound his bleeding feet. Also, he rewrapped the injured ankle and prepared himself for a day of travel. When he came to his pack, he paused long over the squat moose-hide sack, but in the end it went with him.

The snow had melted under the rain, and only the hilltops showed white. The sun came out, and he succeeded in locating the points of the compass, though he knew now that he was lost. Perhaps, in his previous days' wanderings, he had edged away too far to the left. He now bore off to the right to counteract the possible deviation from his true course.

Though the hunger pangs were no longer so exquisite, he realized that he was weak. He was compelled to pause for frequent rests, when he attacked the muskeg berries and rush-grass patches. His tongue felt dry and large, as though covered with a fine hairy growth, and it tasted bitter in his mouth. His heart gave him a great deal of trouble. When he had travelled a few minutes it would begin a remorseless thump, thump, thump, and then leap up and away in a painful flutter of beats that choked him and made him go faint and dizzy.

In the middle of the day he found two minnows in a large pool. It was impossible to bale it, but he was calmer now and managed to catch them in his tin bucket. They were no longer than his little finger, but he was not particularly hungry. The dull ache in his stomach had been growing duller and fainter. It seemed almost that his stomach was dozing. He ate the fish raw, chewing with painstaking care, for the eating was an act of pure reason. While he had no desire to eat, he knew that he must eat to live.

In the evening he caught three more minnows, eating two and saving the third for breakfast. The sun had dried stray shreds of moss, and he was able to warm himself with hot water. He had not covered more than ten miles that day; and the next day, travelling whenever his heart permitted him, he covered no more than five miles. But his stomach did not give him the slightest uneasiness. It had gone to sleep. He was in a strange country, too, and the caribou were growing more plentiful, also the wolves. Often their yelps drifted across the desolation, and once he saw three of them slinking away before his path.

Another night; and in the morning, being more rational, he untied the leather string that fastened the squat moose-hide sack. From its open mouth poured a yellow stream of coarse gold-dust and nuggets. He roughly divided the gold in halves, caching one half on a prominent ledge, wrapped in a piece of blanket, and returning the other half to the sack. He also began to use strips of the one remaining blanket for his feet. He still clung to his gun, for there were cartridges in that cache by the river Dease.

This was a day of fog, and this day hunger awoke in him again. He was very weak and was afflicted with a giddiness which at times blinded him. It was no uncommon thing now for him to stumble and fall; and stumbling once, he fell squarely into a ptarmigan nest. There were four newly hatched chicks, a day old—little specks of pulsating life no more than a mouthful; and he ate them ravenously, thrusting them alive into his mouth and crunching them like egg-shells between his teeth. The mother ptarmigan beat about him with great outcry. He used his gun as a club with which to knock her over, but she dodged out of reach. He threw stones at her and with one chance shot broke a wing. Then she fluttered away, running, trailing the broken wing, with him in pursuit.

The little chicks had no more than whetted his appetite. He hopped and bobbed clumsily along on his injured ankle, throwing stones and screaming hoarsely at times; at other times hopping and bobbing silently along, picking himself up grimly and patiently when he fell, or rubbing his eyes with his hand when the giddiness threatened to overpower him.

The chase led him across swampy ground in the bottom of the valley, and he came upon footprints in the soggy moss. They were not his own—he could see that. They must be Bill's. But he could not stop, for the mother ptarmigan was running on. He would catch her first, then he would return and investigate.

He exhausted the mother ptarmigan; but he exhausted himself. She lay panting on her side. He lay panting on his side, a dozen feet away, unable to crawl to her. And as he recovered she recovered, fluttering out of reach as his hungry hand went out to her. The chase was resumed. Night settled down and she escaped. He stumbled from weakness and pitched head foremost on his face, cutting his cheek, his pack upon his back. He did not move for a long while; then he rolled over on his side, wound his watch, and lay there until morning.

Another day of fog. Half of his last blanket had gone into foot-wrappings. He failed to pick up Bill's trail. It did not matter. His hunger was driving him too compellingly—only—only he wondered if Bill, too, were lost. By midday the irk of his pack became too oppressive. Again he divided the gold, this time merely spilling half of it on the ground. In the afternoon he threw the rest of it away, there remaining to him only the half-blanket, the tin bucket, and the rifle.

An hallucination began to trouble him. He felt confident that one cartridge remained to him. It was in the chamber of the rifle and he had overlooked it. On the other hand, he knew all the time that the chamber was empty. But the hallucination persisted. He fought it off for hours, then threw his rifle open and was confronted with emptiness. The disappointment was as bitter as though he had really expected to find the cartridge.

He plodded on for half an hour, when the hallucination arose again. Again he fought it, and still it persisted, till for very relief he opened his rifle to unconvince himself. At times his mind wandered farther afield, and he plodded on, a mere automaton, strange conceits and whimsicalities gnawing at his brain like worms. But these excursions out of the real were of brief duration, for ever the pangs of the hunger-bite called him back. He was jerked back abruptly once from such an excursion by a sight that caused him nearly to faint. He reeled and swayed, doddering like a drunken man to keep from falling. Before him stood a horse. A horse! He could not believe his eyes. A thick mist was in them, intershot with sparkling points of light. He rubbed his eyes savagely to clear his vision, and beheld, not a horse, but a great brown bear. The animal was studying him with bellicose curiosity.

The man had brought his gun halfway to his shoulder before he realized. He lowered it and drew his hunting-knife from its beaded sheath at his hip. Before him was meat and life. He ran his thumb along the edge of his knife. It was sharp. The point was sharp. He would fling himself upon the bear and kill it. But his heart began its warning thump, thump, thump. Then followed the wild upward leap and tattoo of flutters, the pressing as of an iron band about his forehead, the creeping of the dizziness into his brain.

His desperate courage was evicted by a great surge of fear. In his weakness, what if the animal attacked him? He drew himself up to his most imposing stature, gripping the knife and staring hard at the bear. The bear advanced clumsily a couple of steps, reared up, and gave vent to a tentative growl. If the man ran, he would run after him; but the man did not run. He was animated now with the courage of fear. He, too, growled, savagely, terribly, voicing the fear that is to life germane and that lies twisted about life's deepest roots.

The bear edged away to one side, growling menacingly, himself appalled by this mysterious creature that appeared upright and unafraid. But the man did not move. He stood like a statue till the danger was past, when he yielded to a fit of trembling and sank down into the wet moss.

He pulled himself together and went on, afraid now in a new way. It was not the fear that he should die passively from lack of food, but that he should be destroyed violently before starvation had exhausted the last particle of the endeavor in him that made toward surviving. There were the wolves. Back and forth across the desolation drifted their howls, weaving the very air into a fabric of menace that was so tangible that he found himself, arms in the air, pressing it back from him as it might be the walls of a wind-blown tent.

Now and again the wolves, in packs of two and three, crossed his path. But they sheered clear of him. They were not in sufficient numbers, and besides they were hunting the caribou, which did not battle, while this strange creature that walked erect might scratch and bite.

In the late afternoon he came upon scattered bones where the wolves had made a kill. The debris had been a caribou calf an hour before, squawking and running and very much alive. He contemplated the bones, clean-picked and polished, pink with the cell-life in them which had not yet died. Could it possibly be that he might be that ere the day was done! Such was life, eh? A vain and fleeting thing. It was only life that pained. There was no hurt in death. To die was to sleep. It meant cessation, rest. Then why was he not content to die?

But he did not moralize long. He was squatting in the moss, a bone in his mouth, sucking at the shreds of life that still dyed it faintly pink. The sweet meaty taste, thin and elusive almost as a memory, maddened him. He closed his jaws on the bones and crunched. Sometimes it was the bone that broke, sometimes his teeth. Then he crushed the bones between rocks, pounded them to a pulp, and swallowed them. He pounded his fingers, too, in his haste, and yet found a moment in which to feel surprise at the fact that his fingers did not hurt much when caught under the descending rock.

Came frightful days of snow and rain. He did not know when he made camp, when he broke camp. He travelled in the night as much as in the day. He rested wherever he fell, crawled on whenever the dying life in him flickered up and burned less dimly. He, as a man, no longer strove. It was the life in him, unwilling to die, that drove him on. He did not suffer. His nerves had become blunted, numb, while his mind was filled with weird visions and delicious dreams.

But ever he sucked and chewed on the crushed bones of the caribou calf, the least remnants of which he had gathered up and carried with him. He crossed no more hills or divides, but automatically followed a large stream which flowed through a wide and shallow valley. He did not see this stream nor this valley. He saw nothing save visions. Soul and body walked or crawled side by side, yet apart, so slender was the thread that bound them.

He awoke in his right mind, lying on his back on a rocky ledge. The sun was shining bright and warm. Afar off he heard the squawking of caribou calves. He was aware of vague memories of rain and wind and snow, but whether he had been beaten by the storm for two days or two weeks he did not know.

For some time he lay without movement, the genial sunshine pouring upon him and saturating his miserable body with its warmth. A fine day, he thought. Perhaps he could manage to locate himself. By a painful effort he rolled over on his side. Below him flowed a wide and sluggish river. Its unfamiliarity puzzled him. Slowly he followed it with his eyes, winding in wide sweeps among the bleak, bare hills, bleaker and barer and lower-lying than any hills he had yet encountered. Slowly, deliberately, without excitement or more than the most casual interest, he followed the course of the strange stream toward the skyline and saw it emptying into a bright and shining sea. He was still unexcited. Most unusual, he thought, a vision or a mirage—more likely a vision, a trick of his disordered mind. He was confirmed in this by sight of a ship lying at anchor in the midst of the shining sea. He closed his eyes for a while, then opened them. Strange how the vision persisted! Yet not strange. He knew there were no seas or ships in the heart of the barren lands, just as he had known there was no cartridge in the empty rifle.

He heard a snuffle behind him—a half-choking gasp or cough. Very slowly, because of his exceeding weakness and stiffness, he rolled over on his other side. He could see nothing near at hand, but he waited patiently. Again came the snuffle and cough, and outlined between two jagged rocks not a score of feet away he made out the gray head of a wolf. The sharp ears were not pricked so sharply as he had seen them on other wolves; the eyes were bleared and bloodshot, the head seemed to droop limply and forlornly. The animal blinked continually in the sunshine. It seemed sick. As he looked it snuffled and coughed again.

This, at least, was real, he thought, and turned on the other side so that he might see the reality of the world which had been veiled from him before by the vision. But the sea still shone in the distance and the ship was plainly discernible. Was it reality, after all? He closed his eyes for a long while and thought, and then it came to him. He had been making north by east, away from the Dease Divide and into the Coppermine Valley. This wide and sluggish river was the Coppermine. That shining sea was the Arctic Ocean. That ship was a whaler, strayed east, far east, from the mouth of the Mackenzie, and it was lying at anchor in Coronation Gulf. He remembered the Hudson Bay Company chart he had seen long ago, and it was all clear and reasonable to him.

He sat up and turned his attention to immediate affairs. He had worn through the blanket-wrappings, and his feet were shapeless lumps of raw meat. His last blanket was gone. Rifle and knife were both missing. He had lost his hat somewhere, with the bunch of matches in the band, but the matches against his chest were safe and dry inside the tobacco pouch and oil paper. He looked at his watch. It marked eleven o'clock and was still running. Evidently he had kept it wound.

He was calm and collected. Though extremely weak, he had no sensation of pain. He was not hungry. The thought of food was not even pleasant to him, and whatever he did was done by his reason alone. He slipped off his pants' legs to the knees and bound them about his feet. Somehow he had succeeded in retaining the tin bucket. He would have some hot water before he began what he foresaw was to be a terrible journey to the ship.

His movements were slow. He shook as with a palsy. When he started to collect dry moss, he found he could not rise to his feet. He tried again and again, then contented himself with crawling about on hands and knees. Once he crawled near to the sick wolf. The animal dragged itself reluctantly out of his way, licking its chops with a tongue which seemed hardly to have the strength to curl. The man noticed that the tongue was not the customary healthy red. It was a yellowish brown and seemed coated with a rough and half-dry mucus.

After he had drunk a quart of hot water the man found he was able to stand, and even to walk as well as a dying man might be supposed to walk. Every minute or so he was compelled to rest. His steps were feeble and uncertain, just as the wolf's that trailed him were feeble and uncertain; and that night, when the shining sea was blotted out by blackness, he knew he was nearer to it by no more than four miles.

Throughout the night he heard the cough of the sick wolf, and now and then the squawking of the caribou calves. There was life all around him, but it was strong life, very much alive and well, and he knew the sick wolf clung to the sick man's trail in the hope that the man would be first. In the morning, on opening his eyes, he beheld it regarding him with a wistful and hungry stare. It stood crouched, with tail between its legs, like a miserable and woe-begone dog. It shivered in the still morning wind, and grinned dispiritedly when the man spoke to it in a voice that achieved no more than a hoarse whisper.

The sun rose brightly, and all morning the man tottered and fell toward the ship on the shining sea. The weather was perfect. It was the brief Indian Summer of the high latitudes. It might last a week. Tomorrow or next day it might be gone.

In the afternoon the man came upon a trail. It was of another man, who did not walk, but who dragged himself on all fours. The man thought it might be Bill, but he thought in a dull, uninterested way. He had no curiosity. In fact, sensation and emotion had left him. He was no longer susceptible to pain. Stomach and nerves had gone to sleep. Yet the life that was in him drove him on. He was very weary, but it refused to die. It was because it refused to die that he still ate muskeg berries and minnows, drank his hot water, and kept a wary eye on the sick wolf.

He followed the trail of the other man who dragged himself along, and soon came to the end of it—a few fresh-picked bones where the soggy moss was marked by the foot-pads of many wolves. He saw a squat moose-hide sack, mate to his own, which had been torn by sharp teeth. He picked it up, though its weight was almost too much for his feeble fingers. Bill had carried it to the last. Ha! ha! He would have the laugh on Bill. He would survive and carry it to the ship in the shining sea. His mirth was hoarse and ghastly, like a raven's croak, and the sick wolf joined him, howling lugubriously. The man ceased suddenly. How could he have the laugh on Bill if that were Bill; if those bones, so pinky-white and clean, were Bill?

He turned away. Well, Bill had deserted him; but he would not take the gold, nor would he suck Bill's bones. Bill would have, though, had it been the other way around, he mused as he staggered on.

He came to a pool of water. Stooping over in quest of minnows, he jerked his head back as though he had been stung. He had caught sight of his reflected face. So horrible was it that sensibility awoke long enough to be shocked. There were three minnows in the pool, which was too large to drain; and after several ineffectual attempts to catch them in the tin bucket he forbore. He was afraid, because of his great weakness, that he might fall in and drown. It was for this reason that he did not trust himself to the river astride one of the many drift-logs which lined its sand-spits.

That day he decreased the distance between him and the ship by three miles; the next day by two—for he was crawling now as Bill had crawled; and the end of the fifth day found the ship still seven miles away and him unable to make even a mile a day. Still the Indian Summer held on, and he continued to crawl and faint, turn and turn about; and even the sick wolf coughed and wheezed at his heels. His knees had become raw meat like his feet, and though he padded them with the shirt from his back it was a red track he left behind him on the moss and stones. Once, glancing back, he saw the wolf licking hungrily his bleeding trail, and he saw sharply what his own end might be—unless—unless he could get the wolf. Then began as grim a tragedy of existence as was ever played—a sick man that crawled, a sick wolf that limped, two creatures dragging their dying carcasses across the desolation and hunting each other's lives.

Had it been a well wolf, it would not have mattered so much to the man; but the thought of going to feed the maw of that loathsome and all but dead thing was repugnant to him. He was finicky. His mind had begun to wander again, and to be perplexed by hallucinations, while his lucid intervals grew rarer and shorter.

He was awakened once from a faint by a wheeze close in his ear. The wolf leaped lamely back, losing its footing and falling in its weakness. It was ludicrous, but he was not amused. Nor was he even afraid. He was too far gone for that. But his mind was for the moment clear, and he lay and considered. The ship was no more than four miles away. He could see it quite distinctly when he rubbed the mists out of his eyes, and he could see the white sail of a small boat cutting the water of the shining sea. But he could never crawl those four miles. He knew that, and was very calm in the knowledge. He knew that he could not crawl half a mile. And yet he wanted to live. It was unreasonable that he should die after all he had undergone. Fate asked too much of him. And, dying, he declined to die. It was stark madness, perhaps, but in the very grip of Death he defied Death and refused to die.

He closed his eyes and composed himself with infinite precaution. He steeled himself to keep above the suffocating languor that lapped like a rising tide through all the wells of his being. It was very like a sea, this deadly languor, that rose and rose and drowned his consciousness bit by bit. Sometimes he was all but submerged, swimming through oblivion with a faltering stroke; and again, by some strange alchemy of soul, he would find another shred of will and strike out more strongly.

Without movement he lay on his back, and he could hear, slowly drawing near and nearer, the wheezing intake and output of the sick wolf's breath. It drew closer, ever closer, through an infinitude of time, and he did not move. It was at his ear. The harsh dry tongue grated like sandpaper against his cheek. His hands shot out—or at least he willed them to shoot out. The fingers were curved like talons, but they closed on empty air. Swiftness and certitude require strength, and the man had not this strength.

The patience of the wolf was terrible. The man's patience was no less terrible. For half a day he lay motionless, fighting off unconsciousness and waiting for the thing that was to feed upon him and upon which he wished to feed. Sometimes the languid sea rose over him and he dreamed long dreams; but ever through it all, waking and dreaming, he waited for the wheezing breath and the harsh caress of the tongue.

He did not hear the breath, and he slipped slowly from some dream to the feel of the tongue along his hand. He waited. The fangs pressed softly; the pressure increased; the wolf was exerting its last strength in an effort to sink teeth in the food for which it had waited so long. But the man had waited long, and the lacerated hand closed on the jaw. Slowly, while the wolf struggled feebly and the hand clutched feebly, the other hand crept across to a grip. Five minutes later the whole weight of the man's body was on top of the wolf. The hands had not sufficient strength to choke the wolf, but the face of the man was pressed close to the throat of the wolf and the mouth of the man was full of hair. At the end of half an hour the man was aware of a warm trickle in his throat. It was not pleasant. It was like molten lead being forced into his stomach, and it was forced by his will alone. Later the man rolled over on his back and slept.

There were some members of a scientific expedition on the whale-ship *Bedford*. From the deck they remarked a strange object on the shore. It was moving down the beach toward the water. They were unable to classify it, and, being scientific men, they climbed into the whale-boat alongside and went ashore to see. And they saw something that was alive but which could hardly be called a man. It was blind, unconscious. It squirmed along the ground like some monstrous worm. Most of its efforts were ineffectual, but it was persistent, and it writhed and twisted and went ahead perhaps a score of feet an hour.

Three weeks afterward the man lay in a bunk on the whale-ship *Bedford*, and with tears streaming down his wasted cheeks told who he was and what he had undergone. He also babbled incoherently of his mother, of sunny Southern California, and a home among the orange groves and flowers.

The days were not many after that when he sat at table with the scientific men and ship's officers. He gloated over the spectacle of so much food, watching it anxiously as it went into the mouths of others. With the disappearance of each mouthful an expression of deep regret came into his eyes. He was quite sane, yet he hated those men at mealtime. He was haunted by a fear that the food would not last. He inquired of the cook, the cabin-boy, the captain, concerning the food stores. They reassured him countless times; but he could not believe them, and pried cunningly about the storeroom to see with his own eyes.

It was noticed that the man was getting fat. He grew stouter with each day. The scientific men shook their heads and theorized. They limited the man at his meals, but still his girth increased and he swelled prodigiously under his shirt.

The sailors grinned. They knew. And when the scientific men set a watch on the man, they knew too. They saw him slouch for'ard after breakfast, and, like a mendicant, with outstretched palm, accost a sailor. The sailor grinned and passed him a fragment of sea biscuit. He clutched it avariciously, looked at it as a miser looks at gold, and thrust it into his shirt bosom. Similar were the donations from other grinning sailors.

The scientific men were discreet. They let him alone. But they secretly examined his bunk. It was lined with hardtack; the mattress was stuffed with hardtack; every nook and cranny was filled with hardtack. Yet he was sane. He was taking precautions against another possible famine—that was all. He would recover from it, the scientific men said; and he did, ere the *Bedford's* anchor rumbled down in San Francisco Bay.

Reading for Understanding

Main Idea

1. Which of the following expressions best sums up the main idea of the story?
   (a) Never fry a fish till it's caught.
   (b) Never leave till tomorrow what you can do today.
   (c) A burnt child dreads the fire.
   (d) Never say die.

Details

2. Bill (a) sprained his ankle (b) abandoned his companion (c) came back for his companion (d) was in excellent shape.
3. The muskeg berries (a) were delicious (b) grew in dry country (c) were not nutritious (d) satisfied the hungry man's appetite.
4. The moose-hide sack contained (a) gold (b) food (c) ammunition (d) maps.
5. A ptarmigan is obviously a kind of (a) fish (b) small mammal (c) insect (d) bird.
6. What the man thought was a horse proved to be a (a) moose (b) wolf (c) deer (d) bear.

7. The caribou calf had been (a) killed by wolves (b) seen following its mother (d) mixed with a band of elk (d) able to elude its attackers.
8. The ship was lying in (a) Hudson Bay (b) Coronation Gulf (c) the Mackenzie (d) the Dease Divide.
9. The ship that saved him was a(n) (a) steamship out of Vancouver (b) Eskimo canoe (c) whaler (d) fur-trader.

Inferences

10. At the start of the story, the season was (a) spring (b) summer (c) autumn (d) winter.
11. The two men had obviously been in the Far North to (a) trap bear (b) fish for salmon (c) find gold (d) survey the territory for the government.
12. The fear that remained with the man after he had been rescued was the fear of (a) freezing (b) getting lost (c) starvation (d) criticism by the sailors.
13. Bill probably (a) made it to the cache (b) came back looking for his partner (c) was rescued by an earlier ship (d) died.

Outcome

14. After the events in the story, the survivor probably (a) outfitted another expedition to the north country (b) set up a memorial for Bill (c) never returned (d) sought a position with the ship that had rescued him.

Fact or Opinion

Tell whether the following is a fact or an opinion.

15. If Bill and his partner had stayed together, they would both have survived.

Words in Context

1. "The first man, limping into the milky stream that foamed over the rocks, *vouchsafed* no reply." **Vouchsafed** (226) means (a) granted (b) rejected (c) confirmed (d) disregarded.

2. "The man watched him go, limping grotesquely and *lurching* forward with stammering gait up the slow slope toward the soft skyline of the low-lying hill." **Lurching** (227) means (a) hastening (b) staggering (c) crawling (d) traveling.
3. "Near the horizon the sun was smouldering dimly, almost *obscured* by formless mists and vapors." **Obscured** (227) means (a) accentuated (b) vividly colored (c) shadowed (d) concealed.
4. "He cowered in the midst of the milky water, as though the vastness were pressing in upon him with overwhelming force, brutally crushing him with its *complacent* awfulness." **Complacent** (227) means (a) hideous (b) obvious (c) unconcerned (d) repeated.
5. "Then he proceeded, slowly and carefully, *wincing* with pain, to the bank." **Wincing** (227) means (a) walking (b) flinching (c) succeeding (d) stopping.
6. "Here he would find a *cache* under an upturned canoe and piled over with many rocks." A **cache** (228) is a (a) metal safe (b) moose-hide sack (c) pile of gold (d) hiding place.
7. "It was a slow and *arduous* task." **Arduous** (229) means (a) important (b) repeated, (c) strenuous (d) enjoyable.
8. "He was compelled to wait until the *sediment* had settled." A **sediment** (231) is a (a) deposit (b) moss (c) wave (d) stone.
9. "*Sensibility,* as far as concerned the yearning for food, had been exhausted." **Sensibility** (232) means (a) sensitivity (b) worry (c) determination (d) curiosity.
10. "He now bore off to the right to counteract the possible *deviation* from his true course. **Deviation** (232) means (a) acute angle (b) compass reading (c) departure (d) poorly-marked trail.
11. "There were four newly hatched chicks, a day old—little specks of *pulsating* life." **Pulsating** (233) means (a) joyous (b) throbbing (c) fragile (d) recently born.
12. "At times his mind wandered farther afield, and he plodded on, a mere automaton, strange *conceits* and *whimsicalities* gnawing at his brain." **Conceits** and **whimsicalities** (234) are (a) fanciful ideas (b) bitter disappointments (c) happy memories (d) headaches.
13. "The animal was studying him with *bellicose* curiosity." **Bellicose** (234) means (a) mild (b) aggressive (c) concealed (d) sympathetic.
14. "He, too, growled, savagely, terribly, voicing the fear that is to life *germane* and that lies twisted about life's deepest roots." **Germane** (235) means (a) foreign (b) a puzzle (c) closely related (d) disconnected.

15. "But the sea still shone in the distance and the ship was plainly *discernible.*" **Discernible** (237) means (a) recognizable (b) at rest in the harbor (c) reachable (d) in distress.
16. "In the morning, on opening his eyes, he beheld it regarding him with a *wistful* and hungry stare." **Wistful** (238) means (a) aggressive and impatient (b) keen and unchanging (c) warm and sympathetic (d) sad and yearning.
17. "His mirth was hoarse and ghostly, like a raven's croak, and the sick wolf joined him, howling *lugubriously.*" **Lugubriously** (238) means (a) noisily (b) mournfully (c) joyously (d) uninterruptedly.
18., 19. "After several *ineffectual* attempts to catch them in the tin bucket, he *forbore.*" **Ineffectual** (238) means (a) futile (b) continuing (c) repeated (d) partially successful. **Forbore** (238) means (a) wept (b) made a last attempt (c) gave up (d) slept.
20., 21. "The thought of going to feed the maw of that *loathsome* and all but dead thing was *repugnant* to him." **Loathsome** (239) means (a) covered with hair (b) cruel (c) hateful (d) watchful. **Repugnant** (239) means (a) revolting (b) alarming (c) absurd (d) meaningful.
22. "It was *ludicrous,* but he was not amused." **Ludicrous** (239) means (a) surprising (b) reasonable (c) thought-provoking (d) laughable.
23. "But the man had waited long, and the *lacerated* hand closed on the jaw." **Lacerated** (240) means (a) powerful (b) lightly scratched (c) mangled (d) impatient.
24. "He also babbled *incoherently* of his mother, of sunny Southern California, and a home among the orange groves and flowers." **Incoherently** (240) means (a) joyfully (b) sadly (c) disjointedly (d) tearfully.
25. "They saw him slouch for'ard after breakfast, and like a *mendicant,* with outstretched palm, accost a sailor." A **mendicant** (241) is a (a) seaman (b) friar (c) beggar (d) police officer.
26. He clutched it *avariciously,* looked at it as a miser looks at gold, and thrust it into his shirt bosom." **Avariciously** (241) means (a) slyly (b) angrily (c) swiftly (d)greedily.

Thinking Critically About the Story

1. The title applies to the wolf as well as to the man. Why does London show the wolf to be a parallel sufferer? What is gained by this

subtle comparison? Did you feel any sympathy for the wolf? Did London expect that?

2. What motivates Bill to leave his partner behind? What clues does London provide to explain in some way, if not excuse, Bill's apparent treachery?
3. Would Bill probably have survived if he had stayed with his partner, instead of abandoning him? Explain.
4. In the ancient story of King Midas, everything he touches turns to gold, but the gold almost destroys him. How does that story apply to "Love of Life"?
5. The word *panic*, from the Greek forest god Pan, was coined to suggest the anxiety that overcomes a traveler lost in the woods, not knowing which way to turn. Have you ever been lost, even momentarily, in the woods? Can you suggest the terror you felt?
6. Why was the survivor so abnormal in his attitude toward food?
7. How is the fate of the moose-hide pack a barometer of the man's changing attitude toward gold?
8. Of the many harrowing experiences, which seemed to you the bleakest, most horrifying?

Language in Action

Noah Webster and American Spelling

> He went back to put his pack into shape for travelling.

If you check the spelling of *traveling* in an American dictionary, you'll find the single-*l* spelling first. The second spelling, with two *l*'s as above tends to be used in England. There are many differences between English and American English. Someone once humorously called England and America "Two countries separated by a common language!"

Differences in spelling can often be traced to the efforts of one man: Noah Webster. During the early years of the United States, Webster was a scholar, a compiler of dictionaries and spelling books. Indeed, his name is often used as a prestige name for a dictionary. After Webster's death in 1843, George and Charles Merriam took on the task of keeping the dictionaries up to date. The flow of new words into the language requires frequent updating.

Webster's influence upon American English is deep and extensive. In his famous *Spelling Book*, he eliminated the *u* from almost every *our* word: *ardor*, *favor*, and *honor*. He substituted single consonants for unnecessarily doubled consonants. *Jeweller* became *jeweler*. *Frolick* became *frolic*. *Waggon* became *wagon*. Webster used a single instead of a double consonant in words like *kidnaped* (British *kidnapped*)and *traveler* (*traveller*). Many of the rejected spellings are still retained in British English.

The list goes on and on. Many *ce* words were spelled *se*. *Offence*, *defence*, and *suspence* became *offense*, *defense*, and *suspense*. *Re* words became *er* words, as *theater*, *center*, and *caliber*.

Further drastic change in American spelling has been urged for centuries. Why not make English phonetic? Why not change *head* to *hed*, *thumb* to *thum*, *women* to *wimmen*, and *tongue* to *tung*? Webster tried but failed. Americans will accept some simplification, but reject a spelling that looks "too strange" to them. Massive efforts have been made to change *night* to *nite*, for example, but except for a few unsuccessful attempts, *night* retains its old spelling.

"Changes like these destroy the language!" the critics cry. Proponents say, "Think of all the time lost to misspellings due to nonphonetic spelling." What do you think?

The Sorrel Colt

Benito Lynch
Argentinian

"Now you're in for it!" his mother said very excitedly. "Yes, you'll catch it now! Have you seen your colt?"

Mario turned red, then pale.

"What's wrong? What's happened, Mama?"

"Your colt is running loose in the garden and he has damaged lots of things."

How many children have dreamed of owning a pony or a colt of their own? This most universal of children's daydreams comes true for Mario. He is given a beautiful sorrel (light brown) colt that captures his heart. Unfortunately, the colt is a headstrong animal, not easily tamed. As the story progresses, we begin to sense why its original owner had gladly given it away.

The author, the Argentinian Benito Lynch, has looked into the heart of a boy and provided a convincing picture for his readers. Mario is an ordinary boy, interested in the normal things of childhood like taunting his little brother. But the arrival of the colt changes Mario from a carefree eight-year-old into a concerned colt owner—with reason for concern. For Mario, however, the balance clearly tilts toward the joy of owning the free-spirited, independent colt.

The Sorrel Colt

MARIO WAS TIRED of "Tiger," a game of his own invention, played by pursuing through the tree-tops his brother Leo who was supposed to defend himself bravely by using green figs as projectiles. So Mario strolled to the backyard gate behind the vegetable and flower garden. Under the noon sun, leaning against one of the old posts, he looked up and down the street, waiting patiently in the hope that his little brother, still eager to continue the fight up there on the highest branch of the fig-tree, would get tired in his turn of taunting him with shouts of "stupid carrot" and "obstinate mule." Suddenly an unexpected sight filled him with happy surprise.

Turning the corner of the garden, a man was entering the lane and slowly approaching. He was mounted on a big-bellied mare which was followed by a tiny colt.

"Say!"

And Mario, his eyes wide open and his face flushed, walked over to the edge of the path to get a better view of the procession.

A colt! To understand his emotion, one must figure out what a colt meant to Mario at this time in his life, what it meant to have a colt of his own, that is to say a real horse proportioned to his size.

It was his hobby, his passion, his constant dream. But unfortunately, he knew from experience that his parents didn't want animals in the garden because they ate plants and scraped the bark off the trees.

Way off on the Ranch, they said he could have anything he wanted, that is to say, some docile little pony, but here in the garden, back of the house, no animals were permitted!

That's why Mario was going to be a good boy, as usual, just watching with suppressed desire the passing of that little miracle. But unexpectedly something extraordinary happened.

When he reached Mario, without stopping his trotting mare and hardly turning his head, the strapping rider with sullen face under his red beret let fly at Mario a stupendous offer.

"Say, kid! If you want this colt, you can have it! I'm taking it to the field to kill it!"

As he listened, Mario felt the ground heaving under his feet. His eyes grew misty, all his blood rushed to his head. But alas! He knew all the laws of his home with such finality that he didn't hesitate a second. Red as a tomato, he refused, shame-faced.

"No! Thanks! No!"

The robust young fellow shrugged his shoulders slightly and without adding a word continued along under the sunlight that filled the street. He whisked away with him, following the weary pace of the mare, that gem of a sorrel colt which trotted gracefully after. With its fluffy light-colored tail it flicked the flies off as if it were a big horse.

"Mama!"

Mario rushed headlong toward the house like a colt, without speaking to his brother who, unaware of anything new and still mounted on his fig-tree, took advantage of his brother's hasty passing to pelt him with some figs. Mario arrived under the arbor, blurting out, "Oh, Mama! Oh, Mama!"

The mother, busy at her sewing, seated in an armchair under the young vines, got up startled.

"Holy Virgin! What's the matter, son?"

"Nothing, Mama, nothing—just that a man—"

"Well what, son, what is it?"

"A man passed with a wonderful little colt and he wanted to give it to me!"

"What a scare you gave me!" The mother smiled with relief; but he, excited, continued without listening to her.

"A wonderful colt, Mama, a sorrel colt, small, this high—and the man said he was going to kill him, Mama!"

And now another amazing thing happened. Contrary to all logic and to what would seem normal, Mario heard his mother say to him in a grieved tone, "Really? Good Heavens! Why didn't you accept? Silly boy! We shall soon be going to the Ranch!"

In the face of that extraordinary, unexpected and astounding remark, the boy opened his mouth wide. But he was so crazy about the colt that he didn't stop for questions. With an "I'll call him, then!"—as excited and resonant as a neigh, the boy darted for the door.

"Be careful, son!" shouted the mother.

Careful my eye! Mario was running so fast that his brother couldn't hit him with a single fig as he flashed by.

When he dashed out into the street, the glare of the sun dazzled him. No colt, no mare, no man to be seen anywhere! But presently his straining eyes made out over there in the distance the red beret dancing to the rhythm of a trot in the midst of a cloud of dust.

The clods of dry mud made him stumble and fall several times, his emotion almost choked him, the hateful yapping dogs of the laundress got in his way, but nothing mattered. Nothing, nobody could stop Mario in his mad race.

Before he had covered a few hundred yards, he managed to reach with his voice the ears of that supreme master of his joy, who was going along dejectedly on his humble big-bellied mare.

"Ss! Ss!—Man! Man!"

On hearing him, the strapping young fellow stopped his nag and waited for Mario, frowning.

"Well, what do you want?"

"The colt—I want the colt," blurted Mario almost choking, and at the same time he stretched out both arms toward the animal as if he expected them to receive it like a store package.

The man's face wore an uncertain expression.

"Fine," he said, "lead him off, then." And he added quickly, looking at the boy's hands, "Didn't you bring a halter, or anything?"

Once more Mario flushed.

"No, I didn't."

And puzzled, he gazed all around him as if he expected to find halters hidden among the weeds.

"Well, you sure are dumb as a sausage!"

The man dismounted and twisted off a bit of wire that happened to be swinging free by the thorn-hedge. In the meantime, the child watched him in excitement but without any regret, for if a great king once offered his kingdom for a horse, certainly Mario could, without loss of face, accept an insult in exchange for a colt.

Only Mario could realize what this sorrel colt meant to him, although he did damage plants, he bit, he kicked, and he refused to go when it suited him. Once he even yanked a lock of hair from the boy's head with one bite, thinking no doubt that it was hay. But how nicely he ate sugar out of his hand and neighed when he saw him in the distance!

This colt was his love, his worry, his aim in life, his light of the spirit—so much so that his parents had acquired the habit of using the animal as a means of controlling the youngster and making him behave.

"If you don't do your lessons, you can't go out this afternoon on the colt. If you act like that, we'll take away your colt. If you do this or if you fail to do that. . ."

Always the colt standing watch over the misconduct of Mario like the flaming banner of an invincible army in the midst of battle! But at the same time the colt was a delight, so gentle, so fond, so cunning!

The horse-breaker of the Ranch, a skillful leather braider, had made him a marvelous halter. Little by little, the other ranch hands, because they were fond of Mario or wanted to outrival one another, had made all the other equipment, till now the boy had a pretty riding outfit that aroused everyone's admiration.

For Mario, he was the finest of all colts and the handsomest creature in the whole world who some day would be a great race horse. His conviction of this was so firm that when his brother Leo joked and called the sorrel "little donkey" and other complimentary names of the sort, these sounded like true blasphemies to Mario.

On the other hand, when the Ranch foreman said, after squinting at the colt, "In my opinion, he is going to grow up into a beauty," Mario found the foreman the most understanding and intelligent man around.

Mario's father had decided to plant a garden in the grounds near the house. But it happened that this "hateful colt"—that is what some were calling him now, even Mama, perhaps because he stepped on some new chicks—this creature seemed opposed to the idea of a garden. This could be gathered from the determination with which he attacked tender little plants each time he was let loose, so that Mario had been officially notified that it was a rule never to leave him untethered at night. Still Mario forgot, had, in fact, forgotten a number of times, so that finally, one morning, his exasperated father said to him, shaking his index finger a lot and emphasizing by that rhythm the gravity of his warning, "The first day that darned colt ever again damages a single plant, that same day we'll turn him loose in the open country."

"Oh! Oh!" In the open country! Turn him loose! Could Mario's father possibly know what such a threat meant to his boy?

One would have to be eight years old like him, think the way he does and love his sorrel colt just as he loved him, to estimate the enormity of such a menace.

The open country! Turn him loose! The open country was for Mario something infinite, unfathomable; and to send his colt out into that vastness seemed as atrocious and inhuman as throwing a new born babe into the sea.

It was not surprising therefore that Mario had stopped being careless, and a whole long week now had passed without the infliction by the colt of the slightest hurt to the tiniest flower.

Outside, a radiant February morning was dawning. Mario, lying across his bed with his feet against the wall, was confiding to his brother Leo some of his plans for the brilliant future of his sorrel colt. Unexpectedly his mother came into the bedroom.

"Now you're in for it!" she said very excitedly. "Yes, you'll catch it now! Have you seen your colt?"

Mario turned red, then pale.

"What's wrong? What's happened, Mama?"

"Your colt is running loose in the garden and he has damaged lots of things!"

The whole world was tumbling down on Mario.

"But how can that be?" he managed to say. "How?"

"I don't know how," his mother answered, "but you can't say I didn't warn you till I was blue in the face! Now your father . . . "

"But I tied him up! I tied him up!"

And while he hastily put on some clothes with trembling hands, everything about him seemed murky as if the room had filled with smoke.

It was an awful disaster. Never before had the colt managed to create so much devastation. This time he had not only trampled the lawn but had even carried his mischief to the flower-bed. Here, apparently scraping with his hoof, he had torn up by the roots a number of the rare carnations set out carefully in a graceful diamond pattern.

"My goodness, what you've done! What you've done, baby!"

And as in a dream and not knowing what he was doing, Mario knelt down on the moist earth and started feverishly to set the carnations upright, while "Baby" or "The Rascal" stood by motionless, his head lowered, the halter slipped off his muzzle, and an expression of cynical indifference in his whole attitude.

Like a sleep-walker, as if he were stepping in a soft wool-stuffed mattress, Mario led the colt by the halter along the wide way with its border of poplars. At its end yonder was the large cattle gate with its white posts, and outside extended the terrible open country in its desolate immensity.

The poor boy's head throbbed with the rush of blood to his brain and he saw things hazily through a cloud. He still heard ringing in his ears the catastrophic admonition of his father.

"Take that colt and turn him loose in the open!"

Mario did not weep because he couldn't shed tears. But he walked along like a mechanical toy; he walked in such a very queer way that his mother watched anxiously from the garden.

The fact was that for Mario, the other side of that cattle gate with its white posts was the end of everything. It was the vortex into which, in a few more seconds, all his being was going to tumble, his very existence swallowed up with his sorrel colt.

When Mario had covered half the distance, his mother could not bear it any longer and she moaned, nervously pressing the father's arm, "That's enough, John! That's enough!"

"All right! Call him back!"

But just then Leo rushed off quickly, the mother uttered a piercing scream and the father ran desperately in Mario's direction.

There, close to the cattle gate, Mario in his canvas smock had collapsed on the turf like a bird winged by a bullet.

A few days later when Mario could finally sit up in his bed, his parents, smiling, but with eyelids red and faces pale with so much anxious wakefulness, forced the sorrel colt into the bedroom, one tugging at the halter and the other pushing hard behind his rump.

Reading for Understanding

Main Idea

1. The central theme of the story is (a) the difficulty of training a colt (b) the love of a boy for his colt (c) a father's strictness (d) a mother's love.

Details

2. "Tiger" was (a) the name of the sorrel colt (b) Mario's nickname for his brother (c) a game (d) the name of Mario's cat.
3. Mario saved the colt from (a) starvation (b) cruelty (c) neglect (d) death.
4. The man called Mario "dumb" because (a) he didn't have a halter (b) he couldn't make up his mind immediately (c) he had never ridden a horse (d) he didn't offer to pay for the colt.
5. For the parents the last straw was (a) Mario's insolence (b) the destruction of the garden (c) the colt's tendency to run away (d) Mario's destruction of the carnations.
6. The halter was made by (a) the foreman (b) Mario's father (c) the horse-breaker (d) the original owner.

Inferences

7. The story is set in the season of (a) spring (b) summer (c) autumn (d) winter.
8. The threat of punishment was finally overcome by (a) the colt's sudden change for the better (b) Leo's pleading (c) Mario's promise to repair the garden (d) the parents' love.
9. In the future the colt would probably be (a) tied up more securely (b) given to Leo instead of Mario (c) turned loose (d) sold.

Fact or Opinion

Tell whether the following is a fact or an opinion.

10. The colt could be tamed.

Words in Context

1. Mario "waiting patiently in the hope that his little brother . . . would get tired in his turn of *taunting* him with shouts of 'stupid carrot' and 'obstinate mule.'" **Taunting** (248) means (a) getting his attention (b) calling (c) prodding (d) mocking (See also *taunted,* 187).
2. "Way off on the Ranch, they said he could have anything he wanted, that is to say, some *docile* little pony, but here in the garden, back of the house, no animals were permitted!" **Docile** (248) means (a) obedient (b) multicolored (c) inexpensive (d) spirited.
3. Mario's brother "took advantage of his brother's hasty passing to *pelt* him with some figs." **Pelt** (249) means (a) bombard (b) arouse (c) confuse (d) insult.
4. "With an 'I'll call him then!'—as excited and *resonant* as a neigh, the boy darted for the door." **Resonant** (249) means (a) echoing (b) irritating (c) terrifying (d) pleasing.
5. "Always the colt standing watch over the misconduct of Mario like the flaming banner of an *invincible* army in the midst of battle!" **Invincible** (250) means (a) crusading (b) unconquerable (c) enemy (d) retreating.
6. "One would have to be eight years old like him, think the way he does, and love his sorrel colt just as he loved him, to estimate the *enormity* of such a menace." **Enormity** (251) means (a) measured result (b) great wickedness (c) approach (d) pleasing proportions.

7., 8. "The open country was for Mario something infinite, *unfathomable;* and to send his colt out into that vastness seems as *atrocious* and inhuman as throwing a newborn babe into the sea." **Unfathomable** (251) means not (a) manageable (b) workable (c) understandable (d) likable. **Atrocious** (251) means extremely (a) unexpected (b) unreasonable (c) shocking (d) thoughtless.

9. "Everything about him seemed *murky* as if the room had filled with smoke." **Murky** (252) means (a) moist (b) unpleasant (c) odorous (d) hazy.
10. "Never before had the colt managed to create so much *devastation.*" **Devastation** (252) means (a) destruction (b) inconvenience (c) change (d) rearrangement.

11. "It was the *vortex* into which, in a few more seconds, all his being was going to tumble, his very existence swallowed up by his sorrel colt." A **vortex** (252) is a (a) reflex (b) whirlpool (c) surf (d) haven.

Thinking Critically About the Story

1. What is the significance of the last line, with the colt being *forced* into the room? What does this suggest about the future?
2. Why did the young man want to get rid of the sorrel colt? What clues in the story provide a possible answer?
3. What suggests that Mario was a normal boy before the colt came into his life? How did the colt bring adventure into Mario's life?
4. Were Mario's parents good parents? Give examples to prove your point. Are the two different in their reactions to Mario?
5. Have you ever wanted something with all your heart? Did you get it? Was it what you expected?
6. Were you able to answer question 7 on page 253? What was the clue to the correct answer?
7. In addition to the gift of the colt, what act of kindness did the colt's original owner show toward Mario?
8. Mario's parents use the colt as a means of getting Mario to behave. How? Are such parental tactics fair? Explain.

Language in Action

Our Boxing Skills

> Only Mario could realize what this sorrel colt meant to him, although he did damage plants, he bit, he kicked, and he refused to go when it suited him . . . This colt was his love, his worry, his aim in life, his light of the spirit.

The real world is overwhelming. To exercise some control, we put things into mental boxes. When we can put a certain plant into a mental box called *poison ivy,* we can avoid painful rashes in the future.

Tree, table, basketball, snake, computer, car—these are all convenient boxes. There may be little dispute about them, but trouble arises when boxes are abstract like *truth, liberty, beauty,* and *evil.*

Your boxes are not exactly *mine*. When *you* visualize a chair, *you* may see a kitchen chair; *I* may see a recliner. When you visualize a snake, you may see a poisonous rattler about to strike; I may see a harmless garter snake, a household pet. No two boxes are precisely the same, but we manage to communicate fairly well anyway—a miracle. It's those abstract classifications that cause most trouble.

Mario's classification of the colt was different from his parents'. To Mario, the colt was a wonderful, lovable thing of beauty. To his parents, the colt was a major nuisance, destructive and unmanageable. Which classification is right? The colt fits into both boxes! In reality, apparent contradictions sometimes disappear. (See also Paradox, 61).

"The Work of One Day Is Gazed Upon for One Thousand Days"

— Chinese Proverb

Jade Snow Wong
American

As for Jade Snow, she knew that she still had before her a hard upward climb, but for the first time in her life, she felt contentment. She could stop searching for that niche that would be hers alone. She had found herself and struck her speed. And when she came home now, it was to see Mama and Daddy look up from their work, and smile at her, and say, "It is good to have you home again!"

Challenges come in all shapes and sizes. Some are modest. An amateur golfer strives to break a hundred. Candidates for a seat on the city council seek to persuade the voters. Some are more difficult. A professional football player dreams of winning a Super Bowl.

Starting a business afresh is a leap of faith. Since most small businesses fail within the first five years, stepping out on such a venture can be a daunting prospect.

Jade Snow decided to open a pottery store in Chinatown, an area where she expected the residents to applaud her initiative. Acceptance didn't come easily. Rejection led to anxiety and despair. Hers was a challenge that would have defeated many newcomers, but Jade Snow never gave up. She hit upon a dramatic way to demonstrate her skill and promote her product. The tables turned. Hers was not just a physical adventure but an adventure of the spirit.

"The Work of One Day Is Gazed Upon for One Thousand Days"

JADE SNOW TRUDGED the familiar paths of Chinatown, looking for a store location where she could make and sell her pottery. She didn't know any of the owners, but instead of following the traditional, established custom of the Chinese, who handle such transactions through a middleman who knows the people and can bargain over a cup of tea, she explored every store along Grant Avenue herself.

As there was no unleased vacant store in those days, she was forced to abandon her first wish to have her own store. Instead, she considered subrenting a portion of an art-goods store. She started with the best corner locations. Some wanted too much rent; some just shook their heads; others seemed interested and asked her to return, only to report that co-owners or stockholders disapproved. All were amazed but interested in what she wanted to do; some almost wouldn't believe her.

It was a discouraging round, in which hope alternated with disappointment. Jade Snow became less particular about the choice of location, and began to work on the smaller establishments. Still without luck, she came to almost the only store she hadn't approached. The China Bazaar near Clay Street was a neat little place, and she had looked into it a number of times. But the proprietor, who sat at his cash register at the back and only waited on customers if he felt like it, always with an air of dignity and stoicism, had been altogether too formidable a figure for her to face. Now, driven by desperation, she made herself enter and tell the proprietor what she had in mind.

He said, "I notice everything and everyone who passes by my store, and I have seen you look in several times before now. You don't look like an American-Chinese to me, with two braids on your head instead of a permanent wave."

"I was born here," Jade Snow replied. "Our family head is named Wong Hong. Do you know him?"

"Yes, I have heard of him, and I know that he is an honest Christian."

Jade Snow waited, with hope beginning to rise again.

"Now, I am not a Christian," he added. "I wouldn't move out of my way to do a good deed. But if a good deed comes to my front door and asks to be done, I have very little choice. A man can go through life minding his own business only until someone comes along who desperately needs his help. A middleman I could have said 'No' to, but you make it difficult to refuse you personally."

Jade Snow assured him, "Everyone has refused me but you. This is my life purpose. All I am asking is to get a start until I can find a permanent location."

"But you can see that I have very little room and a very narrow store. I like to keep it exactly my way. I wouldn't mind displaying your finished things, but there would be no room for you to work in."

"Oh, I must work too, for as my stock is sold I shall have to be ready with more things. I can't have a hired staff yet, and I must both make and sell the pottery."

They both thought hard. Jade Snow got an idea. "Would you let me use one of your two store windows to install my wheel? Then the clay splatter will be confined to a small area, and perhaps my working there would attract people to your store to buy your own wares."

The proprietor was doubtful. "I have only the two windows."

Jade Snow implored him. "Please, try it. If it isn't good for your business, we'll make other arrangements."

They discussed terms. The proprietor said, "Now to be frank with you, I'll never be able to make much money off you. Suppose we just decide on a percentage commission on the total amount you sell. If I am going to try to help you, we might as well be fair about it. My commission will cover what you use in space and utilities. You don't know yet how much you will sell. The plan is new for both of us."

Jade Snow mulled over that proposition. "You don't quite believe what I say, do you?" the man questioned. "Go home and ask your father; he is a fair business man."

So Jade Snow told her family, all of whom were surprised that she had at last found something. Until now, they had thought she was taking the wrong means to a silly objective which she would have to give up eventually. In true Wong family fashion, they weren't preventing her from having her own way, nor helping.

"Daddy, I have today found a store which offers the greatest possibilities to date." And she described her experience in detail.

Daddy agreed that the proprietor's proposal was fair. "Now, it is right for me to go and thank this gentleman for his courtesy and generosity, and to make his acquaintance."

The next few weeks were busy ones. With the help of Jade Precious Stone and a former Navy co-worker, Jade Snow bustled around, ordering supplies, price-marking the pottery, getting announcements printed and sent out, and caring for all the details of starting a business, no matter how small. Her former architect-boss went over the store-window foundation for her, to determine what additional bracing was required in order to support the weight of the potter's wheel. He designed and drew up plans for a set of redwood shelves and cases with concealed lights, so that in the little six-by-five-foot floor space there was room to work, store drying pottery, and display a few finished items. The window floor was paved with bricks laid in a basket pattern. Altogether, the use of natural materials in keeping with the look of pottery made an attractive whole which was certainly unlike any other store window in Chinatown.

With materials scarce, it took Jade Snow days of hunting to find even the bricks for the floor. A Chinese carpenter, a fellow Wong and Daddy's old friend, was the only person who would consent to build the shelves and bracing for her, and he could hardly understand the architectural notations on the detailed drawings. Jade Snow's shipyard training in getting things done stood her in good stead.

At last everything was completed and she was ready to set up the window. Prosperity, who had been most interested in all the bustle, went with her to the store and helped lay bricks. The shelves fitted in exactly. The wheel was set in place, and a stack of plaster bats, molded in pie tins and used to support pottery while being made, was placed near by. A beautiful large philodendron plant curled up gracefully along one corner of the window, gift of Mama and Daddy in honor of the new enterprise.

Even while the brick flooring was being laid, curious passers-by stopped. Jade Snow discovered that one had only to get into a window to attract spectators. As they worked, Jade Snow saw a few insects crawling around; they looked like white ants, and she called the proprietor.

"That is indeed a good omen," he declared excitedly. "White ants do not appear except on very rare occasions. When they appear for a new business, it means that the business is blessed and will prosper."

"Oh, come now; haven't you seen white ants here before when you dressed the windows?"

The proprietor shook his head solemnly, "No, never!"

Soon the curious spectators began to murmur aloud, conjecturing as to the nature of the equipment in the elevated display.

"She must be planning to make bricks for the housing project in Chinatown."

"No, look at those white pies; she is setting up a model kitchen."

"You are both wrong; this is a rice-threshing machine. See the stick across it? I have seen them in China!"

"Oh, look, and it is a China girl too. Look, she has no permanent wave. Her braids are the way they wear them in Shanghai. Here is a Shanghai girl!"

Prosperity listened in curiosity and mounting indignation. At last he ran out to the street and announced: "You are all wrong. This is my Honey's pottery machine, and she is going to stir mud on it."

The onlookers laughed. "Listen to the child; he doesn't know what he's talking about!"

There was little chance for other spectators not to know what Jade Snow was doing in the days which followed. From the time she first threw down a ball of clay on the wheel, the street was packed. There were even people on the balconies across the street, and clinging to the telephone pole. Passing automobiles on narrow Grant Avenue stopped and held up traffic while the drivers watched. The first day, policemen came because they thought there might be a riot. Jade Snow could have an audience any time of the day or night on that busy street.

The morning paper carried a picture and two-column story of the new enterprise. Jade Snow had become a wonder in the eyes of the Western world. They declared that she had invented a new mousetrap.

Chinatown was agog. A woman in the window, her legs astride a potter's wheel, her hair in braids, her hands perpetually messy with sticky California clay, her finished products such things as coolies used in China, the daughter of a conservative family, running a business alone—such a combination was sure to fail!

When Jade Snow went around Chinatown, many storekeepers laughed at her. "Look, here comes the mud-stirring maiden. Sold a pot today? Ha! Ha!" Strangers turned to stare long and curiously.

Caucasians came from far and near to see her work, and Jade Snow sold all the pottery she could make. Even before it had been fired, the first piece was eagerly spoken for by the man who had kindly found her bricks for the window. But the Chinese did not come to buy one piece from her.

Then those who had laughed hardest stopped. After two months, the mud-stirring maiden was still in business! After three months, she was driving the first postwar automobile in Chinatown. The skeptics knitted their brows. It must be those crazy foreigners, who didn't know any better. Some Chinese approached the proprietor for information. Was it because her clay came from China? Was it because she had invented a new chemical process to make pottery?

The proprietor would smile politely. "Ask her," he would say.

But no one ever asked her. Chinese and Americans alike acted as if they thought she were deaf or dumb or couldn't understand their language. She learned a very curious thing about human beings: they would wonder, guess, speculate, but never question the person who could give them the direct answers.

One day two high-ranking Caucasian Army officers wandered into the store. They stood and watched her patiently putting a handle on a pitcher while she sat at the wheel. Since the wheel was being used for a table it was motionless.

"I wonder how that wheel operates?" one officer asked another.

"Oh, she sits there and kicks it with her feet," the other replied. Jade Snow, not two feet from them, heard them plainly, and was amused that apparently they did not observe the one-third horsepower motor which Daddy had installed on the wheel, hung almost at their eye level.

"That seems to me unnecessarily primitive," returned the first man. "But that's just the trouble, you can't teach the Chinese anything new!"

And they went off without further investigation, nodding their heads in self-satisfaction.

The reaction of her friends and family was different. Friends and fellow guild members sent flowers. Later they sometimes dropped in for tea, which she brewed in the back kitchen. And they told their friends about the new enterprise. Dr. Reinhardt never failed to call whenever she was near the neighborhood.

But it was Mama who epitomized the family's change of heart. Where there was formerly only tolerance toward their peculiar fifth daughter whom no one could understand, the tolerance was now tinged by an attitude of respect. Mama, who would not look at the potter's wheel at home, now came to the store to see what everyone was talking about.

Daddy, typically, touched her heart in another way. First, he was critical of her daring in assuming a position in the window above her spectators' heads. But when he saw that she was getting the prices and the market she wished, he ventured a suggestion. "Perhaps you should drape printed percale around your wheel, so that people will not see how crude a piece of equipment you use to make fine things."

Then one afternoon driving home, he sat beside her, lost in reverie. When they were parked in front of their house, he told her a story: "I told you once that your grandfather would have been glad to see that you had learned a handicraft. I can add now that he would have been happier to see that you have established your own business alone, even though you must begin modestly for lack of capital. Grandfather

Life is an Adventure

ACTIVITIES

Thinking Critically About the Stories

1. The writer Helen Keller was blind and deaf; yet she managed to live a rich and full life, even managing to speak in a strange and singsong way. What does her quotation on page 205 mean to you? How do you personally feel about the quotation?
2. Of the two stories in which a horse plays a major role ("The Horse of the Sword" and "The Sorrel Colt"), which did you prefer? Why?
3. Jade Snow and the survivor of "Love of Life" had wildly dissimilar experiences; yet they showed similar qualities. What characteristics did they share?
4. "All Summer in a Day" has a sad ending. "The Horse of the Sword" has a happy ending. Do you prefer stories or movies with happy endings?
5. "The Horse of the Sword" features an intensely competitive race. How do you feel about competition? Do you enjoy a good contest in which you must pit your skills against those of others? Explain.
6. Readers tend to identify with characters they read about. With which character did you identify most closely? Why?

The Writing Portfolio

Writing the Longer Theme

After the single sentence and the paragraph, you are invited to try your hand at a longer challenge. The basic elements are still the sentence and the paragraph, but these must be welded together into a satisfactory whole.

To link your paragraphs, you will find connectives helpful. The strongest links are conjunctions. Coordinate conjunctions can connect words, phrases, and clauses of equal rank: *and*, *but*, *or*, *nor*.

Sheila plays field hockey, but Laura prefers volleyball.

Other conjunctions connect a dependent clause with an independent clause. A sample of these helpful connectors: *after*, *as*, *because*, *since*, *though*, *unless*, and *until*.

Though the dam hadn't really broken, the townspeople were panicked.

Other helpful connectors include words like these:

after this	therefore	afterward
a day later	otherwise	finally

Try to use some of these connectors in the writing assignments that follow.

Choose those questions you are most interested in. The lengths of your responses will vary. When asked how long a man's legs should be, Abraham Lincoln replied, "Long enough to reach the ground." Your responses should be "long enough to reach the end!" Use these writing activities as warm-ups for assignments to come.

1. As you look ahead, what do you see in your future? What are your goals?
2. How do you plan to follow through, to reach the goals you've set?
3. Would a teen center be an asset to your community? Write an editorial for your school newspaper presenting your own point of view.
4. Compare the two horses in "The Horse of the Sword" and "The Sorrel Colt."
5. Write the diary entry that Margot might have written after the sunshine vanished. ("All Summer in a Day.")
6. If you were the casting director for "Love of Life," which actors would you cast for Bill and the abandoned partner?
7. Why do some people, like Jade Snow ("The Work of One Day. . ."), prefer to run small shops, even though they could earn more money in a different occupation?

Other Areas of Communication

1. Here are two quotations somewhat at odds in their central messages:
   (a) On every side of us are men who hunt for their personal Northwest Passage, too often sacrificing health, strength, and life itself in the search, and who shall say they are happier in their vain but hopeful quest than wiser, duller folks who sit at home, venturing nothing and, with sour laughs, deriding the seekers for their fabled thoroughfare.

   —Kenneth Roberts

   (b) Men will search for starlings in foreign lands and pay no heed to the lark at home.

   —Dagobert D. Runes

   Appoint one student to present the Roberts point of view and another the Runes point of view. Half the class will take one side and half the other. Then decide if, in any sense, both are right.

2. In the essay "On Running After One's Hat," G. K. Chesterton suggests that adventure depends on your point of view. If your hat blows off in the wind, and you run after it in a state of anger and vexation, you are taking the wrong attitude. Look on it as an adventure, not an irritation. An irritation may be only an adventure improperly considered. Set up a class discussion on that theme. Have different class members take opposing points of view.

3. Each of the following quotations comments about adventure. After you have read them, appoint a class leader who will lead the discussion of such questions as these:
   (a) Which seems the best description?
   (b) How would you apply one of the quotations to a story in this unit?
   (c) What is your own personal definition of adventure?

   Adventure is something you seek for pleasure, or even for profit, like a gold rush or invading a country; for the illusion of being more alive than ordinarily, the thing you *will* to occur; experience is what really happens to you in the long run; the truth that finally overtakes you.

   —Katherine Anne Porter

   The greatest adventures are experience in the soul of men, not across oceans or deserts.

   —Dagobert D. Runes

4. "All Summer in a Day" is a representative Ray Bradbury science fiction story. Another story of his, "The Golden Kite, the Silver Wind," appeared on page 149. Read still another Bradbury story or a story by another science fiction author and prepare to report to the class. If you wish, compare your story with one of the many *Star Trek* episodes.

Language in Action—a Review

You may refer to the preceding pages to answer these questions.

1. The incorrect use of the apostrophe is found in (a) ladies' sneakers (b) childrens' department (c) Gladys's performance (d) Robin and Tom's arrival.
2. The apostrophe is NOT used in the possessive of (a) proper names (b) names of cities (c) personal pronouns (d) abstract nouns.
3. Each of the following sentences contains a simile EXCEPT:

   (a) "But my heart is all a-flutter like the washing on the line."
   —Nathalia Crane

   (b) "The road was a ribbon of moonlight over the purple moor."
   —Alfred Noyes, "The Highwayman"

   (c) "Deep in the shady sadness of a vale sat gray-haired Saturn, quiet as a stone."
   —John Keats, "Hyperion"

   (d) "April is like a child that smiles in waking."
   —Nathalia Crane
4. Each of the following is a phonetic spelling EXCEPT (a) favor (b) ardor (c) traveler (d) women.
5. One of Noah Webster's spelling changes survives in (a) jeweller (b) theatre (c) kidnaped (d) tongue.
6. A basic element in all language is (a) simplified spelling (b) classification (c) phonetic spelling (d) eager acceptance of new words.
7. In simile the basic element is (a) comparison (b) criticism (c) personification (d) action verbs.
8. A major obstacle in the way of simplified spelling is (a) computers (b) inadequate printing presses (c) conservatism (d) the heavy hand of Noah Webster.

Word Origins

The following is a list of words derived from the names of real or fictional people. Select three words from the list and research their origins. Be ready to report to the class.

boycott	derrick	juggernaut	spoonerism
calico	epicure	sideburns	thespian
colossal	gerrymander	silhouette	titanic
cynic	Gordian knot	stentorian	vandal

UNIT FOUR

Can It Be Love?

Four of the most difficult words to define are **life** (430), **humor** (373), **poetry** (424), and **love**. This book cannot provide the final answer for each, but it does provide some food for thought. Each of the following is a valiant attempt to define **love**. No single definition can capture all the facets of love, but the definitions below may set you thinking.

Life has taught us that love does not consist of gazing at each other but in looking outward together in the same direction.

Antoine de Saint-Exupéry

Love is the child of freedom, never that of domination.

Erich Fromm

Love that has been given to you is too sacred a thing to be talked of to anyone . . . except just to the person who is like part of you and who will feel it as you do.

Olive Schreiner

We receive love—from our children as well as others—not in proportion to our demands or sacrifices or needs, but roughly in proportion to our own capacity to love.

Rollo May

We find rest in those we love, and we provide a resting place in ourselves for those who love us.

Saint Bernard of Clairvaux

Love is the way it is.

Thaddeus Golas

Love is like butter; it goes well with bread.

Yiddish Proverb

How bold one gets when one is sure of being loved.

Sigmund Freud

The selections that follow show a surprising range from the protective love of a young girl for her handicapped brother to the yearning of a New Yorker for a society belle. The stories involve people of all ages from a shy painter to a father grieving for his son. Love brings forth both tears and laughter. There are many faces of love. This unit provides many examples.

Mammon and the Archer

O. Henry
American

"You didn't notice," said he, "anywhere in the tie-up, a kind of a fat boy without any clothes on shooting arrows around, did you?"

"Why, no," said Kelly, mystified. "I didn't. If he was like you say, maybe the cops pinched him before I got there."

Among O. Henry's narrative qualities were a strong sense of whimsy and a mastery of the surprise ending. The quotation above actually explains half the title: Cupid is the Archer. Mammon, the other half of the title, is the personification of wealth.

There is an old cynical saying: "Dogs offer the only love that money can buy." The traditional wisdom insists that money can't buy love. There is too great a gap. Yet literature has often suggested the opposite: the Princess and the Commoner in many films; or the Prince and the Shopgirl. In *Pride and Prejudice*, Elizabeth and D'Arcy prove that love can prevail. In real life, Edward VIII gave up his throne for a commoner, Mrs. Simpson. *The Merry Widow* toys with the usual scenario. The Widow has the money, and Count Danilo is representing an impoverished little country.

O. Henry couldn't resist getting into the money-love plot. Here the differences in social station are not the problem. Still, our hero is losing the love of his life, disputing his father's insistence that money can solve just about anything. Then at the last minute, the wheels stop turning. Can it be love? Can that love survive?

O. Henry has the answer.

Mammon and the Archer

OLD ANTHONY ROCKWALL, retired manufacturer and proprietor of Rockwall's Eureka Soap, looked out the library window of his Fifth Avenue mansion and grinned. His neighbor to the right—the aristocratic clubman, G. Van Schuylight Suffolk-Jones—came out to his waiting motor-car, wrinkling a contumelious nostril, as usual, at the Italian renaissance sculpture of the soap palace's front elevation.

"Stuck-up old statuette of nothing doing!" commented the ex-Soap King. "The Eden Museé'll get that old frozen Nesselrode yet if he don't watch out. I'll have this house painted red, white, and blue next summer and see if that'll make his Dutch nose turn up any higher."

And then Anthony Rockwall, who never cared for bells, went to the door of his library and shouted "Mike!" in the same voice that had once chipped off pieces of the welkin on the Kansas prairies.

"Tell my son," said Anthony to the answering menial, "to come in here before he leaves the house."

When young Rockwall entered the library the old man laid aside his newspaper, looked at him with a kindly grimness on his big, smooth, ruddy countenance, rumpled his mop of white hair with one hand and rattled the keys in his pocket with the other.

"Richard," said Anthony Rockwall, "what do you pay for the soap that you use?"

Richard, only six months home from college, was startled a little. He had not yet taken the measure of this sire of his, who was as full of unexpectedness as a girl at her first party.

"Six dollars a dozen, I think, dad."

"And your clothes?"

"I suppose about sixty dollars, as a rule."

"You're a gentleman," said Anthony, decidedly. "I've heard of these young bloods spending $24 a dozen for soap, and going over the hundred mark for clothes. You've got as much money to waste as any of 'em, and yet you stick to what's decent and moderate. Now I use the old Eureka—not only for sentiment, but it's the purest soap made. Whenever you pay more than 10 cents a cake for soap you buy bad perfumes and labels. But 50 cents is doing very well for a young man in your generation, position and condition. As I said, you're a gentleman. They say it takes three generations to make one. They're off. Money'll do it as slick as soap grease. It's made you one. By hokey! it's almost made one of me. I'm nearly as impolite and disagreeable and ill-mannered as these two old knickerbockers gents on each side of me that can't sleep of nights because I bought in between'em."

"There are some things that money can't accomplish," remarked young Rockwall, rather gloomily.

"Now, don't say that," said old Anthony, shocked. "I bet my money on money every time. I've been through the encyclopedia down to Y looking for something you can't buy with it; and I expect to have to take up the appendix next week. I'm for money against the field. Tell me something money won't buy."

"For one thing," answered Richard, rankling a little, "it won't buy one into the exclusive circles of society."

"Oho! won't it?" thundered the champion of the root of evil. "You tell me where your exclusive circles would be if the first Astor hadn't had the money to pay for his steerage passage over?"

Richard sighed.

"And that's what I was coming to," said the old man, less boisterously. "That's why I asked you to come in. There's something going wrong with you, boy. I've been noticing it for two weeks. Out with it. I guess I could lay my hands on eleven millions within twenty-four hours, besides the real estate. If it's your liver, there's the *Rambler* down in the bay, coaled, and ready to steam down to the Bahamas in two days."

"Not a bad guess, dad; you haven't missed it far."

"Ah," said Anthony, keenly; "what's her name?"

Richard began to walk up and down the library floor. There was enough comradeship and sympathy in this crude old father of his to draw his confidence.

"Why don't you ask her?" demanded old Anthony. "She'll jump at you. You've got the money and the looks, and you're a decent boy. Your hands are clean. You've got no Eureka soap on 'em. You've been to college, but she'll overlook that."

"I haven't had a chance," said Richard.

"Make one," said Anthony. "Take her for a walk in the park, or a straw ride, or walk home with her from church. Chance! Pshaw!"

"You don't know the social mill, dad. She's part of the stream that turns it. Every hour and minute of her time is arranged for days in advance. I must have that girl, dad, or this town is a blackjack swamp forevermore. And I can't write it—I can't do that."

"Tut!" said the old man. "Do you mean to tell me that with all the money I've got you can't get an hour or two of a girl's time for yourself?"

"I've put it off too late. She's going to sail for Europe at noon day after tomorrow for a two years' stay. I'm to see her alone tomorrow evening for a few minutes. She's at Larchmont now at her aunt's. I can't go there. But I'm allowed to meet her with a cab at the Grand Central Station tomorrow evening at the 8:30 train. We drive down Broadway to Wallack's at a gallop, where her mother and a box party will be waiting for us in the lobby. Do you think she would listen to a declaration from me during that six or eight minutes under those circumstances? No. And what chance would I have in the theatre or afterward? None. No, dad, this is one tangle that your money can't unravel. We can't buy one minute of time with cash; if we could, rich people would live longer. There's no hope of getting a talk with Miss Lantry before she sails."

"All right, Richard, my boy," said old Anthony, cheerfully. "You may run along down to your club now. I'm glad it ain't your liver. But don't forget to burn a few punk sticks in the joss house to the great god Mazuma from time to time. You say money won't buy time? Well, of course, you can't order eternity wrapped up and delivered at your residence for a price, but I've seen Father Time get pretty bad stone bruises on his heels when he walked through the gold diggings."

That night came Aunt Ellen, gentle, sentimental, wrinkled, sighing, oppressed by wealth, in to Brother Anthony at his evening paper, and began discourse on the subject of lovers' woes.

"He told me all about it," said Brother Anthony, yawning. "I told him my bank account was at his service. And then he began to knock money. Said money couldn't help. Said the rules of society couldn't be bucked for a yard by a team of ten-millionaires."

"Oh, Anthony," sighed Aunt Ellen, "I wish you would not think so much of money. Wealth is nothing where a true affection is concerned. Love is all-powerful. If he only had spoken earlier! She could not have refused our Richard. But now I fear it is too late. He will have no opportunity to address her. All your gold cannot bring happiness to your son."

At eight o'clock the next evening Aunt Ellen took a quaint old gold ring from a moth-eaten case and gave it to Richard.

"Wear it tonight, nephew," she begged. "Your mother gave it to me. Good luck in love she said it brought. She asked me to give it to you when you had found the one you loved."

Young Rockwall took the ring reverently and tried it on his smallest finger. It slipped as far as the second joint and stopped. He took it off and stuffed it into his vest pocket, after the manner of man. And then he 'phoned for his cab.

At the station he captured Miss Lantry out of the gabbing mob at eight thirty-two.

"We mustn't keep mamma and the other waiting," said she.

"To Wallack's Theatre as fast as you can drive!" said Richard, loyally.

They whirled up Forty-second to Broadway, and then down the white-starred lane that leads from the soft meadows of sunset to the rocky hills of morning.

At Thirty-fourth Street young Richard quickly thrust up the trap and ordered the cabman to stop.

"I've dropped a ring," he apologized, as he climbed out. "It was my mother's, and I'd hate to lose it. I won't detain you a minute—I saw where it fell."

In less than a minute he was back in the cab with the ring.

But within that minute a crosstown car had stopped directly in front of the cab. The cab-man tried to pass to the left, but a heavy express wagon cut him off. He tried the right and had to back away from a furniture van that had no business to be there. He tried to back out, but dropped his reins and swore dutifully. He was blockaded in a tangled mess of vehicles and horses.

One of those street blockades had occurred that sometimes tie up commerce and movement quite suddenly in the big city.

"Why don't you drive on?" said Miss Lantry impatiently. "We'll be late."

Richard stood up in the cab and looked around. He saw a congested flood of wagons, trucks, cabs, vans and street cars filling the vast space where Broadway, Sixth Avenue, and Thirty-fourth Street cross one another as a twenty-six inch maiden fills her twenty-two inch girdle. And still from all the cross streets they were hurrying and rattling toward the converging point at full speed, and hurling themselves into the straggling mass, locking wheels and adding their drivers' imprecations to the clamor. The entire traffic of Manhattan seemed to have jammed itself around them. The oldest New Yorker among the thousands of spectators that lined the sidewalks had not witnessed a street blockade of the proportions of this one.

"I'm very sorry," said Richard, as he resumed his seat, "but it looks as if we are stuck. They won't get this jumble loosened up in an hour. It was my fault. If I hadn't dropped the ring we—"

"Let me see the ring," said Miss Lantry. "Now that it can't be helped, I don't care. I think theatres are stupid, anyway."

At 11 o'clock that night somebody tapped lightly on Anthony Rockwall's door.

"Come in," shouted Anthony, who was in a red dressing-gown, reading a book of piratical adventures.

Somebody was Aunt Ellen, looking like a gray-haired angel that had been left on earth by mistake.

"They're engaged, Anthony," she said, softly. "She has promised to marry our Richard. On their way to the theatre there was a street blockade, and it was two hours before their cab could get out of it.

"And oh, Brother Anthony, don't ever boast of the power of money again. A little emblem of true love—a little ring that symbolized unending and unmercenary affection—was the cause of our Richard finding his happiness. He dropped it in the street, and got out to recover it. And before they could continue the blockade occurred. He spoke to his love and won her there while the cab was hemmed in. Money is dross compared with true love, Anthony."

"All right," said old Anthony. "I'm glad the boy has got what he wanted. I told him I wouldn't spare any expense in the matter if—"

"But, Brother Anthony, what good could your money have done?"

"Sister," said Anthony Rockwall. "I've got my pirate in a devil of a scrape. His ship has just been scuttled, and he's too good a judge of the value of money to let drown. I wish you would let me go on with this chapter."

The story should end here. I wish it would as heartily as you who read it wish it did. But we must go to the bottom of the well for truth.

The next day a person with red hands and a blue polka-dot necktie, who called himself Kelly, called at Anthony Rockwall's house, and was at once received in the library.

"Well," said Anthony, reaching for his check-book, "it was a good bilin' of soap. Let's see—you had $5,000 in cash."

"I paid out $300 more of my own," said Kelly. "I had to go a little above the estimate. I got the express wagons and cabs mostly for $5; but the trucks and two-horse teams mostly raised me to $10. The motormen wanted $10, and some of the loaded teams $20. The cops struck me hardest—$50 I paid two, and the rest $20 and $25. But didn't it work beautiful, Mr. Rockwall? I'm glad William A. Brady wasn't onto that little outdoor vehicle mob scene. I wouldn't want William to break his heart with jealousy. And never a rehearsal, either! The boys was on time to the fraction of a second. It was two hours before a snake could get below Greeley's statue."

"Thirteen hundred—there you are, Kelly," said Anthony, tearing off a check. "Your thousand, and the $300 you were out. You don't despise money, do you, Kelly?"

"Me?" said Kelly. "I can lick the man that invented poverty."

Anthony called Kelly when he was at the door.

"You didn't notice," said he, "anywhere in the tie-up, a kind of a fat boy without any clothes on shooting arrows around with a bow, did you?"

"Why, no," said Kelly, mystified. "I didn't. If he was like you say, maybe the cops pinched him before I got there."

"I thought the little rascal wouldn't be on hand," chuckled Anthony. "Good-by, Kelly."

Reading for Understanding

Main Idea

1. The main idea is expressed by which of the following statements?
   (a) Love laughs at locksmiths.
   (b) Older women understand love better than young ones.
   (c) An old man's ingenuity and a young man's ardor save the day.
   (d) Too much preoccupation with money makes man a miser.

Details

2. Anthony Rockwall (a) had a house servant named Kelly (b) gave Richard the ring (c) admired one of his neighbors (d) made his fortune in soap.
3. The person who addresses "Brother Anthony" is (a) Miss Lantry (b) Aunt Ellen (c) Mike (d) Richard.
4. The classic tie-up occurred (a) at Forty-second Street (b) at Thirty-fourth Street (c) at Broadway (d) near the Rockwall house.
5. The news of Richard's success was relayed by (a) Richard himself (b) Miss Lantry (c) Aunt Ellen (d) the cop at the blockade.

Inferences

6. The "soft meadows" on page (279) are (a) metaphorical (b) colorful (c) urban in location (d) overgrazed.
7. Anthony's attitude toward his son was one of (a) irritated disapproval (b) indifference (c) friendly fellowship (d) genial acceptance.

Cause and Effect

8. Without the intervention of Anthony Rockwall, it is reasonable to assume that (a) Richard's love would have been unrequited (b) Miss Lantry would have taken the initiative (c) nothing would have been changed (d) Richard would have won his love on his own.

Author's Style

9. O. Henry's style may best be characterized as (a) stilted (b) exotic (c) pedestrian (d) breezy.

Fact or Opinion

Tell whether the following is a fact or an opinion.

10. The traffic blockade was planned.

Words in Context

1. "His neighbor to the right came out to his waiting motor-car, wrinkling a *contumelious* nose, as usual, at the Italian Renaissance sculpture." **Contumelious** (276) means (a) apprehensive (b) aristocratic (c) disdainful (d) expectant.
2. "Anthony Rockwall shouted 'Mike!' in the same voice that had once chipped off a piece of the *welkin* on the Kansas prairie." The **welkin** (276) is (a) a windmill (b) a granary (c) grass (d) the sky.
3. " 'Tell my son,' said Anthony to the answering *menial*, 'to come in here before he leaves the house.' " A **menial** (276) is a (a) chef (b) servant (c) carpenter (d) correspondent.

Thinking Critically About the Story

1. Clearly this story was written in and about an earlier time, most notably because of the prices: six dollars for a dozen soap, sixty dollars for a suit. Even the transportation has the flavor of a century ago. Does this quaint, old-fashioned quality in any way detract from the appeal of the story? Are there universals that fit every age?
2. Is the character of Anthony Rockwall portrayed favorably, or does his love of wealth make him basically unsympathetic? Take a point of view and sustain it.
3. "Whenever you pay more than 10 cents a cake for soap, you buy bad perfume and labels." Certainly, the price is an ancient memory here, but does the same practice prevail today, adding nonessential ingredients to jack up the price and give the illusion of greater value? Explain.
4. "If only he had spoken earlier." How does this quotation suggest that the romantic problem here is not a matter of different levels of society?

5. Once again a ring proves to be a strategic element in the love story. A ring plays a crucial role in the Tolkien stories. What other fables, folk tales, fairy tales, fantasies include a ring as a major element in the plot?
6. How does Miss Lantry give a first impression of indifference to the suitor?
7. A *trap* is defined as a "light, usually one-horse carriage with springs." We are obviously talking about a different New York. Could such a contrived tie-up be possible today?
8. O. Henry mentions William A. Brady (280), a famous theatrical manager and producer of the time. Why would Brady be jealous?
9. O. Henry delights in sly, impish commentary about life, pretense, the relationship between the sexes. In the following quotation, what comment is he making about the tyranny of fashion? He compares the blockade "as a twenty-six inch maiden fills her twenty-two inch girdle."
10. Is there any indication that Miss Lantry may prove a risky choice for Richard? Explain.

Language in Action

Words from Names

> "I'm nearly as impolite and disagreeable and ill-mannered as these two old knickerbocker gents on each side of me that can't sleep of nights because I bought in between 'em."

Washington Irving wrote a fictitious history of New York, supposedly written by Diedrich Knickerbocker. The name caught on—first as a name for New Yorkers, then attached to a professional basketball team, then extended to clothing, finally shortened to *knickers*. Names have added thousands of words to the English language. Here's a sample.

From Classical Mythology:	jovial	martial	colossal
From science:	watt	volt	galvanize
From history:	waterloo	marathon	vandalism
From Norse Mythology:	Tuesday	Wednesday	Thursday
From art:	thespian	silhouette	titian (color)

How many others can you list?

Mr. Cornelius, I Love You

Jessamyn West
American

"What did I say?" Mr. Delahanty asked, "To cause all that?"

Mrs. Delahanty continued without speaking to shake bits of food from the flowers. "Gertrude, did what I said sound cruel and hateful to you?"

"No, John, not to me," she answered. "But then I'm not in love with Mr. Cornelius."

All the stories in this unit deal with love in one form or other; yet this is the only story with **love** in the title. Despite this, there will be some who say, "The love demonstrated in this chapter isn't really love, at all, merely a girlhood crush." You can decide for yourself. Cress Delahanty's adoration of Mr. Cornelius is totally absorbing . . . and extremely vulnerable, but is it love?

Cress's feelings, are, she thinks, little understood or appreciated by her parents or friends. They come at a critical time in her development. Ruthlessly destroyed, this deep affection could cause her pain and hinder her ability to love later in life. Fortunately, there is a key person who sees the love for what it is, understands it, and brings Cress in as a partner in the task of helping Mr. Cornelius to recover.

What seems like a pointless obsession is a step in the growing maturity of a young woman.

Mr. Cornelius, I Love You

MR. AND MRS. DELAHANTY, Cress, and Cress's friends, Jo Grogan and Bernadine Deevers, sat down to the Delahanty dinner table on Wednesday evening. The table was round with a white cloth that dipped at its four corners to the floor, so that in the dusk of the dining room the cloth seemed actually to be supporting the table. Mrs. Delahanty, who hadn't even expected Cress home for dinner, let alone Jo and Bernadine, felt apologetic about the food which, besides being rather uninviting, was skimpy in amount: a small salmon loaf, Harvard beets, mashed potatoes, and for dessert a cabinet pudding which did nothing to redeem the meal that had gone before. But the girls didn't seem to know or care what they put in their mouths and she decided that strawberries and fresh asparagus would have been wasted on them.

A mockingbird was singing in the orange grove outside the opened windows and the girls listened, a spoonful of cabinet pudding lifted to their opened lips—then, as the song ceased, put the spoons down without having tasted a bite. Mr. and Mrs. Delahanty had given up trying to carry on a conversation with them and treated them as so many portraits ranged round their dining room—"Girls at Dusk," or "Reveries of Youth." They talked their own talk and let the girls dream their dreams, wrap their feet around the rungs of their chairs, and listen (mouths open, eyes closed) to the bird song.

"I saw Doc Mendenhall in town today," Mr. Delahanty said.

Mrs. Delahanty said "Yes?" waiting for whatever it was that made this fact worth reporting, but Bernadine interrupted his train of thought, if he had one, by extending her long arms toward the darkening windows and singing very softly, "Oh night of love, oh beauteous night." Bernadine was barefooted (it was the spring's great fad at high school) though she was eighteen, and wore an elaborate blue voile dress which drifted about her like a sky-stained cloud. Bernadine was to be married the day after school was out and sometimes, Mrs. Delahanty felt, overplayed her role of bride-to-be.

It was already, unbelievably, the last week of school which, in Southern California, is the second week in June, a time climatically as well as scholastically neither one thing nor another, neither spring nor summer, neither truly school nor truly vacation. Class routines had been relaxed but not abandoned. Grade-wise, the feeling among the students was that the year was already water over the dam; still they couldn't be positive; some of the teachers were still going through the motions of setting down grades in their record books. Climatically the days started spring-like, damp and gray with threat even of one more unseasonal rain; at 1 P.M. exactly the day did an about-face, took on September inclinations. At that hour the overcast burned away and the tawny grasses, sun-bleached foothills, and smoldering flowers of full summer emerged. It was very confusing after getting up into a dripping cold which made sweaters and open fires necessary, to finish the day barefooted, hot-cheeked, and as naked as possible.

Cress and Jo both wore shorts and halters. Cress had shasta daisies tucked in the V of her halter and Jo Grogan, with those three flame-colored hibiscus in her short dark hair, might have been August itself on any calendar of girls. As the day darkened the white tablecloth grew silvery, the mockingbird retreated deeper into the orchard, and Mrs. Delahanty felt that the whole scene might be unreal, a mirage cast up into the present out of either the past or the future—that girls *had* sat in many a darkening room in years gone by and would so sit in the future; but that "now," the present minute, was unreal, only the past whisking by on its way to the future, or the future casting a long prophetic shadow to rearwards.

"Jo," she said briskly, "if you'll put some more custard on your pudding you might be able to eat it."

"I beg your pardon," said Jo. "Were you speaking to me?"

"Never mind," Mrs. Delahanty told her. "I was only urging you to eat."

"Oh food!" said Cress. "Food. Who cares about food?"

"I do," said Bernadine. "Howie adores puddings. Will you copy down this recipe for me, Mrs. Delahanty? I plan to serve Howie a different pudding every single night for thirty nights. I already have twenty-two recipes."

"Tapioca, jello, and bread," said Jo, sing-songing. "If puddings be the food of love, cook on."

The mockingbird had ceased to sing. The leaves of the bougainvillaea vine which clambered over the dining-room wall rustled faintly. Mrs. Delahanty began taking the spoons from the serving dishes.

Mr. Delahanty remarked in the voice of a man who has had the words in mind for some time, "Doc Mendenhall says that Frank Cornelius had a bad hemorrhage this morning."

Mrs. Delahanty laid the spoons down, clattering. "Oh John!" she said. "I understood he was getting better."

There was a note in her voice of condemnation, as if Mr. Cornelius had not tried hard enough, as if he were a turncoat, a traitor to his generation—and hers. When old people sickened and died, men and women in their seventies and eighties, that was to be expected. But thirty-eight! That was a direct threat to her and John.

"I don't think he's taken very good care of himself," Mr. Delahanty explained. "You can't throw off t.b. just by wishing. You've got to co-operate, rest, stay put. I've seen Cornelius about town off and on all spring. Baseball, things like that. Staggering around half-alive. I saw him yesterday, sitting along the road out by his place. Today, a hemorrhage. He was asking for . . ."

Cress sprang to her feet, interrupting her father. "You mustn't say that. You have no right to say that." She pulled the daisies from the neck of her halter and passed them from hand to hand distractedly. "You don't have any idea what it's like to be dying. Do you?" she insisted.

Mr. Delahanty agreed instantly. "No, I don't, Crescent. The worst I ever had was a touch of shingles."

"Don't be funny," Cress said, her chin quivering. "Don't be funny about death. How can you understand how terrible it is for Mr. Cornelius to think he may die, no matter how much he takes care of himself? And that if he doesn't go out and see the sunshine and people and trees today he may never see them again. Never, never. And you were never a great athlete like Mr. Cornelius, so it's a thousand times worse for him than it would be for you to stay in bed. And you blame him. You blame him for not giving in. You blame him—" She paused, trying to steady her voice. "I hate—I hate *people* who say cruel things like that." She looked at her father and Mr. Delahanty looked back. Then she dropped her daisies onto her plate amidst the uneaten salmon and beets and ran from the room.

Mrs. Delahanty, after the sound of the slammed door had stopped echoing, leaned over and began to gather up the daisies. The two girls excused themselves and left the room.

"What did I say?" Mr. Delahanty asked. "To cause all that?"

Mrs. Delahanty continued without speaking to shake bits of food from the flowers. "Gertrude, did what I said sound cruel and hateful to you?"

"No, John, not to me," she answered. "But then I'm not in love with Mr. Cornelius."

In her bedroom, Cress sat on the floor, her head on the window sill. When she felt an arm about her shoulders, Jo's by the weight and pressure, she said, "Go away, please go away and leave me alone." The arm remained where it was. Jo knew, and so did Bernadine. Not much, because there wasn't much to know, except that she had seen Mr. Cornelius three times to look at him and had spoken to him twice and that she loved him and would willingly die for him.

There was "not much to know" in what was called the outside world; but inside herself, in her dreams and imaginings there was nothing *but* Mr. Cornelius. She had decided out of her experience of loving Mr. Cornelius that the knowledge people had of one another, parents of children, anyway, was almost nothing. She could sit at the dinner table with her father and mother, answering their questions about school, but being in reality thousands of miles away in some hot dry land nursing Mr. Cornelius back to health; and her father and mother never noticed her absence in the least.

In her dreams she and Mr. Cornelius sometimes went away together, Mr. Cornelius saying, "Cress, without knowing it I have been searching for you all of my life. My sickness is no more than the sum of my disappointment, and without you I can never get well."

Sometimes in her dreams Mrs. Cornelius came to her and the gist of what she said was, "My life with Mr. Cornelius has been a failure. He has not many months to live. I do not want to stand between him and his happiness in the little time that is left. Go, with my blessing."

But for the most part Mrs. Cornelius and the Cornelius boys did not exist in her dreams; even the world, as she knew it in what was called "real life," was greatly altered; or, perhaps, simplified. Changed, anyway, so that it consisted of nothing but sunshine, a background of sand or water, and a grassy or sandy bank against which Mr. Cornelius reclined, getting well. And as he got well she waited on him, and talked to him. As a matter of fact, every thought in her mind had become part of an unending monologue directed toward the omnipresent mental image of Mr. Cornelius. Everything she saw immediately became words in a report to Mr. Cornelius; and if, by chance, some experience was so absorbing as to momentarily obscure his image, she made up for it by living the whole scene through once again just for him. Sometimes she imagined that Mr. Cornelius kissed her. She had to be careful about these imaginings however. She had never been kissed, family didn't count, of course, and since she supposed that when you were kissed by the man you loved, the sensations were near to swooning, swooning was what she nearly did whenever she had imaginings of this kind.

Most often she simply helped Mr. Cornelius as he reclined in the midst of the sunny simplified landscape, his thin beautiful face becoming tanned and fuller as his health improved; but not more beautiful. That was impossible. She doted on his hawk-nose and dark crest; she dismissed every other face she saw as pudgy and ill-shaped by comparison. In her dream she picked flowers for Mr. Cornelius, went to the library for him, read to him, smoothed his brow, sometimes kissed him and always, always gazed at him with enraptured eyes. But all the time she was imagining this life with Mr. Cornelius she suffered, because Mr.

Cornelius was dying and there was nothing she could do about it; she suffered because she had feelings which she did not know how to express, suffered because she had put the core of her life outside its circumference.

She sat up, and Jo took her arm away. It was still light enough to see Bernadine on the floor leaning against the bed, and Jo by her side. The pitcher of white stock on her desk reflected what light there was, like a moon. The room was quiet and warm and full of misery.

"There is nothing you can do, Cress," Jo said. "You love him and he is dying. You can't do anything about either one. All you can do is to endure it."

"I can do something," Cress said.

"What?" Jo asked.

"I can go to Mr. Cornelius and tell him I love him."

"Oh no," Bernadine said, very shocked. "You can't do that."

"Why not?" Cress asked.

"You don't know whether he loves you or not."

"What does that have to do with it? I'm not going to him to ask him if he loves me. I'm going to tell him that I love him."

"Is that what you really want to do, Cress?" Jo asked.

"No—if you mean by want to, do I feel good about going. I feel awful about going. It makes me feel sick to my stomach to even think about it. It gives me the shakes."

Jo once again put an arm around Cress's shoulders. "It's a fact," she reported to Bernadine. "She's shaking like a leaf."

"Look, Cress," Bernadine said. "I'm almost married myself. It's just a matter of days. For all practical purposes I *am* married. You must think of Mr. Cornelius, Cress, and what he'd feel. I know if Howie was sick and maybe dying he wouldn't want some other woman coming to his sick bed and saying, 'I love you.' The first thing he'd do, I know, is say to me, 'Bernadine, throw this madwoman out.' And that's exactly what Mr. Cornelius is liable to say to you."

"I know it," Cress said bleakly.

"Well, then?" Bernadine asked, pride of reasoning in her voice. "Are you still going?"

Cress huddled silent, unanswering.

"It's probably not a very kind thing to do," Jo suggested in her deep, thoughtful voice. "Go to see him now when he's so sick."

"Oh I *know* that. If I just asked myself what was kind I would never do it. But what has kindness got to do with love? I'm not doing it to be kind to Mr. Cornelius. I'm doing it because I have to."

"Have to?" Jo reminded her, steadily. "You don't have to. Sit right here. Sit still. By morning everything will be different."

"By morning Mr. Cornelius may be dead."

"Well then," Bernadine said, "all your problems will be over. Mr. Cornelius will be dead and you'll be sad. But you won't have bothered him or made a fool of yourself."

"I don't care about making a fool of myself."

"You do care. You're still shaking. And think about Mrs. Cornelius. How's she going to feel about someone barging in on her sick husband, making passionate declarations of love?"

"It wouldn't be passionate. I would just say, very quietly, the minute I got there, 'I love you, Mr. Cornelius.' Then leave."

"Cress," Bernadine said, "what actually do you see yourself doing? You get there, the whole family is around the bed, and doctors and priests too, maybe. What are your plans? To say 'I beg your pardon but I've a little message for Mr. Cornelius'? Then push your way through them all to the bedside, drop on your knee, kiss his wasted hand and say, 'Mr. Cornelius, I love you.' Is that it?"

"Oh, don't heckle her, Bernadine," Jo said.

"What I see myself doing," said Cress, "is telling Mr. Cornelius something I have to tell him."

"How," asked Bernadine, "do you see yourself getting there?" Bernadine had Howie's car while he was in the army and she had driven the girls home from school. "Do you see yourself walking eight miles?"

"If I have to," Cress said.

"O.K.," Bernadine told her. "I'll drive you. And let's go right away and get it over with."

Mr. Cornelius was still living in the small one-room tent-house at the edge of the walnut grove in which his home stood. Here he was away from the noises of his family and was able to get the fresh air he needed. It was nine o'clock when Bernadine stopped the car in front of the Cornelius ranch. A dim light was burning inside the tent-house, but there was nothing to indicate the presence of the crowd of people she had prophesied. "Here we are," she said, turning off the engine.

Cress wished for any catastrophe, however great, which would prevent her from having to leave the car. She felt real hatred for Bernadine and Jo. Why, if they were convinced that she shouldn't come, hadn't they remained steadfast? What kind of friends were they, to give way to their better judgment so weakly? And what were her parents thinking about? Why had they permitted her to go riding off into the night? To tell a strange man she loved him? True, she hadn't told them where she was going nor that she loved a strange man. But what were parents for if not to understand without being told? She blamed them for her fright and unhappiness.

Still anything that *happened* would be better than continuing to live in a make-believe world in which she only dreamed that she told Mr.

Cornelius she loved him. And she knew that if Bernadine were to start the car now she would jump out and run toward the tent-house and the declaration which would start her to living inside her dream. She opened the car door and stepped out into the night air which, after the warmth of the car, was damp and cold against her bare legs and arms.

"Cheerio," said Bernadine quite calmly as she was walking away from the car under the dark canopy of the big trees toward the dimly lighted room. Why was it so hard to do what she had set her heart on doing?

She stood at the screened door looking into the room as into a picture. Why did it seem like a picture? The small number of furnishings? Their neat arrangement, dresser balanced by table, chair by bed? The light falling from a bulb, shaded by blue paper, so that part of the room was in deep shadow? But most of all, was it picture-like because she had imagined the room and Mr. Cornelius for so long, that a frame had grown up about them in her mind? Now, would it be possible to break that frame? She opened the screen door, stepped into the room and became a part of the picture by that easy act.

Mr. Cornelius lay on a high narrow bed. He lay very straight, his head supported by three or four pillows and his hands folded across an ice pack which he held to his chest. His eyes were closed and his face, in spite of his illness, was warm with color. At the sight of him all of Cress's doubts left her. Oh Mr. Cornelius, she thought, I do truly love you and I have come at last to tell you.

Without opening his eyes Mr. Cornelius said, "Joyce, I think I'm going to be sick."

Joyce. Cress was surprised at the name. It seemed too gentle for the bus driver. "It's not Joyce, Mr. Cornelius," Cress said. "It's me."

Then Mr. Cornelius opened his eyes and Cress was enchanted all over again by the enormous blaze of being alive and searching and understanding which she saw there.

"It's Cress," he said, in a very low careful voice, "the track-meet girl." Then he closed his eyes. "I'm going to be sick," he said. "Hand me the basin."

The basin, Cress saw, was an enamel wash bowl on the night stand by the bed. She got it, put it on the bed beside Mr. Cornelius.

"Help me," Mr. Cornelius said and Cress helped him the way her mother had helped her when she was sick after her tonsils were out, by putting an arm around his shoulders and supporting him.

"Don't be scared," Mr. Cornelius whispered. "It's not a hemorrhage. I'm just going to lose my supper."

He did and afterwards he lay back against his pillows for a minute or two, then he reached up his hand and rang the bell which was suspended from the headboard of his bed.

"A glass of water," he told Cress, and Cress was holding it for him to rinse his mouth when Mrs. Cornelius arrived. Mrs. Cornelius paid no more attention to her than if she'd been some kind of device to help Mr. Cornelius—like the ice pack or the bell. She took the glass from Cress's hand, slipped her arm around her husband's shoulders and said, "Frank, Frank. Oh thank God, Frank, no more blood. Just your supper and that doesn't matter. I made you eat too much. This was to be expected. If you can swallow a bite or two later I'll fix you another. How do you feel now, honey?"

Cress had backed away from the bed. Mrs. Cornelius was wearing a housecoat or dressing gown of deep red, lightened by wreaths of tiny yellow and white flowers. What she looked like now was not a General in the Russian army but Robert Louis Stevenson's wife, "trusty, dusky, vivid and true with eyes of gold and bramble dew." Her bosom, which had spoiled the lines of her chauffeur's coat, was exactly right for pillowing an invalid's head, and her chestnut hair, curled corkscrew crisp, said "Never give up," as plain as any words, said "Fight on," said "Defy the universe." And all the time she was cradling Mr. Cornelius in her arms, and helping him rinse his mouth she was pressing her cheek to his hair and speaking comforting words through which there ran a mixture of laughing and joking.

"Take this to the bathroom and empty it," she said to Cress when Mr. Cornelius had finished rinsing his mouth. She handed the basin to Cress and nodded toward a door at the back of the room. Cress, ordinarily too squeamish to pull off her own Band-Aids, marched away with it without a word.

When she returned Mr. Cornelius was once more against his pillows and Mrs. Cornelius was wiping his face with a damp cloth.

"Where'd you come from?" she asked Cress as she took the basin from her.

"From out there," Cress said, nodding toward the road. "The girls are waiting for me. In the car," she explained.

Mrs. Cornelius paused in her washing. "What did you come *for?*" she asked.

Cress welcomed the question. It was a wonderful help, like the upward spring of the diving board against her feet when she was reluctant to take off into deep water. Though she no longer had so great a need to say what she had come to say, some change had taken place in her since she had come into the room; what had been locked inside her and had been painful, because unsaid, had somehow, without a word being spoken, gotten itself partially expressed. She was not sure how. Nevertheless she had come to speak certain words. They were the answer to Mrs. Cornelius' question. They were *why* she had come.

So, louder than was necessary, and in a voice cracking with strain she said, "I came to tell Mr. Cornelius I loved him." Then she turned, resolutely, and said the words directly to Mr. Cornelius. "Mr. Cornelius, I love you."

At that Mrs. Cornelius laughed, not jeering, not angry, not unbelieving, but in the soft delighted way of a person who has received an unexpected gift, a pleasure never dreamed of but one come in the nick of time and most acceptable.

"Oh, Frankie," she said, running her hand through Mr. Cornelius' thick black hair, "look at what we've got here."

"What *we've* got," was what she'd said as if, Cress thought, I'd said I loved them both. And then, watching Mr. Cornelius reach for his wife's hand, she saw that there was nothing she could give to Mr. Cornelius without giving it also to Mrs. Cornelius. Because they were not two separated people. They were really one, the way the Bible said. It was an astounding discovery. It was almost too much for her. It held her motionless and speculating. She felt as if her mind, by an infusion of light and warmth, was being forced to expand to accommodate this new idea. And it was an idea which, contrary to all her expectations, she liked. It was exactly what she wanted. Not Mr. Cornelius alone on a stretch of desert sand and she kissing his wasted hand—in spite of her six months' dreaming. What she wanted was Mr. and Mrs. Cornelius. She was so happy for Mrs. Cornelius' presence she almost took and kissed *her* plump brown unwasted hand.

Mrs. Cornelius, however, was continuing her laughing murmur to her husband. "Frankie," she said, "oh Frankie, you old jackanapes. You old irresistible. What's all this talk about being on your last legs? Done for? Caved in? With school girls coming with professions of love? Pretty school girls. Boy, we're not cashing in our checks just yet. Not us. What's your name, dear?" she asked Cress.

Mr. Cornelius answered in his low half-whispering voice. "She's John Delahanty's daughter, Crescent. They call her Cress at school."

"Well," said Mrs. Cornelius. "I've heard the boys mention you. Where'd you see Frank?"

"At a track meet."

"I stared at her some," Mr. Cornelius said. "Reminded me of you at her age. So alive."

"Was I ever like that?" Mrs. Cornelius asked her husband.

"That's what *I* thought about Mr. Cornelius," Cress said.

"Alive?" asked Mrs. Cornelius.

"Oh yes. More than anyone there. More than the boys. I thought his eyes fed on the sights," she said, daring the poetry of her thoughts.

"Fed?" Mrs. Cornelius studied the word then accepted it. "I see what you mean. Now, Frank," she said, "will you lie still and take care of yourself? Unknown school girls loving you and wanting you to get well. You do, don't you?" she asked Cress.

"Oh yes," Cress said. "I was willing to die for him."

Her voice evidently convinced Mrs. Cornelius. "Oh, Frank," she said, "school girls willing to die for you and you not half trying."

"Mrs. Cornelius," Cress said, wanting, since even partial confession made her feel so much better, to tell everything, "I ought to tell you something else." She stumbled for words. "I ought to tell you what else I planned."

"I bet you planned to run away with Frank and nurse him back to health."

Cress was amazed. "Yes," she said, her face burning with guilt and foolishness, "yes I did. How did you know?"

"Oh Frank, don't it bring it all back to you? No wonder you were reminded of me. *I* was going to run away with the minister," she said, turning to Cress. "Save him from his wife and family. And he *was* the most beautiful man in the world, Frank. You can't hold a candle to your father—never could."

Cress wanted to say something, but she couldn't settle on what. She had too many emotions to express. Exhilaration at being released from the isolation of her dreaming; relief to find that other girls had loved secretly too, but most of all joy to have acted, to have made for herself a single undivided world in which to live.

"Oh Mrs. Cornelius," she said, "oh Mrs. Cornelius . . ."

"Cress," asked Mrs. Cornelius, "can you play cards? Or checkers?"

"Yes," Cress said, "I can. I like to."

"And read out loud? Of course you can do that, can't you? Why don't you come read to Frank? And play cards with him? It gets so darn lonesome for him. I work. The boys work, and besides they haven't got enough patience to sit still. And the good people come in and tell Frank how their uncles or mothers passed away with consumption and for him to be resigned. He needs somebody interested in living, not dying. Would you come?"

"Oh yes. If you want me—if he wants me. I could come every day all summer."

"O.K.," Mrs. Cornelius said, "we'll plan on it. Now you'd better run on. Frank's had a bad day. He's worn out."

Cress looked at Mr. Cornelius. His eyes were closed but he opened them at Mrs. Cornelius' words and made a good-by flicker with the lids.

"Good night," Cress said.

Mrs. Cornelius went to the door with her. "We'll count on you," she said once again and put a hand on Cress's shoulder and gave her a kind of humorous loving shake before she turned away.

Cress flew to the car propelled, it seemed, by the beat of her heart as a bird is propelled by the beat of its wings. The walnut leaves were alive and fluttering in the warm air and all about her mockingbirds were singing like nightingales. As she emerged from the grove she saw the June stars big and heavy-looking like June roses. This is the happiest hour of my life, she thought, and she yearned to do something lovely for the girls, something beautiful and memorable; but all she could think of was to ask them to go to town for milk shakes.

"I could stand some food," Bernadine said, "after all that waiting."

"He was sick," Cress explained, "and Mrs. Cornelius and I had to take care of him."

"Mrs. Cornelius? Did she come out?"

"Of course," Cress answered. "Wouldn't you, if Howie was sick?"

Bernadine had no answer to this. She started the car and after they had gone a mile or so Jo asked, "Did you tell him?"

"Of course."

"Does he love you?" Bernadine asked.

Cress felt sorry for Bernadine. "You're a fine one to be getting married," she said. "Of course he doesn't. He loves Joyce."

"Joyce? Who's Joyce?"

"Mrs. Cornelius. I remind him some of her. I adore Mrs. Cornelius. She is like Mrs. Robert Louis Stevenson and *they* are one person. Mr. and Mrs. Cornelius, I mean. They are truly married. I don't suppose you understand," she said, arrogant with new knowledge, "but what is for the one is for the other. I am going to help her take care of him this summer. Isn't that wonderful? Maybe I can really help him get well. Isn't this the most gloriously beautiful night? Oh, I think it's the most significant night of my life." The two girls were silent, but Cress was too full of her own emotions to notice.

When they went into the soda fountain, she looked at their reflection in the mirror and liked what she saw. The three of them had always been proud of one another. Bernadine had glamour, Jo character, and Cress personality; that was the division they made of themselves. "Look at Bernadine, listen to Cress, and let Jo act," someone had said. Oh, but I've broken through that, Cress thought, I can act, too. She searched for some understanding of the part Mrs. Cornelius had played in that breakthrough. If she had said, "You wicked girl," or made her feel that loving was a terrible thing, would she have been pushed back, fearful, into the narrowness of dreaming, and into dreaming's untruths? She didn't know. She couldn't hold her mind to such abstractions.

"What we want," she said to Lester Riggins, the boy at the fountain, "is simply the most stupendous, colossal, overpowering concoction you ever served."

"This is a special night?" Lester asked.

"Super-special."

"How come?"

"Bernadine's going to be married."

"Known that for six months."

"Jo's been accepted for Stanford. With special praise."

"Old stuff."

"Then there's me."

"What about you?"

"I'm alive."

"That's different," Lester said. "Why didn't you tell me in the first place? How do you like it?"

"Being alive? Fine," said Cress. "Better than shooting stars."

"O.K., O.K.," Lester said. "This obviously merits the Riggins' special. Expense any issue?"

"No issue," Cress said.

He brought them something shaped, roughly, like the Eiffel Tower, but more dramatically colored.

"Here it is, girls. Here's to being alive!"

They sank their spoons in it and ate it down, their appetites equal to the whole of it, color, size, sweetness and multiplicity of ingredients.

Reading for Understanding

Main Idea

1. The main idea of the story can best be summarized by which of the following?
   (a) Teenage girls spend too much time on futile daydreaming.
   (b) What begins as a superficial attraction can deepen into a more mature love.
   (c) Cress's mother fails to understand her deepest needs.
   (d) Life is a challenge, difficult at best.

Details

2. Cress first saw Mr. Cornelius (a) in a school play (b) in a math class (c) in a supermarket (d) at a track meet.

3. The about-to-be married person is (a) Jo (b) Cress (c) Bernadine (d) Joyce.
4. Howie is (a) a groom-to-be (b) Mr. Cornelius's best friend (c) related to Mrs. Delahanty (d) loved by Jo.
5. Before the visit, Cress had spoken to Mr. Cornelius (a) once (b) twice (c) three times (d) frequently.
6. Mrs. Cornelius (a) scolded Cress for her foolishness (b) tended to be pessimistic about her husband's illness (c) expected Cress's visit (d) put Cress to work.
7. Cress was driven to the Cornelius house by (a) Bernardine (b) Jo (c) Mr. Delahanty (d) Mrs. Delahanty.

Inferences

8. At the dinner table, the girls didn't take part in the adults' conversation because (a) they were totally absorbed in their own interests (b) they were all excited about the coming marriage (c) Jo and Bernadine had all the latest information about Mr. Cornelius's illness (d) the evening was hot and stifling.
9. The one who may have understood Cress best was (a) Jo (b) Bernadine (c) Mrs. Delahanty (d) Mr. Delahanty.
10. Mr. Delahanty made a tactical error in (a) not allowing Cress to drive (b) criticising the custard pudding (c) blaming Mr. Cornelius for his serious plight (d) urging the girls to eat.
11. Joyce was able to take matters in stride because of (a) Cress's reputation as a good nurse (b) Mr. Cornelius's request (c) her downbeat attitude toward Mr. Cornelius (d) the maturity of her love for her husband.

Author's Attitude

12. The attitude of the author toward Cress's love is one of (a) amazement (b) sympathy (c) criticism (d) indifference.

Outcome

13. After the events in the story, Cress probably (a) followed through on her promise (b) went away on vacation (c) decided not to attend the coming wedding (d) had a disagreement with Mrs. Cornelius.

Order of Events

14. Arrange the items in the order in which they occurred. Use letters only.
    A. Cress enters the Cornelius house.
    B. Cress promises to help all summer.
    C. Cress blows up at her father.
    D. Mr. Delahanty mentions Mr. Cornelius's condition.
    E. Cress decides to visit Mr. Cornelius.

Fact or Opinion

Tell whether the following is a fact or an opinion.

15. Cress's infatuation with Mr. Cornelius was immature.

Words in Context

1. "She pulled the daisies from the neck of her halter and passed them from hand to hand *distractedly.*" **Distractedly** (287) means (a) absent-mindedly (b) anxiously (c) quickly (d) angrily.
2. "Sometimes in her dreams Mrs. Cornelius came to her and the *gist* of what she said was, 'My life with Mr. Cornelius has been a failure.' " **Gist** (288) means (a) substance (b) hope (c) heartbreak (d) disagreement.
3. "If, by chance, some experience was so absorbing as to momentarily *obscure* his image, she made up for it by living the whole scene through once again just for him." **Obscure** (288) means (a) enhance (b) replace (c) paint (d) conceal.
4. "She felt as if her mind, by an *infusion* of light and warmth, was being forced to expand to accommodate this new idea." **Infusion** (293) means (a) rejection (b) awareness (c) replacement (d) saturation.
5. "*Exhilaration* at being released from the isolation of her dreaming . . ." **Exhilaration** (294) means (a) irritation (b) surprise (c) negative arousal (d) joy.

Thinking Critically About the Story

1. Coming-of-age is a commonplace expression. Sometimes it has a legal force: "Upon the person's coming-of-age, he/she will become heir to the . . . fortune." Sometimes, it has a less material force: a turning point, a moment that starts a person on the road to maturity. "Mr. Cornelius, I Love You" is a story with a turning point. At the beginning of the story, Cress is a self-obsessed teenager, concerned only with her own life and feelings. At the end, she is becoming a mature young woman, realistically evaluating her own emotions and the emotions of those who surround her. The selfish self-centeredness has been replaced by something finer. At what point does the turning point occur? Explain.
2. Who, in your opinion, is the hero or heroine of the story? Why did you choose this person?
3. Is the relationship between Cress and her parents realistically portrayed? Give examples to prove your point.
4. The girls are alike in many ways, but also profoundly different. Choose Bernadine, Jo, or Cress and provide a thumbnail sketch of the one you choose.
5. Do some people enjoy misery? Though in good health, they rarely smile or take an upbeat attitude. What satisfaction does a feeling of gloom provide for such people?
6. What is Mr. Cornelius's attitude toward Cress?
7. Does Cress show the same attitudes as a modern groupie who is infatuated with a pop singer or other celebrity?
8. Is first love between two young people different from the crush that young people sometimes develop toward an adult? Explain.
9. The role of mental attitude in the treatment of disease is an oft-argued one. How do you feel? Is Mrs. Cornelius's approach to the illness a sound one? Explain.
10. "Cress was too full of her own emotions to notice." (295) Does this sentence suggest that Cress's road to maturity still stretches on? Is true maturity ever attained?
11. At one point, Jo says, "If puddings be the food of love, cook on." This is an adaptation of lines from Shakespeare's *Twelfth Night*. Is Jo showing off or merely joking? Explain.

Language in Action

When Sound Fits the Sense

Mrs. Cornelius, however, was continuing her laughing murmur to her husband.

If you close your eyes and whisper *murmur*, you will notice that the sound of the word *murmur* fits its definition. An oft-quoted pair of lines by Tennyson is a prime example of the marriage of sound and sense:

The moan of doves in immemorial elms,
And murmuring of innumerable bees.

Moan, immemorial, murmuring, innumerable—all the words provide music as well as meaning.

Onomatopoeia is the use of words that by their sounds imitate or suggest their meaning. (See also page 427.) You use onomatopoeia every time you say that soda *fizzes*, fire *crackles*, dishes *clatter*, a fly *buzzes*. Here's a sampling of other onomatopoeic words you use: *bang, boom, blubber, bubble, clank, click, crash, honk, hum, purr, rattle, snap, squeak, thud, twitter, zip, zoom.*

For those poets who would use the language effectively, Alexander Pope, 18th-century poet, has the following advice:

'Tis not enough no harshness gives offense,
The sound must seem an echo to the sense;
Soft is the strain when Zephyr gently blows,
And the smooth stream in smoother numbers flows;
But when the loud surges lash the sounding shore,
The hoarse, rough verse should like the torrent roar.

Contrast the soft, quiet tone of lines 3 and 4 with the roaring sound of lines 5 and 6.

An Independent Thinker

Mary Wilkins Freeman
American

When his mother escorted Esther to the door, as she took leave, there was a marked difference in her manner. "Come again, soon, Mis' Gay," he heard her say, "run up any time you feel like it, an' stay to tea. I'd really love to have you."

It's not *Romeo and Juliet.* This is a simple love story, with the principal characters drawn from a poor rural area, not the noble houses of Verona. Yet there is an eternal quality about a love threatened by parental disapproval. Mary Wilkins Freeman knew her subject well. She too had suffered from poverty and ill-health. This story captures the spoken rhythms, the desperation of poverty, and the prejudices that are not limited to the poor.

The major strand in the story is the heroism of Esther Gay, a frail old lady with the heart of a fighter and the determination of a military strategist. She is the "Independent Thinker" of the title, a woman of strong principles and unwavering adherence to her beliefs.

An Independent Thinker

ESTHER GAY'S HOUSE was little and square, and mounted on posts like stilts. A stair led up to the door on the left side. Morning-glories climbed up the stair-railing, the front of the house and the other side were covered with them, all the windows but one were curtained with the matted green vines. Esther sat at the uncurtained window, and knitted. She perked her thin, pale nose up in the air, her pointed chin tilted upward too; she held her knitting high, and the needles clicked loud, and shone in the sun. The bell was ringing for church, and a good many people were passing. They could look in on her, and see very plainly what she was doing. Every time a group went by she pursed her thin old lips tighter, and pointed up her nose higher, and knitted more fiercely. Her skinny shoulders jerked. She cast a sharp glance at every one who passed, but no one caught her looking. She knew them all. This was a little village. By and by the bell had stopped tolling, and even the late church-goers had creaked briskly out of sight. The street, which was narrow here, was still and vacant.

Presently a woman appeared in a little flower-garden in front of the opposite house. She was picking a nosegay. She was little and spare, and she bent over the flowers with a stiffness as of stiff wires. It seemed as if it would take mechanical force to spring her up again.

Esther watched her. "It's dretful hard work for her to git around," she muttered to herself.

Finally, she laid down her knitting and called across to her. "Laviny!" said she.

The woman came out to the gate with some marigolds and candytuft in her hand. Her dim blue eyes blinked in the light. She looked over and smiled with a sort of helpless inquiry.

"Come over here a minute."

"I—guess I—can't."

Esther was very deaf. She could not hear a word, but she saw the deprecating shake of the head, and she knew well enough.

"I'd like to know why you can't, a minute. You kin hear your mother the minute she speaks."

The woman glanced back at the house, then she looked over at Esther. Her streaked light hair hung in half-curls over her wide crocheted collar, she had a little, narrow, wrinkled face, but her cheeks were as red as roses.

"I guess I'd better not. It's Sunday, you know," said she. Her soft, timid voice could by no possibility reach those deaf ears across the way.

"What?"

"I—guess I'd better not—as long as it's *Sunday*."

Esther's strained attention caught the last word, and guessed at the rest from a knowledge of the speaker.

"Stuff," said she, with a sniff through her delicate, uptilted nostrils. "I'd like to know how much worse 't is for you to step over here a minute, an' tell me how *she* is when I can't hear across the road, than to stop an' talk comin' out o' meetin'; you'd do that quick enough. You're strainin', Laviny Dodge."

Lavinia, as if overwhelmed by the argument, cast one anxious glance back at the house, and came through the gate.

Just then a feeble, tremulous voice, with a wonderful quality of fine sharpness in it, broke forth behind her,

"Laviny, Laviny, where be you goin'? Come back here."

Lavinia, wheeling with such precipitate vigor that it suggested a creak, went up the path.

"I wa'n't goin' anywhere, mother," she called out. "What's the matter?"

"You can't pull the wool over my eyes. I *seed* you a-goin' out the gate."

Lavinia's mother was over ninety and bedridden. That infinitesimal face which had passed through the stages of beauty, commonplaceness, and hideousness, and now arrived at that of the fine grotesqueness which has, as well as beauty, a certain charm of its own, peered out from its great feather pillows. The skin on the pinched face was of a dark-yellow color, the eyes were like black points, the tiny, sunken mouth had a sardonic pucker.

"Esther just wanted me to come over there a minute. She wanted to ask after you," said Lavinia, standing beside the bed, holding her flowers.

"Hey?"

"She *jest* wanted me to come over an' tell her how you was."

"How I was?"

"Yes."

"Did you tell her I was miser'ble?"

"I didn't go, mother."

"I *seed* you a-goin' out the gate."

"I came back. She couldn't hear 'thout I went way over."

"Hey?"

"It's all right, mother," screamed Lavinia. Then she went about putting the flowers in water.

The old woman's little eyes followed her, with a sharp light like steel.

"I ain't goin' to hev you goin' over to Esther Gay's, Sabbath day," she went on, her thin voice rasping out from her pillows like a file. "She ain't no kind of a girl. Wa'nt she knittin'?"

"Yes."

"Hey?"

"Yes, she was knittin', mother."

"Wa'n't knittin'?"

"Y-e-s, she was."

"I knowed it. Stayin' home from meetin' an' knittin'. I ain't goin' to hev you over thar, Laviny."

Esther Gay, over in her window, held her knitting up higher, and knitted with fury. "H'm, the old lady called her back," said she. "If they want to show out they kin, I'm goin' to do what I think's right."

The morning-glories on the house were beautiful this morning, the purple and white and rosy ones stood out with a soft crispness. Esther Gay's house was not so pretty in winter—there was no paint on it, and some crooked outlines showed. It was a poor little structure, but Esther owned it free of encumbrances. She had also a pension of ninety-six dollars which served her for support. She considered herself well to do. There was not enough for anything besides necessaries, but Esther was one who had always looked upon necessaries as luxuries. Her sharp eyes saw the farthest worth of things. When she bought a half-cord of pine wood with an allotment of her pension-money, she saw in a vision all the warmth and utility which could ever come from it. When it was heaped up in the space under the house which she used for a woodshed, she used to go and look at it.

"Esther Gay does think so much of her own things," people said.

That little house, which, with its precipitous stair and festoons of morning-glories, had something of a foreign picturesqueness, looked to her like a real palace. She paid a higher tax upon it than she should have done. A lesser one had been levied, and regarded by her as an insult. "My house is worth more'n that," she had told the assessor with an indignant bridle. She paid the increased tax with cheerful pride, and frequently spoke of it. Today she often glanced from her knitting around the room. There was a certain beauty in it, although it was hardly the one which she recognized. It was full of a lovely, wavering, gold-green light, and there was a fine order and cleanness which gave a sense of peace. But Esther saw mainly her striped rag-carpet, her formally set chairs, her lounge covered with Brussels, and her shining cooking-stove.

Still she looked at nothing with the delight with which she surveyed her granddaughter Hatty, when she returned from church.

"Well, you've got home, ain't you?" she said, when the young, slim girl, with her pale, sharp face, which was like her grandmother's, stood before her. Hatty in her meeting-gown of light-brown delaine, and her white meeting-hat trimmed with light-brown ribbons and blue flowers was not pretty, but the old woman admired her.

"Yes," said Hatty. Then she went into her little bedroom to take off her things. There was a slow shyness about her. She never talked much, even to her grandmother.

"You kin git you somethin' to eat, if you want it," said the old woman. "I don't want to stop myself till I git this heel done. Was Henry to meetin'?"

"Yes."

"His father an' mother?"

"Yes."

Henry was the young man who had been paying attention to Hatty. Her grandmother was proud and pleased; she liked him.

Hatty generally went to church Sunday evenings, and the young man escorted her home, and came in and made a call. Tonight the girl did not go to church as usual. Esther was astonished.

"Why, ain't you goin' to meetin'?" said she.

"No; I guess not."

"Why? why not?"

"I thought I wouldn't."

The old woman looked at her sharply. The tea-things were cleared away, and she was at her knitting again, a little lamp at her elbow.

Presently Hatty went out, and sat at the head of the stairs, in the twilight. She sat there by herself until meeting was over, and the people had been straggling by for some time. Then she went downstairs, and joined a young man who passed at the foot of them. She was gone half an hour.

"Where hev you been?" asked her grandmother, when she returned.

"I went out a little way."

"Who with?"

"Henry."

"Why didn't he come in?"

"He thought he wouldn't."

"I don't see why."

Hatty said nothing. She lit her candle to go to bed. Her little thin face was imperturbable.

She worked in a shop, and earned a little money. Her grandmother would not touch a dollar of it; what she did not need to spend for herself, she made her save. Lately the old woman had been considering the advisability of her taking a sum from the saving's bank to buy a silk dress. She thought she might need it soon.

Monday, she opened upon the subject. "Hatty," said she, "I've been thinkin'—don't you believe it would be a good plan for you to take a little of your money out of the bank an' buy you a nice dress?"

Hatty never answered quickly. She looked at her grandmother, then she kept on with her sewing. It was after supper, her shop-work was done, and she was sitting at the table with her needle. She seemed to be considering her grandmother's remark.

The old woman waited a moment, then she proceeded: "I've been thinkin'—you ain't never had any real nice dress, you know—that it would be a real good plan for you to take some money, now you've got it, an' buy you a silk one. You ain't never had one, an' you're old enough to."

Still Hatty sewed, and said nothing.

"You might want to go somewhar," continued Esther, "an'—well, of course, if anythin' should happen, if Henry—It's jest as well not to hev' to do everythin' all to once, an' it's consider'ble work to make a silk dress—Why don't you say somethin'?"

"I don't want any silk dress."

"I'd like to know why not?"

Hatty made no reply.

"Look here, Hatty, you an' Henry Little ain't had no trouble, hev' you?"

"I don't know as we have."

"Hatty Gay, I know there's somethin' the matter. Now you jest tell me what 'tis. Ain't he comin' here no more?"

Suddenly the girl curved her arm around on the table, and laid her face down on it. She would not speak another word. She did not seem to be crying, but she sat there, hiding her little plain, uncommunicative face.

"Hatty Gay, ain't he comin'? *Why* ain't he comin'?"

Hatty would give the old woman no information. All she got was that obtained from ensuing events. Henry Little did not come; she ascertained that. The weeks went on, and he had never once climbed those vine-wreathed stairs to see Hatty.

Esther fretted and questioned. One day, in the midst of her nervous conjectures, she struck the chord in Hatty which vibrated with information.

"I hope you want too forrard with Henry, Hatty," Said the old woman. "You didn't act too anxious arter him, did you? That's apt to turn fellows."

Then Hatty spoke. Some pink spots flared out on her quiet, pale cheeks.

"Grandma," said she, "I'll tell you, if you want to know, what the trouble is. I wasn't goin' to, because I didn't want to make you feel bad;

but, if you're goin' to throw out such things as that to me, I don't care. Henry's mother don't like you, there!"

"What?"

"Henry's mother don't like you."

"Don't like me?"

"No."

"Why, what hev I done? I don't see what you mean, Hatty Gay."

"Grace Porter told me. Mrs. Little told her mother. Then I asked him, an' he owned up it was so."

"I'd like to know what she said."

Hatty went on, pitilessly, "She told Grace's mother she didn't want her son to marry into the Gay tribe anyhow. She didn't think much of 'em. She said any girl whose folks didn't keep Sunday, an' stayed away from meetin' an worked, wouldn't amount to much."

"I don't believe she said it."

"She did. Henry said his mother took on so he was afraid she'd die, if he didn't give it up."

Esther sat up straight. She seemed to bristle out suddenly with points, from her knitting-needles to her sharp elbows and thin chin and nose. "Well, he kin give it up then, if he wants to, for all me. I ain't goin' to give up my principles fir him, nor any of his folks, an' they'll find it out. You kin git somebody else jest as good as he is."

"I don't want anybody else."

"H'm, you needn't have 'em then, ef you ain't got no more sperit. I shouldn't think you'd want your grandmother to give up doin' what's right yourself, Hatty Gay."

"I ain't sure it is right."

"Ain't sure it's right. Then I s'pose you think it would be better for an old woman that's stone deaf, an' can't hear a word of the preachin', to go to meetin' an' set there, doin' nothin' two hours, instead of stayin' to home an' knittin', to airn a leetle money to give to the Lord. All I've got to say is, you kin think so, then. I'm a-goin' to do what's right, no matter what happens."

Hatty said nothing more. She took up her sewing again; her grandmother kept glancing at her. Finally she said, in a mollifying voice, "Why don't you go an' git you a leetle piece of cake in the cupboard; you didn't eat no supper hardly."

"I don't want any."

"Well, if you want to make yourself sick, an' go without eatin', you kin."

Hatty did go without eating much through the following weeks. She laid awake nights, too, staring pitifully into the darkness, but she did not make herself ill. There was an unflinching strength in that little, meagre body, which lay even back of her own will. It would take long for her lack of spirit to break her down entirely; but her grandmother did not know that. She watched her and worried. Still she had not the least idea of giving in. She knitted more zealously than ever Sundays; indeed, there was, to her possibly distorted perceptions, a religious zeal in it.

She knitted on week-days too. She reeled off a good many pairs of those reliable blue-yarn stockings, and sold them to a dealer in the city. She gave away every cent which she earned, and carefully concealed the direction of her giving. Even Hatty did not know of it.

Six weeks after Hatty's lover left, the old woman across the way died. After the funeral, when measures were taken for the settlement of the estate, it was discovered that all the little property was gone, eaten up by a mortgage and the interest. The two old women had lived upon the small house and the few acres of land for the last ten years, ever since Lavinia's father had died. He had grubbed away in a boot-shop, and earned enough for their frugal support as long as he lived. Lavinia had never been able to work for her own living; she was not now. "Laviny Dodge will have to go to the poorhouse," everybody said.

One noon Hatty spoke of it to her grandmother. She rarely spoke of anything now, but this was uncommon news.

"They say Laviny Dodge has got to go to the poorhouse," said she.

"What?"

"They say Laviny Dodge has got to go to the poorhouse."

"I don't believe a word on't."

"They say it's so."

That afternoon Esther went over to ascertain the truth of the report for herself. She found Lavinia sitting alone in the kitchen crying. Esther went right in, and stood looking at her.

"It's so, ain't it?" said she.

Lavinia started. There was a momentary glimpse of a red, distorted face; then she hid it again, and went on rocking herself to and fro and sobbing. She had seated herself in the rocking-chair to weep. "Yes," she wailed, "it's so! I've got to go. Mr. Barnes come in, an' said I had this mornin', there ain't no other way. I've—got—to go. Oh, what would mother have said!"

Esther stood still, looking. "A place gits run out afore you know it," she remarked.

"Oh, I didn't s'pose it was quite so near gone. I thought mebbe I could stay—as long as I lived."

"You'd oughter hev kept account."

"I s'pose I hed, but I never knew much 'bout money-matters, an' poor mother, she was too old. Father was real sharp, ef he'd lived. Oh, I've got to go! I never thought it would come to this!"

"I don't think you're fit to do any work."

"No; they say I ain't. My rheumatism has been worse lately. It's been hard work for me to crawl round an' wait on mother. I've got to go. Oh, Esther, it's awful to think I can't die in my own home. Now I've got—to die in the poorhouse! I've—got—to die in the poorhouse!"

"I've got to go now," said Esther.

"Don't go. You ain't but jest come. I ain't got a soul to speak to."

"I'll come in agin arter supper," said Esther, and went out resolutely, with Lavinia wailing after her to come back. At home, she sat down and deliberated. She had a long talk with Hatty when she returned. "I don't care," was all she could get out of the girl, who was more silent than usual. She ate very little supper.

It was eight o'clock when Esther went over to the Dodge house. The windows were all dark. "Land, I believe she's gone to bed," said the old woman, fumbling along through the yard. The door was fast, so she knocked. "Laviny, Laviny, be you gone to bed? Laviny Dodge!"

"Who is it?" said a quavering voice on the other side, presently.

"It's me. You gone to bed?"

"It's you, Mis' Gay, ain't it?"

"Yes. Let me in. I want to see you a minute."

Then Lavinia opened the door and stood there, her old knees knocking together with cold and nervousness. She had got out of bed and put a plaid shawl over her shoulders when she heard Esther.

"I want to come in jest a minute," said Esther. "I hadn't any idee you'd be gone to bed."

The fire had gone out, and it was chilly in the kitchen, where the two women sat down.

"You'll ketch your death of cold in your night-gown," said Esther. "You'd better git somethin' more to put over you."

"I don't keer if I do ketch cold," said Lavinia, with an air of feeble recklessness, which sat oddly upon her.

"Laviny Dodge, don't talk so."

"I don't keer. I'd ruther ketch my death of cold than not; then I shouldn't have to die in the poorhouse." The old head, in its little cotton night-cap, cocked itself sideways, with pitiful bravado.

Esther rose, went into the bedroom, got a quilt and put it over Lavinia's knees. "There," said she, "you hev that over you. There ain't no sense in your talkin' that way. You're jest a-flyin' in the face of Providence, an' Providence don't mind the little flappin' you kin make, any more than a barn does a swaller."

"I can't help it."

"What?"

"I—can't help it."

"Yes, you kin help it, too. Now, I'll tell you what I've come over here for. I've been thinkin' on't all the arternoon, an' I've made up my mind. I want you to come over and live with me."

Lavinia sat feebly staring at her. "Live with you!"

"Yes. I've got my house an' my pension, an' I pick up some with my knittin'. Two won't cost much more'n one. I reckon we kin git along well enough."

Lavinia said nothing, she still sat staring. She looked scared.

Esther began to feel hurt. "Mebbe you don't want to come," she said, stiffly, at last.

Lavinia shivered. "There's jest—one thing—" she commenced.

"What?"

"There's jest one thing—"

"What's that?"

"I dunno what—Mother—You're real good; but—Oh, I don't see how I kin come, Esther!"

"Why not? If there's any reason why you don't want to live with me, I want to know what 'tis."

Lavinia was crying. "I can't tell you," she sobbed; "but, mother—If—you didn't work Sundays. Oh!"

"Then you mean to say you'd ruther go to the poorhouse than come to live with me, Lavinia Dodge?"

"I—can't help it."

"Then, all I've got to say is, you kin go."

Esther went home, and said no more. In a few days she, peering around her curtain, saw poor Lavinia Dodge, a little, trembling, shivering figure, hoisted into the poorhouse covered wagon, and driven off. After the wagon was out of sight, she sat down and cried.

It was early in the afternoon. Hatty had just gone to her work, having scarcely tasted her dinner. Her grandmother had worked hard to get an extra one today, too, but she had no heart to eat. Her mournful silence, which seemed almost obstinate, made the old woman at once angry and wretched. Now she wept over Lavinia Dodge and Hatty, and the two causes combined made bitter tears.

"I wish to the land" she cried out loud once—"I wish to the land I could find some excuse; but I ain't goin' to give up what I think's right."

Esther Gay had never been so miserable in her life as she was for the three months after Lavinia Dodge left her home. She thought of her, she watched Hatty, and she knitted. Hatty was at last beginning to show the effects of her long worry. She looked badly, and the neighbors began speaking about it to her grandmother. The old woman seemed to resent it when they did. At times she scolded the girl, at times she tried to pet her, and she knitted constantly, weekdays and Sundays.

Lavinia had been in the almshouse three months, when one of the neighbors came in one day and told Esther that she was confined to her bed. Her rheumatism was worse, and she was helpless. Esther dropped her knitting, and stared radiantly at the neighbor. "You said she was an awful sight of trouble, didn't you?" said she.

"Yes; Mis' Marvin said it was worse than takin' care of a baby."

"I should think it would take about all of anybody's time."

"I should. Why, Esther Gay, you look real tickled 'cause she's sick!" cried the woman, bluntly.

Esther colored. "You talk pretty," said she.

"Well, I don't care; you looked so. I don't s'pose you was," said the other, apologetically.

That afternoon Esther Gay made two visits: one at the selectmen's room, in the town-hall, the other at Henry Little's. One of her errands at the selectmen's room was concerning the reduction of her taxes.

"I'm a-payin' too much on that leetle house," said she, standing up, alert and defiant. "It ain't wuth it." There was some dickering, but she gained her point. Poor Esther Gay would never make again her foolish little boast about her large tax. More than all her patient, toilsome knitting was the sacrifice of this bit of harmless vanity.

When she arrived at the Littles', Henry was out in the yard. He was very young; his innocent, awkward face flushed when he saw Esther coming up the path.

"Good afternoon," said she. Henry jerked his head.

"Your mother to home?"

"Ye—s."

Esther advanced and knocked, while Henry stood staring.

Presently Mrs. Little answered the knock. She was a large woman. The astonished young man saw his mother turn red, in the face, and rear herself in order of battle, as it were, when she saw who her caller was; then he heard Esther speak.

"I'm a-comin' right to the p'int afore I come in," said she. "I've heard you said you didn't want your son to marry my granddaughter because you didn't like some things about me. Now, I want to know if you said it."

"Yes; I did," replied Mrs. Little, tremulous with agitation, red, and perspiring, but not weakening.

"Then you didn't have nothin' again' Hatty, you nor Henry? Twa'n't an excuse?"

"I ain't never had anything against the girl."

"Then I want to come in a minute. I've got somethin' I want to say to you, Mrs. Little."

"Well, you can come in—if you want to."

After Esther had entered, Henry stood looking wistfully at the windows. It seemed to him that he could not wait to know the reason of Esther's visit. He took things more soberly than Hatty; he had not lost his meals nor his sleep; still he had suffered. He was very fond of the girl, and he had a heart which was not easily diverted. It was hardly possible that he would ever die of grief, but it was quite possible that he might live long with a memory, young as he was.

When his mother escorted Esther to the door, as she took leave, there was a marked difference in her manner. "Come again soon, Mis' Gay," he heard her say; "run up any time you feel like it, an' stay to tea. I'd really like to have you."

"Thank ye," said Esther, as she went down the steps. She had an aspect of sweetness about her which did not seem to mix well with herself.

When she reached home she found Hatty lying on the lounge. "How do you feel to-night?" said she, unpinning her shawl.

"Pretty well."

"You'd better go an' brush your hair an' change your dress. I've been over to Henry's an' seen his mother, an' I shouldn't wonder if he was over here to-night."

Hatty sat bolt upright and looked at her grandmother. "What do you mean?"

"What I say. I've been over to Mrs. Little's, an' we've had a talk. I guess she thought she'd been kind of silly to make such a fuss. I reasoned with her, an' I guess she saw I'd been more right about some things than she'd thought for. An' as far as goin' to meetin' an' knittin' Sundays is concerned—Well, I don't s'pose I kin knit any more if I want to. I've been to see about it, an' Laviny Dodge is comin' here Saturday, an' she's so bad with her rheumatiz that she can't move, an' I guess it'll be all I kin do to wait on her, without doin' much knittin'. Mebbe I kin git a few minutes evenin's, but I reckon 't won't amount to much. Of course I couldn't go to meetin' if I wanted to. I couldn't leave Laviny."

"Did she say he—was coming?"

"Yes; she said she shouldn't wonder if he was up."

The young man did come that evening, and Esther retired to her little bedroom early, and lay listening happily to the soft murmur of voices outside. Lavinia Dodge arrived Saturday. The next morning, when Hatty had gone to church, she called Esther. "I want to speak to you a minute," said she. "I want to know if—Mr. Winter brought me over, and he married the Ball girl that's been in the post-office, you know, and somethin' he said—Esther Gay, I want to know if you're the one that's been sendin' that money to me and mother all along?"

Esther colored, and turned to go. "I don't see why you think it's me."

"Esther, don't you go. I know 'twas; you can't say 'twa'n't."

"It wa'n't much, anyhow."

"'T was to us. It kept us goin' a good while longer. We never said anythin' about it. Mother was awful proud, you know, but I dunno what we should have done. Esther, how could you do it?"

"Oh, it wa'n't anythin'. It was extra money. I airn'd it."

"Knittin'?"

Esther jerked her head defiantly. The sick woman began to cry. "If I'd ha' known, I would ha' come. I wouldn't have said a word."

"Yes, you would, too. You was bound to stan' up for what you thought was right, jest as much as I was. Now, we've both stood up, an' it's right. Don't you fret no more about it."

"To think—"

"Land sakes, don't cry. The tea's all steeped, and I'm goin' to bring you in a cup now."

Henry came that evening. About nine o'clock Esther got a pitcher and went down to the well to draw some water for the invalid. Her old joints were so tired and stiff that she could scarcely move. She had had a hard day. After she had filled her pitcher she stood resting for a moment, staring up at the bright sitting-room windows. Henry and Hatty were in there: just a simple, awkward young pair, with nothing beautiful about them, save the spark of eternal nature, which had its own light. But they sat up stiffly and timidly in their two chairs, looking at each other with full content. They had glanced solemnly and bashfully at Esther when she passed through the room; she appeared not to see them.

Standing at the well, looking up at the windows, she chuckled softly to herself. "It's all settled right," said she, "an' there don't none of 'em suspect that I'm a-carryin' out my p'int arter all."

Reading for Understanding

Main Idea

1. Which of the following proverbial expressions best sums up the main idea of the story?
   (a) What is learned in the cradle lasts to the grave.
   (b) A thousand-mile trip begins with a single step.
   (c) Better poor with honor than rich with shame.
   (d) There are many ways of skinning a cat.

Details

2. "The woman came to the gate with some marigolds and candytuft in her hands." The woman is (a) Esther Gay (b) Lavinia (c) Mrs. Little (d) Hatty.
3. The major obstacle facing the young lovers was (a) Mrs. Little's opinion of Esther (b) the death of Mrs. Dodge (c) Esther's disapproval (d) Henry's indifference.
4. "Just then a feeble, tremulous voice, with a wonderful quality of fine sharpness in it, broke forth behind her." The voice belonged to (a) Mrs. Dodge (b) Lavinia (c) Mrs. Hill (d) Esther.
5. The townspeople thought that Esther was (a) too religious (b) stuck-up (c) insane (d) secretly rich.
6. Hatty's income came from (a) a legacy (b) a maiden aunt (c) Henry (d) a shop.
7. Hatty was (a) a natural beauty (b) loquacious (c) plain-looking (d) wasteful.
8. Esther thought that going to the church meeting would be fruitless because of her (a) dislike of the preacher (b) arthritis (c) deafness (d) small financial contribution.

Inferences

9. Which of the following quotations is the best key to Esther's character?
   (a) "You can git somebody else jest as good as he is."
   (b) "I'm goin' to do what I think's right."
   (c) "What hev I done? I don't see what you mean, Hatty Gay."
   (d) "Well, you've got home, ain't you?"
10. Mrs. Hill's objection to Hatty as a match for her son Henry was based on (a) Hatty's work (b) Esther's failure to attend church (c) bad reports given her by Lavinia (d) Esther's snubbing her on the street.
11. Mrs. Hill's change of heart toward Esther was probably brought about by (a) Esther's promise to attend church regularly (b) Esther's explanation of her reasons for her actions (c) Esther's promise never to knit again (d) Hatty's willingness to stop working.

Fact or Opinion

Tell whether the following is a fact or an opinion.

12. Esther persisted in her desire to have Lavinia come to live with her.

Words in Context

1. "She could not hear a word, but she saw the *deprecating* shake of the head, and she knew well enough." **Deprecating** (302) means (a) disapproving (b) uncertain (c) vigorous (d) tentative.

2. "Just then a feeble, *tremulous* voice, with the wonderful quality of fine sharpness in it, broke forth behind her." **Tremulous** (303) means (a) quivering (b) melodic (c) harsh (d) questioning.

3. "Lavinia, wheeling with such *precipitate* vigor that it suggested a creak, went up the path." **Precipitate** (303) means (a) resounding (b) unexpected (c) daring (d) hasty.

4. "That *infinitesimal* face which had passed through the stages of beauty, commonplaceness, and hideousness...peered out from its great feather pillows." **Infinitesimal** (303) means (a) very large (b) very small (c) soft (d) unyielding.

5. "The skin on the pinched face was of a dark-yellow color, the eyes were like black points, the tiny, sunken mouth had a *sardonic* pucker. **Sardonic** (303) means (a) scornful (b) leaden (c) cruel (d) greedy.

6. "Esther owned it free of *encumbrances*." **Encumbrances** (304) are (a) obstructions (b) taxes (c) partnership interests (d) unpleasant neighbors.

7., 8. "That little house, which with its *precipitous* stair and *festoons* of morning glories, had something of a foreign picturesqueness, looked to her like a real palace." **Precipitous** (304) means (a) twisting (b) narrow (c) uneven (d) steep. **Festoons** (304) are (a) knotted vines (b) garlands (c) paintings (d) images.

9. "Her thin little face was *imperturbable*. **Imperturbable** (305) means (a) calm (b) puzzling (c) revealing (d) unpleasant.

10. "All that she got was obtained from *ensuing* events." **Ensuing** (306) means (a) well-advertised (b) serious (c) unexpected (d) following

11. "Henry Little did not come; she *ascertained* that. **Ascertained** (306) means (a) regretted (b) denied (c) found out (d) doubted.

Thinking Critically About the Story

1. This is a love story between Hatty and Henry, two young lovers, but it is also the depiction of another kind of love. How does Esther demonstrate this mature love?
2. How does the description of Esther's house provide a clue to her character?
3. As the people passed by on their way to church, why did Esther pretend not to see them?
4. How does the dialogue between Lavinia and her mother lay bare the old woman's prejudices? How does the last sentence of that dialogue summarize the problem faced by Esther Gay?
5. Esther's knitting on Sundays affected her reputation in the community, but it also almost destroyed the love affair between Hatty and Henry, and affected her relationship with Lavinia. How did Esther's use of the payment for the knitting justify her obstinacy about not going to church?
6. "The skin on the pinched face was of a dark-yellow color, the eyes were like black points, the sunken mouth had a sardonic pucker." This brilliant, concise description is not the only brilliant bit of observation. Point out at least two others.
7. "Esther was one who had always looked upon necessaries as luxuries." What does this observation tell about Esther?
8. How did Lavinia's acceptance of her mother's values prevent her from moving in with Esther at first?
9. How is dating today different from the courtship of Hatty and Henry? How does their behavior suggest a different time?

Language in Action

Dialect

"It's dretful hard work for her to git around."

Esther's first words tells us that we are in a special time and place where standard English is not spoken by the principal characters. The dialogue is peppered with expressions not heard on national television news programs, except in regional reports: *kin* for *can*, *seed* for *saw*, *agoin'* for *going*, *git* for *get*. Some might observe disparagingly that Esther speaks a "dialect," as if her speech were in some way ineffective.

Dialect is a tricky term. To a linguist, a dialect is a specific form of a language, usually geographically determined, which sets it off from the standard or literary form. The word does not necessarily denote a negative form of communication. The Southern dialect is not inferior to the standard. It *is* different, but the difference lends color to language. Of course, certain situations demand an awareness of the differences. In a sense, everyone speaks a "dialect," whether it is the speech of the Midwestern Heartland or the commands of a Maine sea captain.

Esther's speech also raises the issue of levels of usage (506–507). In some situations, Esther's grammatical errors would be a drawback, but in her own little world, she does just fine. Did you notice that Hatty, who has probably had more schooling than her grandmother, speaks more grammatically correct English? She does use *don't* for *doesn't*, but her speech is closer to standard English than Esther's.

Feuille d'Album

Katherine Mansfield
British

Don't let the title frighten you. It means *Album Leaf* or *Page* and suggests a series of snapshots. Here, the events center on Ian French, a desperately shy painter. Not unattractive, he arouses the interest of many women, but French is blind to their charms. Then, one day, he sees, across the way, **the** girl. French romanticizes his neighbor and devises ways to meet her. He sometimes despairs, but he keeps hoping. Then one day he has an opportunity. How he chooses to meet the girl is one of the strangest meetings in literature.

Feuille d'Album

HE REALLY WAS an impossible person. Too shy altogether. With absolutely nothing to say for himself. And such a weight. Once he was in your studio he never knew when to go, but would sit on and on until you nearly screamed, and burned to throw something enormous after him when he did finally blush his way out—something like the tortoise stove. The strange thing was that at first sight he looked most interesting. Everybody agreed about that. You would drift into the café one evening and there you would see, sitting in a corner, with a glass of coffee in front of him, a thin, dark boy, wearing a blue jersey with a little grey flannel jacket buttoned over it. And somehow that blue jersey and the grey jacket with the sleeves that were too short gave him the air of a boy that has made up his mind to run away to sea. Who has run away, in fact, and will get up in a moment and sling a knotted handkerchief containing his nightshirt and his mother's picture on the end of a stick, and walk out into the night and be drowned. . . . Stumble over the wharf edge on his way to the ship, even. . . . He had black close-cropped hair, grey eyes with long lashes, white cheeks and a mouth pouting as though he were determined not to cry. . . . How could one resist him? Oh, one's heart was wrung at sight. And, as if that were not enough, there was his trick of blushing. . . . Whenever the waiter came near him he turned crimson—he might have been just out of prison and the waiter in the know. . . .

"Who is he, my dear? Do you know?"

"Yes. His name is Ian French. Painter. Awfully clever, they say. Someone started by giving him a mother's tender care. She asked him how often he heard from home, whether he had enough blankets on his bed, how much milk he drank a day. But when she went round to his studio to give an eye to his socks, she rang and rang, and though she could have sworn she heard someone breathing inside, the door was not answered. . . . Hopeless!"

Someone else decided that he ought to fall in love. She summoned him to her side, called him "boy," leaned over him so that he might smell the enchanting perfume of her hair, took his arm, told him how marvellous life could be if one only had the courage, and went round to his studio one evening and rang and rang. . . . Hopeless.

"What the poor boy really wants is thoroughly rousing," said a third. So off they went to cafés and cabarets, little dances, places where you drank something that tasted like tinned apricot juice, but cost twenty-seven shillings a bottle and was called champagne, other places, too thrilling for words, where you sat in the most awful gloom, and where someone had always been shot the night before. But he did not turn a hair. Only once he got very drunk, but instead of blossoming forth, there he sat, stony, with two spots of red on his cheeks, like, my dear, yes, the dead image of that ragtime thing they were playing, like a "Broken Doll." But when she took him back to his studio he had quite recovered, and said "good night" to her in the street below, as though they had walked home from church together. . . . Hopeless.

After heaven knows how many more attempts—for the spirit of kindness dies very hard in women—they gave him up. Of course, they were still perfectly charming, and asked him to their shows, and spoke to him in the cafe, but that was all. When one is an artist one has no time simply for people who won't respond. Has one?

"And besides I really think there must be something rather fishy somewhere. . . . don't you? It can't all be as innocent as it looks! Why come to Paris if you want to be a daisy in the field? No, I'm not suspicious. But——"

He lived at the top of a tall mournful building overlooking the river. One of those buildings that look so romantic on rainy nights and moonlight nights, when the shutters are shut, and the heavy door, and the sign advertising "a little apartment to let immediately" gleams forlorn beyond words. One of those buildings that smell so unromantic all the year round, and where the concierge[1] lives in a glass cage on the ground floor, wrapped up in a filthy shawl, stirring something in a saucepan and ladling out tit-bits to the swollen old dog lolling on a bed cushion. . . . Perched up in the air the studio had a wonderful view. The two big windows faced the water; he could see the boats and the barges swinging up and down, and the fringe of an island planted with trees, like a round bouquet. The side window looked across to another house, shabbier still and smaller, and down below there was a flower market. You could see the tops of huge umbrellas, with frills of bright flowers escaping from them, booths covered with striped awning where they sold plants in boxes and clumps of wet gleaming palms in terra cotta jars. Among the flowers the old women scuttled from side to side like crabs. Really there was no need for him to go out. If he sat at the window until his white beard fell over the sill he still would have found something to draw. . . .

How surprised those tender women would have been if they had managed to force the door. For he kept his studio as neat as a pin. Everything was arranged to form a pattern, a little "still life" as it were—the saucepans with their lids on the wall behind the gas stove, the bowl of eggs, milk jug and teapot on the shelf, the books and the lamp with the crinkly paper shade on the table. An Indian curtain that had a fringe of red leopards marching round it covered his bed by day, and on the wall beside the bed on a level with your eyes when you were lying down there was a small neatly printed notice: GET UP AT ONCE.

Every day was much the same. While the light was good he slaved at his painting, then cooked his meals and tidied up the place. And in the evenings he went off to the café, or sat at home reading or making out the most complicated list of expenses headed: "What I ought to be able to do it on," and ending with a sworn statement . . . . "I swear not to exceed this amount for next month. Signed, Ian French."

Nothing very fishy about this; but those far-seeing women were quite right. It wasn't all.

One evening he was sitting at the side window eating some prunes and throwing the stones on to the tops of the huge umbrellas in the deserted flower market. It had been raining—the first real spring rain of the year had fallen—a bright spangle hung on everything, and the air smelled of buds and moist earth. Many voices sounding languid and content rang out in the dusky air, and the people who had come to close their windows and fasten the shutters leaned out instead. Down below in the market the trees were peppered with new green. What kind of trees were they? he wondered. And now came the lamplighter. He stared at the house across the way, the small, shabby house, and suddenly, as if in an-

[1]building superintendent

swer to his gaze, two wings of windows opened and a girl came out on to the tiny balcony carrying a pot of daffodils. She was a strangely thin girl in a dark pinafore, with a pink handkerchief tied over her hair. Her sleeves were rolled up almost to her shoulders and her slender arms shone against the dark stuff.

"Yes, it is quite warm enough. It will do them good," she said, putting down the pot and turning to someone in the room inside. As she turned she put her hands up to the handkerchief and tucked away some wisps of hair. She looked down at the deserted market and up at the sky, but where he sat there might have been a hollow in the air. She simply did not see the house opposite. And then she disappeared.

His heart fell out of the side window of his studio, and down to the balcony of the house opposite—buried itself in the pot of daffodils under the half-opened buds and spears of green. . . . That room with the balcony was the sitting-room, and the one next door to it was the kitchen. He heard the clatter of the dishes as she washed up after supper, and then she came to the window, knocked a little mop against the ledge, and hung it on a nail to dry. She never sang or unbraided her hair, or held out her arms to the moon as young girls are supposed to do. And she always wore the same dark pinafore and the pink handkerchief over her hair. . . . Whom did she live with? Nobody else came to those two windows, and yet she was always talking to some one in the room. Her mother, he decided, was an invalid. They took in sewing. The father was dead. . . . He had been a journalist—very pale, with long moustaches, and a piece of black hair falling over his forehead.

By working all day they just made enough money to live on, but they never went out and they had no friends. Now when he sat down at his table he had to make an entirely new set of sworn statements. . . . Not to go to the side window before a certain hour: signed, Ian French. Not to think about her until he had put away his painting things for the day: signed, Ian French.

It was quite simple. She was the only person he really wanted to know, because she was, he decided, the only other person alive who was just his age. He couldn't stand giggling girls, and he had no use for grown-up women. . . . She was his age, she was—well, just like him. He sat in his dusky studio, tired, with one arm hanging over the back of his chair, staring in at her window and seeing himself in there with her. She had a violent temper; they quarrelled terribly at times, he and she. She had a way of stamping her foot and twisting her hands in her pinafore. . . . furious. And she very rarely laughed. Only when she told him about an absurd little kitten she once had who used to roar and pretend to be a lion when it was given meat to eat. Things like that made her laugh. . . . But as a rule they sat together very quietly; he, just as he was sitting now, and she with her hands folded in her lap and her feet tucked under, talking in low tones, or silent and tired after the day's work. Of course, she never asked him about his pictures, and of course he made the most wonderful drawings of her which she hated, because he made her so thin and so dark. . . . But how could he get to know her? This might go on for years. . . .

Then he discovered that once a week, in the evenings, she went out shopping. On two successive Thursdays she came to the window wearing an old-fashioned cape over the pinafore, and carrying a basket. From where he sat he could not see the door of her house, but on the next Thursday evening at the same time he snatched up his cap and ran down the stairs. There was a lovely pink light over everything. He saw it glowing in the river, and the people walking towards him had pink faces and pink hands.

He leaned against the side of his house waiting for her and he had no idea of what he was going to do or say. "Here she comes," said a voice in his head. She walked very quickly, with small, light steps; with one hand she carried the basket, with the other she kept the cape together. . . . What could he do? He could only follow. . . . First she went into the grocer's and spent a long time in there, and then she went into the butcher's where she had to wait her turn. Then she was an age at the draper's matching something, and then she went to the fruit shop and bought a lemon. As he watched her he knew more surely than ever he must get to know her, now. Her composure, her seriousness and her loneliness, the very way she walked as though she was eager to be done with this world of grown-ups all was so natural to him and so inevitable.

"Yes, she is always like that," he thought proudly. "We have nothing to do with these people."

But now she was on her way home and he was as far off as ever. . . . She suddenly turned into the dairy and he saw her through the window buying an egg. She picked it out of the basket with such care—a brown one, a beautifully shaped one, the one he would have chosen. And when she came out of the dairy he went in after her. In a moment he was out again, and following her past his house across the flower market, dodging among the huge umbrellas and treading on the fallen flowers and the round marks where the pots had stood. . . . Through her door he crept, and up the stairs after, taking care to tread in time with her so that she should not notice. Finally, she stopped on the landing, and took the key out of her purse. As she put it into the door he ran up and faced her.

Blushing more crimson than ever, but looking at her severely he said, almost angrily: "Excuse me, Mademoiselle, you dropped this."

And he handed her an egg.

Reading for Understanding

Main Idea

1. The main thread of the story is (a) advice on how to meet new people (b) the place of art in determining a man's personality (c) a man's attempt to overcome a desperate shyness (d) the negative side of neatness.

Details

2. French's appearance in the cafe reminded some customers of a (a) successful writer (b) seaman (c) waiter (d) sculptor.
3. The major attraction of French's apartment was its (a) spaciousness (b) convenience (c) closeness to transportation (d) view.
4. French did his painting mostly (a) in the morning (b) after dinner (c) at the cafe (d) on weekends.
5. In his daydreams, the girl (a) had an invalid mother (b) took in laundry (c) was a journalist (d) lived with her grandparents.
6. The girl's shopping trips occurred (a) on Tuesdays (b) when she was out of cheese (c) once a week (d) when she knew French would be at the store.

Inferences

7. French's appearance was (a) careless and unattractive (b) frightening (c) strange enough to cause constant scorn (d) pleasant enough to attract women.
8. The terrible quarrels described on page 321 occurred (a) at a cafe (b) in a daydream (c) after French gave his gift (d) over the girl's unchanging outfit.

Outcome

9. After receiving the gift, the girl probably (a) hadn't realized she had dropped the egg (b) gasped in astonishment (c) thanked French warmly (d) told French she had wanted to meet him.

Fact or Opinion

Tell whether the following is a fact or an opinion.

10. French was ridiculous in his associations with women.

Words in Context

1. "Among the flowers the old women *scuttled* from side to side, like crabs." **Scuttled** (320) means (a) shuffled (b) swayed (c) dipped (d) plodded.
2. "Many voices sounding *languid* and content rang out in the dusky air." **Languid** (320) means (a) forceful (b) bitter (c) loud (d) listless.
3. "Her *composure*, her seriousness and her loneliness, the very way she walked as though she was eager to be done with the world of grown-ups all was so natural to him and so inevitable." **Composure** (322) means (a) frailty (b) appearance (c) curiosity (d) poise.

Thinking Critically About the Story

1. What made various women show an interest in French? What killed that interest?
2. Probably, some of the women who took French under their wing were attractive, even beautiful. Yet the girl that French was attracted to was slender, plainly dressed, apparently not a great beauty. What was there about the girl that appealed to French? Are handsome men sometimes attracted to plain women? Are beautiful women sometimes attracted to plain men? How can such things be? Do movies and television sometimes present inaccurate pictures of man-woman relationships? Explain.
3. What might the girl think when presented with an egg she obviously hadn't dropped? Could the very absurdity have helped French's plan?
4. Does the egg gift suggest French's sense of humor or his desperation?
5. What does buying one egg suggest about the financial means of the girl?
6. What do French's daydreams about his hoped-for life with the girl tell about his personality?
7. Why did the author introduce such an absurd gift instead of a realistic gift like a loaf of bread?

8. Sometimes people fall in love with their idea of a person, rather than with a person. Is French's image of the girl likely to reflect the real person? Explain.

Language in Action

The French Contribution

"Feuille d'Album" is French. *Feuille,* the French word for *leaf, page,* has many relatives and ancestors. It is descended from the Latin *folium,* also leaf. The Middle French of centuries ago coined the word *trefeuil,* "Three leafed." The word passed into English as *trefoil,* a three-leafed plant—for example *clover.*

Many *leaf* roots came to English directly from Latin and not through the French. *Foliage,* a combination of *leaves,* is a good example. *Folio,* for *page number,* is another. Note that even in English, a page may be called a *leaf.* We may "*leaf* through a book," turning the pages.

A great many words have come to us through French—for example, *camouflage, chaperon, depot, debutante, fiancée, resume,* and *role.* Language is forever interesting and unpredictable. English has borrowed both *chauffeur* and *garage* from the French. Americans and the British are amusingly different in their pronunciations of these words. Americans use an American pronunciation for *chauffeur* and a French pronunciation for *garage.* The British do the opposite, using a British pronunciation for *garage* and a French pronunciation for *chauffeur.*

See also "The Norman Conquest" (page 559).

Raymond's Run

Toni Cade Bambara
American

"And I've got a roomful of ribbons and medals and awards. But what has Raymond got to call his own?"

"Raymond's Run" is not a story of high adventure, ghosts, or surprise endings. It takes place in an everyday part of Harlem, a section of New York City. The turf could be part of any community anywhere in the world. It is told by a young teenager with the unpleasant nickname of Squeaky. She is anything but a timid mouse.

Squeaky has learned to fight back hard and furious in the complex neighborhood in which she is growing up. Everyone seems ready to pick on her charge, her older brother Raymond who is not bright enough to take care of himself.

This is also a love story—not a romantic boy-girl relationship but an enduring love between brother and sister. Squeaky's protective arms around her mentally disadvantaged brother provides a clue to her character: an inner softness concealed by the tough façade she shows to the world.

The basic action in the story deals with her success as a runner which leads to her winning Gretchen's friendship, but you get much more when you read this story. A clue to the greater impact is in the title. Raymond is the center of the target. Read and at the end see if you can figure out why the author calls it "Raymond's Run" when the big event is a race that Squeaky wins!

Raymond's Run

I DON'T HAVE MUCH WORK to do around the house like some girls. My mother does that. And I don't have to earn my pocket money by hustling; George runs errands for the big boys and sells Christmas cards. And anything else that's got to get done, my father does. All I have to do in life is mind my brother Raymond, which is enough.

Sometimes I slip and say my little brother Raymond. But as any fool can see he's much bigger and he's older too. But a lot of people call him my little brother cause he needs looking after cause he's not quite right. And a lot of smart mouths got lots to say about that too, especially when George was minding him. But now, if anybody has anything to say to Raymond, anything to say about his big head, they have to come by me. And I don't play the dozens or believe in standing around with somebody in my face doing a lot of talking. I much rather just knock you down and take my chances even if I am a little girl with skinny arms and a squeaky voice, which is how I got the name Squeaky. And if things get too rough, I run. And as anybody can tell you, I'm the fastest thing on two feet.

There is no track meet that I don't win the first place medal. I used to win the twenty-yard dash when I was a little kid in kindergarten. Nowadays, it's the fifty-yard dash. And tomorrow I'm subject to run the quarter-meter relay all by myself and come in first, second, and third. The big kids call me Mercury cause I'm the swiftest thing in the neighborhood. Everybody knows that—except two people who know better, my father and me. He can beat me to Amsterdam Avenue with me having a two fire-hydrant headstart and him running with his hands in his pockets and whistling. But that's private information. Cause can you imagine some thirty-five-year-old man stuffing himself into PAL shorts to race little kids? So as far as everyone's concerned, I'm the fastest and that goes for Gretchen, too, who has put out the tale that she is going to win the first-place medal this year. Ridiculous. In the second place, she's got short legs. In the third place, she's got freckles. In the first place, no one can beat me and that's all there is to it.

I'm standing on the corner admiring the weather and about to take a stroll down Broadway so I can practice my breathing exercises, and I've got Raymond walking on the inside close to the buildings, cause he's subject to fits of fantasy and starts thinking he's a circus performer and that the curb is a tightrope strung high in the air. And sometimes after a rain he likes to step down off his tightrope right into the gutter and slosh around getting his shoes and cuffs wet. Then I get hit when I get home. Or sometimes if you don't watch him he'll dash across traffic to the island in the middle of Broadway and give the pigeons a fit. Then I have to go behind him apologizing to all the old people sitting around trying to get some sun and getting all upset with the pigeons fluttering around them, scattering their newspapers and upsetting the waxpaper lunches in their laps. So I keep Raymond on the inside of me, and he plays like he's driving a stagecoach which is O.K. by me so long as he doesn't run me over or interrupt my breathing exercises, which I have to do on account of I'm serious about my running, and I don't care who knows it.

Now some people like to act like things come easy to them, won't let on that they practice. Not me. I'll high-prance down 34th Street like a rodeo pony to keep my knees strong even if it does get my mother uptight so that she walks ahead like she's not with me, don't know me, is all by herself on a shopping trip, and I am somebody else's crazy child. Now you take Cynthia Procter for instance. She's just the opposite. If there's a test tomorrow, she'll say something like, "Oh, I guess I'll play handball this afternoon and watch television tonight," just to let you know she ain't thinking about the test. Or like last week when she won the spelling bee for the millionth time, "A good thing you got 'receive,' Squeaky, cause I would have got it wrong. I completely forgot about the spelling bee." And she'll clutch the lace on her blouse like it was a narrow escape. Oh, brother. But of course when I pass her house on my early morning trots around the block, she is practicing the scales on the piano over and over and over and over. Then in music class she always lets herself get bumped around so she falls accidently on purpose onto the piano stool and is so surprised to find herself sitting there that she decides just for fun to try out the ole keys. And what do you know—Chopin's waltzes just spring out of her fingertips and she's the most surprised thing in the world. A regular prodigy. I could kill people like that. I stay up all night studying the words for the spelling bee. And you can see me any time of day practicing running. I never walk if I can trot, and shame on Raymond if he can't keep up. But of course he does, cause if he hangs back someone's liable to walk up to him and get smart, or take his allowance from him, or ask him where he got that great big pumpkin head. People are so stupid sometimes.

So I'm strolling down Broadway breathing out and breathing in on counts of seven, which is my lucky number, and here comes Gretchen and her sidekicks: Mary Louise, who used to be a friend of mine when she first moved to Harlem from Baltimore and got beat up by everybody till I took up for her on account of her mother and my mother used to sing in the same choir when they were young girls, but people ain't grateful, so now she hangs out with the new girl Gretchen and talks about me like a dog; and Rosie, who is as fat as I am skinny and has a big mouth where Raymond is concerned and is too stupid to know that there is not a big deal of difference between herself and Raymond and that she can't afford to throw stones. So they are steady coming up Broadway and I see right away that it's going to be one of those Dodge City scenes cause the street ain't that big and they're close to the buildings just as we are. First I think I'll step into the candy store and look over the new comics and let them pass. But that's chicken and I've got a reputation to consider. So then I think I'll just walk straight on through them or even over them if necessary. But as they get to me, they slow down. I'm ready to fight, cause like I said I don't feature a whole lot of chit-chat, I much prefer to just knock you down right from the jump and save everybody a lotta precious time.

"You signing up for the May Day races?" smiles Mary Louise, only it's not a smile at all. A dumb question like that doesn't deserve an answer. Besides, there's just me and Gretchen standing there really, so no use wasting my breath talking to shadows.

"I don't think you're going to win this time," says Rosie, trying to signify with her hands on her hips all salty, completely forgetting that I have whupped her behind many times for less salt than that.

"I always win cause I'm the best," I say straight at Gretchen who is, as far as I'm concerned, the only one talking in this ventriloquist-dummy routine. Gretchen smiles, but it's not a smile, and I'm thinking that girls never really smile at each other because they don't know how and don't want to know how and there's probably no one to teach us how, cause grown-up girls don't know either. Then they all look at Raymond who has just brought his mule team to a standstill. And they're about to see what trouble they can get into through him.

"What grade you in now, Raymond?"

"You got anything to say to my brother, you say it to me, Mary Louise Williams of Raggedy Town, Baltimore."

"What are you, his mother?" sasses Rosie.

"That's right, Fatso. And the next word out of anybody and I'll be *their* mother too." So they just stand there and Gretchen shifts from one leg to the other and so do they. Then Gretchen puts her hands on her hips and is about to say something with her freckle-face self but doesn't. Then she walks around me looking me up and down but keeps walking up Broadway, and her sidekicks follow her. So me and Raymond smile at each other and he says, "Gidyap" to his team and I continue with my breathing exercises, strolling down Broadway toward the ice man on 145th with not a care in the world cause I am Miss Quicksilver herself.

I take my time getting to the park on May Day because the track meet is the last thing on the program. The biggest thing on the program is the May Pole dancing, which I can do without, thank you, even if my mother thinks it's a shame I don't take part and act like a girl for a change. You'd think my mother'd be grateful not to have to make me a white organdy dress with a big satin sash and buy me new white baby-doll shoes that can't be taken out of the box till the big day. You'd think she'd be glad her daughter ain't out there prancing around a May Pole getting the new clothes all dirty and sweaty and trying to act like a fairy or a flower or whatever you're supposed to be when you should be trying to be yourself, whatever that is, which is, as far as I am concerned, a poor Black girl who really can't afford to buy shoes and a new dress you only wear once a lifetime cause it won't fit next year.

I was once a strawberry in a Hansel and Gretel pageant when I was in nursery school and didn't have no better sense than to dance on tiptoe with my arms in a circle over my head doing umbrella steps and being a perfect fool just so my mother and father could come dressed up and clap. You'd think they'd know better than to encourage that kind of nonsense. I am not a strawberry. I do not dance on my toes. I run. That is what I am all about. So I always come late to the May Day program, just in time to get my number pinned on and lay in the grass till they announce the fifty-yard dash.

I put Raymond in the little swings, which is a tight squeeze this year and will be impossible next year. Then I look around for Mr. Pearson, who pins the numbers on. I'm really looking for Gretchen if you want to know the truth, but she's not around. The park is jam-packed. Parents in hats and corsages and breast-pocket handkerchiefs peeking up. Kids in white dresses and light-blue suits. The parkees unfolding chairs and chasing the rowdy kids from Lenox as if they had no right to be there. The big guys with their caps on backwards, leaning against the fence swirling the basketballs on the tips of their fingers, waiting for all these crazy people to clear out the park so they can play. Most of the kids in my class are carrying bass drums and glockenspiels and flutes. You'd think they'd put in a few bongos or something for real like that.

Then here comes Mr. Pearson with his clipboard and his cards and pencils and whistles and safety pins and fifty million other things he's always dropping all over the place with his clumsy self. He sticks out in a crowd because he's on stilts. We used to call him Jack and the Beanstalk to get him mad. But I'm the only one that can outrun him and get away, and I'm too grown for that silliness now.

"Well, Squeaky," he says, checking my name off the list and handing me number seven and two pins. And I'm thinking he's got no right to call me Squeaky, if I can't call him Beanstalk.

"Hazel Elizabeth Deborah Parker," I correct him and tell him to write it down on his board.

"Well, Hazel Elizabeth Deborah Parker, going to give someone else a break this year?" I squint at him real hard to see if he is seriously thinking I should lose the race on purpose just to give someone else a break. "Only six girls running this time," he continues, shaking his head sadly like it's my fault all of New York didn't turn out in sneakers. "That new girl should give you a run for your money." He looks around the park for Gretchen like a periscope in a submarine movie. "Wouldn't it be a nice gesture if you were . . . to ahhh . . . "

I give him such a look he couldn't finish putting that idea into words. Grownups got a lot of nerve sometimes. I pin number seven to myself and stomp away, I'm so burnt. And I go straight for the track and stretch out on the grass while the band winds up with "Oh, the Monkey Wrapped His Tail Around the Flag Pole," which my teacher calls by some other name. The man on the loudspeaker is calling everyone over to the track and I'm on my back looking at the sky, trying to pretend I'm in the country, but I can't, because even grass in the city feels hard as sidewalk, and there's just no pretending you are anywhere but in a "concrete jungle" as my grandfather says.

The twenty-yard dash takes all of two minutes cause most of the little kids don't know no better than to run off the track or run the wrong way or run smack into the fence and fall down and cry. One little kid, though, has got the good sense to run straight for the white ribbon up ahead so he wins. Then the second-graders line up for the thirty-yard dash and I don't even bother to turn my head to watch cause Raphael Perez always wins. He wins before he even begins by psyching the runners, telling them they're going to trip on their shoelaces and fall on their faces or lose their shorts or something, which he doesn't really have to do since he is very fast, almost as fast as I am. After that is the forty-yard dash which I use to run when I was in first grade. Raymond is hollering from the swings cause he knows I'm about to do my thing cause the man on the loudspeaker has just announced the fifty-yard dash, although he might just as well be giving a recipe for angel food cake cause you can hardly make out what he's saying for the static. I get up and slip off my sweat pants and then I see Gretchen standing at the starting line, kicking her legs out like a pro. Then as I get into place I see that ole Raymond is on line on the other side of the fence, bending down with his fingers on the ground just like he knew what he was doing. I was going to yell at him but then I didn't. It burns up your energy to holler.

Every time, just before I take off in a race, I always feel like I'm in a dream, the kind of dream you have when you're sick with fever and feel all hot and weightless. I dream I'm flying over a sandy beach in the early morning sun, kissing the leaves of the trees as I fly by. And there's always the smell of apples, just like in the country when I was little and used to think I was a choo-choo train, running through the fields of corn and chugging up the hill to the orchard. And all the time I'm dreaming this, I get lighter and lighter until I'm flying over the beach again, getting blown through the sky like a feather that weighs nothing at all. But once I spread my fingers in the dirt and crouch over the Get on Your Mark, the dream goes and I am solid again and am telling myself, Squeaky you must win, you must win, you are the fastest thing in the world, you can even beat your father up Amsterdam if you really try. And then I feel my weight coming back just behind my knees then down to my feet then into the earth and the pistol shot explodes in my blood and I am off and weightless again, flying past the other runners, my arms pumping up and down and the whole world is quiet except for the crunch as I zoom over the gravel in the track. I glance to my left and there is no one. To the right, a blurred Gretchen, who's got her chin jutting out as if it would win the race all by itself. And on the other side of the fence is Raymond with his arms down to his side and the palms tucked up behind him, running in his very own style, and it's the first time I ever saw that and I almost stop to watch my brother Raymond on his first run. But the white ribbon is bouncing toward me and I tear past it, racing into the distance till my feet with a mind of their own start digging up footfuls of dirt and brake me short. Then all the kids standing on the side pile on me, banging me on the back and slapping my head with their May Day programs, for I have won again and everybody on 151st Street can walk tall for another year.

"In first place . . . " the man on the loudspeaker is clear as a bell now. But then he pauses and the loudspeaker starts to whine. Then static. And I lean down to catch my breath and here comes Gretchen walking back, for she's overshot the finish line too, huffing and puffing with her hands on her hips taking it slow, breathing in steady time like a real pro and I sort of like her a little for the first time. "In first place . . . " and then three or four voices get all mixed up on the loudspeaker and I dig my sneaker into the grass and stare at Gretchen who's staring back, we both wondering just who did win. I can hear old Beanstalk arguing with the man on the loudspeaker and then a few others running their mouths about what the stopwatches say. Then I hear Raymond yanking at the fence to call me and I wave to shush him, but he keeps rattling the fence like a gorilla in a cage like in them gorilla movies, but then like a dancer or something he starts climbing up nice and easy but very fast. And it occurs to me, watching how smoothly he climbs hand over hand and remembering how he looked running with his arms down to his side and with the wind pulling his mouth back and his teeth showing and all, it occurred to me that Raymond would make a very fine runner. Doesn't he always keep up with me on my trots? And he surely knows how to breathe in counts of seven cause he's always doing it at the dinner table, which drives my brother George up the wall. And I'm smiling to beat the band cause if I've lost this race, or if me and Gretchen tied, or even if I've won, I can always retire as a runner and begin a whole new career as a coach with Raymond as my champion. After all, with a little more study

I can beat Cynthia and her phony self at the spelling bee. And if I bugged my mother, I could get piano lessons and become a star. And I have a big rep as the baddest thing around. And I've got a roomful of ribbons and medals and awards. But what has Raymond got to call his own?

So I stand there with my new plans, laughing out loud by this time as Raymond jumps down from the fence and runs over with his teeth showing and his arms down to the side, which no one before him has quite mastered as a running style. And by the time he comes over I'm jumping up and down so glad to see him—my brother Raymond, a great runner in the family tradition. But of course everyone thinks I'm jumping up and down because the men on the loudspeaker have finally gotten themselves together and compared notes and are announcing "In first place—Miss Hazel Elizabeth Deborah Parker." (Dig that.) "In second place—Miss Gretchen P. Lewis." And I look over at Gretchen wondering what the "P" stands for. And I smile. Cause she's good, no doubt about it. Maybe she'd like to help me coach Raymond; she obviously is serious about running, as any fool can see. And she nods to congratulate me and then she smiles. And I smile. We stand there with this big smile of respect between us. It's about as real a smile as girls can do for each other, considering we don't practice real smiling every day, you know, cause maybe we too busy being flowers or fairies or strawberries instead of something honest and worthy of respect . . . you know . . . like being people.

Reading for Understanding

Main Idea

1. Which of the following bits of dialogue best expresses the main idea of the story?
   (a) "And as anybody can tell you, I'm the fastest thing on two feet."
   (b) "All I have to do in life is mind my brother Raymond, which is enough."
   (c) "Now some people like to act like things come easy to them, won't let on that they practice."
   (d) "That new girl should give you a run for your money."

Details

2. Which of the following is not true?
   (a) Squeaky is younger than Raymond.
   (b) Raymond has limited intelligence.
   (c) Squeaky finds Raymond difficult to control.
   (d) Raymond has an odd appearance.

3. The only one who runs faster than Squeaky is (a) Raymond (b) Gretchen (c) the coach (d) her father.
4. Which of the following statements is not true?
   (a) Mary Louise is no longer a friend of Squeaky.
   (b) Mary Louise had been protected by Squeaky.
   (c) Mary Louise defends Squeaky when others talk against her.
   (d) Mary Louise hangs around with Gretchen.

Inferences

5. Squeaky refuses to "let Gretchen win" because (a) it would be cheating (b) Squeaky would lose her protective shield (c) Raymond would object (d) the judges would disqualify her.
6. Others mistreat Raymond because (a) he is too aggressive (b) he is indifferent (c) they can get even with Squeaky through him (d) he avoids them.

Cause and Effect

7. Squeaky has no friends because (a) she is a troublemaker (b) she is scrappy and hard to get along with (c) she has a thin, high-pitched voice (d) she doesn't have the time.
8. Squeaky doesn't enter the May Pole ceremony because (a) she would rather be in the race (b) her last year's dress is too small (c) her mother doesn't want her to (d) the costume is expensive.

Order of Events

9. Arrange the items in the order in which they occurred. Use letters only.
   A. Squeaky discovers what she can do best—run!
   B. Mary Louise is befriended by Squeaky.
   C. The May Pole is set up for the dance.
   D. Gretchen becomes Squeaky's rival.
   E. Squeaky feels that Raymond can become a star runner.

Outcome

10. Which of the following is not true?
   a. Squeaky proves her superiority once again.
   b. Gretchen and Squeaky make up.

c. Raymond's running ability shows that he is typical for his age.
d. Squeaky hopes that Gretchen and she can make a runner out of Raymond.

Words in Context

1. "The big kids call me *Mercury* cause I'm the swiftest thing in the neighborhood." **Mercury** (327) was originally the name of (a) a car (b) a candy bar (c) the local movie house (d) the messenger of the Roman gods.
2. "A regular *prodigy*. I could kill people like that." **Prodigy** (328) means (a) scoundrel (b) show-off (c) highly talented child (d) wealthy storekeeper.
3. "You'd think my mother'd be grateful not to have to make me a white *organdy* dress." **Organdy** (330) means (a) informal (b) of stiff cloth for dress-up clothing (c) of heavy cloth for denims (d) of highly colored cotton fabric.
4. "He wins before he even begins by *psyching* the runners, telling them they're going to trip on their shoelaces and fall on their faces." **Psyching** (331) means (a) hypnotizing (b) putting the hex on (c) defeating (d) using psychology on.

Thinking Critically About the Story

1. How well equipped is Squeaky to survive in her neighborhood? How well is Raymond? Would they survive any better in yours?
2. Why did Squeaky's parents make Raymond her charge? How does this responsibility affect Squeaky? Is it fair to make her her brother's keeper? Explain. How else could they have handled the problem of Raymond?
3. What makes Squeaky so willing to fight? Is she aware of her inner anger? Explain your answer. To what extent is Raymond responsible?
4. What is Squeaky's theory of practice? To what extent do you agree with her and her methods? Why is she such a loner?
5. Did Squeaky know how to win friends and influence people? Would you choose a person like Squeaky as a friend? Explain your answer.

If you were her counselor, what advice would you give her? Will her friendship with Gretchen last? Explain.

Language in Action

Point of View

A story is always told from a point of view. If told in the first person with *I* as the narrator, the story has a sense of directness. "Raymond's Run" is a first-person narrative. Squeaky's forthrightness has a certain charm. Her thoughts, emotions, and aspirations become our own. For the purposes of the narrative, she is articulate, reasonable, sympathetic. This is a convention we accept for the purposes of the narrative.

The first-person narrative may delve beneath the surface. The narrative is Squeaky thinking, but the reader may wonder whether there is more beneath the surface. Is Squeaky overreacting, possible concealing a sense of inferiority overmastered by the skill in running? First-person narratives are not cut-and-dried. The words resonate beyond the speaker's surface message.

Even the dramatic soliloquy, the most self-revelatory of literary forms, suggests layers of meaning not perceived by the speaker. Do we always understand our own motives?

There are other points of view besides the first person. The omniscient point of view is presented in the third person. This all-knowing point of view is a popular method of storytelling, perhaps the easiest. "Once Upon a Time" usually uses the omniscient point of view.

Why not use this strategy all the time? It would be risky in a detective story. The limited third-person point of view tells us only what the principal character (detective, sidekick) knows.

Authors experiment with other techniques, sometimes combining several points of view in a single narrative. The classical novel in the form of letters exploits these possibilities.

The Sojourner

Carson McCullers
American

Elizabeth answered; her familiar voice was a fresh shock to him. Twice he had to repeat his name, but when he was identified, she sounded glad. He explained that he was only in town for that day. They had a theater engagement, she said—but she wondered if he would come by for an early dinner. Ferris said he would be delighted.

The recipe for a successful romance has sometimes been abbreviated to "Boy meets girl. Boy loses girl. Boy gets girl back." Sometimes, though, the third stage is lacking. In this story, John Ferris seizes a moment to see his former wife in her new family situation. The visit is bittersweet.

The title is significant. A sojourner is a temporary resident, one who stays for a short time. Buried in the French origin of the word is the Latin **diurnum—day**. A sojourner "stays for a day" . . . or a brief time. The visit with his ex-wife stirs feelings that John Ferris didn't realize he had, bringing a change in him that might be for the better.

The Sojourner

THE TWILIGHT BORDER between sleep and waking was a Roman one this morning: splashing fountains and arched, narrow streets, the golden lavish city of blossoms and age-soft stone. Sometimes in this semi-consciousness he sojourned again in Paris, or war German rubble, or Swiss skiing and a snow hotel. Sometimes, also, in a fallow Georgia field at hunting dawn. Rome it was this morning in the yearless region of dreams.

John Ferris awoke in a room in a New York hotel. He had the feeling that something unpleasant was awaiting him—what it was, he did not know. The feeling, submerged by matinal necessities, lingered even after he had dressed and gone downstairs. It was a cloudless autumn day and the pale sunlight sliced between the pastel skyscrapers. Ferris went into the next-door drugstore and sat at the end booth next to the window glass that overlooked the sidewalk. He ordered an American breakfast with scrambled eggs and sausage.

Ferris had come from Paris to his father's funeral which had taken place the week before in his home town in Georgia. The shock of death had made him aware of youth already passed. His hair was receding and the veins in his now naked temples were pulsing and prominent and his body was spare except for an incipient belly bulge. Ferris had loved his father and the bond between them had once been extraordinarily close—but the years had somehow unraveled this filial devotion; the death, expected for a long time, had left him with an unforseen dismay. He had stayed as long as possible to be near his mother and brothers at home. His plane for Paris was to leave the next morning.

Ferris pulled out his address book to verify a number. He turned the pages with growing attentiveness. Names and addresses from New York, the capitals of Europe, a few faint ones from his home state in the South. Faded, printed names, sprawled drunken ones. Betty Wills: a random love, married now. Charlie Williams: wounded in the Hürtgen Forest, unheard of since. Grand old Williams—did he live or die? Don Walker: a B.T.O. in television, getting rich. Henry Green: hit the skids after the war, in a sanitarium now, they say. Cozie Hall: he had heard that she was dead. Heedless, laughing Cozie—it was strange to think that she too, silly girl, could die. As Ferris closed the address book, he suffered a sense of hazard, transience, almost of fear.

It was then that his body jerked suddenly. He was staring out of the window when there, on the sidewalk, passing by, was his ex-wife. Elizabeth passed quite close to him, walking slowly. He could not understand the wild quiver of his heart, nor the following sense of recklessness and grace that lingered after she was gone.

Quickly Ferris paid his check and rushed out to the sidewalk. Elizabeth stood on the corner waiting to cross Fifth Avenue. He hurried toward her meaning to speak, but the lights changed and she crossed the street before he reached her. Ferris followed. On the other side he could easily have overtaken her, but he found himself lagging unaccountably. Her fair brown hair was plainly rolled, and as he watched her Ferris recalled that once his father had remarked that Elizabeth had a 'beautiful carriage.' She turned at the next corner and Ferris followed, although by now his intention to overtake her had disappeared. Ferris questioned the bodily disturbance that the sight of Elizabeth aroused in him, the dampness of his hands, the hard heartstrokes.

It was eight years since Ferris had last seen his ex-wife. He knew that long ago she had married again. And there were children. During recent years he had seldom thought of her. But at first, after the divorce, the loss had almost destroyed him. Then after the anodyne of time, he had loved again, and then again. Jeannine, she was now. Certainly his love for his ex-wife was long since past. So why the unhinged body, the shaken mind? He knew only that his clouded heart was oddly dissonant with the sunny, candid autumn day. Ferris wheeled suddenly and, walking with long strides, almost running, hurried back to the hotel.

Ferris poured himself a drink, although it was not yet eleven o'clock. He sprawled out in an armchair like a man exhausted, nursing his glass of bourbon and water. He had a full day ahead of him as he was leaving by plane the next morning for Paris. He checked over his obligations: take luggage to Air France, lunch with his boss, buy shoes and an overcoat. And something—wasn't there something else? Ferris finished his drink and opened the telephone directory.

His decision to call his ex-wife was impulsive. The number was under Bailey, the husband's name, and he called before he had much time for self-debate. He and Elizabeth had exchanged cards at Christmastime, and Ferris had sent a carving set when he received the announcement of her wedding. There was no reason *not* to call. But as he waited, listening to the ring at the other end, misgiving fretted him.

Elizabeth answered; her familiar voice was a fresh shock to him. Twice he had to repeat his name, but when he was identified, she sounded glad. He explained he was only in town for that day. They had a theater engagement, she said—but she wondered if he would come by for an early dinner. Ferris said he would be delighted.

As he went from one engagement to another, he was still bothered at odd moments by the feeling that something necessary was forgotten. Ferris bathed and changed in the late afternoon, often thinking about Jeannine: he would be with her the following night. 'Jeannine,' he would say, 'I happened to run into my ex-wife when I was in New York. Had dinner with her. And her husband, of course. It was strange seeing her after all these years.'

Elizabeth lived in the East Fifties, and as Ferris taxied uptown he glimpsed at intersections the lingering sunset, but by the time he reached his destination it was already autumn dark. The place was a building with a marquee and a doorman, and the apartment was on the seventh floor.

'Come in, Mr. Ferris.'

Braced for Elizabeth or even the unimagined husband, Ferris was astonished by the freckled red-haired child; he had known of the children, but his mind had failed somehow to acknowledge them. Surprise made him step back awkwardly.

'This is our apartment,' the child said politely. 'Aren't you Mr. Ferris? I'm Billy. Come in.'

In the living room beyond the hall, the husband provided another surprise; he too had not been acknowledged emotionally. Bailey was a lumbering red-haired man with a deliberate manner. He rose and extended a welcoming hand.

'I'm Bill Bailey. Glad to see you. Elizabeth will be in, in a minute. She's finishing dressing.'

The last words struck a gliding series of vibrations, memories of the other years. Fair Elizabeth, rosy and naked before her bath. Half-dressed before the mirror of her dressing table, brushing her fine, chestnut hair. Sweet, casual intimacy, the soft-fleshed loveliness indisputably possessed. Ferris shrank from the unbidden memories and compelled himself to meet Bill Bailey's gaze.

'Billy, will you please bring that tray of drinks from the kitchen table?'

The child obeyed promptly, and when he was gone Ferris remarked conversationally, 'Fine boy you have there.'

'We think so.'

Flat silence until the child returned with a tray of glasses and a cocktail shaker of Martinis. With the priming drinks they pumped up conversation: Russia, they spoke of, and the New York rain-making, and the apartment situation in Manhattan and Paris.

'Mr. Ferris is flying all the way across the ocean tomorrow,' Bailey said to the little boy who was perched on the arm of his chair, quiet and well behaved. 'I bet you would like to be a stowaway in his suitcase.'

Billy pushed back his limp bangs. 'I want to fly in an airplane and be a newspaperman like Mr. Ferris.' He added with sudden assurance, 'That's what I would like to do when I am big.'

Bailey said, 'I thought you wanted to be a doctor.'

'I do!' said Billy. 'I would like to be both. I want to be a atom-bomb scientist too.'

Elizabeth came in carrying in her arms a baby girl.

'Oh, John!' she said. She settled the baby in the father's lap. 'It's grand to see you. I'm awfully glad you could come.'

The little girl sat demurely on Bailey's knees. She wore a pale pink crepe de Chine frock, smocked around the yoke with rose, and a matching silk hair ribbon tying back her pale soft curls. Her skin was summer tanned and her brown eyes flecked with gold and laughing. When she reached up and fingered her father's horn-rimmed glasses, he took them off and let her look through them a moment. 'How's my old Candy?'

Elizabeth was very beautiful, more beautiful perhaps than he had ever realized. Her straight clean hair was shining. Her face was softer, glowing and serene. It was a madonna loveliness, dependent on the family ambiance.

'You've hardly changed at all,' Elizabeth said, 'but it has been a long time.'

'Eight years.' His hand touched his thinning hair self-conciously while further amenities were exchanged.

Ferris felt himself suddenly a spectator—an interloper among these Baileys. Why had he come? He suffered. His own life seemed so solitary, a fragile column supporting nothing amidst the wreckage of the years. He felt he could not bear much longer to stay in the family room.

He glanced at his watch. 'You're going to the theater?'

'It's a shame,' Elizabeth said, 'but we've had this engagement for more than a month. But surely, John, you'll be staying home one of these days before long. You're not going to be an expatriate, are you?'

'Expatriate,' Ferris repeated. 'I don't much like the word.'

'What's a better word?' she asked.

He thought for a moment. 'Sojourner might do.'

Ferris glanced again at his watch, and again Elizabeth apologized. 'If only we had known ahead of time—'

'I just had this day in town. I came home unexpectedly. You see, Papa died last week.'

'Papa Ferris is dead?'

'Yes, at Johns-Hopkins. He had been sick there nearly a year. The funeral was down home in Georgia.'

'Oh, I'm so sorry, John. Papa Ferris was always one of my favorite people.'

The little boy moved from behind the chair so that he could look into his mother's face. He asked, 'Who is dead?'

Ferris was oblivious to apprehension; he was thinking of his father's death. He saw again the outstretched body on the quilted silk within the coffin. The corpse flesh was bizarrely rouged and the familiar hands lay massive and joined above a spread of funeral roses. The memory closed and Ferris awakened to Elizabeth's calm voice.

'Mr. Ferris's father, Billy. A really grand person. Somebody you didn't know.'

'But why did you call him *Papa* Ferris?'

Bailey and Elizabeth exchanged a trapped look. It was Bailey who answered the questioning child. 'A long time ago,' he said, 'your mother and Mr. Ferris were once married. Before you were born—a long time ago.'

'Mr. Ferris?'

The little boy stared at Ferris, amazed and unbelieving. And Ferris's eyes, as he returned the gaze, were somehow unbelieving too. Was it indeed true that at one time he had called this stranger, Elizabeth, Little Butterduck during nights of love, that they had lived together, shared perhaps a thousand days and nights and—finally—endured in the misery of sudden solitude the fiber by fiber (jealousy, alcohol and money quarrels) destruction of the fabric of married love.

Bailey said to the children, 'It's somebody's suppertime. Come on now.'

'But Daddy! Mama and Mr. Ferris—I—'

Billy's everlasting eyes—perplexed and with a glimmer of hostility—reminded Ferris of the gaze of another child. It was the young son of Jeannine—a boy of seven with a shadowed little face and knobby knees whom Ferris avoided and usually forgot.

'Quick march!' Bailey gently turned Billy toward the door. 'Say good night now, son.'

'Good night, Mr. Ferris.' He added resentfully, 'I thought I was staying up for the cake.'

'You can come in afterward for the cake,' Elizabeth said. 'Run along now with Daddy for your supper.'

Ferris and Elizabeth were alone. The weight of the situation descended on those first moments of silence. Ferris asked permission to pour himself another drink and Elizabeth set the cocktail shaker on the table at his side. He looked at the grand piano and noticed the music on the rack.

'Do you still play as beautifully as you used to?'

'I still enjoy it.'

'Please play, Elizabeth.'

Elizabeth arose immediately. Her readiness to perform when asked had always been one of her amiabilities; she never hung back, apologized. Now as she approached the piano there was the added readiness of relief.

She began with a Bach prelude and fugue. The prelude was as gaily iridescent as a prism in a morning room. The first voice of the fugue, an announcement pure and solitary, was repeated intermingling with a second voice, and again repeated within an elaborated frame, the multiple music, horizontal and serene, flowed with unhurried majesty. The principal melody was woven with two other voices, embellished with countless ingenuities—now dominant, again submerged, it had the sublimity of a single thing that does not fear surrender to the whole. Toward the end, the density of the material gathered for the last enriched insistence on the dominant first motif and with a chorded final statement the fugue ended. Ferris rested his head on the chair back and closed his eyes.

In the following silence a clear, high voice came from the room down the hall.

'Daddy, how *could* Mama and Mr. Ferris—' A door was closed.

The piano began again—what was this music? Unplaced, familiar, the limpid melody had lain a long while dormant in his heart. Now it spoke to him of another time, another place—it was the music Elizabeth used to play. The delicate air summoned a wilderness of memory. Ferris was lost in the riot of past longings, conflicts, ambivalent desires. Strange that the music, catalyst[1] for this tumultuous anarchy, was so serene and clear. The singing melody was broken off by the appearance of the maid.

'Miz Bailey, dinner is out on the table now.'

Even after Ferris was seated at the table between his host and hostess, the unfinished music still overcast his mood. He was a little drunk.

'*L'improvisation de la vie humaine*,' he said. 'There's nothing that makes you so aware of the improvisation of human existence as a song unfinished. Or an old address book.'

'Address book?' repeated Bailey. Then he stopped, noncommittal and polite.

'You're still the same old boy, Johnny,' Elizabeth said with a trace of the old tenderness.

It was a Southern dinner that evening, and the dishes were his old favorites. They had fried chicken and corn pudding and rich, glazed candied sweet potatoes. During the meal Elizabeth kept alive a conversation when the silences were overlong. And it came about that Ferris was led to speak of Jeannine.

'I first knew Jeannine last autumn—about this time of the year—in Italy. She's a singer and she had an engagement in Rome. I expect we will be married soon.'

The words seemed so true, inevitable, that Ferris did not at first acknowledge to himself the lie. He and Jeannine had never in that year spoken of marriage. And indeed, she was still married—to a White Russian moneychanger in Paris from whom she had been separated for five years. But it was too late to correct the lie. Already Elizabeth was saying: 'This really makes me glad to know. Congratulations, Johnny.'

He tried to make amends with truth. 'The Roman autumn is so beautiful. Balmy and blossoming.' He added, 'Jeannine has a little boy of six. A curious trilingual[2] little fellow. We go to the Tuileries sometimes.'

A lie again. He had taken the boy once to the gardens. The sallow foreign child in shorts that bared his spindly legs had sailed his

[1]agent for change
[2]speaking three languages

boat in the concrete pond and ridden the pony. The child had wanted to go in to the puppet show. But there was not time, for Ferris had an engagement at the Scribe Hotel. He had promised they would go to the guignol[1] another afternoon. Only once had he taken Valentin to the Tuileries.

There was a stir. The maid brought in a white-frosted cake with pink candles. The children entered in their night clothes. Ferris still did not understand.

'Happy birthday, John,' Elizabeth said. 'Blow out the candles.'

Ferris recognized his birthday date. The candles blew out lingeringly and there was the smell of burning wax. Ferris was thirty-eight years old. The veins in his temples darkened and pulsed visibly.

'It's time you started for the theater.'

Ferris thanked Elizabeth for the birthday dinner and said the appropriate good-byes. The whole family saw him to the door.

A high, thin moon shone above the jagged, dark skyscrapers. The streets were windy, cold. Ferris hurried to Third Avenue and hailed a cab. He gazed at the nocturnal city with the deliberate attentiveness of departure and perhaps farewell. He was alone. He longed for flighttime and the coming journey.

The next day he looked down on the city from the air, burnished in sunlight, toylike, precise. Then America was left behind and there was only the Atlantic and the distant European shore. The ocean was milky pale and placid beneath the clouds. Ferris dozed most of the day. Toward dark he was thinking of Elizabeth and the visit of the previous evening. He thought of Elizabeth among her family with longing, gentle envy and inexplicable regret. He sought the melody, the unfinished air, that had so moved him. The cadence, some unrelated tones, were all that remained; the melody itself evaded him. He had found instead the first voice of the fugue that Elizabeth had played—it came to him, inverted mockingly and in a minor key. Suspended above the ocean the anxieties of transience and solitude no longer troubled him and he thought of his father's death with equanimity. During the dinner hour the plane reached the shore of France.

At midnight Ferris was in a taxi crossing Paris. It was a clouded night and mist wreathed the lights of the Place de la Concorde. The midnight bistros gleamed on the wet pavements. As always after a transocean flight the change of continents was too sudden. New York at morning, this midnight Paris. Ferris glimpsed the disorder of his life: the succession of cities, of transitory loves; and time, the sinister glissando[2] of the years, time always.

'*Vite! Vite!*'[3] he called in terror. '*Dépêchez-vous.*'

---

[1]puppet show
[2]glide up or down the musical scale
[3]quick, hurry

Valentin opened the door to him. The little boy wore pajamas and an outgrown red robe. His grey eyes were shadowed and, as Ferris passed into the flat, they flickered momentarily.

'*J'attends Maman.*'[1]

Jeannine was singing in a night club. She would not be home before another hour. Valentin returned to a drawing, squatting with his crayons over the paper on the floor. Ferris looked down at the drawing—it was a banjo player with notes and wavy lines inside a comic-strip balloon.

'We will go again to the Tuileries.'

The child looked up and Ferris drew him closer to his knees. The melody, the unfinished music that Elizabeth had played, came to him suddenly. Unsought, the load of memory jettisoned—this time bringing only recognition and sudden joy.

'Monsieur Jean,' the child said, 'did you see him?'

Confused, Ferris thought only of another child—the freckled, family-loved boy. 'See who, Valentin?'

'Your dead papa in Georgia.' The child added, 'Was he okay?'

Ferris spoke with rapid urgency: 'We will go often to the Tuileries. Ride the pony and we will go into the guignol. We will see the puppet show and never be in a hurry any more.'

'Monsieur Jean,' Valentin said. 'The guignol is now closed.'

Again, the terror the acknowledgment of wasted years and death. Valentin, responsive and confident, still nestled in his arms. His cheek touched the soft cheek and felt the brush of the delicate eyelashes. With inner desperation he pressed the child close—as though an emotion as protean as his love could dominate the pulse of time.

Reading for Understanding

Main Idea

1. A major theme of the story is that (a) ex-husbands and ex-wives cannot truly be friends (b) a return to the past can bring a spiritual change (c) divorces result in lasting unhappiness for both parties (d) children are not truly appreciated.

Details

2. John Ferris was in New York (a) on business (b) to meet his ex-wife (c) after a funeral (d) for a Thanksgiving reunion.

[1] I'm waiting for mama.

3. Betty Wills is mentioned as (a) a friend of Elizabeth's (b) Bailey's sister (c) a close friend, now dead (d) a former love.
4. Ferris hadn't seen his ex-wife (a) since Christmas (b) since her visit to Paris (c) since her wedding (d) for eight years.
5. Jeannine is (a) Ferris's present love (b) the mother of Billy (c) Elizabeth's maid of honor (d) John's father's second wife.
6. To entertain Ferris, Elizabeth (a) played the piano (b) took out an old photo book (c) invited Ferris to join the theater party (d) told of a trip to Europe.
7. At the Baileys', Ferris was surprised by (a) an old diary (b) a birthday cake (c) a recitation by Billy (d) Bailey's rapid-fire quick wit.

Inferences

8. In later years, (a) Ferris's brother had ceased writing (b) Ferris's mother blamed him for her husband's illness (c) Ferris and his father had grown apart (d) Ferris had proposed marriage to several women.
9. The sight of Elizabeth (a) reinforced Ferris's original decision to divorce her (b) heightened Ferris's sense of loneliness (c) aroused feelings of antagonism toward Bill Bailey (d) made him resolve to win her back.
10. Billy was upset to learn that (a) his mother had been married before (b) Ferris was actually his father (c) Ferris was staying on for two more days (d) he couldn't go to the puppet show.

The Mood of the Story

11. The mood of the story is one of (a) well-earned joy (b) deep bitterness (c) gentle sadness (d) unsatisfied curiosity.

Cause and Effect

12. The break-up of the Ferris marriage many years ago can probably be traced to (a) a third person (b) a difference in their incomes (c) Ferris's desire to have children (d) unresolved quarrels.

Outcome

13. As a result of his visit with the Baileys, Ferris will probably (a) change his attitude toward Valentin (b) break off with Jeannine (c) turn around and go back to New York (d) give up his U.S. citizenship.

Order of Events

14. Arrange the events in the order in which they occurred. Use letters only.
    A. Billy greets Ferris at the door.
    B. Ferris's father dies.
    C. Valentin tells Ferris the puppet show is closed.
    D. Ferris sees Elizabeth on the street.
    E. Elizabeth enters with a baby girl.

Fact or Opinion

Tell whether the following is a fact or an opinion.

15. In the past, Ferris has spent little time with Valentin.

Words in Context

1. "His body was spare except for an *incipient* belly bulge." **Incipient** (338) means (a) huge (b) displeasing (c) rounded (d) beginning.
2. "As Ferris closed the address book, he suffered a sense of hazard, *transience,* almost of fear." **Transience** (338) suggests a lack of (a) meaning (b) anger (c) permanence (d) forethought.
3. "Then, after the *anodyne* of time, he had loved again, and then again." **Anodyne** (339) means (a) memory (b) painkiller (c) passage (d) cruelties.
4. "He knew only that his clouded heart was oddly *dissonant* with the sunny, candid autumn day." **Dissonant** (339) means (a) out of tune (b) in harmony (c) unaffected (d) fully aware.
5. "It was a madonna loveliness, dependent on the family *ambiance.*" **Ambiance** (341) means (a) history (b) atmosphere (c) gentleness (d) playfulness.
6. "His hand touched his thinning hair self-consciously while further *amenities* were exchanged." **Amenities** (341) are (a) gifts (b) inquiries (c) ideas (d) pleasantries.
7. "Ferris felt himself suddenly a spectator—an *interloper* among these Baileys." **Interloper** (341) means (a) intruder (b) unwanted relative (c) unhappy guest (d) associate.

8. " 'You're not going to be an *expatriate,* are you?' " An **expatriate** (341) (a) lives away from his native country (b) is unpatriotic (c) never stays in one place long (d) is a former politician on the run.

9., 10. "Ferris was *oblivious to apprehension.*" **Oblivious to** (341) means (a) concerned about (b) attentive to (c) unaware of (d) accepting of. **Apprehension** (341) means (a) being arrested (b) understanding (c) worry (d) good cheer.

11. "Her readiness to perform when asked had always been one of her *amiabilities.*" **Amiabilities** (342) means (a) skills (b) pleasantnesses (c) annoyances (d) anxieties.

12. "The prelude was as gaily *iridescent* as a prism in a morning room." **Iridescent** (342) is used here in a special sense to mean (a) suitable (b) changeable (c) melodic (d) sparkling.

13. "The music, horizontal and *serene,* flowed with unhurried majesty." **Serene** (342) means (a) vertical (b) peaceful (c) colorful (d) animated.

14. "The principal melody was woven with two other voices, *embellished* with countless ingenuities." **Embellished** (342) means (a) decorated (b) repetitious (c) mindful of (d) defined.

15. "It had the *sublimity* of a single thing that does not fear surrender to the whole." **Sublimity** (342) means (a) appeal (b) challenge (c) nobility (d) appearance.

16. "Unplaced, familiar, the *limpid* melody had lain a long while dormant in his heart." **Limpid** (343) means (a) clear and simple (b) complicated and subtle (c) soft and fuzzy (d) loud but pleasant.

17. "Ferris was lost in the riot of past longings, conflicts, *ambivalent* desires." **Ambivalent** (343) means (a) pressing (b) dramatic (c) violent (d) conflicting.

18., 19. "Strange that the music, catalyst for this *tumultuous anarchy,* was so serene and clear." **Tumultuous** (343) means (a) unexpected (b) raging (c) satisfying (d) disagreeable. **Anarchy** (343) means (a) revelation (b) music (c) disorder (d) thoughtfulness.

20. "He gazed at the *nocturnal* city with the deliberate attentiveness of departure and perhaps farewell." **Nocturnal** (344) deals with (a) beauty (b) night (c) traffic (d) light.

21. "The next day he looked down on the city from the air, *burnished* in sunlight, toylike, precise." **Burnished** (344) means (a) reddened (b) outlined (c) polished (d) exposed.

22. "He thought of Elizabeth among her family with longing, gentle envy, and *inexplicable* regret." **Inexplicable** (344) means not able to be (a) explained (b) stated (c) discovered (d) tolerated.

23. "He thought of his father's death with *equanimity*." **Equanimity** (344) means (a) regret (b) sadness (c) happy memory (d) calmness.
24. "Ferris glimpsed the disorder of his life: the succession of cities, of *transitory* loves." **Transitory** (344) means (a) passionate (b) faithless (c) well-remembered (d) short-lived.
25. "Unsought, the load of memory *jettisoned*—this time bringing only recognition and sudden joy." **Jettisoned** (345) means (a) returned (b) discarded (c) pained (d) rejoiced.
26. "With inner desperation he pressed the child close—as though an emotion as *protean* as his love could dominate the pulse of time." **Protean** (345) means (a) sentimental (b) wholesome (c) unique (d) changeable.

Thinking Critically About the Story

1. In J.B. Priestley's play *Dangerous Corner*, the pleasant amiability of a group changes drastically because of one statement. Discord and disintegration follow. Then Priestley takes the readers or listeners back to a moment before the fateful comment, for a second chance. This time, the comment is not made, and the evening proceeds on its quiet, happy way. Priestley seems to say that momentous events sometimes turn on a seemingly innocent word or decision. Apply that idea to "The Sojourner." Suppose that Ferris had not given in to an impulse. Suppose he had not "turned that corner" and called his ex-wife. How would his later life have been different? Was Ferris better for his bittersweet visit to his wife and her new family? Explain.
2. Are there any clues that suggest one party might have been more guilty than the other in the divorce of Ferris and Elizabeth? Explain.
3. How do Ferris and Bailey differ? Why was Elizabeth probably seeking a different type the second time around?
4. "He was alone" (344). What significance does this statement have in the context of the story?
5. "Billy's everlasting eyes—perplexed and with a glimmer of hostility—reminded Ferris of the gaze of another child." Why the hostility? Who was the other child?
6. Why does the author bring in Elizabeth's music? What effect does it have on Ferris?
7. How has the name *sojourner* suited Ferris's life?

8. " 'Address book?' repeated Bailey (343). Then he stopped, noncommittal and polite." Why does Elizabeth understand while her husband does not?
9. Why does Ferris tell Valentin, "We'll never be in a hurry any more."?
10. *Jettison* (345) or *jetsam,* makes an interesting pair with *flotsam.* Look up both and be ready to distinguish between *flotsam* and *jetsam.*

Language in Action

Allusions

Dinosaur hunters search for clues that provide insight into the past. A giant tooth may suggest a Tyrannosaurus rex. Language, too, is filled with hidden clues that reveal our past. A single word can suggest a mythology that has nourished the world's literature. A good example is *protean* (345). The dictionary and the context tell us it means *changeable,* but that's only part of the story. Proteus, the herdsman of Neptune, was a great prophet, but seekers couldn't catch him because he could assume different shapes.

Iridescence (342) suggests Iris, the Greek goddess of the rainbow. *Ocean* (340) comes from a Greek name for the river that supposedly circled the earth. There was also a Greek Titan, Oceanus, whose children were gods of all the world's rivers.

An allusion is an implied or indirect reference, like the allusion to Proteus concealed in *protean.* Many allusions come from mythology. Some are from other literature. The allusion may be obvious as in a *Romeo,* or concealed, as in *lilliputian* (tiny), from *Gulliver's Travels.*

Allusions may come from still other areas. *Bobby,* a familiar name for an English policeman, came from Sir Robert Peel, who organized the London police force. The Christmas flower, *poinsettia,* was brought to this country more than a century ago by Joel Poinsett, the ambassador to Mexico. *Silhouette* was named for Etienne de Silhouette, a French administrative official.

A Cap for Steve

Morley Callaghan
Canadian

The Father

Björnstjerne Björnson
Norwegian

"Well, here you are," Mr. Hudson said, and he put the two bills in Steve's hand. "It's a lot of money. But I guess you had a right to expect as much."

With a dazed, fixed smile, Steve handed the money slowly to his father, and his face was white.

These two stories are paired for obvious reasons: both deal with the relationship between a father and his son. There are similarities in relationships, but there are great dissimilarities too, in setting, mood, and plot.

"The Father" is told in a spare, direct style. The events speak for themselves, and the author doesn't Inject his own thoughts. Where "The Father" is lean and spare, "A Cap for Steve" is emotional and detailed. We are taken into the lives and hearts of Steve and his father in a way quite different from the technique of "The Father."

Both stories reveal a deep love of a father for his son, but that love is demonstrated quite differently in each.

Since both stories were written in an earlier day, you will find the money amounts mentioned much lower than you would expect today. The stories, though, are timeless.

A Cap for Steve

DAVE DIAMOND, a poor man, a carpenter's assistant, was a small, wiry, quick-tempered individual who had learned how to make every dollar count in his home. His wife, Anna, had been sick a lot, and his twelve-year-old son, Steve, had to be kept in school. Steve, a big-eyed, shy kid, ought to have known the value of money as well as Dave did. It had been ground into him.

But the boy was crazy about baseball, and after school, when he could have been working as a delivery boy or selling papers, he played ball with the kids. His failure to appreciate that the family needed a few extra dollars disgusted Dave. Around the house he wouldn't let Steve talk about baseball, and he scowled when he saw him hurrying off with his glove after dinner.

When the Phillies came to town to play an exhibition game with the home team and Steve pleaded to be taken to the ball park, Dave, of course, was outraged. Steve knew they couldn't afford it. But he had got his mother on his side. Finally Dave made a bargain with them. He said that if Steve came home after school and worked hard helping to make some kitchen shelves he would take him that night to the ball park.

Steve worked hard, but Dave was still resentful. They had to coax him to put on his good suit. When they started out Steve held aloof, feeling guilty, and they walked down the street like strangers; then Dave glanced at Steve's face and, half-ashamed, took his arm more cheerfully.

As the game went on, Dave had to listen to Steve's recitation of the batting average of every Philly that stepped up to the plate; the time the boy must have wasted learning these averages began to appal him. He showed it so plainly that Steve felt guilty again and was silent.

After the game Dave let Steve drag him onto the field to keep him company while he tried to get some autographs from the Philly players, who were being hemmed in by gangs of kids blocking the way to the club-house. But Steve, who was shy, let the other kids block him off from the players. Steve would push his way in, get blocked out, and come back to stand mournfully beside Dave. And Dave grew impatient. He was wasting valuable time. He wanted to get home; Steve knew it and was worried.

Then the big, blond Philly outfielder, Eddie Condon, who had been held up by a gang of kids tugging at his arm and thrusting their score cards at him, broke loose and made a run for the club-house. He was jostled, and his blue cap with the red peak, tilted far back on his head, fell off. It fell at Steve's feet, and Steve stooped quickly and grabbed it. "Okay, son," the outfielder called, turning back. But Steve, holding the hat in both hands, only stared at him.

"Give him his cap, Steve," Dave said, smiling apologetically at the big outfielder who towered over them. But Steve drew the hat closer to his chest. In an awed trance he looked up at big Eddie Condon. It was an embarrassing moment. All the other kids were watching. Some shouted. "Give him his cap."

"My cap, son," Eddie Condon said, his hand out.

"Hey, Steve," Dave said, and he gave him a shake. But he had to jerk the cap out of Steve's hands.

"Here you are," he said.

The outfielder, noticing Steve's white, worshipping face and pleading eyes, grinned and then shrugged. "Aw, let him keep it," he said.

"No, Mister Condon, you don't need to do that," Steve protested.

"It's happened before. Forget it," Eddie Condon said, and he trotted away to the club-house.

Dave handed the cap to Steve; envious kids circled around them and Steve said, "He said I could keep it, Dad. You heard him, didn't you?"

"Yeah, I heard him," Dave admitted. The wonder in Steve's face made him smile. He took the boy by the arm and they hurried off the field.

On the way home Dave couldn't get him to talk about the game; he couldn't get him to take his eyes off the cap. Steve could hardly believe in his own happiness. "See," he said suddenly, and he showed Dave that Eddie Condon's name was printed on the sweat-band. Then he went on dreaming. Finally he put the cap on his head and turned to Dave with a slow, proud smile. The cap was away too big for him; it fell down over his ears. "Never mind," Dave said. "You can get your mother to take a tuck in the back."

When they got home Dave was tired and his wife didn't understand the cap's importance, and they couldn't get Steve to go to bed. He swaggered around wearing the cap and looking in the mirror every ten minutes. He took the cap to bed with him.

Dave and his wife had a cup of coffee in the kitchen, and Dave told her again how they had got the cap. They agreed that their boy must have an attractive quality that showed in his face, and that Eddie Condon must have been drawn to him—why else would he have singled Steve out from all the kids?

But Dave got tired of the fuss Steve made over that cap and of the way he wore it from the time he got up in the morning until the time he went to bed. Some kid was always coming in, wanting to try on the cap. It was childish, Dave said, for Steve to go around assuming that the cap made him important in the neighbourhood, and to keep telling them how he had become a leader in the park a few blocks away where he played ball in the evenings. And Dave wouldn't stand for Steve's keeping the cap on while he was eating. He was always scolding his wife for accepting Steve's explanation that he'd forgotten he had it on. Just the same, it was remarkable what a little thing like a ball cap could do for a kid, Dave admitted to his wife as he smiled to himself.

One night Steve was late coming home from the park. Dave didn't realize how late it was until he put down his newspaper and watched his wife at the window. Her restlessness got on his nerves. "See what comes from encouraging the boy to hang around with those park loafers," he said. "I don't encourage him," she protested. "You do," he insisted irritably, for he was really worried now. A gang hung around the park until midnight. It was a bad park. It was true that on one side there was a good district with fine, expensive apartment houses, but the kids from that neighbourhood left the park to the kids from the poorer homes. When his wife went out and walked down to the corner it was his turn to wait and worry and watch at the open window. Each waiting moment tortured him. At last he heard his wife's voice and Steve's voice, and he relaxed and sighed; then he remembered his duty and rushed angrily to meet them.

"I'll fix you, Steve, once and for all," he said. "I'll show you you can't start coming into the house at midnight."

"Hold your horses, Dave," his wife said. "Can't you see the state he's in?" Steve looked utterly exhausted and beaten.

"What's the matter?" Dave asked quickly.

"I lost my cap," Steve whispered; he walked past his father and threw himself on the couch in the living-room and lay with his face hidden.

"Now, don't scold him, Dave," his wife said.

"Scold him. Who's scolding him?" Dave asked, indignantly. "It's his cap, not mine. If it's not worth his while to hang on to it, why should I scold him?" But he was implying resentfully that he alone recognized the cap's value.

"So you are scolding him," his wife said. "It's his cap. Not yours. What happened, Steve?"

Steve told them he had been playing ball and he found that when he ran the bases the cap fell off; it was still too big despite the tuck his mother had taken in the band. So the next time he came to bat he tucked the cap in his hip pocket. Someone had lifted it, he was sure.

"And he didn't even know whether it was still in his pocket," Dave said sarcastically.

"I wasn't careless, Dad," Steve said. For the last three hours he had been wandering around to the homes of the kids who had been in the park at the time; he wanted to go on, but he was too tired. Dave knew the boy was apologizing to him, but he didn't know why it made him angry.

"If he didn't hang on to it, it's not worth worrying about now," he said, and he sounded offended.

After that night they knew that Steve didn't go to the park to play ball; he went to look for the cap. It irritated Dave to see him sit around listlessly, or walk in circles, trying to force his memory to find a particular incident which would suddenly recall to him the moment when the cap had been taken. It was no attitude for a growing, healthy boy to take, Dave complained. He told Steve firmly once and for all that he didn't want to hear any more about the cap.

One night, two weeks later, Dave was walking home with Steve from the shoemaker's. It was a hot night. When they passed an ice-cream parlour Steve slowed down. "I guess I couldn't have a soda, could I?" Steve said. "Nothing doing," Dave said firmly. "Come on now," he added as Steve hung back, looking in the window.

"Dad, look!" Steve cried suddenly, pointing at the window. "My cap! There's my cap! He's coming out!"

A well-dressed boy was leaving the ice-cream parlour; he had on a blue ball cap with a red peak, just like Steve's cap. "Hey, you!" Steve cried, and he rushed at the boy, his small face fierce and his eyes wild. Before the boy could back away Steve had snatched the cap from his head. "That's my cap!" he shouted.

"What's this?" the bigger boy said. "Hey, give me my cap or I'll give you a poke on the nose."

Dave was surprised that his own shy boy did not back away. He watched him clutch the cap in his left hand, half crying with excitement as he put his head down and drew back his right fist: he was willing to fight. And Dave was proud of him.

"Wait, now," Dave said. "Take it easy, son," he said to the other boy, who refused to back away.

"My boy says it's his cap," Dave said.

"Well, he's crazy. It's my cap."

"I was with him when he got this cap. When the Phillies played here. It's a Philly cap."

"Eddie Condon gave it to me," Steve said. "And you stole it from me, you jerk."

"Don't call me a jerk, you little squirt. I never saw you before in my life."

"Look," Steve said, pointing to the printing on the cap's sweatband. "It's Eddie Condon's cap. See? See, Dad?"

"Yeah. You're right, Son. Ever see this boy before, Steve?"

"No," Steve said reluctantly.

The other boy realized he might lose the cap. "I bought it from a guy," he said. "I paid him. My father knows I paid him." He said he got the cap at the ball park. He groped for some magically impressive words and suddenly found them. "You'll have to speak to my father," he said.

"Sure, I'll speak to your father," Dave said. "What's your name? Where do you live?"

"My name's Hudson. I live about ten minutes away on the other side of the park." The boy appraised Dave, who wasn't any bigger than he was and who wore a faded blue windbreaker and no tie. "My father is a lawyer," he said boldly. "He wouldn't let me keep the cap if he didn't think I should."

"Is that a fact?" Dave asked belligerently. "Well, we'll see. Come on. Let's go." And he got between the two boys and they walked along the street. They didn't talk to each other. Dave knew the Hudson boy was waiting to get to the protection of his home, and Steve knew it, too, and he looked up apprehensively at Dave. And Dave, reaching for his hand, squeezed it encouragingly and strode along, cocky and belligerent, knowing that Steve relied on him.

The Hudson boy lived in that row of fine apartment houses on the other side of the park. At the entrance to one of these houses Dave tried not to hang back and show he was impressed, because he could feel Steve hanging back. When they got into the small elevator Dave didn't know why he took off his hat. In the carpeted hall on the fourth floor the Hudson boy said, "Just a minute," and entered his own apartment. Dave and Steve were left alone in the corridor, knowing that the other boy was preparing his father for the encounter. Steve looked anxiously at his father, and Dave said, "Don't worry, Son," and he added resolutely, "No one's putting anything over on us."

A tall balding man in a brown velvet smoking-jacket suddenly opened the door. Dave had never seen a man wearing one of those jackets, although he had seen them in department-store windows. "Good evening," he said, making a deprecatory gesture at the cap Steve still clutched tightly in his left hand. "My boy didn't get your name. My name is Hudson."

"Mine's Diamond."

"Come on in," Mr. Hudson said, putting out his hand and laughing good-naturedly. He led Dave and Steve into his living-room. "What's this about that cap?" he asked. "The way kids can get excited about a cap. Well, it's understandable, isn't it?"

"So it is," Dave said, moving closer to Steve, who was awed by the broadloom rug and the fine furniture. He wanted to show Steve he was at ease himself, and he wished Mr. Hudson wouldn't be so polite. That meant Dave had to be polite and affable, too, and it was hard to manage when he was standing in the middle of the floor in his old windbreaker.

"Sit down, Mr. Diamond," Mr. Hudson said. Dave took Steve's arm and sat him down beside him on the chesterfield. The Hudson boy watched his father. And Dave looked at Steve and saw that he wouldn't face Mr. Hudson or the other boy; he kept looking up at Dave, putting all his faith in him.

"Well, Mr. Diamond, from what I gathered from my boy, you're able to prove this cap belonged to your boy."

"That's a fact," Dave said.

"Mr. Diamond, you'll have to believe my boy bought that cap from some kid in good faith."

"I don't doubt it," Dave said. "But no kid can sell something that doesn't belong to him. You know that's a fact, Mr. Hudson."

"Yes, that's a fact," Mr. Hudson agreed. "But that cap means a lot to my boy, Mr. Diamond."

"It means a lot to my boy, too, Mr. Hudson."

"Sure it does. But supposing we called in a policeman. You know what he'd say? He'd ask you if you were willing to pay my boy what he paid for the cap. That's usually the way it works out," Mr. Hudson said, friendly and smiling, as he eyed Dave shrewdly.

"But that's not right. It's not justice," Dave protested. "Not when it's my boy's cap."

"I know it isn't right. But that's what they do."

"All right. What did you say your boy paid for the cap?" Dave said reluctantly.

"Two dollars."

"Two dollars!" Dave repeated. Mr. Hudson's smile was still kindly, but his eyes were shrewd, and Dave knew the lawyer was counting on his not having the two dollars; Mr. Hudson thought he had Dave sized up; he had looked at him and decided he was broke. Dave's pride was hurt, and he turned to Steve. What he saw in Steve's face was more powerful than the hurt to his pride: it was the memory of how difficult it had been to get an extra nickel, the talk he heard about the cost of food, the worry in his mother's face as she tried to make ends meet, and the bewildered embarrassment that he was here in a rich man's home, forcing his father to confess that he couldn't afford to spend two dollars. Then Dave grew angry and reckless. "I'll give you the two dollars," he said.

Steve looked at the Hudson boy and grinned brightly. The Hudson boy watched his father.

"I suppose that's fair enough," Mr. Hudson said. "A cap like this can be worth a lot to a kid. You know how it is. Your boy might want to sell—I mean be satisfied. Would he take five dollars for it?"

"Five dollars?" Dave repeated. "Is it worth five dollars, Steve?" he asked uncertainly.

Steve shook his head and looked frightened.

"No, thanks, Mr. Hudson," Dave said firmly.

"I'll tell you what I'll do," Mr. Hudson said. "I'll give you ten dollars. The cap has a sentimental value for my boy, a Philly cap, a big-leaguer's cap. It's only worth about a buck and a half really," he added. But Dave shook his head again. Mr. Hudson frowned. He looked at his own boy with indulgent concern, but now he was embarrassed. "I'll tell you what I'll do," he said. "This cap—well, it's worth as much as a day at the circus to my boy. Your boy should be recompensed. I want to be fair. Here's twenty dollars," and he held out two ten-dollar bills to Dave.

That much money for a cap, Dave thought, and his eyes brightened. But he knew what the cap had meant to Steve; to deprive him of it now that it was within his reach would be unbearable. All the things he needed in his life gathered around him; his wife was there, saying he couldn't afford to reject the offer, he had no right to do it; and he turned to Steve to see if Steve thought it wonderful that the cap could bring them twenty dollars.

"What do you say, Steve?" he asked uneasily.

"I don't know," Steve said. He was in a trance. When Dave smiled, Steve smiled too, and Dave believed that Steve was as impressed as he was, only more bewildered, and maybe even more aware that they could not possibly turn away that much money for a ball cap.

"Well, here you are," Mr. Hudson said, and he put the two bills in Steve's hand. "It's a lot of money. But I guess you had a right to expect as much."

With a dazed, fixed smile Steve handed the money slowly to his father, and his face was white.

Laughing jovially, Mr. Hudson led them to the door. His own boy followed a few paces behind.

In the elevator Dave took the bills out of his pocket. "See, Stevie," he whispered eagerly. "That windbreaker you wanted! And ten dollars for your bank! Won't Mother be surprised?"

"Yeah," Steve whispered, the little smile still on his face. But Dave had to turn away quickly so their eyes wouldn't meet, for he saw that it was a scared smile.

Outside, Dave said, "Here, you carry the money home, Steve. You show it to your mother."

"No, you keep it," Steve said, and then there was nothing to say. They walked in silence.

"It's a lot of money," Dave said finally. When Steve didn't answer him, he added angrily, "I turned to you, Steve. I asked you, didn't I?"

"That man knew how much his boy wanted that cap," Steve said.

"Sure. But he recognized how much it was worth to us."

"No, you let him take it away from us," Steve blurted.

"That's unfair," Dave said. "Don't dare say that to me."

"I don't want to be like you," Steve muttered, and he darted across the road and walked along on the other side of the street.

"It's unfair," Dave said angrily, only now he didn't mean that Steve was unfair, he meant that what had happened in the prosperous Hudson home was unfair, and he didn't know quite why. He had been trapped, not just by Mr. Hudson, but by his own life. Across the road Steve was hurrying along with his head down, wanting to be alone. They walked most of the way home on opposite sides of the street, until Dave could stand it no longer. "Steve," he called, crossing the street. "It was very unfair. I mean, for you to say . . . " But Steve started to run. Dave walked as fast as he could and Steve was getting beyond him, and he felt enraged and suddenly he yelled, "Steve!" and he started to chase his son. He wanted to get hold of Steve and pound him, and he didn't know why. He gained on him, he gasped for breath and he almost got him by the shoulder. Turning, Steve saw his father's face in the street light and was terrified; he circled away, got to the house, and rushed in, yelling, "Mother!"

"Son, Son!" she cried, rushing from the kitchen. As soon as she threw her arms around Steve, shielding him, Dave's anger left him and he felt stupid. He walked past them into the kitchen.

"What happened?" she asked anxiously. "Have you both gone crazy? What did you do, Steve?"

"Nothing," he said sullenly.

"What did your father do?"

"We found the boy with my ball cap, and he let the boy's father take it from us."

"No, no," Dave protested. "Nobody pushed us around. The man didn't put anything over us." He felt tired and his face was burning. He told what had happened; then he slowly took the two ten dollar bills out of his wallet and tossed them on the table and looked up guiltily at his wife.

It hurt him that she didn't pick up the money, and that she didn't rebuke him. "It is a lot of money, Son," she said slowly. "Your father was only trying to do what he knew was right, and it'll work out, and you'll understand." She was soothing Steve, but Dave knew she felt that she needed to be gentle with him, too, and he was ashamed.

When she went with Steve to his bedroom, Dave sat by himself. His son had contempt for him, he thought. His son, for the first time, had seen how easy it was for another man to handle him, and he had judged him and had wanted to walk alone on the other side of the street. He looked at the money and he hated the sight of it.

His wife returned to the kitchen, made a cup of tea, talked soothingly, and said it was incredible that he had forced the Hudson man to pay him twenty dollars for the cap, but all Dave could think of was Steve was scared of me.

Finally, he got up and went into Steve's room. The room was in darkness, but he could see the outline of Steve's body on the bed, and he sat down beside him and whispered, "Look, Son, it was a mistake. I know why. People like us—in circumstances where money can scare us. No, no," he said, feeling ashamed and shaking his head apologetically; he was taking the wrong way of showing the boy they were together; he was covering up his own failure. For the failure had been his, and it had come out of being so separated from his son that he had been blind to what was beyond the price in a boy's life. He longed now to show Steve he could be with him from day to day. His hand went out hesitantly to Steve's shoulder. "Steve, look," he said eagerly. "The trouble was I didn't realize how much I enjoyed it that night at the ball park. If I had watched you playing for your own team—the kids around here say you could be a great pitcher. We could take that money and buy a new pitcher's glove for you, and a catcher's mitt. Steve, Steve, are you listening? I could catch you, work with you in the lane. Maybe I could be your coach . . . watch you become a great pitcher." In the half-darkness he could see the boy's pale face turn to him.

Steve, who had never heard his father talk like this, was shy and wondering. All he knew was that his father, for the first time, wanted to be with him in his hopes and adventures. He said, "I guess you do know how important that cap was." His hand went out to his father's arm. "With that man the cap was—well it was just something he could buy, eh Dad?" Dave gripped his son's hand hard. The wonderful generosity of childhood—the price a boy was willing to pay to be able to count on his father's admiration and approval—made him feel humble, then strangely exalted.

The Father

THE MAN WHOSE STORY is here to be told was the wealthiest and most influential person in his parish; his name was Thord Överaas. He appeared in the parson's study one day, tall and earnest.

"I have gotten a son," said he, "and I wish to present him for baptism."

"What shall his name be?"

"Finn—after my father."

"And the sponsors?"

They were mentioned, and proved to be the best men and women of Thord's relations in the parish.

"Is there anything else?" inquired the parson, and looked up. The peasant hesitated a little.

"I should like very much to have him baptized by himself," said he, finally.

"That is to say on a weekday?"

"Next Saturday, at twelve o'clock noon."

"Is there anything else?" inquired the parson.

"There is nothing else," and the peasant twirled his cap, as though he were about to go.

Then the parson rose. "There is yet this, however," said he, and walking toward Thord, he took him by the hand and looked gravely into his eyes: "God grant that the child may become a blessing to you!"

One day sixteen years later Thord stood once more in the parson's study.

"Really, you carry your age astonishingly well, Thord," said the parson, for he saw no change whatever in the man.

"That is because I have no troubles," replied Thord.

To this the parson said nothing, but after a while he asked: "What is your pleasure this evening?"

"I have come this evening about that son of mine who is to be confirmed tomorrow."

"He is a bright boy."

"I did not wish to pay the parson until I heard what number the boy would have when he takes his place in the church tomorrow."

"He will stand number one."

"So I have heard, and here are ten dollars for the parson."

"Is there anything else I can do for you?" inquired the parson, fixing his eyes on Thord.

"There is nothing else."

Thord went out.

Eight years more rolled by, and then one day a noise was heard outside of the parson's study, for many men were approaching; and at their head was Thord, who entered first.

The parson looked up and recognized him.

"You come well attended this evening, Thord," said he.

"I am here to request that the banns[1] may be published for my son; he is about to marry Karen Storliden, daughter of Gudmund, who stands here beside me."

"Why, that is the richest girl in the parish."

"So they say," replied the peasant, stroking back his hair with one hand.

The parson sat awhile as if in deep thought, then entered the names in his book, without making any comments; and the men wrote their signatures underneath. Thord laid three dollars on the table.

"One is all I am to have," said the parson.

"I know that very well, but he is my only child; I want to do it handsomely."

The parson took the money.

"This is now the third time, Thord, that you have come here on your son's account."

"But now I am through with him," said Thord, and folding up his pocketbook he said farewell and walked away.

The men slowly followed him.

A fortnight later, the father and son were rowing across the lake, one calm, still day, to Storliden to make arrangements for the wedding.

"This thwart[2] is not secure," said the son, and stood up to straighten the seat on which he was sitting.

At the same moment the board he was standing on slipped from under him; he threw out his arms, uttered a shriek, and fell overboard.

"Take hold of the oar!" shouted the father, springing to his feet and holding out the oar.

But when the son had made a couple of efforts, he grew stiff.

"Wait a moment!" cried the father and began to row toward his son.

Then the son rolled over on his back, gave his father one long look, and sank.

Thord could scarcely believe it; he held the boat still and stared at the spot where his son had gone down, as though he must surely come

[1]notice of a proposed marriage
[2]a rower's seat

to the surface again. There rose some bubbles, then some more, and finally one large one that burst; and the lake lay there as smooth and bright as a mirror again.

For three days and three nights people saw the father rowing round and round the spot, without taking either food or sleep; he was dragging the lake for the body of his son. And toward morning of the third day he found it and carried it in his arms up over the hills to his gard.[1]

It might have been about a year from that day when the parson, late one autumn evening, heard someone in the passage outside of the door, carefully trying to find the latch. The parson opened the door, and in walked a tall, thin man, with bowed form and white hair. The parson looked long at him before he recognized him. It was Thord.

"Are you out walking so late?" said the parson, and stood still in front of him.

"Ah, yes! It is late," said Thord, and took a seat.

The parson sat down also, as though waiting. A long, long silence followed. At last Thord said:

"I have something with me that I should like to give to the poor; I want it to be invested as a legacy in my son's name."

He rose, laid some money on the table, and sat down again. The parson counted it.

"It is a great deal of money," said he.

"It is half the price of my gard. I sold it today."

The parson sat long in silence. At last he asked, but gently:

"What do you propose to do now, Thord?"

"Something better."

They sat there for a while, Thord with downcast eyes, the parson with his eyes fixed on Thord. Presently the parson said, slowly and softly:

"I think your son has at last brought you a true blessing."

"Yes, I think so myself," said Thord, looking up, while two big tears coursed slowly down his cheeks.

Reading for Understanding

Main Idea

1. The main idea of both stories, though expressed differently, is (a) the uncertainties of life and fate (b) a father's love for his son (c) the lack of understanding between fathers and sons (d) the cruelty of some persons toward others.

[1]farm, our word *garden*

Details

2. Eddie Condon is (a) related to Steve and Dave (b) the wealthy father (c) Dave's idol (d) a baseball player.
3. The boy with Steve's cap said that (a) it was his father's (b) a baseball player had given it to him (c) he had found it (d) he had bought it.
4. Mr. Hudson gave Steve (a) \$2 (b) \$10 (c) \$20 (d) another cap in return.
5. Dave was impressed by Mr. Hudson's (a) smoking jacket (b) baseball skills (c) sleek automobile (d) angry manner.
6. The cap was eventually (a) lost a second time at the park by Steve (b) kept by the Hudson boy (c) returned to the baseball player (d) soon forgotten by Steve.
7. The tragedy that struck Thord was (a) loss of a fortune (b) disrespect by his son (c) an automobile accident (d) a drowning.
8. Gudmund was (a) Thord's brother (b) the son's father-in-law to-be (c) a close friend of the parson (d) the parson.

Inferences

9. At the beginning of the story, Dave (a) did not understand or sympathize with Steve (b) was a model parent unappreciated by his son (c) was a person too much concerned about his large fortune (d) had an interest in baseball that was transmitted to his son.
10. Throughout the bargaining incident, Mr. Hudson was (a) viciously cruel in defense of his son (b) more sympathetic to Steve than to his son (c) pleasant but superior in manner (d) amused by the difficulties over a hat.
11. Which of the following statements can be said about both stories? (a) Through difficulties, both Dave and Thord grew in understanding. (b) The sons in both stories were very similar. (c) Dave and Thord were similar in the way they handled their sons. (d) Children should be allowed to express their viewpoints.
12. The personality of Thord changes from (a) likable to unpleasant (b) gloomy to humorous (c) proud to humble (d) friendly to unfriendly.

Author's Purpose

13. The purpose of the author of "A Cap for Steve" was to show how (a) false values warp personality (b) children ought to obey their par-

ents (c) dissension between husband and wife can influence a son (d) a stressful situation can result in positive growth.

Order of Events

14. Arrange the items in the order in which they occurred. Use letters only.
    A. Steve accepts the money.
    B. Steve acquires his precious cap.
    C. Dave reluctantly takes Steve to a ball game.
    D. Steve sees his hat on another boy's head.
    E. Dave becomes close to Steve.

Fact or Opinion

Tell whether the following is a fact or an opinion.

15. Steve should have refused the money for his hat.

Words in Context

1. "He *swaggered* around wearing the cap and looking in the mirror every ten minutes." **Swaggered** (353) suggests walking with a touch of (a) arrogance (b) uncertainty (c) humility (d) fierceness.
2. "He looked *apprehensively* at Dave." **Apprehensively** (356) means (a) understandingly (b) uneasily (c) reflectively (d) angrily.
3. " 'Good evening,' " he said, making a *deprecatory* gesture at the cap Steve still clutched tightly in his left hand." **Deprecatory** (356) means (a) wistful (b) sharp (c) apologetic (d) humorous.
4. "That meant Dave had to be polite and *affable*, too." **Affable** (357) means (a) gracious (b) uncompromising (c) jocular (d) affectionate.
5. "He looked at his own boy with *indulgent* concern, but now he was embarrassed." **Indulgent** (358) means (a) well-concealed (b) serious (c) fond (d) anxious.
6. "It hurt him that she didn't pick up the money, and that she didn't *rebuke* him." **Rebuke** (359) means (a) scold (b) praise (c) speak to (d) question.

7. "The wonderful generosity of childhood . . . made him feel humble, then strangely *exalted*." **Exalted** (360) means (a) freed of guilt (b) uplifted (c) confused (d) enlightened.

Thinking Critically About the Stories

1. How did the episode with the cap deepen the love and understanding between Steve and Dave?
2. Why was the cap so important to Steve? What did it represent to him?
3. What kind of person was Mr. Hudson? Was he fair in his solution to the cap problem?
4. How does the author contrast Dave and Mr. Hudson?
5. What role does Steve's mother play in the events? How does the author present her?
6. In "The Father," what is the attitude of the parson toward Thord? How does he react to Thord's various requests?
7. Irony (14) says one thing but suggests another. At one point, Thord explains his unchanged appearance by saying, "That is because I have no troubles." Why is this ironic in the light of the later events?
9. How does the tragedy make Thord a better person?
10. *Hubris* is defined as "excessive pride or self-confidence." The word is often used to express the fall of heroes in Greek tragedy. Does the word apply to Thord? Explain.

Language in Action

Subjective, Objective Writing

The two stories show an interesting difference in the writing. "The Father" illustrates objective writing. "A Cap for Steve" illustrates subjective writing. Each is effective in its own way.

Objective writing is a series of reports. It concentrates on the facts and doesn't try to interpret them. It lets the reader do the interpreting. "The Father" contains deep and personal emotion, a crushing anguish at the end. Yet it just reports the events, leaving to the reader the task of deciding how the characters feel. The parson, for example, does not entirely approve of Thord's pride, but the author doesn't label the disapproval. He shows it subtly by the parson's replies to Thord. He doesn't label Thord's arrogance, either. He shows it.

Subjective writing, on the other hand, provides the author's interpretation. It leaves less to the imagination and does more work for the reader. "A Cap for Steve" uses labeling words like *quick-tempered, resentful, half-ashamed, shy, envious.* These occur throughout the story. We don't have to infer that Dave is indignant in saying, "Who's scolding him?" We are given the word itself.

Poetry tends to be subjective. Good news reporting tends to be objective. In some ways, objective writing is harder to master. Writers tend to choose a point of view (336) from which to tell a story. A story may be told from the first-person or third-person point of view (336) in either the subjective or objective mode.

Can It Be Love?

ACTIVITIES

Thinking Critically About the Stories

1. Which definition of *love* on pages 273–274 seems most apt to you? Why?
2. How many different kinds of love are demonstrated in this unit? Identify each. Do you think each qualifies as an example of love?
3. In the past, marriages were not usually based on romantic love. What is romantic love? Is it a good basis for a successful marriage? What else is needed?
4. Tell which story appealed to you most and suggest your reasons for the choice.
5. There are few marriages more romantic than those involving Hollywood stars. Why do so many Hollywood and other celebrity marriages fail?
6. Which stories provide examples of love realized too late? Why?
7. Which character in this unit appealed to you most? Why?
8. When we read fiction, we tend to identify with one of the characters. With which character did you identify most closely? Explain.

The Writing Portfolio

Editing and Revising

Some of the writing in your portfolio may be for you alone: notes, bits of observation, diary entries. Other materials will be for the eyes of others. These should be edited and revised before "publishing" them.

A first draft gets your initial ideas down, suggests the general structure, and clarifies your thinking. Part of the job is checking technical matters like punctuation and spelling. Another part is checking your writing for clarity. Here's a helpful checklist:

1. Do you begin with an interest catcher and hold that interest?

2. Are your paragraphs forceful and complete?
3. Do you make it easy for your readers to follow? Do you use connecting words?
4. Are your sentences effective, clear and varied?
5. Is your ending satisfying?

As you write one or more of the following themes, go carefully over your first draft. Sometimes it's a good idea to double-space that first draft, leaving room for insertions and changes once you print it out.

1. What kind of fiction do you prefer? Romances? Historical novels? Science fiction? Mysteries? Stories of international intrigue? Choose a category and support your choice by citing examples.
2. Write the letter that Ferris might have written from Paris thanking Elizabeth for her hospitality. ("The Sojourner")
3. Does Thord in "The Father" demonstrate a good and wholesome attitude as a father?
4. Chat rooms and blogs are an important part of the youth experience. Evaluate their advantages and dangers.
5. Online dating successes and failures are common these days. What precautions should possible participants take?
6. The traditional formula for an old-fashioned love story is "Boy meets girl. Boy loses girl. Boy wins girl." Apply this formula to a recent film or TV show. (You may switch the order of "boy" and "girl" if you wish.)
7. One definition of true love is the lover's putting the beloved's welfare ahead of his or her own. Do any of the stories in this unit illustrate this? Explain.
8. In the past, most love stories proceeded in a linear fashion. An occasional flashback may have enriched the story. Current films often present a more fragmented approach: flashbacks, disconnected images, and other cinematic tricks. Which kind of presentation do you prefer? Why?

Other Areas of Communication

1. If you were producing "An Independent Thinker" as a teleplay, which actress would you choose to play Esther Gay? Justify your choice.

2. Are blind dates sometimes acceptable? Set up a panel discussion for your class. Set up in advance the topics to be considered—for example, the advantages and disadvantages, promises and perils.
3. Select from the library a collection of Katherine Mansfield's short stories. Be ready to report to the class on one of the stories.
4. Would one of the stories provide enough material for adaptation as a television play? Present your viewpoint in a talk of 3–5 minutes.
5. Set up a panel discussion of six students on the topic "Character Development in Fiction." Each participant will select a story and present a three-minute talk on character development in that story. Each speaker will analyze the methods used: by what the character does, says, or thinks; by the reactions of other characters to him or her; by what other characters say about him or her; by the author's comments on the character.

Language in Action—a Review

You may refer to the preceding pages to answer these questions.

1. The point of view least used by authors of detective stories is (a) the first person (b) the first person unlimited (c) the limited third person (d) the omniscient third-person.
2. *Silhouette*, *marathon*, and *Tuesday* are grouped because they are (a) derived from Latin (b) all related to the calender (c) they are words from names (d) they are all related to historical events.
3. *Garage* and *chauffeur* are cited in the text because of their (a) spelling (b) pronunciation (c) Greek derivation (d) history before the 20th century.
4. The suiting of sound to sense is called (a) onomatopoeia (b) stereotype (c) simile (d) word strategy.
5. The word derived from literature is (a) *poinsettia* (b) *lilliputian* (c) *silhouette* (d) *bobby*.
6. "The stadium began to tremble. The players stood still and looked at the stadium roof. Was this an earthquake?" This is an example of (a) fiction (b) subjective writing (c) objective writing (d) exaggeration.
7. *Dialect* (a) is a form of a foreign language (b) can be applied only to Southern speech (c) is a specific form of a language usually geo-

graphically determined (d) does not appear in any story other than "An Independent Thinker."

8. Another word for allusion is (a) *reference* (b) *deceit* (c) *hallucination* (d) *illustration*.
9. The first-person narrative (a) is the most truthful of all narrative types (b) is rarely used in modern novels (c) often has hidden meaning (d) is used only in collections of letters.
10. Objective writing is preferred in a (a) poem (b) personal essay (c) news report (d) diary.

UNIT FIVE

For the Fun of It

As for life, (430), poetry (424), and love (273), the following quotations provide food for thought, though not final answers. What is humor? What makes something funny? Why is something funny for one person and not for another? Here are some comments and attempts at definitions.

Men will confess to treason, murder, arson, false teeth, or a wig. How many of them will own up to a lack of humor?

Frank Moore Colby

Laughter is the shortest distance between two people.

Victor Borge

I think the next best thing to solving a problem is finding some humor in it.

Frank A. Clark

He who laughs, lasts.

Mary P. Poole

In telling jokes

If you can't remember them,

Don't dismember them.

Anthony J. Pettito

A sense of humor is a sense of proportion.

Kahlil Gibran

Here you will find examples of many types of humor. Saki takes an absurd situation and carries it to an absurd conclusion, logical if we accept the problem. James Thurber retells a funny episode from childhood and glorifies it with some keen but sympathetic insights. Stephen Leacock pokes fun at himself in the great tradition of comedians like Bill Cosby and Bob Newhart, while three vintage newspaper articles poke fun at the human condition in general.

Burdette's "The Simple Story of G. Washington," is in a class by itself.

You will find other ways of achieving humor in the stories that follow.

My Financial Career

Stephen Leacock
Canadian

Kiddie-Kar Travel

Robert Benchley
American

In America there are two classes of travel—first class, and with children. Traveling with children corresponds roughly to traveling third-class in Bulgaria. They tell me there is nothing lower in the world than third-class Bulgarian travel.

These stories have been paired because they use a special kind of exaggeration: good-natured and gentle. Indeed, understatement is often used as well. They were written by two humorists who died more than a half-century ago within a year of each other.

"My Financial Career" is dated in many ways. The sum of money is trivial by today's standards. The innocence of the depositor is far-fetched in today's sophisticated age. The account is still funny, though, because the petty vanities and weaknesses of human nature don't change.

"Kiddie-Kar Travel" was written at a time when train travel was the principal means of transportation. Note, though, that except for a few details, the article might now apply to bus travel and air travel, as well. Children on airplanes are more restricted because of the special requirements of travel, but most seasoned air travelers have met more than one Roger on a flight.

Note how the authors bring characters to life: the clerk and the bank manager in "My Financial Career," and the lady in a black silk dress in "Kiddie-Kar Travel." The authors seem to be saying, "People are endlessly fascinating. Here's a sample."

My Financial Career

WHEN I GO into a bank, I get rattled. The clerks rattle me; the wickets rattle me; the sight of the money rattles me; everything rattles me. The moment I cross the threshold of a bank I am a hesitating jay. If I attempt to transact business there, I become an irresponsible idiot.

I knew this beforehand; but when my salary was raised to fifty dollars a month, I felt that the bank was the only place for it. So I shambled in and looked timidly around at the clerks. I had an idea that a person about to open an account needed to consult the manager. I went up to a wicket marked "Accountant." The accountant was a tall, cool devil—the very sight of him rattled me. My voice was sepulchral.

"May I see the manager?" I said, and added solemnly, "Alone." I don't know why I said "alone."

"Certainly," said the accountant and fetched him. The manager was a grave, calm man. I held my fifty-six dollars clutched in a crumpled ball in my pocket.

"Are you the manager?" I said. Heaven knows I didn't doubt it.

"Yes," he said.

"May I see you?" I asked. "Alone?" I didn't want to say "alone" again, but without it my question seemed self-evident.

The manager looked at me in some alarm. He felt that I had a terrible secret to reveal.

"Come in here," he said, leading the way to a private room and turning the key.

"We are safe from interruption here," he said. "Sit down."

We both sat down and looked at one another. I found no voice to speak.

"You are a Pinkerton detective, I presume," he said.

He had gathered from my mysterious manner that I was a detective. I knew what he was thinking and felt all the worse.

"No, not from Pinkerton's," I said, seemingly to imply that I came from a rival agency. "To tell the truth," I went on, as if I *had* been prompted to lie about the matter, "I am not a detective at all. I have come to open an account. I intend to keep all my money in this bank."

The manager looked relieved, but still serious; he concluded now that I was a son of Baron Rothschild, or a young Gould.

"A very large account, I suppose," he said.

"Fairly large," I whispered. "I propose to deposit fifty-six dollars now, and fifty dollars a month regularly."

The manager got up and opened the door. He called to the accountant.

"Mr. Montgomery," he said, unkindly loud, "this gentleman is opening an account; he will deposit fifty-six dollars. Good-morning."

I rose. A big iron door stood open at the side of the room.

"Good morning," I said and stepped into the safe.

"Come out," said the manager coldly, showing me the other way.

I went up to the accountant's wicket and poked the ball of money at him with a quick, convulsive movement, as if I were doing a trick. My face was ghastly pale.

"Here," I said, "deposit it." The tone of the words seemed to mean, "Let us do this painful business while the fit is on us."

He took the money and gave it to another clerk. He made me write the sum on a slip and sign my name in a book. I no longer knew what I was doing. The bank swam before my eyes.

"Is it deposited?" I asked, in a hollow, vibrating voice.

"It is," said the accountant.

"Then I want to draw a check."

My idea was to draw out six dollars for present use. Someone gave me a checkbook through a wicket, and someone else began telling me how to write the check. The people in the bank had the impression that I was an invalid millionaire. I wrote something on the check and thrust it in at the clerk. He looked at it.

"What! Are you drawing it all out again?" he asked in surprise. Then I realized that I had written fifty-six instead of six. I was too far gone to reason now. I had a feeling that I could not explain my act. All the clerks had stopped writing to look at me.

Reckless with misery, I made a plunge.

"Yes, the whole thing."

"You withdraw your money from the bank!"

"Every cent of it."

"Are you not going to deposit any more?" said the clerk, astonished.

"Never!"

An idiot hope struck me that he might think someone had insulted me while I was writing the check and that I had changed my mind. I made a wretched attempt to look like a man with a fearfully quick temper.

The clerk prepared to pay the money.

"How will you have it?" he said.

"Oh." I caught his meaning and answered without even trying to think, "In fifties."

He gave me a fifty-dollar bill.

"And the six?" he asked dryly.

"In sixes," I said.

He gave me the money, and I rushed out. As the big doors swung behind me, I caught the echo of a roar of laughter that went up to the ceiling of the bank. Since then I bank no more. I keep my money in cash in my trousers pocket, and my savings in silver dollars in a sock.

Kiddie-Kar Travel

IN AMERICA THERE ARE two classes of travel—first class, and with children. Traveling with children corresponds roughly to traveling third-class in Bulgaria. They tell me there is nothing lower in the world than third-class Bulgarian travel.

The actual physical discomfort of traveling with the kiddies is not so great, although you do emerge from it looking as if you had just moved the piano upstairs singlehanded. It is the mental wear and tear that tells and for a sensitive man there is only one thing worse, and that is a church wedding in which he is playing the leading comedy role.

There are several branches of the ordeal of Going on Choo-Choo, and it is difficult to tell which is the roughest. Those who have taken a very small baby on a train maintain that this ranks as pleasure along with having a nerve killed. On the other hand, those whose wee companions are in the romping stage, simply laugh at the claims of the first group. Sometimes you will find a man who has both an infant *and* a romper with him. Such a citizen should receive a salute of twenty-one guns every time he enters the city and should be allowed to wear the insignia of the Pater Dolorosa, giving him the right to solicit alms on the cathedral steps.

There is much to be said for those who maintain that rather should the race be allowed to die out than that babies should be taken from place to place along our national arteries of traffic. On the other hand, there *are* moments when babies are asleep. (Oh, yes, there are. There *must* be.) But it is practically a straight run of ten or a dozen hours for your child of four. You may have a little trouble in getting the infant to doze off, especially as the train newsboy waits crouching in the vestibule until he sees signs of slumber on the child's face and then rushes in to yell, "Copy of *Life,* out today!" right by its pink, shell-like ear. But after it is asleep, your troubles are over except for wondering how you can shift your cramped arm to a new position without disturbing its precious burden.

If the child is of an age which denies the existence of sleep, however, preferring to run up and down the aisle of the car rather than sit in its chair (at least a baby can't get out of its chair unless it falls out and even then it can't go far), then every minute of the trip is full of fun. On the whole, having traveled with children of all the popular ages, I would be inclined to award the Hair Shirt to the man who successfully completes the ride with a boy of, let us say, three.

In the first place, you start with the pronounced ill will of two thirds of the rest of the occupants of the car. You see them as they come in, before the train starts, glancing at you and yours with little or no attempt to conceal the fact that they wish they had waited for the four o'clock. Across from you is perhaps a large man who, in his home town, has a reputation for eating little children. He wears a heavy gold watch chain and wants to read through a lot of reports on the trip. He is just about as glad to be opposite a small boy as he would be if it were a hurdy-gurdy.[1]

In back of you is a lady in a black silk dress who doesn't like the porter. Ladies in black silk dresses always seem to board the train with an aversion to the porter. The fact that the porter has to be in the same car with her makes her fussy to start with, and when she discovers that in front of her is a child of three who is already eating (you simply have to give him a lemon-drop to keep him quiet at least until the train starts) she decides that the best thing to do is simply to ignore him and not give him the slightest encouragement to become friendly. The child therefore picks her out immediately to be his buddy.

For a time after things get to going all you have to do is answer questions about the scenery. This is only what you must expect when you have children, and it happens no matter where you are. You can always say that you don't know who lives in that house or what that cow is doing. Sometimes you don't even have to look up when you say that you don't know. This part is comparatively easy.

---

[1]hand organ

It is when the migratory fit comes on that you will be put to the test. Suddenly you look and find the boy staggering down the aisle, peering into the faces of people as he passes them. "Here! Come back here, Roger!" you cry, lurching after him and landing across the knees of the young lady two seats down. Roger takes this as a signal for a game and starts to run, screaming with laughter. After four steps he falls and starts to cry.

On being carried kicking back to his seat, he is told that he mustn't run down the aisle again. This strikes even Roger as funny, because it is such a flat thing to say. Of course he is going to run down the aisle again and he knows it as well as you do. In the meantime, however, he is perfectly willing to spend a little time with the lady in the black silk dress.

"Here, Roger," you say, "don't bother the lady."

"Hello, little boy," the lady says, nervously, and tries to go back to her book. The interview is over as far as she is concerned. Roger, however, thinks that it would be just dandy to get up in her lap. This has to be stopped, and Roger has to be whispered to.

He then announces that it is about time that he went to the washroom. You march down the car, steering him by the shoulders and both lurching together as the train takes the curves and attracting wide attention to your very obvious excursion. Several kindly people smile knowingly at you as you pass and try to pat the boy on the head, but their advances are repelled, it being a rule of all children to look with disfavor on any attentions from strangers. The only people they want to play with are those who hate children.

On reaching the washroom you discover that the porter has just locked it and taken the key with him, simply to be nasty. This raises quite a problem. You explain the situation as well as possible, which turns out to be not well enough. There is every indication of loud crying and perhaps worse. You call attention to the Burrows Rustless Screen sign which you are just passing and stand in the passageway by the drinking cups, feverishly trying to find things in the landscape as it whirls by which will serve to take the mind off the tragedy of the moment. You become so engrossed in this important task that it is some time before you discover that you are completely blocking the passageway and the progress of some fifteen people who want to get off at Utica. There is nothing for you to do but head the procession and get off first.

Once out in the open, the pride and prop of your old age decides that the thing to do is pay the engineer a visit, and starts off up the platform at a terrific rate. This amuses the onlookers and gives you a little exercise after being cramped up in that old car all the morning. The imminent danger of the train's starting without you only adds to the fun. At that, there might be worse things than being left in Utica. One of them is getting back on the train again to face the old gentleman with the large watch chain.

The final phase of the ordeal, however, is still in store for you when you make your way (and Roger's way) into the diner. Here the plunging march down the aisle of the car is multiplied by six (the diner is never any nearer than six cars and usually is part of another train). On the way, Roger sees a box of animal crackers belonging to a little girl and commandeers it. The little girl, putting up a fight, is promptly pushed over, starting what promises to be a free-for-all fight between the two families. Lurching along after the apologies have been made, it is just a series of unwarranted attacks by Roger on sleeping travelers and equally unwarranted evasions by Roger of the kindly advances of very nice people who love children.

In the diner, it turns out that the nearest thing they have suited to Roger's customary diet is veal cutlets, and you hardly think that his mother would approve of those. Everything else has peppers or sardines in it. A curry of lamb across the way strikes the boy's fancy and he demands some of that. On being told that he has not the slightest chance in the world of getting it but how would he like a little crackers-and-milk, he becomes quite upset and threatens to throw a fork at the Episcopal clergyman sitting opposite. Pieces of toast are waved alluringly in front of him and he is asked to consider the advantages of preserved figs and cream, but it is curry of lamb or he gets off the train. He doesn't act like this at home. In fact, he is noted for his tractability. There seems to be something about the train that brings out all the worst that is in him, all the hidden traits that he has inherited from his mother's side of the family. There is nothing else to do but say firmly: "Very well, then, Roger. We'll go back *without* any nice dinner," and carry him protesting from the diner, apologizing to the head steward for the scene and considering dropping him overboard as you pass through each vestibule.

In fact, I had a cousin once who had to take three of his little ones on an all-day trip from Philadelphia to Boston. It was the hottest day of the year and my cousin had on a woolen suit. By the time he reached Hartford, people in the car noticed that he had only two children with him. At Worcester he had only one. No one knew what had become of the others and no one asked. It seemed better not to ask. He reached Boston alone and never explained what had become of the tiny tots. Anyone who has ever traveled with tiny tots of his own, however, can guess.

Reading for Understanding

Main Idea

1. The main point of "My Financial Career" is (a) the cruelty of bank managers (b) the incompetence of the narrator (c) the mercilessness of banks (d) the importance of financial planning.
2. A major point of "Kiddie-Kar Travel" is that (a) trains are no place for small children (b) train schedules are poorly constructed (c) a child is mean-spirited by nature (d) American trains are better than Bulgarian.

Details

3. Before depositing his money, the narrator (a) counted it in the bank (b) scolded the accountant (c) checked each clerk to find a kind one (d) asked to see the manager.
4. When withdrawing his money, the narrator (a) asked for fifties (b) joked with the clerk (c) thanked the manager (d) left a portion in his account.
5. The narrator of "Kiddie-Kar Travel" thinks the most difficult age for a child on a train is (a) one (b) two (c) three (d) four.
6. Roger had a fight over (a) a box of animal crackers (b) a man's watch chain (c) a lady's book (d) another little boy.
7. At the diner, Roger insisted on (a) crackers-and-milk (b) peppers (c) sardines (d) curry of lamb.

Inferences

8. The manager was respectful to the bank depositor at first because he thought the depositor was (a) a relative of the accountant (b) an inspector from the Treasury Department (c) a Pinkerton detective (d) a celebrity.
9. Despite his dismay at events on the train, the author realizes that (a) people on trains are all kindly (b) his child is a normal active child (c) dining room facilities are generally hopeless (d) the trip is really rather satisfying.

Fact or Opinion

Tell whether the following is a fact or an opinion.

10. In "Kiddie-Kar Travel," the lady in the black silk dress was probably unmarried with no children of her own.

Words in Context

1. "My voice was *sepulchral.*" **Sepulchral** (376) means (a) tinny (b) quivering (c) excited (d) somber.
2. "I went up to the accountant's wicket and poked the ball of money at him with a quick, *convulsive* movement, as if I were doing a trick." **Convulsive** (377) means (a) frantic (b) steady (c) impulsive (d) proud.
3. "Ladies in black silk dresses always seem to board the train with an *aversion to* the porter." **Aversion to** (379) means (a) wave to (b) criticism for (c) dislike of (d) suggestion for.
4. "'Here! Come back here, Roger!'" you cry, *lurching* after him and landing across the knees of the young lady two seats down." **Lurching** (380) means (a) shouting (b) crawling (c) parading (d) staggering.
5. "You become so *engrossed in* this important task that it is some time before you discover that you are completely blocking the passageway and progress of some fifteen people who want to get off at Utica." **Engrossed in** (380) means (a) excited by (b) aware of (c) perplexed by (d) absorbed in.
6. "The *imminent* danger of the train's starting without you only adds to the fun." **Imminent** (380) means (a) obvious (b) overlooked (c) threatening (d) postponed.

7., 8. "It is just a series of *unwarranted* attacks by Roger on sleeping travelers and equally unwarranted *evasions* by Roger of the kindly advances of very nice people who love children." **Unwarranted** (381) means (a) not justified (b) uncertain (c) not available (d) not understandable. **Evasions** (381) are (a) illusions (b) avoidances (c) attacks (d) conversations.

9. "In fact, he is noted for his *tractability.*" **Tractability** (381) means (a) liveliness (b) weariness (c) curiosity (d) obedience.

Thinking Critically About the Selections

1. How does Stephen Leacock reveal his own weaknesses? Why do we laugh when people put themselves down in a gentle way?

2. How does the Leacock selection show that it was written in an earlier day?
3. The bank manager appears in a brief segment; yet he is sharply observed and effectively described. Point out the touches that reveal his personality.
4. One explanation of humor is that it shows us incongruities, contradictions, things that conflict. To see a tiny dog led on a leash by a seven-foot basketball player is funnier than seeing the same dog with a six-year-old. How does Benchley use incongruities in describing the experiences of Roger on the train?
5. Robert Benchley once acted in humorous short films. In one of them, he goes to bed and places his slippers carefully so that he can step into them when he arises. During the night, the slippers turn around by themselves; thus, he's frustrated when he tried to slip them on in the morning without bending. He is demonstrating the "antihuman qualities of inanimate objects." Audiences found the movie hilarious. What was funny? Does Benchley use any of the same techniques in "Kiddie-Kar Travel"?
6. Have you ever traveled with a small child on a bus, train, or plane? Did your experiences resemble Benchley's in any way? How did you manage in a car? Did you yourself ever groan, "Are we there yet?" Why does transportation often bring out the worst in children, expecially traveling brothers and sisters?

Language in Action

Our English Heritage

> I rose. A big iron door stood open at the side of the room. "Good morning," I said.

There is nothing unusual or startling about the three quoted sentences, but they demonstrate one important aspect of our language. They contain only words of Anglo-Saxon, or Old English, derivation. By a dictionary count, words derived from Latin and Greek far outnumber the words that came down to us from Old English, but that fact disguises an important truth: a count of the words we use *in ordinary conversation* would show a great majority of Old English words. If all the words of Old English origin were suddenly eliminated from our language, we'd scarcely be able to say a complete sentence. If all Latin and Greek words disappeared, we'd be sorely handicapped, but we'd still be able to converse.

Everyday words like *man, woman, house, sun, moon, grass, good, child, sleep* and *stone* are of Old English origin, as are the common personal pronouns—*I, we, you, he, she, it.* The constantly used conjunctions and prepositions and the articles *a, an, the* are also of Old English extraction.

In unusual situations we rely on Old English:

Stay away from that stove. It's hot!

I love you.

Let's go to the beach today.

Don't ever ask me to go there again!

Where did you leave the tickets for tonight's meeting? We'll be late.

Old English is related to many other old tongues on the continent of Europe. It represents the strong Germanic basis of our language. The Romance words, especially from French and Latin, represent the other strand. English has both, a source of diversity and richness of synonyms. See also the Norman Conquest (559).

The Background

"Saki"
Scottish

"But he bore on his back the burden of the dead man's genius."

Saki (pen name of H.H. Munro) looks at the arts—an absurdly funny fiction of one man's plight. The master tattoo artist Signor Andreas Pincini decorates the back of Henry Deplis with a magnificent scene from Greek mythology. You might think that Monsieur Deplis owns his back and the masterpiece so glowingly displayed on it. Alas, that work of art is declared a national treasure, and Deplis' life is changed forever.

Saki says, "What if . . ." and carries it to a farcical conclusion.

The Background

"THAT WOMAN'S ART JARGON tires me," said Clovis to his journalist friend. "She's so fond of talking of certain pictures as 'growing on one,' as though they were a sort of fungus."

"That reminds me," said the journalist, "of the story of Henri Deplis. Have I ever told it you?"

Clovis shook his head.

"Henri Deplis was by birth a native of the Grand Duchy of Luxembourg. On maturer reflection he became a commercial traveler. His business activities frequently took him beyond the limits of the Grand Duchy, and he was stopping in a small town of northern Italy when news reached him from home that a legacy from a distant and deceased relative had fallen to his share.

"It was not a large legacy, even from the modest standpoint of Henri Deplis, but it impelled him toward some seemingly harmless extravangances. In particular it led him to patronize local art as represented by the tattoo needles of Signor Andreas Pincini. Signor Pincini was, perhaps, the most brilliant master of tattoo craft that Italy had ever known, but his circumstances were decidedly impoverished, and for the sum of six hundred francs he gladly undertook to cover his client's back, from the collarbone down to the waistline, with a glowing representation of the Fall of Icarus. The design, when finally developed, was a slight disappointment to Monsieur Deplis, who had suspected Icarus of being a fortress taken by Wallenstein in the Thirty Years' War, but he was more than satisfied with the execution of the work, which was acclaimed by all who had the privilege of seeing it as Pincini's masterpiece.

"It was his greatest effort, and his last. Without even waiting to be paid, the illustrious craftsman departed this life, and was buried under an ornate tombstone, whose winged cherubs would have afforded singularly little scope for the exercise of his favorite art. There remained, however, the widow Pincini, to whom the six hundred francs were due. And thereupon arose the great crisis in the life of Henri Deplis, traveler of commerce. The legacy, under the stress of numerous little calls on its substance, had dwindled to very insignificant proportions, and when a pressing wine bill and sundry other current accounts had been paid there remained little more than 430 francs to offer to the widow. The lady was properly indignant, not wholly, as she volubly explained, on account of the suggested writing off of 170 francs, but also at the attempt to depreciate the value of her late husband's acknowledged masterpiece. In a week's time Deplis was obliged to reduce his offer to 405 francs, which circumstances fanned the widow's indignation into a fury. She canceled the sale of the work of art, and a few days later Deplis learned with a sense of consternation that she had presented it to the municipality of Bergamo, which had gratefully accepted it. He left the neighborhood as unobtrusively as possible, and was genuinely relieved when his business commands took him to Rome, where he hoped his identity and that of the famous picture might be lost sight of.

"But he bore on his back the burden of the dead man's genius. On presenting himself one day in the steaming corridor of a vapor bath, he was at once hustled back into his clothes by the proprietor, who was a North Italian, and who emphatically refused to allow the celebrated Fall of Icarus to be publicly on view without the permission of the municipality of Bergamo. Public interest and official vigilance increased as the matter became more widely known, and Deplis was unable to take a simple dip in the sea or river on the hottest afternoon unless clothed up to the collarbone in a substantial bathing garment. Later on the authorities of Bergamo conceived the idea that salt water might be injurious to the masterpiece, and a perpetual injunction was obtained which debarred the muchly harassed commercial traveler from sea bathing under any circumstances. Altogether, he was fervently thankful when his firm of employers found him a new range of activities in the neighborhood of Bordeaux. His thankfulness, however, ceased abruptly at the Franco-Italian frontier. An imposing array of official force barred his departure, and he was sternly reminded of the stringent law which forbids the exportation of Italian works of art.

"A diplomatic parley ensued between the Luxembourgian and Italian governments, and at one time the European situation became overcast with the possibilities of trouble. But the Italian government stood firm; it declined to concern itself in the least with the fortunes or even the existence of Henri Deplis, commercial traveler, but was immovable in its decision that the Fall of Icarus (by the late Pincini, Andreas), at present the property of the municipality of Bergamo, should not leave the country.

"The excitement died down in time, but the unfortunate Deplis, who was of a constitutionally retiring disposition, found himself a few months later once more the storm center of a furious controversy. A certain German art expert, who had obtained from the municipality of Bergamo permission to inspect the famous masterpiece, declared it to be a spurious Pincini, probably the work of some pupil whom he had employed in in his declining years. The evidence of Deplis on the subject was obviously worthless, as he had been under the influence of the customary narcotics during the long process of pricking in the design. The editor of an Italian art journal refuted the contentions of the German expert and undertook to prove that his private life did not conform to any modern standard of decency. The whole of Italy and Germany were drawn into the dispute, and the rest of Europe was soon involved in the quarrel. There were stormy scenes in the Spanish Parliament, and the University of Copenhagen bestowed a gold medal on the German expert (afterward sending a commission to examine his proofs on the spot), while two Polish schoolboys in Paris committed suicide to show what *they* thought of the matter.

"Meanwhile, the unhappy human background fared no better than before, and it was not surprising that he drifted into the ranks of Italian anarchists. Four times at least he was escorted to the frontier as a dangerous and undesirable foreigner, but he was always brought back as the Fall of Icarus (attributed to Pincini, Andreas, early twentieth century). And then one day, at an anarchist congress at Genoa, a fellow worker, in the heat of debate, broke a phial full of corrosive liquid over his back. The red shirt that he was wearing mitigated the effects, but the Icarus was ruined beyond recognition. His assailant was severely reprimanded for assaulting a fellow anarchist and received seven years' imprisonment for defacing a national art treasure. As soon as he was able to leave the hospital Henri Deplis was put across the frontier as an undesirable alien.

"In the quieter streets of Paris, especially in the neighborhood of the Ministry of Fine Arts, you may sometimes meet a depressed, anxious-looking man, who, if you pass him the time of day, will answer you with a slight Luxembourgian accent. He nurses the illusion that he is one of the lost arms of the Venus de Milo, and hopes that the French government may be persuaded to buy him. On all other subjects I believe he is tolerably sane."

Reading For Understanding

Main Idea

1. The major point of the story is (a) the challenges of art (b) the untrustworthiness of new legatees (c) the absurdity of treating a tattoo as a national treasure (d) the many faces of ingratitude.
2. The amount promised Signor Pincini for his work was (a) 179 francs (b) 430 (c) 600 (d) paid in full.
3. Deplis was a native of (a) Italy (b) Luxembourg (c) Denmark (d) Germany.
4. The art work was destroyed by (a) a fellow worker (b) a customs agent (c) a jealous artist (d) an Italian art expert.
5. The plans of Deplis were thwarted (a) by Signor Pincini (b) by the widow Pincini (c) by a trusted friend (d) at the Franco-Italian border.

Inferences

6. The "unhappy human background" refers to (a) Deplis (b) Pincini (c) Pincini's widow (d) the Minister of Fine Arts.
7. At the end of the story, Deplis has (a) recovered the legacy (b) become partially insane (c) sued for damages (d) accepted his fate with grace.
8. The "harmless extravaganza" refers to (a) extensive travel (b) a contribution to the Louvre (c) gambling (d) a tattoo.

Tone of the Story

9. The tone of the story is (a) satirical (b) disagreeable (c) violent (d) melancholy.

Fact or Opinion

Tell whether the following is a fact or an opinion.

10. "The Fall of Icarus" was a "work of art."

Words in Context

1. "It was not a large *legacy*, even from the modest standpoint of Henry Deplis." A **legacy** (386) is (a) an inheritance (b) a strongbox (c) a communication (d) an expectation.
2. "Signor Pincini was, perhaps, the most brilliant master of tattoo craft that Italy has ever known, but his circumstances were decidedly *impoverished*." **Impoverished** (387) means (a) weary (b) disadvantaged (c) unexpected (d) poor.
3. "The illustrious craftsman departed this life and was buried under an *ornate* tombstone." **Ornate** (387) means (a) obviously neglected (b) showily decorated (c) solid granite (d) informative.
4. "When a pressing wine bill and *sundry* other current accounts had been paid off, there remained little more than 430 francs to offer to the widow." **Sundry** (387) means (a) demanding (b) wasteful (c) miscellaneous (d) overlooked.
5. "The lady was properly indignant, not wholly, as she *volubly* explained, on account of the suggested writing off of 170 francs." **Volubly** (387) means (a) talkatively (b) reasonably (c) sternly (d) cheerfully.
6. "A few days later Deplis learned with a sense of *consternation* that she had presented it to the municipality of Bergamo." **Consternation** (387) is (a) false courage (b) amazement (c) dismay (d) relief.
7. "Public interest and official *vigilance* increased as the matter became more widely known." **Vigilance** (387) means (a) interference (b) inactivity (c) willingness (d) watchfulness.
8. "He was sternly reminded of the *stringent* law which forbids the exportation of Italian works of art." **Stringent** (388) means (a) flexible (b) recently enacted (c) strict (d) sometimes overlooked.

9.,10. "The editor of an Italian art journal *refuted* the *contentions* of the German expert." **Refuted** (388) means (a) explored (b) disproved (c) supported (d) elaborated on. **Contentions** (388) means (a) pretenses (b) published letters (c) incorrect opinions (d) debating points.

11. "It was not surprising that he drifted into the ranks of Italian *anarchists.*" **Anarchists** (388) (a) are secret royalists (b) rebel against all authority (c) believe in a strong central government (d) usually unite with Fascists.

Thinking Critically About the Selection

1. Did you notice that almost the entire selection is in quotation marks? Who are the two persons engaged in the conversation? Do you consider this manner of presenting the story effective? Why or why not?
2. Murphy's Law states, "If things can go wrong, they will go wrong." Select an episode from the selection to show that things can indeed go wrong.
3. Note that the central absurdity of "The Background" is a fantasy; yet the writer treats the subject with all seriousness, even to having the critics quarreling over Deplis' tattoo. How does Saki's mock seriousness help the telling?
4. The most outrageous exaggeration is almost understated, as in "There were stormy scenes in the Spanish Parliament." What possible connection could there have been between Deplis' tattoo and the Spanish Parliament? Provide other examples of matter-of-fact exaggerations and absurdity.
5. The Italian government wouldn't let national treasures out of Italy. Other nations have belatedly tried to keep treasures at home. Dozens of museums around the world are filled with treasures from Egypt, for example. Does the precious art belong to Cairo? In 1806, the Earl of Elgin brought sculptures to England from Greece, presumably to save them from destruction. In 1816, the Parthenon frieze and other sculptural elements were purchased by England and displayed in the British Museum. Years later, the Greek government wanted the Elgin marbles back. Should England relinquish these treasures? This was, and is, a knotty problem, still unsolved. Give your views. Consider questions like this: "Does art belong to the nation of origin or to the world?"

Language in Action

The Greek Contribution

> His assailant was severely reprimanded for assaulting a fellow anarchist and received seven years' imprisonment for defacing a national treasure.

Anarchist, a word used more before 1920 than today, is a good introduction to the Greek contribution to English. It is derived from *an—no* and *archos—ruler.* An *anarchist* is one who believes in no governmental authority, no ruler. The word demonstrates a remarkable quality of Greek as a source of English words. The parts of the word join together easily and comfortably. The same negative prefix *an* appears in *anemia* (no blood), *anesthetic* (no feeling), *anonymous* (no name), and *anorexia* (no appetite). Without the *n,* the prefix gives us *amoral, apathy, asocial, aseptic,* and *asymmetrical. Arch,* in its turn, gives us *patriarch* (father as ruler), *matriarch* (mother as ruler), and *monarch* (single ruler).

Greek roots are incredibly useful. The Greek root for *write* gives us *autograph, biography, graphic,* and *telegraph.* The Greek root *cycl* gives us *bicycle, cyclone, cycle, encyclopedia, tricycle.* The Greek root *log* gives us all those ology words: *astrology, biology, geology, meteorology, psychology, zoology.* Science is especially indebted to Greek for the formation of English words: *atmosphere, barometer, cholorophyll, dynamite, electricity, hieroglyphic, hydrogen, phosphorus, planet, proton, telescope.*

It pays to know a few useful roots like *auto*—self, *demo*—people, *erg*—work, *hydr*—water, *lith*—stone, *morph*—form, *neo*—new, *nom*—law, *pan*—all, *phil*—love, *pod*—foot, *proto*—first, *soph*—wise, *tom*—cut, *trop*—turn, and *typ*—print.

Remember: Bills Are People, Too

Mike Royko
American

Parents Should Choose Riskier Names for Babies

Bill Tammeus
American

Banana Popsicles Are Good for You

Benny Smith
American

It is my experience that guys named George and Bill are as solid and reliable and unassuming as a Labrador retriever. And you wear brown. About 70% of all brown suits, topcoats, and shoes are bought by guys named George or Bill. The rest by guys named Ed or Joe.

What's in a name indeed! Mike Royko explores the impact of a name on lifestyles and experiences. Bill Tammeus calls for greater creativity in naming babies.

Benny Smith doesn't bother with names but writes a gentle, bittersweet account of his experience with grandparents and banana popsicles. His low-key but effective tribute stirs our own childhood memories.

These three selections have been grouped together because they were all feature columns from daily newspapers. All three were written under the pressure of a deadline; yet all three bear rereading. Some cheerful prose has been written by exhausted columnists. Perhaps a certain amount of tension spurs creativity.

Remember: Bills Are People, Too

THE MAN ACROSS THE COUNTER in the coffee shop politely said: "Excuse me, but I'd like to chat with you about names and sensitivity."

I hope your name isn't John.

"No," he said, with a chuckle. "I am not a John of any kind."

Good, I've heard from more angry Johns than I can count since I innocently described a men's room as a john.

"Yes, I noticed that," the man said.

Then my guess is that you are a George or a Bill.

"Why do you say that?"

Because you are a solid, reliable, unassuming and friendly looking person. It is my experience that guys named George and Bill are as solid and reliable and unassuming as a Labrador retriever. And you wear brown. About 70 percent of all brown suits, topcoats and shoes are bought by guys named George or Bill. The rest by guys named Ed or Joe.

"Amazing," he said. "You're right. My name is Bill."

Of course. There was no way you could be a Vic or a Nick or a Rick because you aren't wearing a gold chain. And you are too old to be a Kevin or a Shawn. Nor could you have been a Tyrone, a Leroy or a Jawon.

"Yep," he said, as guys named Bill are inclined to do, "I'm just plain Bill."

There is a song by that name, you know. Just Plain Bill. I believe it is the only song written about you Bills.

"No, there is also, 'Won't You Come Home, Bill Bailey,' in which a guilt-laden woman tries to reach out to the man she mistreated. But as wild guys go, Bill Bailey was kind of straight, since all his woman promised to do was wash the dishes and cook his meals. That's really all that we Bills need to live the good life."

Yes, solid, reliable, unassuming. If every man in America was named Bill, this would be Norway.

"I guess that's a compliment."

Whatever. So, I suppose you wanted to talk about how comforting it is to be a Bill, a handle nobody mocks or takes in vain.

"No," he said, becoming somber, as Bills will do whenever the opportunity arises. "Being a Bill isn't without its moments of pain. I think every Bill would tell you that, if we weren't so darned unassuming, pardon my French."

I wasn't aware of that.

"Oh, yes, because of my name, I have psychological wounds that go all the way back to my childhood."

Those are the worst kind.

"Yes, I was a mere lad when one day the mail came and I heard my mother shout: "Bills, bills, nothing but lousy bills. I hate bills."

And you misunderstood?

"Of course. I was a stunned and heartbroken little tyke. And it got worse when my father said, 'Everybody hates bills, but we're stuck with them. And then my mother said, 'I'd like to tear every bill to shreds.' Then I was not only stunned and heartbroken, but I was terrified."

I can imagine. I hope you asked your parents why they hated you.

"No, being a Bill, I was too unassuming to do that. So I just grew morose until a teacher asked me why I wrote so many suicide notes as my English essays. And I told her that my parents hated me and wanted to tear me to shreds."

I hope that this led to understanding.

"No, they sent a social worker to our house. And my parents agreed to take me to see a psychologist."

Good. All's well that ends well.

"But I just thought you might want to tell people that they might give some thought before they talk negatively or venomously about bills. That kind of talk can cause pain and suffering for those of us named Bill, and can even make us wince."

I can understand that and I'll pass your thoughts along. By the way, Bill, what do you do for a living?

"I'm a bill collector. Isn't that a coincidence?"

Parents Should Choose Riskier Names for Babies

NAMES, IT IS CLEAR, go in and out of fashion.

Which explains why it's been at least six months—and probably much longer—since you've heard of anyone naming a baby Bertha or Wilbur.

I do not pick those hopelessly out-of-fashion names out of the empty air utterly at random. It turns out my late father's name was Wilbur and my mother's name is Bertha. Oh, the ignominy of it.

By the 1950s, when I did most of my growing up, they had become as embarrassing a set of parental names as a child was likely to get stuck with. It's hard to imagine a similarly awful thing for a child of the '90s, unless, perhaps, it's a father who still wears burgundy double-knit polyester pants with a white belt or a mother who goes to the store with spoolies in her hair. (Spoolies—you could ask someone over 40.)

I've just read another of those periodic stories about popular names for babies. At the moment, it says, the world is rapidly filling up with crumb-snatchers named Ashley, Austin, Brittany, Caitlyn, Dillon, Michael, Thomas, Brandon and Zachary. Other names on the rise seem to be Hannah, Morgan, (I know at least one of each), Makayla, Justin, Daniel and James.

By the way, the reporter who wrote the story to which I refer is named Stasia, which, in terms of popularity, is either in the early stages of coming or the late stages of going. Stasia works for a Redding, Calif., newspaper with a name as unfamous as the name Stasia—the *Record-Searchlight.*

Which brings me closer to what I'm trying to say about all of this, which is that I think parents should take more risks naming their kids. There are way too many Jennifers, Jasons and whatnot. But, as far as I know, there's not one kid named Record-Searchlight, even though such a name would stand out powerfully throughout a child's life.

Still, even I might acknowledge that naming a kid Record-Searchlight would be too eccentric. And what I mean by taking more risks in naming kids isn't that. It's more that there are perfectly good names out there that have been abandoned for inexplicable reasons. At least I can't explic them.

For instance, what's wrong with Gertrude? It served Gertrude Stein well, not hindering her advancement in the world a bit. Or what's wrong with Olive? Or Hortense? Or Mildred?

And is there something socially putrid about the name Orville? One of the Wright Brothers slid right through life named Orville, and it didn't clip his wings, so to speak. And can you think of any good reason today very few parents are naming children Ralph or Harvey or Earl or Perkins?

I admire the tendency of African-Americans and other ethnic minorities to come up with fresh and unique names for their babies. This is different than reclaiming abandoned names, but at least they've got the right spirit. Most fully assimilated white Americans haven't loosened up enough to do that.

Which is too bad. It would be a better world with more Violas and Archibalds. For one thing, like Bertha and Wilbur, they'd probably deserve each other.

Banana Popsicles Are Good for You

SIX MONTHS AGO I wrote a column about my grandparents which appeared on this page.

It gave me a chance to look back on what they taught me and how important their teachings were to my everyday life.

I am glad I wrote that column because, within those six months, I have lost two of my three grandparents. Fortunately, they got to read that column before their deaths.

But there is one thing I forgot to share with you—the story of the Banana Popsicle.

My grandfather, Benny Smith Sr., was an independent man who loved his family. Sometime in the late 1970s, my two siblings and I went to live with him and my grandmother after my parents divorced.

For most children, divorce can have a major impact. I think living with my grandparents made it a little less traumatic for us.

Of course, my brother, sister and I would have rather stayed with our parents but, because that situation was not working out, staying with grandparents was the next best thing.

Even though my grandparents did not have the space in their two-bedroom home, they took us in without any hesitation.

I remember a lot of things about those early days staying in their Greenville, S.C., home, but what comes to mind most is the silver refrigerator.

To anyone else, it may have seemed like just another appliance, but to me—even now—it means something much greater.

For inside the freezer part of the two-door appliance was always a freshly stocked pile of banana popsicles. Some people say that garlic is a remedy to a lot of physical ailments, but to me a banana popsicle was the remedy to all of my problems.

Of course on hot summer days after I played with the neighboring kids in the park or in the street, the popsicle was a source of relief. It helped to cool me down after playing in 90-degree temperatures.

When I would fall and bruise my knee, my grandparents would use "old timey" remedies, a hug and,—yes—they'd give me a banana popsicle to help ease the pain.

When I would be disciplined by my grandfather, he used to always make me feel bad, but you could always guarantee about 15 minutes later he would say: "Now go on in dere and get you a popsicle."

Even though I would sometimes get mad at him for scolding me, I would gladly jump at his invitation.

Then several years passed. I was in college and was no longer living with my grandparents but would visit them on every opportunity I had.

Many times I knocked on the wooden screen door to their home and one of them would ask, "Who is it?"

"Me," I would answer.

One of them would unlatch the screen door and greet me with a smile and kiss. It always felt so good to sit in the living room, talk with them, and catch up on how people in the community were doing.

"You just come down?" my grandfather would ask.

"Yep and ya'll are my first stop," I would reply.

"You hungry?" he'd ask.

"Well, not really. I ate before I came."

"Why don't you go in dere and get you a popsicle."

That would always do it for me, because I would jump at the chance.

A chapter in the popsicle saga ended in May when my grandfather died. It was very weird to walk into the house and not see him sitting on the couch, looking at television. And believe it or not, it was very different to no longer have anyone to ask me that question that I had heard for at least 20 years: "Do you want a popsicle?"

But I decided that even though he was gone, I had something special that I had shared with him—something that other people never have the opportunity to share with their grandparents. So I just try to remember those times and, when I am down, know that in addition to God there is something else that can help ease my troubles—a banana popsicle.

Reading for Understanding

Main Idea

1. The main idea of the three selections (a) can be found in the first paragraph of each selection (b) are expressed in their titles (c) are essentially the same (d) are totally contradictory.

Details

2. A way to identify people named *Bill* is by (a) their quarrelsome natures (b) asking about childhood experiences (c) noticing their way of speaking (d) their favorite color, brown.
3. The name linked with *Bill* is (a) *Vic* (b) *Rick* (c) *George* (d) *Kevin.*
4. A name praised by Bill Tammeus is (a) Gertrude (b) Brittany (c) Dillon (d) Michael.
5. *Record-Searchlight* is (a) briefly mentioned as a child's name (b) a newspaper from Dearborn, Michigan (c) the newspaper for which Bill Tammeus writes a column (d) a book about naming babies.
6. Benny Smith (a) lived with his divorced mother (b) loves to eat orange popsicles (c) was brought up by grandparents (d) was bitter toward his father.

Inferences

7. Benny Smith's grandfather was (a) not actually related by blood (b) generally cruel to Benny (c) a newspaperman like Benny (d) a kindhearted man.
8. When Royko says, "This would be Norway," he is (a) assuming all the men would be solid, reliable, unassuming (b) paying tribute to Norwegian fashions (c) gently criticizing Europe (d) implying that we've had enough *Bills* already.
9. Tammeus suggests that (a) parents get into a rut in naming babies (b) *Brandon* is a better name than *Wilbur* (c) it's easy to become too weird in naming babies (d) *Bill* is really the perfect name.

Tone of the Selection

10. The tone of "Remember: Bills Are People, Too" is generally (a) serious (b) glum (c) lighthearted (d) smug.

Words in Context

1. "Because you are a solid, reliable, *unassuming* and friendly-looking person." **Unassuming** (394) means (a) unquestioning (b) modest (c) colorful (d) exciting.
2. "So I just grew *morose* until a teacher asked me why I wrote so many suicide notes as my English essays." **Morose** (395) means (a) quiet (b) gloomy (c) high-strung (d) offensive.
3. "That kind of talk . . . can even make us *wince*." **Wince** (395) means (a) stammer (b) rebel (c) agree (d) flinch.
4. "Oh, the *ignominy* of it." **Ignominy** (396) means (a) surprise (b) attractiveness (c) disgrace (d) wonder.
5. "There are perfectly good names out there that have been abandoned for *inexplicable* reasons." **Inexplicable** (397) reasons (a) cannot be explained (b) stimulate curiosity (c) drive a hard bargain (d) do not remain unclear.
6. "My two *siblings* and I went to live with him and my grandmother." **Siblings** (398) are (a) first cousins (b) children with a common parent (c) stepchildren (d) close friends.

7. "For most children, divorce can have a major *impact*." **Impact** (398) means (a) attempt (b) compromise (c) success (d) shock.

Thinking Critically About the Selections

1. An essay has been defined as a "literary composition usually dealing with its subject from a limited or *personal* point of view." An article, by contrast, tends to be factual and *impersonal*. An article may explain global warming, plead for an environmental cause, or support a political candidate. How would you classify the three selections? Why?
2. Which of the three selections was your favorite? Why?
3. In Shakespeare's *Romeo and Juliet*, Juliet says, "What's in a name? That which we call a rose, by any other name would smell as sweet." Do you agree? Does the name given a child play a part in his life? Provide examples.
4. Can you think of two or three names that especially appeal to you? Can you tell why?
5. Why do some names run in cycles of popularity? Do celebrity names often influence the naming of children? Is this wise, unwise, or unimportant?
6. Is Tammeus right? Are exotic names for babies better than more common ones? Can girls' names afford to be more unusual than boys' names? Why or why not?
7. Benny Smith recalls with relish a childhood treat that symbolized a happy home for him. Do you have a favorite dish, dessert, or candy bar that still delights you as much as it did when you were younger? Tell about it.
8. How does Benny Smith reveal the character of his grandfather?

Language in Action

Idioms

Names, it is clear, go in and out of fashion.

"Go in and out of fashion" is an example of an idiom, which has been defined as "a phrase in which the meaning of the whole expression is different from the total meanings of the words of which it is composed." Idioms vary from language to language. Indeed the root of the word is Greek suggesting the *individual.*

As idioms go, the one in the quotation on the previous page is fairly clear. But consider one like "the fat's in the fire." It means that a moment of decision has arrived, but the meaning cannot be derived by looking at the parts of the idiom. One plus one doesn't equal two.

Consider many of our formal idioms like "How do you do?" The speaker isn't really inquiring about the other's health or his activities. If you "keep it under your hat," you may not actually own a hat. When Maya throws "cold water" on the picnic suggestion, she's nowhere near a water fountain. If Ramon "cannot hold a candle to Joe," he needn't light a match. When you "draw the line" at a suggested activity, you needn't use chalk.

Here's a real-life example of how confusing an idiom can be to a non-native speaker. A parkway sign near an airport carried the following message:

> "Give the grass a break."

Foreign visitors looked at the sign and scratched their heads. The English meaning "Stay off the grass" was lost on the newcomers.

The Night the Ghost Got In

James Thurber
American

"What is it?" he asked me.

"It's an old zither our guinea pig used to sleep on," I said. It was true that a pet guinea pig we once had would never sleep anywhere except on the zither, but I should never have said so. Joe and the other cop looked at me a long time. They put the zither back on a shelf.

A guinea pig that would sleep nowhere else but on a zither? In James Thurber's world, anything can happen. A ghost can run around a dining room and start up the steps, only to disappear. A grandfather can relive episodes of the Civil War, to the great discomfort of a startled policeman. A mother can throw a shoe through a neighbor's closed window to attract attention.

Thurber has the uncanny ability to capture a character in a sentence or two: the narrator, Herman, Mother, the Bodwells, Joe, Grandfather. Outrageous events are told with an understated, deadpan sincerity that enriches the events themselves. The matter-of-fact style contrasts with the wild experiences of the author and his unusual family.

Was there really a ghost? Who cares!

The Night the Ghost Got In

THE GHOST that got into our house on the night of November 17, 1915, raised such a hullabaloo of misunderstandings that I am sorry I didn't just let it keep on walking, and go to bed. Its advent caused my mother to throw a shoe through a window of the house next door and ended up with my grandfather shooting a patrolman. I am sorry, therefore, as I have said, that I ever paid any attention to the footsteps.

They began about a quarter past one o'clock in the morning, a rhythmic, quick-cadenced walking around the dining-room table. My mother was asleep in one room upstairs, my brother Herman in another; grandfather was in the attic, in the old walnut bed which, as you will remember, once fell on my father. I had just stepped out of the bathtub and was busily rubbing myself with a towel when I heard the steps. They were the steps of a man walking rapidly around the dining-room table downstairs. The light from the bathroom shone down the back steps, which dropped directly into the dining-room; I could see the faint shine of plates on the plate-rail; I couldn't see the table. The steps kept going round and round the table; at regular intervals a board creaked, when it was trod upon. I supposed at first that it was my father or my brother Roy, who had gone to Indianapolis but were expected home at any time. I suspected next that it was a burglar. It did not enter my mind until later that it was a ghost.

After the walking had gone on for perhaps three minutes, I tiptoed to Herman's room. "Psst!" I hissed, in the dark, shaking him. "Awp," he said, in the low, hopeless tone of a despondent beagle—he always half suspected that something would "get him" in the night. I told him who I was. "There's something downstairs!" I said. He got up and followed me to the head of the back staircase. We listened together. There was no sound. The steps had ceased. Herman looked at me in some alarm: I had only the bath towel around my waist. He wanted to go back to bed, but I gripped his arm. "There's something down there!" I said. Instantly the steps began again, circled the dining-room table like a man running, and started up the stairs toward us, heavily, two at a time. The light still shone palely down the stairs; we saw nothing coming; we only heard the steps. Herman rushed to his room and slammed the door. I slammed shut the door at the stairs top and held my knee against it. After a long minute, I slowly opened it again. There was nothing there. There was no sound. None of us ever heard the ghost again.

The slamming of the doors had aroused mother: she peered out of her room. "What on earth are you boys doing?" she demanded. Herman ventured out of his room. "Nothing," he said, gruffly, but he was, in color, a light green. "What was all that running around downstairs?" said mother. So she had heard the steps, too! We just looked at her. "Burglars!" she shouted intuitively. I tried to quiet her by starting lightly downstairs.

"Come on, Herman," I said.

"I'll stay with mother," he said. "She's all excited."

I stepped back onto the landing.

"Don't either of you go a step," said mother. "We'll call the police." Since the phone was downstairs, I didn't see how we were going to call the police—nor did I want the police—but mother made one of her quick, incomparable decisions. She flung up a window of her bedroom which faced the bedroom windows of the house of a neighbor, picked up a shoe, and whammed it through a pane of glass across the narrow space that separated the two houses. Glass tinkled into the bedroom occupied by a retired engraver named Bodwell and his wife. Bodwell had been for some years in rather a bad way and was subject to mild "attacks." Most everybody we knew or lived near had *some* kind of attacks.

It was now about two o'clock of a moonless night; clouds hung black and low. Bodwell was at the window in a minute, shouting, frothing a little, shaking his fist. "We'll sell the house and go back to Peoria," we could hear Mrs. Bodwell saying. It was some time before mother "got through" to Bodwell. "Burglars!" she shouted. "Burglars in the house!" Herman and I hadn't dared to tell her that it was not burglars but ghosts, for she was even more afraid of ghosts than of burglars. Bodwell at first thought that she meant there were burglars in his house, but finally he quieted down and called the police for us over an extension phone by his bed. After he had disappeared from the window, mother suddenly made as if to throw another shoe, not because there was further need of it but, as she later explained, because the thrill of heaving a shoe through a window glass had enormously taken her fancy. I prevented her.

The police were on hand in a commendably short time: a Ford sedan full of them, two on motorcycles, and a patrol wagon with about eight in it and a few reporters. They began banging at our front door. Flashlights shot streaks of gleam up and down the walls, across the yard, down the walk between our house and Bodwell's. "Open up!" cried a hoarse voice. "We're men from Headquarters!" I wanted to go down and let them in, since there they were, but mother wouldn't hear of it. "You haven't a stitch on," she pointed out. "You'd catch your death." I wound the towel around me again. Finally the cops put their shoulders to our big heavy front door with its thick beveled glass and broke it in: I could hear a rending of wood and a splash of glass on the floor of the hall. Their lights played all over the living-room and crisscrossed nervously in the dining-room, stabbed into hallways, shot up the front stairs and finally up the back. They caught me standing in my towel at the top. A heavy policeman bounded up the steps. "Who are you?" he demanded. "I live here," I said. "Well, whattsa matta, ya hot?" he asked. It was, as a matter of fact, cold; I went to my room and pulled on some trousers. On my way out, a cop stuck a gun into my ribs. "Whatta you doin' here?" he demanded. "I live here," I said.

The officer in charge reported to mother. "No sign of nobody, lady," he said. "Musta got away—whatt'd he look like?" "There were two or three of them," mother said, "whooping and carrying on and slamming doors." "Funny," said the cop. "All ya windows and doors was locked on the inside tight as a tick."

Downstairs, we could hear the tromping of the other police. Police were all over the place; doors were yanked open, drawers were yanked open, windows were shot up and pulled down, furniture fell with dull thumps. A half-dozen policemen emerged out of the darkness of the front hallway upstairs. They began to ransack the floor: pulled beds away from walls, tore clothes off hooks in the closets, pulled suitcases and boxes off shelves. One of them found an old zither that Roy had won in a pool tournament. "Looky here, Joe," he said, strumming it with a big paw. The cop named Joe took it and turned it over. "What is it?" he asked me. "It's an old zither our guinea pig used to sleep on," I said. It was true that a pet guinea pig we once had would never sleep anywhere except on the zither, but I should never have said so. Joe and the other cop looked at me a long time. They put the zither back on a shelf.

"No sign o' nuthin'," said the cop who had first spoken to mother. "This guy," he explained to the others, jerking a thumb at me, "was nekked. The lady seems historical." They all nodded, but said nothing; just looked at me. In the small silence we all heard a creaking in the attic. Grandfather was turning over in bed. "What's 'at?" snapped Joe. Five or six cops sprang for the attic door before I could intervene or explain. I realized that it would be bad if they burst in on grandfather unannounced, or even announced. He was going through a phase in which he believed that General Meade's men, under steady hammering by Stonewall Jackson, were beginning to retreat and even desert.

When I got to the attic, things were pretty confused. Grandfather had evidently jumped to the conclusion that the police were deserters from Meade's army, trying to hide away in his attic. He bounded out of bed wearing a long flannel nightgown over long woolen underwear, a nightcap, and a leather jacket around his chest. The cops must have realized at once that the indignant white-haired old man belonged in the house, but they had no chance to say so. "Back, ye cowardly dogs!" roared grandfather. "Back t' the lines, ye blasted lily-livered cattle!" With that, he fetched the officer who found the zither a flat-handed smack alongside his head that sent him sprawling. The others beat a retreat, but not fast enough; grandfather grabbed Zither's gun from its holster and let fly. The report seemed to crack the rafters; smoke filled the attic. A cop cursed and shot his hand to his shoulder. Somehow, we all finally got downstairs again and locked the door against the old gentleman. He fired once or twice more in the darkness and then went back to bed. "That was grandfather," I explained to Joe, out of breath. "He thinks you're deserters." "I'll say he does," said Joe.

The cops were reluctant to leave without getting their hands on somebody besides grandfather; the night had been distinctly a defeat for them. Furthermore, they obviously didn't like the "layout;" something looked—and I can see their viewpoint—phony. They began to poke into things again. A reporter, a thin-faced, wispy man, came up to me. I had put on one of mother's blouses, not being able to find anything else. The reporter looked at me with mingled suspicion and interest. "Just what the hell is the real lowdown here, Bud?" he asked. I decided to be frank with him. "We had ghosts," I said. He gazed at me a long time as if I were a slot machine into which he had, without results, dropped a nickel. Then he walked away. The cops followed him, the one grandfather shot holding his now-bandaged arm, cursing and blaspheming. "I'm gonna get my gun back from that old bird," said the zither-cop. "Yeh," said Joe. "You—and who else?" I told them I would bring it to the station house the next day.

"What was the matter with that one policeman?" mother asked, after they had gone. "Grandfather shot him," I said. "What for?" she demanded. I told her he was a deserter. "Of all things!" said mother. "He was such a nice-looking young man."

Grandfather was fresh as a daisy and full of jokes at breakfast next morning. We thought at first he had forgotten all about what had happened, but he hadn't. Over his third cup of coffee, he glared at Herman and me. "What was the idee of all them cops tarryhootin' round the house last night?" he demanded. He had us there.

Reading for Understanding

Main Idea

1. The word that best defines the events in this story is (a) courage (b) intelligence (c) cruelty (d) confusion.

Details

2. When the narrator heard the noise, he first awakened (a) mother (b) grandfather (c) Herman (d) Joe.
3. Grandfather thought he was (a) a member of Stonewall Jackson's army (b) attacking deserters from Meade's army (c) a member of General Lee's staff (d) a messenger behind Union lines.
4. The one with just a towel around him was (a) the narrator (b) grandfather (c) Herman (d) Joe.

Inferences

5. When Herman said, "I'll stay with mother," he was (a) looking out for grandfather (b) extraordinarily brave (c) really scared (d) hoping to trap the ghost.
6. Mrs. Bodwell said, "We'll sell the house and go back to Peoria" because (a) of her neighbors (b) her husband had a new job (c) she needed a larger house (d) of her fear of the ghost.
7. Thurber's attitude toward the police in his house was one of (a) uncritical admiration (b) barely controlled anger (c) good-natured amusement (d) bitter contempt.
8. To say the least, grandfather is (a) a heroic veteran (b) a true family man (c) a friend of the police (d) subject to delusions.

Author's Attitude

9. The author's attitude toward his family is one of (a) justifiable irritation (b) affectionate tolerance (c) studied indifference (d) bitter remembrance.

Order of Events

10. Arrange the items in the order in which they occurred. Use letters only.
    A. Mother throws the shoe.
    B. Grandfather says, "What was the idee of all them cops tarryhootin' round the house last night?"
    C. The narrator hears footsteps on the stairs.
    D. The police find the zither.
    E. Grandfather shoots a policeman.

Words in Context

1. " 'Awp,' he said, in the low, hopeless tone of a *despondent* beagle." **Despondent** (404) means (a) depressed (b) multicolored (c) vicious (d) spirited.
2. " 'Burglars!' she shouted *intuitively*." **Intuitively** (405) means (a) expressively (b) instinctively (c) excitedly (d) fearfully.
3. "The police were on hand in a *commendably* short time." **Commendably** (405) means (a) surprisingly (b) measurably (c) suspiciously (d) admirably.

Thinking Critically About the Selection

1. Thurber's language is colorful. Herman wakes up with an "Awp" in "the low, hopeless tone of a despondent beagle." Why a beagle and not a poodle or an Irish setter? Point out other examples of Thurber's vivid pictures.
2. Ordinarily, writers start a new paragraph for each new speaker, but Thurber runs several bits of conversation together in the same paragraph. Do you approve of this technique? Is anything gained?
3. What kind of person is grandfather? How does the last paragraph contradict our earlier picture of him?
4. If you've ever seen the Keystone cops in old silent movies, you know that they are depicted as comic figures, frantically rushing about, often with hilarious results. Are the policemen in this story like Keystone Cops? Why does Thurber describe them as he does?
5. What is the reaction of the police and the reporter to the inhabitants of the Thurber household? Are their reactions justified?

Language in Action

Malapropisms

"This guy," he explained to the others, jerking a thumb at me, "was nekkid. The lady seems historical."

The misuse of *historical* for *hysterical* is labeled a *malapropism*. The name derives from Mrs. Malaprop, a character in Richard Brinsley Sheridan's play *The Rivals*. Sheridan coined the name from the French *mal a' propos*—"out of place." Mrs. Malaprop loved to use big words. Unfortunately, she tended to misuse them: *contagious* for *contiguous, allegory* for *alligator, delusions* for *allusions, felicity* for *facility, prejudice* for *precipice, reprehend* for *apprehend.*

Every area of life is blessed with these humorous errors. A student wrote, "The Constitution of the United States was established to insure domestic hostility." Another wrote, "Emphasis is putting more distress on one word than another." A third, "Louis XVI was gelatined during the French Revolution." A young party hostess suggested that each arriving guest "mangle with the crowd."

Samuel Goldwyn, famous Hollywood producer, was known for his malapropisms, called *Goldwynisms.* Here's a sample. "The man was poised on the brink of an abscess."

Headlines sometimes provide choice examples:

> Infant abdicated from hospital table
>
> Court escapee still on the lamb
>
> Philadelphia aims at illitracy

And some newspaper reports:

> Kurt Beiner won the Middle School's spelling bee after correctly spelling *desicrate.*
>
> Is your back tired? Are your mussels sore?
>
> The sailor was admired by his piers.
>
> When planting, water the seeds before sewing.
>
> He is recovering from a near-fatal accident that sent him into a comma.

Keep your eye out. Those malapropisms are out there!

The Simple Story of G. Washington

Robert J. Burdette
American

We are patient, and we love children, but if Mrs. Caruthers, of Arch Street, hadn't come and got her prodigy at that critical juncture, we don't believe Burlington could have pulled us out of the snarl.

Communication is a tricky business at best. Verbal contact with a young child may tax patience and invite frustration. Retelling the legend of George Washington and the apple tree (often a cherry tree) should be simple. The characters are two: George Washington and his father. The equipment is simple: a hatchet. The setting is unexceptional: George's home. What's the problem? Let's listen as Clarence Fitzherbert Alençon de Marchemont Caruthers learns all about that colorful legend. The pronouns may be confusing at times, but there is a certain logic to the questions when uttered by a five-year-old.

The Simple Story of G. Washington

ONLY YESTERDAY, a lady friend on a shopping excursion left her little toddler of five bright summers in our experienced charge, while she pursued the duties which called her downtown. Such a bright boy; so delightful it was to talk to him! We can never forget the blissful half hour we spent looking that prodigy up in his centennial history.

"Now listen, Clary," we said—his name is Clarence Fitzherbert Alençon de Marchemont Caruthers—"and learn about George Washington."

"Who's he?" inquired Clarence, etc.

"Listen," we said; "he was the father of his country."

"Whose country?"

"Ours; yours and mine—the confederated union of the American people, cemented with the life blood of the men of '76, poured out upon the altars of our country as the dearest libation to liberty that her votaries can offer!"

"Who did?" asked Clarence.

There is a peculiar tact in talking to children that very few people possess. Now most people would have grown impatient and lost their temper when little Clarence asked so many irrelevant questions, but we did not. We knew, however careless he might appear at first, that we could soon interest him in the story, and he would be all eyes and ears. So we smiled sweetly—that same sweet smile which you may have noticed on our photographs, just the faintest ripple of a smile breaking across the face like a ray of sunlight, and checked by lines of tender sadness, just before the two ends of it pass each other at the back of the neck.

And so, smiling, we went on.

"Well, one day George's father—"

"George who?" asked Clarence.

"George Washington. He was a little boy then, just like you. One day his father—"

"Whose father?" demanded Clarence with an encouraging expression of interest.

"George Washington's; this great man we were telling you of. One day George Washington's father gave him a little hatchet for a—"

"Gave who a little hatchet?" the dear child interrupted, with a gleam of bewitching intelligence. Most men would have got mad, or betrayed signs of impatience, but we didn't. We know how to talk to children. So we went on:

"George Washington. His—"

"Who gave him the little hatchet?"

"His father. And his father—"

"Whose father?"

"George Washington's."

"Oh!"

"Yes, George Washington. And his father told him—"

"Told who?"

"Told George."

"Oh, yes, George."

And we went on just as patient and as pleasant as you could imagine. We took up the story right where the boy interrupted, for we could see that he was just crazy to hear the end of it. We said:

"And he told him that—"

"George told him?" queried Clarence.

"No, his father told George—"

"Oh!"

"Yes; told him that he must be careful with the hatchet—"

"Who must be careful?"

"George must."

"Oh!"

"Yes; must be careful with the hatchet—"

"What hatchet?"

"Why George's."

"Oh!"

"Yes; with the hatchet, and not cut himself with it, or drop it in the cistern, or leave it out on the grass all night. So George went round cutting everything he could reach with his hatchet. And at last he came to a splendid apple tree, his father's favorite, and cut it down, and—"

"Who cut it down?"

"George did."

"Oh!"

"But his father came home and saw it the first thing, and—"

"Saw the hatchet?"

"No! Saw the apple tree. And he said: 'Who has cut down my favorite apple tree?'"

"Whose apple tree?"

"George's father's. And everybody said they didn't know anything about it, and—"

"Anything about what?"

"The apple tree."

"Oh!"

"And George came up and heard them talking about it—"

"Heard who talking about it?"

"Heard his father and the men."

"What was they talking about?"

"About the apple tree."

"What apple tree?"

"The favorite apple tree that George cut down."

"George who?"

"George Washington."

"Oh!"

"So George came up, and he said, 'Father, I cannot tell a lie. It was—'"

"His father couldn't?"

"Why, no, George couldn't."

"Oh! George? Oh, yes!"

" 'It was I cut down your apple tree; I did—' "

"His father did?"

"No, no, no; said he cut down his apple tree."

"George's apple tree?"

"No, no; his father's."

"Oh!"

"He said—"

"His father said?"

"No, no, no; George said, 'Father, I cannot tell a lie. I did it with my little hatchet.' And his father said: 'Noble boy, I would rather lose a thousand trees than have you to tell a lie.' "

"George did?"

"No; his father said that."

"Said he'd rather have a thousand trees?"

"No, no, no; said he'd rather lose a thousand apple trees than—"

"Said he'd rather George would?"

"No; said he rather he would than have him tell a lie."

"Oh! George would rather have his father lie?"

We are patient, and we love children, but if Mrs. Caruthers, of Arch Street, hadn't come and got her prodigy at that critical juncture, we don't believe all Burlington could have pulled us out of the snarl. And as Clarence Fitzherbert Alençon de Marchemont Caruthers pattered down the stairs, we heard him telling his ma about a boy who had a father named George, and he told him to cut an apple tree, and said he'd rather tell a thousand lies than cut down one apple tree. We do love children, but we don't believe than either nature or education has fitted us to be a governess.

Reading for Understanding

Main Idea

1. The best word to describe the mood of the author is (a) fascination (b) admiration (c) frustration (d) animation.

Details

2. The narrator preferred to call the boy (a) Fitzherbert (b) George (c) Mr. Caruthers (d) Clary.
3. The boy told his mother that George (a) wouldn't cut down the apple tree (b) told a lie (c) was related to the first President (d) is the son in the story.

Inferences

4. The attitude of the narrator at the beginning of his story is (a) doubtful (b) irritable (c) optimistic (d) uninterested.
5. The story overheard on the stairs (a) showed precocious understanding (b) was hopelessly garbled (c) finally got the story right (d) involved someone other than George Washington.
6. The boy's questions showed (a) some familiarity with the legend (b) a willingness to listen (c) a mother's strong influence (d) instant understanding.
7. In this version of the legend, George (a) goes on a cutting spree (b) shows mature restraint (c) speaks sharply to his father (d) refuses the hatchet.
8. The boy's questions (a) have no relationship to the preceding statements (b) show the boy's inferior intelligence (c) show the boy's prejudices (d) grow out of the preceding statements.

Outcome

9. If Mrs. Caruthers had asked the narrator to mind her son again, the narrator would probably have (a) welcomed the opportunity (b) made some excuse (c) offered to extend the allotted time (d) spoken disrespectfully to her.

Fact or Opinion

Tell whether the following is a fact or an opinion.

10. At first, the narrator spoke proudly of his patience with children.

Words in Context

1. "We can never forget the blissful half hour we spent looking the *prodigy* up in his centennial history." A **prodigy** (412) is (a) talkative (b) reserved (c) highly talented (d) insatiably curious.

2.,3. " 'The confederated union of the American people. . .poured out upon the altars of our country as the dearest *libation* to liberty that her *votaries* can offer!' " A **libation** (412) is (a) a ceremonial drink (b) a precious treasure (c) unrestrained applause (d) deserved recognition. **Votaries** (412) are (a) respected pioneers (b) certified citizens (c) devoted admirers (d) elected officials.

4. "Little Clarence asked so many *irrelevant* questions." **Irrelevant** (412) means NOT (a) obvious (b) connected (c) well-considered (d) fortunate.

5.,6. "We are patient, and we love children, but if Mrs. Caruthers, of Arch Street, hadn't come and got her prodigy at that critical *juncture*, we don't believe all Burlington could have pulled us out of the *snarl*. A **juncture** (414) is a kind of (a) rejection (b) moment (c) turning point (d) opportunity. A **snarl** (414) is a (a) tangle (b) brawl (c) display (d) situation.

Thinking Critically About the Story

1. This little dialogue is saturated with irony (14). Remember: "Irony is a clash between what is and what seems to be." The title itself is ironic. Explain. Point out other examples.
2. There is a humorous contrast between the boy's naïvete and the wordy patriotic tribute. Why does the author insert these statements far beyond Clary's comprehension?
3. How sincere is the "sweet smile" as compared with a smile in the photographs?
4. At one point, the narrator says, "We knew how to talk to children." True or false? Prove your point.
5. At another point , is the narrator beginning to "lose it" in trying to retell the George Washington legend for the sake of young Clary? Explain.

6. How did Clarence demonstrate that he had completely garbled the story told him? Explain.
7. Was Clarence intentionally maddening? How do you know?

Language in Action

Communication–Common Problems

> "We love children, but we don't believe that either nature or education has fitted us to be a governess."

"The Simple Story of George Washington" is a disaster of communication. The narrator's expression of inadequacy shouldn't be surprising. Communication is a miracle. Though Clarence and his adult companions speak the same language, they seem to be on different pages. There are several reasons for failure in this example.

The first misconception was the narrator's assumption that he had common ground with Clarence. Successful communication requires that the speaker (or writer, of course) and the listener have enough in common to have an intelligent dialogue. Note that the root *commun* is Latin for *common*. Clary's world doesn't include votaries and libations. The problem is obvious here, but it is a common obstacle to sharing plans, ideas, points of view.

A related problem is the narrator's erroneous assumptions about his charge. For one thing, he expects Clary to identify the pronouns that pepper his dialogue. "At last he came to a splendid apple tree, his father's favorite, and cut it down." There are two pronouns, *he* and *it*, that seem crystal clear to a mature listener, but Clary has lost track of their antecedents. For the boy's sake, this sentence would have been clearer: "At last George came to a splendid apple tree, his father's favorite, and cut the tree down." Avoiding possibly confusing pronouns and replacing them with nouns would have been clearer for the boy.

Clary's problems resemble in part the difficulties for those who learn a second language. Conversations depend upon assumptions, leaving out segments that listeners fill in, rushing on without connectives that the listener automatically supplies. Listening to a relaxed conversation in your native English is easy. You scarcely notice the omissions. Listening to a strange new language is like Clary's trying to make sense of that confusing story about someone named *George* who did something somehow connected with a father. Communication is a miracle often taken for granted, often misused.

For the Fun of It

ACTIVITIES

Thinking Critically About the Selections

1. Madame de Stael wrote, "Wit consists in knowing the resemblance of things that differ, and the difference of things that are alike." What does this quotation mean to you? Do you agree with the point made?
2. Leigh Hunt wrote, "Wit is the clash and reconcilement of incongruities, the meeting of extremes around a corner." Is this a superior definition? Explain.
3. In science fiction, once you accept the basic idea or premise, things fall into place logically. In "All Summer in a Day" (216), for example, once you accept the basic concept—sunshine once in seven years—the story follows logically. Similarly, in "The Simple Story of G. Washington," once you accept the premise that Clarence is going to subject every statement to his literal, logical, five-year-old brain, everything falls into place. Choose another selection in this unit. Point out the basic premise and show how all the rest follows from it.
4. The poet William Wordsworth wrote, "Poetry is emotion recollected in tranquility." James Thurber wrote, "Humor is emotional chaos remembered in tranquility." How does the Thurber story show that Thurber practiced what he preached?
5. Which story especially appealed to your own sense of humor? Why? What kinds of comedy do you especially enjoy?
6. Don Herold wrote, "A humorist is a man who feels bad but who feels good about it." What do you suppose the writer meant?
7. H. L. Mencken wrote, "Human life is basically a comedy. Even the tragedies often seem comic to the spectator, and not infrequently they actually have comic touches for the victim. Happiness probably consists largely in the capacity to detect and relish them." Does this unusual quotation seem reasonable to you? What do you think Mencken had in mind?

The Writing Portfolio

Purposes of Writing

Writing may be classified by the purpose of the writer. Writing tends to demonstrate one of the following purposes:

1. Writing to inform (directions, explanations, reports)
2. Writing to persuade (editorials, letters to the editor, argumentative essays)
3. Writing to entertain (narrative, description, character sketch)
4. Writing to express oneself (diary, autobiography, poem, personal experience)
5. Writing to remember (notes, summaries, outlines, research papers)

As you look over the following suggestions, choose those you are most interested in.

1. The first chapter of Charles Dickens's *David Copperfield* has the title "I Am Born." Then it begins: "Whether I shall turn out to be the hero of my own life, or whether that station will be held by anybody else, these pages must show."

   Taking a cue from David Copperfield, begin an autobiography that you might complete some day.
2. Write a letter to the editor of your school newspaper suggesting a change of procedure in the cafeteria or some other area of school life.
3. Write a character sketch of Thurber's grandfather ("The Night the Ghost Got In.") Make up any traits needed to round out a picture of that colorful character.
4. Do you agree that parents should choose riskier names for babies (396)? Write a light essay with the title "What's in a Name?".
5. Why do some television sitcoms have an afterlife, long after the final program has aired? Even programs that have had successful runs die in syndication. Why do programs like *Seinfeld*, *Friends*, and *Everybody Loves Raymond* survive in syndication for a longer period than their original runs? What special qualities do shows like these have? Select one for your analysis.
6. Benny Smith (397) pays tribute to his beloved grandfather. Is there an older member of your own family who has played a major role in your life? Share your experiences and feelings with others.

Other Areas of Communication

1. If you enjoyed Leacock and Benchley, you may enjoy a book by another humorist of their generation. From the library, borrow a book by Clarence Day, Corey Ford, Jean Kerr, Ring Lardner, S. J. Perelman, Ruth McKenney, Alexander Woollcott, or E. B. White. Report to the class. Consider whether the topics chosen by these writers are different from those chosen by modern-day humorists.

2. *Comic* and *comedian* have sometimes been distinguished by definition. One says funny things; the other says things which are funny. Which is which? Choose a favorite TV program and decide which definition fits the central character. Compare your choices with other students'.

3. The stories of Saki make for good oral reading. Find "The Open Window" or another Saki story and prepare to read it aloud to the class. Or choose another Thurber story, perhaps from *My Life and Hard Times.*

4. Tape an old sitcom from the 1950's or '60's like *I Love Lucy* or *The Dick Van Dyke Show.* Ask the class to critique it, pointing out good and bad points. What is the source of the humor? Slapstick? Characterization? Witty dialogue?

5. "The Simple Story of G. Washington" provides a kind of classic comic dialogue in which one listener consistently misunderstands the other person. One of the most famous is the old "Who's on first?" dialogue of Abbott and Costello. Try to locate a tape of this routine. See if its similarity with "The Simple Story" strikes you as funny. If you can't find the tape, ask somebody older if they've seen it, and what they thought of it.

Language in Action—a Review

You may refer to the preceding sections to answer these questions.

1. By actual count of words in conversation, the majority of words come originally from (a) Latin (b) Greek (c) French (d) Old English.

2. "Let's all go to the matinee today and meet Sally and Luis there." The word that is probably not of Old English origin is (a) *all* (b) *go* (c) *matinee* (d) *meet*.
3. A basic necessity for effective communication is (a) good will (b) smooth articulation (c) something in common (d) a large vocabulary.
4. The word *malapropism* is named for (a) a fictional character (b) a Greek author (c) an historical character (d) an early television personality.
5. A common culprit hindering effective conversation is the (a) adjective (b) pronoun (c) interjection (d) preposition.
6. Anglo-Saxon is most closely related to the (a) Slavic (b) Romanic (c) Greek (d) Germanic.
7. The major function of the hyphen is to (a) separate words in series (b) make quotations clearer (c) join parts of a compound sentence (d) link words.
8. The idioms of a language (a) mean the same in other languages (b) are especially difficult for a foreigner (c) can be understood by studying each word individually (d) play a tiny role in communication.
9. Of the following examples, idiom is best illustrated by (a) The Andersons are well off. (b) I own a Yorkshire terrier. (c) The math test is tomorrow (d) Manny is going to Toledo tomorrow.
10. Of the following, the one that does NOT contain a malapropism is (a) Bruce won the tennis tourniquet (b) Julius Seized was assassinated on the steps of the Capitol. (c) Three counter fitters were arrested for passing money obviously not genuine. (d) Our cat Spots is sneaky, crafty, and demanding.

UNIT SIX

The Power of Poetry

Carlyle once said of Tennyson: "Alfred is always carrying a bit of chaos around with him, and turning it into a cosmos." Well, that is poetry's job, and it is amazingly like the enterprise of life.

John Livingstone Lowes

The rituals of the earliest people seem to be in a form we might label **poetry**. Primitive chants as well as modern hymns have a special quality that might be called **poetic**. Like Samuel Johnson on page (427), a student once said, "I know what poetry is until you ask me. Then I'm not sure just what it means."

When you hear something you particularly enjoy, you might say, "That's poetry." Just what the quality is that makes it poetry is difficult to explain. Poetry has meant different things to different people.

In this unit, you'll meet different kinds of poetry: narrative, dramatic, lyric, and humorous. There will be some overlapping, since all classifications are matters of convenience and not written in stone. You will also read an opening essay: "Poetry . . . What Is It?" After you have finished the unit, you may have a better idea of how selections may be classified as poetry. You will also meet some poems that will amuse you, entertain you, and touch you.

Poetry. . . What Is It?

The most beautiful, impressive, and widely effective mode of saying things.

—Matthew Arnold

Robert Frost, Emily Dickinson, Walt Whitman, and Alfred, Lord Tennyson are considered great poets. Are they? Why? What is poetry anyway? How can you tell? Would you like to decide for yourself?

Six Selections

Here are six selections. Are they all poetry? Some? Which?

1. A flea and fly in a flue
   Were imprisoned, so what could they do?
   "Let us fly," said the flea.
   Said the fly, "Let us flee."
   So they flew through a flaw in the flue.

2. This goodly frame, the earth, seems to me a sterile promontory, this most excellent canopy, the air, look you, this brave o'erhanging firmament, this majestical roof fretted with golden fire, why, it appears no other thing to me than a foul and pestilent congregation of vapors.

3. The pedigree of honey
   Does not concern the bee;
   A clover, any time, to him
   is aristocracy.

4. Now you will feel no rain
   For each of you will be shelter to the other.
   Now you will feel no cold
   For each of you will be warmth to the other.

Now there is no loneliness. Now there is no loneliness.
Now you are two persons but there is but one life before you.
Go now to your dwelling place
To enter into the days of your togetherness
And may your days be good and long upon the earth.

5. Snow
  in the northern hills . . .
Rain
  in the coastal valleys . . .
Fog
  along the
        shores . . .
Today.

6. Peonies scattering,
two or three petals
  lie on one another.

Poetry . . . or Not?

Well, what did you think? How do you rate these as poetry? Let's identify them and find out whether you change your rating after you discover who wrote them. Does a selection become a poem because a famous poet wrote it?

The first is a limerick that has come down to us from an uncertain source and authorship. The second is a quotation from Shakespeare's *Hamlet.* It is written in the form of prose, but it is often considered "poetic." The third is a brief poem written by Emily Dickinson. The fourth is an Apache wedding blessing. The fifth is a weather report taken from the newspaper and arranged in "poetic" form. The sixth is a haiku by the famous Japanese poet, Buson.

Are all of these poetry? Any of them? How can you tell? There is, in truth, no final answer. There is no one in a position to say, for example, "The second selection is true poetry, but selection six is not."

Defining Poetry

To make such a statement, we must first define *poetry,* but no one has yet succeeded in doing that successfully. There have been many attempts, as we shall see below, but there has never been precise agreement on what constitutes poetry. Even if we were able to arrive at such an agreement, we'd soon find that the application would present problems. We might, for example, arbitrarily define poetry as "a selection composed of four-line stanzas, with alternating lines of four feet and three feet. In each stanza, lines 2 and 4 must rhyme." We have, in fact, actually defined the *ballad* (443).

So far so good, but such a narrow, mechanical definition of poetry would not satisfy most people. They would consider such a definition too rigid. They might suggest that there must be an emotional content, use of visual imagery, clever use of sound effect.

Note the following attempts at a definition of poetry.

(a) "Poetry is . . . the spontaneous overflow of powerful emotions recollected in tranquillity."

—William Wordsworth

(b) "Poetry is at bottom a biography, the life of a man."

—Thomas Carlyle

(c) Poetry is "the language of feeling."

—Benedetto Croce

(d) "Prose is words in their best order; poetry, the best words in the best order."

—Samuel Taylor Coleridge

(e) "Poetry is the lava of imagination, whose eruption prevents the earthquake."

—Lord Byron

(f) "Poetry is not a science, it is an act of faith."

—Robert Graves

(g) "A poem should not mean
But be."

—Archibald MacLeish

(h) "Like a piece of ice on a hot stove, the poem must ride on its own melting."

—Robert Frost

(i) "If poetry comes not as naturally as the leaves to a tree, it had better not come at all."

—John Keats

(j) Poetry is "imaginary gardens with real toads in them."

—Marianne Moore

(k) "Every poem says much in little. It packs into the fewest possible words—by means of their sound, their sense, and their companionship—a wide or rare experience."

—Walter de la Mare

The preceding definitions are but a sample of descriptions of poetry that have come down to us through the years. A. E. Housman suggested, "Poetry seems to me more physical than intellectual." Robert Frost seemed to agree when he said a poem begins "as a lump in the throat, a sense of wrong, a homesickness, a lovesickness." Emily Dickinson said, "If I read a book and it makes my whole body so cold no fire can warm me, I know that is poetry."

Samuel Johnson said, "What is poetry? Why, Sir, it is much easier to say what it is not. We all know what light is, but it is not easy to tell what it is."

The Four Ingredients

Perhaps when you were young, you thought that poetry had to have rhyme because so many poems for children do rhyme. Then you learned that the poetry in Shakespeare's plays rarely does rhyme. Or perhaps you felt that poems ought to have a definite rhythm. Then you came across the free verse of Walt Whitman, poetry without a regular rhythm. Whenever one ingredient is suggested as an essential part of poetry, you come upon a perfectly respectable poem without it.

There are, however, four basic ingredients which seem to be a part of most works classified as poetry. These ingredients can be remembered easily by recalling the key word TIME. Each letter refers to an important ingredient.

*T*hought
*I*magery
*M*usic
*E*motion

Thought refers to the intellectual content of a poem, the idea that the poet seeks to present. *Imagery* refers to the figures of speech and to the appeals to the senses frequently used in poetry. *Music* refers to the poet's use of sound to gain an effect. Rhythm, rhyme, and onomatopoeia (use of words to suggest the sounds themselves) are some of the "musical" devices that poets call upon. *Emotion* is often the driving force behind the poem. Indignation, grief, and the joy of living are often portrayed in poetry. Picasso once said, "The artist is a receptacle for emotions that come from everywhere: from the sky, from the earth, from a scrap of paper, from a spider's web."

There is a fifth element, compression, which is usually characteristic of poetry. Poems condense experience. An old ballad like "Lord Randal" (443) tells a tragedy that could fill a volume—and it tells the tale in a handful of stanzas. Notice the compression in Emily Dickinson's poem on pedigrees (424). In four lines she ridicules snobbish claims to extra worth because of illustrious ancestors. Note, too, that she uses a comparison—the honey and the bee—to make her point.

Poetry and Everyday Life

The poet uses words in special ways, but such skill is not confined to the poet. Everyday speech is filled with touches of poetry. Think of these flower names: *baby's breath, Lady's slipper orchid, foxglove, love-in-a-mist, butter-and-eggs, forget-me-not, crown of thorns, adder's tongue, bird-foot violet, bluebonnet, Dutchman's breeches.* Some names may conceal the poetic meanings. *Dandelion* means "lion's tooth." A *daisy* is "the day's eye." An *aster* is "a star."

Two Ways of Writing a Poem

Compare the following two selections:

(a) Flower in the crannied wall,
I pluck you out of the crannies:—
Hold you here, root and all, in my hand,
Little flower—but if I could understand
What you are, root and all, and all in all,
I should know what God and Man is.

—Alfred, Lord Tennyson
British

(b) When I looked under the hedge—
the little grass called a shepherd's purse
was flowering.

—Basho
Japanese

The first is by one of the greatest English poets, Alfred, Lord Tennyson, once Poet Laureate of England. The second is by Basho, a great seventeenth-century Japanese poet. He perfected the haiku, a Japanese poem with seventeen syllables. You'll find more examples on pages 460–461.

The most striking similarity is the setting of the poems. In both, the poet sees a flower, and in both he tries to capture the scene for us. In both, the flower itself is inconspicuous. There is a gentle quiet mood in both poems.

There the similarities end, however, and the differences appear. There is an obvious difference in the length: three lines by Basho and six by Tennyson. The central difference is the attitude of the poet toward the flower. Basho notes it and captures it in a few syllables. He doesn't philosophize about it. He usually avoids philosophizing about life or seeking deeper meanings in symbols. In one haiku, he says,

How admirable:
to see lightning and not think
life is fleeting.

He seems to say, "Get away from excessive reliance on symbols. Life is life, not a flash of lightning, a pathless wood, or a great sea." His approach cuts through many of the symbolic devices that poets have relied upon. Basho's flower is a flower, not a symbol of the puzzle of life.

Tennyson, by contrast, uses the flower as a reason for commenting upon the mystery of life. Basho doesn't touch the flower. Tennyson uproots it. Basho doesn't exert domination over nature. Tennyson does. Nature is secondary to his musing about the meaning of life.

Which is the greater poem? As we have already seen, such a question is almost meaningless. Which do you prefer? That, at least, is a question that can be answered.

Even if we could define *better,* there would be little point in trying to decide which is better, since they are so different in style and approach. They demonstrate two altogether different approaches to poetry and, as such, deserve our attention.

Basho's approach tends to be more characteristic of some Eastern poetry, particularly of the haiku. Even in Japanese haiku, however, philosophy sometimes appears. And there are many touches in most Western poets that remind us of Basho's writing and of the Japanese haiku.

Note how the following lines from Shakespeare's *A Midsummer Night's Dream* resemble the haiku in the direct observation of flowers without pondering what they might mean.

I know a bank where the wild thyme blows,
Where oxlips and the nodding violet grows
Quite over-canopied with luscious woodbine,
With sweet musk-roses, and with eglantine.

The most famous haiku, possibly one of the most famous poems in the world, is by Basho.

The old pond—
a frog jumps in,
sound of water.

If you've ever had the experience, these few syllables will bring it back to you.

That's Life

As we have seen, poets have two quite different ways of presenting an experience. They also have two distinguishable ways of reacting to life itself. They may accept life as it is, without attempting to judge, bless, criticize, or praise it. Or they may seek to evaluate life, to appraise it, put it into manageable boxes. The approach is often dictated by culture rather than conscious choice.

Some Eastern philosophies, notably Taoism and Zen, accept life and avoid making judgments and generalizations. Most Western philosophies seek to discover "the meaning of life" and to relate people to themselves, their fellows, their society, and the universe. Most Westerners agree with Socrates, who said, "An unexamined life is not worth living."

Western philosophies often stress action, doing. Eastern philosophies often stress quiet awareness and meditation. Westerners have a way of saying, "Don't just stand there; do something." Eastern philosophies may suggest, "Don't just do something; stand there." These different philosophies are reflected in the poetry in this unit.

Poets vary in their approach to the problems of life just as they vary in their re-creation of vivid experiences.

For Longfellow (*American*):

Life is real! Life is earnest!
   And the grave is not its goal;
Dust thou are, to dust returnest,
   Was not spoken of the soul.

For Shelley (*British*):

Life, like a dome of many-colored glass,
Stains the white radiance of Eternity,
Until Death tramples it to fragments.

For Issa (*Japanese*):

   The world of dew
is the world of dew,
   And yet, and yet—

Even a writer of haiku dealing with simple observations allows himself an occasional comment about life's brevity. This haiku of Issa's is sometimes translated as "Dew evaporates, and all our world is dew."

How have the writers defined life? Samuel Butler said, "Life is playing a violin solo in public and learning the instrument as one goes on." Life has been called a "disease" (Alexander Pope), a "vapor that appeareth for a little time, and then vanisheth away" (James 4:14), a "march" (John Fletcher), a "winter's day" (Francis Quarles), a "flight of a sparrow" (the Venerable Bede), a "jest" (John Gay), a "fatal complaint" (O.W. Holmes), "a long lesson in humility" (J. M. Barrie), a "long headache" (John Masefield), a "gleam of time between two eternities" (Thomas Carlyle), a "fairy tale" (Hans Christian Andersen), a "series of surprises" (R. W. Emerson), the "art of avoiding pain" (Thomas Jefferson), a "game that must be played" (E. A. Robinson).

The musical *Fiddler on the Roof* has a memorable song, "L'chayim," meaning "To life!" Poets have been singing this song since the dawn of history.

Understanding a Challenging Poem

The haiku are simple, easily understandable, but not superficial. They capture a moment in time like a three-dimensional snapshot. But they don't require some hard thinking to ferret out their meanings. Occasionally a poem is more difficult, more complex. Part of the pleasure lies in digging out the meaning. A poem that is perhaps most often misunderstood or only partially understood is Shelley's "Ozymandias."

> I met a traveler from an antique land
> Who said: "Two vast and trunkless legs of stone
> Stand in the desert . . . Near them, on the sand,
> Half sunk, a shattered visage lies, whose frown,
> And wrinkled lip, and sneer of cold command
> Tell that its sculptor well those passions read
> Which yet survive, stamped on these lifeless things,
> The hand that mocked them, and the heart that fed;
> And on the pedestal these words appear;
> 'My name is Ozymandias, king of kings;
> Look on my works, ye Mighty, and despair!'
> Nothing beside remains. Round the decay
> Of that colossal wreck, boundless and bare
> The lone and level sands stretch far away."

Most readers understand the theme of the poem without difficulty: the futility of earthly ambition in the setting of eternity. Great Ozymandias, despite his boast, is all but forgotten. His empire has disappeared and his fame is a mockery. His fallen statue symbolizes his lost wealth, power and fame.

Most readers are content to stop here, but if they do, they miss a delightful story concealed in lines 3–8. There is a little human drama revealed there for us—of a domineering, powerful king and an unimportant artist, but in the end the artist has the last word. The story is all there. It's a kind of puzzle. After you have studied lines 3–8 to your own satisfaction, consider these questions:

1. Whose hand and whose heart are mentioned in line 8?
2. Who did the sneering and who did the mocking? What was the sculptor's attitude toward the king?
3. What has survived (line 7)? What is the object of *survive*?
4. What was "stamped on these lifeless things"? What are the "lifeless things"? Who did the stamping?
5. How does the word *well* (line 6) tell us that the sculptor has psychological insight?
6. What passions are referred to in line 6?
7. What is the subject of *survive,* line 7?

How well did you understand lines 3–8? Now consider these possible answers to the questions.

1. It was the sculptor's hand and the king's heart.
2. Ozymandias did the sneering, and the sculptor did the mocking. The sculptor obviously disliked the king.
3. The passions have survived. They have survived both "the hand that mocked them" (the sculptor's) and "the heart that fed [them]" (the king's). They have survived because they have been stamped on stone.
4. The passions have been stamped on stone ("lifeless things") by the sculptor.
5. He "read those passions well," that is, with keen insight, for he was able to reproduce the passions in stone by means of the "frown," the "wrinkled lip," and the "sneer of cold command."
6. The passions are those of self-indulgence, a sense of power and one's own importance, an arrogant way of dealing with subordinates.
7. The subject is *which.* The antecedent of *which* is *passions.*

These questions and answers have illuminated the scene, with its two characters: the cruel king and the irreverent sculptor. Though the king has used his power to force the sculptor to do his bidding, the sculptor has made a lasting comment about the king. He has captured the king's worst qualities in stone. It is these that have survived.

Understanding this little scene within the poem deepens the irony of the poem. Not only do we learn that the king's fame, power, wealth, and empire have disappeared, but we also learn that something personal *has* survived after all. And what is that legacy to posterity? The artist's rendering of the tyrant's true character—frown, wrinkled lip, and sneer of cold command! Any interpretation of "Ozymandias" which overlooks the subtle irony of the sculptor's victory over temporal power misses half the enjoyment of the poem. Some poems, like the humorous poems on pages 471–483, can be enjoyed on the first reading. Others, like "My Last Duchess" (pages 441–443), call for closer reading. The poems that follow in this unit will provide a cross-section of poetic types. For convenience, the labels *Poem* and *Poetry* will be used throughout the unit.

Reading for Understanding

Main Idea

1. A major idea of this essay is that (a) all poetry, however varied in content, has the same style (b) the haiku is a verse form that is superior to the ballad (c) poetry defies an exact definition (d) a selection needs to have a strong rhythm to qualify as poetry.

Details

2. Two Shakespearean quotations mentioned in the essay are from (a) *Hamlet* and *Julius Caesar* (b) "*Ozymandias*" and *A Midsummer Night's Dream* (c) *Julius Caesar* and "Ozymandias" (d) *Hamlet* and A *Midsummer Night's Dream.*
3. The flower poem was written by (a) Tennyson (b) Shelley (c) Keats (d) Dickinson.
4. The person who called poetry "imaginary gardens with real toads in them" is (a) Robert Frost (b) Marianne Moore (c) Lord Byron (d) Thomas Carlyle.
5. All the following are mentioned as creators of haiku except (a) Basho (b) Buson (c) Onitsura (d) Issa.

Inferences

6. If we judge by the example on page (424), a limerick tends to be (a) humorous (b) intense (c) unrhymed (d) serious.
7. According to Housman, Frost, and Dickinson (427), poetry leads to (a) unquestioned joy (b) a physical reaction (c) an extreme curiosity (d) a mellow sadness.
8. Picasso's quotation (427) (a) applies only to painters (b) reflects a narrow point of view (c) is too far-fetched to be taken seriously (d) explains a source of poetry.

Author's Purpose

9. The author's purpose in providing the six selections on pages 424–425 is to (a) show the difference between poetry and mere verse (b) introduce readers to a beautiful Apache blessing (c) challenge readers to consider their ideas of poetry (d) compare Dickinson and Shakespeare.

Fact or Opinion

Tell whether the following is a fact or an opinion.

10. The most satisfying poetry uses rhyme for a special effect.

Words in Context

1. "We might, for example, *arbitrarily* define poetry as a 'selection composed of four-line stanzas, with alternating lines of four feet and three feet.'" **Arbitrarily** (426) means (a) high-handedly (b) unintentionally (c) accurately (d) humorously.
2. "Flower in the crannied wall, I pluck you out of the *crannies.*" **Crannies** (428) are (a) pockets of earth (b) cracks (c) stone faces (d) varieties of vegetation.
3. "Even a writer of haiku dealing with simple observations allows himself an occasional comment about life's *brevity.*" **Brevity** (430) means (a) bitterness (b) confusion (c) briefness (d) challenge.
4. "Life is 'a long lesson in *humility.*' " **Humility** (431) means (a) patience (b) love (c) disappointment (d) humbleness.

5. "The haiku are simple, easily understandable, but not *superficial.*" **Superficial** (431) means (a) intentionally confusing (b) shallow (c) imitative (d) obscure.
6. "The passions are those of *self-indulgence*, a sense of power and one's own importance, an arrogant way of dealing with subordinates." **Self-indulgence** (432) is opposed to (a) self-control (b) self-criticism (c) self-satisfaction (d) selfishness.

Thinking Critically About the Essay

1. If it is difficult to define poetry exactly and finally, what is the point of using the label *poetry* at all?
2. If you were asked to apply a label to each of the six selections on pages 424–425, to which ones would you apply the label poetry? Why?
3. If you compare the Tennyson poem and the Basho haiku on page 428, which appeals to you more? Why? How does your choice suggest your own philosophy of life?
4. How does Lord Byron's definition of poetry (*e* on page 426) differ from Robert Frost's (*h* on page 426)? What point of similarity is there?
5. *Colossal* (431) comes from the Greek legend of the Colossus of Rhodes, a giant statue at the entrance to the harbor. How did the word acquire its present meaning? What other legends are suggested in the following words? Choose four to look up. A good dictionary will supply the answers.

atlas	hygiene	mercurial	stentorian
aurora	iridescent	music	tantalize
cereal	January	odyssey	Thursday
echo	jovial	panic	titanic
Friday	labyrinth	protean	Tuesday
helium	martial	saturnine	volcano
hyacinth	mausoleum	siren	Wednesday

See also Allusions (350).

6. How do you rate Matthew Arnold's definition of poetry (424) with those listed on page 426? If you had to choose one, which would you choose?

7. Another famous Basho haiku is the following:

    A crow
has settled on a bare branch—
    autumn evening.

   What picture does this suggest to you? What is the mood of the selection? What words suggest that mood?

8. Many flower names are metaphors (). Parts of the body also suggest metaphors; for example, a *leg* of the chair, a *head* of cabbage. How many more can you suggest?

9. "I was embarrassed" is a literal expression. "I nearly died from embarrassment" is figurative (224). *Literally* and *figuratively* are sometimes used incorrectly. Point out the absurdity of the following expression:

   When Bud tried to fill Dad's ears with a lame excuse, Dad's eyes popped, his cheeks flamed, and he literally hit the ceiling.

Language in Action

Figures of Speech (Figurative Language)

If we call a football lineman a *tiger,* we know that he's not a tiger, merely being compared with a tiger. The list of poetic flower word names on page (428) suggests many comparisons. An implied comparison like these is called a *metaphor.* Metaphors are common in everyday speech. A bowler *runs up* a score. We hate to *catch* a cold. He *caught* her warning glance.

A *simile* is also a comparison, but it is more obvious, using *like* or *as.* Ted is *like a bulldog* when he sets his mind on something. (Note also the metaphor *sets.*)

Personification gives human traits to things not human, animate or inanimate. Duty *calls.* Injustice *cries out.*

Metonymy substitutes one word for another closely associated with it. The kettle *boils.* (The water in the kettle boils, not the kettle itself.)

Synecdoche substitutes a part for the whole or a whole for the part. The Adamses have 40 *head* of cattle. (They own the cattle as well as the heads!) Kentucky defeated Syracuse. (The basketball teams, not the universities, won and lost.)

Though the names may fade away, keep in mind that figurative language is a major thread in all communication. Figurative language says "It is what it isn't," and we all enjoy using it.

Narrative and Dramatic Poetry

I gave commands;

Then all smiles stopped together.

—Robert Browning

This, one of the most chilling quotations in all of poetry, suggests some of the range of poetry. In later chapters, you'll meet lyric and humorous poetry. Here, poetry tells a story, sometimes a dark one, as in "My Last Duchess;" sometimes a light one, as in "The Passionate Shepherd" and "The Nymph's Reply." Poetry, because of its compression, can say much in little. Sometimes mere suggestion can tell volumes.

Narrative poetry is ancient. The urge to tell a story before enchanted listeners inspired bards to tell and retell great legends. Sometimes these narratives flowered in the great epics:

Gilgamesh—Sumer
Beowulf—England (and Northern Europe)
The Odyssey and the Iliad of Homer—Ancient Greece
The Aeneid—Rome

The line between narrative and dramatic poetry blurs. There are dramatic elements in the epics. The confrontation between Hector and Achilles, for example, is filled with the elements of strong characterization, sharp dialogue, potential action. The Iliad is filled with other dramatic encounters. Similarly, there are narrative elements in dramatic poetry. The story of the Duke of Ferrara and his "last duchess" has a plot, motivation, conflict, and resolution. The high point of dramatic poetry, according to many critics, is the poetry of Shakespeare's plays, as in the quotation on page (424).

Old ballads are often cast in dramatic form. "Lord Randal" (443) is presented simply as a dialogue between a son and his mother. There are no extraneous elements, no opinions, no interpretations. The story is presented as simply and directly as it's possible to do. The simplicity intensifies the impact.

In addition to the dramatic poems, this section contains a sampling of narrative poems. Here the story is the important element, but compression is still the essential characteristic.

The Passionate Shepherd to His Love

Christopher Marlowe
British

The Nymph's Reply to the Shepherd

Attributed to Sir Walter Raleigh
British

Why So Pale and Wan?

Sir John Suckling
British

In the long history of poetry, few poems interlock with each other as the first two do. In a spirit of romantic enthusiasm, Christopher Marlowe pens an invitation that is timeless. Why not give in to pleasure, taking no thought of tomorrow? Why not indulge every impulse? Why not?

Why not, indeed! Sir Walter Raleigh bends a hard and skeptical eye on the invitation. He matches a realistic probability with every inviting inducement in the first poem. These were written over four hundred years ago, but the sentiments and humor speak to us across the centuries. It also has a bit of advice for young women!

To balance this advice, Sir John Suckling provides some practical advice to a lovelorn young man. Here, *fond* means foolish. The three poems suggest that love and infatuation haven't changed in over 400 years!

The Passionate Shepherd to His Love

Come live with me and be my love,
And we will all the pleasures prove
That hills and valleys, dales and fields,
Or woods or steepy mountain yields.

And we will sit upon the rocks
And see the shepherds feed their flocks
By shallow rivers, to whose falls
Melodious birds sing madrigals.[1]

And I will make thee beds of roses
And a thousand fragrant posies;
A cap of flowers, and a kirtle[2]
Embroidered all with leaves of myrtle;

A gown made of the finest wool
Which from our pretty lambs we pull;
Fair-linèd slippers for the cold,
With buckles of the purest gold;

A belt of straw and ivy buds
With coral clasps and amber studs—
And if these pleasures may thee move,
Come live with me and be my love.

The shepherd swains[3] shall dance and sing
For thy delight each May morning—
If these delights thy mind may move,
Then live with me and be my love.

The Nymph's Reply to the Shepherd

If all the world and love were young,
And truth in every shepherd's tongue,

[1]**madrigals**: lyrics adapted to a musical setting [2]**kirtle:** gown [3]**swains:** young gallants

These pretty pleasures might me move,
To live with thee and be thy love.

But time drives flocks from field to fold,
When rivers rage, and rocks grow cold;
And Philomel[1] becometh dumb;
The rest complains of cares to come.

The flowers do fade, and wanton[2] fields
To wayward winter reckoning yields;
A honey tongue, a heart of gall,[3]
Is fancy's spring, but sorrow's fall.

Thy gowns, thy shoes, thy beds of roses,
Thy cap, thy kirtle, and thy posies,
Soon break, soon wither, soon forgotten,
In folly ripe, in reason rotten.

Thy belt of straw and ivy buds,
Thy coral clasps and amber studs,
All these in me no means can move,
To come to thee and be thy love.

But could youth last, and love still breed,
Had joys no date,[4] nor age no need,
Then these delights my mind might move,
To live with thee and be thy love.

Why So Pale and Wan?

Why so pale and wan, fond lover?
   Prithee, why so pale?
Will, when looking well can't move her,
   Looking ill prevail?
   Prithee, why so pale?

Why so dull and mute, young sinner?
   Prithee, why so mute?
Will, when speaking well can't win her,
   Saying nothing do't?
   Prithee, why so mute?

Quit, quit, for shame; this will not move,
   This cannot take her.

[1]**Philomel:** the nightingale [2]**wanton:** unrestrained [3]**gall:** bitterness [4]**date:** end

If of herself she will not love,
  Nothing can make her:
  The devil take her!

My Last Duchess

Robert Browning
British

The previous poems were light and humorous, but this poem is quite the opposite. Put in the form of a dramatic monologue, the poem tells the story of an arrogant duke and his unfortunate wife. In a dramatic monologue, we must imagine a dialogue, but we hear only one speaker. It's much like listening to someone receiving a telephone call. From the one speaker we can hear, we must construct the conversation and the setting. In a play, a soliloquy involves a character speaking directly to the audience, thinking out loud. A dramatic monologue, on the other hand, suggests a listener, here an emissary to the Duke from a neighboring Count.

Imagine the two men walking along admiring the Duke's works of art. Perhaps the emissary sees a beautiful painting on the wall. The Duke replies, "That's my last Duchess painted on the wall." The poem takes off from there.

As you read, note that the Duke monopolizes the conversation. In his own mind, he is a man of good taste and fine sensibility, but the poem reveals him as a monster. Look for clues.

My Last Duchess

Scene: Ferrara

That's my last Duchess painted on the wall,
Looking as if she were alive. I call
That piece a wonder, now: Frà Pandolf's[1] hands
Worked busily a day, and there she stands.
Will't please you sit and look at her? I said

[1]**Frà Pandolf:** a fictitious painter and monk of the Italian Renaissance. "Frà" means "Brother."

"Frà Pandolf" by design, for never read
Strangers like you that pictured countenance,
The depth and passion of its earnest glance,
But to myself they turned (since none puts by
The curtain I have drawn for you, but I)
And seemed as they would ask me, if they durst,
How such a glance came there; so, not the first
Are you to turn and ask thus. Sir, 'twas not
Her husband's presence only, called that spot
Of joy into the Duchess' cheek: perhaps
Frà Pandolf chanced to say, "Her mantle laps
Over my Lady's wrist too much," or "Paint
Must never hope to reproduce the faint
Half-flush that dies along her throat"; such stuff
Was courtesy, she thought, and cause enough
For calling up that spot of joy. She had
A heart—how shall I say?—too soon made glad,
Too easily impressed; she liked whate'er
She looked on, and her looks went everywhere.
Sir, 'twas all one! My favor[2] at her breast,
The dropping of the daylight in the West,
The bough of cherries some officious fool
Broke in the orchard for her, the white mule
She rode with round the terrace—all and each
Would draw from her alike the approving speech,
Or blush, at least. She thanked men—good; but thanked
Somehow—I know not how—as if she ranked
My gift of a nine-hundred-years-old name
With anybody's gift. Who'd stoop to blame
This sort of trifling? Even had you skill
In speech (which I have not) to make your will
Quite clear to such an one, and say, "Just this
Or that in you disgusts me; here you miss,
Or there exceed the mark"—and if she let
Herself be lessoned so, nor plainly set
Her wits to yours, forsooth, and made excuse
—E'en then would be some stooping, and I choose
Never to stoop. Oh sir, she smiled, no doubt,
Whene'er I passed her; but who passed without
Much the same smile? This grew; I gave commands;
Then all smiles stopped together. There she stands
As if alive. Will 't please you rise? We'll meet

[2]**favor:** gift

The company below, then. I repeat,
The Count your master's known munificence
Is ample warrant that no just pretense
Of mine for dowry will be disallowed;
Though his fair daughter's self, as I avowed
At starting, is my object. Nay, we'll go
Together down, sir. Notice Neptune, though,
Taming a sea horse, thought a rarity,
Which Claus of Innsbruck cast in bronze for me!

Lord Randal

Anonymous
English Ballad

For incredible compression, few poems can match folk ballads. These wonderful little poems have come down to us from the past without ascribed authorship. Each one tells a story. Sometimes the tale is humorous like that wifely victory in "Get Up and Bar the Door" (475). Sometimes, though, the story is a dark and violent one, as in "Lord Randal."

The ballad is in the form of a dramatic dialogue between a young man and his mother. The first two lines of each stanza present the mother's questions. The second two lines present the son's answers. The first stanza is a neutral one. A young man is tired and seeks rest. But as the poem develops, we learn of foul play—first hinted at and then admitted. At what point does the mother begin to suspect foul play? How does the son finally tell of the plot against him, suggesting who his murderer is?

Note that the ballad implies much more than it says. The young man's deceptive calm conceals a horrible tragedy. Here we have enough material for a full-length motion picture, but it's all contained in five simple stanzas. We are left to ponder characterization and motive.

Lord Randal

15th Century

"O where hae ye been, Lord Randal, my son?
O where hae ye been, my handsome young man?"

"I hae been to the wild wood; mother, make my bed soon,
For I'm weary wi' hunting, and fain wald lie down."

"Where gat ye your dinner, Lord Randal, my son?
Where gat ye your dinner, my handsome young man?"
"I dined wi' my true love; mother, make my bed soon,
For I'm weary wi' hunting, and fain wald lie down."

"What gat ye to your dinner, Lord Randal, my son?
What gat ye to your dinner my handsome young man?"
"I gat eels boiled in broo;[1] mother, make my bed soon,
For I'm weary wi' hunting, and fain wald lie down."

"What became of your bloodhounds, Lord Randal, my son?
What became of your bloodhounds, my handsome young man?"
"O they swelled and they died; mother, make my bed soon,
For I'm weary wi' hunting, and fain wald lie down."

"O I fear ye are poisoned, Lord Randal, my son!
O I fear ye are poisoned, my handsome young man!"
"O yes! I am poisoned; mother, make my bed soon,
For I'm sick at the heart, and I fain wald lie down."

Lochinvar

Sir Walter Scott
Scottish

The previous four poems all dealt with love or its counterfeit. "Lochinvar" is a story of true love, complete with a young couple in love about to be thwarted by the young lady's father. Once again, poetry shows its skill in compression. There is a plot. There are well-drawn characters: fearless Lochinvar, his shy love, the unworthy groom-to-be, the overbearing father. There is a whirlwind narrative, as Lochinvar takes his fate in his own hands. A rollicking rhythm carries the story along. There is suspense as the lovers try to make their escape.

[1]**broo:** broth

This seems the kind of story that belongs only to an age of romanticism when gallant young men dared everything for love. Actually, though, the same story line is used in Dustin Hoffman's early hit movie, *The Graduate*. Like Lochinvar, Hoffman steals the beautiful bride, Katharine Ross, from under the noses of the bride's family, at the altar.

Lochinvar

Oh, young Lochinvar is come out of the West,—
Through all the wide Border his steed was the best,
And, save his good broadsword, he weapon had none,—
He rode all unarmed, and he rode all alone.
So faithful in love, and so dauntless in war,
There never was knight like the young Lochinvar.

He stayed not for brake, and he stopped not for stone,
He swam the Eske river where ford there was none,
But, ere he alighted at Netherby gate,
The bride had consented, the gallant came late:
For a laggard in love, and a dastard in war,
Was to wed the fair Ellen of brave Lochinvar.

So boldly he entered the Netherby hall,
Among bridesmen, and kinsmen, and brothers, and all.
Then spoke the bride's father, his hand on his sword,
(For the poor craven bridegroom said never a word),
"Oh, come ye in peace here, or come ye in war,
Or to dance at our bridal, young Lord Lochinvar?"

"I long wooed your daughter, my suit you denied;—
Love swells like the Solway, but ebbs like its tide;—
And now am I come, with this lost love of mine,
To lead but one measure, drink one cup of wine.
There are maidens in Scotland more lovely by far,
That would gladly be bride to the young Lochinvar."

The bride kissed the goblet, the knight took it up,
He quaffed off the wine, and he threw down the cup.
She looked down to blush, and she looked up to sigh,
With a smile on her lips, and a tear in her eye.
He took her soft hand ere her mother could bar:
"Now tread we a measure," said young Lochinvar.

So stately his form, and so lovely her face,
That never a hall such a galliard did grace;
While her mother did fret, and her father did fume,

And the bridegroom stood dangling his bonnet and plume,
And the bridemaidens whispered, "'Twere better by far
To have matched our fair cousin with young Lochinvar."

One touch to her hand, and one word in her ear,
When they reached the hall-door, and the charger stood near;
So light to the croupe the fair lady he swung,
So light to the saddle before her he sprung!
"She is won! we are gone! over bank, bush, and scaur;[1]
They'll have fleet steeds that follow," quoth young Lochinvar.

There was mounting 'mong Graemes of the Netherby clan;
Forsters, Fenwicks, and Musgraves, they rode and they ran;
There was racing and chasing on Cannobie Lee,
But the lost bride of Netherby ne'er did they see.
So daring in love, and so dauntless in war,
Have ye e'er heard of gallant like young Lochinvar?

The River Merchant's Wife: A Letter

Li T'ai Po
Chinese

A dramatic poem can take many forms, as we have seen. One of the most effective is a simple letter. The following poem has a dramatic setting. The husband of a young Chinese wife has gone away. We know something about her life through the descriptive opening stanzas. She has been faithful and loving, but her husband has suddenly left her.

The poem leaves us with many tantalizing questions. Why did the husband leave his young wife? What were his intentions in going? Will he ever return? Why did the husband drag his feet when he left? Now the mosses are growing by the gate. Do the mosses symbolize the wife's fate—to be abandoned?

This poem touches our emotions and leaves us with many tantalizing unanswered questions.

[1]**scaur:** bare place on a mountainside

While my hair was still cut straight across my forehead
I played about the front gate, pulling flowers.
You came by on bamboo stilts, playing horse,
You walked about my seat, playing with blue plums.
We went on living in the village of Chokan:
Two small people, without dislike or suspicion.

At fourteen I married My Lord you.
I never laughed, being bashful.
Lowering my head, I looked at the wall.
Called to, a thousand times, I never looked back.

At fifteen I stopped scowling,
I desired my dust to be mingled with yours
Forever and forever and forever.
Why should I climb the look out?

At sixteen you departed,
You went into far Ku-to-yen, by the river of swirling eddies.
And you have been gone five months.
The monkeys make sorrowful noise overhead.

You dragged your feet when you went out.
By the gate now, the moss is grown, the different mosses,
Too deep to clear them away!
The leaves fall early this autumn, in wind.
The paired butterflies are already yellow with August
Over the grass in the West garden;
They hurt me. I grow older.
If you were coming down through the narrows of the river Kiang,
Please let me know beforehand,
And I will come out to meet you
As far as Cho-fu-sa.

The Destruction of Sennacherib

Lord Byron
British

This poem shows another aspect of poetry: the ability to illuminate a Biblical incident in a handful of vivid lines. Sennacherib was a powerful king of Assyria, conqueror of Babylon, scourge of his neighbors. At one point, he mounted an attack on Jerusalem. The Biblical account provides a bloody fate for the forces of Sennacherib: "The angel of the Lord went out, and smote in the camp of the Assyrians an hundred fourscore and five thousand."

Lord Byron took the spare description in *2 Kings* and *Isaiah* and painted a picture of proud magnificence crushed in a night. Note the contrast between the gorgeously attired attackers and the distorted bodies after the terrible onslaught. Note, too, the galloping rhythm that carries the poem along, much as it did the saga of Lochinvar (445). See pages 452–453 for further comment about poetic rhythm.

The Destruction of Sennacherib

The Assyrian came down like the wolf on the fold,
And his cohorts[1] were gleaming in purple and gold,
And the sheen of their spears was like stars on the sea,
When the blue wave rolls nightly on deep Galilee.

Like the leaves of the forest when summer is green,
That host with their banners at sunset were seen:
Like the leaves of the forest when autumn hath blown,
That host on the morrow lay wither'd and strown.

For the Angel of Death spread his wings on the blast,
And breathed in the face of the foe as he pass'd
And the eyes of the sleepers wax'd deadly and chill,
And their hearts but once heaved, and forever grew still!

And there lay the steed with his nostril all wide,
But through it there roll'd not the breath of his pride;
And the foam of his gasping lay white on the turf,
And cold as the spray of the rock-beating surf.

And there lay the rider distorted and pale,
With the dew on his brow, and the rust on his mail:
And the tents were all silent, the banners alone,
The lances unlifted, the trumpet unblown.

And the widows of Ashur are loud in their wail,
And the idols are broke in the temple of Baal;
And the might of the Gentile, unsmote by the sword,
Hath melted like snow in the glance of the Lord!

[1]**cohorts:** forces

Reading for Understanding

Main Idea

1. Which of the following best expresses the main idea?
   a. Dramatic poetry in purest form is preferable to simple narrative poetry.
   b. Both dramatic and narrative poetry can present a story in compressed form.
   c. Dramatic poetry tends to be downbeat and pessimistic, emphasizing the negative.
   d. English ballads are superior to the poetry of named poets.

Details

2. All the following were mentioned as great epic poems EXCEPT (a) the *Aeneid* (b) *Beowulf* (c) *Gilgamesh* (d) *Paradise Lost.*
3. Lord Randal's mother notices that (a) the dogs are not with her son (b) her son has brought a token from his true love (c) her son refuses to answer her questions (d) he has a wound in his side.
4. As part of his escape plan, Lochinvar uses (a) a fight with the prospective groom (b) the dance (c) the groom's protectiveness (d) a friend.
5. The Assyrians were defeated by (a) the Babylonians (b) the Israelites (c) a terrible change of weather (d) an angel.

Inferences

7. "The Nymph's Reply to the Shepherd" (439) is an example of (a) wide-eyed innocence (b) bitter, bitter denunciation (c) logical argument (d) limited agreement.
8. When the Duke says (line 11, page 442), "If they durst," (a) he is revealing his own cruelty (b) the emissary from the Count is favorably impressed (c) he is stopping the emissary from drawing the curtain (d) he is demonstrating a sly sense of humor.
9. Lord Randal (a) is showing his independence in his relationship with his mother (b) cannot understand why he feels so ill (c) realizes his true love has poisoned him (d) seeks vengeance.
10. The bride-to-be in "Lochinvar" (a) openly defied her father (b) was happy to join Lochinvar's plan (c) hated to lose her groom (d) had the same personality as her mother.

11. The setting of "Lochinvar" is (a) Scotland (b) Canada (c) southern England (d) not suggested.

Tone of the Selection

12. The tone of the "Nymph's Reply" (439) is one of (a)indignation (b) passionate disagreement (c) gentle humor (d) unreasonable demand.

Author's Attitude

13. The poet's attitude toward the Duke of Ferrara (442) is one of (a) affection (b) cheerful acceptance (c) amazement (d) intense dislike.

Outcome

14. As a result of the emissary's visit to the Duke (442), (a) the emissary will report a murder (b) the Duke will imprison the emissary (d) the Duke will lower his demand for a dowry (d) the Count's daughter will be delivered to the Duke.

Fact or Opinion

Tell whether the following is a fact or an opinion.

15. John Suckling (440) offers "Advice to the Lovelorn."

Words in Context

1. "The story of the Duke of Ferrara and his 'Last Duchess' has a plot, motivation, conflict, and *resolution*." **Resolution** (437) means (a) solving of the problem (b) determination to act (c) humorous commentary (d) subtle humor.
2. "There are no *extraneous* elements, no opinions, no interpretations." **Extraneous** (437) means (a) not essential (b) expert (c) unestablished (d) meager.
3. "The three poems suggest that love and *infatuation* haven't changed in over 400 years." **Infatuation** (439) means (a) jealousy (b) happiness (c) envy (d) foolish attachment.

4. "The bough of cherries some *officious* fool broke in the orchard for her." **Officious** (442) means (a) vigorous (b) official (c) meddlesome (d) efficient.

5., 6. "The Count your master's known *munificence* is ample *warrant* that no just pretense of mine for dowry will be disallowed." **Munificence** (443) means (a) good nature (b) generosity (c) intelligence (d) friendliness. **Warrant** (443) means (a) release (b) guarantee (c) search (d) prize.

7. "These wonderful little poems have come down to us from the past without *ascribed* authorship." **Ascribed** (443) means (a) the usual (b) written down (c) satisfactory (d) credited.

8. " 'Lochinvar' is a story of true love, complete with a young couple in love about to be *thwarted* by the young lady's father." **Thwarted** (444) means (a) defeated (b) supported (c) misunderstood (d) examined.

9. "A laggard in love and a *dastard* in war was to wed the fair Ellen of brave Lochinvar." **Dastard** (445) means (a) respected leader (b) fearless knight (c) nasty coward (d) unfriendly comrade.

10. "He *quaffed* off the wine, and he threw down the cup." **Quaffed** (445) means drank (a) proudly (b) casually (c) deeply (d) noisily.

11. "So daring in love, and so *dauntless* in war, have you e'er heard of gallant like young Lochinvar?" **Dauntless** (446) means (a) inventive (b) fearless (c) respected (d) beloved.

12. Sennacherib was a powerful king of Assyria, conqueror of Babylon, *scourge* of his neighbors." **Scourge** (447) means (a) destructive enemy (b) envy (c) constant protector (d) persistent observer.

13. "The *sheen* of their spears was like stars on the sea." **Sheen** (448) means (a) appearance (b) great number (c) threat (d) brightness.

Thinking Critically About the Selections

1. In the pair of "Shepherd" poems, the stanzas are balanced. Stanza 1 in the Marlowe poem is matched by stanza 1 in the Raleigh poem. Reread the poems and point out how Raleigh answers Marlowe point by devastating point.
2. What question has the emissary asked the Duke that brings forth the response in lines 5–13, pages 441–442? How does the Duke's response show his evil arrogance? Point to lines to prove your point.

3. What has so enraged the Duke? His wife was faithful, lovely, pleasant, appreciative, friendly to all. What "fault" did she have that so enraged the Duke?
4. Although we don't know for certain what happened to the Duchess, we can make a reasonable guess. Why is the poem more effective if the Duchess's fate is not spelled out in detail?
5. How does the Duke's obvious love of art contrast with his character?
6. How does the rollicking rhythm of "Lochinvar" complement the romantic story?
7. "The Destruction of Sennacherib" begins with a vivid image. The Assyrian assault is compared with the attack of a wolf on a sheepfold. What points of similarity make this comparison effective?

Language in Action

Poetic Rhythms

Even if you were unaware of the technique, you could feel the powerful rhythms of "Lochinvar" and "The Destruction of Sennacherib." That feeling of being swept along is no accident. The poets cleverly devised their sentences to sweep the reader or, preferably, listener along. If you read the poems aloud, you'll appreciate the poet's mastery of his medium. *Meter,* as it is called, is a repeated basic pattern. The elements of meter are called *feet.* These are the four most common metrical feet.

Name of Foot	*Number of Syllables*	*Syllable Accented*	*Example*
iamb	two	second	Marié
trochee	two	first	Máry
anapest	three	third	Gabriellé
dactyl	three	first	Gábriel

A poetic line is sometimes identified by the number of metrical feet. The most common are *trimeter* (three feet), *tetrameter* (four feet), *pentameter* (five feet) and *hexameter* (six feet). Both "Lochinvar" and "Sennacherib" have four feet and can be identified as *anapestic tetrameter.* Both "Shepherd" poems are written in *iambic tetrameter.* "My Last Duchess" is written in *iambic pentameter,* as are the great works of Shakespeare. The Suckling poem is written in alternating trochaic tetrameter and trochaic trimeter. The poet allows variations in the rhythm, but usually one of the types predominates.

These may seem at first like forbidding terms, but an awareness of the poet's technique can add a measure of enjoyment to the reading of a poem. The marching rhythm of the iamb is quite different from the galloping rhythm of the anapest. Appreciating the technical skills of the poet adds a grace note to contacts with poetry.

Lyric Poetry

> **I believe a leaf of grass is no less than the journeywork of the stars.**
> **And the running blackberry would adorn the parlors of heaven,**
> **And the narrowest hinge in my hand puts to scorn all machinery,**
> **And the cow crunching with depress'd head surpasses any statue,**
> **And a mouse is miracle enough to stagger sextillions of infidels.**

—From "Song of Myself"

These lines by Walt Whitman suggest the power of poetry to open doors to new experiences and new ways of thinking.

> **The sea is calm tonight,**
> **The tide is full, the moon lies fair**
> **Upon the straits;—on the French coast the light**
> **Gleams and is gone: the cliffs of England stand,**
> **Glimmering and vast, out in the tranquil bay.**

—From "Dover Beach"

These lines by Matthew Arnold suggest the power of poetry to transport the reader or listener to another place, both emotionally and physically. Both of these selections belong to that type of poetry often called **lyric**. The dictionary definition of **lyric** suggests a means of identifying it: "expressing direct, usually intense, personal emotion, especially in a manner suggestive of song."

The selections in this chapter display a variety of emotions and style, from the delicate, introspective, sensitive lyrics of Emily Dickinson to the more objective observations of the haiku poets. Yet even in the latter, a certain personal style comes through, in varying degrees. The haiku of Issa, for example, tend to be more personal than those of Basho.

The lyrics of country music tend to be deeply personal. They often sing of heartbreak and loss, yearning and joy, even as do the lyrics of an earlier day.

Four Representative Short Lyrics

The following four selections are a good introduction to the lyric. They're quite brief; yet each one presents a mood, a picture, a philosophical idea. Each is a complete poem. Little more can be said.

The Eagle

He clasps the crag with crooked hands;
Close to the sun in lonely lands,
Ringed with the azure world, he stands.

The wrinkled sea beneath him crawls;
He watches from his mountain walls,
And like a thunderbolt he falls.

—Lord Tennyson
British

Heaven-Haven

I have desired to go
   Where springs not fail,
To fields where flies no sharp and sided hail
   And a few lilies blow.

And I have asked to be
   Where no storms come,
Where the green swell is in the havens dumb,
   Out of the swing of the sea.

—Gerard Manley Hopkins
British

Memory

My mind lets go a thousand things,
Like dates of wars and deaths of kings,

And yet recalls the very hour—
'Twas noon by yonder village tower,
And on the last blue moon in May—
The wind came briskly up this way,
Crisping the brook beside the road;
Then, pausing here, set down its load
Of pine-scents, and shook listlessly
Two petals from that wild-rose tree.

—Thomas Bailey Aldrich
American

Outwitted

He drew a circle that shut me out—
Heretic, rebel, a thing to flout.
But Love and I had the wit to win:
We drew a circle that took him in.

—Edwin Markham
American

Poetic impulses are universal. The next selections come, respectively, from Africa and from China. The former poems suggest the writer's love for Africa. The latter poems provide a bitterly ironic pair. The poet almost resents having a daughter, not a son. He thinks of the problems ahead, but the problems are removed in a way he deeply regrets.

Up-Country

Then I came back
Sailing down the Guinea coast,
Loving the sophistication
Of your brave new cities:
Dakar, Accra, Cotonou,
Lagos, Bathurst, and Bissau,
Freetown, Libreville.
Freedom is really in the mind.

Go up-country, they said,
To see the real Africa.
For whomsoever you may be,
That is where you come from.
Go for bush—inside the bush

You will find your hidden heart,
Your mute ancestral spirit.

And so I went,
Dancing on my way.

—Abioseh Nicol
African

On An African Beach

Here I stand
On the white-fringed edge of the world:
Its limits are my mind.
Let your white sun
Wash my strong brown body.

I feel the crinkle of your golden sands
Under the yellow soles of my feet.
If I lose this certain grip,
If this blue sea washes all of you away,
I will have been widowed
By the moon's rising tide.

I have taken you for better or for worse,
Yet between the thick and the thin
Of this ebbing flow I cannot form a whole.

But if with love again
I turn my face towards you, Africa,
Turning away from the faithless horizon,
Your green mountains will give me
My fulfillment.

—Abioseh Nicol
African

Golden Bells

When I was almost forty
I had a daughter whose name was Golden Bells.
Now it is just a year since she was born;
She is learning to sit and cannot yet talk.
Ashamed—to find that I have not a sage's heart:
I cannot resist vulgar thoughts and feelings.
Henceforward I am tied to things outside myself:

My only reward—the pleasure I am getting now.
If I am spared the grief of her dying young,
Then I shall have the trouble of getting her married.
My plan for retiring and going back to the hills
Must now be postponed for fifteen years!

—Po Chü-i
Chinese

Remembering Golden Bells

Ruined and ill—a man of two score;
Pretty and guileless—a girl of three.
Not a boy—but still better than nothing:
To soothe one's feeling—from time to time a kiss!
There came a day—they suddenly took her from me;
Her soul's shadow wandered I know not where.

And when I remember how just at the time she died
She lisped strange sounds, beginning to learn to talk,
Then I know that the ties of flesh and blood
Only bind us to a load of grief and sorrow.
At last, by thinking of the time before she was born,
By thought and reason I drove the pain away.
Since my heart forgot her, many days have passed
And three times winter has changed to spring.
This morning, for a little, the old grief came back,
Because, in the road, I met her foster-nurse.

—Po Chü-i
Chinese

Poetry has been used effectively for social protest. The following two poems, written by black women poets, have a central core of social concern, but they are vastly different, especially in tone. The first, written more than two centuries ago by a slave, is a gentle prayer for the spread of freedom. The second, by Alice Walker, is a powerful and loving tribute to the black mothers of a previous generation. Strong, loving, undaunted, and unselfish, these women kept their strong convictions and self-respect—and never yielded.

from *To the Right Honorable William, Earl of Dartmouth*

Should you, my lord, while you pursue my song,
Wonder from whence my love of *Freedom* sprung,

Whence flow these wishes for the common good,
By feeling hearts alone best understood,
I, young in life, by seeming cruel fate
Was snatch'd from *Afric's* fancy'd happy seat:
What pangs excruciating must molest,
What sorrows labour in my parent's breast?
Steel'd was the soul and by no misery mov'd
That from a father seiz'd his babe belov'd.
Such, such my case. And can I then but pray
Others may never feel tyrannic sway?

—Phillis Wheatley
American

Women

They were women then
My mama's generation
Husky of voice—Stout of
Step
With fists as well as
Hands
How they battered down
Doors
And ironed
Starched white
Shirts
How they led
Armies
Headragged Generals
Across mined
Fields
Booby-trapped
Ditches
To discover books
Desks
A place for us
How they knew what we
Must know
Without knowing a page
Of it
Themselves.

—Alice Walker
American

A Gathering of Haiku

The haiku is not confined to Japan. Many persons write haiku for personal enjoyment. Some writers in English restrict themselves to 17 syllables, as in Japanese. They find that writing a haiku sharpens perceptions and challenges ingenuity to work within the space limitations. The first three haiku that follow are by Buson, who was born in 1716, 22 years after the death of Basho. The second three are by Issa. Issa was born in 1763, 20 years before Buson's death, so that the two were contemporaries for a while. They flourished almost three centuries ago; yet their haiku seem contemporary. The third three are by Stewart W. Holmes, a contemporary American writer of haiku.

Butterfly
sleeping—
on the temple bell.

Sudden shower—
a flock of sparrows
clinging to the grasses

Before the white Chrysanthemums
the scissors hesitate
a moment.

—Buson
Japanese

Under my house
an inchworm
measuring the joists

That wren—
looking here, looking there,
You lose something?

Don't kill that fly!
Look—it's wringing its hands,
Wringing its feet

—Issa
Japanese

In the chill spring air
clouds white with the full moon's light
move slowly, slowly.

The moon, the mountains, the leaves
are silent,
The churr of a katydid.

Chickadees come to the feeder
in vain this morning.
A hungry squirrel?

—Stewart W. Holmes
American

An Indian Prayer

Though written as prose, the following selection has all the qualities of great lyric poetry.

An Indian Prayer

Oh Father whose voice I hear in the wind and whose breath gives
life to all the world, hear me. I am a man before you, one of
your many children. I am small and weak, I need your strength
and wisdom.
Let me walk in beauty and make my eyes ever behold the red
and purple sunset. Make my hands respect the things you
have made, my ears sharp to hear your voice. Make me
wise, so that I may know the things you have taught my
people, the lessons you have hidden in every leaf and rock.
I seek strength, Father . . . not to be superior to my brothers,
but to be able to fight my greatest enemy . . . myself.
Make me ever ready to come to you with clean hands and
straight eyes so that when life fades as the fading sunset,
my spirit may come to you without shame.

—Tom Whitecloud
Native American

Nine by Emily Dickinson

The American poet with perhaps the greatest lyric voice was a recluse who seldom left her Amherst home. In secret, she wrote over a thousand poems, but her reputation had to wait until many of the poems were published after her death. Her physical world was narrow, but her spiritual world was wide and deep. You may find these poems a little strange at first. You may, for example, expect rhyme, but Dickinson doesn't always worry about exact rhymes. Sometimes the end words don't seem to rhyme at all, like *whole* and *tell* in Poem 6. No matter. The poems deserve quiet reading and rereading. There are no finer examples of lyric poetry in all of literature.

1

I taste a liquor never brewed,
From tankards scooped in pearl;
Not all the vats upon the Rhine
Yield such an alcohol!

Inebriate of air am I,
And debauchee of dew,
Reeling, through endless summer days,
From inns of molten blue.

When landlords turn the drunken bee
Out of the foxglove's door,
When butterflies renounce their drams,
I shall but drink the more!

Till seraphs[1] swing their snowy hats,
And saints to windows run,
To see the little tippler
Leaning against the sun!

2

He ate and drank the precious words,
His spirit grew robust;
He knew no more that he was poor,
Nor that his frame was dust.
He danced along the dingy days,
And this bequest of wings
Was but a book. What liberty
A loosened spirit brings!

[1]**seraphs:** angels

3

A light exists in spring
  Not present on the year
At any other period.
  When March is scarcely here

A color stands abroad
  On solitary hills
That science cannot overtake,
  But human nature *feels.*

It waits upon the lawn;
  It shows the furthest tree
Upon the furthest slope we know;
  It almost speaks to me.

Then, as horizons step,
  Or noons report away,
Without the formula of sound,
  It passes, and we stay:

A quality of loss
  Affecting our content,
As trade had suddenly encroached
  Upon a sacrament.

4

Dear March, come in!
How glad I am!
I looked for you before.
Put down your hat—
You must have walked—
How out of breath you are!
Dear March, how are you?
And the rest?
Did you leave Nature well?
Oh, March, come right upstairs with me,
I have so much to tell!

5

Have you got a brook in your little heart,
Where bashful flowers blow,
And blushing birds go down to drink,
And shadows tremble so?

And nobody knows, so still it flows,
That any brook is there;
And yet your little draught of life
Is daily drunken there.

Then look out for the little brook in March,
When the rivers overflow,
And the snows come hurrying from the hills,
And the bridges often go.

And later, in August it may be,
When the meadows parching lie,
Beware, lest this little brook of life
Some burning noon go dry!

6

The skies can't keep their secret!
They tell it to the hills—
The hills just tell the orchards—
And they the daffodils!

A bird, by chance, that goes that way
Soft overheard the whole.
If I should bribe the little bird,
Who knows but she would tell?

I think I won't, however,
It's finer not to know;
If summer were an axiom,
What sorcery had snow?

So keep your secret, Father!
I would not, if I could,
Know what the sapphire fellows do,
In your new-fashioned world!

7

Two butterflies went out at noon
And waltzed above a stream,
Then stepped straight through the firmament
And rested on a beam;

And then together bore away
Upon a shining sea,—
Though never yet, in any port,
Their coming mentioned be.

If spoken by the distant bird,
If met in ether sea
By frigate or by merchantman,
Report was not to me.

8

I started early, took my dog,
And visited the sea;
The mermaids in the basement
Came out to look at me,

And frigates in the upper floor
Extended hempen hands,
Presuming me to be a mouse
Aground, upon the sands.

But no man moved me till the tide
Went past my simple shoe,
And past my apron and my belt,
And past my bodice too,

And made as he would eat me up
As wholly as a dew
Upon a dandelion's sleeve—
And then I started too.

And he—he followed close behind;
I felt his silver heel
Upon my ankle,—then my shoes
Would overflow with pearl.

Until we met the solid town,
No man he seemed to know;
And bowing with a mighty look
At me, the sea withdrew.

9

Arcturus is his other name,—
I'd rather call him star!
It's so unkind of science
To go and interfere!

I pull a flower from the woods,—
A monster with a glass
Computes the stamens in a breath,
And has her in a class.

Whereas I took the butterfly
Aforetime in my hat,
He sits erect in cabinets,
The clover-bells forgot.

What once was heaven, is zenith now.
Where I proposed to go
When time's brief masquerade was done,
Is mapped, and charted too!

What if the poles should frisk about
And stand upon their heads!
I hope I'm ready for the worst,
Whatever prank betides[1]!

Perhaps the kingdom of Heaven's changed!
I hope the children there
Won't be new-fashioned when I come,
And laugh at me, and stare!

I hope the father in the skies
Will lift his little girl,—
Old-fashioned, naughty, everything,—
Over the stile of pearl!

---

[1]**betides:** happens

Reading for Understanding

Main Idea

1. In general, lyric poetry is characterized by (a) personal emotion (b) narrative skill (c) understated humor (d) dramatic monologues.

Details

2. The poem about miracles was written by (a) Lord Tennyson (b) Emily Dickinson (c) Walt Whitman (d) Matthew Arnold.
3. Modern examples of lyric poetry can be found in (a) opera (b) rock (c) musical comedy (d) country music.
4. The two writers who were partial contemporaries are (a) Basho and Holmes (b) Buson and Issa (c) Basho and Issa (d) Issa and Holmes.
5. In "Memory," Thomas Bailey Aldrich especially remembers (a) dates of wars (b) deaths of kings (c) an early snow (d) rose petals.
6. *Golden Bells* is the name of (a) a young girl (b) temple bells (c) a house in the country (d) a love song.

Inferences

7. The poem that calls for release from the problems of life is (a) "Outwitted" (b) "Heaven-Haven" (c) "Memory" (d) "An Indian Prayer."
8. Edwin Markham's poem (456) displays (a) a sneaky spirit (b) a great soul (c) revenge (d) intense curiosity.
9. The poem "Up-Country" (456) suggests the author's (a) search for roots (b) despair over his past (c) disillusion with the up-country (d) desire to settle in one of the cities mentioned.
10. In "Remembering Golden Bells" (458), the poet meets a foster nurse and (a) greets the woman coldly (b) may feel some regret (c) decides to adopt another child (d) is elated by the experience.

Poet's Attitude

11. The poet's attitude in the two "Golden Bells" poems (457–458) may be characterized as (a) joyous (b) charitable (c) carefree (d) selfish.

Tone of the Selection

12. The tone of "An Indian Prayer" (461) can be characterized as one of (a) despair (b) self-pity (c) reverence (d) relief.

Author's Language

13. The extended image in Emily Dickinson's first poem is one of pretended (a) intoxication (b) hunger (c) story-telling (d) indifference.

Author's Attitude

14. Emily Dickinson's attitude toward the "light in spring," Poem 3 (463), is one of (a) happiness at the extent of that light (b) obvious irritation at its arrival (c) sadness and a sense of loss (d) curiosity about its nature.

Fact or Opinion

Tell whether the following is a fact or an opinion.

15. Japanese haiku are superior to those of any other culture.

Words in Context

1. The selections in this chapter display a variety of emotions and style, from the delicate, *introspective,* sensitive lyrics of Emily Dickinson to the more objective observations of the haiku poets. **Introspective** (454) means (a) colorful (b) thoughtful (c) critical (d) rebellious.

2.,3. "He drew a circle that shut me out—*heretic,* rebel, a thing to *flout.*" A major characteristic of a **heretic** (456) is (a) insincerity (b) weakness (c) disagreement (d) doubt. **Flout** (456) means treat with (a) contempt (b) respect (c) disbelief (d) kindness.

4. "Ashamed—to find that I have not a *sage's* heart: I cannot resist vulgar thoughts and feelings." A **sage** (457) is a (a) merchant (b) writer (c) wise man (d) wistful clown.

5. "They find that writing a haiku sharpens *perceptions* and challenges ingenuity to work within the space limitations." **Perceptions** (460)

suggests (a) awareness (b) critical feelings (c) dramatic incidents (d) wittiness.

6. "The American poet with perhaps the greatest lyric voice was a *recluse* who seldom left her Amherst home." A **recluse** (461) is a kind of (a) poet (b) actor (c) hermit (d) social climber.

7.,8. "*Inebriate* of air am I, and *debauchee* of dew." **Inebriate** (462) suggests (a) inspiration (b) drunkenness (c) keenness of inspiration (d) vigor. By using **debauchee** (462) humorously, Emily Dickinson is suggesting (a) evil motives (b) antagonism (c) immobility (d) loss of control.

9. "When butterflies *renounce* their drams, I shall but drink the more!" **Renounce** (462) means (a) consume (b) refuse (c) discover (d) decorate.

10. "This *bequest* of wings was but a book." **Bequest** (462) means (a) matched pair (b) inheritance (c) library (d) foretelling.

11. "Trade had suddenly encroached upon a sacrament." **Encroached** (463) means (a) entered (b) happened (c) relied (d) trespassed.

12. "If summer were an *axiom,* what sorcery had snow?" An **axiom** (464) is a (a) self-evident truth (b) false principle (c) legal agreement (d) brief moment.

13. "The butterflies . . . stepped straight through the *firmament* and rested on a beam." **Firmament** (465) refers to (a) a meadow (b) a weeded area (c) the sky (d) a garden.

Thinking Critically About the Selections

1. Lord Tennyson chooses an unusual adjective to describe the sea (455): *wrinkled.* Is this an appropriate word? How can water be wrinkled? Did the description appeal to you? Why?
2. Thomas Bailey Aldrich describes a common mystery: the inconsistency of memory. Are there incidents in your own life that remain with you even though they seemed insignificant at the time? Suggest an example.
3. How much time elapses between the first and second poems in the Golden Bells poems? What clues tell you exactly? What has happened in the intervening time? How do the poems reveal that father's character?

4. What requests does Tom Whitecloud make of his God (461)? How do these requests reveal something about the author?
5. In Poem 1 (462) what is Emily Dickinson drinking that causes her giddy state? Note that she keeps the image of exhilaration and intoxication throughout. How can anyone "lean against the sun"? Is this a vivid image for you?
6. Which three poems mention March, a month that usually has few champions? What special qualities does March have, at least in the eyes of Emily Dickinson?
7. In Poem 9, the poet takes sides against the preciseness and labeling of science. Why?
8. Lyric poetry often selects some insignificant object or incident and makes it beautiful. Select a poem from this chapter. Tell why you think it successfully brings to life an image we might otherwise overlook.

Language in Action

Rhyme

Rhyme depends upon a similarity in sound. Young lovers have been rhyming *June* and *moon* for centuries. Shakespeare sometimes ends a scene with a rhyme, as in these lines from *Hamlet:*

The play's the thing
Wherein I'll catch the conscience of the king.

Letters are often used to indicate a rhyme scheme. The rhyme scheme in "The Eagle" (455), for example, can be designated aaa bbb; in "Heaven-Haven" (455), abba cddc; in "Memory" (455), aabbccddee; and in "Outwitted" (456), aabb. By contrast, Walt Whitman's poetry (454), called *free verse,* has neither a set rhythm nor rhyme. Except for an occasional song or scene ending as above, Shakespeare's plays have a recognizable rhythm but not rhyme. This form of poetry is called *iambic pentameter* (452), or blank verse.

Most amateur writers tend to use rhyme in their poetry. There is something satisfying in the recognition of a familiar sound at the end of a line.

Note that "The Destruction of Sennacherib" (448) has not only a galloping rhythm but a recognizable rhyme scheme. The rhyme scheme of the first stanza is aabb. How would you designate the rhymes of the remaining stanzas? And "Lochinvar" (445)?

Humorous Poetry

Stick close to your desks and never go to sea,
And you all may be rulers of the Queen's Navee.

—W. S. Gilbert

Poetry seems especially able to handle absurdity. The songs of Gilbert and Sullivan are prime examples of that skill, but other writers, too, have tried their hand at fun in verse.

Humor seems to be as difficult to define as poetry. "I know what it is, but I can't tell you" is a typical response to a question about humor. Understatement, exaggeration, incongruity all contribute to a sense of fun, and poets use all three. Incongruity depends upon absurdity, on contrast, on something out of place. A powerfully built athlete leading a tiny dog on a chain is incongruous, likely to provoke laughter. See also pages 373–374.

The poems in this section rely on a variety of methods to bring forth a smile. The unexpected plays a role in "Twins," and "Elegy on the Death of a Mad Dog." Exaggeration is used in "The Height of the Ridiculous." Sheer nonsense is the appeal of "Jabberwocky." The joy of recognizing humorous human failings in others is the appeal of "Get Up and Bar the Door." "Sir Joseph Porter's Song" from **H.M.S. Pinafore** is, of course, sung in the operetta, but the humor comes through in the verse itself. Two haiku also demonstrate that this simple poetic form can contain humor along with keen observation.

Elegy on the Death of a Mad Dog

Oliver Goldsmith
British

The Twins

Henry S. Leigh
British

These two poems make an interesting pair. They show similar approaches to humorous poetry, but with several differences. Both pretend to be quite serious, a frequent device in humorous poetry. Both present a reasonable situation and then turn it topsy-turvy. Oliver Goldsmith makes the poem seem more serious than it otherwise might be by using the formal word *elegy*, a song of sorrow or lamentation. To tell the story, he uses a simple ballad stanza, with alternating rhyming lines. Henry S. Leigh addresses the reader directly and thus emphasizes the absurdity of the last line. He seems to have written ballad stanzas (443) and then joined two together to make the longer stanzas of the poems.

Elegy on the Death of a Mad Dog

Good people all, of every sort,
   Give ear unto my song;
And if you find it wondrous short—
   It cannot hold you long.

In Islington there was a man,
   Of whom the world might say,
That still a godly race he ran—
   Whene'er he went to pray.

A kind and gentle heart he had,
   To comfort friends and foes;
The naked every day he clad—
   When he put on his clothes.

And in that town a dog was found,
As many dogs there be,
Both mongrel, puppy, whelp, and hound,
And cur of low degree.

This dog and man at first were friends;
But when a pique began,
The dog, to gain some private ends,
Went mad, and bit the man.

Around from all the neighboring streets,
The wondering neighbors ran,
And swore the dog had lost his wits,
To bite so good a man.

The wound it seemed both sore and sad
To every Christian eye;
And while they swore the dog was mad,
They swore the man would die.

But soon a wonder came to light,
That showed the rogues they lied;
The man recovered of the bite,
The dog it was that died.

The Twins

In form and feature, face and limb,
I grew so like my brother
That folks got taking me for him,
And each for one another.
It puzzled all our kith and kin,
It reached an awful pitch;
For one of us was born a twin,
Yet not a soul knew which.

One day (to make the matter worse),
Before our names were fixed,
As we were being washed by nurse
We got completely mixed;
And thus, you see, by Fate's decree,
(Or rather nurse's whim),
My brother John got christened *me*,
And I got christened *him*.

This fatal likeness even dogged
  My footsteps when at school,
And I was always getting flogged,
  For John turned out a fool.
I put this question hopelessly
  To every one I knew—
What *would* you do, if you were me,
  To prove that you were *you*?

Our close resemblance turned the tide
  Of my domestic life;
For somehow my intended bride
  Became my brother's wife.
In short, year after year the same
  Absurd mistakes went on;
And when I died—the neighbors came
  And buried Brother John!

The Height of the Ridiculous

Oliver Wendell Holmes
American

In many collections of light verse, "The Height of the Ridiculous" has an honored place. Understatement is a form of humor. When someone says, "I had a bit of trouble" after running into gridlock traffic and missing an important appointment, he is using understatement. Mark Twain's famous "Journalism in Tennessee" is an example of sustained humorous understatement. Exaggeration, the other side of the coin, is often used for humorous effect, as here.

The Height of the Ridiculous

I wrote some lines once on a time
  In wondrous merry mood,
And thought, as usual, men would say
  They were exceeding good.

They were so queer, so very queer,
  I laughed as I would die;
Albeit, in the general way,
  A sober man am I.

I called my servant, and he came;
  How kind it was of him
To mind a slender man like me,
  He of the mighty limb!

"These to the printer," I exclaimed,
  And, in my humorous way,
I added, (as a trifling jest,)
  "There'll be the devil[1] to pay."

He took the paper, and I watched,
  And saw him peep within;
At the first line he read, his face
  Was all upon the grin.

He read the next; the grin grew broad,
  And shot from ear to ear;
He read the third; a chuckling noise
  I now began to hear.

The fourth; he broke into a roar;
  The fifth; his waistband split;
The sixth; he burst five buttons off,
  And tumbled in a fit.

Ten days and nights, with sleepless eye,
  I watched that wretched man,
And since, I never dare to write
  As funny as I can.

Get Up and Bar the Door

Although most old English and Scottish ballads are grim tales of heartbreak and tragedy, a few are bright, filled with humorous observation. Here's an all-too-human situation. Husband and wife get into a disagreement about who is to bar the cottage door. Neither one will give

[1]**devil:** a pun; a "printer's devil" is an apprentice printer

in: two supposedly mature persons who let stubborn pride get them into a situation that could have been avoided. Who will outlast the other and who will "get up and bar the door"?

It fell about the Martinmas time,
  And a gay time it was then,
When our goodwife got puddings to make,
  And she's boiled them in the pan.

The wind so cold blew south and north,
  And blew into the floor;
Quoth our goodman to our goodwife,
  "Go out and bar the door."

"My hand is in my hussyfskap,[1]
  Goodman, as you may see;
If it should not be barred this hundred year,
  It's no be barred for me."

They made a pact between the two,
  They made it firm and sure,
That the first word whoe'er should speak
  Should rise and bar the door.

Then by there came two gentlemen,
  At twelve o'clock at night,
And they could neither see house nor hall,
  Nor coal nor candle-light.

"Now whether is this a rich man's house,
  Or whether is it a poor?"
But ne'er a word would one of them speak,
  For barring of the door.

And first they ate the white puddings,
  And then they ate the black;
Though much thought the goodwife to herself,
  Yet ne'er a word she spake.

Then said the one unto the other,
  "Here, man, take you my knife;
Do you take off the old man's beard,
  And I'll kiss the goodwife."

"But there's no water in the house,
  And what shall we do than?"
"What ails thee at the pudding-broo,
  That boils into the pan?"

[1]**hussyfskap:** kneading-trough

O up then started our goodman,
  An angry man was he:
"Will you kiss my wife before my eyes,
And scald me with pudding-bree?"

Then up and started our goodwife,
  Gave three skips on the floor:
"Goodman, you've spoken the foremost word.
  Get up and bar the door."

Sir Joseph Porter's Song

W. S. Gilbert
British

The operettas of W. S. Gilbert and Arthur Sullivan were outstandingly successful when they first appeared over a century ago. They have retained a solid popularity ever since. For his efforts, Sullivan was knighted in 1883 by Queen Victoria. Gilbert was also knighted—by Edward VII in 1907, 24 years later. Gilbert was not happy at the slight, and his verse showed his annoyance.

Gilbert was not one of the Queen's favorites. Time and again, in his operettas he poked fun at her government. In *Iolanthe*, for example, he poked fun at the House of Lords. The verse that may have irritated the Queen most is the song in *H.M.S. Pinafore* by Sir Joseph, the First Lord of the Admiralty. Though the Lord's position may not actually require nautical skills, the tone of the song is mocking . . . and the Queen "was not amused."

Sir Joseph Porter's Song from *H.M.S. Pinafore*

When I was a lad I served a term
As office boy to an Attorney's firm.
I cleaned the windows and I swept the floor,
And I polished up the handle of the big front door,
  I polished up that handle so carefullee
  That now I am the Ruler of the Queen's Navee!

As office boy I made such a mark
That they gave me the post of a junior clerk.
I served the writs with a smile so bland,
And I copied all the letters in a big round hand—
  I copied all the letters in a hand so free,
  That now I am the Ruler of the Queen's Navee.

In serving writs I made such a name
That an articled clerk I soon became;
I wore clean collars and a brand-new suit
For the pass examination at the Institute,
  And that pass examination did so well for me,
  That now I am the Ruler of the Queen's Navee.

Of legal knowledge I acquired such a grip
That they took me into the partnership,
And that partnership, I ween,
Was the only ship that I ever had seen.
  But that kind of ship so suited me,
  That now I am the Ruler of the Queen's Navee.

I grew so rich that I was soon sent
By a pocket borough into Parliament
I always voted at my party's call,
And I never thought of thinking for myself at all.
  I thought so little, they rewarded me
  By making me the Ruler of the Queen's Navee.

Now Landsmen all, whoever you may be,
If you want to rise to the top of the tree,
If your soul isn't fettered to an office stool.
Be careful to be guided by this golden rule—
  Stick close to your desks and never go to sea,
  And you all may be Rulers of the Queen's Navee.

Jabberwocky

Lewis Carroll
British

Lewis Carroll is immortal because of the Alice books: *Alice in Wonderland* and *Through the Looking-Glass.* However, he also wrote much humorous verse, as well as some serious books in mathematics. You may already have met "The Walrus and the Carpenter" and "Father William." Of all the humorous verse, perhaps the most unusual is "Jabberwocky."

This is obviously the tale of a heroic young man who set out to slay a fearsome monster and succeeded. This is a hackneyed plot, found in old English tales of heroism, in stories of King Arthur, and in legends and fairy tales everywhere. The plot is used in science fiction, too, though the monster is often not of this world. Remember the *Alien* movies? What makes "Jabberwocky" so special is the language. Carroll has invented a great many nonsense words. Some of these have entered the language as blends (483). Who knows what borogoves are or what a frumious Bandersnatch might do! Some words have recognizable parts. *Slithy* is a blend (483) of *lithe* and *slimy.* No matter where the words came from, the poem makes a kind of sense. Each reader or listener sees a different Jabberwock, but nobody fails to see the hero galumphing back home.

Jabberwocky

'Twas brillig, and the slithy toves
Did gyre and gimble in the wabe:
All mimsy were the borogoves,
And the mome raths outgrabe.

"Beware the Jabberwock, my son!
The jaws that bite, the claws that catch!
Beware the Jubjub bird, and shun
The frumious Bandersnatch!"

He took his vorpal sword in hand;
Long time the manxome foe he sought—
So rested he by the Tumtum tree,
And stood awhile in thought.

And, as in uffish thought he stood,
The Jabberwock, with eyes of flame,
Came whiffling through the tulgey wood,
And burbled as it came!

One, two! One, two! And through and through
The vorpal blade went snicker-snack!
He left it dead, and with its head
He went galumphing back.

"And hast thou slain the Jabberwock?
Come to my arms, my beamish boy!

O frabjous day! Callooh! Callay!"
He chortled in his joy.

'Twas brillig, and the slithy toves
Did gyre and gimble in the wabe:
All mimsy were the borogoves,
And the mome raths outgrabe.

Anon

R. J. Lowenherz
American

In Budapest there is a statue of an early Hungarian hero. No one knows much about him. There is no record of his appearance. As a result, the statue has a hood over the face, concealing those unknown features.

There are unknown elements in literature, too. Literary works whose authors are unknown are always attributed to *Anonymous,* or *Anon* as it is usually abbreviated. The author of the following poem playfully imagines that Anon is a person who has been cruelly blamed for all those inferior works ascribed to him.

Of all the bards of song and verse,
What Jennifer or John
Right from the first has suffered worse
Than he they call *Anon?*

The feeble fable, murky myth,
Or legendary lay
Lies never with a Jones or Smith:
"It's by *Anon,*" they say.

If minstrels drone a dreary tale,
Disclaiming they first said it,
Whose name goes on that weary wail?
Anon gets all the credit.

No vulgar verse, low limerick,
Or witticism lame
Is left to stick a Tom or Dick:
Anon gets all the blame.

Of all the bards of song and verse,
None lives so put upon
As that poor lad whose cruel curse
Was to be named *Anon.*

Two Haiku

The haiku, so impressive in capturing a moment in a few syllables, is sometimes used for humor. The first, by a contemporary writer of haiku, uses a colloquial pun. The second, by a fourth-grade elementary school student, contrasts beauty and work.

Waiting in the darkness
I hear nothing.
Owl, why don't you give a hoot?

—Stewart W. Holmes

The leaves are falling,
They look like a new rainbow.
Aw! Where is the rake?

—Thomas F. Christ

Reading for Understanding

Main Idea

1. A major idea of the chapter is contained in which of the following sentences?
   (a) The greatest humorous poems contain nonsense words.
   (b) Three major ingredients of humorous poetry are understatement, exaggeration, absurdity.
   (c) The greatest humorous poets are happy in their own lives, secure in their accomplishments.
   (d) Old English ballads often have tragic themes unrelieved by humor.

Details

2. Exaggeration is mentioned as a major appeal of (a) "Get Up and Bar the Door" (b) the Owl haiku (c) "The Height of the Ridiculous" (d) "Elegy on the Death of a Mad Dog."
3. In "The Twins," the fool is (a) John (b) the speaker (c) the wife (d) the doctor.
4. In "The Height of the Ridiculous," the poor victim is (a) the printer (b) a stranger (c) a relative (d) a servant.
5. In "Get Up and Bar the Door," the husband was finally prompted to action by (a) the threatened kiss (b) the loss of the puddings (c) the arrival of strangers (d) his wife's surrender.

6. Sir Joseph Porter started out in life as (a) a junior clerk (b) an articled clerk (c) a junior partner (d) an office boy.

Inferences

7. When the husband said, "Go out and bar the door," (a) he didn't expect his wife to do it (b) his wife resented the order (c) he expected visitors (d) the door was closed but not barred.
8. *Manxome* (479, line 10) probably means something like (a) "sluggish" (b) "invisible" (c) "terrifying" (d) "cowardly."

Author's Attitude

9. The author's attitude toward political appointees in "Sir Joseph Porter's Song" is one of (a) ridicule (b) awe (c) approval (d) hatred.

Fact or Opinion

Tell whether the following is a fact or an opinion.

10. "Get Up and Bar the Door" is the finest humorous ballad in existence.

Words in Context

1. "A powerfully built athlete leading a tiny dog on a chain is *incongruous,* likely to provoke laughter." **Incongruous** (471) means (a) insulting (b) out of place (c) charming (d) not understandable.
2. "The Lord's position may not actually require *nautical* skills." **Nautical** (477) pertains to (a) magic (b) artisans (c) puzzles (d) ships.
3. "If your soul isn't *fettered to* an office stool, be careful to be guided by this golden rule." **Fettered to** (478) means (a) associated with (b) chained to (c) dissatisfied with (d) separated from.
4. "This is a *hackneyed* plot." **Hackneyed** (479) means (a) sparkling (b) original (c) overused (d) ancient.

Thinking Critically About the Selections

1. In "Elegy on the Death of a Mad Dog," is the poet making a sly, unexpected comment about the character of the man? Explain.

2. In "The Twins," how does the poet pile absurdity on absurdity? How does he cap the list at the end?
3. In "The Height of the Ridiculous," the poet writes completely objectively about the servant's comical disintegration. Point out the specific observations that convince the poet that his verses are dangerous.
4. Why are untested, inexperienced, unready persons often appointed to positions for which they are unsuited?
5. In "Get Up and Bar the Door," stubbornness almost turns into disaster. Why do people sometimes stubbornly refuse to take actions obviously beneficial, preferring instead to embark on a self-destructive course?
6. Which of the poems in this section seem to you most humorous? Can you tell why?

Language in Action

Blends

When Lewis Carroll joined *lithe* and *slimy* to make *slithy,* he was using a process that has given us many words in English. The results of such coinages are often called *portmanteau words,* or *blends.* Also in "Jabberwocky," Carroll combined *snort* and *chuckle* to produce *chortle,* a word found in most dictionaries. When Carroll wanted to create a name for another monster, he took two words that were unpleasant to him: *snake* and *shark.* He created *snark* and a masterpiece to go with it: "The Hunting of the Snark."

Lewis Carroll was only one source of blends. *Motor* plus *hotel* provides *motel. Agriculture* plus *business* equals *agribusiness.* The hybrid offspring of a lion and tiger is called a *ligon. Information* plus *commercial* provides *infomercial.* A *port* for a *helicopter* is a *heliport. Breakfast* plus *lunch* equals *brunch. Electric* and *execute* blend to form *electrocute.* The *World Almanac* published a visual encyclopedia for students and titled it *infopedia (information* plus *encyclopedia*).

Science and technology provide many blends. The common computer word *modem* is actually a blend of *modulator* and *demodulator.* A *pixel* is *pix* plus *element. Electronic* plus *mail* equals *e-mail.* New blends are constantly entering the language.

The Power of Poetry

ACTIVITIES

Thinking Critically About the Selections

1. After reading the poems and the various definitions of poetry, how has your understanding of poetry been changed? Which poem or poems seem closest to your own feelings about poetry?

2. Does poetry tend to strike deeper into your inner feelings than prose? Explain.

3. Now that you've read many poems, return to the Issa haiku on page 430. Why has this poem been put with the other two? How is it different? Similar? Why does Issa make *dew* the key word? What is characteristic of dew?

4. "Ozymandias" on page 431 is analyzed in some detail. How can the analysis of a poem deepen appreciation and understanding?

5. Who is the most villainous person presented in the poems? Why did you choose this person?

6. Now that you've experienced a variety of poetic types, do you still prefer your poems with a set rhythm and rhyme? Explain.

7. What are the special appeals of the haiku?

8. W. S. Gilbert (477) was a master of satire, a literary form characterized by scorn and ridicule. Satire need not be in the form of poetry. *Gulliver's Travels* is one of the world's greatest satirical works, poking fun at mankind's stupidities. But satire does appear in poetry too, as in "Sir Joseph Porter's Song." Gilbert is being fairly good-humored here, but satire can be deadly. Some television comics rely on satire for their humor. Jon Stewart is a good example. Can you think of others? Is their satire good-natured or bitter? The characters in sitcoms are often portrayed satirically. Can you suggest one or more examples?

The Writing Portfolio

Writing Original Poetry

Poetry is sometimes unfairly criticized. Many young people think that poetry is only for the few. Yet, throughout history, poetry has been for the many. Bards and storytellers often recited in poetry. Perhaps the greatest epics ever created, the *Iliad* and the *Odyssey*, were created in poetic form.

Even today, popular songs create poetic verse. The ballads of country music are modern equivalents of the poems the troubadours once sang to their lady loves. Poetry is not dead. The impulses are all around us. Writing an original poem can be fun—and sometimes good therapy. Try your hand at one or more of the following. If you wish, start with the deceptively simple haiku and then attempt slightly longer poems.

1. A number of haiku have been included in this unit because they are deceptively simple, yet powerful in their impact. Even if longer poems intimidate you, you'll enjoy creating a haiku. The following haiku were all written by high school students.

   A wet spider web
   sagging from weight of raindrops
   sparkles in the sun.

   —Gigi Garrido

   Gazing at the sky,
   so bright is the rising moon
   above the mountains.

   —Frances DiGioia

   All is quiet now,
   The night is like a heavy curtain.
   The day's act is done.

   —Priscilla George

   The house I live in . . .
   the house, the grass, and the street
   all belong to me.

   —Nelson Jenkins

Try your hand. For an extra challenge, keep the haiku to 17 syllables, in lines of 5, 7, and 5 syllables. Nature, school, the city, people, travel . . . the possibilities are everywhere. Don't be "profound" or philosophical. For the haiku, just capture what you see.

2. One of the simplest poetic forms is the couplet: two rhyming lines. Couplets often appear on commercial greeting cards. The couplet

has been used for many purposes: Satire, social commentary, philosophy of life, humor, and character description. Shakespeare often used a couplet to conclude a scene in his plays. At the end of Act One, Hamlet cries,

> The time is out of joint; O cursed spite,
> That ever I was born to set it right.

The following samples suggest the range of the simple couplet.

> Oh, what a tangled web we weave,
> When first we practice to deceive.
>
> —Sir Walter Scott

> Hope springs eternal in the human breast;
> Man never is, but always to be blest.
>
> —Alexander Pope

> Swans sing before they die; 'twere no bad thing
> Should certain persons die before they sing.
>
> —Samuel Taylor Coleridge

> Seven wealthy towns contend for Homer dead,
> Through which the living Homer begged his bread.
>
> —John Dryden

> Slowly, silently, now the moon
> Walks the night in her silver shoon.
>
> —Walter de la Mare

Now try your hand at writing a couplet. Use any subject that comes to mind. Perhaps you'll create a humorous couplet like the following by Dorothy Parker.

> Four be the things I'd been better without:
> Love, curiosity, freckles, and doubt.

3. A quatrain is a stanza of four lines, with many varieties of rhyme scheme. A representative quatrain is "Outwitted" by Edwin Markham (456). The ballad stanza is a special form of the quatrain. The first and third rhymes are typically in unrhymed iambic tetrameter (452). The second and fourth lines are in rhymed iambic trimeter (452).

> There lived a wife at Usher's Well,
>   And a wealthy wife was she;
> She had three stout and stalwart sons,
>   And sent them o'er the sea.
>
> —Early English Ballad

For other examples, see "The Height of the Ridiculous" (474) and "Get Up and Bar the Door" (475). Create a quatrain of your own.

4. The limerick is an old favorite. This five-line form tends to be humorous, often with a surprising last line. One of the masters of the limerick was Edward Lear, who lived a century and a half ago:

 There was an old man with a beard,
 Who said, "It is just as I feared;
  Two owls and a hen
  Four larks and a wren.
 Have all built their nests in my beard."

 Write a humorous limerick, and share it with your classmates.

5. If you wish, try a longer poem, either in traditional form or free verse. Use the suggestions in this chapter for guidance.

Other Areas of Communication

1. Try your hand at analyzing the following short poem. With a student selected as class leader, prepare to discuss what the poet is suggesting. What does the puddle symbolize? What are those black pearls? Warm ooze of mud? What is the poet talking about?

 Poetry

 Yes, you can
 talk about it
 as you could
 walk in dry boots
 circumspectly
 around a justfound puddle.

 But what is that
 to the joyful splash,
 black pearls flying
 in the startled air,
 and the warm ooze of mud
 between your bare toes?

 —R. J. Lowenherz

2. Several poems are ideal for choral reading: "The Twins," The Destruction of Sennacherib," "Lochinvar," among others. With your

teacher's guidance, break these poems into parts for a narrator and one or more choruses.

3. If you can borrow *H.M.S. Pinafore* from the library, bring it to school and play "Sir Joseph Porter's Song." If you have facilities for video, so much the better.
4. In the library, find "The Hunting of the Snark" by Lewis Carroll and prepare to read it aloud to the class.
5. A poet who resembles Emily Dickinson in some ways is A.E. Housman. Take a Housman volume from the library and prepare to read aloud to the class.
6. There are many fine collections of lyric poetry. Palgrave's *Golden Treasury* is one of the most famous. Select a volume from the library and select a poem to present to the class. Read it and tell why you chose it.
7. The interaction of students and teacher of poetry was the central theme of *The Dead Poets Society* with Robin Williams. It is available on DVD. If you have access to it, view it and report on it. Does the story seem plausible to you? Explain.
8. For the next week, keep a notebook of all the metaphors you hear, then share them with classmates. Be aware of metaphors so common you may tend to overlook them, like *drop a hint, hit a blank wall,* and *frosty reception.*
9. Keep an eye out for blends (483), words formed by cementing two other words together. List them.
10. From country music, select a song that has strong narrative elements. If possible, bring to class the song's verses. Is this poetry?

Language in Action—a Review

You may refer to the preceding pages to answer these questions.

1. *Eye of the hurricane* is an example of (a) a simile (b) literal language (c) metonymy (d) metaphor.
2. Which of the following is an example of personification?

   (a) The district attorney took strong action.
   (b) Duty whispers low, but we must listen.
   (c) The fullback took the ball and rushed for three yards over tackle.
   (d) Our mother and father are coming for Thanksgiving.

3. The pattern of poetic feet is called (a) rhythm (b) rhyme (c) meter (d) free verse.
4. The name *Marie* is given as an example of a(n) (a) iambic foot (b) trochaic foot (c) anapestic foot (d) dactylic foot.
5. Shakespeare's poetry was written in (a) trochaic trimeter (b) iambic pentameter (c) the ballad form (d) none of these.
6. The poetry of Emily Dickinson often (a) deals with political topics (b) follows a standard stanza length (c) avoids metaphors (d) uses imperfect rhymes.
7. Shakespeare sometimes uses rhyming lines (a) to end a scene (b) to reveal character (c) for purely decorative reasons (d) to speed the action.
8. *Motel* is an example of a (a) metaphor (b) personification (c) blend (d) synecdoche.
9. One pleasure of rhyme is the feeling of (a) recognition (b) sympathy (c) excitement (d) contemplation.
10. The poet who wrote free verse is (a) Thomas Bailey Aldrich (b) Lord Tennyson (c) Walt Whitman (d) Oliver Wendell Holmes.

UNIT SEVEN

Actions and Motivations

I have always thought the actions of men the best interpreters of their thoughts.

John Locke

Have you ever done something that surprised you? Afterwards you may have said, "Did I say that?" Or "Did I do that?" If our own motivation is often so confusing to us, how much more complex and puzzling is the motivation of others. Human beings are complicated creatures. Novelists, playwrights, poets all try to reveal to us the motivations of a cross-section of people.

This unit provides a treasure trove of interesting actions and sometimes baffling motivations. "A Quarter's Worth of Fireworks" reaches into the heart of a troubled teenager while studying the interplay of a teenager and his peers, a teenager and his parents. "The Lottery Ticket" could be played out in a modern living room.

The remaining selections reveal a variety of motivations. "A Story Told to the Dark" carries an inspirational message and reveals positive motivation. "The Rising of the Moon" deals with conflicting emotions and motivations in a setting that breeds confusion and conflict. "Never" is a depiction of passivity and indecision.

Two stories similar in many ways close the unit. "A Worn Path" and "Thank You, M'am" have at their centers two strong old women. The life-affirming motivations of Phoenix and Luella reveal that strength of character may be found in the city or the deep woods.

A Quarter's Worth of Fireworks

Norman Katkov
American

Will I ever forget the feeling of desperate doom falling upon us as Sid dropped to the ground and the bag slipped out of my hands? Will I ever forget—can I forget—the panic as the light blazed suddenly in the house and we heard her hobbling across the bare floor of the sleeping porch upstairs?

Peer pressure. Few words hold as much meaning, heartache, and often disaster as these. Peer pressure suggests an overpowering yearning to be part of a group, to be accepted, to be like the rest of the crowd. Though peer pressure wields its influence throughout life, it is especially strong during the teen years when young people are trying to find out who they are. Smoking is a sad example. Many young people who know the deadly results of smoking begin because others in the crowd are smoking. Motivation has many sources.

"A Quarter's Worth of Fireworks" follows a young man through an escapade that grew out of peer pressure. Though unpleasant, the experience has an unexpected result, helping him toward greater maturity. It proves a turning point in the relationship of a father and a son.

A Quarter's Worth of Fireworks

IN THOSE DAYS in our house we each got a dime for the Fourth of July: a nickel for ice cream and a nickel for the afternoon movie on Concord Street: Tom Mix in one feature and Hoot Gibson in the other. Louie would have his dime in his back pocket because there wasn't room for anything more in the front pocket. Joey, the baby, would have ten pennies in his handkerchief in his fist because he liked money. I, Danny, the eldest, would have mine in my stash pocket as I walked between them, holding a hand of each, because that was orders from pa. We were the three Lombardi kids from Colorado Street whose ma sewed for money and whose pa worked in the Great Northern yards, walking back and forth every day to save trolley fare.

In those days everything was orders in our house. It was orders to go to the movies to celebrate the Fourth of July. It was orders to come straight home, with me responsible. It was orders to cross the street before coming to the house with the high black fence where Harry Connery's mother lived. They said he had something to do with moonshine. They said he was bad. When he came to visit his mother, the men from Colorado Street would stand on the corner and guess how much his long touring car cost.

For me it was also orders to keep clear of the bluff where the other guys were shooting off the Minnesota Salutes: three-and five-inch firecrackers as big around as a penny. They were against the law to sell in the city limits, so the guys bought them up on Dodd Road in Dakota County.

Everything was an order from pa, who called us into the living room that one night before the Fourth, the evening paper spread on the couch and the citizenship certificates, his and ma's, hanging on the wall above his head in the double frame she had bought on Robert Street.

He sat like a kid—I can see him yet, with one leg under him. We could hear the money in his fist as he smiled at us.

"Dan, how you feel, eh?" he asked, as though we hadn't been eating supper together in the kitchen half an hour ago.

"I feel fine, pa," I said, because you had to do it this way, like he had done for his pa in Sicily.

Pa said, "Louie, everything O.K. with you?"

"Sure, pa," Louie said, and I had the idea then. As I heard the coins, I thought of it. My heart caught so that for an instant it hurt when I breathed.

I watched pa, who said, "Hey, you, Joey," as I stood there feeling all the danger of what I was going to say before I even knew if I was going to say it. I waited, biting my lip for guts as pa pulled Joey forward, bending to kiss the uncombed black hair. "How is my baby?" he asked. Joey nodded, waiting patiently for his due.

"All right," pa said. "So. Tomorrow is Fourth of July. Larry Ho says please make safe-and-sane holiday. Newspaper says all should be careful."

Larry Ho was the nickname of our mayor, whom pa had never seen, but never called anything else because he had voted for the man.

"Movies is safe and sane," pa said. "Movies, and for each ice cream and, later, when night comes, sparklers."

Sparklers again!

Sitting on the front-porch steps below ma and pa, as I had last year, watching the sparklers he had stuck in the ground, waiting for them to burn out, so I could go up to the corner where the guys were. I almost said it then, because I had said it three times to myself, but only stood quiet as pa counted pennies aloud, dropping each one into Joey's cupped hands.

When pa got to ten, he said, "Louie," and handed over a dime.

"Thanks," Louie said, as pa looked up at me. He smiled at me and I saw the dime in his hand.

He said, "Danny," and I couldn't hold it back.

"No," I said, instead of the speech I had repeated to myself three times.

"Take your dime," pa said. He hadn't even heard me. "For movies tomorrow."

"No," I said. He heard me that time. "I don't want——"

"Take, mister," pa said.

"I don't want a dime," I announced, stepping back from the couch. "I don't want to go to the movies," I said. "I don't want to watch sparklers. I want a quarter."

"A quarter?" he repeated, moving on the couch so both legs were swung over the side now, the stockinged feet touching the floor. "Why a quarter?" he asked. "You tell me, please," he said.

"Why a quarter?"

I could feel my fingernails all the way into my palms, but I said it. "Minnesota Salutes," I said. "I want to buy two packs like the rest of the——"

"——guys in block," pa finished for me. "And if they smoke, mister? Then will you smoke? And if they will hitch a ride to a truck to go——"

"Peter," ma said, but he didn't even look up at her.

"——downtown and be bums on the streets?"

"I'm no bum," I said. I was in it now, I guess, talking to him as I had never talked to him before. "I don't smoke," I continued. "You know that. Do you think I smoke?" I demanded, and he reached out on the couch for the newspaper.

"You heard Larry Ho of this safe-and-sane holiday," he declared. "You know of this terrible burn and explosion from big firecrackers, eh? You know I like if you take Louie and Joey to the movies?"

"How about what I like?" I asked.

"Daniel," ma said.

I turned my head, but she said no with her lips.

"Here, you," pa said. He was holding the dime out. I turned to ma again, but she said no again without saying anything, and then I didn't care.

I grabbed the dime and threw with all my might, and then I ran. I banged the swinging door into the kitchen so that it slammed the sink, and the dishes in the dryer rattled, but I kept going, down the back steps, over our yard, through Morgan's yard and Dwyer's yard. When I reached the sidewalk I turned right, and slowed down a little.

Robert Street was a shopping street. A shopping street was trouble where pa was concerned, so it was against orders. He didn't want his kids there. I was never going back home, so I didn't care. Five minutes later I was on it, with all the lights in the world burning at once, and enough people to fill the ball park just walking along.

I walked with them, my hands in my pockets and wondering where I would sleep. I wondered where I would eat and what kind of a job I should look for. I wondered if pa and ma would go to the cops. There was a cop on the corner ahead of me. Behind him, leaning against the windows of a fruit-and-vegetable store, I saw Sid Glotter and Gutless Wonder, whose real name was Tommy Richards. I turned quick, taking big steps to the curb. I was waiting for the traffic light to change when I heard Sid.

"Hey, Dan!" he said. "Get home before I tell your old man."

I walked back slow, wanting to see Sid's nose splattered over his face, my hands loose at my sides and the fingers curled just a little.

"Tell him," I said.

Sid sneered at me. "Does he know you're out, baby boy?"

"Yeh," Gutless put in, "ain't mamma gonna spank when mamma gets you home?"

I wasn't afraid of him. I looked right at him. "What's it to you, Gutless?" I asked. "What business is it of yours?"

Sid put his hand on my arm. "Take it easy, Dan," he said.

I pushed his hand off me. "Just mind your business," I said. I was mad and I was afraid. I had seen Sid give it to Joe Grabowski, and Joe was bigger too. But I couldn't back away. Gutless Wonder would never let me forget it.

"Beat it," Gutless said. "Go on, beat it."

"When I'm ready," I said. By busting in, Gutless had stopped anything happening between Sid and me. I could get away now, but I had to wait a minute, so it wouldn't look like they were chasing me. I opened my belt and pulled it tight, looking down to get it right, taking as much time as a pitcher.

"I'll see you guys," I said, and felt Sid's hand on my arm again.

"Where you headed for, Dan?" he said.

"To get some Minnesota Salutes," I told him. I moved his hand off me, turning away from them, my hands in my pockets lifting my pants high off my shoes, swearing at myself for saying what I did. I don't know why I said it. Tomorrow they would be waiting on the bluff. I'd be the bum of the street.

I crossed with the light, walking with my head down. I'd never been so alone in my life. I guess I'd never really felt hopeless. I would just have to keep going and hitch a ride on a truck. I headed out toward the Flats, where Robert Street ended and the highway began. I was down near the license-plate factory when they caught up with me. They ran around in front of me, walking backward.

"There ain't no Salutes out here," Sid said. "There's nothing but potato farms out here. You ain't got money, Dan."

"I'll get it," I said. "I'll get it." Why had I stopped to talk with them in the first place?

"Where?" Sid asked.

"Don't worry."

"Where?"

"Don't worry!"

That's when Sid stopped walking backward. He stopped—boom, like that—putting his hands against my chest and pushing. "I know where," he said. He was pushing backward, not hard, but the way a friend pushes. Now I was walking backward while they were going forward until we were all in the dark, against the wall of the license-plate factory. "Do you want to know where?" Sid asked.

"Maybe," I said.

He put his face right up to mine. "Harry Connery's mother is where," he said, and I shivered.

I felt it cold all across my back. I felt it hurt in my chest. "You're crazy," I whispered.

"Unh-uh," he said. He shook his head real slow. "I'm smart, Dan."

"Yeh," Tommy said, giggling. He was nervous. I could tell he was nervous. "Yeh, Sid's smart," Gutless said.

"Ah, you shut up," Sid said. He looked at me again. "There's a tree in the alley behind Harry Connery's house," he whispered. "We go up the tree, swing out over the fence, drop down into the yard. We got three empty bags here. We fill them full of tomatoes out of old lady Connery's garden. We take them up on Robert Street to the fruit-and-vegetable store. We get a quarter a box. We send Gutless Wonder up on Dodd Road. He comes back with two packs each of Minnesota Salutes."

"You're crazy," I said. "What about Harry Connery?"

"He's not there," Sid assured me.

"How do you know there's tomatoes?" I asked.

"Quit stalling," Sid said. "I need somebody to——"

"I got to be home," I said.

"——come into the yard with me. Gutless Wonder will stand watch outside. That's the most you can expect from Gutless Wonder. What are you, Dan, another one?"

"I got to be——"

"Gutless," Sid said, and took his hands from my chest. "I knew it." He started walking toward the lighted end of Robert Street. I ran ahead of him and turned. I said, "I never stole before. Nothing."

"This ain't stealing, for Pete's sake," he said. "Old lady Connery all alone. Nutty as a hoot owl. What's she going to do with all those tomatoes?"

It was pa's fault. One stinking quarter! He could have done that. He didn't have to order my whole life!

"O.K.," I said. I put my hands in my pockets, lifting my pants high above my shoes. "Come on."

"Yeh, that's the stuff," Gutless said. He started to come up beside me. Sid didn't even look. He just reached over and pushed Gutless. "Behind us," he said. "You can't walk with the men."

That was all he or any of us said until we were in the alley behind the block old lady Connery lived in.

There he whispered, "Give me the bags, Gutless." He got the bags. "We'll fill 'em together, Dan. We'll stack 'em against the tree. I'll go up. You hand 'em to me. I'll go over with 'em, one at a time. Gutless will run 'em up here." He pointed at the grassy slope behind Eli Watkins' house. "When you hand me the third bag, follow me out. O.K.?"

I wanted to say no, but I nodded. I was in it, nodding at Sid Glotter, whom I didn't even like. Whom I was afraid of, really.

I can never remember all of it. I remember going up in the tree. I don't remember coming down into the garden. I can remember the ground smell still, and on a clear summer night, wherever I am, I can still see the tomato vines in the moonlight, yet I can't remember picking the tomatoes. I can't remember filling the bags, or carrying the bags, or handing the bags up to Sid, but I remember the tree groaning with his weight. I remember Sid leaning forward for the third bag, and will I ever forget the terrifying moment when the branch broke?

Will I ever forget the feeling of desperate doom falling upon us as Sid dropped to the ground and the bag slipped out of my hands? Will I ever forget—can I forget—the panic as the light blazed suddenly in the house and we heard her hobbling across the bare floor of the sleeping porch upstairs?

"Sid?" I said. I couldn't find him. I tried to whisper. "Sid, are you all right? Where are you, Sid?"

"Shut up and come on," he whispered. "Come on," he whispered, reaching for a branch, swinging with his legs free like a man on a trapeze.

For a crazy second I was paralyzed until another light flashed on in the house, and a third. I jumped and grabbed and was kicked in the ribs as Sid struggled upward. I saw the lights going on in the house and twisted like a monkey from side to side moving up, up, up until I was even with the fence, reaching, holding, climbing higher than the fence and then pushing away from the tree with all my might, falling over and down.

Over the fence with palms out into the dry, rocky, hard-as-cement alley, feeling the rocks cut, feeling my pants rip at the knees, feeling my ribs hurt, crawling forward as I moved, even while I tried to straighten up, like a sprinter after the starting gun sounds.

I passed Sid. I was running with all my might, but I couldn't pass Gutless, who was waiting for us when we got to the grass behind Eli Watkins' house.

"Get the two bags," Sid said, but he was through bossing me. He took one. I got Gutless Wonder by the shoulder, shoving him so he almost fell.

"Go on," I said. I was shaking. I was sick from what had happened. "Go on, Gutless. Running Gutless. Worrying about yourself. Go on, take——"

"Watch yourself, Dan," Sid said.

"And you," I said, turning to him. "Thief," I called him. "What are you going to do, thief? I'm a thief, so what do you think you'll do? Come on, then," I said. "Come on," as Gutless backed off, cradling his bag of tomatoes.

"I'll see you later," Sid warned me.

"Now," I said. "Now if you want it, or tomorrow, or whenever you think you're big enough." I was ready. I didn't care if he beat me up. I just wanted to be clean of him. He made me sick, and what I had done made me more sick.

"O.K.," Sid said. He was hurrying off, carrying the tomatoes. "O.K., Dan, I'll remember."

I watched them go. Then I turned toward home.

Don't you see? It was like I wanted a licking. I wanted pa to beat me up. It would be kind of payment for what I did.

He didn't even say hello. He looked at me over the rim of the glass of soda water he was drinking, sitting across the kitchen table from ma. I got one look before he went back to the newspaper.

"Good morning," ma said. I saw it was five minutes to ten.

"Hi," I said, starting for my bedroom.

Ma dropped her sewing. "Dan!" she cried. I had forgotten my hands. My hands, my knees, the ripped pants, and the ribs she couldn't see.

"Daniel Lombardi, you hurt!"

"No, I'm not, ma." I was looking at him, but he kept reading the newspaper.

"Hitched a ride by a truck," ma decided, "and fell."

I wanted to tell him then. I wanted him to share it with me, I guess, and take some of the sickness away, but as ma grabbed me my knees hurt so much I almost cried out.

"Look, Peter; from truck," she said.

"I didn't fall off no truck, ma," I said. "We were scaling the fire-barn wall. I fell off."

"Peter, look here on Dan," ma said.

He folded the newspaper real slow. He got up. He put the newspaper under his arm. He looked at me. Looked through me. Then he walked out.

"Come on, come on," ma said, pulling me to the sink.

"I'm no baby," I said. "I can wash myself." He had never done anything like that: just walked out when one of us was hurt. While I was washing and ma was bandaging, I waited for him to come into the kitchen. All I heard was the turning of the newspaper pages. When I was finished, when ma had poured me milk and given me three cookies, I said, "Pa never did that."

"What?" She was busy with the needle once more.

"Paid no attention if someone was hurt."

"Pa hurts, too, Dan."

"What are you talking about?" I demanded.

"Hurts here," she said, pressing her heart.

"What if I don't want to go to the movies?" I asked. "Is that so wrong?"

"Wrong for pa," she said. "Dan, you don't know hows pa feel about Fourth of July? Pa feels like go to church on Fourth of July. Pa feels this is the most important day, Independence Day."

I got up, leaving the milk and cookies. I ran into the living room, stopping in front of him. I moved the papers with my hand so he could see me, and I said, "I'm sorry, pa."

"M'm'm'm'm," he said.

"I didn't mean it."

"M'm'm'm'm'm."

"Pa, please."

"All right, mister. Now maybe I finish this newspaper."

I almost ripped the paper. I almost kicked it like you would punt a football. I wanted to do something, anything, to get rid of all the feelings inside of me, but I could only walk back into the kitchen to dunk my cookies.

"What's the matter with him?" I asked ma.

"He hurts," ma announced again.

"I hurt, too," I said. "Haven't I got feelings?"

Ma smiled, shaking her head. "Someday you be a papa, Danny. Someday you have a oldest son. Oldest son can hurt like nothing can hurt."

"Is that a reason to——"

"Listen, you," ma said. She wasn't sewing now. "Finish milk and go to bedroom."

On my way to bed I went into the living room for a book I didn't want. After I was in my pajamas, I came back and got another book I didn't want, but he didn't even look up. I waited about five minutes and went back.

"Can I have the funnies?" I asked.

Pa went through the paper like each sheet was a thousand dollars. When he gave me the funnies, I said, "Thanks."

"M'm'm'm'm," he said. I went to sleep with that. That's what my pa gave me for good night. Long afterward, when the lights were out in the house, when I could hear the floor boards creaking and I seemed all alone in the world, I got to sleep by telling myself he would make up in the morning. He would grab my neck, cup my neck in his hand like he always had done, pulling me forward to knock my head against his head so lightly it was like a leaf falling to the ground.

I was wrong. I couldn't have been wronger. Pa was gone.

He came in while I was finishing my toast. He carried a bag under his arm. I said, "Hi, pa. Is it hot out?" but he only turned to ma.

"Where are the boys?" he asked. "I don't see Louie or Joey."

"I can't tell," she said. "My nurse is off today."

Pa went through the kitchen as she shook her head. "Sicilians," ma said. "Stay 'way from him, Danny."

"Yes," I said. "I can do it now," I said. I slid out from behind the kitchen table. I got my cap from the peg as I went out into the sun. I guess I was just tired of begging. Of begging, of being kicked around, of being brushed off. I went down Colorado Street to the playgrounds to shag flies for an hour. Afterward I watched a scrub game between two teams of older guys. Then Herman Simon wanted to see some planes take off, so we walked to the airport. The sun was almost straight over us, so we sat alongside the hangar in the shade for a while. Coming back, we cut across the old city dump before returning over the State Street Bridge. I left Herman there to walk to the top of the Ohio Street hill, which looked down on half of the city. That's where Louie found me—sitting on the ground and leaning against a tree.

"Dan?"

"What?"

"Can I sit with you?" he asked, sitting with me.

"All right."

"The movies were terrible," Louie said.

"All right."

"You would have hated them, Dan."

"O.K."

"Do you want my ice-cream nickel?" he asked.

"No," I said. "Thanks."

"You can have it."

"No!"

"Dan," Louie said, "I'm supposed to bring you home for supper. Ma said to find you."

"You didn't find me," I said.

"Yes, I did." He was worried. "Here you are."

"I'm not hungry," I said. "Go on home."

"Come with me, Dan." He was standing now. "Please, Dan."

"I'm not hungry! Can't you understand English?" I asked, and saw he was going to cry. I got to my feet, brushing my pants. "Come on, I'll walk with you, but I'm not going home."

We came down the hill without talking. We went past the playground so we could come into Colorado Street from the near side. I said, "I'm going down to the bluff."

"Please, Dan," Louie said. He took my hand. "I'm supposed to bring you home."

"No," I said. Pa wouldn't even look at me. "No, I'm not hungry." I shook myself free, walking toward the bluff.

He walked beside me, half running to keep up with me. I could hear the Salutes going a block away. When I got there, Gutless Wonder was touching a long piece of smoking punk to a firecracker Sid Glotter held. As the wick smoldered, Sid lunged forward. Gutless Wonder said, "Sid, don't!" There was real fear in his voice as he jumped away. Sid saw me and said, "Here, Dan," motioning with the Salute. Louie jumped. Eli Watkins, on the other side of me, jumped while I stood there.

"Guts," said Sid, throwing it over the bluff. "You got guts, ain't you, Dan?"

"Enough for you."

He took a Salute from a pack. "Here," he said.

Louie tugged at my sleeve. I pushed him away as Sid came forward. "Take it," Sid insisted, holding the firecracker in front of him. "Let's be divvies. Partners."

I said, "Beat it," and behind me, a man said, "Hi, Sid."

I turned to see Harry Connery. I knew it was Harry. He was looking at me. He was big. He was taller than anybody I had ever seen. He was wearing brown-and-white shoes, and my chest hurt. I wanted a drink of water as he said, "How are you, Sid?" talking to me.

I knew then. His mother had heard me calling Sid in the darkness in the garden last night.

"I'm not Sid," I said, while Louie started to run. Louie, who couldn't look at anyone who was in trouble. I was alone now, all right. All of them around me had spread out, stepping back or to either side until there were only Harry Connery and me.

"You're not, eh? What do they call you, kid?"

"I'm Dan. Dan Lombardi." My whole back was wet. I could feel my shirt sticking to me. Then a breeze came, blowing his pants back. His legs were as big around as lampposts.

"Who's Sid?" Harry Connery asked me. He reached down to take my arm in his hand. He held my arm until it began to hurt. He said, "Come on, kid, which one? If he isn't here, where does he live? What's his last name? I'm telling you, kid, don't make me——"

"That's him!"

Harry Connery released me and I turned to see Gutless Wonder. He was already over the side of the bluff, pointing at Sid.

"There he is, mister," said Gutless Wonder. "That's the guy, Sid Glotter," and he disappeared.

Harry Connery moved, but Sid was too fast. He leaped like a broad jumper going after Gutless Wonder, and as Harry Connery stood with his back to me, I said, "Me too. I was with them, Mr. Connery."

He stopped dead, boom, like he had run against a wall. He had his back to me. I wasn't running, that's all. I had to get it over with, that's all. I didn't care what he did or what happened, I had to get it out of my head.

I had my hand to my face, feeling his five fingers on my cheek like five whips before I believed it. He had turned and come ahead and grabbed me, holding my shirt with one hand, slapping me with the other.

"Lousy little punk," he said, holding me. My face hurt so I could hardly see. "No-good, thieving punk," he said, hitting me again, on the same side again. I had to bite my lips or I would have cried. I would have just screamed, it hurt so. He had his hand up and I was trying to hide my face when Pa grabbed his arm.

"My boy," he said. "That's my boy you hit," he said, holding Harry Connery's arm in both his hands, his undershirt over his pants and his bedroom slippers on his bare feet. "You stop now," pa said.

Harry Connery stopped. He let me go and turned to pa. He looked pa up and down. He said, "Your kid?"

"Bet my life," pa said, and Harry Connery hit pa with his fist. He got him on the side of the face below the eye, and pa went on his back on the ground. His bedroom slipper fell off. I was crying then, all right. I couldn't stand it to see him on the ground. He was on his back, and he turned and pushed himself. He was on his hands and knees then, shaking his head, and when he saw me, he said, "Don't cry here," he said. "This is America. Don't have to be afraid here!"

"I stole tomatoes," I said. "Pa, I stole." And I told him.

"Will be all right," he said, and got to his feet then. He stood before Harry Connery, and he said, "Is just a boy, mister. I 'pologize for my boy. I pay hows much you say," and as he reached for his coin purse, with his hand in his pocket, Harry Connery hit him again, right under the same eye.

When he fell—when pa fell this time, he didn't lie on the ground. He got up and backed away, and he said, "You don't do nice, mister." He shook his head. "If my boy do wrong, he's a boy. I teach him," and Harry Connery swung.

But pa swung. Pa had closed his right hand, which all week used a sledge and a crowbar in the Great Northern Railroad shops, and as pa got hit, his fist found Harry Connery. Pa closed his left fist, swinging with that, and that found Harry Connery. Harry Connery went back against the big round disk on the fence that lit up to show drivers it was a dead end. He was hanging there a minute with pa in front of him and both bedroom slippers were off.

"Now you stop, mister," pa said in his bare feet. "Now you finish. I don't care if you real tough guy; you don't hit boys. Not kids. My kid. My Dan," pa said, and I could see him beginning to shake. I saw him shake, which was the real sign he was mad. I had only seen him like that once, when an uncle of ma's in Naples wrote a letter and sent a picture of Benito Mussolini.

"I don't care who you bootleg, you hear me, mister," pa said. "You don't touch kids. I go tomorrow. I 'pologize to your mamma. Sweet woman, your mamma; always say hello with my wife. I bring him," pa said, gesturing at me, "and he 'pologize. And whatever she say, he do: plant tomato, sweep sidewalk, shovel snow all winter, what ever. But you don't hit, mister. Not in America. . . . Dan, bring slippers," pa said. He turned to Harry Connery again. "Not in America," pa repeated.

I dropped the slippers on the ground, because he would yell if I bent to help him. He said that nobody had to bend. He got his slippers on and he turned to me.

"You stay, Dan?" he asked. "Stay or come home?" he asked.

I wanted to grab his hand. I wanted to swing on his arm and jump on his back, like I used to, but I was too old now. I just wanted to hold him, but I said, "I'll go home."

That's all I said and that's all he said. We walked in the street. His eye was beginning to puff. He was going to have some shiner. We passed Clinton Avenue without talking, and Greenwood Street, and there, halfway down the block, when I could see the chairs on our front porch, pa stopped. He turned to me in the street, reaching into his pocket.

He had his hand in his pocket and he said, "Dan, you listen." He said, "Dan, I am——You too old——I do——" He took a deep breath. "No," he said. "Start over." I saw the quarter in his hand. "Here, Dan," he said. "You buy Minnesota Salutes," and I shook my head.

Shook my head and stepped back, turning away, or I would cry and he couldn't stop me.

"Here, take," pa said.

He stepped toward me with the quarter out, and I said, "I don't want it, pa."

"Take, son," he said, and I grabbed it. I wanted only to end this.

"I want to go home with you," I said, and pulled back my arm. I couldn't stand it about the money any longer. As I started to throw, pa grabbed me.

He was laughing and holding me, and he said, "Whoa! Whoa, Dan, I don't make these quarters." He held me to him, with my head in his chest, rubbing my hair until, in a minute, he said, "All right?" He nodded at me. "Are you all right, my son?"

"Yes," I said. "Yes, I'm all right, pa," and he took the quarter. He put the quarter in my stash pocket and he cupped my neck. He was bending forward and he moved me forward until our heads touched.

"Come on, Dan," he said. "We go light our sparklers for safe-and-sane Fourth."

Reading for Understanding

Main Idea

1. The central problem of the story is (a) Sid's lack of responsibility (b) the danger in playing with fireworks (c) the value of friendship (d) Dan's self-image.

Details

2. Harry Connery's mother (a) was a criminal (b) lived near the movie theater (c) grew tomatoes (d) disowned her son.
3. Gutless Wonder is (a) Sid's brother (b) Harry Connery (c) Louie (d) Tommy Richards.
4. The lights went on in the house because (a) Sid cried out (b) a branch broke (c) Harry arrived home (d) Gutless hurt himself.
5. Larry Ho was (a) a seller of firecrackers (b) an owner of a restaurant in town (c) the mayor (d) chief of police.

Inferences

6. Pa acted as he did because he (a) was deeply concerned about his children (b) had a streak of cruelty in him (c) was indifferent about the younger children (d) had lost the respect of his wife.
7. Harry Connery (a) was probably engaged in a shady business (b) enjoyed meeting with the young people of the community (c) made Danny's father run away from him (d) had little respect for his mother.

Author's Attitude

8. The author's attitude toward pa was one of (a) coldness (b) respect (c) disapproval (d) bafflement.

Order of Events

9. Arrange the items in the order in which they occurred. Use letters only.
   A. Pa strikes Connery.
   B. Danny runs away from home.
   C. The boys steal tomatoes.
   D. Pa and Danny walk off together.
   E. Connery hurts Danny.

Outcome

10. At the end of the story, (a) Sid gets Danny to go on another tomato raid (b) Danny refuses to apologize to Mrs. Connery (c) Danny and his father get along better together (d) Danny is punished severely by his father.

Thinking Critically About the Story

1. Why did the author choose the title "A Quarter's Worth of Fireworks"? Why not choose a title more directly associated with the robbery?
2. Why was Dan led to do something he basically disapproved of?
3. Was Danny's father a good one? Explain.
4. How did Sid's attitude toward Dan change when Dan began to challenge him?
5. A story may have what is often called a *turning point* or a *defining moment.* What episode in "A Quarter's Worth of Fireworks" proved to be the turning point of the story?
6. What is the strength of peer pressure, a power that makes people do what they really don't want to do? Do people respect those who don't always run with the crowd? Explain.
7. Why did Dan say, "Me, too. I was with them, Mr. Connery"? At that point, Dan seemed to be safe from Connery. Why did he jeopardize himself?
8. How does the author contrast Harry Connery and Dan's father?
9. Motivations are a major consideration in this unit. What makes Gutless act the way he does?
10. *Gutless* is a cruel nickname. Why do people often commit little acts of cruelty in dealing with each other?

Language in Action

Levels of Usage

> Sid put his hand on my arm. "Take it easy, Dan," he said.
>
> "Beat it," Gutless said. "Go on, beat it."
>
> "This ain't stealing, for Pete's sake," he said.

You wouldn't wear a tux or evening dress to a picnic, nor would you wear jeans or sports gear to a wedding. There's a time and place for everything—including words.

The three statements above have a slightly different flavor. The first is colloquial English, the language we use nearly all the time. If you listen to conversations at a party, you'll notice they tend to use colloquial English.

The second example is also colloquial, but it uses the slang expression *beat it*. Slang expressions dominate some conversations. They can be colorful, but often die out when the fad has passed. Some slang words like *fun* and *stingy* eventually made it into the language.

The third expression, with its use of *ain't*, is considered incorrect English. Though a long resident in the English language, *ain't* has still not gained acceptance as a good word choice. When Dan says, "I didn't fall off no truck, ma," he is using the double negative, another unacceptable usage in situations where language counts—as in a job interview.

Formal English, or literary English, is reserved for more serious occasions: a scholarly book, a funeral oration, a wedding ceremony. Some words that appear in literary English—like *confront*, *relegate*, and *compliance*—seldom find their way into colloquial English. The Declaration of Independence and the Constitution of the United States are written in formal English.

Formal: "We hold these truths to be self-evident, that all men are created equal, that they are endowed by their Creator with certain unalienable rights . . ."

Colloquial: "It's pretty clear to us that people are really equal and have some rights that can't be taken away from them."

The seriousness of the Declaration of Independence calls for impressive, formal language. The colloquial counterpart lacks grandeur and is inappropriate for the occasion. As a paraphrase on another occasion though, it's good. It avoids the now-disapproved use of *men* for *humankind*. The Declaration was written in a much earlier time.

A good rule is to use language that doesn't call attention to itself. Don't use formal English in a friendly conversation. Don't use slang in a formal situation. Avoid incorrect English in any situation that affects your future.

The Lottery Ticket

Anton Chekhov
Russian

"Masha, 9,499 is there!" he said in a hollow voice.

His wife looked at his astonished and panic-stricken face, and realized that he was not joking.

"9,499?" she asked, turning pale and dropping the folded tablecloth on the table.

"Yes, yes . . . it really is there!"

Whatever you may think of lotteries, they are a fact of life in many states. Millions of people check television and newspaper reports, hoping that their special numbers will turn up. Heavy advertising promotions add fuel to the fire by picturing what life would be like for a lottery winner. "The Lottery Ticket" was written more than a century ago, but the plot is timeless. The characters' actions and motivations are recognizable.

Ivan and Masha may have a ticket to luxury. The first part of the problem has been solved. They have a ticket with the first four numbers, but what of the remaining two? Why does Ivan delay checking the remaining two numbers? How does this delay reveal character and sum up two lives?

The Lottery Ticket

IVAN DMITRITCH, a middle-class man who lived with his family on an income of twelve hundred a year and was very well satisfied with his lot, sat down on the sofa after supper and began reading the newspaper.

"I forgot to look at the newspaper today," his wife said to him as she cleared the table. "Look and see whether the list of drawings is there."

"Yes, it is," said Ivan Dmitritch; "but hasn't your ticket lapsed?"

"No; I took the interest on Tuesday."

"What is the number?"

"Series 9,499, number 26."

"All right . . . we will look . . . 9,499 and 26."

Ivan Dmitritch had no faith in lottery luck, and would not, as a rule, have consented to look at the lists of winning numbers, but now, as he had nothing else to do and as the newspaper was before his eyes, he passed his finger downwards along the column of numbers. And immediately, as though in mockery of his skepticism, no further than the second line from the top, his eye was caught by the figure 9,499! Unable to believe his eyes, he hurriedly dropped the paper on his knees without looking to see the number of the ticket, and, just as though some one had given him a douche of cold water, he felt an agreeable chill in the pit of the stomach; tingling and terrible and sweet!

"Masha, 9,499 is there!" he said in a hollow voice.

His wife looked at his astonished and panic-stricken face, and realized that he was not joking.

"9,499?" she asked, turning pale and dropping the folded tablecloth on the table.

"Yes, yes. . . it really is there!"

"And the number of the ticket?"

"Oh, yes! There's the number of the ticket too. But stay. . .wait! No, I say! Anyway, the number of our series is there! Anyway, you understand . . . ."

Looking at his wife, Ivan Dmitritch gave a broad, senseless smile, like a baby when a bright object is shown it. His wife smiled too; it was as pleasant to her as to him that he only mentioned the series, and did not try to find out the number of the winning ticket. To torment and tantalize oneself with hopes of possible fortune is so sweet, so thrilling!

"It is our series," said Ivan Dmitritch, after a long silence. "So there is a probability that we have won. It's only a probability, but there it is!"

"Well, now look!"

"Wait a little. We have plenty of time to be disappointed. It's on the second line from the top, so the prize is seventy-five thousand. That's not money, but power, capital! And in a minute I shall look at the list, and there—26! Eh? I say, what if we really have won?"

The husband and wife began laughing and staring at one another in silence. The possibility of winning bewildered them; they could not have said, could not have dreamed, what they both needed that seventy-five thousand for, what they would buy, where they would go. They thought only of the figures 9,499 and 75,000 and pictured them in their imagination, while somehow they could not think of the happiness itself which was so possible.

Ivan Dmitritch, holding the paper in his hand, walked several times from corner to corner, and only when he had recovered from the first impression began dreaming a little.

"And if we have won," he said—"why, it will be a new life, it will be a transformation! The ticket is yours, but if it were mine I should, first of all, of course, spend twenty-five thousand on real property in the shape of an estate; ten thousand on immediate expenses, new furnishing . . . travelling . . . paying debts, and so on. . . . The other forty thousand I would put in the bank and get interest on it."

"Yes, an estate, that would be nice," said his wife, sitting down and dropping her hands in her lap.

"Somewhere in the Tula or Oryol provinces. . . . In the first place we shouldn't need a summer villa, and besides, it would always bring in an income."

And pictures came crowding on his imagination, each more gracious and poetical than the last. And in all these pictures he saw himself well-fed, serene, healthy, felt warm, even hot! Here, after eating a summer soup, cold as ice, he lay on his back on the burning sand close to a stream or in the garden under a lime-tree. . . . It is hot. . . . His little boy and girl are crawling about near him, digging in the sand or catching ladybirds in the grass. He dozes sweetly, thinking of nothing, and feeling all over that he need not go to the office today, tomorrow, or the day after. Or, tired of lying still, he goes to the hayfield, or to the forest for mushrooms, or watches the peasants catching fish with a net. When the sun sets he takes a towel and soap and saunters to the bathing-shed, where he undresses at his leisure, slowly rubs his bare chest with his hands, and goes into the water. And in the water, near the opaque soapy circles, little fish flit to and fro and green water-weeds nod their heads. After bathing there is tea with cream and milk rolls. . . . In the evening a walk or *vint* with the neighbours.

"Yes, it would be nice to buy an estate," said his wife, also dreaming, and from her face it was evident that she was enchanted by her thoughts.

Ivan Dmitritch pictured to himself autumn with its rains, its cold evenings, and its St. Martin's summer.[1] At that season he would have to take longer walks about the garden and beside the river, so as to get thoroughly chilled, and then drink a big glass of vodka and eat a salted mushroom or a soused cucumber, and then—drink another. . . . The children would come running from the kitchen-garden, bringing a carrot and a radish smelling of fresh earth. . . . And then, he would lie stretched full length on the sofa, and in leisurely fashion turn over the pages of some illustrated magazine, or, covering his face with it and unbuttoning his waistcoat, give himself up to slumber.

The St. Martin's summer is followed by cloudy, gloomy weather. It rains day and night, the bare trees weep, the wind is damp and cold. The dogs, the horses, the fowls—all are wet, depressed, downcast. There is nowhere to walk; one can't go out for days together; one has to pace up and down the room, looking despondently at the grey window. It is dreary!

Ivan Dmitritch stopped and looked at his wife.

"I should go abroad, you know, Masha," he said.

And he began thinking how nice it would be in late autumn to go abroad somewhere to the South of France . . . to Italy . . . to India!

"I should certainly go abroad too," his wife said. "But look at the number of the ticket!"

"Wait, wait! . . ."

He walked about the room and went on thinking. It occurred to him: what if his wife really did go abroad? It is pleasant to travel alone, or in the society of light, careless women who live in the present, and not such as think and talk all the journey about nothing but their children, sigh, and tremble with dismay over every farthing. Ivan Dmitritch imagined his wife in the train with a multitude of parcels, baskets, and bags; she would be sighing over something, complaining that the train made her head ache, that she had spent so much money. . . . At the stations he would continually be having to run for boiling water, bread and butter. . . . She wouldn't have dinner because of its being too dear. . . .

"She would begrudge me every farthing," he thought, with a glance at his wife. "The lottery ticket is hers, not mine! Besides, what is the use of her going abroad? What does she want there? She would shut herself up in the hotel, and not let me out of her sight. . . . I know!"

And for the first time in his life his mind dwelt on the fact that his wife had grown elderly and plain, and that she was saturated through and through with the smell of cooking, while he was still young, fresh, and healthy, and might well have got married again.

"Of course, all that is silly nonsense," he thought; "but . . . why should she go abroad? What would she make of it? And yet she would

[1]Usually around November 11, St. Martin's Day. It is a European term for our *Indian Summer.*

go, of course. . . . I can fancy . . . In reality it is all one to her, whether it is Naples or Klin. She would only be in my way. I should be dependent upon her. I can fancy how, like a regular woman, she will lock the money up as soon as she gets it. . . . She will hide it from me. . . . She will look after her relations and grudge me every farthing."

Ivan Dmitritch thought of her relations. All those wretched brothers and sisters and aunts and uncles would come crawling about as soon as they heard of the winning ticket, would begin whining like beggars, and fawning upon them with oily, hypocritical smiles. Wretched, detestable people! If they were given anything, they would ask for more; while if they were refused, they would swear at them, slander them, and wish them every kind of misfortune.

Ivan Dmitritch remembered his own relations, and their faces, at which he had looked impartially in the past, struck him now as repulsive and hateful.

"They are such reptiles!" he thought.

And his wife's face, too, struck him as repulsive and hateful. Anger surged up in his heart against her, and he thought malignantly:

"She knows nothing about money, and so she is stingy. If she won it she would give me a hundred roubles, and put the rest away under lock and key."

And he looked at his wife, not with a smile now, but with hatred. She glanced at him too, and also with hatred and anger. She had her own daydreams, her own plans, her own reflections; she understood perfectly well what her husband's dreams were. She knew who would be the first to try and grab her winnings.

"It's very nice making daydreams at other people's expense!" is what her eyes expressed. "No, don't you dare!"

Her husband understood her look; hatred began stirring again in his breast, and in order to annoy his wife he glanced quickly, to spite her at the fourth page on the newspaper and read out triumphantly:

"Series 9,499, number 46! Not 26!"

Hatred and hope both disappeared at once, and it began immediately to seem to Ivan Dmitritch and his wife that their rooms were dark and small and low-pitched, that the supper they had been eating was not doing them good, but lying heavy on their stomachs, that the evenings were long and wearisome. . . .

"What the devil's the meaning of it?" said Ivan Dmitritch, beginning to be ill-humoured. "Wherever one steps there are bits of paper under one's feet, crumbs, husks. The rooms are never swept! One is simply forced to go out. Damnation takes my soul entirely! I shall go and hang myself on the first aspen-tree!"

Reading for Understanding

Main Idea

1. The central point of the story can best be expressed by the phrase (a) What if? (b) A penny saved (c) Time and tide (d) Not worth a farthing.

Details

2. The prize was for (a) 9,499 (b) 10,000 (c) 25,000 (d) 75,000.
3. All of the following are Ivan's daydreams EXCEPT (a) watching peasants fishing (b) going into the water (c) buying an expensive colt (d) traveling abroad.
4. The remaining winning number was (a) 16 (b) 26 (c) 36 (d) 46.
5. The ticket actually belonged to (a) Masha (b) Ivan (c) the oldest daughter (d) a favorite aunt.

Inferences

6. The one who would be most affected by a winning lottery ticket is probably (a) Masha (b) Ivan (c) the son (d) the daughter.
7. A possible misfortune of a winning lottery ticket is (a) extra money (b) bothersome relatives (c) cruelty to the children (d) giving up a job.

Outcome

8. At the conclusion of the story, Masha and Ivan probably (a) were closer than ever (b) went abroad (c) continued as before (d) divorced.

Author's Attitude

9. The author's attitude toward Ivan is probably one of (a) restrained enthusiasm (b) awed admiration (c) mild dislike (d) envy.

Fact or Opinion

Tell whether the following is a fact or an opinion.

10. Ivan and Masha would have been better off winning the lottery.

Words in Context

1. "In all these pictures he saw himself well-fed, *serene,* healthy, felt warm, even hot!" **Serene** (510) means (a) unhurt (b) bold (c) wealthy (d) peaceful.
2. "In the water, near the *opaque* soapy circles, little fish flit to and fro and green water-weeds nod their heads." **Opaque** (510) is the opposite of (a) transparent (b) dark (c) filmy (d) swiftly running
3. "'She would *begrudge* me every farthing.'" **Begrudge** (511) means (a) allot (b) give reluctantly (c) take away (d) count.
4. "All those wretched brothers and sisters and aunts and uncles would come crawling about as soon as they heard of the winning ticket, would begin whining like beggars, and *fawning* upon them with oily, hypocritical smiles." **Fawning** (512) upon means (a) addressing openly (b) commenting critically to (c) bowing to (d) asking opinions of.
5. "Anger surged up in his heart against her, and he thought *malignantly.*" **Malignantly** (512) means (a) hatefully (b) thoughtlessly (c) quickly (d) wearily.

Thinking Critically About the Story

1. The opening sentences tell us that Ivan "was very well satisfied with his lot." In the last paragraph, Ivan is "beginning to be ill-humoured." Why? Nothing has really happened. Ivan is no richer and no poorer than at the beginning. What has changed Ivan's mood?
2. Would Ivan and Masha have been better off if their ticket hadn't come close? Explain.
3. Why does Ivan delay so long in looking for the winning number in the lottery series 9,499?
4. How does Chekhov reveal the lifestyle of Masha and Ivan? Is it a purely materialistic way of life? Explain.
5. We learn more of Ivan's innermost feelings than of Masha's. Why doesn't the author give them "equal time"?
6. How do *you* personally feel about state-run lotteries? What are the arguments usually used in favor? Against?

7. What is the significance of the statement "Hatred and hope both disappeared at once"?
8. How does the lottery experience focus a lifetime of little irritations and hatreds ordinarily buried in the business of living?

Language in Action

Tracing Word Origins

She would begrudge me every farthing.

Every word has a story to tell, and *farthing* is no exception. A farthing is a former British coin worth a fourth of a penny. It took on the meaning *of little value*. The expression *not worth a farthing* expressed scorn for this forgotten coin. When you pronounce *farthing* and *fourthing* in turn, you can guess the origin: *fourth*. Language scholars, however, don't jump to conclusions. They know that explanations that seem obvious are often wrong.

Sometimes a colorful guess is correct. *Caterpillar* is indeed derived from *cat. A caterpillar is a hairy cat.* Sometimes though, the guess is incorrect. A *pantry* is not connected to the word *pan* but ultimately to the Latin *panis, bread*. Such a mistake is often called *folk etymology*.

Scholars have traced *farthing* back to Old English *feortha*, meaning a *fourth*. The Middle English form was *ferthing*. The word is related to *vierdunc* (*fourth part*) in Middle High German. For most purposes, that information is enough, but for scholars, the road extends farther back. There are related words in Gothic, Old Norse, Latin, Greek, and even Sanskrit. These languages are all part of the great Indo-European family.

Some students collect interesting word origins, or etymologies, as others collect stamps. Following the trail of word's history opens doors to many exciting new areas.

A Story Told to the Dark

Rainer Maria Rilke
German

In the night, unable to sleep in the overcrowded train, it became clear to him that he was really going for the sake of his childhood, hoping to rediscover something in those old streets: a doorway, a tower, a fountain, anything to induce some joy or some sorrow by which he might recognize himself again.

In Thomas Wolfe's novel **You Can't Go Home Again**, the title suggests the theme of the book. In this story, Dr. Lassmann can't exactly go home again, either, but he finds something more precious than he could ever have anticipated.

In search of Klara, a childhood friend, Dr. Lassmann learns what seems to be a sordid story of abandonment and possible betrayal. Expecting to find his friend miserable, beaten down, pessimistic, he is amazed to find the opposite.

Klara is radiantly happy. She has had a spiritual awakening that has changed her life. The explanation of that experience will challenge you.

The word **dark** in the title has rich connotations discussed in the last paragraph of the story.

A Story Told to the Dark

I WANTED to put on my coat and go to my lame friend Ewald. But I had lingered over a book, an old book at that, and evening had come, as in Russia spring comes. A moment ago the room had been distinct, even to its remotest corners, and now all the things in it were as though they had never known anything but twilight; everywhere large dark blossoms opened, and luminous gleams slipped about their velvet calyxes as on dragonfly wings.

The lame man would surely no longer be at his window. So I stayed at home. What was it I had wanted to tell him? I no longer knew. But after a while I felt that someone was entreating me for this lost story—some lonely soul, perhaps, standing far away at the window of his dusky chamber, or perhaps this very darkness itself, that surrounded me and him and all things. So it happened that I told my story to the dark. And it leaned ever closer to me so that I could speak more and more softly, quite as befits my story. It takes place in the present and begins:

After a long absence Doctor Georg Lassmann was returning to the home of his birth. He had never possessed much there, and now he had only two sisters left in his native city, both married, apparently well married; to see them again after twelve years was the purpose of his visit. So he himself believed. But in the night, unable to sleep in the over-crowded train, it became clear to him that he was really going for the sake of his childhood, hoping to rediscover something in those old streets: a doorway, a tower, a fountain, anything to induce some joy or some sorrow by which he might recognize himself again. One gets so lost in life. And then he remembered many things: the little apartment in the Heinrichsgasse with the shiny door-latch and the dark-coated tiles, the well-cared-for furniture and his parents, those two threadbare beings, standing almost awed beside it; the swift and harassed week-days and the Sundays that were like emptied rooms, the rare visitors whom one received laughing and embarrassed, the out-of-tune piano, the old canary, the heirloom armchair in which one might not sit, a birthday, an uncle who came from Hamburg, a puppet-show, a barrel-organ, a children's party, and someone calling: "Klara." The doctor had almost dropped off. They were in a station, lights went by and the listening hammer went ringing along the wheels. And that was like. Klara, Klara "Klara," the doctor reflected, now wide awake, "who was Klara anyway?" And immediately he became aware of a face, a child's face with blond, straight hair. Not that he could have described it, but he had a sense of something quiet, helpless, resigned, and of a pair of narrow childish shoulders drawn still more together by a washed-out little dress, and he began to imagine a face to go with them—but then he knew that he need not imagine it. It was there—or rather, it had been there, then. So the doctor recalled his single playfellow Klara, not without effort. Until the day he went to boarding-school, at the age of about ten, he had shared with her everything that happened to him, little that it was (or was it much?). Klara had no sisters or brothers, and he had as good as none; for his older sisters did not concern themselves with him. But since then he had never asked anyone about her. How had that been possible?—He leaned back. She had been a pious child, he still remembered, and then he asked himself: "What can have become of her?" For a time the thought frightened him that she might have died. An immeasurable dread overcame him in the closely packed compartment; everything seemed to confirm this assumption: she had been a sickly child, she hadn't been very well off at home, she had often cried; undoubtedly, she was dead. The doctor could not stand it any longer; he disturbed certain of the sleepers, shoving his way between them into the corridor of the car. There he opened a window and gazed out into the blackness with the dancing sparks. That quieted him. And when he returned to the compartment later, despite the uncomfortable position, he soon went to sleep.

The reunion with his two married sisters passed off not without embarrassment. The three had forgotten how far apart, notwithstanding their close relationship, they had always remained, and endeavored for a while to act like brother and sisters. But they soon silently agreed to take refuge behind that polite mediate tone which social intercourse has invented for all occasions.

He dined at his younger sister's, whose husband was in particularly comfortable circumstances, a manufacturer with the title of Imperial Councilor; and it was after the fourth course that the doctor asked:

"Tell me, Sophie, what's become of Klara?"

"Klara who?"

"I don't remember her name. The little one, you know, a neighbor's daughter, with whom I played as a child."

"Oh, you mean Klara Söllner?"

"Söllner, that's it, Söllner. Now I remember: old Söllner was that awful old man—but what of Klara?"

His sister hesitated. "She married—and now she lives altogether in retirement."

"Yes," went on the Imperial Councilor, and his knife slid rasping across his plate, "quite retired."

"You know her too?" The doctor turned to his brother-in-law.

"Y-ye-es—just slightly; she's pretty well known here, of course."

Husband and wife exchanged a look of understanding. The doctor noticed that for some reason they did not care to say more on the subject, and he let it drop.

The more eagerness to pursue it did the Councilor show when the lady of the house had left them to their coffee.

"This Klara," he asked with a sly smile, watching the ash that fell from his cigar into a silver bowl, "wasn't she supposed to be a quiet child and homely too?"

The doctor said nothing. The Councilor moved confidentially closer.

"That was a story!—Did you never hear of it?"

"But I haven't seen anybody to talk to."

"Talk to?" the Councilor laughed cunningly. "You could have read it in the papers."

"What?" asked the doctor nervously.

"Why, she ran off and left him—" From behind a cloud of smoke the manufacturer discharged this astonishing sentence and waited in unconfined well-being for the effect. But the effect did not seem to please him. He took on a businesslike manner, sat up straight and began to report in another, an injured tone, as it were: "Well, they had married her to Lehr, of the building council. You wouldn't have known him. Not an old man—my age. Rich, thoroughly respectable, you know, thoroughly respectable. She hadn't a penny and in addition she had no looks, no bringing-up, etc. Still, Lehr didn't want a great lady, just a modest housekeeping wife. But Klara—she was taken into society all over, everybody was kindly disposed towards her—really, they acted—well, you know, she could easily have made a position for herself—when one day, hardly two years after the wedding, off goes Klara. Can you imagine it: gone. Where? To Italy. A little pleasure-trip, not alone, naturally. All that last year we hadn't invited them—as though we had suspected! Lehr, a good friend of mine, a man of honor, a man—"

"And Klara?" the doctor broke in, rising.

"Oh, yes—well, the chastisement of heaven fell upon her. You see, the man in question—an artist, they say, you know—a casual sort of bird, naturally, just—well, when they got back from Italy, to Munich: goodbye, and she saw him no more. Now she's sitting there with her child!"

Doctor Lassmann strode excitedly up and down: "In Munich?"

"Yes, in Munich," replied the Councilor and also rose. "They say she's having a pretty miserable time—"

"How miserable?"

"Well," the Councilor gazed at his cigar, "peculiarly, and then anyhow—God, what an existence—"

Suddenly he laid his well-groomed hand on his brother-in-law's shoulder and clucked with pleasure: "You know they also used to say that she lived on—"

The doctor turned short about and walked out of the door. The Councilor, whose hand had fallen from the other's shoulder, needed ten minutes to recover from his astonishment. Then he went in to his wife and said angrily:

"I've always said so, your brother is decidedly strange."

And she, having just dozed off, yawned lazily: "Oh, Lord yes."

A fortnight later the doctor departed. He knew all at once that he must seek his childhood elsewhere. In the Munich directory he found: Klara Söllner, the name of a suburb, the street and number. He announced his coming and drove out. A slender woman greeted him in a room full of light and kindliness.

"Georg, and you remember me?"

The doctor stood still in amazement. At last he said: "So this is you, Klara."

She held her calm face with its clear brow quite still, as though to give him time to recognize her. It took long. Finally the doctor seemed to have found something that proved to him that his old playfellow really stood before him. He sought her hand again and pressed it; then slowly let it go and looked about the room. It seemed to contain nothing superfluous. At the window a desk with papers and books, at which Klara must just have been sitting. The chair had been pushed back.

"You were writing?" . . . and the doctor felt how silly the question was.

But Klara answered, unconcernedly: "Yes, I'm doing some translating."

"For publication?"

"Yes," Klara said simply, "for a publishing house."

Georg noticed some Italian photographs on the walls. Among them Giorgione's "Concert."

"You are fond of this?" He stepped nearer to the picture.

"And you?"

"I have never seen the original; it's in Florence, isn't it?"

"In the Pitti. You must go there."

"For the purpose?"

"For the purpose." There was a free and simple serenity about her. The doctor looked up thoughtfully.

"What's the matter, Georg? Won't you sit down?"

"I'm upset," he faltered. "I thought—but you aren't in the least miserable—!" he suddenly exclaimed.

Klara smiled. "You have heard my story?"

"Yes, that is—"

"Oh," she interrupted quickly, as she saw his brow darken, "it's not people's fault if they speak differently of it. The things we experience are often inexpressible, and any one who insists on telling them nevertheless, necessarily makes mistakes—" A pause.

And the doctor: "What has made you so kind?"

"Everything," she said softly and warmly. "But why do you say: kind?"

"Because—because you really ought to have grown hard. You were such a weak, helpless child; children of that sort later either grow hard or—"

"Or they die, you mean. Well, I died too. I died for many years. From the time I last saw you at home, until—" She took up something from the table. "See, this is his picture. It flatters him a little. His face is not so clear-cut, but—nicer, simpler. I'll show you our child in a moment, it's asleep in the next room. It's a boy. Called Angelo, like him. He is away now, traveling, far away."

"And you are all alone?" asked the doctor absently, still absorbed in the photograph.

"Yes, I and the child. Isn't that enough? I will tell you how it is. Angelo is a painter. His name is little known; you would never have heard it. Until lately he had been struggling with the world, with his plans, with himself and with me. Yes, with me too; because for a year I've been begging him to travel. I felt how much he needed it. Once he asked jokingly: 'Me or a child?' 'A child,' said I, and then he went."

"And when will he come back?"

"When the child can say his name, that's how we arranged it." The doctor was about to say something, but Klara laughed: "And as it's a difficult name, it will take a while yet. Angelino won't be two till summer."

"Extraordinary," said the doctor.

"What, Georg?"

"How well you understand life. How big you have grown, how young! What have you done with your childhood? We were both such—such helpless children. But that can't be altered or made never to have happened."

"You mean, we ought to have suffered from our childhood, by rights?"

"Yes, I mean just that. From that heavy darkness behind us with which we preserve such feeble, vague relations. There comes a time when we deposit in it all our firstlings, all beginning, all confidence, the seeds of all that which might perhaps some day come to be. And suddenly we realize that the whole thing has sunk in a deep sea, and we don't even know just when. We never noticed it. As though some one were to gather in all his money and buy with it a feather to stick in his hat: whish!—the first breeze carries it away. Naturally he arrives home without his feather, and nothing remains for him but to look back and think when it could have flown off."

"You are thinking of that, Georg?"

"Not any more. I've given it up. I begin somewhere behind my tenth year, at the point where I stopped praying. The rest doesn't belong to me."

"And how is it, then, that you remember me?"

"That is just why I have come to you. You are the only witness to that time. I believed I could find again in you—that which I cannot find in myself. Some gesture, some word, some name, that has significance—some enlightenment—" The doctor's head sank into his cold, uneasy hands.

Frau Klara pondered. "I remember so little of my childhood, as though there were a thousand lives between. But now that you remind me of it so, something comes back to me. One evening. You came to us, unexpectedly; your parents had gone out, to the theater or something of the sort. Our house was all lit up. My father was expecting a guest, a relative, a distant wealthy relative, if I remember rightly. He was coming from, from—I don't know where, but in any case from some distance. We had already been awaiting him for two hours. The doors were open, the lamps were burning, my mother went over from time to time and smoothed an antimacassar[1] on the sofa, father stood at the window. Nobody dared sit down for fear of displacing a chair. As you happened to come, you waited with us. We children listened at the door. And the later it grew, the more marvelous a guest did we expect. Yes, we even trembled lest he come before he should have attained that last degree of gloriousness to which with every minute of his not-coming he drew nearer. We were not afraid that he might not appear at all; we knew for certain he would come, but we wanted to leave him time to grow great and mighty."

Suddenly the doctor raised his hand and said sadly: "So we both know that—that he didn't come. I had not forgotten it either."

"No," Klara corroborated, "he didn't come—" And after a pause: "But it was lovely all the same!"

"What?"

"Oh, well—the waiting, the many lamps—the stillness—the festive spirit."

Something stirred in the next room. Frau Klara excused herself for a moment; and as she came brightly and serenely back, she said: "We can go in now. He's awake and smiling.—But what was it you wanted to say just now?"

[1]chair-back cover

"I was just wondering what could have helped you to—to yourself, to this calm possession of yourself. Life certainly hasn't made it easy for you. Evidently something helped you that I haven't got?"

"What might that be, Georg?" Klara sat down beside him.

"It is strange; when I first remembered you again, one night, three weeks ago, on the train, I thought: She was a pious child. And now, since I have seen you, although you are so entirely different from what I had expected—in spite of that, and yet, I would like to say, only the more surely, I believe I feel that what led you through all dangers was—your piety."

"What do you call piety?"

"Well, your relation to God; your love of God, your belief."

Frau Klara closed her eyes. "Love of God? Let me think." The doctor watched her tensely. She seemed to speak her thoughts slowly, as they came to her: "As a child—did I love God? I don't believe so. Why, I never even—it would have seemed to me insane presumption—that isn't the right word—like the worst sin, to think: *he is*. As though I had thereby compelled him to be in me, in that weak child with the absurdly long arms, in our poor apartment where everything was imitation and false, from the bronze wall-plaques of papier mâché to the wine in the bottles that bore such expensive labels. And later—" Klara made a defensive gesture with her hands, and her eyes closed tighter, as though she feared to see something dreadful through the lids—"why, I would have had to drive him out of me if he had been living in me then. But I knew nothing about him. I had quite forgotten him. I had forgotten everything.—It was in Florence, when for the first time in my life I saw, heard, felt, realized and simultaneously learned to be thankful for all those things, that I first thought of him again. There were traces of him everywhere. In all the pictures I found bits of his smile, the bells were still alive with his voice, and on the statues I saw the imprints of his hands."

"And you found him there?"

Klara looked at the doctor with large, happy eyes: "I felt that he had been—somewhere, once, had been . . . why should I have felt more? That was already more than enough."

The doctor got up and went to the window. From it one could see a stretch of field and the little old village church, and above it sky, no longer quite untouched by evening. Suddenly Doctor Lassmann asked, without turning round:

"And now?"

Receiving no answer, he came softly back again.

"Now—" Klara faltered as he stood before her, and then raised her eyes full to his face, "now I sometimes think: he will be."

The doctor took her hand and kept it a moment. He seemed to gaze into the unknown.

"What are you thinking of, Georg?"

"I'm thinking that it's like that evening once more: you are again waiting for the wonderful guest, for God, and know that he will come. And I have joined you by chance—"

Klara rose, calm and happy. She looked very young. "Well, this time we'll really wait until it happens." She said it so joyfully and so simply that the doctor had to smile. And so she led him into the adjoining room, to her child—

In this story there is nothing that children may not know. Still, the children haven't heard it. I have told it only to the dark, to no one else. And the children are afraid of the dark, and run away from it, and if some time they have to stay in it, they press their eyes shut and put their fingers in their ears. But for them also the time will come when they love the dark. From it they will learn my story, and then they will understand it better, too.

Reading for Understanding

Main Idea

1. A principal idea of the story is that (a) train travel is irritating (b) hardships may lead to spiritual awakenings (c) the more life changes, the more it remains the same (d) art is eternal.

Details

2. Dr. Lassmann hadn't seen his sisters (a) since he first met Klara (b) since his graduation (c) after a disagreement (d) in 12 years.
3. The Imperial Councilor was (a) Klara's father (b) the village schoolteacher (c) the doctor's brother-in-law (d) an artist.
4. The doctor found Klara (a) in Florence (b) in Munich (c) in his hometown (d) on the train.

Inferences

5. Which of the following best symbolizes Klara's personality?
   (a) "A room full of light and kindliness."
   (b) "Goodbye, and she saw him no more."
   (c) "She had been a sickly child."
   (d) "Rich, thoroughly respectable, you know, thoroughly respectable."

6. A major quality displayed by Klara was (a) a witty tongue (b) a sensitivity to criticism (c) a love of life (d) an artistic talent.
7. When the expected guest didn't arrive, Klara felt (a) it didn't matter (b) her life was shattered (c) Georg should have gone for him (d) something crucial was missing.
8. The doctor's trip to see Klara was really (a) a rest from his family (b) to find material for a book (c) to repay a loan from long ago (d) a spiritual quest.
9. When the Imperial Councilor says (518) that Klara is "quite retired," he is being (a) kindly (b) sarcastic (c) neighborly (d) curious.

Fact or Opinion

Tell whether the following is a fact or an opinion.

10. The doctor left the Councilor's presence without waiting for him to finish his conversation.

Words in Context

1. "Luminous gleams slipped about their velvet *calyxes* as on dragonfly wings." **Calyxes** (517) are (a) dragonflies (b) cushions (c) flower parts (d) kinds of sewing material.
2. "There was a free and simple *serenity* about her." **Serenity** (520) means (a) inquisitiveness (b) shyness (c) peacefulness (d) tactlessness.

Thinking Critically About the Story

1. This story could have omitted the first two paragraphs and the last. The story itself is complete without them. Why did the author provide this framework? Are the three paragraphs essential to the story, helping to emphasize the author's point? Explain.
2. Was the child Klara different from the woman she became, or were the bases of her personality already evident in childhood? Explain.
3. What is Georg looking for in his return to his hometown? Does he find it?

4. The expected guest at the childhood party did not come, but Klara says, "It was lovely all the same." What did Klara mention to support her statement that "it was lovely all the same"?
5. "It was in Florence, when for the first time in my life I saw, heard, felt, realized, and simultaneously learned to be thankful for all those things, that I first thought of him again. There were traces of him everywhere. In all the pictures I found bits of his smile, the bells were still alive with his voice, and on the statues I saw the imprints of his hands."

    Here Klara seems to be expressing her philosophy of life. What does that self-revelation mean to you?
6. Klara says, "I felt that he had been—somewhere, once, had been . . . why should I have felt more? That was already more than enough."

    How does this statement reflect Klara's reactions to the failure of the visitor to appear (question 4)?
7. How is Georg affected by the expression of Klara's philosophy?
8. "Live in the moment and accept all our blessings with gratitude and humility." Would Klara agree with this statement? Why or why not?
9. What does the author mean by saying, "The time will come when they (the children) love the dark"? What does the dark symbolize for the author?
10. Trying to put matters of the spirit into words, into a story, is a difficult feat. Do you think the author has successfully suggested a spiritual quest and a possible solution? Explain.
11. In a painting in the Boston Museum of Fine Arts, the artist Paul Gauguin wrote three basic questions asked by people since ancient times:

    Whence do we come?

    Who are we?

    Whither are we going?

    Does "A Story Told to the Dark" ask similar questions?

Language in Action

Punctuation: the Semicolon

The doctor could not stand it any longer; he disturbed certain of the sleepers, shoving his way between them into the corridor of the car.

This is a good example of the way in which a semicolon (;) is used. There are two independent clauses that have to be connected in some way. A comma after *longer* would produce an unacceptable run-on sentence. A conjunction, *and*, might be used.

> The doctor could not stand it any longer, and so he disturbed certain of the sleepers, shoving his way between them into the corridor of the car.

The author chose to use a semicolon, often used between two independent clauses that are closely related in meaning. Sometimes the semicolon joins two short clauses.

> Prentice voted for the resolution; Fazio voted against it.

Sometimes the conjunction is used in a sentence with more than two independent clauses. The following long sentence contains four independent clauses. The semicolon links the first two independent clauses with the second two.

> A moment ago the room had been distinct, even to its remotest corners, and now all the things in it were as though they had never known anything but twilight; everywhere large dark blossoms opened, and luminous gleams slipped about their velvet calyxes as on dragonfly wings.

The author might have used a period after *twilight,* but he preferred the semicolon.

The colon, a related punctuation mark, is discussed on page 534.

Never

H. E. Bates
British

"No one will believe I've gone. But it's true—I'm going at last."

Are we architects of our own destinies? Or, like prisoners, do we sometimes fall in love with our chains? "Never" is a deceptively simple story, with a single character and shadowy figure in the background. Yet in the space of a few pages, it sums up a life, lays bare a character, and raises questions about human motivation.

For a long time, Nellie has planned to break away from a stifling routine, freeing herself from the boring restraints of everyday life. The solution, she thinks, is simple: taking the train to London and freedom. Or so she has daydreamed. At last, the time is right. The clothes are packed. The timetable has been checked. Nellie starts out on the first step to a new life. How does she fare? What happens? Why? The answers probe the depths of a human personality.

Never

IT WAS AFTERNOON: great clouds stumbled across the sky. In the drowsy, half-dark room the young girl sat in a heap near the window, scarcely moving herself, as if she expected a certain timed happening, such as a visit, sunset, a command. Slowly she would draw the fingers of one hand across the back of the other, in the little hollows between the guides, and move her lips in the same sad, vexed way in which her brows came together. And like this too, her eyes would shift about, from the near, shadowed fields, to the west hills, where the sun had dropped a strip of light, and to the woods between, looking like black scars one minute, and like friendly sanctuaries the next. It was all confused. There was the room, too. The white keys of the piano would now and then exercise a fascination over her which would keep her whole body perfectly still for perhaps a minute. But when this passed, full of hesitation, her fingers would recommence the slow exploration of her hands, and the restlessness took her again.

It was all confused. She was going away: already she had said a hundred times during the afternoon—'I am going away, I am going away. I can't stand it any longer.' But she had made no attempt to go. In this same position, hour after hour had passed her and all she could think was: 'Today I'm going away. I'm tired here. I never do anything. It's dead, rotten.'

She said, or thought it all without the slightest trace of exultation and was sometimes even methodical when she began to consider: 'What shall I take? The blue dress with the rosette? Yes. What else? what else?' And then it would all begin again: 'Today I'm going away. I never do anything.'

It was true: she never did anything. In the mornings she got up late, was slow over her breakfast, over everything—her reading, her mending, her eating, her playing the piano, cards in the evening, going to bed. It was all slow—purposely done, to fill up the day. And it was true, day succeeded day and she never did anything different.

But today something was about to happen: no more cards in the evening, every evening the same, with her father declaring: 'I never have a decent hand, I thought the ace of trumps had gone! It's too bad!!' and no more: 'Nellie, it's ten o'clock—Bed!' and the slow unimaginative climb of the stairs. Today she was going away: no one knew, but it was so. She was catching the evening train to London.

'I'm going away. What shall I take? The blue dress with the rosette? What else?'

She crept upstairs with difficulty, her body stiff after sitting. The years she must have sat, figuratively speaking, and grown stiff! And as if in order to secure some violent reaction against it all she threw herself into the packing of her things with a nervous vigour, throwing in the blue dress first and after it a score of things she had just remembered. She fastened her bag: it was not heavy. She counted her money a dozen times. It was all right! It was all right. She was going away!

She descended into the now dark room for the last time. In the dining-room someone was rattling tea-cups, an unbearable, horribly domestic sound! She wasn't hungry: she would be in London by eight—

eating now meant making her sick. It was easy to wait. The train went at 6.18. She looked it up again: 'Elden 6.13, Olde 6.18, London 7.53.'

She began to play a waltz. It was a slow, dreamy tune, ta-tum, tum, ta-tum, tum, ta-tum, tum, of which the notes slipped out in mournful, sentimental succession. The room was quite dark, she could scarcely see the keys, and into the tune itself kept insinuating: 'Elden 6.13, Olde 6.18,' impossible to mistake or forget.

As she played on she thought: 'I'll never play this waltz again. It has the atmosphere of this room. It's the last time!' The waltz slid dreamily to an end: for a minute she sat in utter silence, the room dark and mysterious, the air of the waltz quite dead, then the teacups rattled again and the thought came back to her: 'I'm going away!'

She rose and went out quietly. The grass on the roadside moved under the evening wind, sounding like many pairs of hands rubbed softly together. But there was no other sound, her feet were light, no one heard her, and as she went down the road she told herself: 'It's going to happen! It's come at last!'

'Elden 6.13. Olde 6.18.'

Should she go to Elden or Olde? At the crossroads she stood to consider, thinking that if she went to Elden no one would know her. But at Olde someone would doubtless notice her and prattle about it. To Elden, then, not that it mattered. Nothing mattered now. She was going, was as good as gone!

Her breast, tremulously warm, began to rise and fall as her excitement increased. She tried to run over the things in her bag and could remember only 'the blue dress with the rosette,' which she had thrown in first and had since covered over. But it didn't matter. Her money was safe, everything was safe, and with that thought she dropped into a strange quietness, deepening as she went on, in which she had a hundred emotions and convictions. She was never going to strum that waltz again, she had played cards for the last, horrible time, the loneliness, the slowness, the oppression were ended, all ended.

'I'm going away!'

She felt warm, her body tingled with a light delicious thrill that was like the caress of a soft night-wind. There were no fears now. A certain indignation, approaching fury even, sprang up instead, as she thought: 'No one will believe I've gone. But it's true—I'm going at last.'

Her bag grew heavy. Setting it down in the grass she sat on it for a brief while, in something like her attitude in the dark room during the afternoon, and indeed actually began to rub her gloved fingers over the backs of her hands. A phrase or two of the waltz came back to her. . . . That silly piano! Its bottom G was flat, had always been flat! How ridiculous! She tried to conjure up some sort of vision of London, but it was difficult and in the end she gave way again to the old cry: 'I'm going away.' And she was pleased more than ever deeply.

On the station a single lamp burned, radiating a fitful yellowness that only increased the gloom. And worse, she saw no one and in the cold emptiness traced and retraced her footsteps without the friendly assurance of another sound. In the black distance all the signals showed hard circles of red, looking as if they could never change. But she nevertheless told herself over and over again: 'I'm going away—I'm going away.' And later: 'I hate everyone. I've changed until I hardly know myself.'

Impatiently she looked for the train. It was strange. For the first time it occurred to her to know the time and she pulled back the sleeve of her coat. Nearly six-thirty! She felt cold. Up the line every signal displayed its red ring, mocking her. 'Six-thirty, of course, of course.' She tried to be careless. 'Of course, it's late, the train is late,' but the coldness, in reality her fear, increased rapidly, until she could no longer believe those words. . . .

Great clouds, lower and more than ever depressing, floated above her head as she walked back. The wind had a deep note that was sad too. These things had not troubled her before, now they, also, spoke failure and foretold misery and dejection. She had no spirit, it was cold, and she was too tired even to shudder.

In the absolutely dark, drowsy room she sat down, telling herself: 'This isn't the only day. Some day I shall go. Some day.'

She was silent. In the next room they were playing cards and her father suddenly moaned: 'I thought the ace had gone.' Somebody laughed. Her father's voice came again: 'I never have a decent hand! I never have a decent hand! Never!'

It was too horrible! She couldn't stand it! She must do something to stop it! It was too much. She began to play the waltz again and the dreamy, sentimental arrangement made her cry.

'This isn't the only day,' she reassured herself. 'I shall go. Some day!'

And again and again as she played the waltz, bent her head and cried, she would tell herself that same thing:

'Some day! Some day!'

Reading for Understanding

Main Idea

1. The main idea of the story is best expressed in (a) the opening three sentences (b) the second paragraph (c) the title (d) the father's comments about cards.

Details

2. The central character, Nellie, emphasized packing (a) cards (b) the blue dress (c) the waltz (d) the London address.
3. Elden and Olde are (a) train stations (b) German cities (c) London contacts (d) helpful relatives.
4. One train left the station at (a) 6:13 (b) 6:30 (c) 7:53 (d) 8:07.

Inferences

5. The "hard circles of red" (531) indicated that (a) the trains were delayed (b) the train had already left (c) there was an accident down the road (d) the London trains had been detoured.
6. The father's attitude seemed (a) vicious (b) insane (c) loving (d) dictatorial.
7. The timetables suggest that London was about (a) a half hour away (b) an hour away (c) an hour and a half away (d) three hours away.

Tone of the Story

8. The tone of the story is (a) cheerful (b) angry (c) confused (d) melancholy.

Outcome

9. Probably a year later, Nellie would be saying, (a) "Happy at last." (b) "Events are for the best." (c) "I owe my father a debt of gratitude." (d) "Some day! Some day!"

Fact or Opinion

Tell whether the following is a fact or an opinion.

10. Nellie missed her train.

Words in Context

1. "Slowly she would draw the fingers of one hand across the back of the other in the little hollows between the guides, and move her lips in the same, sad, *vexed* way in which her brows came together." **Vexed** (529) means (a) inquisitive (b) ugly (c) picturesque (d) irritated.
2. "She said, or thought it all without the slightest trace of *exultation*." **Exultation** (529) means (a) blame (b) rejoicing (c) gloom (d) interference.

Thinking Critically About the Story

1. What kind of person is Nellie? How is her character revealed?
2. What kind of person is the father? How do his few comments provide a clue to Nellie's unhappiness?
3. What does playing the waltz symbolize in the development of the story?
4. Why did Nellie miss the train?
5. Nellie is called "the young girl." How young do you think she is? 12? 16? 20? How does her age affect the impact of the story? If she were 50, would the impact be different? How?
6. Define *habit*. Has Nellie fallen into a bad habit? Explain.
7. Is it more difficult to break a perennial lateness habit than a smoking habit? Explain.
8. Are some habits good and desirable? Mention several examples.

Language in Action

Punctuation: the Colon

And then it would all begin again: "Today I'm going away. I never do anything."

One of the most useful—and neglected—punctuation marks is the colon. It appears in certain formal situations, like the salutation of a business letter.

Dear Mr. Hopkins:

It separates hours and minutes in expressing time.

6:37 P.M.

It separates numbers of a Biblical chapter and verse.

Genesis 1:17

Perhaps its most useful rule, though, is in compound sentences. The semicolon (526) helps to join together two independent clauses without a conjunction. The colon goes further: it does link the two clauses together, like a semicolon. It also introduces the clause or statement that explains, restates, or proves the statement in the first clause. (Did you notice the use of a colon in the third sentence of this paragraph?) In the example at the head of this section, the colon is used to introduce a quotation that explains the pronoun *it* in the main clause.

Unlike many other authors, H. E. Bates seems especially fond of the colon. Point out another example from the story and decide whether that colon is justified, or whether a semicolon or comma might have served as well.

The Rising of the Moon

Lady Gregory
Irish

One word more, for signal token,
Whistle up the marching tune,
With your pike upon your shoulder,
At the Rising of the Moon.

In 1907, when this play was written, Ireland was still an unhappy part of the United Kingdom. For 700 years, the Anglo-Irish struggle had continued, with bitter rebellions and equally bitter countermeasures. The Easter Monday Rising in 1916 failed but was followed by guerrilla warfare and harsh British reprisals. A succession of events led to the formation of the Irish Free State as part of the British Commonwealth. In 1937, the name changed to **Éire**, with a new constitution. In 1948, Éire became a republic and withdrew from the British Commonwealth.

Six northern counties, however, remained part of the United Kingdom. Peace did not come to Northern Ireland at that time, and peace has remained elusive ever since.

As noted above, "The Rising of the Moon" was written in 1907, during the troubles. Irish policemen, still part of the British structure, are being asked to capture a member of the Irish underground. The sergeant, in particular, is torn by opposing motivations. Where will he be at "the rising of the moon"?

The Rising of the Moon

Scene: Side of a quay in a seaport town. Some posts and chains. A large barrel. Enter three policemen. Moonlight.

SERGEANT, *who is older than the others, crosses the stage to right and looks down steps. The others put down a pastepot and unroll a bundle of placards.*

POLICEMAN B. I think this would be a good place to put up a notice. (*He points to barrel.*)

POLICEMAN X. Better ask him. (*Calls to* SERGEANT.) Will this be a good place for a placard? (*No answer.*)

POLICEMAN B. Will we put up a notice here on the barrel? (*No answer.*)

SERGEANT. There's a flight of steps here that leads to the water. This is a place that should be minded well. If he got down here, his friends might have a boat to meet him; they might send it in here from outside.

POLICEMAN B. Would the barrel be a good place to put a notice up?

SERGEANT. It might; you can put it there. (*They paste the notice up.*)

SERGEANT (*reading it*). Dark hair—dark eyes, smooth face, height five feet five—there's not much to take hold of in that—It's a pity I had no chance of seeing him before he broke out of gaol.[1] They say he's a wonder, that it's he makes all the plans for the whole organization. There isn't another man in Ireland would have broken gaol the way he did. He must have some friends among the gaolers.

POLICEMAN B. A hundred pounds is little enough for the Government to offer for him. You may be sure any man in the force that takes him will get promotion.

SERGEANT. I'll mind this place myself. I wouldn't wonder at all if he came this way. He might come slipping along there (*points to side of quay*), and his friends might be waiting for him there (*points down steps*), and once he got away it's little chance we'd have of finding him; it's maybe under a load of kelp he'd be in a fishing boat, and not one to help a married man that wants it to the reward.

---

[1]jail

POLICEMAN X. And if we get him itself, nothing but abuse on our heads for it from the people, and maybe from our own relations.

SERGEANT. Well, we have to do our duty in the force. Haven't we the whole country depending on us to keep law and order? It's those that are down would be up and those that are up would be down, if it wasn't for us. Well, hurry on, you have plenty of other places to placard yet, and come back here then to me. You can take the lantern. Don't be too long now. It's very lonesome here with nothing but the moon.

POLICEMAN B. It's a pity we can't stop with you. The Government should have brought more police into the town, with *him* in gaol, and at assize[2] time too. Well, good luck to your watch. (*They go out.*)

SERGEANT (*walks up and down once or twice and looks at placard*). A hundred pounds and promotion sure. There must be a great deal of spending in a hundred pounds. It's a pity some honest man not to be the better of that.

(A ragged man appears at left and tries to slip past. SERGEANT *suddenly turns.)*

SERGEANT. Where are you going?

MAN. I'm a poor ballad-singer, your honor. I thought to sell some of these (*holds out bundle of ballads*) to the sailors. (*He goes on.*)

SERGEANT. Stop! Didn't I tell you to stop? You can't go on there.

MAN. Oh, very well. It's a hard thing to be poor. All the world's against the poor!

SERGEANT. Who are you?

MAN. You'd be as wise as myself if I told you, but I don't mind. I'm one Jimmy Walsh, a ballad-singer.

SERGEANT. Jimmy Walsh? I don't know that name.

MAN. Ah, sure, they know it well enough in Ennis. Were you ever in Ennis, Sergeant?

SERGEANT. What brought you here?

MAN. Sure, it's to the assizes I came, thinking I might make a few shillings here or there. It's in the one train with the judges I came.

[2]court proceeding

SERGEANT. Well, if you came so far, you may as well go farther, for you'll walk out of this.

MAN. I will, I will; I'll just go on where I was going. (*Goes toward steps.*)

SERGEANT. Come back from those steps; no one has leave to pass down them tonight.

MAN. I'll just sit on the top of the steps till I see will some sailor buy a ballad off me that would give me my supper. They do be late going back to the ship. It's often I saw them in Cork carried down the quay in a hand-cart.

SERGEANT. Move on, I tell you. I won't have any one lingering about the quay tonight.

MAN. Well, I'll go. It's the poor have the hard life! Maybe yourself might like one, Sergeant. Here's a good sheet now. (*Turns one over.*) "Content and a pipe"—that's not much. "The Peeler and the Goat"—you wouldn't like that. "Johnny Hart"—that's a lovely song.

SERGEANT. Move on.

MAN. Ah, wait till you hear it. (*Sings.*)

There was a rich farmer's daughter
lived near the town of Ross;
She courted a Highland soldier,
his name was Johnny Hart;
Says the mother to her daughter,
"I'll go distracted mad
If you marry that Highland soldier
dressed up in Highland plaid."

SERGEANT. Stop that noise.

(MAN *wraps up his ballads and shuffles toward the steps.*)

SERGEANT. Where are you going?

MAN. Sure you told me to be going, and I am going.

SERGEANT. Don't be a fool. I didn't tell you to go that way; I told you to go back to the town.

MAN. Back to the town, is it?

SERGEANT (*taking him by the shoulder and shoving him before him*). Here, I'll show you the way. Be off with you. What are you stopping for?

MAN (*who has been keeping his eye on the notice, points to it*). I think I know what you're waiting for, Sergeant.

SERGEANT. What's that to you?

MAN. And I know well the man you're waiting for—I know him well—I'll be going. (*He shuffles on.*)

SERGEANT. You know him? Come back here. What sort is he?

MAN. Come back is it, Sergeant? Do you want to have me killed?

SERGEANT. Why do you say that?

MAN. Never mind. I'm going. I wouldn't be in your shoes if the reward was ten times as much. (*Goes on off stage to left.*) Not if it was ten times as much.

SERGEANT (*rushing after him*). Come back here, come back. (*Drags him back.*) What sort is he? Where did you see him?

MAN. I saw him in my own place, in the County Clare. I tell you you wouldn't like to be looking at him. You'd be afraid to be in the one place with him. There isn't a weapon he doesn't know the use of, and as to strength, his muscles are as hard as that board. (*Slaps barrel.*)

SERGEANT. Is he as bad as that?

MAN. He is then.

SERGEANT. Do you tell me so?

MAN. There was a poor man in our place, a sergeant from Ballyvaughan.—It was with a lump of stone he did it.

SERGEANT. I never heard of that.

MAN. And you wouldn't, Sergeant. It's not everything that happens gets into the papers. And there was a policeman in plain clothes, too . . . It is in Limerick he was. . . . It was after the time of the attack on the police barrack at Kilmallock. . . . Moonlight . . . just like this . . . waterside. . . . Nothing was known for certain.

SERGEANT. Do you say so? It's a terrible county to belong to.

MAN. That's so, indeed! You might be standing there, looking out that way, thinking you saw him coming up this side of the quay (*points*), and he might be coming up this other side (*points*), and he'd be on you before you knew where you were.

SERGEANT. It's a whole troop of police they ought to put here to stop a man like that.

MAN. But if you'd like me to stop with you, I could be looking down this side. I could be sitting up here on this barrel.

SERGEANT. And you know him well, too?

MAN. I'd know him a mile off, Sergeant.

SERGEANT. But you wouldn't want to share the reward?

MAN. Is it a poor man like me, that has to be going the roads and singing in fairs, to have the name on him that he took a reward? But you don't want me. I'll be safer in the town.

SERGEANT. Well, you can stop.

MAN (*getting up on barrel*). All right, Sergeant. I wonder, now, you're not tired out, Sergeant, walking up and down the way you are.

SERGEANT. If I'm tired I'm used to it.

MAN. You might have hard work before you tonight yet. Take it easy while you can. There's plenty of room up here on the barrel, and you see farther when you're higher up.

SERGEANT. Maybe so. (*Gets up beside him on barrel, facing right. They sit back to back, looking different ways.*) You made me feel a bit queer with the way you talked.

MAN. Give me a match, Sergeant (*he gives it and* MAN *lights pipe*); take a draw yourself? It'll quiet you. Wait now till I give you a light, but you needn't turn around. Don't take your eye off the quay for the life of you.

SERGEANT. Never fear, I won't. (*Lights pipe. They both smoke.*) Indeed it's a hard thing to be in the force, out at night and no thanks for it, for all the danger we're in. And it's little we get but abuse from the people, and no choice but to obey our orders, and never asked when a man is sent into danger, if you are a married man with a family.

MAN (*sings*).

As through the hills I walked to view the hills and shamrock plain,
I stood awhile where nature smiles to view the rocks and streams,
On a matron fair I fixed my eyes beneath a fertile vale,
As she sang her song it was on the wrong of poor old Granuaile.

SERGEANT. Stop that; that's no song to be singing in these times.

MAN. Ah, Sergeant, I was only singing to keep my heart up. It sinks when I think of him. To think of us two sitting here, and he creeping up the quay, maybe, to get to us.

SERGEANT. Are you keeping a good lookout?

MAN. I am; and for no reward too. Amn't I the foolish man? But when I saw a man in trouble, I never could help trying to get him out of it. What's that? Did something hit me? (*Rubs his heart.*)

SERGEANT (*patting him on the shoulder*). You will get your reward in heaven.

MAN. I know that, I know that, Sergeant, but life is precious.

SERGEANT. Well, you can sing if it gives you more courage.

MAN (sings).

Her head was bare, her hands and feet with iron bands were bound,
Her pensive strain and plaintive wail mingles with the evening gale,
And the song she sang with mournful air, I am old Granuaile.
Her lips so sweet that monarchs kissed . . .

SERGEANT. That's not it. . . . "Her gown she wore was stained with gore." . . . That's it—you missed that.

MAN. You're right, Sergeant, so it is; I missed it. (*Repeats line.*) But to think of a man like you knowing a song like that.

SERGEANT. There's many a thing a man might know and might not have any wish for.

MAN. Now, I daresay, Sergeant, in your youth, you used to be sitting up on a wall, the way you are sitting up on this barrel now, and the other lads beside you, and you singing "Granuaile"? . . .

SERGEANT. I did then.

MAN. And the "Shan Bhean Bhocht"? . . .

SERGEANT. I did then.

MAN. And the "Green on the Cape"?

SERGEANT. That was one of them.

MAN. And maybe the man you are watching for tonight used to be sitting on the wall, when he was young, and singing those same songs. . . . It's a queer world.

SERGEANT. Whisht! . . . I think I see something coming. . . . It's only a dog.

MAN. And isn't it a queer world? . . . Maybe it's one of the boys you used to be singing with that time you will be arresting today or tomorrow, and sending into the dock.

SERGEANT. That's true inded.

MAN. And maybe one night, after you had been singing, if the other boys had told you some plan they had, some plan to free the country, you might have joined with them . . . and maybe it is you might be in trouble now.

SERGEANT. Well, who knows but I might? I had a great spirit in those days.

MAN. It's a queer world, Sergeant, and it's little any mother knows when she sees her child creeping on the floor what might happen to it before it has gone through its life, or who will be who in the end.

SERGEANT. That's a queer thought now, and a true thought. Wait now till I think it out. . . . If it wasn't for the sense I have, and for my wife and family, and for me joining the force the time I did, it might be myself now would be after breaking gaol and hiding in the dark, and it might be him that's hiding in the dark and that got out of gaol would be sitting up where I am on this barrel. . . . And it might be myself would be creeping up trying to make my escape from himself, and it might be himself would be keeping the law, and myself would be breaking it, and myself would be trying maybe to put a bullet in his head, or to take up a lump of a stone the way you said he did . . . no, that myself did. . . . Oh! (*Gasps. After a pause*) What's that! (*Grasps* MAN'S *arm.*)

MAN (*jumps off barrel and listens, looking out over water*). It's nothing, Sergeant.

SERGEANT. I thought it might be a boat. I had a notion there might be friends of his coming about the quays with a boat.

MAN. Sergeant, I am thinking it was with the people you were, and not with the law you were, when you were a young man.

SERGEANT. Well, if I was foolish then, that time's gone.

MAN. Maybe, Sergeant, it comes into your head sometimes, in spite of your belt and your tunic, that it might have been as well for you to have followed Granuaile.

SERGEANT. It's no business of yours what I think.

MAN. Maybe, Sergeant, you'll be on the side of the country yet.

SERGEANT (*gets off barrel*). Don't talk to me like that. I have my duties and I know them. (*Looks round.*) That was a boat; I hear the oars. (*Goes to the steps and looks down.*)

MAN (*sings*).

O, then, tell me, Shawn O'Farrell,
Where the gathering is to be.
In the old spot by the river
Right well known to you and me!

SERGEANT. Stop that! Stop that, I tell you!

MAN (*sings louder*).

One word more, for signal token,
Whistle up the marching tune,
With your pike upon your shoulder,
At the Rising of the Moon.

SERGEANT. If you don't stop that, I'll arrest you. (*A whistle from below answers, repeating the air.*)

SERGEANT. That's a signal. (*Stands between him and steps.*) You must not pass this way. . . . Step farther back. . . . Who are you? You are no ballad-singer.

MAN. You needn't ask who I am; that placard will tell you. (*Points to placard.*)

SERGEANT. You are the man I am looking for.

MAN (*takes off hat and wig.* SERGEANT *seizes them*). I am. There's a hundred pounds on my head. There is a friend of mine below in a boat. He knows a safe place to bring me to.

SERGEANT (*looking still at hat and wig*). It's a pity! It's a pity. You deceived me. You deceived me well.

MAN. I am a friend of Granuaile. There is a hundred pounds on my head.

SERGEANT. It's a pity, it's a pity!

MAN. Will you let me pass, or must I make you let me?

SERGEANT. I am in the force. I will not let you pass.

MAN. I thought to do it with my tongue. (*Puts hand in breast.*)What is that? (*Voice of* POLICEMAN X *outside.*) Here, this is where we left him.

SERGEANT. It's my comrades coming.

MAN. You won't betray me . . . the friend of Granuaile. (*Slips behind barrel.*)

(*Voice of* POLICEMAN B.) That was the last of the placards.

POLICEMAN X (*as they come in*). If he makes his escape it won't be unknown he'll make it.

(SERGEANT *puts hat and wig behind his back.*)

POLICEMAN B. Did any one come this way?

SERGEANT (after a pause). No one.

POLICEMAN B. No one at all?

SERGEANT. No one at all.

POLICEMAN B. We had no orders to go back to the station; we can stop along with you.

SERGEANT. I don't want you. There is nothing for you to do here.

POLICEMAN B. You bade us to come back here and keep watch with you.

SERGEANT. I'd sooner be alone. Would any man come this way and you making all that talk? It is better the place to be quiet.

POLICEMAN B. Well, we'll leave you the lantern anyhow. (*Hands it to him.*)

SERGEANT. I don't want it. Bring it with you.

POLICEMAN B. You might want it. There are clouds coming up and you have the darkness of the night before you yet. I'll leave it over here on the barrel. (*Goes to barrel.*)

SERGEANT. Bring it with you I tell you. No more talk.

POLICEMAN B. Well, I thought it might be a comfort to you. I often think when I have it in my hand and can be flashing it about into every dark corner (*doing so*) that it's the same as being beside the fire at home, and the bits of bogwood blazing up now and again. (*Flashes it about, now on the barrel, now on* SERGEANT.)

SERGEANT (*furious*). Be off the two of you, yourselves and your lantern!

(*They go out.* MAN *comes from behind barrel. He and* SERGEANT *stand looking at one another.*)

SERGEANT. What are you waiting for?

MAN. For my hat, of course, and my wig. You wouldn't wish me to get my death of cold?

(SERGEANT gives them.)

MAN (*going toward steps*). Well, good night, comrade, and thank you. You did me a good turn tonight, and I'm obliged to you. Maybe I'll be able to do as much for you when the small rise up and the big fall down . . . when we all change places at the Rising (*waves his hand and disappears*) of the Moon.

SERGEANT (*turning his back to audience and reading placard*). A hundred pounds reward! A hundred pounds! (*Turns toward audience.*) I wonder, now, am I as great a fool as I think I am?

CURTAIN

Reading for Understanding

Central Theme

1. The central theme of this play is (a) man's inhumanity to man (b) police brutality (c) conflicting loyalties (d) Irish humor.

Details

2. The ragged man says he is there (a) to help the Sergeant (b) to sell ballads (c) as a representative of local government (d) to fish.
3. "Johnny Hart" is (a) the balladeer's brother (b) Policeman B (c) a British folk hero (d) a song title.
4. The reward has been set at (a) 25 pounds (b) 50 pounds (c) 75 pounds (d) 100 pounds.

Inferences

5. When the ragged man tells what a fiend the wanted man is, he is (a) talking about himself (b) understating the truth (c) hoping to make the Sergeant laugh (d) frightening the other two policemen.
6. The Sergeant's mood throughout is one of (a) nervousness (b) great joy (c) assurance (d) indifference.

7. "The Rising of the Moon" is a symbol of (a) peace and contentment (b) rebellion (c) a renewed interest in the drama (d) the brotherhood of man.
8. The ragged man is a (a) coward (b) good psychologist (c) vicious killer (d) secret member of the British police.

Outcome

9. The ragged man will (a) charge the Sergeant with treason (b) give himself up (c) flee to safety (d) be captured soon after leaving the wharf.

Author's Attitude

10. The author's attitude toward the Sergeant and the ragged man is one of (a) stunned disbelief (b) antagonism (c) misplaced sentiment (d) sympathetic understanding.

Words in Context

1. "Will this be a good place for a *placard?*" A **placard** (536) is a (a) barrel (b) guard post (c) poster (d) meeting.
2. "Points to side of *quay.*" A **quay** (536) is (a) a stairway (b) an entrance to a shack (c) a houseboat (d) a wharf.

Thinking Critically About the Play

1. At the very beginning, the Sergeant doesn't answer two of his assistants' questions. What does this lack of attention suggest about the Sergeant's thoughts?
2. How does the Sergeant differ from the two policemen? How would the policemen have handled the meeting with the ragged man?
3. How significant is the fact that the Sergeant seems to know a revolutionary ballad better than the ragged man does? Was the man trying to test the Sergeant? How?
4. What does the Sergeant mean when he says (541), "There's many a thing a man might know and might not have any wish for"?

5. Why does the ragged man say, "You needn't ask who I am; that placard will tell you"? Why is the man willing to take the risk at that point?
6. When the Sergeant answers, "No one," he has made a decision. What was it?
7. How great a sacrifice did the Sergeant make in letting the wanted man escape? What does this sacrifice tell us about the character of the Sergeant?
8. At what point did you realize that the ragged man was also the wanted man? What clues helped you?
9. Why has the Sergeant changed over the years from a potential young revolutionary to a representative of the hated government? Is the change complete? Explain.
10. Could this play have been written today, in a different setting, but with the same impact? Explain.

Language in Action

Dialogue in a Play

> POLICEMAN B. I think this would be a good place to put up a notice. (*He points to barrel.*)
>
> POLICEMAN X. Better ask him. (*Calls to* SERGEANT.) Will this be a good place for a placard? (*No answer.*)

How do you indicate dialogue in a printed play? It would obviously be inconvenient to keep using quotation marks. Over the years, certain conventions have prevailed. Notice the two bits of dialogue above. The speaker is indicated by capital letters followed by a period. Then the words follow. If there are any stage directions, they are included in parentheses, usually in *italics*. Nothing could be simpler. You will have an opportunity to try your hand at some dialogue or a short play at the end of this unit.

In addition to providing dialogue, the playwright may also set the scene, using italics for this helpful information. In our play, italics are used for the stage directions at the beginning. Italics are also used, here, as they would be in any written material, for the quotations from patriotic Irish songs.

Some playwrights use extended stage directions, providing an almost novel-style presentation . . . subjective rather than objective (366–367). When Eugene O'Neill set the scene for the opening pages of

Strange Interlude, he used a page and a half. George Bernard Shaw used his plays to express his personal philosophy, some of which found its way into extended stage directions. Shaw visualized his plays being read as well as acted. At times he introduced humor into these stage directions, obviously never to be used in the play itself. In the opening stage directions for *Saint Joan,* Shaw describes one of the characters, a handsome military squire, as "the sort of man whom age cannot wither because he has never bloomed."

The dramatis personae (cast of characters usually listed at the beginning of the play) may have identifying labels, as in this from Oscar Wilde's *The Importance of Being Earnest:*

MERRIMAN, *butler to Mr. Worthing*

A Worn Path

Eudora Welty
American

Old Phoenix would have been lost if she had not distrusted her eyesight and depended on her feet to know where to take her.

The traditional favorite Christmas story in America is O. Henry's "Gift of the Magi," in which the exchange of gifts creates the magical O. Henry touch. "A Worn Path" also takes place at Christmastime, and it also centers around gifts, but that is where the resemblance ends.

"A Worn Path" is told from the point of view of an elderly back-country woman, Phoenix Jackson. She has left her simple cabin deep in the mountains and is walking through the winter woods to Natchez to get the medicine needed by her ailing grandson. The deep pine and oak forest is inhabited by a fascinating variety of creatures that Phoenix either encounters or imagines she encounters.

Phoenix reaches the city filled with Christmastime spirit and decorations. She gets the medicine and decides to buy a gift for the grandchild. There is no mystery or high adventure in this tale.

Be patient with the story. Let the author weave her magic, and your reward will be the same emotional impact and enjoyment you should be finding in stories with more definite plots. Read it to understand not only the action, but more important, the people in it.

The key to the story is in its title. What is the Worn Path? Is it Phoenix's continuing quiet acceptance of life and its hardships? Is it the recurring Christmas season? Is it the gift-giving from one generation to another? Is it . . ., but read and find out for yourself. This is a Christmas story, but different!

A Worn Path

IT WAS DECEMBER—a bright frozen day in the early morning. Far out in the country there was an old black woman with her head tied in a red rag, coming along a path through the pinewoods. Her name was Phoenix Jackson. She was very old and small and she walked slowly in the dark pine shadows, moving a little from side to side in her steps, with the balanced heaviness and lightness of a pendulum in a grandfather clock. She carried a thin, small cane made from an umbrella, and with this she kept tapping the frozen earth in front of her. This made a grave and persistent noise in the still air, that seemed meditative, like the chirping of a solitary little bird.

She wore a dark striped dress reaching down to her shoetops, and an equally long apron of bleached sugar sacks, with a full pocket; all neat and tidy, but every time she took a step she might have fallen over her shoelaces, which dragged from her unlaced shoes. She looked straight ahead. Her eyes were blue with age. Her skin had a pattern all its own of numberless branching wrinkles and as though a whole little tree stood in the middle of her forehead, but a golden color ran underneath, and the two knobs of her cheeks were illuminated by a yellow burning under the dark. Under the red rag her hair came down on her neck in the frailest of ringlets, still black, and with an odor like copper.

Now and then there was a quivering in the thicket. Old Phoenix said, "Out of my way, all you foxes, owls, beetles, jack rabbits, coons, and wild animals! . . . Keep out from under these feet, little bobwhites . . . Keep the big wild hogs out of my path. Don't let none of those come running my direction. I got a long way." Under her small black-freckled hand her cane, limber as a buggy whip, would switch at the brush as if to rouse up any hiding things.

On she went. The woods were deep and still. The sun made the pine needles almost too bright to look at, up where the wind rocked. The cones dropped as light as feathers. Down in the hollow was the mourning dove—it was not too late for him.

The path ran up a hill. "Seem like there is chains about my feet, time I get this far," she said, in the voice of argument old people keep to use with themselves. "Something always take a hold on this hill—pleads I should stay."

After she got to the top she turned and gave a full, severe look behind her where she had come. "Up through pines," she said at length. "Now down through oaks."

Her eyes opened their widest and she started down gently. But before she got to the bottom of the hill a bush caught her dress.

Her fingers were busy and intent, but her skirts were full and long, so that before she could pull them free in one place they were caught in another. It was not possible to allow the dress to tear. "I in the thorny bush," she said. "Thorns, you doing your appointed work. Never want to let folks pass—no sir. Old eyes thought you was a pretty little *green* bush."

Finally, trembling all over, she stood free, and after a moment dared to stoop for her cane.

"Sun so high!" she cried, leaning back and looking, while the thick tears went over her eyes. "The time getting all gone here."

At the foot of this hill was a place where a log was laid across the creek.

"Now comes the trial," said Phoenix.

Putting her right foot out, she mounted the log and shut her eyes. Lifting her skirt, leveling her cane fiercely before her, like a festival figure in some parade, she began to march across. Then she opened her eyes and she was safe on the other side.

"I wasn't as old as I thought," she said.

But she sat down to rest. She spread her skirts on the bank around her and folded her hands over her knees. Up above her was a tree in a pearly cloud of mistletoe. She did not dare to close her eyes, and when a little boy brought her a little plate with a slice of marble cake on it she spoke to him. "That would be acceptable," she said. But when she went to take it there was just her own hand in the air.

So she left that tree, and had to go through a barbed wire fence. There she had to creep and crawl, spreading her knees and stretching her fingers like a baby trying to climb the steps. But she talked loudly to herself: she could not let her dress be torn now, so late in the day, and she could not pay for having her arm or her leg sawed off if she got caught fast where she was.

At last she was safe through the fence and risen up out in the clearing. Big dead trees, like black men with one arm, were standing in the purple stalks of the withered cotton field. There sat a buzzard.

"Who you watching?"

In the furrow she made her way along.

"Glad this not the season for bulls," she said, looking sideways, "and the good Lord made his snakes to curl up and sleep in the winter. A pleasure I don't see no two-headed snake coming around that tree, where it come once. It took a while to get by him, back in the summer."

She passed through the old cotton and went into a field of dead corn. It whispered and shook, and was taller than her head. "Through the maze now," she said, for there was no path.

Then there was something tall, black, and skinny there, moving before her.

At first she took it for a man. It could have been a man dancing in the field. But she stood still and listened, and it did not make a sound. It was as silent as a ghost.

"Ghost," she said sharply, "who be you the ghost of? For I have heard of nary death close by."

But there was no answer, only the ragged dancing in the wind.

She shut her eyes, reached out her hand, and touched a sleeve. She found a coat and inside that an emptiness, cold as ice.

"You scarecrow," she said. Her face lighted. "I ought to be shut up for good," she said with laughter. "My senses is gone. I too old. I the oldest people I ever know. Dance, old scarecrow," she said, "while I dancing with you."

She kicked her foot over the furrow, and with mouth drawn down shook her head once or twice in a little strutting way. Some husks blew down and whirled in streamers about her skirts.

Then she went on, parting her way from side to side with the cane, through the whispering field. At last she came to the end, to a wagon track, where the silver grass blew between the red ruts. The quail were walking around like pullets, seeming all dainty and unseen.

"Walk pretty," she said. "This the easy place. This the easy going."

She followed the track, swaying through the quiet bare fields, through the little strings of trees silver in their dead leaves, past cabins silver from weather, with the doors and windows boarded shut, all like old women under a spell sitting there. "I walking in their sleep," she said, nodding her head vigorously.

In a ravine she went where a spring was silently flowing through a hollow log. Old Phoenix bent and drank. "Sweetgum makes the water sweet," she said, and drank more. "Nobody knows who made this well, for it was here when I was born."

The track crossed a swampy part where the moss hung as white as lace from every limb. "Sleep on, alligators, and blow your bubbles." Then the track went into the road.

Deep, deep the road went down between the high green-colored banks. Overhead the live oaks met, and it was as dark as a cave.

A black dog with a lolling tongue came up out of the weeds by the ditch. She was meditating, and not ready, and when he came at her she only hit him a little with her cane. Over she went in the ditch, like a little puff of milkweed.

Down there, her senses drifted away. A dream visited her, and she reached her hand up, but nothing reached down and gave her a pull. So she lay there and presently went to talking. "Old woman," she said to herself, "that black dog came up out of the weeds to stall you off, and now there he sitting on his fine tail, smiling at you."

A white man finally came along and found her—a hunter, a young man, with his dog on a chain.

"Well, Granny!" he laughed. "What are you doing there?"

"Lying on my back like a june bug waiting to be turned over, mister," she said, reaching up her hand.

He lifted her up, gave her a swing in the air, and set her down, "Anything broken, Granny?"

"No sir, them old dead weeds is springy enough," said Phoenix, when she had got her breath. "I thank you for your trouble."

"Where do you live, Granny?" he asked, while the two dogs were growling at each other.

"Away back yonder, sir, behind the ridge. You can't even see it from here."

"On your way home?"

"No, sir, I going to town."

"Why, that's too far! That's as far as I walk when I come out myself, and I get something for my trouble." He patted the stuffed bag he carried, and there hung down a little closed claw. It was one of the bob-whites, with its beak hooked bitterly to show it was dead. "Now you go on home, Granny!"

"I bound to go to town, mister," said Phoenix. "The time come around."

He gave another laugh, filling the whole landscape. "I know you black people! Wouldn't miss going to town to see Santa Claus!"

But something held Old Phoenix very still. The deep lines in her face went into a fierce and different radiation. Without warning she had seen with her own eyes a flashing quarter fall out of the man's pocket on to the ground.

"How old are you, Granny?" he was saying.

"There is no telling, mister," she said, "no telling."

Then she gave a little cry and clapped her hands, and said, "Git on away from here, dog! Look! Look at that dog!" She laughed as if in admiration. "He ain't scared of nobody. He a big black dog." She whispered, "Sic him!"

"Watch me get rid of that cur," said the man. "Sic him, Pete! Sic him!"

Phoenix heard the dogs fighting and heard the man running and throwing sticks. She even heard a gunshot. But she was slowly bending forward by that time, further and further forward, the lids stretched down over her eyes, as if she were doing this in her sleep. Her chin was lowered almost to her knees. The yellow palm of her hand came out from the fold of her apron. Her fingers slid down and along the ground under the piece of money with the grace and care they would have in lifting an egg from under a sitting hen. Then she slowly straightened up, she stood erect, and the quarter was in her apron pocket. A bird flew by. Her lips moved. "God watching me the whole time. I come to stealing."

The man came back, and his own dog panted about them. “Well, I scared him off that time,” he said, and then he laughed and lifted his gun and pointed it at Phoenix.

She stood straight and faced him.

“Doesn’t the gun scare you?” he said, still pointing it.

“No, sir, I seen plenty go off closer by, in my day, and for less than what I done,” she said, holding utterly still.

He smiled, and shouldered the gun. “Well, Granny,” he said, “you must be a hundred years old, and scared of nothing. I’d give you a coin if I had any money with me. But you take my advice and stay home, and nothing will happen to you.”

“I bound to go on my way, mister,” said Phoenix. She inclined her head in the red rag. Then they went in different directions, but she could hear the gun shooting again and again over the hill.

She walked on. The shadows hung from the oak trees to the road like curtains. Then she smelled wood smoke, and smelled the river, and she saw a steeple and the cabins on their steep steps. Dozens of little black children whirled around her. There ahead was Natchez shining. Bells were ringing. She walked on.

In the paved city it was Christmas time. There were red and green electric lights strung and crisscrossed everywhere, and all turned on in the daytime. Old Phoenix would have been lost if she had not distrusted her eyesight and depended on her feet to know where to take her.

She paused quietly on the sidewalk, where people were passing by. A lady came along in the crowd, carrying an armful of red-, green-, and silver-wrapped presents; she gave off perfume like the red roses in hot summer, and Phoenix stopped her.

“Please, missy, will you lace up my shoe?” She held up her foot.

“What do you want, Grandma?”

“See my shoe,” said Phoenix. “Do all right for out in the country, but wouldn’t look right to go in a big building.”

“Stand still then, Grandma,” said the lady. She put her packages down carefully on the sidewalk beside her and laced and tied both shoes tightly.

“Can’t lace’ em with a cane,” said Phoenix. “Thank you, missy. I doesn’t mind asking a nice lady to tie up my shoe when I gets out on the street.”

Moving slowly and from side to side, she went into the stone building and into a tower of steps, where she walked up and around and around until her feet knew to stop.

She entered a door, and there she saw nailed up on the wall the document that had been stamped with the gold seal and framed in the gold frame which matched the dream that was hung up in her head.

“Here I be,” she said. There was a fixed and ceremonial stiffness over her body.

"A charity case, I suppose," said an attendant who sat at the desk before her.

But Phoenix only looked above her head. There was sweat on her face; the wrinkles shone like a bright net.

"Speak up, Grandma," the woman said. "What's your name? We must have your history, you know. Have you been here before? What seems to be the trouble with you?"

Old Phoenix only gave a twitch to her face as if a fly were bothering her.

"Are you deaf?" cried the attendant.

But then the nurse came in.

"Oh, that's just old Aunt Phoenix," she said. "She doesn't come for herself—she has a little grandson. She makes these trips just as regular as clockwork. She lives away back off the Old Natchez Trace." She bent down. "Well, Aunt Phoenix, why don't you just take a seat? We won't keep you standing after your long trip." She pointed.

The old woman sat down, bolt upright in the chair.

"Now, how is the boy?" asked the nurse.

Old Phoenix did not speak.

"I said, how is the boy?"

But Phoenix only waited and stared straight ahead, her face very solemn and withdrawn into rigidity.

"Is his throat any better?" asked the nurse. "Aunt Phoenix, don't you hear me? Is your grandson's throat any better since the last time you came for medicine?"

With her hand on her knees, the old woman waited, silent, erect and motionless, just as if she were in armor.

"You mustn't take up our time this way, Aunt Phoenix," the nurse said. "Tell us quickly about your grandson, and get it over. He isn't dead, is he?"

At last there came a flicker and then a flame of comprehension across her face, and she spoke.

"My grandson. It was my memory had left me. There I sat and forgot why I made my long trip."

"Forgot?" The nurse frowned. "After you came so far?"

Then Phoenix was like an old woman begging a dignified forgiveness for waking up frightened in the night. "I never did go to school—I was too old at the Surrender," she said in a soft voice. "I'm an old woman without an education. It was my memory fail me. My little grandson, he is just the same, and I forgot it in the coming."

"Throat never heals, does it?" said the nurse, speaking in a loud, sure voice to Old Phoenix. By now she had a card with something written on it, a little list. "Yes. Swallowed lye. When was it—January—two—three years ago—"

Phoenix spoke unasked now. "No, missy, he not dead, he just the same. Every little while his throat begin to close up again, and he not able to swallow. He not get his breath. He not able to help himself. So the time come around, and I go on another trip for the soothing medicine."

"All right. The doctor said as long as you came to get it you could have it," said the nurse. "But it's an obstinate case."

"My little grandson, he sit up there in the house all wrapped up, waiting by himself," Phoenix went on. "We is the only two left in the world. He suffer and it don't seem to put him back at all. He got a sweet look. He going to last. He wear a little patch quilt and peep out, holding his mouth open like a little bird. I remembers so plain now. I not going to forget him again, no, the whole enduring time. I could tell him from all the others in creation."

"All right." The nurse was trying to hush her now. She brought her a bottle of medicine. "Charity," she said, making a check mark in a book.

Old Phoenix held the bottle close to her eyes and then carefully put it into her pocket.

"I thank you," she said.

"It's Christmas time, Grandma," said the attendant. "Could I give you a few coins out of my purse?"

"Five nickels is a quarter," said Phoenix stiffly.

"Here's a quarter," said the attendant.

Phoenix rose carefully and held out her hand. She received the quarter and then fished the other quarter out of her pocket and laid it beside the new one. She stared at her palm closely, with her head on one side.

Then she gave a tap with her cane on the floor.

"This is what come to me to do," she said. "I going to the store and buy my child a little windmill they sells, made out of paper. He going to find it hard to believe there such a thing in the world. I'll march myself back where he waiting, holding it straight up in this hand."

She lifted her free hand, gave a little nod, turning round, and walked out of the doctor's office. Then her slow step began on the stairs, going down.

Reading for Understanding

Main Idea

1. The characters in this story reveal (a) a distrust of other people (b) a feeling of superiority over others (c) a disregard of the Christmas spirit (d) different aspects of giving and sharing.

Details

2. Which one of the following is not true of Phoenix?

(a) She lives alone with her grandson.
(b) She is afraid to be alone in the woods.
(c) Her mind plays tricks on her.
(d) She is unaware of her odd appearance.

3. The black dog (a) wants to be petted (b) rushes at her (c) wants to be friendly (d) is hungry.
4. Which one of the following statements is not true?
   (a) The hunter arrives in time to save Phoenix from being hurt.
   (b) The hunter gives Phoenix a coin as a present.
   (c) The hunter and his dog chase the black dog.
   (d) The hunter may have shot at the black dog.
5. The little boy who brings her a plate with a slice of marble cake in the woods is (a) her grandchild (b) imaginary (c) related to the hunter (d) the farmer's son.

Cause and Effect

6. To get to Natchez, Phoenix trespasses on private land because (a) she missed the bus (b) the owners give her permission (c) she enjoys doing so (d) she has always done so.
7. Phoenix buys the windmill (a) to enjoy it herself (b) as a Christmas present (c) to please the storekeeper (d) because the nurse suggests that she do so.

Inference

8. The attendant gives Phoenix the quarter (a) to pay for the medicine (b) to give to her grandchild (c) as a holiday gift (d) to buy some food.

Order of Events

9. Arrange the items in the order in which they occurred. Use letters only.
   A. The grandchild is having difficulty swallowing.
   B. Phoenix is frightened by the scarecrow.
   C. Phoenix buys a Christmas present.
   D. Up through the pines. Now down through the oaks.
   E. Phoenix sees Christmas decorations.

Outcome

10. At the end of the story, we know that (a) the grandchild recovers (b) Phoenix goes to church (c) Phoenix is too weak to travel (d) Phoenix will reach home safely.

Words in Context

1., 2. "This made a grave and *persistent* noise in the still air that seemed *meditative*, like the chirping of a solitary little bird." **Persistent** (550) means (a) loud (b) frightening (c) steady (d) penetrating. **Meditative** (550) means (a) thoughtful (b) bothersome (c) immediate (d) unrehearsed.

3. "There was a fixed and *ceremonial* stiffness over her body." **Ceremonial** (554) means (a) artificial (b) solemn (c) ostentatious (d) understated.

4. "At last there came a flicker and then a flame of *comprehension*." **Comprehension** (555) means (a) agreement (b) coherence (c) gentleness (d) understanding.

5. "But it's an *obstinate* case." **Obstinate** (556) means (a) challenging (b) stubborn (c) impossible (d) recent.

Thinking Critically About the Story

1. Which details did the author add to emphasize Phoenix's age? Her poverty? Her acceptance of life? Her love for her grandchild? Why did she emphasize these aspects?
2. Throughout her journey, not once did Phoenix complain. What are some happenings she could have railed against? What makes her a memorable character? Is her attitude typical of most people? Explain. Is it typical of most elderly people? Of poor people? Of the people you know?
3. How does the author convey to us Phoenix's attitude toward nature as she walks through the woods? How does her attitude toward "wild nature" compare with yours?
4. How does the attitude of the nurse differ from that of the attendant when Phoenix enters the doctor's office? Why is there this sharp difference? How do most young people react to elderly people whom they meet for the first time? To elderly people whom they have grown up with? Why is there such a difference? Do we react differently toward people our own age and those 10, 20, 40, 60 years older? Explain your answers.
5. What aspects of Christmas are present in this story? Why is there no snow mentioned? How will Phoenix be celebrating Christmas? To what extent does she reveal her sense of Christmas spirit?

Language in Action

The Norman Conquest

"At the foot of the hill was a *place* where a log was laid across the creek."

In 1066, William the Conqueror, from Normandy, defeated King Harold and placed himself on the English throne. The changes had far-reaching political results, but the changes in language were perhaps even more important in the long run. The invasion changed English from a relatively "pure" Germanic tongue, with close links to Northern Europe, to a mixed Germanic-Romance language. Though the Anglo-Saxon underclass deeply resented the arrival of their new overlords, they began, inevitably, to adopt some Norman-French words. These words were of Latin origin. The Norman invaders stayed on in their new home until through intermarriage they became part of the English people. The Norman language, like the Norman rulers, was absorbed into English.

In *Ivanhoe*, Sir Walter Scott points out how the new language emphasized class distinctions. The Old English words *sheep*, *deer*, *calf*, and *ox* dealt with animals on the hoof. The French equivalents *mutton*, *veal*, *venison*, and *beef* dealt with meat on the table. Scott asked, "Who did the hard work?" The Old English *house*, suggesting a modest dwelling, was matched by the Norman French *mansion*, suggesting wealth and power. The Old English *ask* was matched by the Norman French *demand*.

Mario Pei, author of *The Story of Language*, makes an interesting point. Family names are part of a language's fundamental stock of words. *Mother*, *father*, *daughter*, *son*, *sister* and *brother* come down straight from Old English. More distant relationships have come to us from the Norman Conquest: *uncle*, *aunt*, *nephew*, *niece*, and *cousin*. English combined the Norman *grand* with the Old English *father* to create *grandfather*. Of course, if we go far enough back into the past, both Germanic and Romance roots will turn out to be related. They are both part of the Indo-European family.

If it were not for the Norman invasion, *place* in the quotation above would probably have been replaced by an old Germanic equivalent like *spot*. The union of the two major strands, Germanic and Romance, has enriched the language beyond all imagining.

"A Worn Path" is written simply, with a preponderance of Old English words. The speech of Phoenix is laden with incorrect English, but it has a direct power partly traceable to her use of simple Anglo-Saxon English, with a small percentage of Romance words.

(Review pages 384–385 for the other half of the story: "Our English Heritage.")

Thank You, M'am

Langston Hughes
American

The water dripping from his face, the boy looked at her. There was a long pause. A very long pause. After he had dried his face and, not knowing what else to do, dried it again, the boy turned around, wondering what next. The door was open. He could make a dash for it down the hall. He could run, run, run, *run*.

A classic old movie, *Brief Encounter,* suggests how crucial a short interlude in a person's life can be. Throughout our lives, we all experience brief encounters, moments spent with others, often strangers. Fellow travelers on a bus or plane, persons who help with directions in a strange city, conversations while waiting in line at a supermarket—these often have some impact on our lives, however slight.

"Thank You, M'am" describes a brief encounter that may well have had a critical impact on a young life. We meet Mrs. Jones all too briefly, but we are likely to remember her after many other characters in this book have been forgotten. Has she helped change a potential criminal's direction in life? The money amounts mentioned show that this story was written in an earlier day, but the problem described is contemporary.

Thank You, M'am

SHE WAS A LARGE WOMAN with a large purse that had everything in it but a hammer and nails. It had a long strap, and she carried it slung across her shoulder. It was about eleven o'clock at night, dark, and she was walking alone, when a boy ran up behind her and tried to snatch her purse. The strap broke with the sudden single tug the boy gave it from behind. But the boy's weight and the weight of the purse combined caused him to lose his balance. Instead of taking off full blast as he had hoped, the boy fell on his back on the sidewalk and his legs flew up. The large woman simply turned around and kicked him right square in his blue-jeaned sitter. Then she reached down, picked the boy up by his shirt front, and shook him until his teeth rattled.

After that the woman said, "Pick up my pocketbook, boy, and give it here."

She still held him tightly. But she bent down enough to permit him to stoop and pick up her purse. Then she said, "Now ain't you ashamed of yourself?"

Firmly gripped by his shirt front, the boy said, "Yes'm."

The woman said, "What did you want to do it for?"

The boy said, "I didn't aim to."

She said, "You a lie!"

By that time two or three people passed, stopped, turned to look, and some stood watching.

"If I turn you loose, will you run?" asked the woman.

"Yes'm," said the boy.

"Then I won't turn you loose," said the woman. She did not release him.

"Lady, I'm sorry," whispered the boy.

"Um-hum! Your face is dirty. I got a great mind to wash your face for you. Ain't you got nobody home to tell you to wash your face?"

"No'm," said the boy.

"Then it will get washed this evening," said the large woman, starting up the street, dragging the frightened boy behind her.

He looked as if he were fourteen or fifteen, frail and willow-wild, in tennis shoes and blue jeans.

The woman said, "You ought to be my son. I would teach you right from wrong. Least I can do right now is to wash your face. Are you hungry?"

"No'm," said the being-dragged boy. "I just want you to turn me loose."

"Was I bothering *you* when I turned that corner?" asked the woman.

"No'm."

"But you put yourself in contact with *me*," said the woman. "If you think that that contact is not going to last awhile, you got another thought coming. When I get through wih you, sir, you are going to remember Mrs. Luella Bates Washington Jones."

Sweat popped out on the boy's face and he began to struggle. Mrs. Jones stopped, jerked him around in front of her, put a half nelson[1] about his neck, and continued to drag him up the street. When she got to her door, she dragged the boy inside, down a hall, and into a large kitchenette-furnished room at the rear of the house. She switched on the light and left the door open. The boy could hear other roomers laughing and talking in the large house. Some of their doors were open, too, so he knew he and the woman were not alone. The woman still had him by the neck in the middle of her room.

She said, "What is your name?"

"Roger," answered the boy.

"Then, Roger, you go to that sink and wash your face," said the woman, whereupon she turned him loose—at last. Roger looked at the door—looked at the woman—looked at the door—*and went to the sink.*

"Let the water run until it gets warm," she said. "Here's a clean towel."

"You gonna take me to jail?" asked the boy, bending over the sink.

"Not with that face, I would not take you nowhere," said the woman. "Here I am trying to get home to cook me a bite to eat, and you snatch my pocketbook! Maybe you ain't been to your supper either, late as it be. Have you?"

"There's nobody home at my house," said the boy.

"Then we'll eat," said the woman. "I believe you're hungry—or been hungry—to try to snatch my pocketbook!"

"I want a pair of blue suede shoes," said the boy.

"Well, you didn't have to snatch *my* pocketbook to get some suede shoes," said Mrs. Luella Bates Washington Jones. "You could of asked me."

"M'am?"

The water dripping from his face, the boy looked at her. There was a long pause. A very long pause. After he had dried his face and, not knowing what else to do, dried it again, the boy turned around, wondering what next. The door was open. He could make a dash for it down the hall. He could run, run, run, *run*!

[1]term in wrestling. One arm is thrust under the corresponding arm of the opponent and the hand is placed on the back of the neck.

The woman was sitting on the day bed. After a while she said, "I were young once and I wanted things I could not get."

There was another long pause. The boy's mouth opened. Then he frowned, not knowing he frowned.

The woman said, "Uh-hum! You thought I was going to say *but*, didn't you? You thought I was going to say, *but I didn't snatch people's pocketbooks.* Well, I wasn't going to say that." Pause. Silence. "I have done things, too, which I would not tell you, son—neither tell God, if He didn't already know. Everybody's got something in common. So you set down while I fix us something to eat. You might run that comb through your hair so you will look presentable."

In another corner of the room behind a screen was a gas plate and an icebox. Mrs. Jones got up and went behind the screen. The woman did not watch the boy to see if he was going to run now, nor did she watch her purse, which she left behind her on the day bed. But the boy took care to sit on the far side of the room, away from the purse, where he thought she could easily see him out of the corner of her eye if she wanted to. He did not trust the woman *not* to trust him. And he did not want to be mistrusted now.

"Do you need somebody to go to the store," asked the boy, "maybe to get some milk or something?"

"Don't believe I do," said the woman, "unless you just want sweet milk yourself. I was going to make cocoa out of this canned milk I got here."

"That will be fine," said the boy.

She heated some lima beans and ham she had in the icebox, made the cocoa, and set the table. The woman did not ask the boy anything about where he lived, or his folks, or anything else that would embarrass him. Instead, as they ate, she told him about her job in a hotel beauty shop that stayed open late, what the work was like, and how all kinds of women came in and out, blondes, redheads, and Spanish. Then she cut him a half of her ten-cent cake.

"Eat some more, son," she said.

When they were finished eating, she got up and said, "Now here, take this ten dollars and buy yourself some blue suede shoes. And next time, do not make the mistake of latching onto[1] *my* pocketbook *nor nobody else's*—because shoes got by devilish ways will burn your feet. I got to get my rest now. But from here on in, son, I hope you will behave yourself."

She led him down the hall to the front door and opened it. "Good night! Behave yourself, boy!" she said, looking out into the street as he went down the steps.

The boy wanted to say something other than, "Thank you, m'am," to Mrs. Luella Bates Washington Jones, but although his lips

[1]dialectal expression meaning seizing, grasping.

moved, he couldn't even say that as he turned at the foot of the barren stoop and looked up at the large woman in the door. Then she shut the door.

Reading for Understanding

Main Idea

1. The author may be suggesting that (a) petty criminals are not worth saving (b) an act of kindness may change a person's life (c) yearning for new clothes may lead to crime (d) young people should respect their elders.

Details

2. Mrs. Jones lives in a (a) condominium (b) one-family house (c) rooming house (d) hotel.
3. Mrs. Jones worked in a (a) grocery store (b) bank (c) clothing store (d) beauty parlor.

Inferences

4. When Mrs. Jones asked Roger if he would run if she released him, he (a) lied (b) refused to answer (c) nodded (d) told the truth.
5. When Roger "looked at the door—looked at the woman—looked at the door," he was (a) considering his chances of getting away (b) being grateful for her kindly treatment of him (c) listening to the sound of the other roomers laughing and talking (d) noticing that the door was closer than the sink.
6. Throughout the episode, Roger's mental condition was one of (a) bafflement (b) bitterness (c) fear for his life (d) relaxation.
7. Mrs. Jones may be characterized as (a) strong but wishy-washy (b) firm but fair (c) well-intentioned but fallible (d) egotistical but generous.
8. Roger is described as (a) tall and muscular (b) squat and heavy (c) slight and slender (d) lame and pathetic.

Outcome

9. At the end of the story, Roger probably (a) realized he hated Mrs. Jones (b) didn't reflect upon his experience (c) spent the $10 on shoes (d) tried stealing someone else's purse.

Fact or Opinion

Tell whether the following is a fact or an opinion.

10. Mrs. Jones could have called the police.

Words in Context

1. "Mrs. Jones stopped, jerked him around in front of her, put a *half-nelson* around his neck and continued to drag him up the street." A **half-nelson** (562) is a (a) ballet move (b) friendly embrace (c) wrestling hold (d) braided rope.
2. "And he did not want to be *mistrusted* now." **Mistrusted** (563) means (a) doubted (b) disliked (c) disregarded (d) disrespected.

Thinking Critically About the Story

1. What kind of woman was Mrs. Jones? What clues to her personality does the author provide?
2. What kind of life does Mrs. Jones lead? Consider where she works, where she lives, how she reacts to Roger.
3. Do you think that Mrs. Jones's treatment of Roger has made a positive impression on him? Explain.
4. "He did not trust the woman *not* to trust him. And he did not want to be mistrusted now." In your own words, tell what you think the sentences mean. Try eliminating both negatives in the first sentence to see if the omissions help the sense.
5. What are the clues that explain the boy's actions?

Language in Action

Stories in Words

Kitchenette (562) can be traced back to the Latin *coquere*, "to cook." The same root gives us *cook*, *culinary*, *precocious*, and *cuisine*. A *kitchen* is a place for *cooking*. Our word has a suffix, *ette*, meaning "little, small." This suffix, called a *diminutive*, appears in a great many words: *ringlet*, *cabinet*, *dinette*, *closet*, *drum majorette*. By an odd process of language, *superette* is sometimes used for a small supermarket. Here the two elements—*super* and *ette*—seem to contradict each other.

Suede (562) comes directly from the French *gants de Suède*, or *Swedish gloves*. Many nations have given their names to the English language. Some retain their capitals: *French* horn, *Danish* pastry, *Russian* roulette, *Brazil* nut, *Irish* stew, *German* shepherd, *Persian* cat. Other words have been in the language long enough to lose their capital letters: *china*, *morocco* (leather), *japan* (varnish), *roman* type, and *lima* bean (563). Some words are written either way—for example *Brussels* sprouts or *brussels* sprouts.

Cocoa (563), like the product itself, comes to us from the Aztec people of Mexico. The Spanish first borrowed the word as *cacao*. That spelling is retained for the dried fatty seeds of the cocoa tree. *Cocoa* was once pronounced with three syllables: *KO-ko-a*.

Actions and Motivations

ACTIVITIES

Thinking Critically About the Selections

1. Which story had the greatest emotional impact on you? Why?
2. Was your choice in #1 your favorite story? Why or why not?
3. Do you agree with John Locke's statement at the beginning of the unit (491)? Why or why not?
4. In the "The Black Cat," Edgar Allan Poe wrote, "Who has not, a hundred times, found himself committing a vile or a stupid action, for no other reason than because he knows he should *not?*" Is this rather pessimistic view of human nature true, perhaps in part? Does experimenting with smoking as a teenager qualify as an example of such an action? Explain.
5. In contrast to #4, La Rochefoucauld wrote, "There are countless actions which appear ridiculous, whose hidden motives are very wise and weighty." What does this mean? Do you agree? Are both #4 and #5 accurate? Explain.
6. In Shakespeare's *Henry IV, Part 2,* Prince Hal knows his father is dying. He tries on the crown and later says to his father, "I never thought to hear you speak again." The King, thinking Hal couldn't wait to be king, replies, "Thy wish was father to that thought." Is the King's statement accurate? Do our wishes influence our thoughts? Do our thoughts influence our wishes? Can they be separated?
7. Here's a real-life problem for you, one that is very much involved with actions and motivations. In the 1996 Olympic Games at Atlanta, the great athlete Carl Lewis won his ninth career gold medal in the broadjump, tying the achievement of several other athletes. Then he began campaigning for a place on the 400-meter relay team, thus giving him a chance for a unique tenth gold medal. The problem was that the relay team had already been set after qualifying and practicing together. A substantial number of people said, "Put Carl in; he's the best." An equal number of people said, "Don't take away another runner's dream unfairly by replacing him at the last moment.

The team members earned their places." If you were the coach, what would be your decision? Why? What are the two ideals being balanced and contrasted here?

After you have made your decision and discussed the possibilities, turn to page 571 to find out what actually happened. Then tell whether the actual result made you change your opinion.

8. The central characters of "A Worn Path" and "Thank You, M'am" have many points in common. Suggest at least three ways in which the women resemble each other. Select two characters from other selections in the unit and compare them.
9. Select two selections in this unit and provide for each an adjective that you think best describes the tone. Here are some suggestions to start you thinking. You may prefer others. Justify your choices.

angry	haunting	reflective
anguished	humorous	romantic
bittersweet	inspiring	satirical
depressing	ironical	scholarly
despairing	jittery	solemn
gloomy	joyous	upbeat
grim	menacing	uneasy

The Writing Portfolio

Types of Writing

You have undoubtedly had experience with a variety of writing types: business and friendly letters, narratives, descriptions, explanations, essays, articles, various kinds of persuasion and argumentation, research papers. Many of these will be duplicated in the college and working years ahead.

This section is a continuation of the activities in Unit 5 (419). As you look over the following suggestions, choose those that you are most interested in.

1. Write a short one-act play based on a school experience. Follow the suggestions for "Dialogue in a Play," (547). Perhaps it was a cafeteria episode, a conversation just before health class, dialogue in the school bus, or some other situation. If you can add a touch of humor, so much the better.

2. Try your hand at a short story, using "A Quarter's Worth of Fireworks" (493) as a model. Provide these six elements: situation, complication, conflict, development, climax, and outcome. Preferably, take an episode from your own experience, but if your interests run to fantasy or science fiction, why not!
3. Write a character sketch of someone you know. These are ways of revealing character: by dialogue, by actions, by the person's thoughts, by the reactions of other persons, by others' opinions, and by your own direct statements.
4. In a letter to a friend, review one of the selections in this unit. Among possible areas of comment are these: general effect, setting, plot, an effective scene, use of dialogue, central idea, effectiveness of beginning and ending, clarity, progress of the plot.
5. Watch a TV movie, and then write a review. Some of the elements mentioned in #4 apply here, as well.
6. Write a summary of one of the selections in this unit. Condense the plot to a page or two. Try to use your own words rather than the words of the original.

Other Areas of Communication

1. Are you a video-game enthusiast? Are there any selections in this unit that might serve as the basis of a video game? If not, what essential qualities do the selections lack?
2. Several of the stories suggest the position of women in their society. Masha Dmitrich in "The Lottery Ticket" and the girl in "Never" show women in unhappy situations, born to a special role. Be ready to set up a panel discussion considering these points and any others that seem relevant.
   (a) The Position of Women Throughout History
   (b) Major Gains in Recent Years
   (c) Current Inequities That Need Correction
   (d) The Portrayal of Women on TV Sitcoms
   (e) Strategies for Further Improvement
3. "The Rising of the Moon" makes a suitable class play. With the help of your teacher, cast the play and choose a student director. Present it with the book as a script. An unusually energetic cast might prefer to memorize the parts.

4. Writers weave their stories from life experiences and a keen imagination. Many writers get story ideas from the newspapers. Find a newspaper article that resembles, in one or more respects, one of the selections in this unit. Perhaps it's the experience of a lottery winner or a boy saved from a gang. Bring the article to class and prepare to tell about it.
5. Choose a partner in the class. Prepare to present an interview originating from a selection in this unit. For example, a reporter interviews the Sergeant of "The Rising of the Moon" after it's discovered that the wanted man has escaped.
6. A major legal problem is what to do with preteen and teenage criminals, often perpetrators of major crimes like assault, theft, arson, and murder. Debate the following resolution in class. Divide the class into two groups, one taking the positive and one the negative:

   Resolved: That teenagers who are major offenders should be treated in court as adults.

Language in Action—a Review

You may refer to the preceding pages to answer these questions.

1. In talking about levels of usage, to replace the word *colloquial,* we might choose (a) *slang* (b) *incorrect* (c) *informal* (d) *formal.*
2. As a general rule, the best language to use (a) is standard formal English (b) doesn't call attention to itself (c) is colloquial with a touch of slang (d) is slang that is lively, colorful, and striking.
3. The word *farthing* is related to (a) four (b) far (c) fear (d) fire.
4. All the following are listed as part of the Indo-European family EXCEPT (a) Gothic (b) Old Norse (c) Sanskrit (d) Finnish.
5. Both the colon and the semicolon are used to (a) introduce quotation marks (b) join together adjectives in a series (c) replace the exclamation point (d) join independent clauses together.
6. A person who loved to introduce long stage directions to help a play's readers is (a) William Shakespeare (b) Lady Gregory (c) George Bernard Shaw (d) Moss Hart.
7. In a printed play, the parentheses include words that (a) are not actually said in the play itself (b) often distract from an understanding of the play (c) contradict what the character has just said (d) provide

an opportunity for the principal actor to present the theme of the play.

8. A major contribution of William the Conqueror was (a) a generous sharing of his wealth with the conquered people (b) willingness to set up democratic institutions (c) a rich new strand in the English language (d) fierce devotion to his new subjects.
9. The *-ette* suffix in *kitchenette* is related to (a) color (b) culinary art (c) size (d) verbs.
10. *Cocoa*, both name and product, came from (a) French colonialism (b) the American Indian (c) Cajun cooking (d) the Aztecs.

Atlanta Olympics problem, page (567):

The coach did not put Carl Lewis into the relay.

The team did not win the gold medal, won by Canada.

The team did win the silver medal, however.

UNIT EIGHT

The World Over

If civilization is to survive, we must cultivate the science of human relationships—the ability of all peoples, of all kinds, to live together, in the same world at peace.

Franklin Delano Roosevelt

A major purpose of this book has been to provide a cross-section of writing around the world. If we are ever to live safely in one world, we need to recognize the things we all have in common. There are obvious cultural differences, and these can make for a varied and colorful world. But the similarities are profound, more important than the superficial differences.

In addition to selections by American authors, you have already met Chinese, Irish, English, German, Hungarian, Norwegian, Japanese, African, Filipino and Russian writers. This unit will add selections by Chilean, Egyptian, Indian, Polish, and Syrian writers. The settings are different, but they all reveal a common humanity.

This unit concludes with stories by American authors. "He" and "The Person of the Moment" tell of two young people with critically different experiences. These extremes are mirrored throughout the unit. The sadness of "My Lord, the Baby" is matched by the gentle humor of "Bontshe the Silent." The two young people in "Hill-bred" will seem familiar and recognizable to young lovers anywhere in the world. Politically, we are far from living in "One World," but emotionally we are all kin.

My Lord, the Baby

Rabindranath Tagore
Indian

The baby saw the river rushing by, splashing and gurgling as it went. . . . At the sight, the heart of the human child grew excited and restless. He got down stealthily from the go-cart and toddled off toward the river. On his way he picked up a small stick and leaned over the bank of the stream, pretending to fish.

World travelers are always impressed when they hear children laughing and playing in a schoolyard or park. Differences in language disappear. The cries and shouts sound the same in Bombay and Nairobi as they do in Nashville and Seattle. Children are children around the world. They tend to play together without awareness of religion or the political backgrounds of their parents. For a while, they are citizens of the world. As they grow older, differences and prejudices begin to appear.

The child in "My Lord, the Baby" is a typical child, recognizable by anyone who has been with a baby for a time. He is happy, demanding, willful, and utterly defenseless. The person assigned to take care of him is loving, careful, thoughtful . . . and unlucky. Though the setting is India, the mother's grief knows no national boundaries.

My Lord, the Baby

I

RAICHARAN WAS TWELVE YEARS OLD when he came as a servant to his master's house. He belonged to the same caste as his master and was given his master's little son to nurse. As time went on the boy left Raicharan's arms to go to school. From school he went on to college, and after college he entered the judicial service. Always, until he married, Raicharan was his sole attendant.

But, when a mistress came into the house, Raicharan found two masters instead of one. All his former influence passed to the new mistress. This was compensated for by a fresh arrival. Anukul had a son born to him, and Raicharan by his unsparing attentions soon got a complete hold over the child. He used to toss him up in his arms, call to him in absurd baby language, put his face close to the baby's, and draw it away again with a grin.

Presently the child was able to crawl and cross the doorway. When Raicharan went to catch him, he would scream with mischievous laughter and make for safety. Raicharan was amazed at the profound skill and exact judgment the baby showed when pursued. He would say to his mistress with a look of awe and mystery: "Your son will be a judge someday."

New wonders came in their turn. When the baby began to toddle, that was to Raicharan an epoch in human history. When he called his father Ba-ba and his mother Ma-ma and Raicharan Chan-na, then Raicharan's ecstasy knew no bounds. He went out to tell the news to all the world.

After a while Raicharan was asked to show his ingenuity in other ways. He had, for instance, to play the part of a horse, holding the reins between his teeth and prancing with his feet. He had also to wrestle with his little charge, and if he could not, by a wrestler's trick, fall on his back defeated at the end, a great outcry was certain.

About this time Anukul was transferred to a district on the banks of the Padma. On his way through Calcutta he bought his son a little go-cart. He bought him also a yellow satin waistcoat, a gold-laced cap, and some gold bracelets and anklets. Raicharan was wont to take these out and put them on his little charge with ceremonial pride whenever they went for a walk.

Then came the rainy season, and day after day the rain poured down in torrents. The hungry river, like an enormous serpent, swallowed down terraces, villages, cornfields, and covered with its flood the tall grasses and wild casuarinas on the sandbanks. From time to time there was a deep thud, as the riverbanks crumbled. The unceasing roar of the main current could be heard from far away. Masses of foam, carried swiftly past, proved to the eye the swiftness of the stream.

One afternoon the rain cleared. It was cloudy, but cool and bright. Raicharan's little despot did not want to stay in on such a fine afternoon. His lordship climbed into the go-cart. Raicharan, between the shafts, dragged him slowly along till he reached the rice fields on the banks of the river. There was no one in the fields, and no boat on the stream. Across the water, on the farther side, the clouds were rifted in the west. The silent ceremonial of the setting sun was revealed in all its glowing splendor. In the midst of that stillness the child, all of a sudden, pointed with his finger in front of him and cried: "Chan-na! Pitty fow."

Close by on a mud flat stood a large *Kadamba* tree in full flower. My lord, the baby, looked at it with greedy eyes, and Raicharan knew his meaning. Only a short time before he had made, out of these very flower balls, a small go-cart; and the child had been so entirely happy dragging it about with a string, that for the whole day Raicharan was not made to put on the reins at all. He was promoted from a horse into a groom.

But Raicharan had no wish that evening to go splashing, knee-deep through the mud to reach the flowers. So he quickly pointed his finger in the opposite direction, calling out: "Oh, look, baby, look! Look at the bird." And with all sorts of curious noises he pushed the go-cart rapidly away from the tree.

But a child destined to be a judge cannot be put off so easily. And besides, there was at the time nothing to attract his eyes. And you cannot keep up forever the pretense of an imaginary bird.

The little Master's mind was made up, and Raicharan was at his wits' end. "Very well, baby," he said at last, "you sit still in the cart, and I'll go and get you the pretty flower. Only mind you don't go near the water."

As he said this, he made his legs bare to the knee and waded through the oozing mud toward the tree.

The moment Raicharan had gone, his little Master went off at racing speed to the forbidden water. The baby saw the river rushing by, splashing and gurgling as it went. It seemed as though the disobedient wavelets themselves were running away from some greater Raicharan with the laughter of a thousand children. At the sight of their mischief, the heart of the human child grew excited and restless. He got down stealthily from the go-cart and toddled off toward the river. On his way he picked up a small stick and leaned over the bank of the stream pretending to fish. The mischievous fairies of the river with their mysterious voices seemed to be inviting him into their playhouse.

Raicharan had plucked a handful of flowers from the tree and was carrying them back in the end of his cloth, with his face wreathed in smiles. But when he reached the go-cart, there was no one there. He looked on all sides and there was no one there. He looked back at the cart and there was no one there.

In that first terrible moment his blood froze within him. Before his eyes the whole universe swam round like a dark mist. From the depth of his broken heart he gave one piercing cry: "Master, Master, little Master!"

But no voice answered "Chan-na." No child laughed mischievously back; no scream of baby delight welcomed his return. Only the river ran on, with its splashing, gurgling noise as before—as though it knew nothing at all and had no time to attend to such a tiny human event as the death of a child.

As the evening passed by, Raicharan's mistress became very anxious. She sent men out on all sides to search. They went with lanterns in their hands and reached at last the banks of the Padma. There they found Raicharan rushing up and down the fields, like a stormy wind, shouting the cry of despair: "Master, Master, little Master!"

When they got Raicharan home at last, he fell prostrate at his mistress' feet. They shook him, and questioned him, and asked him repeatedly where he had left the child; but all he could say was that he knew nothing.

Though everyone held the opinion that the Padma had swallowed the child, there was a lurking doubt left in the mind. For a band of gypsies had been noticed outside the village that afternoon, and some suspicion rested on them. The mother went so far in her wild grief as to think it possible that Raicharan himself had stolen the child. She called him aside with piteous entreaty and said: "Raicharan, give me back my baby. Oh! give me back my child. Take from me any money you ask, but give me back my child!"

Anukul tried to reason his wife out of this wholly unjust suspicion: "Why on earth," he said, "should he commit such a crime as that?"

The mother only replied: "The baby had gold ornaments on his body. Who knows?"

It was impossible to reason with her after that.

II

RAICHARAN WENT BACK to his own village. Up to this time he had had no son, and there was no hope that any child would now be born to him. But it came about before the end of a year that his wife gave birth to a son and died.

An overwhelming resentment at first grew up in Raicharan's heart at the sight of this new baby. At the back of his mind was resentful suspicion that it had come as a usurper in place of the little Master. He also thought it would be a grave offense to be happy with a son of his own after what had happened to his master's little child. Indeed, if it had not been for a widowed sister, who mothered the new baby, it would not have lived long.

But a change gradually came over Raicharan's mind. A wonderful thing happened. This new baby began to crawl about and cross the doorway with mischief in its face. It also showed an amusing cleverness in making its escape to safety. Its voice, its sounds of laughter and tears, its gestures, were those of the little Master. On some days, when Raicharan listened to its crying, his heart suddenly began thumping wildly against his ribs, and it seemed to him that his former little Master was crying somewhere in the unknown land of death because he had lost his Chan-na.

Phailna (for that was the name Raicharan's sister gave to the new baby) soon began to talk. It learned to say Ba-ba and Ma-ma with a baby accent. When Raicharan heard those familiar sounds the mystery suddenly became clear. The little Master could not cast off the spell of his Chan-na, and therefore he had been reborn in his own house.

The arguments in favor of this were, to Raicharan, altogether beyond dispute:

(i) The new baby was born soon after his little Master's death.

(ii) His wife could never have accumulated such merit as to give birth to a son in middle age.

(iii) The new baby walked with a toddle and called out Ba-ba and Ma-ma. There was no sign lacking which marked out the future judge.

Then suddenly Raicharan remembered that terrible accusation of the mother. "Ah," he said to himself with amazement, "the mother's heart was right. She knew I had stolen her child." When once he had come to this conclusion, he was filled with remorse for his past neglect. He now gave himself over, body and soul, to the new baby, and became its devoted attendant. He began to bring it up as if it were the son of a rich man. He bought a go-cart, a yellow satin waistcoat, and a gold-embroidered cap. He melted down the ornaments of his dead wife and made gold bangles and anklets. He refused to let the little child play with anyone of the neighborhood and became himself its sole companion day and night. As the baby grew up to boyhood, he was so petted and spoiled and clad in such finery that the village children would call him "Your Lordship," and jeer at him; and older people regarded Raicharan as unaccountably crazy about the child.

At last the time came for the boy to go to school. Raicharan sold his small piece of land and went to Calcutta. There he got employment with great difficulty as a servant and sent Phailna to school. He spared no pains to give him the best education, the best clothes, the best food. Meanwhile he lived himself on a mere handful of rice and would say in secret: "Ah! my little Master, my dear little Master, you loved me so much that you came back to my house. You shall never suffer from any neglect of mine."

Twelve years passed away in this manner. The boy was able to read and write well. He was bright and healthy and good-looking. He paid a great deal of attention to his personal appearance and was specially careful in parting his hair. He was inclined to extravagance and finery, and spent money freely. He could never quite look on Raicharan as a father, because, though fatherly in affection, he had the manner of a servant. A further fault was this, that Raicharan kept secret from everyone that he himself was the father of the child.

The students of the hostel, where Phailna was a boarder, were greatly amused by Raicharan's country manners, and I have to confess that behind his father's back Phailna joined in their fun. But, in the bottom of their hearts, all the students loved the innocent and tenderhearted old man, and Phailna was very fond of him also. But, as I have said before, he loved him with a kind of condescension.

Raicharan grew older and older, and his employer was continually finding fault with him for his incompetent work. He had been starving himself for the boy's sake. So he had grown physically weak and was no longer up to his work. He would forget things, and his mind became dull and stupid. But his employer expected a full servant's work out of him and would not brook excuses. The money that Raicharan had brought with him from the sale of his land was exhausted. The boy was continually grumbling about his clothes and asking for more money.

III

RAICHARAN MADE UP HIS MIND. He gave up the situation where he was working as a servant, and left some money with Phailna and said: "I have some business to do at home in my village and shall be back soon."

He went off at once to Baraset, where Anukul was magistrate. Anukul's wife was still broken down with grief. She had had no other child.

One day Anukul was resting after a long weary day in court. His wife was buying, at an exorbitant price, an herb from a mendicant quack, which was said to ensure the birth of a child. A voice of greeting was heard in the courtyard. Anukul went out to see who was there. It was Raicharan. Anukul's heart was softened when he saw his old servant. He asked him many questions and offered to take him back into service.

Raicharan smiled faintly and said in reply: "I want to make obeisance to my mistress."

Anukul went with Raicharan into the house, where the mistress did not receive him as warmly as his old master. Raicharan took no notice of this, but folded his hands, and said: "It was not the Padma that stole your baby. It was I."

Anukul exclaimed: "Great God! Eh! What! Where is he?"

Raicharan replied: "He is with me. I will bring him the day after tomorrow."

It was Sunday. There was no magistrate's court sitting. Both husband and wife were looking expectantly along the road, waiting from early morning for Raicharan's appearance. At ten o'clock he came, leading Phailna by the hand.

Anukul's wife, without question, took the boy into her lap, and was wild with excitement, sometimes laughing, sometimes weeping, touching him, kissing his hair and his forehead, and gazing into his face with hungry, eager eyes. The boy was very good-looking and dressed like a gentleman's son. The heart of Anukul brimmed over with a sudden rush of affection.

Nevertheless, the magistrate in him asked: "Have you any proofs?"

Raicharan said: "How could there be any proof of such a deed? God alone knows that I stole your boy, and no one else in the world."

When Anukul saw how eagerly his wife was clinging to the boy, he realized the futility of asking for proofs. It would be wiser to believe. And then—where could an old man like Raicharan get such a boy from? And why should his faithful servant deceive him for nothing?

"But," he added severely, "Raicharan, you must not stay here."

"Where shall I go, Master?" said Raicharan, in a choking voice, folding his hands. "I am old. Who will take an old man as a servant?"

The mistress said: "Let him stay. My child will be pleased. I forgive him."

But Anukul's magisterial conscience would not allow him. "No," he said, "he cannot be forgiven for what he has done."

Raicharan bowed to the ground and clasped Anukul's feet. "Master," he cried, "let me stay. It was not I who did it. It was God."

Anukul's conscience was worse stricken than ever, when Raicharan tried to put the blame on God's shoulders.

"No," he said, "I could not allow it. I cannot trust you anymore. You have done an act of treachery."

Raicharan rose to his feet and said: "It was not I who did it."

"Who was it then?" asked Anukul.

Raicharan replied: "It was my fate."

But no educated man could take this for an excuse. Anukul remained obdurate.

When Phailna saw that he was the wealthy magistrate's son, and not Raicharan's, he was angry at first, thinking that he had been cheated all this time of his birthright. But seeing Raicharan in distress, he generously said to his father: "Father, forgive him. Even if you don't let him live with us, let him have a small monthly pension."

After hearing this, Raicharan did not utter another word. He looked for the last time on the face of his son; he made obeisance to his old master and mistress. Then he went out and was mingled with the numberless people of the world.

At the end of the month Anukul sent him some money to his village. But the money came back. There was no one there of the name of Raicharan.

Reading for Understanding

Main Idea

1. The best word to describe the central theme of the story is (a) oppression (b) devotion (c) absurdity (d) selfishness.

Details

2. Raicharan became a servant at (a) 10 (b) 12 (c) 14 (d) 16.
3. Ba-ba was another name for (a) Raicharan (b) Chan-na (c) Anukul (d) Phailna.
4. Tragedy was caused by (a) Raicharan's complaints (b) a loss of the Master's fortune (c) the mother's indifference (d) carelessness at the swollen river.

Inferences

5. The "playhouse" mentioned on page 576 is really (a) the depths of the river (b) a treehouse (c) a spot at the foot of the rainbow (d) a glen in the forest.
6. Raicharan repeatedly said that he knew nothing about the disappearance because (a) he had secretly kidnaped the boy (b) he was in league with gypsies (c) he wanted to punish the Master's wife (d) it was true.

7. It seems safe to assume that the baby (a) had indeed been kidnaped (b) was taken to Calcutta (c) had drowned (d) disliked Raicharan.
8. At story's end, Raicharan's son was (a) forgiving (b) actually Anukul's child (c) proud of Raicharan (d) a servant.
9. At first, when Raicharan said that Phailna was really the couple's son, (a) the mother refused to believe it (b) Phailna himself objected (c) Anukul was not convinced (d) Raicharan withdrew the claim.

Outcome

10. At the end of the story, Phailna (a) went back with Raicharan (b) was raised as a wealthy boy (c) actually struck his father (d) proved to be the baby lost earlier.

Words in Context

1. "When the baby began to toddle, that was to Raicharan an *epoch* in human history." An **epoch** (575) is (a) a setback (b) an important period of time (c) a period of turmoil (d) a paradise.
2. "Raicharan's little *despot* did not want to stay in on such a fine afternoon." A **despot** (576) is a (a) child (b) neighbor (c) responsibility (d) tyrant.
3. "When they got Raicharan home at last, he fell *prostrate* at his mistress' feet." **Prostrate** (577) means (a) stretched out (b) weeping (c) protesting (d) rapidly.
4. "At the back of his mind was a resentful suspicion that it had come as a *usurper* in place of the little Master." A **usurper** (578) is one who (a) claims special privileges (b) is constantly dictatorial (c) takes on a demon's form (d) takes the place of another.
5. "But, as I have said before, he loved him with a kind of *condescension*." **Condescension** (579) arises from (a) kindness (b) a feeling of superiority (c) bitterness and dread (d) awe and mystery.

6., 7. "His wife was buying, at an *exorbitant* price, an herb from a *mendicant* quack, which was said to ensure the birth of a child." **Exorbitant** (579) means (a) advertised (b) excessive (c) bartered (d) honest. A **mendicant** (579) is a (a) medical expert (b) qualified salesperson (c) beggar (d) circus performer.

8. " 'I want to make *obeisance* to my mistress.' " **Obeisance** (579) is (a) a communication (b) a mark of respect (c) payment (d) discovery.
9. "Anukul remained *obdurate*." **Obdurate** (580) means (a) stubborn (b) interested (c) agreeable (d) violent.

Thinking Critically About the Story

1. What little touches does Tagore include to show that he has observed babies?
2. "He belonged to the same caste as his master." What does that mean? Does the caste system survive in modern India?
3. Some people have an uncanny ability to relate to children, to meet them on their level, and provide enlightened companionship. Was Raicharan such a person? Point out examples.
4. Why did Anukul finally decide to accept Phailna as his son despite his early misgivings?
5. How was Raicharan's act in giving up his own son characteristic of him throughout the story?
6. What happened to Raicharan? Why?

Language in Action

Nonverbal Communication

> When they got Raicharan home at last, he fell prostrate at his mistress' feet. They shook him, and questioned him, and asked him repeatedly where he had left the child; but all he could say was that he knew nothing.

The essential element in communication is the word. As we write and speak, we use these marvelous tools that have been given to us. But communication is more than words. In the quotation above, Raicharan's actions display his grief more than any words could do.

Facial expressions are rich with meaning. "Delilah is a great tennis player" can be destroyed with a wink. "I'm happy to see you" can be reversed with a pained expression. A smile can take the sting out of a gentle criticism. It's difficult to suppress an expression of surprise if the news is unexpected. Lady Macbeth says to her husband, "Your face, my thane, is as a book where men may read strange matters."

Bodily attitude is as revealing as the face. When two tennis players leave the court, their bodily attitudes usually tell which won and which lost. The loser's shoulders may slump. His eyes may be downcast. The very picture tells a story.

Gestures are rich elements in communication. Sign languages are obvious examples. Even though we have a rich store of words at our command, we cannot refrain from *pointing* when giving directions. Ask someone to describe a spiral staircase without using hands. In some cultures, gestures play a stronger part than in our culture. A traveler abroad should refrain from gestures. He or she may be using an apparently innocent gesture that is insulting in the foreign culture.

Silence can also convey a message. "How did you enjoy the new reality show?" No reply may speak volumes. Silence can also signal to a friend, "I'd like to have some quiet time."

Signs and graphic symbols are also effective nonverbal communicators. Street signs, traffic signs, protesters' placards, parking spaces with pictures of a wheelchair—all convey a message without a word.

Taken altogether, you have a vast array of elements to use in communicating.

Hillbred

Arreph El-Khoury
Syrian

The Clerk went inside his office and faced them across a wide desk. He sat on a chair.

"Now," he said, business-like, "what can we do for you?"

"We want a marriage license," announced Kasid, his face flushing darkly. Hind giggled.

Young love is the theme of Shakespeare's **Romeo and Juliet**, as well as stories derived from it—like the musical **West Side Story**. Older adults sometimes fail to understand the depth of feeling that even first love can inspire. This lack of sympathy is the core of many stories, novels, and films.

Kasid and Hind are in love. They travel down from their native hills to secure a marriage license. They are intimidated by the strangeness of their surroundings but are finally taken to his office by a gentle clerk. The clerk is eager to help these frightened lovers, but he has bad news for them.

Another time, another place, other lovers, but this story by a Syrian author has an immediacy that will put you into the story, wishing you could help.

Hillbred

HASBAYA IS A NICE little city—"The Biggest Little City Between Mount Hermon and the Mediterranean," as it is called by its inhabitants. Squatting on its two slopes around the banks of its river, its gray and white stone houses with their flat or pyramidal roofs among the trees give the appearance of bas-relief on emerald-green, deep-sea majolica.[1] The most noticeable building in Hasbaya, next to the ancient crusaders' castle, is the courthouse, which was built by the Turks, to be inherited by the Arabs when His Majesty King Faisal was the head of the Syrian government after the World War, and most recently by the Lebanese government after the French had added Hasbaya to Mount Lebanon.

On a warm and sunny spring day in which the glorious Syrian sun was bathing in a sea of jade and the warm wind was racing over the purple and blue hills, a young man by the name of Kasid and a girl by the name of Hind were seen entering the high archway gate of the courthouse, in front of which a Lebanese soldier with a fixed bayonet stood motionless as if carved of rock.

They were dressed in homespun clothes and wore native shoes, black and hobnailed. A black *ighal* of coiled goat's hair encircled Kasid's white muslin headkerchief. Under the tight-fitting red *aba* which reached to his knees, he wore an embroidered jacket and vest of black cloth and a shirt of effulgent white. A peach-colored silk sash around his waist held a curved dagger. His trousers were voluminous and indigo-dyed. As for Hind, her gentle, brown eyes were heavily loaded with kohl and her fingertips dyed red with henna. The white muslin *mandil* over her head fell in folds to her ankles, partially obscuring her blue dress and black coat.

The eyes of this young pair were scrutinizing every object around them as they proceeded forward. Silently they advanced toward the inner courtyard where a number of soldiers were basking in the sun. They turned their eyes away from the soldiers as if these were gray *jin* of evil and looked to the left, knowing not what to do. On the wall they saw a number of bulletins on blackboards. Kasid advanced toward the bulletins, read a while, turned his head away from them and came back to Hind. He motioned her to follow him. She obeyed, and they walked to the end of the corridor, glanced to the left and right. Kasid, seeing a few doors at their right, motioned Hind to follow him a second time, walked toward

[1]a kind of earthenware

these doors and began to read the signs on them. He read the sign on the first, the second, the third, and, seeing that none of these doors was that of the office he sought, he advanced to the foot of a winding stairway which led to the second story.

Kasid looked at the grim, ghastly walls and the disconsolate steps and paused for a moment. Finally he told Hind to follow him and began to climb the stairs with the uncertain, suspicious step of the hillbred who reckons with the inequalities of the land. Hind followed him in silence. Sometimes he was looking at the walls, at other times glancing over his shoulder at Hind behind him, and with added mistrust at the higher steps. Finally they reached a door at their left with the Clerk's sign on it. Here they stood firm—their eyes like those of a cat confronted by a mastiff.

"Enter," Kasid ordered Hind with a motion of his head.

"You enter—you who are armed with a dagger!" retorted Hind.

Kasid stood his ground. Hind looked at him. He grinned childishly. She turned her head away from him and stared at the wall. Kasid drew his head close to her. She turned facing him. She was the first to speak. "What shall we do?"

"I do not know, by Allah!" replied Kasid with an awkward shrug of his broad shoulders. They looked at each other helplessly. Kasid ventured a step forward toward the door of the Clerk's office. Hind followed him with her eyes as her red lips opened with a sardonic smile. Suddenly he stopped, pondered a while and as suddenly sat down on the steps. Hind came and sat beside him as if they were on the steps of their respective houses.

"Why don't you enter?" asked Kasid.

"Why don't you enter first and bring it?" she snapped at him.

Kasid shook his head disapprovingly.

At that moment they heard footsteps coming toward them from the higher part of the steps and in unison they looked over their shoulders. A man, dressed in European clothes, came down toward them. They turned their heads away from him. The man continued to descend until he was two steps from them.

"What are you doing here?" the man asked. They did not answer but smiled. "What are you doing here—what do you want?" he asked impatiently.

They stood up. "We want to enter this room," Kasid said, pointing to the door of the Clerk's office.

"Come on," said the man, smiling, "I am the Clerk." He walked to the door and pushed it open. He entered. Kasid and Hind followed him inside with a shambling gait.

The Clerk went inside his office and faced them across a wide desk. He sat on a chair. "Now," he said, business-like, "what can we do for you?"

"We want a marriage license," announced Kasid, his face flushing darkly. Hind giggled.

The Clerk smiled broadly, opened a drawer and produced a sheet of paper which he handed to Kasid across the table, saying, "Fill it in."

Kasid took the sheet of paper with a shaky hand, looked at Hind, motioned her to follow him and went to another desk in the room and sat down on a chair. There were penholders, inkwells and blotters on the desk. Kasid began to read and write without asking Hind a question. She stood looking at him and smiling sarcastically. Finally, he stood up, breathed contentedly, motioned Hind to follow him and came toward the Clerk. He handed him the sheet of paper. The Clerk began to read what Kasid had written in an exceptionally poor penmanship; he read their names, ages, conditions, birthplaces, the names of their parents, their occupations, their addresses and the date. Glancing at the sheet of paper for a second time, the Clerk smiled and shook his head.

"My lad," said the Clerk sympathetically, "you are not old enough nor is she!"

"*Allahu Akbar!* (God is Greater!)" Kasid and Hind exclaimed in unison. "How old do we have to be?" asked Kasid with a dark frown on his highly hawkish face.

The Clerk told him the age required by the law.

"But we are not that and we want to marry each other," argued Kasid, vehemently.

"It is necessary, then, to have your parents sign this sheet of paper before we can issue a license for you," the Clerk informed him as he handed him the sheet of paper.

"We are orphans. Our parents were killed by the French in the last uprising against them," pronounced Kasid with a pain in his heart.

"It is regrettable; you have to wait until you are old enough!" said the Clerk.

Kasid made a wry face. He looked at Hind beside him and suddenly his face became haggard, passionate and tragic. Quickly he returned the sheet of paper to the Clerk, and, with his right hand on the haft of his dagger and his left grasping Hind by the arm, he went out of the room, whispering in her ears, "Allah did not say so in the Book!"

Reading for Understanding

Main Idea

1. The main theme of the story is (a) military cruelty (b) the stupidity of children (c) frustrated love (d) devouring distrust.

Details

2. The original disagreement between Kasid and Hind was over (a) clothes to be worn (b) who was to enter first (c) the actual date (d) Hind's parents.
3. The act of kindness was shown to them by (a) a soldier (b) a relative of Kasid's (c) a court judge (d) the Clerk.
4. Besides their age, the barrier to the marriage of Kasid and Hind was (a) the lack of parents to approve (b) the Clerk's hidden attraction to Hind (c) Kasid's timid behavior (d) the closeness of the holiday season.

Inferences

5. When Kasid and Hind entered the courthouse, they were exceptionally (a) shy (b) confident (c) rude to an old man (d) well prepared.
6. The Clerk's behavior toward the pair was (a) mean (b) indifferent (c) irritating (d) sympathetic.
7. Kasid's temperament could be characterized as (a) calm (b) hotheaded (c) stable (d) mature.
8. The clothing of the two lovers could be described as (a) ugly (b) unfashionable (c) oppressively hot (d) stylish.
9. The word *Hillbred* is meant to convey (a) a sense of long-held superiority (b) stability, like the rock-ribbed peaks (d) a slightly negative suggestion (d) a source of revolutionary zeal.

Fact or Opinion

Tell whether the following is a fact or an opinion.

10. The marriage license regulations were unfair.

Words in Context

1. "He wore an embroidered jacket and vest of black cloth and a shirt of *effulgent* white." **Effulgent** (586) means (a) brilliant (b) subdued (c) eggshell (d) threadbare.
2. "The eyes of this young pair were *scrutinizing* every object around them as they proceeded forward." **Scrutinizing** (586) means (a) envying (b) pricing (c) touching (d) examining.
3. "Kasid looked at the grim, ghastly walls and the *disconsolate* steps and paused for a moment." **Disconsolate** (587) means (a) steep (b) colorful (c) cheerless (d) partly broken.
4. "At that moment they heard footsteps coming toward them from the higher part of the steps and *in unison* they looked over their shoulders." **In unison** (587) means (a) at the same time (b) with fear (c) smiling with relief (d) in succession.
5. "Kasid and Hind followed him inside with a *shambling* gait." **Shambling** (587) means (a) rushing (b) walking awkardly (c) tiptoeing carefully (d) stately.
6. " 'But we are not that and we want to marry each other,' argued Kasid *vehemently*." **Vehemently** (588) means (a) reasonably (b) quietly (c) forcefully (d) breathlessly.
7. "Kasid made a *wry* face." **Wry** (588) means (a) sour (b) funny (c) teary (d) twisted.
8. "He looked at Hind beside him and suddenly his face became *haggard,* passionate and tragic." **Haggard** (588) means (a) alert (b) angry (c) careworn (d) animated.

Thinking Critically About the Story

1. What is the significance of the title of the story?
2. Do Kasid and Hind show signs of maturity sufficient to make a successful marriage?
3. At what age should young people be allowed to marry without parental consent?
4. Why were Kasid and Hind particularly unfortunate?

5. Most areas of the world have regulations for issuing marriage licenses. Why should the state control the issuance of licenses? What stake do nations have in the control of marriages?
6. Could this story be set in the United States without losing credibility? Explain.

Language in Action

Synonyms: No Two Alike

> Kasid looked at the grim, ghastly walls and the disconsolate steps and paused for a moment.

In one sense *grim* and *ghastly* are synonyms. They both suggest the dreadful appearance of the walls. They also suggest a basic truth about synonyms. Though synonyms are words that mean approximately the same, no two words are interchangeable in any and all situations. A beautiful woman's facial expression may be grim . . . but not ghastly.

In addition to their commonly accepted meanings, words also have connotations that help to distinguish them. *Abode, house, dwelling, habitation, domicile* and *home* can be interchanged in some situations but not all.

"The dwelling on 108 Maple Drive is for sale." *House* and perhaps even *home*—can be substituted for *dwelling* without a problem.

> "When I've been away for a week or more, I can't wait to go home again."

Not a single synonym can be substituted for *home* here without destroying the feel of the sentence.

Home is an emotional word, rich with connotations. *House* is rather neutral and colorless. *Dwelling* is a bland word used in real estate. *Habitation* carries no warmth. *Abode* might be used in a scientific article:

> The *abode* of the cliff dwellers seems cold and cheerless to us today.

How do the following synonyms for a "country retreat" suggest different qualities: *shack, shanty, ranch, hut, cabin, hunting lodge?*

from The Stream of Days

Taha Hussein
Egyptian

He hurried along nervously at his companion's side, breathing the nauseous smells, and half-deafened by the medley of sounds that came from all sides at once, left and right, above and below, to meet in midair, where they seemed to unite above the boy's head, layer upon layer, into a single fine mist.

Many young people of the industrial nations take education for granted. It's there. It's free. It's nearly universal. In the United States, education through the secondary school is provided for everyone to take advantage of. Even college is available for most motivated students. Sometimes those things made available are not appreciated.

In third world countries, education is a precious and often limited commodity. An education is a ticket to a better life, but it is not easily obtainable universally. Students who attend the schools and colleges realize how precious the gift is.

In this story, a young man comes in from the countryside to the overpopulated capital of Egypt: Cairo. He is overwhelmed by the sights, sounds, and smells of the poverty-stricken area he must live in, but it's all worthwhile when he reaches the lecture halls and hears messages that sometimes bewilder him but always excite him.

Nothing dramatic happens in this story, by an Egyptian author, but it gives the flavor of life in a poor nation. Visualize the scenes: the crowded streets, alleys, and stairways near his lodgings; the more spacious rooms of the lecture halls. Share the experiences of the young student . . . and get a renewed appreciation of your own school setting.

from The Stream of Days

I

FOR THE FIRST TWO or three weeks of his stay in Cairo he was lost in bewilderment. All he knew was that he had left the country behind him and settled in the capital as a student attending lectures at the Azhar. It was more by imagination than by sense that he distinguished the three phases of his day.

Both the house he lived in and the path that led to it were strange and unfamiliar. When he came back from the Azhar he turned to the right through a gateway which was open during the daytime and shut at night; after evening prayer there was only a narrow opening left in the middle of the door. Once through it, he became aware of a gentle heat playing on his right cheek, and a fine smoke teasing his nostrils; while on the left he heard an odd gurgling sound which at once puzzled and delighted him.

For several days, morning and evening, he listened curiously to this sound, but lacked the courage to inquire what it might be. Then one day he gathered from a chance remark that it came from the bubbling of a *narghile*[1] smoked by tradesmen of the district. It was provided for them by the proprietor of the café from which the gentle heat and the fine smoke cloud issued.

He walked straight on for a few steps before crossing a damp, roofed-in space in which it was impossible to stand firmly because of the slops thrown there by the café proprietor. Then he came out into an open passageway; but this was narrow and filthy and full of strange, elusive smells, which were only moderately unpleasant early in the day and at nightfall, but as the day advanced and the heat of the sun grew stronger, became utterly intolerable.

He walked straight on through this narrow passage; but rarely did he find it smooth or easy. More often than not his friend would have to push him either this way or that so as to avoid some obstacle or other. Then he would continue in the new direction, feeling his way toward a house either to left or right, until he had passed the obstacle and taken the old direction again. He hurried along nervously at his companion's side, breathing the nauseous smells, and half-deafened by the medley of sounds that came from all sides at once, left and right, above and below,

[1]a water pipe, similar to a hookah

to meet in midair, where they seemed to unite above the boy's head, layer upon layer, into a single fine mist.

There was in fact a remarkable variety of sounds. Voices of women raised in dispute, of men shouting in anger or peaceably talking together; the noise of loads being set down or picked up; the song of the water carrier crying his wares; the curse of a carter to his horse or mule or donkey; the grating sound of cart wheels; and from time to time this confused whirl of sounds was torn by the braying of a donkey or the whinnying of a horse.

As he passed through this babel,[1] his thoughts were far away, and he was scarcely conscious of himself or of what he was doing; but at a certain point on the road he caught the confused sound of conversation through a half-open door on the left; then he knew that a pace or two further on he must turn to the left up a staircase which would bring him to his lodging.

It was an ordinary sort of staircase, neither wide nor narrow, and its steps were of stone; but since it was used very frequently in both directions, and no one troubled to wash or sweep it, the dirt piled up thickly and stuck together in a compact mass on the steps, so that the stone was completely covered up, and whether you were going up or coming down the staircase appeared to be made of mud.

Now whenever the boy went up or down a staircase he was obliged to count the steps. But long as were the years he stayed in this place, and countless the times he negotiated this staircase, it never occurred to him to count the number of its steps. He learned at the second or third time of climbing it that after going up a few steps he had to turn a little to the left before continuing his ascent, leaving on his right an opening through which he never penetrated, though he knew that it led to the first floor of the building in which he lived for so many years.

This floor was not inhabited by students, but by workers and tradesmen. He left the entrance to it on his right, and went on up to the second floor. There his harassed spirit found rest and relief; lungfuls of fresh air drove away the sense of suffocation with which he had been oppressed on that filthy staircase, and then too there was the parrot, whistling on without a break, as if to testify before all the world to the tyranny of her Persian master, who had imprisoned her in an abominable cage, and would sell her tomorrow or the day after to another man who would treat her in exactly the same way. And when he was rid of her and had laid hands on the cash, he would buy a successor for her who would be cooped up in the same prison pouring forth the same curses on her master, and waiting as her sister had waited to be passed on from hand

[1]scene of confusion

to hand, and from cage to cage, while everywhere she went that plaintive cry of hers would delight the hearts of men and women.

When our friend reached the top of the staircase he breathed in the fresh air that blew on his face, and listened to the voice of the parrot calling him toward the right. He obeyed, turning through a narrow corridor, past two rooms in which two Persians lived. One of these was still a young man, while the other was already past middle age. The one was as morose and misanthropic as the other was genial and good-natured.

At last the boy was home. He entered a room like a hall, which provided for most of the practical needs of the house. This led on to another room, large but irregular in shape, which served for social and intellectual needs. It was bedroom and dining room, reading room and study, and a room for conversation by day or by night. Here were books and crockery and food; and here the boy had his own particular corner, as in every room he occupied or visited at all frequently.

This place of his was on the left inside the door. After advancing a pace or two he found a mat spread on the ground, and above that an old but quite serviceable carpet. Here he sat in the daytime, and here he slept at night, with a pillow for his head and a rug to cover him. On the opposite side of the room was his elder brother's pitch, a good deal higher than his own. He had a mat spread on the ground, and a decent carpet on top of that, then a felt mattress, and above that a long, wide piece of bedding stuffed with cotton, and finally, crowning all, a coverlet. Here the young sheikh[1] would sit with his close friends. They were not obliged to prop up their backs against the bare wall, as the boy did, having cushions to pile up on the rugs. At night this couch was transformed into a bed on which the young sheikh slept.

II

THIS WAS ALL the boy ever learned about his immediate surroundings. The second phase of his life consisted in the tumultuous journey between his home and the Azhar. He went out through the covered passage till he felt the heat of the café on his left cheek, and heard the bubbling of the *narghile* on his right. In front of him was a shop which played an important part in his life; it belonged to El-Hagg Firûz, who supplied the neighborhood with most of the necessities of life. In the morning he sold boiled beans, prepared in the usual variety of ways. But El-Hagg Firûz used to boast the special virtues of his beans—and raise their prices accordingly. He had plain beans, beans in fat, beans in butter, beans in every kind of oil; he added, if required, all sorts of spices. As for the students,

[1]The word *sheikh* meant originally "old man" or "elder." In this translation it is used in two senses: (1) as more or less equivalent to *âlim*, "doctor," and so teacher at the Azhar; (2) "scholar" or aspirant to learning, as here.

they adored these beans, and often made far too large a meal of them. So by mid-morning they were already dull in the head, and at the noon lecture they slept.

When evening came El-Hagg Firûz sold his customers their supper: cheese, olives, milled sesame, or honey. To the more luxurious he supplied boxes of tuna or sardines. And to a few of them perhaps, as night approached, he sold things which have no name, and nothing to do with food, things spoken of in a whisper, yet passionately vied for.

The boy used to overhear these whisperings; sometimes he half understood, but as a rule the whole transaction was a mystery to him. As the days passed by and he grew older, he came to see through these subtle hints and ambiguities. What he learned then obliged him to overhaul his standards of judgment, and to revise his valuation both of people and of things.

El-Hagg Firûz held a unique position in the neighborhood and among the students especially. It was to him that they went when their money ran out toward the end of the month, or when their remittances were overdue. He it was who gave them food on credit, lent them a piaster or two from time to time, and helped them out in all kinds of emergencies. No wonder his name was as often on their lips as those of the most learned sheikhs of the Azhar.

But this was not all. El-Hagg Firûz was essential to the students in yet another way. It was to him that were addressed all the letters bringing them news of their families, or enclosing flimsy notes which they took to the post office with empty pockets, to return with the jingle of silver falling cheerily on their ears and into their very hearts.

Naturally not a single student missed an opportunity of passing the time of day morning and evening at El-Hagg Firûz' shop, or of casting a quick furtive glance at the spot where letters were waiting to be collected. How often one of them would go home grasping a sealed envelope which was spotted with oil and butter stains; yet despite its greasiness that envelope was more precious in his eyes than any composition or textbook on law, grammar or theology.

On leaving the covered passage, then, the boy found himself in front of El-Hagg Firûz' shop; his friend would take him a few paces in that direction to greet El-Hagg Firûz and to inquire if there was a letter for him or not; the reply would bring either smiles or frowns to his face. Then he turned away to the left, and walked straight forwards down the long narrow street crowded with passersby. It was full of students, merchants, tradesmen, laborers; carts drawn by donkeys, horses or mules; carters shouting out warnings or curses at the men, women or children blocking their path. Then on each side of the street were different kinds of shops, in many of which was prepared the meager diet of the poor. The smells that issued from them were abominable, but that did not prevent them from delighting most of the passersby, whether they were students, laborers or porters. Some of them turned aside to these shops and bought a scrap of food to gulp down on the spot, or take home and eat, either alone or with others. And some of them, assailed by this battery of smells, remained unmoved. They were tempted but did not yield. Their eyes saw, their nostrils smelled, their appetite was stirred; but, alas, their pockets were empty. They passed on with yearning in their souls and with bitterness and resentment in their hearts; yet at the same time they were content with their lot and accepted it with resignation.

In some other shops a quiet, unhurried trade was transacted, almost without any words passing at all. If anything was said, it was under the breath, so as scarcely to be heard. In spite of this—or perhaps for this very reason—the trade in question brought great wealth and prosperity to those who practiced it. To all appearances the majority of these shops dealt only in coffee and soap, though some of them also sold sugar and rice.

As he passed through all this a warm interest stirred in the boy. But he would have understood practically nothing had not his friend from time to time volunteered an explanation. He continued on his way, sometimes walking firmly forwards, sometimes swerving aside. When the road was clear he marched with a sure step, but stumbled and faltered on its edges when it was crowded or twisty. At last he came to a spot where he had to turn a little to the left and then plunge into a lane as narrow and crooked and filthy as could be. Its atmosphere was foul with an abominable medley of smells, and from time to time weak, hollow voices which reflected its misery and wrong echoed back cries for charity to the footfalls of passersby, begging at the sound of steps, as if life had only been perceptible through the ears. They were answered by other voices: the thin, harsh, strangled cries of those winged creatures which love darkness and desolation and ruins. Often enough these noises were accompanied by the flutter of wings, which sometimes, to his horror, shaved past his ear or his face. Instinctively his hand would fly up for protection, and for sometime afterwards his heart would be throbbing with apprehension.

On he walked with his friend along this narrow, dark, twisting alley, now rising, now descending, now going straight on, now turning to left or right. And all the time these loathsome sounds assailed him, sometimes from in front, and sometimes from behind, but never without dismaying him. After a time he felt his heart lighten and his lungs expand, and knew that the moment of release had come. He heaved one sigh of relief, loaded with all the weight of his anxiety and distress.

Now he breathed freely and easily, as if he were taking in great drafts of life from the fresh air which flowed over him as he left the bat-ridden alley. On he went along the road, which twisted treacherously under his feet for a few moments, then became firm again so that he could step forward easily and with confidence. His heart thrilled with joy at the strange harmony of sounds which came to his ears as he walked along the pleasant, peaceful street. On one side of him was the Mosque of Sayyidna-l-Hussein, and on the other a series of small shops. How often he would stop at one of these during the days that followed, and what good things he tasted there! Soaked figs and their juice in summertime, and in winter *bassbûssa*,[1] which diffused a warm glow of well-being through the body. Sometimes he would stop at a Syrian retailer's to choose from a variety of foods, hot or cold, salt or sweet. Their taste gave him inexpressible pleasure, yet if they were offered him now he would be afraid they might make him ill, or even poison him.

He continued along this street until he came to a place where the voices grew louder and more numerous. He realized that the roads divided here and that he could branch right or left, go straight on, or turn about. "Here are the crossroads," said his companion. "If you go right you reach the Sikka El-Gadida, then the Musky, then 'Ataba El-Khadra. To the left you have Sharia El-Darrâssa. But we must go straight on into Sharia El-Halwagi, the street of learning and hard work. It is so narrow that if you stretched out your arms left and right you could almost touch both walls. Now you are walking between a number of small bookshops. There are books of every kind in them, new and old, good and bad, in print of manuscript."

How many a pleasant and rewarding halt did our friend make in that narrow street, which remained fixed in his memory later on, after his life had changed its course.

But this time he must hurry past. His guide had to be at the Azhar before the lecture began. Here they were, arrived at the Barbers' Gate. He took off his sandals, laid them one on top of the other, then picked them up in his hand as he followed his companion. A little further on he stepped over a shallow threshold into the quiet courtyard of the Azhar, and felt a cool morning breeze blow refreshingly upon his face. And so he entered the third phase of this new life of his.

III

THIS THIRD PHASE of his existence was the one he loved best of all. In his own room he endured all the pains of exile. It was like a foreign country to him, and he never became familiar with its contents, except perhaps those nearest to him. He did not live in it in the same sense that he had lived in his country home or in other familiar rooms where nothing was unknown to him. He passed his days there in exile from people and things alike, and in such anguish of heart that the oppres-

[1]nut-cake of Syrian origin

sive air he breathed there brought him no rest or refreshment, but only heaviness and pain.

Nor was there any doubt of his preferring these hours in the Azhar to the agitated journey back and forth, whose hazards drove him almost to despair. It was not only his steps that were confused and unsteady; his very heart was overwhelmed by that unnerving perplexity which perverts a man's purposes and drives him blindly onwards, not only along the material road which he needs must follow, but also along the free paths of the mind, feckless and without a plan. Not only was he distracted by the hubbub and tumult that eddied around him. He was distressed at the unsteadiness of his walk and the impossibility of harmonizing his own quiet, faltering steps with the firm and even brutal pace of his companion.

It was only in the third phase of his day that he found rest and security. The fresh breeze that blew across the court of the Azhar at the hour of morning prayer met him with a welcome and inspired him with a sense of security and hope. The touch of this breeze on his forehead, damp with sweat from that feverish journey, resembled nothing so much as the kisses his mother used to give him during his early years, when he chanted verses from the Koran to her or entertained her with a story he had heard at the village school; or when, as a pale, delicate infant, he abandoned the corner in which he had been reciting the litany from the *sura* Ya-Sin to go and carry out some household task or other.

Those kisses revived his heart and filled him not only with tenderness but with hope and confidence. The breeze which welcomed him in the court of the Azhar, no less, brought rest after weariness, calm after tumult, a smile after gloomy looks. However, he as yet knew nothing of the Azhar, and had not the least idea what he would find there. But it was enough for him to brush with his bare feet the ground of that court, to feel on his face the caress of its morning breeze, and to realize that around him the Azhar was preparing to awake from its drowsiness, that its inertia would soon give place to activity. He began to recover consciousness of himself, as life returned to him. He felt the conviction of being in his own country, among his own people, and lost all sense of isolation, all sadness. His soul blossomed forth, and with every fiber of his being he yearned to discover . . . well, what? Something he was a stranger to, though he loved it and felt irresistibly drawn toward it—knowledge. How many times had he heard this word, and longed to find out its hidden meaning! His impression of it was vague enough, to be sure; but of this he was convinced, that knowledge had no limits and that people might spend their whole lives in acquiring a few drops of it. He too wished to devote his whole life to it and to win as much of it as he could, however little that might be. His father and the learned friends who came to visit him had spoken of knowledge as a boundless ocean, and the child had never taken this expression for a figure of speech or a metaphor, but as the simple truth. He had come to Cairo and to the Azhar with the intention of throwing himself into this ocean and drinking what he could of it, until the day he drowned. What finer end could there be for a man of spirit than to drown himself in knowledge? What a splendid plunge into the beyond!

All these thoughts suddenly thronged into his young spirit, filling it and taking possession of it, blotting out the memory of that desolate room, of the turbulent, twisty road, and even of the country and its delights. They convinced him that it was no mistake or exaggeration to be consumed with love for the Azhar as well as with regret for the country.

The boy paced on with his companion until he had crossed the court and mounted the shallow step which is the threshold of the Azhar itself. His heart was all modesty and humility, but his soul was filled with glory and pride. His feet stepped lightly over the worn-out mats that were laid out across the floor, leaving a bare patch here and there, as if on purpose to touch the feet which passed over them with something of the benediction attached to that holy ground. The boy used to love the Azhar at this moment, when worshipers were finishing their early-morning prayer and going away, with the marks of drowsiness still in their eyes, to make a circle round some column or other and wait for the teacher who was to give a lecture on tradition or exegesis, first principles or theology.[1]

At this moment the Azhar was quiet, and free from the strange intermingled murmurs that filled it from sunrise until evening prayer. You could only hear the whispered conversations of its inmates or the hushed but steady voice of some young man reciting the Koran. Or you might come upon a worshiper who had arrived too late for the common service, or had gone on to perform extra prayers after completing the statutory number. Or maybe you would hear a teacher beginning his lecture in the languid tone of a man who has awakened from sleep and said his prayers but has not yet eaten anything to give him strength and energy. He starts in a quiet, husky voice: "In the name of God, the merciful, the compassionate: Praise be to God, father of the worlds: May His peace and blessing be upon our lord Muhammad, the most noble of the prophets, upon his family and his companions. These are the words of the author of the Book, may God rest his soul and grant us the fruits of his learning. Amen!"

The students listened to the lecture with the same quiet languor in which it was given. There was a striking contrast between the different tones the sheikhs used at the early-morning and midday lectures. At dawn their voices were calm and gentle, with traces of drowsiness in them. At noon they were strong and harsh, but fraught too with a certain sluggishness induced by the lunch they had just eaten, the baked beans and pickles and so on which made up the usual fare of an Azharite at this time. At dawn

[1]These are the four primary subjects of the traditional Azharite course.

the voices seemed to beg humbly for favor from the great authorities of the past, while by noon they were attacking them almost as if they were adversaries. This contrast always astonished and delighted the boy.

On he went with his friend up the two steps leading into the *liwân*.[1] There beside one of those sacred pillars, to which a chair was bound by a great chain, our friend was deposited by his companion, who left him with these words: "Wait there and you will hear a lecture on tradition; when mine is over I will return and fetch you." His companion's lecture was on the first principles of Islamic law, given by Sheikh Râdy, God rest his soul. The textbook was the *Tahrîr* of El-Kemal Ibn El-Humam. When the boy heard this sentence, every word filled him at once with awe and curiosity. First principles of law? What science was this? Sheikh Râdy? Who could he be? *Tahrîr?* What was the meaning of this word? El-Kemal Ibn El-Humam? Could there be a more wonderful pair of names? How true it was that knowledge is a boundless ocean, full of unimaginable benefit for any thoughtful being who is ready to plunge into it. The boy's admiration for this lecture especially grew deeper every day as he listened to his brother and his brother's friends studying their lesson beforehand. What they read sounded very strange, but there was no doubt of its fascination.

As he listened the boy used to burn with longing to grow six or seven years older, so that he might be able to understand it, to solve its riddles and ambiguities, to be master of the whole subject as those distinguished young men were, and to dispute with the teachers about it as they did. But for the present he was compelled to listen without understanding. Time and again he would turn over some sentence or other in his mind on the chance of finding some sense in it. But he achieved nothing by all this, except perhaps a greater respect for knowledge and a deeper reverence for his teachers, together with modesty as to his own powers and a determination to work harder.

There was one sentence in particular. How many sleepless nights it cost him! How many days of his life it overcast! Sometimes it tempted him to miss an elementary lecture—for he had understood his first lessons without difficulty—and so led him on to playing truant from the sheikh's lecture on tradition, in order to speculate on what he had heard from the lips of those older students.

The sentence which took possession of him in this way was certainly a remarkable one. It would fall echoing in his ears as he lay on the threshold of sleep, and drag him back to a wakefulness which lasted all night through. This was the sentence: "Right is the negation of negation." What could these words mean? How could negation be negated? What might such negation be? And how could the negation of negation

[1] colonnade surrounding the central court of the mosque

be right? The sentence began to whirl round in his head like the ravings of delirium in a sick man's brain, until one day it was driven out of his mind by one of El-Kafrawy's *Problems.* This problem he understood at once and was able to argue about. Thus he came at last to feel that he had begun to taste the water of the boundless ocean of knowledge.

The boy sat beside the pillar, toying with the chain and listening to the sheikh on tradition. He understood him perfectly, and found nothing to criticize in his lesson except the cascade of names which he poured forth on his listeners in giving the source and authorities for each tradition. It was always "so-and-so tells us" or "according to so-and-so." The boy could not see the point of these endless chains of names, or this tedious tracing of sources. He longed for the sheikh to have done with all this and come down to the tradition itself. As soon as he did so the boy listened with all his heart. He memorized the tradition and understood it, but showed not the slightest interest in the sheikh's analysis, which reminded him too well of the explanations given by the Imam of the mosque in his country village and the sheikh who used to teach him the elements of law.

While the sheikh proceeded with his lesson the Azhar began gradually to wake up, as if stirred out of its torpor by the voices of the teachers holding forth, and by the discussions which arose between them and the students, amounting sometimes almost to quarrels. The students came closer, the voices rose higher, the echoes intermingled and the sheikhs raised their voices again, so that the students might be able to hear them, ever higher and higher, up to the final climax of the words "God is all-wise." For meanwhile other students had come up to wait for a lecture on law by another sheikh, or maybe the same one; so he had no choice but to end the early-morning lecture and begin the next. Then the boy's companion would return, take him by the hand without a word and drag him off all ungently to another place, where he dumped him like a piece of luggage and abandoned him again.

The boy realized that he had been transferred to the law class. He would listen to this lecture until it came to an end and both sheikhs and students went off. Then he would stay rooted to the spot until his friend came back from Sayyidna-l-Hussein, where he had been attending a lecture on law given by Sheikh Bakhît, God rest his soul.

Now Sheikh Bakhît was prolix in the extreme, and his students used to harass him with objections. So he never finished the lesson until the middle of the morning. Then the boy's companion would return to where he was, take him by the hand without a word and lead him out of the Azhar. And so back he went through the second phase along the road between the Azhar and his lodgings into the third and final phase, where he was left alone in his place in the corner on the old carpet stretched out over a rotten worn-out mat.

Reading for Understanding

Main Idea

1. The main point of the story is (a) the sights and sounds of a crowded inner city (b) a boy's thirst for knowledge (c) a greedy tradesperson (d) a hopeless situation.

Details

2. The first portion of the story describes in detail the boy's (a) return to his lodgings (b) stay at the school (c) departure for the school (d) reactions to the lectures.
3. The smells in the narrow, filthy passageway (a) were strongest in the morning (b) were almost universally pleasant (c) reminded the boy of home (d) were most unpleasant in the heat.
4. The filthiest part of his dwelling was (a) the gateway (b) the study (c) the staircase (d) his own room.
5. The boy owed a special debt to (a) the two Persians (b) the owner of the parrot (c) the mayor of Cairo (d) his friend.

Inferences

6. The impression given by the neighborhood in which the boy lived was that of (a) intellectual curiosity (b) poverty (c) elegance (d) protest.
7. The story is being told (a) as a reminiscence in later years (b) to criticize the lecturers at the Azhar (c) to warn others of the problems of Egyptian education (d) in the form of an extended letter.
8. The boy disapproved of (a) his brother (b) his friend's interference in his life (c) teaching by just pouring forth names (d) the custom of removing shoes on entering the Azhar.
9. The style of the story is (a) indifferent and uninvolved (b) bitter and pessimistic (c) frivolous and rigid (d) calm and factual.

Fact or Opinion

Tell whether the following is a fact or an opinion.

10. Conditions in the boy's home area were unlivable.

Words in Context

1. "There was the parrot, whistling on without a break, as if to testify before all the world to the tyranny of her Persian master, who had imprisoned her in an *abominable* cage." **Abominable** (594) means (a) disgusting (b) narrow (c) strong metal (d) carelessly constructed.
2. "Everywhere she went that *plaintive* cry of hers would delight the hearts of men and women." **Plaintive** (595) means (a) loud (b) chattering (c) mournful (d) repeated.

3., 4. "The one was as *morose* and *misanthropic* as the other was genial and good-natured." **Morose** (595) means (a) cruel (b) gloomy (c) nervous (d) thoughtful. **Misanthropic** (595) means (a) misunderstood (b) quiet and reserved (c) disbelieving (d) unsociable.

5. "The second phase of his life consisted in the *tumultuous* journey between his home and the Azhar." **Tumultuous** (595) means (a) turbulent (b) long and boring (c) daily (d) enjoyable.
6. "Naturally not a single student missed an opportunity . . . of casting a quick *furtive* glance at the spot where letters were waiting to be collected." **Furtive** (596) means (a) unashamed (b) secret (c) longing (d) conspicuous.
7. "They were content with their lot and accepted it with *resignation*." **Resignation** (597) means (a) despair (b) disapproval (c) surrender (d) high spirits.

8., 9. And all the time these *loathsome* sounds *assailed* him, sometimes from in front, and sometimes from behind, but never without dismaying him." **Loathsome** (597) means (a) loud and constant (b) unexpected (c) disgusting (d) harmonious. **Assailed** (597) means (a) amused (b) stimulated (c) wearied (d) attacked.

10. "He passed his days there in exile from people and things alike and in such *anguish* of heart that the oppressive air he breathed there brought him no rest or refreshment, but only heaviness and pain." **Anguish** (598) means (a) distress (b) tightness (c) alertness (d) death.
11. "His heart was all modesty and *humility*, but his soul was filled with glory and pride." **Humility** (600) means (a) fury (b) humbleness (c) wonder (d) mirth.
12. "Or maybe you would hear a teacher beginning his lecture in the *languid* tone of a man who has awakened from sleep and said his prayers

but has not yet eaten anything to give him strength and energy." **Languid** (600) means (a) oppressive (b) unattractive (c) listless (d) curious.

13. "By noon they were attacking them almost as if they were *adversaries.*" **Adversaries** (601) are (a) unbelievers (b) criminals (c) monsters (d) enemies.
14. "The Azhar began gradually to wake up, as if stirred out of its *torpor* by the voices of the teachers holding forth." **Torpor** (602) means (a) debate (b) sluggishness (c) exercises (d) disagreements.
15. "Now Sheikh Bakhit was *prolix* in the extreme, and his students used to harass him with objections." **Prolix** (602) means (a) belligerent (b) unpleasant (c) inconsistent (d) wordy.

Thinking Critically About the Selection

1. This selection is a masterpiece of vivid description. The author captures the setting by appealing to the senses of smell, taste, sight, and sound. Point out some of the vivid descriptions that bring the setting to life.
2. Was El-Hagg Firûz a good influence, a friend of the students? Explain.
3. Did the boy love learning for learning's sake? Point to the story to prove your point.
4. How did the boy react to all the difficulties he faced in seeking to get an education?
5. The author talks about the three phases of the boy's life. What were they?
6. Does the method of lecture and challenge seem like a good one to you? Why or why not?
7. "How many a pleasant and rewarding halt did our friend make in that narrow street, which remained fixed in his memory later on, after his life had changed its course."

   Do you think the author is talking about his own boyhood? If so, why would he choose the third person (336) instead of the first person to tell the story?

Language in Action

Antonyms

> At dawn their voices were calm and gentle, with traces of drowsiness in them. At noon, they were strong and harsh.

Calm and *gentle* are here contrasted with *strong* and *harsh.* A pair like *gentle* and *harsh* are called *antonyms:* words opposed in meaning. The roots distinguish them:

anti—against	*onym*—name
syn—with, together	*onym*—name

Antonyms are extremely useful. They help us to define: for example, *discordant* means *not harmonious.* They enrich our speech by introducing contrasts: "India is a land of unbelievable *poverty* and *wealth.*" They help us to build vocabularies; for example, we can remember easily what *humility* means if we recall it is the opposite of *pride.*

Many common expressions include pairs of opposites: *feast* or *famine, thick* or *thin, friend* or *foe, ups* and *downs, win* or *lose.* A word may have both a synonym and an antonym. *Banquet,* for example, is a synonym of *feast,* an antonym of *fasting.*

Since words have different meanings in different contexts, a single word may have many antonyms. *Clear* is such a word. We may talk about a *clear* day, a *clear* conscience, or a *clear* style of writing. Obviously one antonym will not do for all of these. The antonym of the first might be *overcast* or *cloudy.* Of the second it might be *troubled.* Of the third it might be *confused.*

Lucero

Oscar Castro Z.
Chilean

In fact, this pass was one of the most impressive in the mountain chain. The path at that point was only eighty centimeters wide, just enough to let an animal get by between the stone wall and the abrupt drop. One false step . . . and that would be the end till Judgment Day.

Rarely does a setting play a more important role in a story than in "Lucero." The towering Andes mountains with their snow-clad peaks and awesome abysses, are at the very heart of the story, a tale of a mountain guide and his beloved horse Lucero.

Ruben must catch up with four companions, who left the ranch an hour before him. The trail is treacherous, as the quotation vividly makes clear, but Ruben has his old friend, his horse Lucero, who has traveled the mountains with him for many years. The two face Vulture's Pass, whose name suggests its soaring height. Then, the unexpected happens. Ruben and Lucero are not alone.

Few stories set the stage so briefly and skillfully for the shattering climax. Few people have had to make a decision so quickly and painfully as Ruben. You will not soon forget the gallant Lucero and his loving master in this tale by a Chilean author.

Lucero

OUTLINED ONE AGAINST THE OTHER, the crests of the mountain chain seemed shuffled like a deck of stony cards as far as Ruben Olmos' eyes could travel. Dazzling white peaks, bluish dips, upjutting points arose before his gaze, constantly shifting, more inaccessible as the traveler mounted. Before starting on an abrupt and tiring descent, he decided to give a rest to his mount panting like bellows. During the pause, he crossed his left leg over the saddle and let his eyes wander down toward the valley. The first thing that attracted his gaze was the mirrorlike glitter of the river stretching with reluctance its capricious windings among pastures and filled fields. Then his view shifted over beyond some rectangular enclosures, and sought the village he had left that morning. There it was framed in the distance like the toys in a shop window with its tiny houses and the dim ravines of its streets. A few zinc plate roofs darted back the sun's brilliance, cutting the air with streaks of violent silvery radiance.

With a flutter of his eyelids Ruben Olmos rubbed out the picture of the valley and now examined his mount, whose damp flanks rose and fell in rhythmical movement.

"So you're getting old, Lucero?" he asked in an affectionate tone. And the animal, as if it understood, turned toward him its face, black with a white star on its forehead.

"Well, it's a sure thing that you have worked plenty, but you have many years of travel ahead of you yet. At least, while there are still some mountains around here."

He turned to gaze at the Andean massiveness, familiar and friendly to him and Lucero. They hadn't crossed and recrossed it for nothing during these eleven years. Ruben Olmos, a bit dazzled by the white blaze of the sun on the snow, thought of his travel comrades and of the lead they had over him. But he didn't pay much attention to this detail, for he was certain he would overtake them before nightfall.

"So long as you go along with me, we won't have to spend the night alone," he declared to his horse, finishing his thought.

Ruben Olmos was an experienced mountain guide. He had learned his difficult art from his father who had taken him along even as a child over these precipices and ravines in spite of his unwillingness and the mistrust that the mountains at first had roused in him. When the old man had died, peacefully in his bed, the ranch owner had appointed the young man as successor. He had crossed at least a hundred times this mountain barrier which, in his young days, had seemed to him impassable, and had led over numerous herds of cattle from Cuyó, always with good luck on his side.

He chose Lucero when the animal was still a frisking colt and had broken him in himself. After that the rider had never been willing to use another mount although his boss had presented him with two other horses apparently more powerful and from better breeds. Lucero had become for him a mascot to which he clung with a sort of superstition induced by a hazardous life.

The guide, accustomed to the epic struggle against the elements, loved danger more than women. With instinctive wisdom he centered his devotion on a beast, perhaps with the feeling that from it he need expect no rebuff or treason. If some day he were asked to choose between losing his brother or Lucero, he would hesitate before making up his mind, because this creature, more than a mere conveyance, inspired in him from the beginning the feeling of a friend. He was in a sense an extension of his own being, as if the push of his muscles flowed into the tendons of Lucero.

Ruben Olmos was born with flesh fashioned out of hard substance. He felt life in a rush of tides throbbing along the passages of his being. On horseback he was always the leader, not one to be led. And this energy needed space to exert itself; no place could seem more favorable or more adapted to his talents than the tumultuous heights of the Andes.

If observed superficially, the guide looked like an ordinary fellow. At the best, he gave the impression of self-confidence. His coppery skin and flattened nose evoked the Indian in his ancestry. His smile had no brightness, it was dimmed by his eyes, at most it gleamed momentarily at the edge of his teeth. A herdsman amidst solitudes, he had learned from them silence and penetration. He had a deeper tie with Lucero than with human beings. It must have been because the horse did not answer, or because he always said "yes" with his loving moist eyes. There was no telling.

"Fine, now we must be moving."

Setting his iron shoes into the cracks, the horse ascended toward heaven. The rider, bent forward, moved with the rhythmic sway of each step. Pebbles rolled down into the depths and the rings on the reins tinkled. And Lucero—toc, toc, toc—was finally there on the crest after toiling upwards for a quarter-hour.

Upon the heights the wind flowed more constant, bearing more cold moisture. It glided over the face of the guide. It sought some opening in his cloak, in order to grasp it with its teeth. However, long practice made this man safe from its attack, and although the blast persisted, it did not succeed in altering his course.

With several crests of mountains crossed, the valley was no longer visible. There were hills ahead, toward which the eye looked. And above stretched a thin sky, pure, more blue than the cold of the wind, hardly speckled by the flashing flight of an eagle, sole possessor of this unattainable space.

The loneliness of the heights was so immense, so clearly desolate, that the traveler sometimes had the swift impression of drowning in the wind, as if he were swirling in the depths of treacherous waters. But this man did not have time to admire the magnificent stretches of the landscape. The atmosphere, like a transparent bubble, the deep orchestral tones of the verdure,[1] the symphony of birds and insects which mounted upwards in delicate surges—none of these things found an echo in his spirit, formed as it was out of the dark substances of struggle and decision.

From a rise which gave a clear view of the near-by heights, Ruben Olmos scanned the path in the hope of seeing those who had gone ahead of him. But he perceived nothing but emptiness during this exploration. The man pursed his lips. The four companions who had left the ranch an hour ahead of him had gained quite a lead. He would have to press his horse.

On he went past the familiar landmarks, the Lion's Cave, the Condor's Perch, the Black Gap. "My comrades must be waiting for me in the Muleteer Shelter," he thought, and sank his spurs into Lucero's ribs.

The path was hardly more than a vague track from whose line other eyes less experienced than his might stray. But Ruben Olmos couldn't go wrong. This slight rut over which he was traveling was, for him, a wide and spacious thoroughfare leading to one goal: the pueblo of Cuyó.

As he reached higher land, vegetation became tougher and more twisted to resist the attacks of the storms. Hawthorn, rosemary, sharp-edged cactus loomed up like dark splashes of a painter's brush against the pale snow. The solitudes began to get whiter and deeper, clothed with a dignified serenity. Ruben Olmos imagined that it was five o'clock in the afternoon. The sun, already slipping into the West, was struggling to sift its warmth through the wind.

The setting suddenly changed as the horse of the guide emerged into an immense stadium of stone. Two enormous mountains framed it, each with its half parenthesis circling a crevice whose depths could not be plumbed. It seemed as if an immense cataclysm had severed the mountain chain at a blow.

The rider stopped Lucero. The Vulture Pass exerted a strange fascination on his mind. When he was fifteen and had crossed it for the first

[1]green vegetation

time, he had had a whim to look down into it in spite of his father's warning, and after a moment he had noticed that the ravine began to whirl around like a blue funnel. Something like an invisible claw was pulling him into the abyss and he was letting himself go. Fortunately his father had observed the danger and shouted, "Turn your head around, you fool!" From that time on, in spite of all his calm control, he had not dared to let his gaze wander down that unfathomable depth.

Moreover, the Vulture's Pass had its legends. No herd of cattle could cross it on Good Friday, without some terrible misfortune. It was his father who had given him this information, illustrating with stories of various incidents when cattle or horses had been swallowed up in some mysterious way by this chasm.

In fact, this pass was one of the most impressive in the mountain chain. The path at that point was only eighty centimeters[1] wide, just enough to let an animal get by between the stone wall and the abrupt drop. One false step . . . and that would be the end till Judgment Day.

Before venturing along that shelf suspended who knew how many feet above the depth, Ruben Olmos complied scrupulously with the agreement established among those who crossed the mountains: he took his pistol out of his holster and fired two shots into the air to give warning to any possible traveler that the route was being used and that he was to wait. The explosions sent their waves into the clear air. They rebounded against the rocks and returned multiplied to the ears of the guide. After a little pause, the rider decided to resume his journey. Lucero, carefully setting his iron shoes on the rocky road was apparently unaware of any change in the aspect of the route. "Splendid horse!" mused the rider, summing up in these words all his affection for the animal.

Ruben Olmos will never be able to forget what was about to happen. Upon emerging from an abrupt turn, his heart gave one wild leap in his breast. From the opposite direction, less than twenty paces away, appeared a man mounted on a dark sorrel-colored nag. Amazement, frustration, and anger flashed across the faces of the travelers. Both, with an instinctive pull, reined in their horses. The first to break the anguished silence was the rider on the sorrel. After a growling curse, he shouted, "And how did you ever presume to start on this way without giving warning?"

Ruben Olmos knew that mere words would not help. He kept on advancing till the heads of the two horses almost touched. Then in a quiet firm voice that seemed to come from way down in his chest, he said, "It was you, my friend, who didn't give the signal shots."

The other drew his revolver and Ruben did likewise, with a promptness unsuspected in him. They looked at each other fixedly for a moment, with a spark of defiance in their eyes. The stranger had steely

[1]a little over 30 inches

cold eyes and features that betrayed will-power and decisiveness. In his aspect, his assurance, he revealed that he was a mountaineer accustomed to danger. Both realized that they were worthy adversaries.

Ruben Olmos finally decided to prove that he was in the right. Grasping his weapon with the barrel pointed to the abyss so as not to arouse distrust, he drew out the bullets, presenting a pair of empty cartridges.

"Here are my two shots," he declared.

The stranger imitated him, likewise offering as proof two leadless shells.

"Tough luck, my friend; we fired at the same time," declared the guide.

"That's how it was, comrade. And now what are we going to do?"

"As for going back, it just can't be done."

"Well then, one of us will have to get along on foot."

"Yes, that's so, but which one of us?"

"Luck will have to decide that."

And without any other comment the sorrel rider took a coin out of his pocket, and put it between his two hands without looking.

"You say which," he said.

There was a terrible hesitation in Ruben's mind. Those two clamped hands which he beheld hid the secret of an unalterable verdict. They represented more power than all the laws written by men. Fate would speak through them in its inexorable, impartial voice. And, as Ruben Olmos never defied the decrees of uncertain Fate, he pronounced the word that someone whispered in his brain.

"Heads!"

The other then slowly uncovered the coin and the oblique afternoon sun lit up a laurel wreath circling a sickle and hammer: Ruben had lost. He did not betray by the slightest gesture his inner dismay. His eyes turned softly and slowly toward the head and neck of Lucero. Presently, his hand gestured the caress that burst from his heart. And finally, as if to free himself from the fatality bearing down on him, he let himself drop to the path over the shining croup of his horse. He untied the gun and the provision-bag attached to the saddle. Then he slipped off the blanket roll resting on the animal's haunch. And all this slowly created between the two men a silence more dreadful than the Andean solitude.

During these preparations, the stranger seemed to suffer as much as the loser. Pretending to see nothing, he was busy braiding and unbraiding the thongs of his whip. Ruben Olmos was deeply grateful to him for this feigned indifference. When his painful work was done, he said to the other in a voice which preserved an inexpressibly desperate firmness, "Did you happen to meet four herdsmen with two mules on the way?"

"Yes, they're resting at the Refuge. Are they your companions?"

"Yes, it happens they are."

Lucero, perhaps surprised to be freed from the saddle in such an inappropriate spot, turned his head, and Ruben gazed for a moment upon his eyes, gentle as dark pools. The star on his forehead. His ears erect. His nostrils quivering. To gather his determination, Ruben uttered into the air in a voice laden with secret sorrow, "Keep a close rein on your beast, friend."

The other pulled in the reins, turning the head of his sorrel toward the rocky wall.

Only then Ruben Olmos, his heart dissolved in agony, lightly patted Lucero's neck once more, and with an immense shove sent him rolling into the abyss.

Reading for Understanding

Main Idea

1. The main idea of the story can best be summed up in the phrase (a) mountain problems (b) a faithful friend lost (c) careless planning (d) an act of evil.

Details

2. Ruben and Lucero had worked together (a) since the previous spring (b) six years (c) eleven years (d) for half of Ruben's lifetime.
3. Ruben (a) was trying to reach four companions (b) planned to return to the ranch the next day (c) dreaded crossing the Andes (d) took Lucero along as a last thought.
4. All the following are mentioned as part of the Andes mountains EXCEPT (a) Lion's Cave (b) Eagle's Nest (c) Black Gap (d) Condor's Perch.
5. Ruben fired two shots to (a) prove his manhood (b) try to bring down a deer (c) warn that he was crossing the Pass (d) break the boredom.

Inferences

6. If Ruben were asked to choose between Lucero and his brother, he'd (a) be almost persuaded by his love for Lucero (b) immediately

choose his brother as his closest friend (c) refuse to answer such a foolish question (d) choose Lucero without another thought.

7. Apparently, the two men (a) were convinced the other was dishonest (b) hadn't heard the others' shots (c) decided to return the way they had come (d) fought hand to hand.
8. The laurel wreath on the coin indicated that (a) there was still glory in Ruben's decision (b) the coin was not a perfect one (c) Ruben had made a lucky decision (d) the coin was tails.
9. Ruben felt that the outcome (a) proved his own manhood (b) was fate (c) left the other traveler untouched (d) was somehow dishonest.

Fact or Opinion

Tell whether the following is a fact or an opinion.

10. One of the animals had to die.

Words in Context

1. "Dazzling white peaks, bluish dips, upjutting points arose before his gaze, constantly shifting, more *inaccessible* as the traveler mounted." **Inaccessible** (608) means (a) unreachable (b) invisible (c) unsettling (d) uninviting.
2. "The first thing that attracted his gaze was the mirror-like glitter of the river stretching with reluctance its *capricious* windings among pastures and tilled fields." **Capricious** (608) means (a) gradual (b) striking (c) erratic (d) picturesque.
3. "With instinctive wisdom he centered his devotion on a beast, perhaps with the feeling that from it he need expect no *rebuff* or treason." **Rebuff** (609) means (a) repetition (b) disagreement (c) illness (d) rejection.
4. "The solitudes began to get whiter and deeper, clothed with a dignified *serenity*." **Serenity** (610) means (a) intensity (b) vividness (c) tranquility (d) abundance of color.
5. "It seemed as if an immense *cataclysm* had severed the mountain chain at a blow." A **cataclysm** (610) is a (a) violent upheaval (b) strong thunderstorm (c) blizzard with hail (d) giant.

6. "Ruben Olmos complied *scrupulously* with the agreement established among those who crossed the mountains." **Scrupulously** (611) means (a) reluctantly (b) precisely (c) willingly (d) undoubtfully.
7. "The first to break the *anguished* silence was the rider on the sorrel." **Anguished** (611) means (a) embarrassed (b) hostile (c) long (d) tortured.
8. "Grasping his weapon with the barrel pointed to the *abyss* so as not to arouse distrust, he drew out the bullets, presenting a pair of empty cartridges." An **abyss** (612) is a (a) pleasant valley (b) deep gorge (c) gentle slope (d) lofty peak.

Thinking Critically About the Story

1. How does the author emphasize the closeness between Ruben and Lucero? How does this make the final tragedy stronger?
2. Show how the author suggests that the other traveler keenly feels the tragedy that is about to unfold.
3. How does the author build suspense, leading to the final event?
4. Why was Ruben grateful to the other traveler for his "feigned indifference"?
5. What descriptive touches suggest that the author himself loved the mountains?
6. How does the following sentence show irony (14–15)?

   "Well, it's a sure thing that you have worked plenty, but you have many years of travel ahead of you yet."

7. What incredible coincidence necessitated the tragic decision?

Language in Action

E-Prime

> The loneliness of the heights was so immense, so clearly desolate, that the traveler sometimes had the swift impression of drowning in the wind.

The word *is* in all its forms has come in for criticism from students of language, especially when it passes subjective judgments (166) as in "Adrienne is too vain." A form of writing, called *E-Prime,* has been devised to eliminate *is* in its many forms.

If the quoted text sentence had been written in E-Prime, it might have looked like this: "The immense and desolate loneliness of the heights sometimes gave the traveler the swift impression of drowning in the wind." Because the original sentence communicated the picture effectively, the E-Prime sentence may not strike you as a great improvement. Sometimes, though, the recast sentence makes a point directly, clearly, and more objectively:

> With *is:* The ant is an excellent preacher because she is not talkative.

> Without *is:* None preaches better than the ant, and she says nothing.

Convenience will probably not eliminate *is* and other linking verbs from the language. But occasionally trying to write and speak in E-Prime sharpens perceptions and gives users additional awareness of the ways in which language may mislead us.

Except for quoted passages and the word *is* used as an example, this section has been written in E-Prime. Did you notice?

Bontshe the Silent

Isaac Peretz
Polish

"Gentlemen judges," begins a strident, incisive, and stinging voice—but stops short.

"Gentlemen," he begins again, this time more softly but once more he interrupts himself.

And at last, very soft, a voice issues from the throat of the accuser:

"Gentlemen judges! He was silent! I shall be silent too."

"Bontshe the Silent" begins in tears and ends in joy and laughter. In his lifetime, Bontshe was a lost soul. Few knew and no one cared that he existed. He lived a simple life as a poor man—not a giant of intellect or a powerful leader of others. He was merely "Bontshe the Silent."

On his death, Bontshe appears before the heavenly tribunal for judging. What does this poor soul have to offer in his own behalf? By most of the standards of the world, Bontshe is a failure. What can he expect from the tribunal where there can be no delusion, no deception, no pretense, no self-promotion?

This lovely fanciful tale was written in Yiddish by the Polish author Isaac Peretz. It raises questions about what is "most worth," how a person should be judged. It uses a trial to determine whether Bontshe will receive in heaven the kind of mistreatment and negative evaluation he suffered on earth.

The story has been cited for its perfect example of a "characteristic last act." Even in heaven, it seems, Bontshe is still Bontshe.

Bontshe the Silent

HERE, IN THIS WORLD below, the death of Bontshe produced no impression whatever. In vain you will ask: "Who was Bontshe? How did he live? What did he die of? Was it his heart that burst, his strength that gave out, or his dorsal spine that broke under a burden too heavy for his shoulders?" No one knows. Maybe it was hunger that killed him.

Had a dray horse fallen dead in the street, people would have displayed much more interest than they did in this case of a poor man. The newspapers would have reported the incident, and some of us would have hurried to the spot to look at the carcass and examine the place where the accident had occurred. But were there as many horses as there were men—a thousand millions—then even a horse would not have received such distinction.

Bontshe had lived quietly, and quietly died; like a shadow he passed over the face of the earth. When he celebrated his confirmation he made no brilliant speech. He lived, a grain of sand on the sea shore, among the millions of its kind. And when the wind at last carried him off to the other side, no one noticed it. In his life-time the dust of the roads kept no impression of his footsteps, and after his death the wind swept away the small board over his grave. The grave-digger's wife found it at some distance from the grave and made a fire with it to boil a pot of potatoes. Three days after Bontshe's death you would ask the grave-digger in vain to show you the spot where he had buried him.

Had there been a tombstone over Bontshe's grave, a learned archaeologist might have discovered it after a century, and once more the name of Bontshe would have been heard among us. He was only a shadow. No head or heart preserved his image, and no trace remained of his memory.

He left behind neither child nor property. He had lived miserably, and miserably he died. Had it not been for the noise of the crowd, someone might, by accident, have heard how Bontshe's vertebral column was snapping under a too heavy burden. Had the world had more time, someone might have noticed that during his life Bontshe's eyes were already dim and his cheeks terribly hollow. He might have noticed that even when he was not carrying loads on his shoulders his head was always bent to the ground, as if he were looking for his grave. Had there been as few poor people as there are horses someone might, perhaps, have asked: "What has become of Bontshe?"

When they took him to the hospital, Bontshe's corner in his basement hovel did not for long remain unoccupied; ten people of his kind were already waiting for it, and they knocked it down among themselves to the highest bidder. When they carried him from his hospital bed to the mortuary chamber, twenty poor patients were already waiting for the place vacated. And scarcely had Bontshe left the morgue, when twenty corpses extricated from underneath the ruins of a fallen house were brought in.

Who knows how long he will remain undisturbed in his grave? Who knows how many corpses are already waiting for the piece of ground he is buried in? Born quietly, he lived in silence, died in silence, and was buried in a silence even greater.

But it was not thus that things happened in the *other* world. There, the death of Bontshe produced a deep impression, a veritable sensation. The bugle-call of the Messiah, the sound of the ram's horn, was heard throughout the seven heavens: "Bontshe the Silent has died." Broad-winged archangels were flying about, announcing to each other that Bontshe had been summoned to appear before the Supreme Judgment Seat. In Paradise there was a noise, an excitement, and one could hear the joyful shout: "Bontshe the Silent! Just think of it! Bontshe the Silent!"

Very young angels, with eyes of diamond, gold-threaded wings, wearing silver slippers, were rushing out, full of joy, to meet Bontshe. The buzzing of their wings, the clatter of their small slippers, and the merry laughter of those dainty, fresh, and rosy little mouths, filled the heavens and reached the throne of the Most High. God himself knew that Bontshe was coming—

The Patriarch Abraham stationed himself at the gate of heaven, stretching out his right hand to Bontshe in cordial welcome: "Peace be with you," a sweet smile illuminating his delighted old countenance.

What means this rumbling and rolling here in heaven? Two angels were rolling an armchair of pure gold for Bontshe. Whence this luminous flash of light? It was a golden crown, set with the most precious stones, that they were carrying—for Bontshe!

"But the Supreme Court has not yet pronounced judgment?" ask the astonished saints, not without a tinge of jealousy.

"Bah!" reply the angels, "that will only be a formality. Against Bontshe, even the attorney for the prosecution himself will not find a word to say. The case will not last five minutes. Don't you know who Bontshe is? He is of some importance, this Bontshe."

When the little angels seized Bontshe in mid air and played a sweet tune to him; when the Patriarch Abraham shook hands with him as if he had been an old comrade; when he learned that his chair was ready for him in Paradise and that a crown was waiting for his head, that before the Celestial Tribunal not one superfluous word would be spoken in his case, Bontshe, as once upon earth, was frightened into silence. He was sure that it could only be a dream from which he would soon awake, or simply a mistake.

He was used to both. More than once, when he was still on earth, he had dreamed of picking up money from the ground. Veritable treasures were lying there!—and yet—when he awoke in the morning, he was more miserable and poorer than ever. More than once it had happened to him that someone in the street had smiled at him and spoken a kind word to him. But when he found out his mistake, the stranger turned and spat out in disgust, full of contempt. "Just my luck," thought Bontshe, scarcely daring to raise his eyes, afraid lest the dream should disappear. He trembles at the thought of suddenly waking up in some horrible cavern full of serpents and lizards. He is careful not to let the slightest sound escape his mouth, to stir or move a limb for fear of being recognized and hurled into the abyss. He trembles violently, and does not hear the compliments paid him by the angels, nor does he notice how they are dancing around him. He pays no heed to the Patriarch's cordial "Peace be with you," nor does he even wish good-morning to the celestial court when he is at last brought in. He is simply beside himself with fear.

His fear increased greatly when his eyes involuntarily fell upon the flooring of the Supreme Court of Justice. It was of pure alabaster, inset with diamonds. "And my feet," thought Bontshe, "are treading such a floor!" He grew quite rigid. "Who knows," he thought, "what rich man, what Rabbi, what saint they are expecting? He will soon arrive and mine will be a sad end!"

Terror-stricken, he did not even hear the President of the Court call out in a loud voice: "The case of Bontshe the Silent!" He did not hear how, handing over a dossier to the counsel for the defence, he commanded: "Read, but briefly." All around Bontshe the whole hall seemed to be turning. A muffled noise reached his ears, but in the midst of the din he began to distinguish more clearly and sharply the voice of the angelic advocate—a voice as sweet as a violin:

"His name," the voice was saying, "suited him even as a gown made by an artist's hand suits a graceful body."

"What is he talking about?" Bontshe asks himself. And then he heard an impatient voice interrupting the speaker:

"No metaphors, please."

"Never," continues the advocate, "never has he uttered a complaint against God or men. Never has a spark of hatred flamed up in his eyes, never has he lifted his eyes with pretensions to heaven."

Again Bontshe fails to understand what it is all about, but once more the stern voice interrupts the speaker:

"No rhetoric, please."

"Job succumbed, but Bontshe has suffered more than Job."

"Facts, bare facts, please," the President emphatically calls again.

"He was always silent," the advocate proceeds, "even when his mother died and at the age of thirteen there came a stepmother, a serpent, a wicked woman."

"Perhaps after all he means me," thinks Bontshe to himself.

"No insinuations, please, against third persons," angrily says the President.

"She used to begrudge him a piece of bread; throw him a few musty crusts three days old and a mouthful of gristle for meat, whilst she herself drank coffee with cream."

"Come to business!" cries the President.

"She never spared him her fingernails, blows, or cuffs, and through the holes of his miserable musty rags there peeped out the blue and black body of the child. Barefooted he used to chop wood for her in winter, in the biting frost. His hands were too young and too weak to wield the dull ax, and the blocks were too big. More than once did he sprain his wrists, more than once were his feet frozen, but he remained silent. He was silent even before his father—"

"Oh, yes, the drunkard," laughs the accusing attorney, and Bontshe feels cold all over.

"Even to his father he never complained," the advocate concludes.

"He was always miserable and alone, had no friends, no schooling, no religious instruction, no decent clothes and not a minute of respite."

"Facts, facts," the President once more interrupts.

"He was silent even later, when his own father, the worse for drink, seized him by the hair and threw him out of the house on a bitterly cold and snowy winter night. He picked himself up from the snow, without weeping, and ran whither his eyes carried him. He was silent during his lonely walk, and when the pangs of hunger began to torture him, he begged only with his eyes.

"On a wet and foggy spring night he reached a large town. He entered it like some drop of water that is falling into the ocean, but he nevertheless passed his first night in the police jail. He was silent, without asking the why or wherefore. Set free, he started to look for work, for the hardest work possible; but he was silent. What was even harder than work itself, was the finding of it, and he was silent. He was always silent. Splashed by the mud thrown at him by strangers, spat upon by strangers, driven with his heavy load from the sidewalk into the midst of the road, among cabs, cars, coaches, and vehicles of every sort—at every instant looking death in the face, he remained silent. Bathed in a cold sweat, crushed under the heavy loads he was carrying, his stomach empty and tortured, he was silent.

"He never calculated how many pounds he was carrying for a farthing, how often he stumbled for a penny and how many errands he had to run, how many times he almost breathed his last when going to collect his pay. He was always silent. He never dared to raise his voice when asking for his pay, but like a beggar or a dog he stood at the door and his dumb and humble request could only be read in his eyes. 'Come later,' he was told, and he disappeared like a shadow until later, when he would ask even more quietly, nay *beg* for his due. He was silent even when people haggled over his pay, knocked off something from it, or slipped a counterfeit coin into his hand. He was always silent!"

"Then after all it is me that they mean," Bontshe consoles himself.

"One wonderful day Bontshe's fortune changed," proceeded the advocate, after taking a drink of water. "Two spirited, frightened, runaway horses were rushing by, dragging a rich coach with rubber wheels. With a broken skull the driver lay way back on the pavement. Foam was spurting from the mouths of the animals, sparks flew from their hoofs, and their eyes shone like glowing coals on a dark night. In the coach, there sat a man, more dead than alive. Bontshe stopped the runaway horses. The man whose life he had thus saved was a Jew; he proved to be of a charitable disposition and was grateful to Bontshe. He handed over to him the whip of his dead coachman, and Bontshe became a coachman. The charitable man even found him a wife. He did more: he provided Bontshe with a child. And Bontshe always kept silent."

"They mean me; they mean me!" thought Bontshe, strengthening himself in his belief; but nevertheless he dared not raise his eyes on the august tribunal. Still he listened to his angelic advocate.

"Bontshe was silent," continued the latter, "even when his benefactor became bankrupt and neglected to pay Bontshe his wages. He was silent when his wife ran away from him, leaving him alone with an infant in arms. He was silent even fifteen years later, when the same child grew up till he was strong enough to throw the father out of his own house."

"They mean me, they mean me!" Bontshe thinks joyfully.

"He was silent," continued the defending angel, as his voice grew still softer and more sad, "when his former benefactor paid all his creditors except Bontshe, to whom he did not give a penny. And when, riding again in his coach with rubber tires and with horses like lions, the benefactor one day ran over him, Bontshe still kept silent. He did not even tell the police. Even in the hospital where one is allowed to cry, he kept silent! He was silent even when the house physician refused to approach his bed unless he had paid him fifteen coppers, or when the attendant refused to change his bed linen unless he gave him five coppers.

"He was silent in his death agony, he was silent in his last hour.

Never did he utter a word against God, never a word against man. . . . I have spoken!"

Bontshe began to tremble in his whole body. He knew that after the speech for the defence it was the turn of the prosecution. "What will the prosecuting counsel say now?" Bontshe did not remember his life. Down *below* he used to forget everything the moment it occurred. The angel advocate had recalled to his mind all his past. Who knows what the prosecuting angel will recall to his memory?

"Gentlemen judges," begins a strident, incisive, and stinging voice—but stops short.

"Gentlemen," he begins again, this time more softly but once more he interrupts himself.

And at last, very soft, a voice issues from the throat of the accuser:

"Gentlemen judges! He was silent! I shall be silent too."

Profound silence fell over the assembly. Then from above a new soft, sweet, and trembling voice is heard:

"Bontshe, my child, Bontshe," said the voice, and it sounded like a harp. "Bontshe, my well-beloved child."

And Bontshe's heart begins to weep for joy. He would like to raise his eyes, but they are dimmed by tears. Never in his life had he felt such joy in weeping.

"My child, my well-beloved!" Since his mother's death he had never heard such a voice or such words.

"My child," continues the President of the Celestial Tribunal, "you have suffered everything in silence. There is not a limb in your body that is whole, not a bone that is intact, not a corner in your soul that is not bleeding—and you have always kept silent.

"Down below upon the earth they never understood such things. You yourself were not aware of your power; you did not know that you could cry and that your cries would have caused the very walls of Jericho to tremble and tumble down. You yourself did not know what strength lay hidden in you. Down below, your silence was not rewarded, but down below is the world of delusion, whilst here in heaven is the world of truth, here you will reap your reward.

"The Supreme Tribunal will never pass sentence against you; it will never judge and condemn you, nor will it mete out to you such and such a reward. Everything here belongs to you; take whatever your heart desires."

For the first time Bontshe ventures to lift his eyes. He is dazzled by so much light and splendor. Everything is sparkling, everything around him is flashing, beams are issuing from all sides, and he droops his weary eyes once more.

"Really?" he asks, still doubting and embarrassed.

"Yes, really," replies the President of the Celestial Tribunal; "verily I tell you that it is so indeed, and that everything here is yours; everything in heaven belongs to you. All the brightness and the splendor you perceive is only the reflection of your own silent goodness of heart, the reflection of your own pure soul. You will only be drawing from your own source."

"Really?" Bontshe asks again, but this time his voice sounds more firm and assured.

"Certainly, certainly, certainly," he is assured on all sides.

"Then, if such is the case," says Bontshe with a happy smile, "I should like to have every morning a hot roll with fresh butter."

Abashed, angels and judges drooped their heads; while the accuser burst out into loud laughter.

Reading for Understanding

Main Idea

1. This is the story of (a) a truly good man (b) a life of no accomplishment (c) revenge (d) misunderstandings.

Details

2. "Serpent, wicked woman" is used to describe Bontshe's (a) wife (b) ungrateful son (c) stepmother (d) benefactor.
3. For saving the life of a wealthy man, Bontshe was at first (a) sent to Warsaw (b) made a coachman (c) given no reward (d) given half the man's fortune.
4. Bontshe was owed money by his (a) father (b) son (c) runaway wife (d) benefactor.

Inferences

5. Bontshe's death caused a stir in heaven because of his (a) blameless life (b) forgiveness of his wife (c) heroic death (d) confidence in his own saintliness.
6. Which of the following is an example of irony (14–15)?
   (a) Barefooted he used to chop wood for her in winter, in the biting frost.
   (b) He was always miserable and alone.
   (c) He was silent, without asking the why or wherefore.
   (d) "Who knows what rich man, what Rabbi, what saint they are expecting?"

7. The prosecuting angel (a) disapproved of Bontshe (b) had no evil deeds to report (c) used trickery in his attack (d) was shouted down by other angels.
8. Bontshe's request was (a) expected by the angels (b) excessive (c) ridiculously modest (d) never made orally.
9. The best adjective to apply to Bontshe is (a) grasping (b) uncomplaining (c) proud (d) dissatisfied.

Fact or Opinion

Tell whether the following is a fact or an opinion.

10. Bontshe should have stood up for himself when he was poorly treated.

Words in Context

1. "And scarcely had Bontshe left the morgue, when twenty corpses *extricated* from underneath the ruins of a fallen house were brought in." **Extricated** (619) means (a) discovered (b) abandoned (c) toppled (d) freed.
2. "There, the death of Bontshe produced a deep impression, a *veritable* sensation." **Veritable** (619) means (a) true (b) uncommon (c) understated (d) brief.
3. "He did not hear how, handing over a *dossier* to the counsel for the defense, he commanded: 'Read, but briefly.' " A **dossier** (620) is a(a) legal complaint (b) kind of fiction (c) challenge (d) bundle of documents.
4. " 'Never has he lifted his eyes with *pretensions* to heaven.' " **Pretensions** (620) means (a) pleadings (b) complaints (c) cries of rage (d) claims.
5. " 'Job *succumbed*, but Bontshe has suffered more than Job.' " **Succumbed** (621) means (a) prevailed (b) rejoiced (c) was defeated (d) relayed.
6. " 'She used to *begrudge* him a piece of bread; throw him a few musty crusts.' " **Begrudge** (621) means (a) allot (b) dislike giving (c) give with ceremony (d) share fairly.

7., 8. " 'Gentlemen judges,' begins a *strident*, *incisive*, and stinging voice—but stops short." **Strident** (623) means (a) harsh-sounding

(b) low key (c) repressed (d) colorless. **Incisive** (623) means (a) pleasant (b) penetrating (c) thoughtful (d) unfriendly.

9. " 'There is not a limb in your body that is whole, not a bone that is *intact*.'" **Intact** (623) means (a) reinforced (b) unharmed (c) useful (d) stressed.

10. " 'The Supreme Tribunal will never pass sentence against you; it will never judge and condemn you, nor will it *mete* out to you such and such a reward.' " **Mete** (623) means (a) measure (b) transfer (c) confirm (d) reserve.

11. " 'Yes, really,' replies the President of the Celestrial Tribunal; '*verily* I tell you that it is so indeed, and that everything here is yours; everything in heaven belongs to you.'" **Verily** (623) means (a) hesitantly (b) loudly (c) carefully (d) truly.

12. "*Abashed*, angels and judges drooped their heads; while the accuser burst out into loud laughter." **Abashed** (624) means (a) amazed (b) pleased (c) embarrassed (d) momentarily angry.

Thinking Critically About the Story

1. Of the following world figures, which one most closely accepted a philosophy similar to Bontshe's: Bill Clinton, John Lennon, Bono, Mother Theresa, Colin Powell, Princess Di? Justify your choice.
2. What do you think the author's purpose was in writing "Bontshe the Silent"?
3. Why do good people suffer? In the Bible, Job is a symbol of suffering virtue. He becomes a test of righteousness in the face of despair. Because of a debate between God and Satan, Job's family and possessions are taken from him. He is covered with sores and suffers physical torment. Though Job eventually comes through his troubles and finds wealth and happiness, there were times when he bewailed his fate. Why does the story mention Job (621)? How does Bontshe differ from Job?
4. At what point does Bontshe begin to realize that the trial is going his way?
5. Some plays and stories end with a "characteristic last act," an action typical of the central character. Episodes of *Murder, She Wrote*, for example, ended with Angela Lansbury's gentle laughter after the resolution of the problem. What is Bontshe's last action? Is it typical?

6. In the face of life's problems, does your own philosophy lean toward acceptance and pacifism or struggle and activism? Which seems to you a better course? Is a blend sometimes best?

Language in Action

Homonyms and Related Words

> "The Supreme Tribunal will never pass sentence against you; it will never judge and condemn you, nor will it mete out to you such and such a reward."

Mete belongs to a common class of words in English: words that are spelled differently but pronounced alike: *mete, meet, meat.* The word *homonym* has won wide acceptance to mean "one of two or more words pronounced alike but having different spellings and meanings." Such words are also sometimes called *homophones.* Words that are spelled and pronounced alike but with different meanings are also called *homonyms:* bear—carry; bear—animal. Pairs like lead (metal)—lead (guide) and tear (drop)—tear (rip), which are spelled alike but differ in meaning and pronunciation, are called heteronyms or homographs.

The Greek roots help you to remember the meanings:

homonym = *homo,* same + *onym,* name
homophone = *homo,* same + *phon,* sound
homograph = *homo,* same + *graph,* writing (spelling)
heteronym = *hetero,* other + *onym,* name

Can you distinguish the meaning of each word in the following pairs?

ascent, assent
capital, capitol
coarse, course
fair, fare
groan, grown
hail, hale
hear, here
hew, hue
it's, its
main, mane
muscle, mussel
ode, owed
plain, plane
profit, prophet
rap, wrap
read, reed
stationary, stationery
steal, steel
thyme, time
yolk, yoke

He

Katherine Anne Porter
American

She mustn't make a sound nor a move; she mustn't get the bull started. The bull heaved his head aside and horned the air at a fly. Her voice burst out of her in a shriek, and she screamed at Him to come on, for God's sake. He didn't seem to hear her clamor, but kept on twirling His switch and limping on, and the bull lumbered along behind Him as gently as a calf.

This is a tale of hardship and tenderness. The Whipples lead a poverty-stricken life on a farm that barely keeps them going. They have two sons and a daughter. Adna and Emly are normal, but the second son is simple-minded. This son, always referred to as *He*, is in many ways more complex than the Whipples can imagine.

Mrs. Whipple's efforts to care for her son and to keep up appearances are sad, understandable, but doomed. Mr. Whipple, a shadowy figure in the background, is in many ways a tragic figure. This story is told directly, objectively, with revealing dialogue. You may find the Whipples remaining in your memory long after you have finished the story.

He

LIFE WAS VERY HARD for the Whipples. It was hard to feed all the hungry mouths, it was hard to keep the children in flannels during the winter, short as it was: "God knows what would become of us if we lived North," they would say: keeping them decently clean was hard. "It looks like our luck won't never let up on us," said Mr. Whipple, but Mrs. Whipple was all for taking what was sent and calling it good, anyhow when the neighbors were in earshot. "Don't ever let a soul hear us complain," she kept saying to her husband. She couldn't stand to be pitied. "No, not if it comes to it that we have to live in a wagon and pick cotton around the country," she said, "nobody's going to get a chance to look down on us."

Mrs. Whipple loved her second son, the simple-minded one, better than she loved the other two children put together. She was forever saying so, and when she talked with certain of her neighbors she would even throw in her husband and her mother for good measure.

"You needn't keep on saying it around," said Mr. Whipple; "you'll make people think nobody else has any feeling about Him but you."

"It's natural for a mother," Mrs. Whipple would remind him. "You know yourself it's more natural for a mother to be that way. People don't expect so much of fathers, some way."

This didn't keep the neighbors from talking plainly among themselves. "A Lord's pure mercy if He should die," they said. "It's the sins of the fathers," they agreed among themselves. "There's bad blood and bad doings somewhere, you can bet on that." This behind the Whipples' backs. To their faces everybody said, "He's not so bad off. He'll be all right yet. Look how He grows!"

Mrs. Whipple hated to talk about it, she tried to keep her mind off it, but every time anybody set foot in the house, the subject always came up, and she had to talk about Him first, before she could get on to anything else. It seemed to ease her mind. "I wouldn't have anything happen to Him for all the world, but it just looks like I can't keep Him out of mischief. He's so strong and active, He's always into everything; He was like that since He could walk. It's actually funny sometimes, the way He can do anything, it's laughable to see Him up to His tricks. Emly has more accidents, I'm forever tying up her bruises, and Adna can't fall a foot without cracking a bone. But He can do anything and not get a scratch. The preacher said such a nice thing once when he was here. He said, and I'll remember it to my dying day, 'The innocent walk with

God—that's why He don't get hurt.'" Whenever Mrs. Whipple repeated these words, she always felt a warm pool spread in her breast, and the tears would fill her eyes, and then she could talk about something else.

He did grow and He never got hurt. A plank blew off the chicken house and struck Him on the head and He never seemed to know it. He had learned a few words, and after this He forgot them. He didn't whine for food as the other children did, but waited until it was given Him; He ate squatting in the corner, smacking and mumbling. Rolls of fat covered Him like an overcoat, and He could carry twice as much wood and water as Adna. Emly had a cold in the head most of the time—"She takes after me," said Mrs. Whipple—so in bad weather they gave her the extra blanket off His cot. He never seemed to mind the cold.

Just the same, Mrs. Whipple's life was a torment for fear something might happen to Him. He climbed the peach trees much better than Adna and went skittering along the branches like a monkey, just a regular monkey. "Oh, Mrs. Whipple, you hadn't ought to let Him do that. He'll lose His balance sometime. He can't rightly know what He's doing."

Mrs. Whipple almost screamed out at the neighbor. "He *does* know what He's doing! He's as able as any other child! Come down out of there, you!" When He finally reached the ground she could hardly keep her hands off Him for acting like that before people, a grin all over His face and her worried sick about Him all the time.

"It's the neighbors," said Mrs. Whipple to her husband. "Oh, I do mortally wish they would keep out of our business. I can't afford to let Him do anything for fear they'll come nosing around about it. Look at the bees, now. Adna can't handle them, they sting him up so; I haven't got time to do everything, and now I don't dare let Him. But if He gets a sting He don't really mind."

"It's just because He ain't got sense enough to be scared of anything," said Mr. Whipple.

"You ought to be ashamed of yourself," said Mrs. Whipple, "talking that way about your own child. Who's to take up for Him if we don't, I'd like to know? He sees a lot that goes on, He listens to things all the time. And anything I tell Him to do He does it. Don't never let anybody hear you say such things. They'd think you favored the other children over Him."

"Well, now, I don't, and you know it, and what's the use of getting all worked up about it? You always think the worst of everything. Just let Him alone, He'll get along somehow. He gets plenty to eat and wear, don't He?" Mr. Whipple suddenly felt tired out. "Anyhow, it can't be helped now."

Mrs. Whipple felt tired too, she complained in a tired voice. "What's done can't never be undone, I know that good as anybody; but

He's my child, and I'm not going to have people say anything. I'm sick of people coming around saying things all the time."

In the early fall Mrs. Whipple got a letter from her brother saying he and his wife and two children were coming over for a little visit next Sunday week. "Put the big pot in the little one," he wrote at the end. Mrs. Whipple read this part out loud twice, she was so pleased. Her brother was a great one for saying funny things. "We'll just show him that's no joke," she said; "we'll just butcher one of the suckling pigs."

"It's a waste, and I don't hold with waste the way we are now," said Mr. Whipple. "That pig'll be worth money by Christmas."

"It's a shame and a pity we can't have a decent meal's vittles once in a while when my own family comes to see us," said Mrs. Whipple. "I'd hate for his wife to go back and say there wasn't a thing in the house to eat. My God, it's better than buying up a great chance of meat in town. There's where you'd spend the money!"

"All right, do it yourself then," said Mr. Whipple. "No wonder we can't get ahead!"

The question was how to get the little pig away from his ma, a great fighter, worse than a Jersey cow. Adna wouldn't try it; "That sow'd rip my insides out all over the pen." "All right, old fraidy," said Mrs. Whipple, "*He's* not scared. Watch *Him* do it." And she laughed as though it was all a good joke and gave Him a little push towards the pen. He sneaked up and snatched the pig right away from the teat and galloped back and was over the fence with the sow raging at His heels. The little black squirming thing was screeching like a baby in a tantrum, stiffening its back and stretching its mouth to the ears. Mrs. Whipple took the pig with her face stiff and sliced its throat with one stroke. When He saw the blood He gave a great jolting breath and ran away. "But He'll forget and eat plenty, just the same," thought Mrs. Whipple. Whenever she was thinking, her lips moved making words. "He'd eat it all if I didn't stop Him. He'd eat up every mouthful from the other two if I'd let Him."

She felt badly about it. He was ten years old now and a third again as large as Adna, who was going on fourteen. "It's a shame, a shame," she kept saying under her breath, "and Adna with so much brains!"

She kept on feeling badly about all sorts of things. In the first place it was the man's work to butcher; the sight of the pig scraped pink and naked made her sick. He was too fat and soft and pitiful-looking. It was simply a shame the way things had to happen. By the time she had finished it up, she almost wished her brother would stay at home.

Early Sunday morning Mrs. Whipple dropped everything to get Him all cleaned up. In an hour He was dirty again, with crawling under fences after a possum, and straddling along the rafters of the barn looking for eggs in the hayloft. "My Lord, look at you now after all my trying! And here's Adna and Emly staying so quiet. I get tired trying to keep you decent. Get off that shirt and put on another, people will say I don't half dress you!" And she boxed Him on the ears, hard. He blinked and blinked and rubbed His head, and His face hurt Mrs. Whipple's feelings. Her knees began to tremble, she had to sit down while she buttoned His shirt. "I'm just all gone before the day starts."

The brother came with his plump healthy wife and two great roaring hungry boys. They had a grand dinner, with the pig roasted to a crackling in the middle of the table, full of dressing, a pickled peach in his mouth and plenty of gravy for the sweet potatoes.

"This looks like prosperity all right," said the brother; "you're going to have to roll me home like I was a barrel when I'm done."

Everybody laughed out loud; it was fine to hear them laughing all at once around the table. Mrs. Whipple felt warm and good about it. "Oh, we've got six more of these; I say it's as little as we can do when you come to see us so seldom."

He wouldn't come into the dining room, and Mrs. Whipple passed it off very well. "He's timider than my other two," she said, "He'll just have to get used to you. There isn't everybody He'll make up with; you know how it is with some children, even cousins." Nobody said anything out of the way.

"Just like my Alfy here," said the brother's wife. "I sometimes got to lick him to make him shake hands with his own grandmammy."

So that was over, and Mrs. Whipple loaded up a big plate for Him first, before everybody. "I always say He ain't to be slighted, no matter who else goes without," she said, and carried it to Him herself.

"He can chin Himself on the top of the door," said Emly, helping along.

"That's fine, He's getting along fine," said the brother.

They went away after supper. Mrs. Whipple rounded up the dishes, and sent the children to bed and sat down and unlaced her shoes. "You see?" she said to Mr. Whipple. "That's the way my whole family is. Nice and considerate about everything. No out-of-the-way remarks—they *have* got refinement. I get awfully sick of people's remarks. Wasn't that pig good?"

Mr. Whipple said, "Yes, we're out three hundred pounds of pork, that's all. It's easy to be polite when you come to eat. Who knows what they had in their minds all along?"

"Yes, that's like you," said Mrs. Whipple. "I don't expect anything else from you. You'll be telling me next that my own brother will be saying around that we made Him eat in the kitchen! Oh, my God!" she rocked her head in her hands, a hard pain started in the very middle of her forehead. "Now it's all spoiled, and everything was so nice and easy. All right, you don't like them and you never did—all right, they'll not come here again soon, never you mind! But they *can't* say He wasn't dressed every lick as good as Adna—oh, honest, sometimes I wish I was dead!"

"I wish you'd let up," said Mr. Whipple. "It's bad enough as it is."

It was a hard winter. It seemed to Mrs. Whipple that they hadn't ever known anything but hard times, and now to cap it all a winter like this. The crops were about half of what they had a right to expect; after the cotton was in it didn't do much more than cover the grocery bill. They swapped off one of the plow horses, and got cheated, for the new one died of the heaves. Mrs. Whipple kept thinking all the time it was terrible to have a man you couldn't depend on not to get cheated. They cut down on everything, but Mrs. Whipple kept saying there are things you can't cut down on, and they cost money. It took a lot of warm clothes for Adna and Emly, who walked four miles to school during the three-months session. "He sets around the fire a lot, He won't need so much," said Mr. Whipple. "That's so," said Mrs. Whipple, "and when He does the outdoor chores He can wear your tarpaullion coat. I can't do no better, that's all."

In February He was taken sick, and lay curled up under His blanket looking very blue in the face and acting as if He would choke. Mr. and Mrs. Whipple did everything they could for Him for two days, and then they were scared and sent for the doctor. The doctor told them they must keep Him warm and give Him plenty of milk and eggs. "He isn't as stout as He looks, I'm afraid," said the doctor. "You've got to watch them when they're like that. You must put more cover onto Him too."

"I just took off His big blanket to wash," said Mrs. Whipple, ashamed. "I can't stand dirt."

"Well, you'd better put it back on the minute it's dry," said the doctor, "or He'll have pneumonia."

Mr. and Mrs. Whipple took a blanket off their own bed and put His cot in by the fire. "They can't say we didn't do everything for Him," she said, "even to sleeping cold ourselves on His account."

When the winter broke He seemed to be well again, but He walked as if His feet hurt Him. He was able to run a cotton planter during the season.

"I got it all fixed up with Jim Ferguson about breeding the cow next time," said Mr. Whipple. "I'll pasture the bull this summer and give Jim some fodder in the fall. That's better than paying out money when you haven't got it."

"I hope you didn't say such a thing before Jim Ferguson," said Mrs. Whipple. "You oughtn't to let him know we're so down as all that."

"That ain't saying we're down. A man is got to look ahead sometimes. *He* can lead the bull over today. I need Adna on the place."

At first Mrs. Whipple felt easy in her mind about sending Him for the bull. Adna was too jumpy and couldn't be trusted. You've got to be steady around animals. After He was gone she started thinking, and after awhile she could hardly bear it any longer. She stood in the lane and watched for Him. It was nearly three miles to go and a hot day, but He oughtn't to be so long about it. She shaded her eyes and stared until colored bubbles floated in her eyeballs. It was just like everything else in life, she must always worry and never know a moment's peace about anything. After a long time she saw Him turn into the side lane, limping. He came on very slowly, leading the big hulk of an animal by a ring in the nose, twirling a little stick in His hand, never looking back or sideways, but coming on like a sleepwalker with His eyes half shut.

Mrs. Whipple was scared sick of bulls; she had heard awful stories about how they followed on quietly enough, and then suddenly pitched on with a bellow and pawed and gored a body to pieces. Any second now that black monster would come down on Him, my God, He'd never have sense enough to run.

She mustn't make a sound nor move; she mustn't get the bull started. The bull heaved his head aside and horned the air at a fly. Her voice burst out of her in a shriek, and she screamed at Him to come on, for God's sake. He didn't seem to hear her clamor but kept on twirling His switch and limping on, and the bull lumbered along behind him as gently as a calf. Mrs. Whipple stopped calling and ran towards the house, praying under her breath: "Lord, don't let anything happen to Him. Lord, you *know* people will say we oughtn't to have sent Him. You *know* they'll say we didn't take care of Him. Oh, get Him home, safe home, safe home, and I'll look out for Him better! Amen.

She watched from the window while He led the beast in, and tied him up in the barn. It was no use trying to keep up, Mrs. Whipple couldn't bear another thing. She sat down and rocked and cried with her apron over her head.

From year to year the Whipples were growing poorer. The place just seemed to run down of itself, no matter how hard they worked. "We're losing our hold," said Mrs. Whipple. "Why can't we do like other people and watch for our best chances? They'll be calling us poor white trash next."

"When I get to be sixteen I'm going to leave," said Adna, "I'm going to get a job in Powell's grocery store. There's money in that. No more farm for me."

"I'm going to be a school-teacher," said Emly. "But I've got to finish the eighth grade, anyhow. Then I can live in town. I don't see any chances here."

"Emly takes after my family," said Mrs. Whipple. "Ambitious every last one of them, and they don't take second place for anybody."

When fall came Emly got a chance to wait on table in the railroad eating-house in the town near-by, and it seemed such a shame not to take it when the wages were good and she could get her food too, that Mrs. Whipple decided to let her take it, and not bother with school until the next session. "You've got plenty of time," she said. "You're young and smart as a whip."

With Adna gone too, Mr. Whipple tried to run the farm with just Him to help. He seemed to get along fine, doing His work and part of Adna's without noticing it. They did well enough until Christmas time, when one morning He slipped on the ice coming up from the barn. Instead of getting up He thrashed round and round, and when Mr. Whipple got to Him, He was having some sort of fit.

They brought Him inside and tried to make Him sit up, but He blubbered and rolled, so they put Him to bed and Mr. Whipple rode to town for the doctor. All the way there and back he worried about where the money was to come from: it sure did look like he had about all the troubles he could carry.

From then on He stayed in bed. His legs swelled up double their size, and the fits kept coming back. After four months, the doctor said, "It's no use, I think you'd better put him in the County Home for treatment right away. I'll see about it for you. He'll have good care there and be off your hands."

"We don't begrudge Him any care, and I won't let Him out of my sight," said Mrs. Whipple. "I won't have it said I sent my sick child off among strangers."

"I know how you feel," said the doctor. "You can't tell me anything about that, Mrs. Whipple. I've got a boy of my own. But you'd better listen to me. I can't do anything more for Him, that's the truth."

Mr. and Mrs. Whipple talked it over a long time that night after they went to bed. "It's just charity," said Mrs. Whipple, "that's what we've come to, charity! I certainly never looked for this."

"We pay taxes to help support the place just like everybody else," said Mr. Whipple, "and I don't call that taking charity. I think it would be fine to have Him where He'd get the best of everything. . . and besides, I can't keep up with these doctor bills any longer."

"Maybe that's why the doctor wants us to send Him—he's scared he won't get his money," said Mrs. Whipple.

"Don't talk like that," said Mr. Whipple, feeling pretty sick, "or we won't be able to send Him."

"Oh, but we won't keep Him there long," said Mrs. Whipple. "Soon's He's better, we'll bring Him right back home."

"The doctor has told you and told you time and again He can't ever get better, and you might as well stop talking," said Mr. Whipple.

"Doctors don't know everything," said Mrs Whipple, feeling almost happy. "But anyhow, in the summer Emly can come home for a vacation and Adna can get down for Sundays: we'll all work together and get on our feet again, and the children will feel they've got a place to come to."

All at once she saw it full summer again, with the garden going fine, and new white roller shades up all over the house, and Adna and Emly home, so full of life, all of them happy together. Oh, it could happen, things would ease up on them.

They didn't talk before Him much, but they never knew just how much He understood. Finally the doctor set the day, and a neighbor who owned a double-seated carryall offered to drive them over. The hospital would have sent an ambulance, but Mrs. Whipple couldn't stand to see Him going away looking so sick as all that. They wrapped Him in blankets, and the neighbor and Mr. Whipple lifted Him into the back seat of the carryall beside Mrs. Whipple, who had on her black shirtwaist. She couldn't stand to go looking like charity.

"You'll be all right, I guess I'll stay behind," said Mr. Whipple. "It don't look like everybody ought to leave the place at once."

"Besides, it ain't as if He was going to stay forever," said Mrs. Whipple to the neighbor. "This is only for a little while."

They started away, Mrs. Whipple holding to the edges of the blankets to keep Him from sagging sideways. He sat there blinking and blinking. He worked His hands out and began rubbing His nose with His knuckles, and then with the end of the blanket. Mrs. Whipple couldn't believe what she saw; He was scrubbing away big tears that rolled out of the corners of His eyes. He sniveled and made a gulping noise. Mrs. Whipple kept saying, "Oh, honey, you don't feel so bad, do you? You don't feel so bad, do you?" for He seemed to be accusing her of something. Maybe He remembered that time she boxed His ears, maybe He had been scared that day with the bull, maybe He had slept cold and couldn't tell her about it; maybe He knew they were sending Him away for good and all because they were too poor to keep Him. Whatever it was, Mrs. Whipple couldn't bear to think of it. She began to cry, frightfully, and wrapped her arms tight around Him. His head rolled on her shoulder: she had loved Him as much as she possibly could, there were Adna and Emly who had to be thought of too, there was nothing she could do to make up to Him for His life. Oh, what a mortal pity He was ever born.

They came in sight of the hospital, with the neighbor driving very fast, not daring to look behind him.

Reading for Understanding

Main Idea

1. The main thread of the story is (a) the contrast between Adna and Him (b) the burdens of entertaining relatives (c) Mr. Whipple's domination of his family (d) Mrs. Whipple's efforts on behalf of Him.

Details

2. An accident that caused Him to forget His few words was (a) being gored by a bull (b) falling off the barn roof (c) being struck by a plank (d) being cut by a butcher's knife.
3. The one who took the suckling pig away from its mother was (a) Mrs. Whipple (b) He (c) Mr. Whipple (d) Adna.
4. Emly's goal was to (a) be a teacher (b) be a farm wife (c) be a waitress (d) make money to send her brother to a mental institution.

Inferences

5. A dominating force in Mrs. Whipple's personality was (a) cruelty (b) humor (c) pride (d) serenity.
6. In acting as hostess for her brother and his family, Mrs. Whipple was most concerned to (a) have Him wait on tables (b) conceal any evidence of poverty (c) keep Mr. Whipple happy (d) irritate her brother's wife.
7. The decision to send Him to the hospital (a) was against Mr. Whipple's wishes (b) made Him happy (c) was suggested by Mrs. Whipple's brother (d) was unavoidable.
8. The personality of Him can be characterized as (a) pleasant (b) vicious (c) dominating (d) insincere.

Cause and Effect

9. He suffered the serious illness at the end of the story because of (a) poor nutrition (b) an infection from Emly (c) a fall (d) Mrs. Whipple's neglect of Him.

Order of Events

10. Arrange the items in the order in which they occurred. Use letters only.
    (A) He leads the bull.
    (B) The family of Mrs. Whipple's brother visits.
    (C) The sow chases Him.
    (D) He leaves for the hospital.
    (E) He becomes ill but recovers.

Words in Context

1. "'We don't *begrudge* Him any care, and I won't let Him out of my sight,' said Mrs. Whipple.'" **Begrudge** (635) means (a) give up reluctantly (b) deprive thoughtlessly (c) foster intentionally (d) reject absolutely.
2. "He *sniveled* and made a gulping noise." **Sniveled** (636) means (a) objected loudly (b) protested silently (c) sniffed repeatedly (d) turned His head.

Thinking Critically About the Story

1. How does the first line set the mood of the story and provide essential information for what's to come?
2. Mrs. Whipple was a compassionate mother, but part of her concern was not for the well being of Him but for something else. What was it? Explain.
3. What kind of person was Mr. Whipple? What was his relationship with his wife? Who is the more to be pitied, Mr. Whipple or Mrs. Whipple?
4. Point out examples to show how Katherine Anne Porter piles detail upon detail to emphasize the Whipples' poverty.
5. Was He better off growing up in a normal family, or would He have been better in an institution from the start?
6. Families with disadvantaged children like Him often say that the child is a blessing, a model for the rest of the family, a treasured

member. Have you found similar experiences among friends, acquaintances or even on TV? Tell about them.

7. The two other children are slighted in this story; yet we have clues to their personalities. Choose Adna or Emly and tell what kind of person he/she was.

Language in Action

Stories in Words

Pneumonia (633) has as its basic root *pneuma*, "wind, breath." *Pneumon* means "lung." *Pneumonia* is thus a disease of the *lungs*. A *pneumatic* device works by compressed air (breath). *Pulmonary* comes from the original Greek through Latin. It still retains the meaning of *breath, lung*. A *pulmonary* artery carries blood from the heart to the *lungs*.

Ambitious (635) comes from the Latin verb *ambire*, "to go around." *Ambire* itself contains the verb *ire*, "go" and the prefix *around*. An *ambitious* person *goes around* soliciting votes, seeking favor. At one time the word had a negative connotation, but in recent years it has become neutral or even positive. The *ambi* root appears in such words as *ambidextrous* and *ambiguous*. The *ire* root appears in *exit* and *itinerant*. *Initial* meant "a going into, a beginning." From this came the sense of the *beginning* letter.

Sniveled (636) probably comes from an ancient root meaning "to flow." *Snivel* is extremely interesting as one of a large number of words beginning with *sn*. Many of these words have to do with activities associated with the nose: *snarl*, *sneer*, *sneeze*, *sniff*, *snore*, *snort*, *snout*, and *snuff*. What is even more surprising is the number of negative words beginning with *sn*: *snag*, *snake* (for some people), *snappish*, *snarl*, *snatch*, *sneak*, *snide*, *snit*, *snitch*, *snob* and *snoop*. As proof that all-embracing generalizations in language are tricky, here are some *sn* words that are neutral or even positive: *snail*, *snip*, *snack*, and *snow*. Still, all those negative words may suggest an interesting association.

The Person of the Moment

from I Know Why the Caged Bird Sings

Maya Angelou
American

The white kids were going to have a chance to become Galileos and Madame Curies and Edisons and Gaughins, and our boys (the girls weren't even in on it) would try to become Jesse Owenses and Joe Louises.

In *I Know Why the Caged Bird Sings*, of which this selection is a part, Maya Angelou presents her spiritual journey to become one of the leading spokespersons for African-American causes. Born in 1928 in St. Louis, Missouri, she moved with her family to Stamps, Arkansas. She saw first-hand the spiritual cost of segregation.

Biographical information on her Web site lists her as author, poet, historian, songwriter, playwright, dancer, stage and screen producer, director, performer, singer, and civil rights activist. Throughout her busy life, she has remained a leader in the cause of equal opportunity for all groups.

"The Person of the Moment" tells of a turning point in her life. The opening pages are aglow with the excitement of graduation, but the commencement address turns her bitter. A dramatic moment turns that hatred and bitterness to pride and eagerness to meet the challenges of life.

The Person of the Moment

THE CHILDREN IN STAMPS trembled visibly with anticipation. Some adults were excited too, but to be certain the whole young population had come down with graduation epidemic. Large classes were graduating from both the grammar school and the high school. Even those who were years removed from their own day of glorious release were anxious to help with preparations as a kind of dry run. The junior students who were moving into the vacating classes' chairs were tradition-bound to show their talents for leadership and management. They strutted through the school and around the campus exerting pressure on the lower grades. Their authority was so new that occasionally if they pressed a little too hard it had to be overlooked. After all, next term was coming, and it never hurt a sixth grader to have a play sister in the eighth grade, or a tenth-year student to be able to call a twelfth grader Bubba. So all was endured in a spirit of shared understanding. But the graduating classes themselves were the nobility. Like travelers with exotic destinations on their minds, the graduates were remarkably forgetful. They came to school without their books, or tablets or even pencils. Volunteers fell over themselves to secure replacements for the missing equipment. When accepted, the willing workers might or might not be thanked, and it was of no importance to the pregraduation rites. Even teachers were respectful of the now quiet and aging seniors, and tended to speak to them, if not as equals, as beings only slightly lower than themselves. After tests were returned and grades given, the student body, which acted like an extended family, knew who did well, who excelled, and what piteous ones had failed.

Unlike the white high school, Lafayette County Training School distinguished itself by having neither lawn, nor hedges, nor tennis court, nor climbing ivy. Its two buildings (main classrooms, the grade school and home economics) were set on a dirt hill with no fence to limit either its boundaries or those of bordering farms. There was a large expanse to the left of the school which was used alternately as a baseball diamond or a basketball court. Rusty hoops on the swaying poles represented the permanent recreational equipment, although bats and balls could be borrowed from the P.E. teacher if the borrower was qualified and if the diamond wasn't occupied.

Over this rocky area relieved by a few shady tall persimmon trees the graduating class walked. The girls often held hands and no longer bothered to speak to the lower students. There was a sadness about them, as if this old world was not their home and they were bound for higher ground. The boys, on the other hand, had become more friendly, more outgoing. A decided change from the closed attitude they projected while studying for finals. Now they seemed not ready to give up the old school, the familiar paths and classrooms. Only a small percentage would be continuing on to college—one of the South's A & M (agricultural and mechanical) schools, which trained Negro youths to be carpenters, farmers, handymen, masons, maids, cooks and baby nurses. Their future rode heavily on their shoulders, and blinded them to the collective joy that had pervaded the lives of the boys and girls in the grammar school graduating class.

Parents who could afford it had ordered new shoes and ready-made clothes for themselves from Sears and Roebuck or Montgomery Ward. They also engaged the best seamstresses to make the floating graduating dresses and to cut down secondhand pants which would be pressed to a military slickness for the important event.

Oh, it was important, all right. Whitefolks would attend the ceremony, and two or three would speak of God and home, and the Southern way of life, and Mrs. Parsons, the principal's wife, would play the graduation march while the lower-grade graduates paraded down the aisles and took their seats below the platform. The high school seniors would wait in empty classrooms to make their dramatic entrance.

In the Store I was the person of the moment. The birthday girl. The center. Bailey had graduated the year before, although to do so he had had to forfeit all pleasures to make up for his time lost in Baton Rouge.

My class was wearing butter-yellow piqué dresses, and Momma launched out on mine. She smocked the yoke into tiny crisscrossing puckers, then shirred the rest of the bodice. Her dark fingers ducked in and out of the lemony cloth as she embroidered raised daisies around the hem. Before she considered herself finished she had added a crocheted cuff on the puff sleeves, and a pointy crocheted collar.

I was going to be lovely. A walking model of all the various styles of fine hand sewing and it didn't worry me that I was only twelve years old and merely graduating from the eighth grade. Besides, many teachers in Arkansas Negro schools had only that diploma and were licensed to impart wisdom.

The days had become longer and more noticeable. The faded beige of former times had been replaced with strong and sure colors. I began to see my classmates' clothes, their skin tones, and the dust that waved off pussy willows. Clouds that lazed across the sky were objects of great concern to me. Their shiftier shapes might have held a message that in my new happiness and with a little bit of time I'd soon decipher. During that period I looked at the arch of heaven so religiously my neck kept a steady ache. I had taken to smiling more often, and my jaws hurt from the unaccustomed activity. Between the two physical sore spots, I suppose I could have been uncomfortable, but that was not the case. As a member of the winning team (the graduating class of 1940) I had outdistanced unpleasant sensations by miles. I was headed for the freedom of open fields.

Youth and social approval allied themselves with me and we trammeled memories of slights and insults. The wind of our swift passage remodeled my features. Lost tears were pounded to mud and then to dust. Years of withdrawal were brushed aside and left behind, as hanging ropes of parasitic moss.

My work alone had awarded me a top place and I was going to be one of the first called in the graduating ceremonies. On the classroom blackboard, as well as on the bulletin board in the auditorium, there were blue stars and white stars and red stars. No absences, no tardinesses, and my academic work was among the best of the year. I could say the preamble to the Constitution even faster than Bailey. We timed ourselves often:

"WethepeopleoftheUnitedStatesinordertoformamoreperfectunion. . ." I had memorized the Presidents of the United States from Washington to Roosevelt in chronological as well as alphabetical order.

My hair pleased me too. Gradually the black mass had lengthened and thickened, so that it kept at last to its braided pattern, and I didn't have to yank my scalp off when I tried to comb it.

Louise and I had rehearsed the exercises until we tired out ourselves. Henry Reed was class valedictorian. He was a small, very black boy with hooded eyes, a long, broad nose and an oddly shaped head. I had admired him for years because each term he and I vied for the best grades in our class. Most often he bested me, but instead of being disappointed I was pleased that we shared top places between us. Like many Southern Black children, he lived with his grandmother, who was as strict as Momma and as kind as she knew how to be. He was courteous, respectful and soft-spoken to elders, but on the playground he chose to play the roughest games. I admired him. Anyone, I reckoned, sufficiently afraid or sufficiently dull could be polite. But to be able to operate at a top level with both adults and children was admirable.

His valedictory speech was entitled "To Be or Not to Be." The rigid tenth-grade teacher had helped him write it. He'd been working on the dramatic stresses for months.

The weeks until graduation were filled with heady activities. A group of small children were to be presented in a play about buttercups and daisies and bunny rabbits. They could be heard throughout the building practicing their hops and their little songs that sounded like silver bells. The older girls (nongraduates, of course) were assigned the task of making refreshments for the night's festivities. A tangy scent of ginger, cinnamon, nutmeg and chocolate wafted around the home economics building as the budding cooks made samples for themselves and their teachers.

In every corner of the workshop, axes and saws split fresh timber as the woodshop boys made sets and stage scenery. Only the graduates were left out of the general bustle. We were free to sit in the library at the back of the building or look in quite detachedly, naturally, on the measures being taken for our event.

Even the minister preached on graduation the Sunday before. His subject was, "Let your light so shine that men will see your good works and praise your Father, Who is in Heaven." Although the sermon was purported to be addressed to us, he used the occasion to speak to backsliders, gamblers and general ne'er-do-wells. But since he had called our names at the beginning of the service we were mollified.

Among Negroes the tradition was to give presents to children going only from one grade to another. How much more important this was when the person was graduating at the top of the class. Uncle Willie and Momma had sent away for a Mickey Mouse watch like Bailey's. Louise gave me four embroidered handkerchiefs. (I gave her three crocheted doilies.) Mrs. Sneed, the minister's wife, made me an underskirt to wear for graduation, and nearly every customer gave me a nickel or maybe even a dime with the instruction "Keep on moving to higher ground," or some such encouragement.

Amazingly the great day finally dawned and I was out of bed before I knew it. I threw open the back door to see it more clearly, but Momma said, "Sister, come away from that door and put your robe on."

I hoped the memory of that morning would never leave me. Sunlight was itself still young, and the day had none of the insistence maturity would bring it in a few hours. In my robe and barefoot in the backyard, under cover of going to see about my new beans, I gave myself up to the gentle warmth and thanked God that no matter what evil I had done in my life He had allowed me to live to see this day. Somewhere in my fatalism I had expected to die, accidentally, and never have the chance to walk up the stairs in the auditorium and gracefully receive my hard-earned diploma. Out of God's merciful bosom I had won reprieve.

Bailey came out in his robe and gave me a box wrapped in Christmas paper. He said he had saved his money for months to pay for it. It felt like a box of chocolates, but I knew Bailey wouldn't save money to buy candy when we had all we could want under our noses.

He was as proud of the gift as I. It was a soft-leatherbound copy of a collection of poems by Edgar Allan Poe, or, as Bailey and I called him, "Eap." I turned to "Annabel Lee" and we walked up and down the garden rows, the cool dirt between our toes, reciting the beautifully sad lines.

Momma made a Sunday breakfast although it was only Friday. After we finished the blessing, I opened my eyes to find the watch on my plate. It was a dream of a day. Everything went smoothly and to my credit. I didn't have to be reminded or scolded for anything. Near evening I was too jittery to attend to chores, so Bailey volunteered to do all before his bath.

Days before, we had made a sign for the Store, and as we turned out the lights Momma hung the cardboard over the doorknob. It read clearly: CLOSED. GRADUATION.

My dress fitted perfectly and everyone said that I looked like a sunbeam in it. On the hill, going toward the school, Bailey walked behind with Uncle Willie, who muttered, "Go on, Ju." He wanted him to walk ahead with us because it embarrassed him to have to walk so slowly. Bailey said he'd let the ladies walk together, and the men would bring up the rear. We all laughed, nicely.

Little children dashed by out of the dark like fireflies. Their crepe-paper dresses and butterfly wings were not made for running and we heard more than one rip, dryly, and the regretful "uh uh" that followed.

The school blazed without gaiety. The windows seemed cold and unfriendly from the lower hill. A sense of ill-fated timing crept over me, and if Momma hadn't reached for my hand I would have drifted back to Bailey and Uncle Willie, and possibly beyond. She made a few slow jokes about my feet getting cold, and tugged me along to the now-strange building.

Around the front steps, assurance came back. There were my fellow "greats," the graduating class. Hair brushed back, legs oiled, new dresses and pressed pleats, fresh pocket handkerchiefs and little handbags, all homesewn. Oh, we were up to snuff, all right. I joined my comrades and didn't even see my family go in to find seats in the crowded auditorium.

The school band struck up a march and all classes filed in as had been rehearsed. We stood in front of our seats, as assigned, and on a signal from the choir director, we sat. No sooner had this been accomplished than the band started to play the national anthem. We rose again and sang the song, after which we recited the pledge of allegiance. We remained standing for a brief minute before the choir director and the principal signaled to us, rather desperately I thought, to take our seats. The command was so unusual that our carefully rehearsed and smooth-running machine was thrown off. For a full minute we fumbled for our chairs and bumped into each other awkwardly. Habits change or solidify under pressure, so in our state of nervous tension we had been ready to follow our usual assembly pattern: the American national anthem, then the pledge of allegiance, then the song every Black person I knew called the Negro National Anthem. All done in the same key, with the same passion and most often standing on the same foot.

Finding my seat at last, I was overcome with a presentiment of worse things to come. Something unrehearsed, unplanned, was going to happen, and we were going to be made to look bad. I distinctly remember being explicit in the choice of pronoun. It was "we," the graduating class, the unit, that concerned me then.

The principal welcomed "parents and friends" and asked the Baptist minister to lead us in prayer. His invocation was brief and punchy, and for a second I thought we were getting back on the high road to right action. When the principal came back to the dais, however, his voice had changed. Sounds always affected me profoundly and the principal's voice was one of my favorites. During assembly it melted and lowed weakly into the audience. It had not been in my plan to listen to him, but my curiosity was piqued and I straightened up to give him my attention.

He was talking about Booker T. Washington, our "late great leader," who said we can be as close as the fingers on the hand, etc. . . . Then he said a few vague things about friendship and the friendship of kindly people to those less fortunate than themselves. With that his voice nearly faded, thin, away. Like a river diminishing to a stream and then to a trickle. But he cleared his throat and said, "Our speaker tonight, who is also our friend, came from Texarkana to deliver the commencement address, but due to the irregularity of the train schedule, he's going to, as they say, 'speak and run.'" He said that we understood and wanted the man to know that we were most grateful for the time he was able to give us and then something about how we were willing always to adjust to another's program, and without more ado— "I give you Mr. Edward Donleavy."

Not one but two white men came through the door offstage. The shorter one walked to the speaker's platform, and the tall one moved over to the center seat and sat down. But that was our principal's seat, and already occupied. The dislodged gentlemen bounced around for a long breath or two before the Baptist minister gave him his chair, then with more dignity than the situation deserved, the minister walked off the stage.

Donleavy looked at the audience once (on reflection, I'm sure that he wanted only to reassure himself that we were really there), adjusted his glasses and began to read from a sheaf of papers.

He was glad "to be here and to see the work going on just as it was in the other schools."

At the first "Amen" from the audience I willed the offender to immediate death by choking on the word. But Amens and yes, sir's began to fall around the room like rain through a ragged umbrella.

He told us of the wonderful changes we children in Stamps had in store. The Central School (naturally, the white school was Central) had already been granted improvements that would be in use in the fall. A well-known artist was coming from Little Rock to teach art to them. They were going to have the newest microscopes and chemistry equipment for their laboratory. Mr. Donleavy didn't leave us long in the dark over who made these improvements available to Central High. Nor were we to be ignored in the general betterment scheme he had in mind.

He said that he had pointed out to people at a very high level that one of the first-line football tacklers at Arkansas Agricultural and Mechanical College had graduated from good old Lafayette County Training School. Here fewer Amen's were heard. Those few that did break through lay dully in the air with the heaviness of habit.

He went on to praise us. He went on to say how he had bragged that "one of the best basketball players at Fisk sank his first ball right here at Lafayette County Training School."

The white kids were going to have a chance to become Galileos and Madame Curies and Edisons and Gauguins, and our boys (the girls weren't even in on it) would try to be Jesse Owenses and Joe Louises.

Owens and the Brown Bomber were great heroes in our world, but what school official in the white-goddom of Little Rock had the right to decide that those two men must be our only heroes? Who decided that for Henry Reed to become a scientist he had to work like George Washington Carver, as a boot-black, to buy a lousy microscope? Bailey was obviously always going to be too small to be an athlete, so which concrete angel glued to what country seat had decided that if my brother wanted to become a lawyer he had to first pay penance for his skin by picking cotton and hoeing corn and studying correspondence books at night for twenty years?

The man's dead words fell like bricks around the auditorium and too many settled in my belly. Constrained by hard-learned manners I couldn't look behind me, but to my left and right the proud graduating class of 1940 had dropped their heads. Every girl in my row had found something new to do with her handkerchief. Some folded the tiny squares into love knots, some into triangles, but most were wadding them, then pressing them flat on their yellow laps.

On the dais, the ancient tragedy was being replayed. Professor Parsons sat, a sculptor's reject, rigid. His large, heavy body seemed devoid of will or willingness, and his eyes said he was no longer with us. The other teachers examined the flag (which was draped stage right) or their notes, or the windows which opened on our now-famous playing diamond.

Graduation, the hush-hush magic time of frills and gifts and congratulations and diplomas, was finished for me before my name was called. The accomplishment was nothing. The meticulous maps, drawn in three colors of ink, learning and spelling decasyllabic words, memorizing the whole of *The Rape of Lucrece*—it was for nothing. Donleavy had exposed us.

We were maids and farmers, handymen and washerwomen, and anything higher that we aspired to was farcical and presumptuous.

Then I wished that Gabriel Prosser and Nat Turner had killed all whitefolks in their beds and that Abraham Lincolon had been assassinated before the signing of the Emancipation Proclamation, and that Harriet Tubman had been killed by that blow on her head and Christopher Columbus had drowned in the *Santa Maria*.

It was awful to be Negro and have no control over my life. It was brutal to be young and already trained to sit quietly and listen to charges brought against my color with no chance of defense. We should all be dead. I thought I should like to see us all dead, one on top of the other. A pyramid of flesh with the white folks on the bottom, as the broad base, then the Indians with their silly tomahawks and teepees and wigwams and treaties, the Negroes with their mops and recipes and cotton sacks and spirituals sticking out of their mouths. The Dutch children should all stumble in their wooden shoes and break their necks. The French should choke to death on the Louisiana Purchase (1803) while silkworms ate all the Chinese with their stupid pigtails. As a species, we were an abomination. All of us.

Donleavy was running for election, and assured our parents that if he won we could count on having the only colored paved playing field in that part of Arkansas. Also—he never looked up to acknowledge the grunts of acceptance—also, we were bound to get some new equipment for the home economics building and the workshop.

He finished, and since there was no need to give any more than the most perfunctory thank-you's, he nodded to the men on the stage, and the tall white man who was never introduced joined him at the door. They left with the attitude that now they were off to something really important. (The graduation ceremonies at Lafayette County Training School had been a mere preliminary.)

The ugliness they left was palpable. An uninvited guest who wouldn't leave. The choir was summoned and sang a modern arrangement of "Onward, Christian Soldiers," with new words pertaining to graduates seeding their place in the world. But it didn't work. Elouise, the daughter of the Baptist minister, recited "Invictus," and I could have cried at the impertinence of "I am the master of my fate, I am the captain of my soul."

My name had lost its ring of familiarity and I had to be nudged to go and receive my diploma. All my preparations had fled. I neither marched up to the stage like a conquering Amazon, nor did I look in the audience for Bailey's nod of approval. Marguerite Johnson, I heard the name again, my honors were read, there were noises in the audience of appreciation, and I took my place on the stage as rehearsed.

I thought about colors I hated: ecru, puce, lavender, beige and black.

There was shuffling and rustling around me, then Henry Reed was giving his valedictory address, "To Be or Not to Be." Hadn't he heard the whitefolks? We couldn't *be*, so the question was a waste of time. Henry's voice came out clear and strong. I feared to look at him. Hadn't he got the message? There was no "nobler in the mind" for Negroes because the world didn't think we had minds, and they let us know it. "Outrageous fortune"? Now, that was a joke. When the ceremony was over I had to tell Henry Reed some things. That is, if I still cared. Not "rub," Henry, "erase." "Ah, there's the erase." Us.

Henry had been a good student in elocution. His voice rose on tides of promise and fell on waves of warnings. The English teacher had helped him to create a sermon winging through Hamlet's soliloquy. To be a man, a doer, a builder, a leader, or to be a tool, an unfunny joke, a crusher of funky toadstools. I marveled that Henry could go through with the speech as if we had a choice.

I had been listening and silently rebutting each sentence with my eyes closed; then there was a hush, which in an audience warns that something unplanned is happening. I looked up and saw Henry Reed, the conservative, the proper, the A student, turn his back to the audience and turn to us (the proud graduating class of 1940) and sing, nearly speaking,

> "Lift ev'ry voice and sing
> Till earth and heaven ring
> Ring with the harmonies of Liberty. . ."[1]

---

[1] "Lift Ev'ry Voice and Sing"—words by James Weldon Johnson and music by J. Rosamond Johnson. Copyright by Edward B. Marks Music Corporation. Used by permission.

It was the poem written by James Weldon Johnson. It was the music composed by J. Rosamond Johnson. It was the Negro national anthem. Out of habit we were singing it.

Our mothers and fathers stood in the dark hall and joined the hymn of encouragement. A kindergarten teacher led the small children onto the stage and the buttercups and daisies and bunny rabbits marked time and tried to follow:

"Stony the road we trod
Bitter the chastening rod
Felt in the days when hope, unborn, had died.
Yet with a steady beat
Have not our weary feet
Come to the place for which our fathers sighed?"

Every child I knew had learned that song with his ABC's and along with "Jesus Loves Me This I Know." But I personally had never heard it before. Never heard the words, despite the thousands of times I had sung them. Never thought they had anything to do with me.

On the other hand, the words of Patrick Henry had made such an impression on me that I had been able to stretch myself tall and trembling and say, "I know not what course others may take, but as for me, give me liberty or give me death."

And now I heard, really for the first time:

"We have come over a way that with tears
has been watered,
We have come, treading our path through
the blood of the slaughtered."

While echoes of the song shivered in the air, Henry Reed bowed his head, said "Thank you," and returned to his place in the line. The tears that slipped down many faces were not wiped away in shame.

We were on top again. As always, again. We survived. The depths had been icy and dark, but now a bright sun spoke to our souls. I was no longer simply a member of the proud graduating class of 1940; I was a proud member of the wonderful, beautiful Negro race.

Oh, Black known and unknown poets, how often have your auctioned pains sustained us? Who will compute the lonely nights made less lonely by your songs, or by the empty pots made less tragic by your tales?

If we were a people much given to revealing secrets, we might raise monuments and sacrifice to the memories of our poets, but slavery cured us of that weakness. It may be enough, however, to have it said that we survive in exact relationship to the dedication of our poets (include preachers, musicians and blues singers).

Reading for Understanding

Main Idea

1. The main idea can best be expressed by which of the following quotations?
   (a) "We were on top again. As always, again. We survived."
   (b) "The ugliness they left was palpable."
   (c) "The school blazed without gaiety."
   (d) "The weeks until graduation were filled with heady activities."

Details

2. Bailey is the (a) valedictorian (b) school principal (c) narrator's brother (d) guest speaker.
3. The speaker used Booker T. Washington as a/an (a) senatorial candidate (b) role model (c) personal friend (d) author of inspirational texts.
4. The narrator was a/an (a) expert in martial arts (b) twelfth-grade graduate (c) backup speaker to Henry (d) eighth-grade student.
5. The title, "The Person of the Moment," refers to (a) James Weldon Johnson (b) Mr. Donleavy (c) Henry Reed (d) the narrator.
6. The narrator's anticipation of the ceremony can be labeled (a) lukewarm (b) curious (c) excited (d) uncertain.

Inferences

7. A decided change in the tone of the narrative could be blamed on (a) Mr. Donleavy (b) the principal (c) the behavior of the senior class (d) the immaturity of the eighth-graders.
8. Mr. Donleavy's speech can be characterized as (a) hard-hitting (b) sympathetic (c) superficial (d) perceptive.

The Author's Tone

9. The final tone of this story is (a) angry but determined (b) joyously accepting (c) sad (d) calm.

Fact or Opinion

Tell whether the following is a fact or an opinion.

10. Mr. Donleavy was thoughtless and violently racist.

Words in Context

1. "Youth and social approval allied themselves with me and we *trammeled* memories of slights and insults." **Trammeled** (643) means (a) reinforced (b) retold (c) restrained (d) reawakened.
2. "The *meticulous* maps, drawn in three colors of ink. . .it was for nothing. Donleavy had exposed us." **Meticulous** (648) means extremely (a) vivid (b) careful (c) creative (d) well-researched.
3. "We were maids and farmers, handymen and washerwomen, and anything higher that we aspired to was farcical and *presumptuous.* **Presumptuous** (648) means (a) bold (b) disputed (c) easygoing (d) unlikely.

Thinking Critically About the Story

1. The introduction mentions a turning point in Maya Angelou's life. At what point in the narrative does this crucial moment occur? What brought it on?
2. Was Mr. Donleavy's speech extemporaneous? What evidence supports your evaluation?
3. "But Amens and Yes, sir's began to fall around the room like rain through a ragged umbrella." What mood is the narrator trying to suggest?
4. The "ragged umbrella" image in the preceding question is an example of Maya Angelou's skill with words. Point out other examples.
5. Maya Angelou finds humor in small things, like the minister's using the occasion with a captive audience to "speak to backsliders, gam-

blers, and general ne'er-do-wells." What other humorous touches can you find?

6. The book's title, *I Know Why the Caged Bird Sings*, comes from a poem "Sympathy," by Paul Laurence Dunbar. Find a copy of the poem on the Internet, or in the library. Why do you think Maya Angelou chose this title?
7. Why was the speaker's extravagant praise of black athletes distasteful to the narrator?
8. Point out examples of closeness in the narrator's comments about her family members, especially Bailey.

Language in Action

Our Latin Heritage

> The English teacher had helped him to create a sermon winging through Hamlet's soliloquy.

There are four major strands of English: the Anglo-Saxon or Old English (384); the Norman French (559); the Greek; and the Latin. Words of Latin origin dominate the dictionary, though we must remember that ordinary speech is richest in words that go back before the Norman Conquest.

In the quotation, *create* and *sermon* are ultimately of Latin derivation, but *soliloquy* is a relative latecomer. It is traceable to the time of Shakespeare. It is an excellent example of the way in which Latin merges two roots: *solus*—alone; *loqu*—to speak.

For building a vocabulary, knowing Latin roots can help. A sample of such roots would include *ali*—other, *aqu*—water, *aud*—hear, *brev*—short, *cred*—believe, *doc*—teach, and others too numerous for mention here.

Because of the Latin influence on Old English, we now have pairs of words with useful distinctions. In the following list, the first word is Old English; the second is the Latin origin. Can you distinguish between them?

eat, devour	small, diminutive
fall, collapse	stir, commotion
illness, disease	strike, collide

learner, student	tarnish, stain
scare, terrify	wise, intelligent

The influence of Latin upon the basic English tongue is far-reaching and continuing. Latin entered the language at many different periods and is still active as a source of new words.

The World Over

ACTIVITIES

Thinking Critically About the Stories

1. Select a non-American story that could be transferred to an American setting without loss of effectiveness. Justify your choice.
2. In the movie *Independence Day,* all nations join against the common enemy, the alien invaders. Is not the common enemy of all nations hunger, poverty, hatred? How far should the United States go in assuming world leadership against the common enemies?
3. Several stories had settings that were exotic, quite different from the settings of "He" and "The Person of the Moment." What were some of the ways in which your chosen stories seemed strange and alien?
4. "They shall beat their swords into plowshares and their spears into pruning-hooks; nation shall not lift up sword against nation, neither shall they learn war any more."

   —Isaiah 2:4

   How does this statement compare with Franklin Delano Roosevelt's (573)? Is the goal attainable? What are some of the obstacles to overcome?
5. "If there is righteousness in the heart there will be beauty in the character. If there be beauty in the character, there will be harmony in the home. If there is harmony in the home, there will be order in the nation. When there is order in the nation, there will be peace in the world."

   —Chinese proverb

   Is the proverb a realistic blueprint for world peace? Present your own viewpoint.
6. "It is better to be a dog in peaceful times than a man in times of unrest."

   —Chinese proverb

   Another proverb says, "May you live in uninteresting times!" What do these two mean? Would you prefer to live in "uninteresting times"?

7. Which story could best be expanded into a novel? Justify your choice.

Other Areas of Communication

1. The trial scene of "Bontshe the Silent" lends itself to dramatization. Cast the little play and perform it in class. One character will be needed for the nonspeaking part.
2. The name *Job* appears in certain expressions like *poor as Job* and *the patience of Job. Job's tears* are seeds sometimes used as beads. The most interesting allusion is *Job's comforter.* Your dictionary will provide a simple definition, but for a more complete and helpful description, consult *The Encyclopedia of Word and Phrase Origins,* by Robert Hendrickson, published by Facts on File, or another book of allusions.
3. Which story is the one you'll be likely to remember for some time to come? Why? Hold a class discussion on enduring elements in fiction.
4. "The Stream of Days" could be the basis of a television documentary on life as a student in Cairo, Egypt. If you were filming the documentary, how would you go about it? What features would you emphasize? Present your plan to the class.
5. If you have CDs of music from other lands, prepare to bring one to class. Point out elements you consider different from those the class is familiar with.

The Writing Portfolio

A Look Back and a Look Ahead

If you have followed the units in this anthology in sequence, you now have a considerable body of writing in your portfolio. Even if you have skipped here and there, you will have valuable samples of your writing ability. Do not discard your work. You will find yourself referring to the portfolio from time to time. Whatever you have learned can be kept fresh by looking back now and then at this important achievement.

For this final unit, suggestions will help you review all your writing and all your reading. The following ideas for follow-up should provide a fitting climax to the book.

1. Complete three of the following sentences, keeping in mind the suggestions on pages 141–143. Give reasons. Be specific.

   (a) For me, the most memorable character in this anthology was . . .
   (b) The story that surprised me most was . . .
   (c) In general, the type of story I prefer is . . .
   (d) In poetry, I was surprised to learn that . . .
   (e) The unit that most appealed to me was . . .
2. Complete the paragraph (201) of which the following is the topic sentence:

   The computer and the Internet has (or has not) ultimately destroyed the effectiveness and value of the written word.
3. Can you suggest a better title for this book? Give your views in three or four well developed paragraphs. Demonstrate your acquaintance with several selections.
4. Recall the setting of each selection in this unit. Which seemed to you most exotic, least like the world you live in? Develop your point in three or four well-structured paragraphs.
5. Did something you learned in another school subject deepen your appreciation and understanding of a selection in this book? For example, did a knowledge of Indian life and history deepen your appreciation of "My Lord, the Baby"?
6. How do you picture yourself five or ten years in the future? Write a description of that future scenario.
7. Write an essay listing your present goals. Save it and read it again years hence to see how well you achieved those goals.

SAVE YOUR PORTFOLIO!

Language in Action—a Review

You may refer to the preceding pages to answer these questions.

1. All these are examples of nonverbal communication EXCEPT (a) gestures (b) facial expressions (c) exclamations (d) silence.

2. In traveling abroad, tourists should be particularly careful in using (a) questions (b) foreign road maps (c) clothing (d) gestures.
3. Of the following, the word that usually holds the warmest feelings is (a) *abode* (b) *home* (c) *dwelling* (d) *house.*
4. It may truthfully be said about synonyms that (a) no two are interchangeable in all contexts (b) every word has a dozen synonyms in English (c) *grim* and *ghastly* are exact synonyms (d) the wealth of synonyms in English can be a disadvantage for writers.
5. *Troubled* is (a) a possible antonym of *clear* (b) a synonym of *humble* (c) a word without an antonym (d) rarely used outside medical situations.
6. E-Prime (a) is a term used in mathematics (b) recommends a flowery style of writing (c) avoids the use of *is* (d) is desirable but impossible to use.
7. Words of Latin derivation (a) occur in spoken language more than Old English words do (b) outnumber all other word sources in the dictionary (c) stopped entering the language in Shakespeare's time (d) are less frequent than those of Greek derivation.
8. All the following are homonyms EXCEPT (a) *hear—here* (b) *bass* (voice)—*bass* (fish) (c) *eight—ate* (d) *pine* (tree)—*pine* (long for).
9. *Stationery* means *letter paper; stationary* means (a) not movable (b) cardboard envelope (c) pertaining to a train (d) faithful to a cause.
10. Two words often paired are (a) *heteronym* and *homonym* (b) *homophone* and *homograph* (c) *homonym* and *homophone* (d) *heteronym* and *homophone.*

Glossary

The best way to build a vocabulary is to meet new words in helpful contexts. A word's context is the setting it appears in, all the other words around it. The following list contains a great many new words that are worth adding to your word store.

All the words in the list appear in the stories you have read. Here you will find helpful definitions. In addition, you will meet the words in new contexts, sentences designed to suggest the meaning of the listed words. These sentences, together with the contexts in which the words originally appeared, will help you add the words to your vocabulary.

A

abashed (624) embarrassed, ashamed, dismayed.
Though he tripped on the steps to the stage, Fred was not abashed and proceeded on with a firm step to receive his diploma.

abominable (594) repulsive, hateful, horrible.
Conditions in the Rwandan refugee camp were abominable until international agencies stepped in.

abstracted (48) inattentive, thoughtful, absentminded.
Lil may seem abstracted at times, but she is rarely unaware of the conversations around her.

abyss (612) gulf, gorge, ravine, void.
The cable car hung limply over the abyss until the power was restored.

acclaimed (151) applauded, approved, praised.
Casablanca has been acclaimed as one of the ten best pictures of all times.

adversaries (601) foes, enemies, opponents.
The two adversaries shook hands before the boxing match.

affable (52, 357) agreeable, gracious, friendly.
Underneath his hypocritically affable manner, Uriah Heep was a hard and vicious person.

agog (261) excited, eager, expectant.
Kayla was agog at the prospect of using her first scuba equipment.

allusion (23) implied reference.
The works of John Milton have many allusions to Greek and Roman mythology.

ambiance (341) atmosphere, environment, mood.

There is a certain ambiance in the gathering of a happy family at Thanksgiving.

ambivalent (343) uncertain, conflicting, unsure.

Sinbad was ambivalent about leaving his home again, but the lure of the sea sent him forth on another voyage.

amenities (341) pleasantries, contributions to social gatherings.

The buyer and seller of the house exchanged amenities before beginning the hard bargaining.

amiable (26, 51) pleasant, good-natured, agreeable.

In the short story "The Most Dangerous Game," the outwardly amiable manner of General Zaroff concealed a killer instinct.

amiabilities (342) pleasantnesses, friendlinesses.

The amiabilities of the Palmer family have won them a legion of friends.

anarchists (388) rebels against all authority.

In Russia before World War I, the Anarchists helped pave the way for revolution.

anarchy (343) lawlessness, disorder, chaos.

For a brief period during every civil riot, anarchy reigns and shows what can happen when lawlessness rules.

anguish (598) agony, misery, distress.

The disappearance of the cat Muffy caused the family as much anguish as losing a close friend.

anguished (611) distressed, tormented.

When Angela came upon the smoldering ruins of her house, she gave an anguished cry.

anodyne (339) painkiller, relief, balm.

When Jeremy is troubled by his many problems, he uses detective stories as an anodyne.

aperture (25) open space, opening.

The castle wall was solid except for a small aperture near one of the top turrets.

apprehension (134, 341) worry, dread, concern.

When Jason heard the doorbell ring, a shiver of apprehension went through him.

apprehensively (356) uneasily, fearfully, anxiously.

After he was caught cheating on the exam, Justin waited apprehensively outside the principal's office.

arbitrarily (426) high-handedly, obstinately, willfully.

Josef Stalin arbitrarily decided to eliminate millions of peasant farmers.

ardor (89) warmth, intensity, enthusiasm.

The ardor of football fans has provided a twelfth player for the home team.

arduous (229) strenuous, exhausting, difficult.

Replacing the roof timbers blown off by the hurricane was a long and arduous task.

ascertained (306) established, determined, made certain.

Before leaving for the airport, Irina ascertained that her flight was on time.

ascribed (443) credited, assigned, attributed.
Poems ascribed to the Celtic poet Ossian were later shown to have been written by an 18th-century poet, James MacPherson.

asinine (65) stupid, silly, unintelligent.
At first, Carla's suggestion seemed almost asinine, but the more we thought about it, the better it sounded.

assailed (597) attacked, assaulted, charged.
The judge assailed Charles Darnay for his lineage, not for any evil actions.

astute (187) shrewd, cunning, crafty.
Sherlock Holmes in noted for his astute observations and keen deductions.

atrocious (251) horrible, shocking, dreadful.
News of the atrocious events at the Nazi extermination camps began to leak to the outside world.

autocrat (48) dictator, absolute ruler.
In his own household, Father Clarence Day was an autocrat, but a kindly one.

avariciously (241) greedily, selfishly, stingily.
At first, Silas Marner avariciously guarded his wealth, but the physical wealth was replaced for him by the child Eppie.

averse (24) unfavorably inclined, opposed.
I'm not averse to hard work as long as it isn't boring.

aversion to (379) dislike of, hatred for, prejudice against.
Larry loves sweet pickles but has an aversion to dill.

axiom (464) self-evident truth.
The American Constitutional system of checks and balances demonstrates an axiom of good government.

B

begrudge (511, 621, 635) resent, grudge, envy.
Scrooge was so greedy, he would begrudge his employees the slightest pleasure.

belied (48) contradicted, misrepresented, denied.
The modest car driven by John Shubert belied his great wealth and power.

bellicose (234) aggressive, hostile, warlike.
The tyrant's bellicose attacks on neighboring countries preceded his invasion of their homelands.

benighted (108) unenlightened, overtaken by darkness or night.
At times, Father Clarence Day considered his sons benighted idiots, but he never lost his great love for them.

bequest (462) inheritance, legacy.
Part of the philanthropist's bequest was a substantial grant to our town library.

beseechingly (73) imploringly, in a begging manner.
The actor beseechingly asked his agent to find him a part in a new TV series.

blanched (22) become ashen or pale.
She blanched at the sight, and all the blood drained from her face.
blight (107) disease, affliction, sickness.
A blight destroyed most of America's elm trees.
bludgeon (151) club, cudgel, heavy stick.
The victim had obviously been struck by a bludgeon wielded with great force.
brevity (430) briefness, shortness, conciseness.
President Calvin Coolidge was famous for the brevity of his speech . . . in conversation or on public occasions.
broached (85) suggested, introduced, opened.
When the idea of women's suffrage was broached for the first time, most people were amused but opposed.
burnished (344) made shiny, polished.
The burnished shields dazzled the Gauls as the Roman army advanced in disciplined formation.

C

cache (228) hiding place, vault, repository.
When discovered, the cache of the pack rat included many lost household items.
calyxes (517) flower parts.
The calyxes of the poinsettia were a beautiful green.
capricious (608) fanciful, erratic, fickle.
The building of the Taj Mahal was considered a capricious whim by Shah Jahan's subjects.
cataclysm (610) a sudden upheaval that destroys or changes drastically.
The 1908 earthquake was a cataclysm that destroyed much of San Francisco.
ceremonial (554) conventional, formal, solemn, stately.
Graduation from high school is a ceremonial occasion, worthy of celebration.
commendably (405) admirably, in a manner worthy of praise.
The teacher was commendably generous in the extra time she put in to help students.
complacency (73) self-satisfaction, smugness
Maureen's complacency remained untouched, though all the other candidates were worried and uneasy.
complacent (6, 227) smug, self-satisfied, at ease.
Despite the early returns from urban areas, the senatorial candidate remained complacent, certain that the rural vote would turn the tide.
composure (322) poise, level-headedness, self-control.
The witness lost his composure on the witness stand and forfeited the sympathy of the previously well-disposed jurors.
comprehension (555) enlightenment, realization, understanding.
Drawing proper inferences from a story is a test of reading comprehension.

conceits (234) fanciful ideas, concepts, imagination.
The conceits of television's *The X-Files* have stirred the imagination of millions.

condescension (579) patronizing attitude or behavior, snobbery.
The aristocracy looked with condescension on the laboring classes that made their luxuries possible.

consternation (387) dismay, confusion, bewilderment.
To the astronauts' consternation, a hatch on the Shuttle was stuck, forcing NASA to cancel the space walk.

consummate (109) complete, total, perfect.
Though some people criticize Pablo Picasso's subject matter, all agree that he was a consummate craftsman.

contentions (388) struggles, conflicts, debating points.
The defense attorney disputed the detectives' contentions that her client was at the scene of the crime.

contrived (101) planned, schemed, designed.
Nedra cleverly contrived to bring the hostile former partners together again.

contumelious (276) disdainful, scornful, denouncing.
The leading character had a contumelious attitude toward his supposed social inferiors.

convulsive (377) agitated, unsettled, agonized.
With a convulsive movement, Leona grasped her prepared speech and ran off the stage.

covert (125) hidden, secretive, concealed, disguised.
The covert actions of the CIA were criticized by members of Congress who objected to unchecked secrecy.

crannies (428) cracks, grooves, clefts, gaps.
Mountain laurel somehow grows out of crannies in a rock face in the Appalachian Mountains.

D

dappled (209) spotted, mottled, variegated.
The colt's hide was a dappled pattern of brown and white.

dastard (445) coward, weakling.
Though Shakespeare's John Falstaff was a dastard in war, his sense of humor makes audiences love him.

dastardly (100) cowardly, underhanded, deceitful.
Mussolini's dastardly attack on Ethiopia aroused the world's conscience, but nothing was done to stop him.

dauntless (446) fearless, courageous, daring.
Marcia's dauntless scaling of the cliff at El Capitan aroused the admiration of her fellow climbers.

debauchee (462) ne'er-do-well, one who is corrupted.
In *Dr. Jekyll and Mr. Hyde,* the principal character turns from a respected physician to a debauchee of the worse kind.

defray (19) reimburse, pay.

The award will defray all the winner's expenses, but a husband or wife will have to pay full fare.

delectable (180) delicious, delightful, pleasing to the taste.
The delectable desserts at the beginning of the cafeteria line tempted diners to leave room for dessert.

deprecating (302) belittling, pleading against, urging reasons against.
A lack of self-confidence caused Dan to adopt a deprecating manner when presenting one of his opinions.

deprecatory (356) apologetic, disapproving, belittling.
Whenever he was praised for his heroic act, Carl always made a deprecatory gesture as though the incident were trivial.

despondent (404) depressed, dejected, downhearted.
Ophelia became despondent over the death of her father at the hands of Hamlet.

despot (576) dictator, tyrant, ruler with absolute authority.
In a land ruled by a despot, free speech is outlawed.

desultory (6) aimless, erratic, sluggish.
Ramon made a few desultory comments to start the conversation, but when no one picked up the threads, he have up altogether,

devastation (252) destruction, desolation, ruin.
During the blitz, the devastation in the city of London was extensive.

deviation (232) swerve, departure, turning.
Because of irregularities in the earth's magnetic field, the compass direction of north is a deviation from true north.

discernible (237) recognizable, apparent, visible.
With no discernible reason or explanation, Charlotte broke off the conversation and stormed out of the house.

disconsolate (587) heartbroken, dejected, despondent.
Romeo was disconsolate when he came upon the apparently lifeless body of Juliet.

dispel (36) drive away, scatter, banish.
A Will Ferrell comedy is guaranteed to dispel the gloom.

dissipated (66) driven off, scattered, vanished.
His peaceful feeling was dissipated by the children's raucous laughter.

dissolute (19) corrupt, immoral, wicked.
Many of the Roman emperors were dissolute dictators, excelling in evil without restraint.

dissonant (339) out of tune, discordant, grating.
The heckler's insistent interruptions of the candidate's speech provided a dissonant note in an otherwise happy occasion.

distended (76) expanded, stretched, swollen.
After the snake had swallowed the rat, its body looked abnormally distended.

distractedly (287) confusedly, absent-mindedly, excitedly.
When Hamlet spoke distractedly, Polonius thought the Prince had gone mad over love of his daughter Ophelia.

docile (248) passive, gentle, easily led.

In the story of Andocles and the lion, the lion is docile so that Androcles can remove a thorn from his forepaw.

dossier (620) bundle of documents, detailed records.
To expose the spy, the CIA built a dossier of treasonous actions.

dote on (109) love excessively, adore, pamper.
How can Angela dote on that ill-tempered, mangy, ugly mongrel?

dumbfounded (105) confused, astonished, bewildered.
When I saw some pictures by the Hubble telescope, I was dumbfounded to see galaxies billions of light years away.

E

effulgent (586) radiant, brilliant, shining.
Joseph, in his coat of many colors, was effulgent, the envy of his brothers.

effusively (10) generously, enthusiastically, exuberantly.
Mrs. Bennet effusively greeted the young guests in the hope of finding a husband for one of her daughters.

embellished (342) adorned, decorated, enriched.
The medieval Books of Hours were embellished with fine decorations in gold and lapis lazuli.

encroached (463) intruded, moved in on, trespassed.
The airport runways illegally encroached upon the wildlife preserve and had to be rerouted.

encumbrances (304) burdens, hindrances, impediments.
Mothers and fathers who consider the children mere encumbrances may lack the skills needed for successful parenting.

engrossed in (380) absorbed in, preoccupied with, involved with.
When Daphne becomes engrossed on the Internet, the house could almost burn down around her with scarcely any notice.

enormity (251) wickedness, cruelty, dreadfulness.
In *Hamlet,* Queen Gertrude seems unaware of the enormity of Claudius's crime.

ensuing (306) following.
The construction work will be completed in the ensuing weeks.

epitomized (262) summarized, served as an example of, summed up.
The seeing-eye dog epitomized the best results of obedience training.

epoch (575) era, important period of time.
The epoch of westward expansion in the United States ended with the 19th century.

equanimity (344) calmness, coolness, poise.
The seasoned investor took the loss of her fortune with equanimity.

evade (101) avoided, shunned.
In *Much Ado about Nothing,* the villains couldn't evade capture by the silliest, most inept constable in all of Shakespeare.

evasion (109) avoidance, escape.
The fox used many evasion tactics to throw the hounds off the scent.

evasions (381) avoidances, bypasses, escapes.
Most tax evasions are quickly uncovered by the IRS.

evoked (121) brought out, summoned, called forth.
Falstaff's antics evoked much laughter in Shakespeare's day.

exalted (360) uplifted, inspired, jubilant.
After working with the Habitat crew for a week, Sharon felt both proud and exalted.

exhaustive (75) thorough, complete.
An exhaustive analysis of the accident showed that the driver of the sedan had been careless in making a left turn.

exhilaration (294) high spirits, light-heartedness, elation.
When the roller coaster begins its breathtaking drop, Bev and Stan feel a special sense of exhilaration.

exorbitant (579) excessive, unreasonable, too expensive.
Some companies charge young customers exorbitant prices for common stamps.

expatriate (341) exile, one who lives outside his native country.
An expatriate in Venice for years, George longed to go home.

extraneous (437) nonessential, irrelevant, inappropriate.
Solving a crime requires eliminating all extraneous clues and focusing on those that seem relevant.

extricated (619) disentangled, freed.
After filing bankruptcy, Dana extricated herself from many old debts.

exultation (529) rejoicing, gladness, joy.
After crossing the goal line, the running back lifted his arms in a gesture of wild exultation.

F

facetiously (128) jokingly, wittily, amusingly.
To downplay his achievement, Todd spoke facetiously about his luckily being in the right place at the right time.

fawning (512) flattering, insincere.
A strong, confident leader does not like to be surrounded by fawning assistants who never provide contradictory insights.

feigned (89) pretended
When Andre heard his mother coming to the bedroom, he put out the light and feigned sleep.

festoons (304) garlands, wreaths, decorative chains.
Festoons of colored lights decorated the entrance to the prom.

fettered (478) chained, shackled, bound, hampered.
When the defendant entered the courtroom, he was fettered, hands and feet.

firmament (465) the sky.
At sunset, the entire firmament was aglow with radiance.

flout (456) disdain, scorn, denounce.
Terence's tendency to flout rules of sensitive behavior has lost him most of his friends.

forbore (238) ceased, gave up, refrained.
After five useless attempts at solving the puzzle, Dick finally sighed and forbore.

formidable (6, 47, 258) feared, menacing, powerful.
Though the Carolina Panthers were formidable opponents, in Superbowl 38, the Patriots still won by three points.

fretful (47) irritable, ill-tempered, sulky.
Maurya was fretful because she hadn't heard from Tim in over a month.

furtive (596) secret, sly, stealthy.
Elizabeth Bennet stole furtive glances at the proud but handsome Mr. Darcy.

G

germane (235) closely related, relevant, allied.
Unless the matter was proved germane to the trial, the judge did not allow the evidence to be used.

gist (288) substance, essence, core.
Edward Everett spoke at length, but Abraham Lincoln in his brief Gettysburg Address better summed up the spirit of the occasion.

grotesque (63) weird, abnormal, repulsive.
In the Disney version, the grotesque image of the Hunchback of Notre Dame was modified by the character's warmth.

H

hackneyed (479) overdone, commonplace, shopworn.
The humorous poet Ogden Nash poked fun at hackneyed experiences and expressions.

haggard (18, 588) gaunt, emaciated, exhausted.
After a week wandering around the forest, the two boys emerged looking haggard.

half-nelson (562) a wrestling hold.
After a few moments of sparring, one wrestler was able to control the match with a sudden half-nelson.

heinousness (46) nastiness, viciousness, sinfulness.
The heinousness of Macbeth's crimes eventually turned former friends against him.

heretic (456) nonbeliever, skeptic, freethinker.
Joan of Arc, who was burnt at the stake as a heretic, was canonized in 1920.

hue (169) color.
The dominant hue of the wild rose is red, but the color is not pure.

humility (431, 600) humbleness, meekness, mildness.
Mahatma Gandhi showed true humility of spirit in all his actions.

I

ignominy (396) dishonor, disgrace, shame.
The so-called ignominy of defeat is often a harmful and needless emotion.

imminent (380) approaching, impending, threatening.

The imminent arrival of the French ambassador had the entire White House staff on red alert.

impact (398) shock, clash, collision.

Scientists around the world watched the impact of the comet's crash into the surface of Jupiter.

impending (22) menacing, threatening, about to occur.

The impending takeover of the company by a corporate giant will throw many employees out of work.

imperturbable (305) even-tempered, calm, easygoing.

Dad can remain imperturbable in a household of active children.

imperturbably (26) serenely, coolly, tranquilly.

The speaker answered the heckler imperturbably, even though he was seething inside.

implored (259) appealed to, begged, entreated.

In *Othello*, Desdemona implored her husband not to hurt her.

impoverished (387) poor, poverty-stricken, strained.

Sir Walter Scott's efforts to earn enough money to get out of bankruptcy almost impoverished him.

improvised (89) without extensive preparation, spur of the moment.

When Telia sprained her ankle while camping, she improvised a crutch from a tree branch.

impunity (103) lack of punishment, immunity, reprieve.

In India, Mother Teresa walked into the most dangerous areas with impunity.

inaccessible (608) unapproachable, impassable, unreachable.

The Spanish parador near Cadiz was perched on a seemingly inaccessible mountain crag.

incarceration (65) imprisonment, confinement.

The incarceration of the Count of Monte Cristo made him bitter toward his enemies outside the prison.

incipient (338) beginning, becoming apparent.

An incipient sore throat often warns of a cold to come.

incisive (623) penetrating, sharp, piercing.

The reviewer's incisive criticism of the play helped the performer to improve.

incoherently (80, 240) in a wild, rambling disconnected way.

In *Treasure Island,* Ben Gunn's voice rambled incoherently, but throughout could be heard the word *cheese.*

incongruous (471) inappropriate, out of place, conflicting.

At the White House, Woody Allen's sneakers seemed incongruous with his formal attire.

indignant (188) angry, exasperated, offended.

When Rico realized he hadn't been sent an invitation to the wedding, he was indignant at the apparent thoughtlessness.

indulgent (358) tolerant, pampering, permissive.

The children of parents who are too indulgent often cry out for help and discipline.

inebriate (462) drunken, intoxicated.

In *Arthur*, Dudley Moore plays a character who is inebriate through a good part of the film.

ineffectual (238) ineffective, useless, fruitless.
After an ineffectual attempt to lock the door, Alice realized that she had been using the wrong key.

inexplicable (78, 344, 397) unexplainable, baffling, bewildering.
The inexplicable outbreak of certain diseases presents an unending challenge for research scientists.

infatuation (439) loss of sound judgment, foolish attachment, unwise passion.
What seemed at first, to friends of Romeo, like a mere infatuation with Juliet proved to be a profound love.

infinitesimal (303) tiny, diminutive, microscopic.
The sun is but an infinitesimal part of the Milky Way galaxy.

infusion (293) saturation, immersion, injection.
An infusion of new blood into South Florida revitalized many older quiet areas.

intact (623) unbroken, perfect, whole.
If the package is returned intact, you will be entitled to a full refund.

interloper (341) intruder, interferer, trespasser.
In Cinderella's family, she felt alone, an interloper.

introspective (454) thoughtful, meditative, reflective.
Geraldine is an outgoing extrovert; Beth is more introspective.

intuitively (405) instinctively, spontaneously, involuntarily.
In general, animals seem to select intuitively the foods that are best for them

invincible (250) unconquerable, invulnerable.
The invincible armies of the invading Tartars swept across Europe to the gates of Vienna.

iridescent (342) shimmering, glittering, lustrous.
A drop of rain on a window pane can cast an iridescent glow when the sun appears.

irrelevant (412) inappropriate, unrelated, off-the-topic.
One obnoxious member of the audience asked a completely irrelevant question to sidetrack the discussion.

J

jettisoned (345) discarded, tossed out, expelled.
When Jack heard the previous speaker's talk, he jettisoned his prepared speech and decided to talk without notes.

juncture (414) turning point, connection.
At a critical juncture in the Revolutionary War, General Washington survived a bitter winter.

L

lacerated (240) torn, mangled, wounded.
An examination after the accident showed that Larry's forearm was lacerated, but no bones had been broken.

laconic (105) concise, brief, to the point.
When asked by the press for particulars about the crime, the detectives remained laconic and noncommittal.
languid (320, 600) listless, inactive, sluggish.
Wealthy young ladies in Jane Austen's novels often strike a languid pose around potential suitors.
legacy (386) inheritance, heirloom, bequest.
The conspirators' assassination of Julius Caesar left a legacy of hate that eventually proved their undoing.
libation (412) ceremonial drink, toast.
At the Bicentennial celebration, the speaker offered a libation to all those who had contributed to the making of this nation.
limpid (343) clear, transparent, straightforward.
The limpid turquoise waters of Lake Louise have provided inspiration for photographers for over a century.
loathsome (239, 597) disgusting, offensive, vile.
Certain special effects in horror movies are loathsome but impressive.
lowering (48) gloomy, dismal, threatening.
The lowering clouds on the western horizon were motivation enough to turn the sailboat around and head for the dock.
ludicrous (239) ridiculous, amusing, laughable.
Some of Garry's solutions for the budget deficit were ludicrous to the members of the Camera Club.
lugubriously (238) mournfully, gloomily, sadly.
Rex howled lugubriously at being put out into the cold.
lurching (227, 380) staggering, swerving, tottering.
The sudden turn on the narrow-gauge railway to Skagway had us all lurching and grabbing for something to hold onto.

M

malignantly (512) evilly, hatefully.
He looked at me so malignantly, I felt chills up my spine.
meditative (550) pensive, thoughtful, pondering, lost in thought.
Sitting by a quiet stream can foster a meditative mood.
mendicant (241, 579) beggar, member of a certain religious order.
In oriental society, a mendicant is often a holy man, not an outcast.
menial (276) servant, person of lesser degree.
Though he was a menial in his employer's household, he kept a fierce sense of pride and dignity.
Mercury (327) Roman god; messenger of the gods.
With his winged shoes, Mercury would outrace the clouds and sun.
mete (623) allot, distribute, apportion.
In his decisions, King Arthur tried to mete out justice to his subjects.
meticulous (648) precise, exact, conscientious.
His meticulous calculations convinced Clyde Tombaugh that the new planet Pluto would be found just about where he looked.

misanthropic (595) cynical, unsociable, antisocial.
The misanthropic ways of Ebenezer Scrooge were altered when the ghosts of Christmas appeared to him.
mistrusted (563) doubted, distrusted.
David Copperfield mistrusted the motives of Uriah Heep.
morose (20, 395, 595) gloomy, somber, melancholy.
Tad's morose disposition made him an unpopular member of the birdwatching expedition.
munificence (443) generosity, extravagance.
In Shakespeare's play *Timon of Athens,* the central character showers his munificence upon his friends, only to be scorned by them in his later hour of need.
murky (252) gloomy, dismal, bleak, hazy.
The murky interior of the cafe was heavy with smoke.

N

nautical (477) naval, maritime, pertaining to the sea.
A nautical mile is slightly longer than the unit used on land.
nettled (66) annoyed, irritated, provoked.
The debater's direct attack nettled his weaker opponent.
nocturnal (25, 344) pertaining to night.
Though the raccoon is generally a nocturnal animal, a family of raccoons struts in our backyard in the late afternoon.
nomenclature (63) name designation, process of naming.
George Stewart, a student of nomenclature, wrote several books on names.
notorious (23) outstanding and well-known in an unfavorable sense.
The notorious Jesse James gang was finally destroyed on the death of the leader in 1882.

O

obdurate (580) obstinate, stubborn, unbending.
King Claudius urged Hamlet to look upon him as a father, but Hamlet remained obdurate in his rejection.
obeisance (579) mark of respect or submission.
The curtsy ladies give before the queen is a form of obeisance.
oblivious (341) unaware, unmindful, distracted.
When Norma works at her PC, she is oblivious to outside noises.
obscure (288) conceal, hide, cloak.
To obscure his true motives, Fernando said he was there for the job interview.
obscured (227) concealed, hidden, overshadowed.
When, during the total solar eclipse, the moon had completely obscured the disk of the sun, an eerie twilight awed the noisy crowd.
obsession (136) a controlling or fixed idea, a compelling motivation.

Charles Babbage's obsession with mechanical calculating machines foreshadowed the rise of electronic computers a century after his death.

obstinate (556) immovable, stubborn, unbending, uncompromising.
In his refusal to go out for football, Glenn remains obstinate.

officious (442) interfering.
The officious clerk at the motor vehicle bureau was a source of irritation to those waiting on line.

opaque (510) nontransparent, impervious to light.
The neighboring chimneys had poured forth so much soot, the house windows were almost opaque.

organdy (330) very stiff, transparent cotton fabric.
Graduation dresses traditionally were made with an organdy shell.

ornate (387) showily decorated, elaborate, luxurious.
The ornate details of New Orleans's French Quarter houses never fail to charm tourists.

P

pallet (160) small, hard, temporary bed.
When the family arrives for Thanksgiving, someone has to sleep on a pallet in the TV room.

pallor (63) paleness.
Too many days cooped up inside his tiny office had given Brad's face an unhealthy pallor.

pandemonium (151) confusion, turmoil, uproar.
Pandemonium occurred when the snakes escaped from their cage.

pelt (249) bombard, beat steadily, assail.
From the window, we watched the hailstorm pelt the land with golf-ball-sized stones.

perceptions (460) sensations, impressions, insight.
False perceptions of Adolf Hitler's motives gave him a head start in rebuilding his powerful army.

peremptorily (101) dictatorily, arrogantly, autocratically.
James Bond's voice rang out peremptorily, "Stand where you are!"

perpetrated (19) committed, performed.
It was discovered that the convicted criminal had perpetrated even more crimes than those for which he was charged.

perpetual (63) continuing, incessant, constant.
Mr. Eller's face wore a perpetual frown which even laughter around him could not erase.

perplexed (194) puzzled, confused, bewildered.
When Lourdes was perplexed by a question on the SAT, she wasted no time on it but went on to another.

persistent (550) determined, purposeful, untiring, steadfast.
Despite setbacks, Sir Edmund Hilary remained persistent in his goal to scale Mt. Everest.

perturbation (72) restlessness, alarm, turmoil.
There was perturbation in the locker room when it was announced that the star player would be suspended for the next two games.

petulantly (64) crossly, crankily, irritably.
When Jeb's wishes were not followed, he always reacted petulantly and peevishly.
placard (536) poster, notice posted in a public place.
After election, candidates are supposed to remove all placards from public buildings.
plaintive (595) sad, melancholy, sorrowful.
The plaintive call of the mourning dove has given the bird its name.
precipitate (303) hasty, hurried, headlong.
When the celebrity arrived, the fans broke rank in a precipitate rush.
precipitated (87) caused, provoked, stimulated.
Rapidly rising oil prices precipitated a crisis in the American economy.
precipitous (304) sheer, steep, abrupt.
Some of Colorado's most precipitous slopes entice the most adventurous skiers.
prepossessing (103) attractive, pleasing, charming.
The famous architect Frank Lloyd Wright made a prepossessing appearance with his high collar, porkpie hat, and dramatic cape.
presumptuous (648) arrogant, impertinent, taking liberties.
It isn't presumptuous to seek to earn a fair wage for a good job.
pretensions (620) claims.
The pretensions of Bonnie Prince Charlie to the British throne eventually came to nothing.
prodigy (328, 412) a highly talented child.
Too few prodigies at four are labeled geniuses at twenty.
prolix (602) wordy, long-winded, rambling.
The prolix report of the membership committee soon had the other members nodding.
propitiate (49) soothe, conciliate, appease.
When the god Thor sent his thunderbolts crashing over the land, the Norse sought to propitiate him.
prostrate (577) stretched out, lying flat, completely overcome.
The nervous councillor fell prostrate at the feet of the shogun and began to speak.
protean (345) changeable, variable, flexible.
Marilyn Monroe was noted for her protean moods, some negative, others leading to some of her finest acting moments.
psyching (331) using psychology to defeat.
Jim was psyching out Jamal when he told him the game was cancelled.
pulsating (233) throbbing, beating, palpitating.
Doctors studied the pulsating of the man's heart on the electrocardiograph.

Q

quaffed (445) drank deeply.
John Falstaff quaffed a pint of ale before setting out to war.

quay (536) wharf, landing place.
The high tides associated with the hurricane caused beach erosion and damaged the quay.

R

rebuff (609) rejection, refusal, snub.
Despite many rebuffs, Margaret Mitchell persisted and finally sold the manuscript of *Gone With the Wind.*
rebuke (87, 359) scold, reprimand, reproach.
King Arthur had to rebuke Sir Bedivere for not tossing the sword Excalibur back into the lake as he had been ordered.
recapitulated (106) summarized, reviewed, restated.
After discussing all safety precautions for the hike, the leader recapitulated what he had said just to make sure.
recluse (461) hermit, loner, solitary person.
Until the arrival of the little girl Eppie, Silas Marner was a recluse, avoiding other people.
recumbent (78) lying down, resting.
The recumbent figure on the lawn proved to be Tanya, who rose to greet us as we approached.
reiterated (65) repeated, restated.
The candidate reiterated several times his contention that his opponent's voting record was very poor.
refuted (388) disproved, discredited, denied.
Galileo refuted the popular belief that the sun revolves around the earth.
relentlessly (170) strictly, harshly, ruthlessly.
For three days, the northeast wind relentlessly attacked the sand dunes and caused considerable beach erosion.
renounce (462) give up claim or right to, give up, refuse.
Edward VIII renounced the throne of England because of his love for an American divorcée.
repercussions (219) reactions, recoils, rebounds.
The repercussions of his assassination were felt around the world.
reproach (124) to blame, criticize, to condemn, shame.
His older brother reproached him for his rude behavior and compelled him to apologize.
repugnance (136) disgust, queasiness, revulsion.
It took a full week for Caroline to overcome her repugnance at dissecting a frog in the biology lab.
repugnant (239) repulsive, disagreeable, offensive.
At first, the thought of leaving home for college was repugnant to Marianne, but she gradually warmed to the idea.
repulsively (70) in a way that arouses disgust.
He repulsively slurped the greasy soup.
resignation (597) surrender, submission, yielding.
Charles Darnay accepted with resignation his condemnation to death.
resolution (437) solving of the problem.

There was no resolution to the brothers' conflict until they stopped sharing a bedroom.

resonant (249) resounding, echoing, full-bodied.
James Earl Jones' resonant voice can reach the top seats in any theater without amplification.

résumé (106) summary, synopsis, digest.
Sheila presented her résumé to the human resources director and waited for her first question.

revel (170) celebrate, enjoy, carouse.
Romeo and Juliet reveled in their love, but feared for the future.

reverie (31) daydream, fantasy.
When the teacher called on him, Todd was jolted from his reverie.

rigorous (101) strict, relentless, severe.
More crimes are solved by rigorous police work than by intuition.

S

sage (457) wise man, master, authority.
Lao-tzu, a possibly legendary sage of ancient China, is the father of Taoism.

sallow (103) sickly, pale, unhealthy-looking.
The liberated prisoners emerged into the sunlight, sallow, and wasted in frame.

sardonic (303) scornful, disdainful, contemptuous.
Iago's sardonic grin belied the honesty of his speech.

scourge (447) affliction, misfortune, someone or something to inflict pain.
The nomadic Mongols rode west, becoming the scourge of eastern and central Europe.

scrupulously (611) precisely, extremely carefully.
The referee followed the rule book scrupulously.

scrutinizing (586) examining, inspecting, studying.
After scrutinizing the stamp with the inverted center, the experts pronounced it a fake.

scuttled (320) hurried, scurried, shuffled.
The cattle egrets scuttled through the field, looking for insects.

sedentary (63) inactive, settled.
Exercise is important for those who otherwise live a sedentary life.

sediment (231) deposit, dregs, grounds.
The sediment at the bottom of the water boiler proved to be mostly iron.

self-indulgence (432) pursuit of pleasure, dissipation, selfishness.
The self-indulgence of Roman Emperors like Caligula finally destroyed them.

sensibility (232) sensitivity, acuteness, awareness.
Jane Austen's *Sense and Sensibility* contrasts the common elements: reason and emotion.

sepulchral (376) mournful, woeful, gloomy.
In his black clothes and hat and with his sallow complexion, Mr. Dolby gave a sepulchral appearance.

serene (342, 510) peaceful, calm, at peace.
Our cat Tammy rules the entire family with serene self-assurance.

serenity (520, 610) peacefulness, calmness, stillness.
Though Terry's business world was hectic, his own home provided the serenity that refreshed his spirit.

shambling (587) shuffling, tottering, walking awkwardly.
Shambling footsteps outside the door announced the arrival of the hunchback of Notre Dame.

sheen (448) brilliance, glow, luster.
Metallic paints have a sheen that ordinary paints cannot produce.

siblings (398) children having a common parent.
Elizabeth Bennet lives with her siblings in a house they are destined to lose upon their father's death.

singular (17) unusual, peculiar, odd.
The lawyer had a singular way of using his hands, a habit that constantly called attention to itself.

singularly (108) exceptionally, uniquely, remarkably.
With his height and great reflexes, Michael Jordan was singularly adept in the game of basketball.

skeptics (261) disbelievers, doubters, questioners.
The skeptics who scoffed at wireless technology were proved wrong.

snarl (414) tangle, snare.
The usual traffic snarl during the rush hour was worsened by an accident at the corner of Main Street and Fourth Avenue.

sniveled (636) sniffed repeatedly, whimpered, whined, sniffled.
When his drum was taken away to give his parents peace, the child sniveled and left the room.

sorrel (209) light chestnut horse.
Among the pure-white Arabians was a lively sorrel, conspicuous by his color.

stealthily (78) slyly, secretly, cautiously.
The cat stealthily approached the bird, but a sudden motion frightened its prey away.

stodgy (100) dull, boring, tiresome.
On first meeting, Dan seemed a stodgy, uninteresting fellow, but once on the topic of music, he became a spellbinder.

strident (623) harsh-sounding, shrill, rasping.
The strident voice of the speaker reached every corner of the huge auditorium.

stringent (388) strict, severe, demanding.
In an effort to curb drunk driving, states issued stringent regulations involving the amount of alcohol in the blood.

sublimity (342) nobility, grandeur, loftiness.
The sublimity of the message in the Twenty-third Psalm chokes me with emotion.

succumbed (621) surrendered, admitted defeat, died.
In about 1670 B.C., the Egyptian forces succumbed to the Hyksos, who are known as the "shepherd kings."

sundry (387) miscellaneous, assorted, diversified.
Shopping with Leo means coming home with chocolates, hard candies, and sundry other sweets.
superficial (431) shallow, trivial, without substance.
A con artist's superficial charm can trick innocent victims.
surmises (85) guesses, beliefs, opinions.
We must get more facts; surmises are not enough.
swaggered (353) walked in an arrogant, pompous manner.
When Jason swaggered into the room, all conversation ceased.
swarthy (46) dark-complexioned, dark-skinned.
Years under the desert sun had turned her blond brother into a swarthy stranger.

T

taunted (187) mocked, reproached, ridiculed, scoffed at.
The linebacker taunted the quarterback after knocking down the pass intended for a wide receiver.
taunting (248) mocking, ridiculing, insulting.
After taunting Romeo and Mercutio, Tybalt kills Mercutio in a duel and is then slain by Romeo.
terminating (68) ending, ceasing, finishing.
The flight from St. Louis will be terminating at La Guardia Airport, New York City.
tersely (67) briefly, crisply, pointedly.
When questioned about the accident, Mark replied tersely, but his facial expression spoke volumes.
thwarted (444) frustrated, foiled, checked.
In England, Guy Fawkes Day celebrates the day the authorities thwarted the Gunpowder Plot to blow up the Houses of Parliament.
torpor (602) inactivity, sluggishness, lethargy.
During the rain and heat of the monsoon season, travelers to India experience an overwhelming torpor.
tractability (381) obedience, willingness, submissiveness.
Many mustangs when treated gently and calmly become models of tractability.
trammeled (643) restrained, curbed, confined.
Too often we are trammeled by fear of failure, thus missing out on many opportunities.
transience (338) impermanence, briefness, brevity.
Great art is often concerned with the brevity of life and the transcience of beauty.
transitory (344) temporary, short-lived, fleeting.
Some celebrities discover too late that fame can be transitory.
tremulous (303) trembling, shivering, quivering.
In a tremulous voice, Oliver Twist asked for more food.
trivial (19) commonplace, unimportant, slight.

Sometimes a trivial event triggers a serious result.

tumultuous (343, 595) agitated, wild, boisterous.
The tumultuous crowd decided to storm the Bastille and set the prisoners free.

tumultuously (220) wildly, turbulently, fiercely.
The soccer fans celebrated tumultuously when England defeated Italy.

U

unassuming (394) modest, humble, low-key.
In the *Star Trek* series, Mr. Spock's generally unassuming manner underplayed his technical skill and profound understanding of his fellow staff members.

unfathomable (251) past understanding, unknowable, profound.
The best literature gives readers a glimpse into the unfathomable depths of the human soul.

unhinged (104) unbalanced, unnerved, confused.
Ophelia thought that Hamlet's mind had become unhinged because of unrequited love for her.

unison (587) at the same time, in perfect agreement.
When Mark entered, the guests lit the lights and shouted "Surprise!" in unison.

unobtrusive (48) inconspicuous, modest, shy.
The journalist's unobtrusive manner won over the interviewer's confidence and produced a lively dialogue.

unwarranted (381) uncalled for, not justified, inappropriate.
To his loyal soldiers, any attack on their leader Robert E. Lee was unwarranted.

urchin (53) mischievous youngster.
Whenever Sherlock Holmes had a special assignment in London, he called upon a streetwise urchin.

usurper (578) one who takes the place of another, often without right.
The defeated Yorkist factions in England after Bosworth Field considered Henry VII a usurper.

V

veered (107) turned, swerved, changed direction.
Just when the forest fires seemed out of control, the wind veered and eased the threat.

vehemently (588) forcefully, with intense emotion.
Though the suspect vehemently protested his innocence, he was taken to the station house for questioning.

verily (623) certainly, truly in fact.
Harold chuckled: "Verily I say unto you that we'll win tonight's hockey game."

veritable (619) real, genuine.
Before the battle of Agincourt, King Henry V was a veritable tower of strength for his men.

vexed (529) irritated, angered, annoyed.
The witness was vexed by the probing questions the plaintiff's lawyer kept asking him.
vigil (34) watch, watchfulness, period of wakefulness.
The guard dog keeps his lonely vigil inside the chain-link fence.
vigilance (387) watchfulness, wariness, caution.
Every scholar of history knows that eternal vigilance is the price of liberty.
voluble (50, 179) talkative, fluent, glib.
The suspect was voluble in his protestations of innocence.
volubly (387) talkatively, wordily, fluently.
Though eyewitnesses put the suspect at the crime scene, he volubly protested his innocence.
vortex (252) whirlpool, eddy.
The threatening vortex of the approaching tornado sent everyone scurrying to the safest places to wait out the storm.
votaries (412) devoted admirers.
Sam and LeToya are votaries of Aristotle's philosophy.
vouchsafed (226) granted, bestowed, allowed.
The authorities vouchsafed Anderson's return to America.

W

warrant (443) guarantee, authorization, approval.
Cindy's charisma and charm are warrant that she will be nominated prom queen.
welkin (276) sky, firmament.
The news of the end of the war made the welkin resound with cheers and rejoicing.
whimsicalities (234) fanciful ideas, absurdities.
The whimsicalities of Ogden Nash's mind are displayed in the humorous verse he created.
wince (395) flinch, draw back, shrink.
The long-suffering members of the Cotter family wince when Dan begins to practice his violin.
wincing (227) flinching, recoiling, cringing.
Though wincing with pain from a foot blister, Sampras played out the match.
wistful (238) yearning, touched with melancholy.
With a wistful look back at his native land, Robert Louis Stevenson set out for the South Seas.
writhed (22) distorted, twisted, wrenched.
Laocoön writhed in pain as the serpents attacked him and his sons.
wry (588) twisted, lopsided, witty.
Samantha's wry expression suggested that she disagreed with Meg's comments.

Index to Language in Action

U

W